Law and Language

The International Library of Essays in Law and Legal Theory

Second Series

Series Editor: Tom D. Campbell

Titles in the Series:

Freedom of Speech, Volumes I and II
Larry Alexander

Privacy
Eric M. Barendt

Comparative Legal Cultures
John Bell

Contract Law, Volumes I and II
Brian Bix

Corporate Law
William W. Bratton

Legal Positivism
Tom D. Campbell

International Trade Law
Ronald A. Cass and Michael S. Knoll

Sociological Perspectives on Law, Volumes I and II
Roger Cotterrell

Intellectual Property
Peter Drahos

Family, State and Law, Volumes I and II
Michael D. Freeman

Natural Law
Robert P. George

Commercial Law
Clayton P. Gillette

Competition Law
Rosa Greaves

Chinese Law and Legal Theory
Perry Keller

International Law, Volumes I and II
Martti Koskenniemi and David Kennedy

Constitutional Law
Ian D. Loveland

Interpretation of Law
D. Neil MacCormick and Fernando Atria

Human Rights
Robert McCorquodale

Anti-Discrimination Law
Christopher McCrudden

Medical Law and Ethics
Sheila McLean

Mediation
Carrie Menkel-Meadow

Environmental Law
Peter Menell

Criminal Law
Thomas Morawetz

Law and Language
Thomas Morawetz

Law and Anthropology
Martha Mundy

Gender and Justice
Ngaire Naffine

Law and Economics
Eric A. Posner

Japanese Law
J. Mark Ramseyer

Justice
Wojciech Sadurski

The Rule of Law
Frederick Schauer

Restitution
Lionel D. Smith

Company Law
David Sugarman

Freedom of Information
Robert G. Vaughn

Tort Law
Ernest J. Weinrib

Rights
Robin West

Welfare Law
Lucy A. Williams

Law and Language

Edited by

Thomas Morawetz

University of Connecticut, USA

Routledge
Taylor & Francis Group
LONDON AND NEW YORK

First published 2000 by Ashgate Publishing

Published 2016 by Routledge
2 Park Square, Milton Park, Abingdon, Oxon OX14 4RN
711 Third Avenue, New York, NY 10017, USA

Routledge is an imprint of the Taylor & Francis Group, an informa business

British Library Cataloguing in Publication Data
Law and language. – (International library of essays in law
and legal theory. Second series)
1. Law – Language 2. Law – Language – Philosophy 3. Language
and languages – Philosophy
I. Morawetz, Thomas
340.1'4

Library of Congress Cataloging-in-Publication Data
Law and language / edited by Thomas Morawetz.
p. cm. — (The International library of essays in law and
legal theory. Areas ; 2nd ser., 6)
Includes index.
ISBN 1 84014 770 9
1. Law—Language. 2. Law—United States—Language. 3. Law—
Interpretation and construction. 4. Jurisprudence. I. Morawetz,
Thomas, 1942– . II. Series.
K213.L39 2000
340'.01'4—dc21 99-38742
CIP

ISBN 9781840147704 (hbk)

Transfered to Digital Printing in 2012

Contents

Acknowledgements

The editor and publishers wish to thank the following for permission to use copyright material.

Boston University Law Review and J.A. Christian Limited for the essay: Catharine A. MacKinnon (1991), 'Pornography as Defamation and Discrimination', *Boston University Law Review*, **71**, pp. 793–815. Reprinted by permission from the *Boston University Law Review*, **71** (1991). Copyright © 1991 Catharine A. MacKinnon.

Cardozo School of Law for the essay: Richard Hyland (1990), 'Babel: a She'ur', *Cardozo Law Review*, **11**, pp. 1585–612. This essay originally appeared in *Cardozo Law Review*, **11** (1990) at p. 1585.

Columbia University for the essay: Louis Henkin (1963), 'Morals and the Constitution: The Sin of Obscenity', *Columbia Law Review*, **63**, pp. 391–414. Reprinted by permission.

The Michigan Law Review Association for the essay: J.M. Balkin (1994), 'Transcendental Deconstruction, Transcendent Justice', *Michigan Law Review*, **92**, pp. 1131–86.

Oxford University Press for the essay: Timothy A.O. Endicott (1996), 'Linguistic Indeterminacy', *Oxford Journal of Legal Studies*, **16**, pp. 667–97. Copyright © 1996 Oxford University Press.

Southern California Law Review for the essays: Thomas C. Grey (1985), 'The Hermeneutics File', *Southern California Law Review*, **58**, pp. 211–36; David Couzens Hoy (1985), 'Interpreting the Law: Hermeneutical and Poststructuralist Perspectives', *Southern California Law Review*, **58**, pp. 135–76. Reprinted with permission of the Southern California Law Review. Page 135, the Contents page of this essay, has not been reproduced in this volume.

Texas Law Review for the essay: Sanford Levinson (1982), 'Law as Literature', *Texas Law Review*, **60**, pp. 373–403. Copyright © 1982 Texas Law Review Association. Reprinted by permission.

University of California Press for the essay: Robert C. Post (1988), 'Cultural Heterogeneity and Law: Pornography, Blasphemy, and the First Amendment', *California Law Review*, **76**, pp. 297–335. Copyright © 1988 California Law Review, Inc.

University of Chicago Law Review for the essay: James Boyd White (1985), 'Law as Rhetoric, Rhetoric as Law: The Arts of Cultural and Communal Life', *University of Chicago Law Review*, **52**, pp. 684–702. A revised version of this essay appears in *Heracles' Bow: Essays in the Rhetoric and Poetics of the Law*, (University of Wisconsin Press, 1986).

Washington & Lee University for the essay: Stanley E. Fish (1988), 'The Annual John Randolph Tucker Lecture – Force', *Washington and Lee Law Review*, **45**, pp. 883–902.

Yale Law Journal Co. and Fred B. Rothman & Co. for the essay: James Boyd White (1987), 'Thinking About Our Language', *Yale Law Journal*, **96**, pp. 1960–83. A revised version of this essay appears in *Justice as Translation: An Essay in Cultural and Legal Criticism*, (University of Chicago Press, 1990).

Yale Law & Policy Review for the essay: Thomas I. Emerson (1984), 'Pornography and the First Amendment: A Reply to Professor MacKinnon', *Yale Law and Policy Review*, **3**, pp. 130–43.

Every effort has been made to trace all the copyright holders, but if any have been inadvertently overlooked the publishers will be pleased to make the necessary arrangement at the first opportunity.

Preface to the Second Series

The first series of the International Library of Essays in Law and Legal Theory has established itself as a major research resource with fifty-eight volumes of the most significant theoretical essays in contemporary legal studies. Each volume contains essays of central theoretical importance in its subject area and the series as a whole makes available an extensive range of valuable material of considerable interest to those involved in research, teaching and the study of law.

The rapid growth of theoretically interesting scholarly work in law has created a demand for a second series which includes more recent publications of note and earlier essays to which renewed attention is being given. It also affords the opportunity to extend the areas of law covered in the first series.

The new series follows the successful pattern of reproducing entire essays with the original page numbers as an aid to comprehensive research and accurate referencing. Editors have selected not only the most influential essays but also those which they consider to be of greatest continuing importance. The objective of the second series is to enlarge the scope of the library, include significant recent work and reflect a variety of editorial perspectives.

Each volume is edited by an expert in the specific area who makes the selection on the basis of the quality, influence and significance of the essays, taking care to include essays which are not readily available. Each volume contains a substantial introduction explaining the context and significance of the essays selected.

I am most grateful for the care which volume editors have taken in carrying out the complex task of selecting and presenting essays which meet the exacting criteria set for the series.

TOM CAMPBELL
Series Editor
The Faculty of Law
The Australian National University

Introduction

I

Law has always made special demands on language. Legal positivists remind us that law consists, at least in significant part, of general rules put forward and enforced by persons with power over others. Rules are expressed in language. The effective transmission and understanding of such rules depends on the clarity and transparency of language.

Of course, transparency may be an ideal that is most honoured in the breach. The language of law and its processes throughout history is notoriously formalized and hermetic. Specialized usages are often accessible only to a trained mandarinate. From Aristophanes to Kafka, writers mock law as a paradigm of linguistic inaccessiblity.

Thus, the relationship of law and language has a paradoxical aspect. Law involves performative uses of language – most notably, the enactments of laws and the passing of judgments by courts – that marry words to action. Lives are significantly ordered and altered by these kinds of linguistic acts. Therefore, a domain of language in which transparency is most to be desired is among those in which it is least likely to be found.

Given the fact that law consists in specialized linguistic usages, one must assume that those trained in law have always been self-conscious about language. What is new in the contemporary period is that understandings about language drawn from *other* disciplines – philosophy, literature, anthropology – have coloured law's understanding of itself. Self-consciousness about language in the history of law seems to have coexisted with naiveté. Law, in at least some of its manifestations and institutions, has aspired to a kind of precision and a kind of imperviousness to interpretative variability that is impossible for any form of communication, for any institution that relies on the retrieval of meaning from texts.

Given the complexity of the relationship between its elements, one can hardly expect the phrase 'law and language' to demarcate a discrete field of interest and study. It is both too vague and too inclusive: virtually all of contemporary jurisprudence fits within its embrace. Positivism, Dworkinian naturalism, legal hermaneutics and critical theory all put forth theses about the use and abuse of language in law and legal institutions. Cultural anthropology and literary theory offer relevant and engaging hypotheses about how language works and how it affects the balance of order and disorder.

Any selection of essays for a volume on law and language is bound to be more than ordinarily arbitrary. Mindful of the focus of other volumes in this series, I have tried to avoid turning it into a volume predominantly on contemporary analytical jurisprudence, critical jurisprudence or legal hermeneutics. Even so, it is neither possible nor desirable to sidestep the preoccupations of these disciplines. These essays address them, but often obliquely.

The essays in Parts I and II fall within the inchoate discipline that has come to be known as 'law and literature'. To students, the phrase typically connotes works of fiction about law and lawyers. To scholars, it has come to designate the lessons to be learned about law from the study of literature, literary theory and linguistics. Literary theory, in turn, has come to embrace a general inquiry into the nature and constraints of understanding and communication. The essays in these two Parts hint at the scope, ambition and diversity of these writings.

The essays in Part III shift attention to the law *of* language and literature. The earlier essays pay deference to the notion that all thought and all language use are constrained processes – constrained by our capacities, our experiences, our assumptions, and our aims. By contrast, the essays in this Part consider the deliberate constraint of language through legal rules. It has long been recognized that government, through law, has the power to affect the expression of ideas. Law may shape and limit expression either through explicit prohibitions or through implicit subsidies, taxes and other forms of encouragement and discouragement. It may also protect speech and other forms of expression. Any legal system that identifies and rests on fundamental rights is likely to accord the right of expression a prominent place.

II

In his distinguished introduction to critical legal theory, *Critical Legal Histories*, Robert Gordon remarks, in an aside, that 'the law schools tend to pick up mainstream intellectual opinion ten to fifteen years late'. Perhaps Gordon is being generous. The essays by James Boyd White and Richard Hyland in Part I admonish legal theorists to take seriously intellectual ideas that have been around for a long time. Some may trace these ideas to romanticism and Hegelianism, others to the sociology of knowledge, and still others to the Wittgenstinian and Kuhnian revolutions in philosophy.

White's first essay (Chapter 1) advises us that:

> . . . habits of thought and language have tendencies, pressures of their own, that can perhaps be checked or controlled, but ought certainly be reckoned with: how language has real power over the mind that uses it, even the mind that contributes to its reformulation. The cultural implications of one's language can be addressed, perhaps even overcome; but the tendencies are there, and have a force of their own. (this volume, p. 11)

He describes an understanding of thought and language that conjures with *concepts*, and he opposes it to a literary understanding. His point seems to be that if we assume that thought involves the manipulation of concepts and that language involves the representation of concepts with words, we fall prey to all the fallacies of naive Platonism. The main fallacy is that words pick out concepts whose parameters are fixed for all time and across the speakers, across all communities of speakers. This fallacy afflicts both legal philosophers, who speak about such concepts as law, justice and desert, and practising lawyers and law-makers, who may assume the fixity of such concepts as property, contract, intention and due process.

White wants us to approach these Platonic assumptions with informed scepticism. We must be mindful of the fact that the experiences, beliefs, interests, and criteria of one historical period, one intellectual community or one individual will not necessarily, or even probably, be those of another. Far from assuming that concepts are timeless and part of a store of common meanings, we must see every act of communication as an act of translation fraught with the possibility of a breakdown in meaning. That our utterances have common meanings is not so much a foregone conclusion as an act of faith to be examined and validated in each instance of expression.

White sees hope and opportunity in the fact that communities and individuals reappropriate language in new ways over time. Thus, what Wittgenstein's followers call a 'language-game' evolves. What Kuhn describes as a 'paradigm shift', whereby our ways of thinking about a domain of experience change to accommodate new kinds of experience and new criteria of truth, may in law and other social practices be a characteristic and a constant rather than a rare feature of language use and understanding. In other words, the institutions that make decisions – in particular the appellate courts – are self-conscious about using paradigms and about rethinking them.

Like White, Richard Hyland (Chapter 2) is also concerned with meaning and the perils of translation. But his attention is focused not on translation between individuals, but between national cultures. Again like White, Hyland is wary of conceptualism, the assumption that such concepts as 'law' cross cultural boundaries unscathed. Rather, he sees national cultures as representing diverse and irreconcilable ways of understanding and expressing experience. A culture's language, its legal system, and its pedagogy cohere and have a distinctive, describable character. What this means, for Hyland, is that the habitué of one culture risks the kind of blindness that White also fears, the blind assumption that one's own language, one's own legal system, one's own ways of understanding are the only valid system and represent determinate concepts in themselves. The remedy, for Hyland, is to come to know other cultures and to see one's own as an outsider. In this way, one comes to see communication properly as translation.

Hyland's conclusion that one cannot look critically at one's culture, language, and legal system except from the standpoint of a different culture may be debatable. Complex cultures and systems of understanding arguably have their own internal methods and traditions of self-scrutiny. The clash of insights and points of view may proceed as productively within a culture as between national cultures. For White, it is the job of each individual to turn communication into such an opportunity.

III

Whereas the three essays in Part I offer an overview of a linguistic and conceptual issue that lies at the heart of every contemporary movement in legal theory – the determinacy and indeterminacy of language, both general and legal – those in Part II delve into its implications.

In Chapter 4 Timothy Endicott makes clear that much nonsense attends the discussion of determinacy. Two extreme positions are plainly untenable. The idea that language is perfectly determinate, an assumption that undergirds many formalistic accounts of legal (and other kinds of) reasoning, is hardly supportable. It is clear that at least some questions of meaning are matters of debate and that we lack decision procedures for resolving such debates; language, as H.L.A. Hart reminds us in *The Concept of Law*, has open texture. Of course, the degree of uncertainty that attends determinations of meaning is a matter of text and context. A STOP sign may be a paradigm of determinate, unnuanced meaning, but even that is true only insofar as we have a shared practice within which the functions of such simple texts are learned.

If it is absurd to claim that all texts in all contexts have determinate meaning, it is equally so to claim that every reader gives unique meaning to each text in the light of her idiosyncratic background, experiences and purposes. The final insight of hermeneutics is not solipsism. Any remotely adequate theory of interpretation must account for both the centrifugal and the centripetal aspects of the process. It must also explain both the fact that we are part of what Stanley Fish calls an 'interpretive community', that we play language-games whose rules we share with others, and the fact that each of us necessarily plays our own variations on a common theme. In other words, it must explain how agreement *and* disagreement are both possible, and how disagreement is itself the occasion for indulging a shared practice involving guidelines for how to disagree.

Sanford Levinson's essay, 'Law as Literature' (Chapter 5), describes the range of interpretative theories that have been crafted to respond to the challenge of indeterminacy in judicial interpretation. Drawing on literary theory, he stresses the felicity of the metaphor of *constructing* meaning rather than *finding* it. In particular, he raises questions about the role of the author's own understanding of his text. Arriving at meaning, Levinson suggests, is hardly a matter of merely discovering (*finding* out) what the author intended. Even though one must be cognizant of the intentional character of all texts and of the fact that the author had relevant intentions, one must also be prepared to see the author, after the event of writing, as potentially just one more reader of the text.

These possibilities are explored in a particularly fecund parable that constitutes Tom Grey's 'The Hermeneutics File' (Chapter 6) in which Grey confronts his protagonist, a law professor, with an interpretative task that is idiosyncratic and, at the same time, a metaphor for interpretation in general. The task itself requires the protagonist/narrator to reflect upon and revise his own closely held position about text creation and interpretation. The next essay, 'Interpreting the Law', by David Hoy offers a more systematic and formal account of the constraints on legal interpretation. Hoy defends Hans-Georg Gadamer's hermeneutic theory and compares it with the work of Jürgen Habermas.

In Chapter 8 J.M. Balkin tackles the same issues from a different perspective, claiming 'to integrate deconstructive insights about language and meaning with the reality of individual subjects and the claims of individual responsibility' (this volume: 264). In other words, he tries to show how the nihilistic or solipsistic implications of deconstruction can be transcended by an understanding of persons as subjects who can only achieve justice through the recognition and reconciliation of others' points of view.

In the last essay in Part II, Stanley Fish raises political questions about the constraints on interpretation. Is law a limitation on force or merely a manifestation of it – that is, force by another name? To the extent that law is indeterminate, it arguably forfeits its claim as a bulwark against force. It threatens to become a rhetorical tool that lends force the camouflage of legitimacy.

IV

In the liberal tradition, two justifications for a right of free expression coexist. On one hand, a so-called free market of ideas is said to be the best guarantor, or at least the most fertile ground, for good politics and good government. Free speech is a manifestation of democracy and a check on authoritarianism. This justification relies to some extent on the good sense of persons, on their ability to distinguish better ideas from worse and to adopt those better ideas.

On the other hand, even if persons lack good sense and if free expression does not lead to greater general beneficence, free expression can be justified as a manifestation of personal autonomy and, therefore, a fundamental right. Complete personhood, on this theory, cannot be realized without it.

Every society has taboos. Even in a legal system that recognizes a robust right of free expression, certain uses of language are marginal and controversial. The language of sex, violence, and especially sex-and-violence-together typically has this status. In part the reason is that such expressions have a performative aspect in that these uses of language itself are intended to arouse, coerce or harm. Such language may simultaneously express ideas and be performative. (Indeed, the philosopher, J.L. Austin, points out that language typically involves what he calls locutionary and perlocutionary acts simultaneously.)

The last three decades have seen a renaissance of scholarship about free expression. In the American context, this takes the form of debates over the scope of the first amendment to the Constitution; in the international arena, it is often a discussion about fundamental human rights. The American debates show an erosion and confusion of traditional political categories. Critics on both the left and the right of the political spectrum argue that the scope of free expression should be reconsidered and circumscribed. On the left, scholars mindful of feminist and race issues suggest that traditionally protected speech can and does perpetuate a culture in which groups are harmed and silenced. Hate speech and pornography are said to be flagrant examples of this. On the right, critics argue that some protected speech subverts social harmony. At the same time, proponents of a robust and broad understanding of the first amendment also have disparate political orientations, from the libertarian on the traditional right to the liberal on the left.

Louis Henkin's classic essay (Chapter 10) acknowledges the links between expression and action, but locates the core of First Amendment protection in the ideational content of the expression. He suggests that debates about limiting the scope of protection characteristically label some ideas as corrupt and immoral. Such ideas, it is said, corrupt us with their immorality. Henkin argues that these categories and causal accounts are based on simplistic and outdated assumptions about human nature and that they have their root in a view of government that gives it a quasi-religious role, a role incompatible with constitutional principles.

Catharine MacKinnon's familiar and highly influential essay (Chapter 11) sets out the radical feminist argument for balancing the right of free expression against the right of discrimination, and thus reversing the discriminatory effect of expressions and ideas that harm, objectify and silence women. Thomas Emerson's response in Chapter 12 summarizes the liberal answer to such arguments. Liberals identify the ideals of the American Constitution with a system in which the remedy for harmful ideas and speech is more speech, responsive speech, rather than less, and in which government is not in the business of selecting among ideas on the basis of harmful or benign content and effects.

The persuasiveness of the liberal argument relies on the distinction between a public domain in which all ideas are equally protected and a private domain in which some ideas dominate the social and cultural context. Thus a liberal must have faith that governmental neutrality achieves a common good and is more than a tacit subsidization of the most powerful voices in the private domain, as MacKinnon assumes and fears. Liberals fear that a government that openly and officially embraces the power to endorse some ideas and censor others will inevitably be authoritarian and corrupt.

In 'Cultural Heterogeneity and Law' (Chapter 13) Robert Post finds a controversial assumption about the First Amendment at the core of the arguments of those who would limit it. For them, the politics of free expression is fuelled by a pluralist ideal whereby the values of competing groups are balanced in the prevailing culture. Law and politics must be adjusted to achieve that balance. MacKinnon's agenda commends such an adjustment. Other critical theorists clearly accept this assumption. For Post, the First Amendment stands not for pluralism but individualism, a system in which each individual may choose her own values in reaction to, and preference to, those of any group.

Debates about free expression are broadly relevant to any system of law and rights. The issues raised in the American constitutional context can be generalized. Ultimately they involve a notion of the conditions of human flourishing. The liberal ideal is that these conditions require exposure to as unconstrained a panoply of ideas and thoughts as possible and the opportunity to express one's own conclusions. Underlying the ideal is optimism – the optimism that individuals can be trusted to use these opportunities to live well and harmoniously.

Part I
Law as Expression

[1]

Thinking About Our Language

James Boyd White†

Except for one meeting, which I will describe below, I knew Bob Cover only through his writings. This circumstance was of course a disappointment to me, for our interests were similar, and his death now makes the loss irreparable. But perhaps this is less of a limitation than would normally be the case, for as much as any one in the law Bob was, and is, actively present in his writing, both as a person and as a mind.—But that dichotomy of person and mind gets it wrong, for what I would like to catch is a sense of fusion or integration: of intellect and passion, sympathy and objectivity, politics and thought, all suffused with the sense that law has meaning, whether we like it or not, and meaning at many different levels—for the slave, or master, or other victim of the law, for the judge torn apart by the injustice of the laws he is sworn to apply, for the student and professor and community whose lives are so largely defined by the law they have not made. But the meanings of the law do not just lie inertly out there in the world. They must be actively created and sustained, for the most part by the people of the law, who live in the great paradox of human life that implicates us all in the systems of belief and action we seek to criticize and change. Bob Cover's great gift was for seeing law not simply as a set of rules, nor as an instrument for social control, nor as the expression of policy, but as a system of meaning in its own right. In this he spoke to those of use who are drawn to the law as a life not merely of power but of significance.

The only occasion I spent time with Bob was at a conference, where we both made presentations and talked about our papers afterwards. He criticized mine, I remember, for being too harsh in its judgment of the opinion of Chief Justice Taft in *Olmstead v. United States.*[1] This was an authoritarian and rigid opinion towards which he was in no way naturally inclined; yet his capacity for sympathetic understanding led him to see in this unexpected place if not merit or virtue at least humanity struggling with its own limits.

This essay, which is dedicated to him, is about language, one of his

---

† Hart Wright Professor of Law, Professor of English, and Adjunct Professor of Classical Studies, The University of Michigan. I wish to thank Rudolf Arnheim, Terence Ball, Alton Becker, Lee Bollinger, Kenneth DeWoskin, Thomas Eisele, Paul Friedrich, Lemuel Johnson, Bruce Mannheim, Terrance Sandalow, Frederick Schauer, Domna Stanton, Joseph Vining, and Christina Whitman for their very helpful comments on an earlier draft.

1. 277 U.S. 438, 455 (1928).

Thinking About Our Language

interests as well as my own. It is intended to assert the value and primacy of what I call literary discourse over a certain kind of academic language, and in doing so to suggest a possibility for more fully integrated and living speech, in the law and elsewhere. In it I set forth a view of language, and its relation both to the individual mind and to the community, that underlies my own investigation of law as a system of meaning, as a culture at once literary and political, and I do so with the hope that it may also be of use to others similarly occupied. While I am sure Bob would have had much to criticize in it, I also like to think that he would have found its basic thrust congenial.

* * *

In a famous passage Thucydides says that during the wave of civil wars that followed the Corcyrean revolution words themselves lost their meaning. In the Crawley translation the passage reads as follows:

> Words had to change their ordinary meaning and to take that which was now given them. Reckless audacity came to be considered the courage of a loyal ally; prudent hesitation, specious cowardice; moderation was held to be a cloak for unmanliness; ability to see all sides of a question inaptness to act on any. Frantic violence became the attribute of manliness; cautious plotting, a justifiable means of self-defence. The advocate of extreme measures was always trustworthy; his opponent a man to be suspected. . . . Oaths of reconciliation, being only proffered on either side to meet an immediate difficulty, only held good so long as no other weapon was at hand; but when opportunity offered, he who first ventured to seize it and to take his enemy off his guard, thought this perfidious vengeance sweeter than an open one, since, considerations of safety apart, success by treachery won him the palm of superior intelligence. . . . [T]he moderate part of the citizens perished between the two, either for not joining in the quarrel, or because envy would not suffer them to escape.[2]

Here Thucydides talks about social collapse in terms that will seem all too familiar to us—think of Lebanon, for example—but what is most interesting to me is that he focuses attention on a verbal or linguistic deterioration that he finds associated with the social and political one. He does not claim that the shift in language causes the change in behavior; on the other hand, for him that shift does reflect a change in culture that makes certain kinds of speech and conduct—those we associate with civilized life—increasingly impossible.

For me this passage is a kind of emblem, defining a topic and sug-

2. Thucydides, The Peloponnesian War 189-91 (Crawley trans. 1951).

The Yale Law Journal Vol. 96: 1960, 1987

gesting a view of life that directs attention to the relation between language, on the one hand, and both the individual self and collective life on the other. Without attempting to argue for them here, I shall begin by sketching out some views about the nature of language that suggest the importance of rendering our languages and their uses self-conscious, so that we may criticize them; I shall then, in a spirit of experiment, try to make conscious, and to criticize, that part of our own language that is centered on the word "concept" and its cognates.

I. Reciprocity

The essential feature of human life exemplified in the passage from Thucydides is the structural reciprocity between language and the individual character (or what we call personality or identity): Each of us is partly made by our language, which gives us the categories in which we perceive the world and which form our motives; but we are not simply that, for we are users and makers of our language too; and in remaking our language we contribute to the remaking of our characters and lives, for good or ill. This remaking is necessarily a shared or collective process, for language itself is socially constructed. The reciprocity I speak of thus exists at the collective as well as at the individual level, for our community is defined by our language—our language *is* the set of shared expectations and common terms that enable us to think of ourselves as a "we"—and that language too can be transformed.

This implies that on some occasions at least we may be able to contribute to the remaking of our shared resources of meaning, and thus of our public or communal lives. This is obviously the case with great artists and thinkers—their work changes the terms in which we think and talk, the ways in which we imagine and constitute ourselves—and upon reflection we can see a similar process at work in ordinary life as well, as we make and remake our own languages in our written and oral conversations with one another. Language, and the world it constitutes, are thus forever changing—"moderate prudence" loses its force as an appeal and thus as a socially validated possibility—and we change with them, both as individuals and as communities. The ineradicable flux of language, and of the world, so recently "discovered" and lamented by the modernist who learns at last that the language and methods of science are after all not good for all forms of thought and life, is actually structural to human experience, a condition of life that has been addressed again and again by our predecessors. What is required to face this circumstance is not a science in the usual sense but an art—the art of reconstituting language, self, and community under conditions of ontological relativism, an art that is literary and rhetorical in character and of which we ourselves are the most important subject.

But what kind of art is this and where can we learn it? Here my own answer has been to turn to our predecessors and betters, to see what they have done. How do Homer and Thucydides, how do Swift and Jane Austen, how do Burke and the framers of the Constitution, address the circumstance I have described, that language constantly changes meaning and that we change too? If words lose their meaning, they also get new meanings, and what is the art by which that is done and done well?

In reading and rereading these and other texts with such questions in mind, while writing *When Words Lose Their Meaning*, I gradually worked out—in fact largely learned from these texts—what I call a "way of reading," which I could then bring back to them in an organized way. This way of reading proceeds by focusing attention on three places: (1) On the nature of the language a particular writer or speaker has inherited—the language that gives her some things to say and do with words and denies her others, the language that constitutes her natural and social world and gives it meaning. (This is a species of cultural and rhetorical analysis.) (2) On the way he or she acts upon this language, for good or ill, modifying its central terms, or reducing it to cliche, enriching or impoverishing it. (This is a species of literary analysis.) And (3), in a different dimension, on the nature of the social and ethical relations that the writer establishes with his reader, with the people he speaks about, and with the natural world. This can range from the relationship of two that is implied in the making of any text to a set of relationships that creates a whole world: Burke's attempt to create a constitution in his text that will be a constitution for Great Britain—a way of talking that defines a community and its relation to nature—is one example; our own Constitution and certain public and legal texts made under it are others. (Here the analysis is ethical and political.)

From this point of view, the law offers an especially interesting form of life, for at its central moment, the legal hearing, it works by testing one version of its language against another, one way of telling a story and thinking about it against another, and by then making a self-conscious choice between them. It is an institution that remakes its own language and it does this under conditions of regularity and publicity that render the process subject to scrutiny of an extraordinary kind. As an ethical or political matter, the structure of the legal process entails remarkable possibilities—little enough realized in the event—for thinking about and achieving that simultaneous affirmation of self and recognition of other that many (I among them) think is the essential ethical task of a discoursing and differing humanity. These ethical possibilities arise from the fact that the premises of the legal hearing commit it to a momentary equality among its speakers and to the recognition that all ways of talking, including its own, may be subject to criticism and change.

The larger public world provides a less formally structured version of the same process, for language and politics work reciprocally, each changing the other, with no dominant partner. I do not think, that is, that one sphere of life, say the economic or the intellectual, determines all the others; thus I think that there is no privileged ground of analysis upon which we can stand, no privileged subject by explaining which we can explain—or ought to try to explain—everything else. The student of politics and society must thus face at the official and collective level exactly the same reciprocity that exists in the relation between the individual self and its culture more generally. We are always making ourselves, as individuals and communities, always making our language; yet we are always being made by our language, by our past, and by the actions of others, and the line between the making and the made is never clear. This means, among other things, that our own habits of mind, of perception, and of feeling are contingent and changeable; they are thus a central part of our proper subject, and this is true for us not only as citizens, or cultural actors more generally, but in our professional lives, as lawyers and teachers and writers. Our work cannot claim to be the kind of science that assumes a validity beyond culture, beyond language, but should hope to be a literary or rhetorical art, a way of working with and within our language.

Once one looks to the languages in which community and character are constituted, one suddenly sees that political and social analysis involves the understanding of a whole set of things not normally thought to belong to it: language, mind, and the reciprocal relation between them; the way language is made and changed, by individuals and by communities; and the way language resists change. To think about language, especially about language change, is to require attention to the processes of speaking and reading more generally, to composition and interpretation. This in turn brings into our field of concern the nature of the ethical and political relations that are appropriate to people who conceive of themselves as language-users and language-makers.

Talking about "politics" itself thus becomes a species of what it describes: How ought we to talk in our own performances? About those performances? These questions invite us to be self-reflective, to make our own processes of thought and speech the subject of our critical attention—for whatever we claim to believe about others must also be true for us. They invite us to resist the fallacies of reductionist theories that can on their own terms account for everything in the world but themselves.

Thinking About Our Language

This means that as we talk about politics or law we shall be taking positions, implicitly or explicitly, on certain large questions about the nature of language and its relation both to culture and to the individual self. To ask, "What are the proper expectations to bring to the political and linguistic activities of others?" is to ask also, "What are the proper expectations to bring to what we ourselves say and do?"

II. The Language of Concepts

I want to start to work out a line of response to that question by thinking of some of the implications of the word "concept" (and its cognates) especially as it is used in thought and writing about language and politics. I choose this word because it is a central term in our discourse, and one that for most people seems to be completely unproblematic, a perfectly natural way to talk. But for me it is problematic in the extreme: It has overtones and implications that I find difficult, and it is these difficulties that I wish to explain.

A.

In what follows I shall describe two rather extreme types or models of thought, the "conceptual" and the "linguistic" (or "literary") and I shall argue for the latter and against the former. These will be somewhat caricatured positions—you may even think I am attacking a straw man—but I think it may be useful to pursue them nonetheless. I should say at the outset that the position I mean to support is not the traditional "middle view," but the extreme position on the linguistic end, or what might be called a literary-rhetorical view of intellectual and cultural life.

Although I focus attention on what I see to be the dangers of the word "concept" it is not my object to eliminate the term from our language but rather to identify certain assumptions about language and life that are often associated with its use—assumptions that I think false or misleading, but that can exist, I hasten to add, without its help, and that can also be at least partly denied or resisted by one who uses the term with appropriate qualifications. I seek to use this word, that is, as a way into certain larger qualities of our culture, certain habits of our own minds that are so firmly fixed that they may easily seem to inhere in the nature of thought itself.[3]

In talking about this word and its associations I speak simply as a local informant about my own language, without any claims to knowledge beyond those of my reader, whose language it also is. I do not ask that what

3. Other terms could afford similar access to this region of our culture and of our minds: the word "theory," for example, or "problem" or "knowledge" or "reason" or even "fact."

I say be taken on faith or authority, but that it be checked against the reader's own experience; and I speak out of the recognition not only that my account of my language may be wrong but that even if it is right it may not, indeed will not, wholly correspond with the experience of another, for there is a sense in which all of our languages are different, none of them identical.

I begin, then, with a statement of my own experience of our language, and I recognize that it has something of the character of an admission: the admission that as I have read articles, mainly in journals of law and philosophy, but in other fields too, that use the word "concept"—the concept of law, the concept of right, the concept of equality—I have found myself repeatedly saying that I simply do not know what this word means. I keep wishing that the writer would use another word—like "word"—or just drop the term entirely. As I say, I do not think that the word "concept" and all its derivatives should be driven from the language. "Conception" as a word for "understanding"—as in "my conception" of law or legal argument, "my conception" of good teaching—seems to me useful; and I suppose I would use "concept" in mathematics and perhaps some other similar fields, as in the "concept of a triangle," or the "concept of a carburetor." And since it is part of my view that writers remake their languages all the time, there is no reason in principle why "concept" could not be used by one writer or another in a way that is adequately, even beautifully, controlled or qualified.

For all language, not just the language of concepts, has its dangers: All languages threaten to take over the mind and to control its operation, with all this implies for one's feelings, for one's sense of self, and for the possibilities of meaning in one's actions and relations.[4] The art of all speech, all expression, thus lies in learning to qualify a language while we use it: in finding ways to recognize its omissions, its distortions, its false claims and pretensions, ways to acknowledge other modes of speaking that qualify or undercut it. The art of expression is the art of talking two ways at once: the art of many-voicedness.[5] So it is with the word "concept": Its more appropriate uses, in science and mathematics say, might remain unchanged, for there perhaps it is properly qualified and controlled by the rest of the relevant discourse; but I think its use in linguistics, law, politics, and so forth should be more fully and explicitly controlled by arts of qualification, including those of irony, ambiguity, and contrast, than is

4. Terms that present similar dangers in the field of literary criticism are such nouns as "symbol," or "meaning," or the verb "represent," or the preposition "about" (as in "this poem is about . . .").

5. This view is developed at length in J.B. White, The Legal Imagination (1973) and J.B. White, Heracles' Bow 77-106 (1985).

now usually the case. I am speaking, then, not of necessities but of tendencies, of the forces a particular mode of speaking seems to generate, the directions it moves us, or what might be called its cultural implications. These are the pressures with which our art must come to terms.

B.

But to say this is to invite the question, What can I mean by the "tendency" of a particular form of speech, or its "moving us" in certain directions? Let us consider as an example the language and culture of contemporary economics. Of course economics is a useful, legitimate, and interesting field of inquiry, but it is also a culture, and a culture shaped in part by the implications of its intellectual and verbal habits. Suppose you decided to study the way wealth is created by exchanges, and for purposes of analysis you posited a set of actors, of equal age and competence, each with some control over the material of the universe—called resources—and you assumed as a fundamental psychological principle an unlimited acquisitiveness on the part of each, and therefore, with respect to the resources, a severe structural scarcity. Suppose further you assumed that each agent was interested in its own welfare only, and thus perceived itself to be in permanent competition with all other agents (except those whom it chose to make the object of what economists call altruism). Next you assumed a medium in which surplus could be accumulated without limit. Then you began to see what flowed from these assumptions and tried to analyze real world events in these terms.

If you actually did this you would find yourself caught in a game, perhaps a fascinating game, testing your capacity to draw certain kinds of logical conclusions from the premises stated, a game with a force and life of its own. You would become a player, an economist; you would inhabit a world with its own values, its own realities, its own rewards. From such simplicity, such complexity! And such fun, too, though for me of rather an empty kind (at least until an attempt was made to connect the economic language and its culture to others). For good or ill, the language and its practices would gradually start to shape the way you saw the world and felt about it, your sense of yourself and of others. You might find yourself, for example, thinking and talking too much as if people really were the objects or calculating machines that economics assumes them to be or accepting "GNP" as a measure of a nation's economic health.

Of course one could claim that the language of economics is a scientific theory and as such wholly value-neutral. An economic theory is a simplified version of reality, meant, as all such theories are, not to be a full picture of anything but to permit the organization of data in simplified forms so that predictions can be made, assumptions tested, and so on. (Not

The Yale Law Journal Vol. 96: 1960, 1987

to worry, says Milton Friedman, economic theory is merely a filing system, to be proved or falsified by experiment. We don't *mean* what we say: We speak always in hypotheses.[6]) It is also conceivable that the language and culture of contemporary economics, and the body of knowledge they generate, could be subordinated to another culture, another set of values—say concern for the environment or for the welfare of those who seem least able to help themselves. But to achieve such a subordination is for the economic culture as a whole impossible, and for the individual economist difficult indeed: The premises of the discipline to which she has given herself are inconsistent with the premises of the uses to which she wishes to put what she discovers. In the end, despite its claims to be merely hypothetical, economic theory becomes a culture of its own and can be studied and judged as such.[7]

My present point is not to criticize economics—similar analyses, with similarly distressing conclusions, could be made of the cultures of other disciplines, including literary criticism and law—but to suggest how habits of thought and language have tendencies, pressures of their own, that can perhaps be checked or controlled, but ought certainly be reckoned with: how language has real power over the mind that uses it, even the mind that contributes to its reformulation. The cultural implications of one's language can be addressed, perhaps even overcome; but the tendencies are there, and have a force of their own.

C.

To return to our particular subject, then, we can ask, What are the subcultural implications of the word "concept"? Its first pressure, I think, is to direct attention away from language to something else: to the realm of ideas, to what is in the mind, or to some field of intellectual reality, and in each instance to something that is assumed to exist in a realm apart from language. "Concepts" are not words; they are the internal or intellectual phenomena that words are thought to label, as markers, or towards which words are thought to point. To talk about concepts is thus to take a step in the direction of talking as if words have no force of their own, as if they are transparent or discardable once the idea or concept is apprehended. On this view, in its extreme form, the function of words is either

6. *See* M. FRIEDMAN, *The Methodology of Positive Economics*, in ESSAYS IN POSITIVE ECONOMICS 3, 7 (1953).

7. My remarks are most true of a particular branch of economics, neoclassical microeconomics of the sort especially associated with Chicago, but I think other forms of contemporary economic thought present their own versions of these difficulties. For elaboration of these points, see White, *How Should We Talk About Corporations? The Languages of Economics and of Citizenship*, 94 YALE L.J. 1416 (1985); White, *Economics and Law: Two Cultures in Tension*, 54 TENN. L. REV. (forthcoming 1987).

Thinking About Our Language

to identify external phenomena that can be observed or apprehended without the use of language—that rock, or tree, or person—or to define or clarify concepts, which also exist outside language and beyond culture. ("He has a concept in his mind." Is that statement true or false? Neither: It is dangerous.)

One extreme form of the kind of discourse that talk about concepts invites is what I call theoretical, by which I mean that it is definitional, deductive, and empirical in nature. We define our terms on the assumption that they can be reduced to phrases that could substitute for them; rationality consists in manipulating these definitions either in patterns of deductive coherence or in hypothetically descriptive patterns that will be tested by reference to extralinguistic phenomena, which will in turn establish whether they are true or false. Rational discourse, so conceived, is propositional in character; and knowledge, whether factual or conceptual, is of necessity propositional too. Propositions are what we reason about and reason with. (Hence all the talk in the philosophy journals about P and P'.)

This set of assumptions derives from the model of "science" that has so powerfully dominated our intellectual life in this century. But the habit of mind and language that I wish to identify is far deeper in our intellectual culture than the disciplines that explicitly model themselves on science. We see it also when a classicist talks about the Greek "concept" of honor, when an analytic philosopher talks about the "concept" of a right, when an anthropologist talks about the Hopi "concept" of time, when a linguist reduces utterances to propositions that have the "same," ultimately conceptual, meaning to be expressed variously in different languages (or "codes"), when a lawyer talks about the "concept" of freedom of speech, when a sociologist or psychologist represents social or psychological "types" as if they corresponded with reality, when someone establishes a department in "The History of Ideas," or when a teacher of writing praises a text for the clarity with which it "gets its basic concepts across." People may of course resist the implications of their usage—by thinking of conceptual variety or change or instability, for example—but this can be done only against the force of the term itself.[8]

8. Consider the following quotation from a writer I admire, composed as part of an effort that I also admire, namely, to insist that modern philosophy recognize the differences that characterize different cultures and languages:

> In fact, of course, moral concepts change as social life changes. I deliberately do not write "because social life changes," for this might suggest that social life is one thing, morality another, and that there is merely an external, contingent causal relationship between them. This is obviously false. Moral concepts are embodied in and are partially constitutive of forms of social life. One key way in which we may identify one form of social life as distinct from another is by identifying differences in moral concepts. So it is an elementary commonplace to point out that there is no precise English equivalent for the Greek word δικαιοσυνη, usually

One particular danger presented by such locutions is that we may find ourselves speaking as if there were no reason why people in different cultures cannot have the same concepts, no reason why different languages cannot express the same concepts. To the part of our mind that works this way, indeed, variety of language may come to seem mainly a nuisance, a bother to be eliminated if possible in the interest of what we conceive of as "more efficient communication." For implicit in most talk of this sort is the premise or claim that concepts can be wholly restated, and restated in various languages. Underlying this is the assumption that "communication" occurs not when we speak the same languages—when we understand each other's utterances in the sense that we know how to respond to them, but when we have the same concepts. Although the conceptual world is communicable only *through* language, it is supposed to exist on a plane above and beyond language, which disappears when its task is done.

While the conceptual view is in principle neutral among languages, and thus would concede that the Chinese translation of our concepts could be as accurate as any statement of our own, in practice it is imperialistic. On this view of language there is no reason why we should learn any other language, any other habits of thought, than our own. At the practical level there is the implied claim that our own language is or can be a metalanguage, in which all propositions can be uttered, all truths stated. And the sense that our language—whether we mean by this English, or economics, or law—is the language into which all others can be translated presents the dangers of linguistic imperialism familiar to us from the ex-

---

translated justice. And this is not a mere linguistic defect, so that what Greek achieves by a single word English needs a periphrasis to achieve. It is rather that the occurrence of certain concepts in ancient Greek discourse and of others in modern English marks a difference between two forms of social life. To understand a concept, to grasp the meaning of the words which express it, is always at least to learn what the rules are which govern the use of such words and so to grasp the role of the concept in language and social life. This in itself would suggest strongly that different forms of social life will provide different roles for concepts to play. Or at least for some concepts this seems likely to be the case. There certainly are concepts which are unchanging over long periods, and which must be unchanging for one of two reasons. Either they are highly specialized concepts belonging within stable and continuing disciplines, such as geometry; or else they are highly general concepts necessary to any language of any complexity. I have in mind here the family of concepts expressed by such words as *and*, *or*, and *if*. But moral concepts do not fall into either of these two classes.

A. MacIntyre, A Short History of Ethics 1-2 (1966).

Even this writer speaks of "understand[ing] a concept," of "grasp[ing] the meaning of words which express it," and of "rules governing the use of such words." For me these formulations draw attention away from the reality of text and language to another plane, which I think does not exist. I do not think words "express concepts"; I think that utterances or texts made of words have meanings, a rather different thing. I do not think that the use of words is reducible to "rules" (though of course we do have expectations, partly shared, to some degree expressible, which a particular use may confirm or disappoint). Finally, I think that even the key terms in our logic—"if," "and," "or"—shift from language to language too. Of course the analytic philosopher can insist upon the possibility of translating other locutions into his language, but that is to make exactly the sort of assertion that I think conceptual talk typically makes, and which I oppose.

perience of many colonial countries—the imposition, say, of English law on the Hindus or the Burmese, or the insistence that all that really needs to be said in Indonesia can be said in Dutch.[9]

Another danger, very widespread in our own world, is that talk about concepts tends to nominalize, and hence to reify, everything. The verb, the adverb, the adjective all give way to the noun. The effect is to create a universe of imagined intellectual objects arranged in quantitative or spatial relations to each other, but without the principle of life that is found in the active verb. Imagine a language that emphasized the verb instead of the noun and copula; our thought would be full of a sense of movement, life, and change, of actors engaged in action.

One who uses the word "concept" in the way I mean, then, is on his way towards making the error of the bureaucrat who can only imagine the world in the terms of his institution; of the Dean who thinks that the merits of any question can be made plain to her in the language of academic planning, without any shift of mind; of the lawyer who thinks that the world comes in legal categories; of the doctor who thinks that the definitions of disease in terms of physical cause and modes of treatment correspond perfectly to the experience of his or her patients; and so on. It is the error of thinking that one's own habits of mind and expression are not to be questioned, that they simply define rationality and coherence. One cannot use a language of concepts, after all, to reflect upon and criticize any of the languages that shape one's mind and world.[10]

D.

Talk about concepts is also intimately, though perhaps not inextricably, tied to dichotomous and linear thinking, to a commitment to a kind of coherence that denies that our terms have shifting and contrasting uses. The most fundamental rule of logic, that of noncontradiction, requires it: Each term in a logical system must be used in such a way that it either is or is not the case that it applies to the world, and, if the system is to be coherent, the word must be used in ways that are at least consistent and preferably identical. This is a struggle for the univocal, for the proposition

9. Consider here Robinson Crusoe's famous account of his relation to the person he found on the island: "[I]n a little time I began to speak to him, and teach him to speak to me; and first, I made him know his name should be Friday, which was the day I sav'd his life; . . . I likewise taught him to say Master, and then let him know, that was to be my name . . . ." D. DEFOE, ROBINSON CRUSOE 150 (Everyman's Library ed. 1975) (I owe this reference to Lemuel Johnson.).

10. Of course one can talk about the "concepts" of others with an emphasis on the differences, in an effort to recognize and value another way of thought and life. But I think that to use the term "concept" as a central part of one's vocabulary in such an enterprise is to undercut the enterprise itself, to move oneself and one's reader in the direction of thinking that the concepts exist apart from language and that they can thus be seen by us directly and talked about in our language without loss.

that is true or false, entailed or not entailed, and it works by propounding questions that must be answered yes or no. This mode of thought is thus not only dichotomous, it is inherently aggressive and defensive, for its claim is to mark out the terrain of truth.

But only one sort of truth. In ordinary language we use our words in richly overlapping, sometimes contrastive ways, and we know that we define our terms partly in the way we use them. The lawyer, for example, can use "jurisdiction," "equity," or "common law" in the most radically different ways without confusion. And, more deeply, poets have always known that life cannot be reduced to systems and schemes. In their poems they often seek to capture assertion and denial at once, to carry the reader to the point where her languages break down. Toleration of ambivalence has long been thought to be an essential ingredient of intellectual, emotional, and political maturity: the capacity to see, with Virgil for example, at once the greatness of Rome and its terrible cost, or with Wallace Stevens at once the fictional character of the poetic world and its reality. The comprising of contrary tendencies, the facing of unresolved tensions, is an essential part of the art of life, as our artists repeatedly teach us. This is one reason why the poem or the drama or the novel, or any other piece of living speech, cannot be adequately represented in a paraphrase, for the paraphrase will normally speak with a single voice, with a confidence of characterization that the poem itself undercuts or qualifies; to the extent that the paraphrase catches the contrasting forces of the poem, its multiplicity of voice and value, the paraphrase approaches the status of a poem itself.

All this is something of a truism as said of poetry, but I think it is true of philosophy too. One of the great vices of much philosophic talk is the assumption that the texts made by Hobbes or Locke, or Plato or Aristotle, can on this point or that be reduced to an outline of an argument.[11] That of course is not what the writers wrote, but we are terribly tempted—one sees it in student papers and professional essays alike—to reduce intellectual texts to rationalistic outlines. Yet as Plato taught us, and Hobbes certainly knew, all philosophy must in part be about the language in which it is composed, and so too must all law, all history, all linguistics, all criticism. What we know of poetry, that it is not paraphrasable or subject to translation, is true as well of all of our texts, formal and informal. Each speech act has its own meaning.[12]

11. Consider especially the efforts of modern analytic philosophers to translate into propositional and conceptual forms Wittgenstein's *Philosophical Investigations*, a text that is meant to undermine those very forms. For a good discussion, see Stroud, *An End to Anxiety* (Book Review), LONDON REV. OF BOOKS July 18, 1985, at 14.

12. This is not to say, with the deconstructionists and other moderns, that there is therefore no meaning, that language "doesn't work," or anything like that. Language has meaning, but not of the

Thinking About Our Language

Under these circumstances the great task is to train the imagination to bring within its field of attention the language through which it functions as well as the non-linguistic world within which it seeks to act. One central difficulty with talk about "concepts" is that it directs attention in just the wrong way, away from language to something that is thought to exist apart from language. And when attention is in fact directed to the problematic character of one particular term, or "concept," as it sometimes is, the rest of the language used is assumed to have perfect stability and soundness. Actually all of our language, not just certain terms within it, is in constant flux. Our use of it, and our talk about it, should alike reflect this fact.

III. Literary Language

But how is this to be done? What view are we to take of language and its meaning?

Let me start with the way in which words mean. For me words are not discrete and definable entities, as much of our talk about them (especially when we are thinking conceptually) seems to assume. They do not carry their meanings like pieces of freight, which the competent reader can pick up perfectly, nor are they reducible to ideas that can be regarded as having some existence beyond or behind language. Any use of language assumes a competence in the audience that the utterance itself does not confer. Much of the meaning of words therefore lies in silence, in the unstated but accepted background against which they have their meaning. Even mathematics is deeply cultural and communal, for its definitions rest on inherently unstable cultural assumptions—e.g., about the meaning of the "shortest distance" in Euclid's famous definition of a straight line. (Can we think of the use of language as teaching one who already knows his or her language how else it may be used?)

What is more, in our actual speech words normally do not exist as units, as I have been assuming and as much of our talk seems necessarily to assume, but as parts of sentences or other expressions, each of which is located in a particular linguistic, intellectual, social and cultural context.[13] It is not the words themselves but their various uses—or the ways they have been used—that have meaning, and these uses occur in sentences and other gestures that serve the widest range of human purposes. The "pro-

---

kind implied in most conceptual and analytic talk; it works and works well, but on its own terms, not those of scientific rationalism.

13. For an especially rich statement of the ways in which context gives meaning, see Becker, *The Biography of a Sentence: A Burmese Proverb*, in TEXT, PLAY, AND STORY: THE CONSTRUCTION AND RECONSTRUCTION OF SELF AND SOCIETY 136 (E. Bruner ed. 1984) (1983 Proceedings of the American Ethnological Society).

The Yale Law Journal Vol. 96: 1960, 1987

position," which academics often assume serves as the standard form of thought, is in real speech more rare than one might think. Sentences are perhaps better thought of as "practices" than propositions—including sentences meant to be propositions, for they too exemplify a set of social and rhetorical practices, and do not merely succeed or fail to state the truth. (All this was well known by Samuel Johnson, the great lexicographer, who defined English words not only by substitutive phrases—"X means Y"—but much more richly by their actual and diverse uses in sentences made by eminent writers.) Similarly, the metaphors of a "range of meaning" or a "semantic field," which suggest that words have meanings that can be represented as both two-dimensional and contiguous, like strips of tape or patches of cloth, are utterly misleading, for different uses appear in contexts that are socially, emotionally, and culturally different from each other. It is an abuse of language to try to reduce its meaning to the restatable, the propositional. Our talk about language should reflect the various ways in which it has simultaneous meanings. A better metaphor for the way words mean might be that of neurological ganglia, making up three-dimensional, organic, interactive patterns, which work by processes we know we do not understand, even though they directly coincide, as language also does with our own processes of understanding.

Language has an ineradicably individual character. Words, and other language forms, simply do not mean—not ever—exactly the same things to all users of them, as the builders of intellectual systems must claim or at least hope to achieve. Each of us loads any expression with significances that derive from our prior experience of language and of life, an experience that is obviously different for each of us. And it is not only words that mean differently to different people, but the sentences or other utterances in which they appear, the cultural background against which they acquire their meaning, the silences into which they are intrusions. What is behind the shimmering and fluid world of language is not a world of potentially clear and in principle shareable ideas or understandings, as talk about concepts assumes, but a world of private meanings, radical silences, incommunicable sensations, experiences, and images. Each of us is a circle of experiences and meanings that can occasionally, through language, meet or overlap with others, at least at the edges. Talk about concepts seems to assume that language can be pierced and some underlying reality exposed. I think that cannot be done. What lies beyond language is real all right, but it is not communicable, certainly not in a language of concepts.

I do not mean that meaning is completely private, which would obviously make social and linguistic life impossible, but that for each of us there is always an element or dimension of meaning—perhaps a residuum, though from our point of view it doesn't feel like it—that is irremediably personal. It could hardly be otherwise when each of us brings to every utterance such widely differing sets of prior experiences, such different aims and wishes. What we call the self is in part the history of a perpetual, and in principle unstable, negotiation between the languageless experience of the organism and its language, a negotiation parallel to those between self and nature, self and other. This history will be different for each of us.

Think here of conversation and life on a law school or college faculty. We can if we are lucky create a world that we can inhabit with confidence and some comfort, upon which we can build much of our lives. Yet despite the sense we sometimes have that the shared world of meanings in such a place is permanent and natural—especially by comparison with such places as Thucydides' Corcyra, torn by civil war—at moments we see that even this world will be maintained only by perpetual and imperfect negotiation. It can always collapse; and at its most healthy much of its meaning is radically different for its different members, and different in ways that never find expression. For one person the school may be a refuge, for another a cosmic challenge; for a devout Catholic the whole process would have meaning of a kind it could not for the atheist; and so on. Part of maintaining a community is maintaining the agreement not to speak or ask about the ways in which its language means differently for different members. And those differences can be so enormous that in listening to the talk one is often surprised that it can go on at all.[14]

I have said that language is more personal or individual than conceptual talk allows, but there is one sense in which it is less so, for conceptual talk assumes that the speaker "has" a concept, indeed must have a concept in order to speak. In fact, of course, we learn our language in large part by imitation, often with a sense only of what is appropriate to specific kinds of occasion. Much of the meaning of what we say is not to be found in our minds or intentions at all, but in the language itself.[15] We always say more than we know. This means that learning a language is partly learning from it the meaning of what we already know how to say, which has, without our knowing it, marked our world, our mind. This is why

14. Or think of the formation of a friendship: how wonderful it is to find someone whose language speaks to you, and to whom your language speaks, below the explicit level.

Or think of the task of the lawyer interviewing a client: The story she has just been told makes sense of a kind, no doubt, it may even be compelling and vivid; yet the lawyer never accepts it in its first form but goes on to ask questions the function of which is to make explicit the language behind the language, the context that gives the utterances the meaning they have for the client. She tries to retrieve and make conscious as much of the context as she can in order to discover the range of ways the story can be told, its set of potential meanings.

15. Consider here the meaning of Robinson Crusoe's name, "Master," to "Friday" as he learns it and in the language he is learning. See *supra* note 9.

The Yale Law Journal Vol. 96: 1960, 1987

the study of our language is at once a study of ourselves and of our culture.

The difference between conceptual and literary uses of language is especially sharp on the question of definition. As I suggested above, conceptual talk seems to proceed on the assumption that its terms can be stipulatively defined in phrases that could substitute for them, while literary definitions occur in the working of the text itself.

This is of course a commonplace with respect to poetry: We know that the poet creates webs of significance that define one thing in terms of another: the rose in sexual terms, for example, or the spider in theological ones. But the same thing can be seen in texts thought to be intellectual rather than poetic, including legal texts. The good writer knows that she cannot just use the word "privacy" or "foreseeability," for example, as though "everyone knows what it means," and also that a one-line definition will not do. You must give your terms meaning in your use of them, a meaning that will be somewhat different from the meaning that is given them in any other text.[16] The literary mind thus takes the words and sentences that surround it in the culture as defining incomplete possibilities for expression and action, ways of locating the self and the audience in relation to the culture; it then uses them in ways that transform them, for good or ill, in the relation that the text creates with its reader.

Let me call upon an example here, and one familiar to lawyers. Think of the first sentence of ***Federalist*** No. 1, which reads: "After an unequivocal experience of the inefficacy of the subsisting federal government, you are called upon to deliberate on a new Constitution for the United States of America."[17] The central word in that sentence is "deliberate," for this is what the text "calls upon" its reader to do; and for another reason too, since this invitation is also a promise, a promise that the text will participate in the deliberation, and do so in such a way as to exemplify its proper form. To this much at least the text is committed.

How is "deliberate" defined? Never by explicit description or distinction, never conceptually or stipulatively. The text does not say, for example, "by deliberation we mean the serious and sustained application of open-minded attention," or something equally thrilling, and then go on to use the term as if it automatically meant what the text declared it to mean. Instead, the term is given meaning by a kind of performance or enactment. This begins, indeed, in this opening sentence, where we learn, perhaps disconcertingly, that "deliberate" does not mean open-mindedness on all topics, as we might be inclined to think, but in this instance takes as

16. More extended discussion of this point in connection with particular texts can be found in J.B. White, When Words Lose Their Meaning (1984), in particular *id.* at 153-60, 217-19.
17. The Federalist No. 1, at 33 (A. Hamilton) (C. Rossiter ed. 1961).

a given that the existing government is "inefficacious." Even more, the text is willing to bury that assumption in a subordinate clause, almost as if hoping that the reader, in a hurry to reach the main subject, verb, and object, will slide over it without objecting. We are at once invited to "deliberate" and thrown off balance by the evident commitment of the writer on the question in issue.

But is this so bad? Just because we are undecided does not mean that everyone need be; indeed have we not something to learn from those whose opinions are settled, so long as they are put before us in a candid way? As the writer will say towards the end of the paper, "I frankly acknowledge to you my convictions, and I will freely lay before you the reasons on which they are founded."[18] By this time, through a process described below, we have come to see the existence of "conviction" in our interlocutor not as a deliberative vice but as a virtue, as a benefit to us; and perhaps we have come to see as well that a similar state of conviction—based on "reasons"—is what we should aspire to ourselves.

Back to the beginning: In the first paragraph the writer tells us that what will be decided by this process of deliberation is "whether societies of men are really capable or not of establishing good government from reflection and choice, or whether they are forever destined to depend for their political constitutions on accident and force."[19] Whatever "deliberation" is, then, it is of the gravest importance; it is opposed to "accident and force," and it involves "reflection," or as he soon says, a "judicious estimate of our true interests, unperplexed and unbiased by considerations not connected with the public good."[20]

But such "reflection" is most difficult indeed, for the nature of mankind is against it: most obviously because the conduct of those selfishly opposed to the Constitution, who will resist it for reasons of interest or passion, and not fairly participate in debate.[21] This the writer starts to say, but then corrects himself: many of the opponents are motivated by "upright intentions,"[22] though perhaps subject to "honest errors";[23] more than that, in fact, for there are often "wise and good men on the wrong as well as on the right side of questions of the first magnitude to society"[24] and "we are not always sure that those who advocate the truth are influenced by purer principles than their antagonists."[25] The fault is on both sides. The result

18. *Id.* at 36.
19. *Id.* at 33.
20. *Id.*
21. *Id.* at 33–34.
22. *Id.* at 34.
23. *Id.*
24. *Id.*
25. *Id.*

will be that a "torrent of angry and malignant passions will be let loose."[26] We can expect both sides to seek to persuade "by the loudness of their declamations and by the bitterness of their invectives."[27]

The writer is here imagining a world in which the reader, like other citizens, will necessarily be confused: good men and bad on both sides of the question, everyone out of intellectual and rhetorical control, speakers proceeding by "declamation" and "invective," and so on. This set of circumstances gives rise to the felt need for something else, for what the text calls deliberation—for what it promises to offer us—and in doing so begins to give it meaning. In this context of uncertainty it is a real virtue for the voice of *The Federalist* to speak out of "conviction." Only the voice of this text, committed to the point of bias but self-corrective too, and utterly candid about its commitments, has the stability and maturity required to think its way through the questions before it. Thank heavens, the reader is led to say, someone knows his own mind, and is willing to speak in such a way as to assist our own "deliberation," and to do so by explaining his "reasons," which are offered to us for our acceptance or rejection on the merits.

This is only the beginning of what could be said on this subject about *Federalist* No. 1, let alone about the Papers as a whole, one central achievement of which is to work out an extended definition by performance of "deliberation" and "reason" alike, but perhaps it suggests how such an analysis might proceed. And I might add one final point: In defining the conditions of deliberation, of its own utterance, *The Federalist* describes a discursive world dominated by selfishness, passion, shortsightedness, manipulativeness, and so on. This is just the conception of human nature upon which it ultimately rests the need for the national government, just the ground upon which it resists the republicans, who believe in the possibility of civic virtue. In accepting it as the condition of deliberation the reader is likely to be accepting it in deeper ways as well. The terms upon which *The Federalist* offers itself, that is, as a place and occasion for "reasoned" talk, distanced from the confusion and irrationality of ordinary life, are precisely the terms upon which it offers the Constitution. Both create the possibility of a new kind of community, based upon a new kind of conversation, of which one central term is "deliberation," as defined in this text.

26. *Id.* at 35.

27. *Id.*

IV. Translation

What I think is called for in our talk about our common life and language, then, is not conceptual talk but what I call a literary discourse, by which I mean language uses that are self-conscious of the limits—of the over-commitments, of the dead spots—in the language itself.[28]

Because concepts are abstract, and because in this paper I oppose the "literary" to the "conceptual," it might be thought that for me literary language has to be concrete or particular. But a resolutely particular language would in its own way be as bad as a conceptual one, at least if it assumed the perfect adequacy of its terms and categories. Instead, what I call literary texts are characteristically marked by a tension between languages, between the concrete and the abstract, say, or between a language of nature and one of morality; the effect is to qualify each language while using it. Their art lies in writing two ways at once. In this respect law is naturally literary, for the legal case as we normally think of it can be neither an exercise in abstract analysis nor the presentation of mere particulars, but requires the interaction of both modes of discourse.

The modern philosopher's question is, "What proposition are you advancing?" Mine is, "What text are you making?" I mean this question to reach the language used, its particular formulation, its relation to its context, the voice of the speaker, his or her definition of audience, and so on. "Who are you in this text, who am I, and what kind of conversation do you seek to establish between us?"

All of this has consequences for one's view of human reason, and for the expectations and standards that one should bring to texts that purport to be "rational," including the present one. Rationality is not the manipulation or explication of ideas or concepts, assumed to have some extralinguistic reality and force, but using words well in accordance with the conditions of reality, including: the limits of language and of our own minds; the reality and contingency of the convictions out of which we function; and the silence that bounds everything we say. Reason, on this view, is not reductive or schematic but integrative: saying what we know to be true in light of all else we know to be true at the same time. (This is the opposite of the view of social science as a filing system.)

This view has consequences for ethics as well. I spoke earlier of the ontological relativism of my view, and while that characterization is accurate enough it does not entail what is usually meant by moral relativism,

28. It is possible to have literary uses of what seem to be nonliterary languages, even, as I suggested earlier, of conceptual languages. It is the attitude towards one's language, as that shows up in one's use of it, not the level of one's diction, that counts most deeply. My opposition in this paper is not to abstract words—after all I use such terms as "conceptual" and "literary" myself—but to certain ways of talking about, and using, such terms.

for I do not mean to suggest that we are left without a ground of judgment or conviction. Quite the reverse: It is a claim that we can ground our "intellectual" discourse in our actual convictions, in what we "think" conceived of much more fully than we reveal in our analytic and theoretical discourse; and an appeal for a language of morality that is self-consciously moral, of politics that is political, and so on.

Literary use of language, in fact, has an active ethical significance, for to acknowledge the limits of one's own mind and language is necessarily to acknowledge the existence of the other person as well as of other possible languages. The norm for conceptual talk, indeed for much academic talk more generally, seems to be inherently aggressive: The idea is to stake out certain intellectual terrain with the force of one's logic, or by the demonstration of certain facts, against an audience assumed to be hostile, which will be persuaded only if compelled. The literary method, on the other hand, knows that nothing can be said with certain truth or validity, that no one can be compelled to submit, and that compelled submission is worthless anyway. It proceeds instead on the assumption that our categories and terms are perpetually losing and acquiring meaning, that they mean differently to different people and in different texts. It is not a territorial claim but an invitation to reflection. The implied standards for one's own expressions are thus authenticity, actuality, integration, a commitment to acknowledging the limits both of language and of mind. Concerning others a complementary ethic emerges with similar clarity and simplicity: respect for the other (grounded in a simultaneous recognition of similarity of situation and otherness of experience); allowing the other what we claim for ourselves, the authentic assertion of conviction and judgment; and a willingness to learn the other's language and to undergo the changes we know that will entail. What we ask from others is what we offer to them, a willingness to speak to them as they are actually situated and constituted, with recognition of their claims to a language and a world. The heart of this set of ethical practices is the art of simultaneous affirmation of oneself and recognition of the other.

The tendency of much abstract theoretical and conceptual talk is to appeal to the part of ourselves that wants to be surrounded by linear arguments, always hypothetical and susceptible to summarization in logical outline; that wants to live without the personal or actual voice, and without the responsibility of conviction, in a world reduced to quantitative metaphors; that wants to render the world into certain abstract intellectual forms or claim it to be meaningless. It works by an ideal of the purely rational where "rational" is given a special and rather bloodless significance.[29]

A proper language of reason, by contrast, a proper language of justice, would accept the literary condition on which we live: that while we struggle for coherence in our expression, this coherence will always be tentative, always incomplete, for all that we say, all that we are, is in part a function of the context in which we live, always imperfectly perceived and always changing. As an example of literary discourse one can think not only of poetry but of law, which has survived as well as it has—and has been as important as it has—because it is a discourse constantly in the process of its own transformation, not in part but all at once, in which speakers recognize that their central terms must be defined anew as they are used in new contexts, and in which all speakers recognize that everything is in principle arguable.

* * *

At any given point in time, and place in culture, certain appeals have force—people will listen, feel they must respond, and so on—while certain others do not. As time goes on these appeals, and the contexts from which they arise, shift and grow or wither. (Think for example of the different force of an appeal to the Gospels in the discourse of Harvard University made 100 years ago and today.) This is not merely a matter of intellectual or conceptual, but of cultural change. We can understand much of what the words we translate as "honor" mean in the *Iliad*, or the plays of Corneille, or what "honor" itself once meant in England, or in South Carolina, yet in our world these words cannot mean what they once did. The English word "honor," which once expressed the motives for which people would kill each other, or go to voluntary death, has now lost much of its meaning; this loss is not merely, or primarily, a "conceptual" one but a loss of force and significance, a difference in relation to the unstated backgrounds and to the feelings of the speakers. Who today would ever ground a conviction on "honor"? This is really the point of the famous passage in Thucydides: A resource is gone, and gone forever, except perhaps as it can be revived or recreated by individual speakers, exercising the kind of art that Thucydides himself, other great writers, and perhaps our best judges too, can be seen to practice.

In our own thought and writing about the texts, practices, and cultures

29. Our own language of moral and political philosophy in particular seems to me badly impoverished. The attempt to convert moral and political distinctions into conceptual ones, expressions of conviction into intellectual points, and to make these choices "rational" in the computational sense that is now so natural to us, is to strip our central terms of much of their force and meaning and to destroy a cultural resource of great importance.

of others—and our own, too—we should be aware, then, not only of the reality but of the insurmountability of the differences between languages. This means that we cannot simply construct versions of other people's central terms as if we could understand them perfectly. As with other translations, we have to recognize that the most we can attain is an imperfect understanding and approximation. What is called for is not an attempt to penetrate the other world at the level of idea, behind or beyond language, but the effort to learn the language ourselves, incomplete as that learning must of necessity be.[30]

But, you may say, does this not mean the end of all attempts to generalize—to describe, count, weigh—and of all efforts to analyze the real worlds of different cultures, or the different stages of our own culture? My answer is both yes and no. I do think that it would mean the end of all attempts to treat political or cultural questions as if they were language-free—it would mean the end of pure behaviorism and of the sort of view of individual and collective life that characterizes economics, at least in its unqualified form. But this does not mean that we can say nothing, describe nothing, about these important matters. We can give descriptive, analytic, and comparative accounts of the rhetorical and cultural situations of others; we can study and analyze their responses, creative or not, to their situations as we understand them. We can learn to see and judge their own reconstitutions of their own languages. We can, that is, describe with some accuracy the rhetorical facts (the claims that can and cannot be made); and the literary facts (the ways in which individual speakers and writers remake their languages, for good or ill); and this will go far towards defining the essential ethical and political facts, the ways a particular community is constituted, in a text and in the world. We can identify the appeals and topics that characterize a particular world, and the way they are and can be elaborated. We can do in short what Thucydides has shown us how to do.

But this will not take the form of propositions about concepts or other parts of the nonlinguistic world, which can be elaborated and tested by deduction and induction; nor shall we assume that we can penetrate the minds and languages of others further than we in fact can do. An impor-

30. One's main aim in learning languages—French or Burmese, say—should not be to discover how one can say this or that in French or Burmese, but to learn what one can say and be in those languages that one cannot in one's own. Think of your own first thoughts about learning a language: How different everything would be if you were to greet your neighbor, or your teacher, in French, or order a beer in German, or ask about the weather in Spanish. As sophisticated people we are likely to feel superior to such youthful and romantic expectations, but here, as often, the young and ingenuous have something we should pay attention to. Or think of grammar: Is this the blueprint by which the language is built, the engineer's design document? Much language-teaching seems to assume so, but of course nothing could be further from the truth. Grammar is what we use when we do not have enough experience of a language to make it our own.

tant part of our attention must always be given to our own language, to its preconceptions and its omissions. This is in a sense nothing new, for it has long been said that one of the points of all comparative studies is to make our own world accessible and criticizable in a new way. My point is that this truth is obscured by those aspects of our current discourse that assume that reality can be authoritatively described and understood in our language, whether on the theory that "material" reality can be described as well by "us" as by "them," or on the theory that nonmaterial reality can be represented and understood as concepts that can be translated without loss into any language.

For me the beginning of wisdom—This is what Plato teaches, for example—is to train the mind to be conscious of its formulations just as it is conscious of the intentions it seeks to realize through them, to be as aware of the language we use as we are of the world in which we use it. What stage of intellectual and ethical development such an awareness, properly disciplined and encouraged, might lead to is beyond our full imagining, but it could be as great a shift as the acquisition of language itself has been. What will lead us to it is not further conceptual elaboration, nor an insistence on the transparency of our own languages, nor the delight in meaninglessness—in the loss of one kind of meaning, that is—celebrated by the priests of deconstruction, but an art, slow to develop, of recognizing the other, an art of assertion within acknowledged limits—an art for which the best word, properly used to reflect its impossibilities, may be "translation."

[2]

BABEL: A *SHE'UR*

for Sharka

*Richard Hyland**

Unserem Packmeister sind nun doch noch Bedenken gekommen.

The letter bearing the sentence surfaces again, long afterward, as we leaf through an old correspondence file. She slowly reads the sentence aloud, savoring the surprisingly literary quality of the prose from a German shipping firm, then asks whether it is possible to translate the sentence into English. I stare at it for a moment, and suddenly the little memory floods over me. One of the reasons translation is so time-consuming is that it causes the mind to wander . . . .

We were moving again. We had spent days dragging empty boxes from the market, packing them with books and padding them with crumpled pages from the sports section. Finally, we loaded them into a rented VW van and drove them to the freight forwarder. A worker pointed to a place for the boxes—on a wooden pallet in the middle of a gaping warehouse. The random-size boxes, however, piled high and tilting slightly, did not look stable. Yet the warehouser was confident: the pile would not topple. A month later, back in the U.S., we received the letter telling us that our belongings had been shipped, that everything was in order, except that the boxes of books had had to be adjusted on the pallet and strapped down with wide metal bands . . . .

Unserem Packmeister sind . . . To our packing master are . . . It is not yet the close of business. I call a moving company and ask for the term used to designate the member of the moving team who is in charge of packing. *The packer,* I am told. Is there no name for a specially skilled packer who, because of years of dedicated service and accumulated expertise, is consulted about particularly difficult questions? *You mean a supervisor*? Is there then no word like *packing master* or *master packer*? *Hey, what's this all about*? I manage to extricate myself, offer thanks, and hang up. I then report the results of the conversation. We fall silent. Why, she asks, does the German language have the concept while English does not? And who is the subject of the *our*? To whom in the end does the master packer belong?

nun doch noch . . . now yet again . . . Adverbs, expletives, and

* Professor of Law, University of Miami Law School.

other German particles are packed with meanings as randomly as our boxes were packed with books. Some of the meanings can be approximated in English, but others can be translated only by a gesture—a shrug, a frown, a slap on the knee. The particles mean so much separately that they are able to mean almost anything when strung together.

Bedenken gekommen . . . thoughts-about come . . . Not just thoughts but apprehensions—doubts of some kind. The real question is where do the misgivings come from: What is the point of this odd sentence structure according to which the master packer, the human actor, serves only as the place at which thoughts come to rest?

Of course, the words can be interpreted to make at least some sense in English. *Nun* may well be the key. It seems to invoke a sigh of relief—*now, coming to a conclusion after long reflection*. *Doch* can be taken with *noch* to signify a contrast, to insist that the new conclusion is firm, despite the initial contrary opinion. And perhaps it would be best in English to camouflage somewhat the surprising implication from the sentence structure, namely that thoughts possess their own means of locomotion.

In the end, second thoughts did in fact occur to our master packer. If this is a translation, then I am a translator. And I suppose Gadamer would explain not only that I have thereby interpreted the original but also that my horizon and language have become fused with those of the text. Yet I do not experience the fusion. I experience my translation as a sad and sorry compromise, and one that, far from fusing anything, instead reveals the great distance separating the very different sentences involved in the drama. There is the original. There are the several possible word-for-word renderings. There is my own approximation, together with the numerous alternatives that I have rejected. And there are the various sentences that *I* might have written in American English in such a letter—if the thought had occurred to me and if, in such a situation, I had found it useful to write it down. *Our supervisor had second thoughts about the way your boxes were loaded on the pallet*, I might have written. Or, more likely, I would have been more direct. *We decided that it was necessary, before shipment, to secure your boxes to the pallet*. The fact is, however, that I probably would not have found it necessary to mention the thought at all.

The experience of translating produces in me not the pleasure of merger and comfort but rather the acute distress of things torn apart and a vain and frantic desire to hold them together. In the end, the text entreats *me* to be a master packer. And so I pack my translation, somewhat arbitrarily, with as much meaning as possible. But the translation is, after all, only a sentence, and I am only a packer. Much has found its way into the translation, but as rereading it continually reminds me, much more has been left out—enough, surely, for many other sentences. In contrast to the master packer, I do not feel that I have completed my job, that my horizon is at one with another's.

The notion of translation implies that there is some relationship between languages. The fact that there is difficulty indicates at least that there is no one-to-one correspondence between words in one language and those in another. Since the law is formulated in language, the difficulty of translation suggests a similar lack of continuity from one legal system to another. It might then be asked how exactly to characterize the relationship between one language and another, or between two different legal systems. At least in the West, the discussion about such questions traditionally implicates a Biblical text (Gen. 11: 1-9) that tells the story of the tower of Babel. The object of this essay is to explore the lesson of this story for the appreciation of diversity, particularly the diversity of legal systems.

Of God

There is no way around it: reflection about the meaning of Babel requires recourse to the notion of God. One of the difficulties in thinking about Divinity is that the prevailing tradition offers little margin for error. According to Revelations (3:12), the names of God are literally inscribed in the faithful. As Fray Luis de Léon (*De los nombres de Cristo*) remarked, those names are the essence that God communicates to the fortunate—brief ciphers wherein God miraculously encapsulates all that human understanding can and may perceive of Godhood. Since, in this tradition, all names of God partake of Divinity, the stakes in theological discussion are high: any assertion may not only be challenged as incorrect, but also branded as blasphemy. Even English, despite its extravagantly rich resources, lacks the necessary vocabulary for a completely open discussion about the nature of God.

Hebrew offers a convenient distinction—one which might easily be incorporated into English—that serves to relax the tension in theological discussion. Hebrew distinguishes between those names used exclusively when addressing the Holy One and others that may be employed in both discussion and everyday conversation.

Though there is some dispute about whether Hebrew contains a single word for *God*, it does contain numerous names *of* God. There is a twelve-letter name, and there is also a forty-two letter name, both long since forgotten. There is the word that was spoken to Moses when he inquired of the name he was to tell to the Children of Israel. In fact, it is said that the Torah contains nothing other than the names of God. Seven of these names are distinguished by the fact that, once written, they may not be erased. The first of these, the ineffable Tetragrammaton, may no longer be pronounced—a prohibition that leads to some confusion, since the true pronunciation has been forgotten. Even in the days of the priests, it was spoken aloud only in the Temple, most notably by the High Priest, after ritual purification on the holiest of days, in a whisper muffled by song. The six remaining names are used today when directly addressing the Holy One and may not be uttered outside of prayer or blessing. When, even in study, reference is made to these names, their pronunciation is altered, slightly but perceptibly, in order to avoid sacrilege.

In discussion or conversation about God, use is made of other names—oblique references, really. One such name is *HaShem*, which means simply *The Name*. It refers not directly to God, but rather to the Holy Name. Names such as this create space between the signifier and the signified and are therefore sufficiently removed from the name of God that their inadvertent misuse must not necessarily be considered irreverent. That is why they are needed here.

Even once a name has been agreed upon, the preliminaries are not over. A form must be found in which to discuss such matters. Theological discussion almost necessarily assumes that there is a fundamental ordering to the universe and thus does not proceed as though it involved a typical question from the law or politics. The Talmudic tradition offers a form for this sort of disputation. It is called the *she'ur*. The word *she'ur* may well be derived from a Hebrew verb signifying *to measure* or *estimate*. On one level, it indicates the measured or circumscribed time available between religious services for such discussions. Yet the idea of measurement reveals something of the substantive goal as well, the desire to open the nature of Divine order to human understanding—to demonstrate that, at least to some extent, humanity can grasp something about infinity. The *she'ur* begins by revealing a puzzle—usually an apparent inconsistency between two texts of the Written or Oral Laws. Since it is assumed that both texts were transcribed from Divine dictation, and since it is further assumed that Divine texts do not contain inconsistencies, the problem is to resolve the dissonance and restore meaning to the Holy Text. At the same time, precisely because the topic is the infinite and the Divine, no *she'ur* claims to be absolutely right, and none need fear being absolutely wrong. It is clear from the outset that every suggestion will enrich the discussion and equally clear that none will ever close it.

Though the *she'ur* was developed as a form for discussing the *Chumash* (the Five Books or Torah) and the Talmudic texts, its usefulness is not limited to that context. It may be understood more broadly to offer form to a discussion about the relationship between harmony and diversity—to the investigation of the affinities between empirically existing activities once it is assumed that there is order in the cosmos. The question here, for example, involves the relationship between homogeneity and diversity with respect to the human languages—and with respect to the various systems of law. The name *HaShem* is meant to serve here as a convenient reference to the idea of reason in diversity. The *she'ur* is employed as a mode for its elaboration.

Of History

The story of the tower built at Babel is based on the assumption that humanity once shared a single language. It was the language of Noah's family, for only Noah and his wife, together with their three sons and their wives, survived the Flood. According to the *Chumash*, all nations are descended from this family. After the death of Noah, as humankind journeyed from Ararat, the mountain of the East where the ark of Noah had come to rest, it came upon the plain of Shinar. As the group looked out onto the plain, everything about the place must have reminded them of death, for the bodies of those who had died in the Flood had washed down onto Shinar. Perhaps it was the very proximity of the plain to death, together with humanity's desire to conquer mortality, that convinced the group to settle there and to build a city and a tower. Because of the events that soon transpired, the city became known as Babel, which may be derived from *Bab-ilu* (*Gate of God* in Assyrian, perhaps signifying the portals through which the nations were to go out), and, at least by popular etymology, is related to *balal*, the Hebrew for *to mix up* or *confuse*. The tower to be built there was designed to reach to Heaven. After construction of the tower was well along, *HaShem* came down to examine it. Upon seeing the tower, the Holy One destroyed it, confounded the speech of the various nations so that they could no longer understand one another, and scattered them over the face of the earth.

Tradition has had much to say about the tower. It is said to have contained two sets of stairs. The eastern stairs were used by workers carrying bricks to the top, while the stairs to the west were used by those who returned for new bricks. The tower was tremendously tall, so much so that its top appeared to touch the sky. When the tower was destroyed, the bottom third of it sank into the ground, the top third was consumed by fire, and only the middle third remained. Yet what remained of the tower was so immense that one might have walked for three days without leaving its shadow. (Some of the traditional stories about the tower are collected in *The Torah Anthology* [*MeAm Lo'ez*].)

From Rashi to Derrida (Des Tours de Babel, in *Difference in Translation* (Graham ed. 1985)), the scholars have unanimously interpreted the confusion of language as a well-deserved punishment, one particularly designed to prevent the completion of the tower. The diversity of language and the inevitability of mutual misunderstanding have been considered elements of a curse brought on by Divine annoyance at human pride, particularly at the vanity implicit in the conception of the tower—the belief that human beings might reach Heaven, and therefore immortality, without the journey through death.

Despite its persistence, there is something peculiarly unsatisfying about this interpretation of the story. The tower, of course, could never have reached Heaven. The Holy One had no reason for concern. Moreover, pride of accomplishment and the desire to postpone or transcend death are constant elements of the human condition and certainly not its least attractive ones. Furthermore, though *HaShem* is capable of rage (metaphorically understood), the Rambam demonstrated that not every human failing is capable of inducing Divine anger: an examination of the incidents of wrath in both the Torah and the prophetic writings reveals that only one very particular sin provokes the Holy One, and that is idolatry. And finally, the confusion of language involves much more than the simple creation of a barrier to communication. If all that *HaShem* had desired was to obstruct human discourse, that could have been achieved by hindering the human ear or by slowing the tongue. In other words, the building of the tower seems to provide little enough reason for punishment at all, let alone for a punishment of this particular type. The difficulty then becomes to discover a connection between the confusion of language and the building of the tower than can be reconciled with the all-encompassing wisdom of the Holy One.

Once the problem is posed in this manner, the story of Babel is so evocative that numerous resolutions suggest themselves. My own favorite interprets the story as a fable of post modernism. The first step in conceiving of the story in this way is to reexamine its status as history. In my view, none of the stories recounted at the beginning of the *Chumash* need be interpreted as history, at least not history as we are used to conceiving of it. Though the sages do not deny the historicity of these stories, a few of their sentences seem to point to the possibility of a nonhistorical reading. Woe unto them, remarked Rabbi Shimon bar Yochai in the *Zohar,* who see in the Torah merely worldly stories and history. To Rabbi Yaakov Culi, the few stories retold in the Torah are really mysteries, enshrouded in words that make them appear like history. For the nonhistorical reading, it is irrelevant whether the incidents described in those stories actually took place, whether a tower was actually built or human language actually confused as described in the Torah. Rather the stories present analysis in the *form* of history. To decipher this curious form, the story of Babel must be read in context.

The *Chumash* presents a code of laws—613 commandments, 248 mandating some positive act, the remaining 365 enumerating the prohibitions—interspersed with what appears to be an historical narrative. The culmination of the narrative is the recounting of the single Divine revelation in human history, the appearance of the Holy One and the giving of the Law at Sinai. What precedes the giving of the Law is an account of the formation and education of the people chosen to receive it, which begins with the story of Abraham our Father. Before beginning the story of Abraham and his descendants, the *Chumash* focuses on three events—the stories of Eden, the Flood, and Babel.

The three stories may be read as the preface to a legal text, a reminder of the three preconditions that are necessary for a functioning legal system. These stories describe not the past but the present, each designating a necessary element of the whole. Each story illustrates one of the prerequisites by means of an *as though* analysis, what Hans Vaihinger (*The Philosophy of "As If"*) might have called a heuristic fiction. The very possibility of the law is rooted in these three aspects of the human condition, yet they seem so natural that they are virtually imperceptible until they have been problematized—scandalized really—by ascribing to them fictional origins: it is *as though* humanity had been Divinely created and then suffered a Fall, *as though* it had received a covenant from the Lord after a terrible destruction, *as though* an original common language had been fragmented. The challenge is to redeem the wisdom sealed in the metaphors.

In Eden, our first ancestors tasted of the forbidden fruit, and thereby gained the ability to distinguish between good and evil. The story of the Fall recognizes in human nature an attraction to evil as well as an understanding of good, together with the ability to distinguish between the two, and the insight that they are often intertwined. The story describes one aspect of the human condition that serves as a prerequisite for a functioning legal system, a feature so essential that it is difficult to conceive of a legal system without it. If human beings did not both recognize the good and yet, at the same time, desire evil, the notion of a legal prohibition backed by coercion would be incoherent. There is also something more to the story. The teller of the tale must have marveled at the human ability to appreciate the distinction between right and wrong. It may have seemed that the knowledge of good and evil results not from reasoned inquiry but rather from a quality innate in human nature. And yet human beings are clearly not predetermined to do good. The knowledge of good seems to be Divinely inspired, as though the human race initially had been Divinely created and subsequently had fallen from the perfect identification with Divine will that constituted grace.

Unfortunately, the knowledge of good and evil, unguided by morality, did not prove sufficient to overcome temptation. Beginning with Cain and Abel, what resulted was such human iniquity that the Holy One decided to drown the world. After the Flood, *HaShem* covenanted with Noah that the world would never again be destroyed by calamity. By making the promise, the Lord demonstrated to Noah the nature of obligation and thereby initiated him and his family into the concept of duty. The sense of duty or morality is the second prerequisite of a legal system, for there can be law only if humanity struggles to comply with the demands of duty. The daily, heroic, and largely successful human struggle to overcome desire makes it seem as though humankind is attempting to fulfill promises made in exchange for the Lord's own covenant.

An understanding that right differs from wrong and a moral commitment to the good are still not sufficient for the establishment of a legal system, at least according to the author of the *Chumash*. The final requirement is an understanding of the necessity of particularity. The Divine Text expressed the requirement by portraying the fragmentation of a single original language. This account raises two difficulties. The first is to make sense of the claim that the various natural languages have a common origin. The second is to understand why the notion of particularity is a necessary prerequisite for a code of laws.

Of Language

As our ancestors were resolving to build the city and the tower of

Babel, it is written that they also decided to make for themselves a name, in order to avoid being scattered over the face of the earth. Confronted by the splendid yet frightening multifariousness of existence, they wished to prevent their dispersion by gathering together, by reducing everything to a unique name, to a single understanding. They sought transcendence beyond the realm of diversity in a unique foundational principle. The idea of the single name influenced the conception of the tower. Finding no stones, we are told, they made bricks and burnt them thoroughly. The tower's foundation was thus a human construction. Yet the tower builders believed that, if they were to construct a tower, even on such foundations, on a plain encountered by chance, they would be able to dominate Creation and, from the top of the tower, enter into Eternity.

The story of the tower of Babel suggests how easily the human mind can be seduced by reductionism. The story expresses the frantic yet persistent hope that it is possible to escape uncertainty by glorifying the theory of the moment: if only the tower is tall enough, our ancestors thought, it can reach to Heaven. The story reminds us that human intuition seeks truth in unity, in monocausal explanation, rather than in multiplicity. If humanity were possessed of but a single language, it would inevitably believe that there is but a single valid understanding. In the end, Babel reveals the limitation of the human imagination, its difficulty in conceiving of infinite possibility.

This is an important limitation, because the ability to conceive of possibility is the difference between Divine and human understanding. The Holy One understands the world as it is, both in its existence and in its potential. That is what Heidegger called original being (*das ursprüngliche Sein*). Humankind, on the other hand, tends to focus on the given and the finite and to reduce it to a single explanation. However great its comprehension, no human mind can ever discover more than an extremely limited number of the possible alternatives.

Hashem destroyed the tower and scrambled language not to punish those who had sought to reach Heaven, but rather to open the human mind to the appreciation of possibility. For this purpose it was necessary to establish at least some of those possibilities empirically and to permit them to flourish independently. The confusion of language, by making it difficult for one nation to communicate with the next, permitted each group to develop relatively autonomously the possibilities inherent in the language it received.

The development of a particular language over time is a cultural tradition. There is of course never homogeneity within a tradition. For one, languages are often composed of numerous competing dialects. Moreover, each cultural tradition is the expression of a debate—at times only an unvoiced tension—between the rulers and the ruled, between sexes and races and religions, majorities and minorities of all kinds. There is also constant Babel or confusion even within the same language. And, of course, history matters too. To begin with, the tradition is constantly reorganizing itself, emphasizing today what it yesterday rejected. Moreover, at some point, cultural developments that occurred much earlier may prove difficult to interpret, so that, like Middle English, they are no longer fully able to contribute to the contemporary discussion. Yet despite the internal conflict and confusion, each tradition shares a common understanding. In fact, what distinguishes one tradition from another are the terms in which the various conflicts are fought out.

From the standpoint of Babel, in other words, language is not transparent. If the various languages were merely neutral instrumentalities for the communication of thought, it would be impossible to explain their extraordinary multiplicity and diversity. The tradition is that seventy nations received languages at Babel. These languages ultimately differentiated themselves into what may have been as many as ten thousand languages, of which possibly five thousand survive today. The reason for the diversity is that each language is constituted by, expresses, and reproduces a particular intelligibility. In Heidegger's phrase, language is *die redende Gliederung*, speaking articulation. Since each language represents only one of the many possible understandings, the existence of thousands of languages confirms the possibility of at least so many lived articulations of meaning. In fact, the number of possibilities may well be endless. The mission confided by the Holy One to human hands is to discover, explore, and develop these endless possibilities. It is *as though* an original common language had once been fragmented.

Of Translation

The Babelian understanding of language irrevocably alters the notion and goal of translation. Translation as traditionally understood—the phrase-by-phrase rendering of a message from one language into another while *retaining the sense* (Samuel Johnson)—proves to be impossible. The problem is not that languages are totally incommensurable with each other. It is not that it is inherently impossible to express in one language the meaning of a word or phrase from another. Language determines not, as Benjamin Lee Whorf seems to have believed, what it is *possible* to see and understand, but rather what *easily* can be grasped and what, in contrast, requires more effort. If languages were impregnable fortresses, nothing could be learned from a foreign culture.

The principal problem is rather that languages communicate simultaneously on various levels. On one level, language is a tool by which human beings attempt to come to terms with their world, either by attempting to describe or represent the world that they perceive to be external to them or by seeking to express their inner awareness and conflicts. The question about whether language is adequate to the task, an issue about which Richard Rorty has expressed doubts, does not bar human beings from the attempt. Even on this level, no message can be comprehensively translated from one language into another without constant resort to asterisks and extensive explanatory notes.

This is not a problem that affects only a few well-known untranslatables, such as *Aufhebung* or the pair *langue/parole*. Even the English word *bread* does not have the same meaning as the French word *pain*. Though there are dozens of differences, the easiest to explain are found on the side of the signified. Not only are the breads referred to by the two words significantly different in form, texture, and taste, but also bread in America is usually bought pre-packaged, pre-sliced, and even pre-frozen and is rarely eaten with the main course, while French bread is bought fresh in bakeries shortly before it is to be consumed at the main meal. On the side of the signifier, the differences are just as stark. Though the two words share many connotations, such as the notion of *daily bread* (*pain quotidien*), colloquial English has developed the metaphor to produce the idea of the *breadwinner* and even equates *bread* with *money*, while French tends to use *pain* in metaphors related to the shape of the loaf, such as *pain de viande* (meat loaf) and *pain à cacheter* (sealing wax), and colloquial French even arrives somehow at having *pain* mean a slap in the face. Moreover, the literary associations of the two words are completely diverse. *Pain* rhymes with *sain* (healthy), *pin* (pine tree), and *vin* (wine), while *bread* rhymes with *dead*, *head*, and *said*. Upon hearing the word *bread*, it is unlikely that anyone but those with a childhood in English will recall the verse *"A loaf of bread," the Walrus said*, and suddenly feel the tug from the far side of the looking glass.

Language as a tool—the use human beings make of words—is not all there is to language. Languages, too, communicate. They speak through those who are attempting to use them in their own communication. As John Sallis notes, language is not primarily an articulation of meaning that we perform, but rather one that is always already performed for us, one we have already assumed inadvertently by virtue of our life in language. (Language and reversal, in *Martin Heidegger: in Europe and America* (Ballard & Scott eds. 1973)). The particular intelligibility that a language conveys may be at cross purposes with the intent of the individual speaker. If, as we are used to saying, language is a game, it is not a game that we play with language, but rather one that language plays with us. This is one of the senses in which one might say, with Heidegger, that it is actually language that speaks (*Denn eigentlich spricht die Sprache*).

The consequences for translation are considerable. The problem is not simply that the meaning of a particular word or phrase in one language cannot find an exact equivalent in another. The problem is rather that there is nothing identical across languages. Languages are simply not equivalents as media for communication. The different understandings implicit in the natural languages render every one of their words, phrases, and sentences untranslatable—unless the translation in accompanied by an absurdly compendious and extraordinarily subtle textual apparatus.

Thus, if there is a relationship at all among languages—and only then would translation even be conceivable—it arises only in terms of the whole that, together, the various languages may have constituted. If the Holy Name is in fact the organizing principle of the universe, and if all of the world's languages are fragments of the original language spoken at Babel, then each language represents a piece of a much larger jigsaw puzzle. No piece can reveal its meaning alone, but each may acquire coherency when examined together with some of the other pieces. One problem, of course, is that, by now, we have lost half the pieces, even assuming that we ever once had them all. As a result, whatever the whole may once have signified will remain forever concealed from us.

The absence of a direct relationship among languages provides reason for skepticism about Gadamer's confidence in translation. For Gadamer, translation is simply a particular kind of understanding. All understanding is interpretation, the fusion of the reader's language and horizon with the language and horizon of a text. Since translation involves a similar fusion, it too would be merely interpretation. It would represent both an extreme form of and a model for understanding. Gadamer's confidence would be warranted if the task were merely to understand what human beings do with words. But his method is unable to account for what is communicated by the language itself. Another and very different strategy is needed in order to reproduce in one language the understanding constituted by another. As Walter Benjamin was probably the first to note, translation could solve this problem only by importing from one language into another an entire fragment of the foreign culture, and not merely the thing meant. In this sense, successful translation not only enriches the target language but also reminds us of its limitations.

Of Law and Legal Education

The story of Babel is particularly important as the preface to a legal text. It emphasizes the particularity of any single code of laws. No code promulgated in a post-Babelian language—even if conceived in Divine inspiration—can be universal. Every law is a particular law. It is part of a particular language, embedded in a particular cultural tradition, and designed for a particular people. The laws codified in the *Chumash*—the 613 *mitzvos*, including the Ten Commandments—apply directly only to the people in whose language the code is written.

Like languages, legal systems express particular understandings. And as with languages, the particular understandings are constituted in conflict and debate, are what the debaters share. Thus, no matter how successful, no particular legal system can make a direct claim to universality—none can overcome the particularity of the language in which it is formulated. Each legal system articulates the meaning of law and justice in a particular way. Wisdom in the law is not located within any particular understanding, but results rather from grasping all of these articulations at once.

The understandings incorporated in the numerous particular systems of law and justice may be accessed in several ways, but it may be easiest to begin at what might be called the beginning: not a beginning buried in the past but rather the beginning all new jurists experience as they are initiated into their craft—the various and extraordinarily diverse systems of legal education. Intuition suggests that legal education will differ greatly between traditions that are geographically dispersed and culturally disparate. But even a common cultural heritage does not prevent difference. For this reason, in order to suggest the range of methods in legal education, it is especially important to consider legal education in countries whose traditions seem to be closely related. Those established in West Germany, France, and the United States will be examined here. Though the skills taught in the three systems may seem to overlap somewhat, there is something very different about the manner in which they are articulated. The focus here is on those differences. In order to avoid a much more extensive discussion, I ignore other related processes in the law, such as the manner in which cases are decided and the methods of legal scholarship.

The principal object of German legal education is to develop the skill of the *Fallösung* or case resolution, a particular method for finding a legal solution to a hypothetical fact situation. It is the skill required for success at the German state examination, which is given at the conclusion of law school and which alone determines a student's final grade and rank in class. The technique of the *Fallösung* is considered so important that upper-level German law students often abandon university instruction entirely for the year or two prior to their state exam and follow courses taught by one of the many private tutors, the *Repetitoren*, who relentlessly drill and develop the skills required.

Substantively, German legal education tends to center in the private law, especially the law of contracts, particularly of sales contracts. The focus there is on questions of remedy, specifically on the relationship between the remedies and defenses available under general contract law and those provided by sales law. The complex set of rules provided in the German Civil Code and in the relevant case law to govern these matters involves elaborate cross-references, repeated resort to the interaction of principle, exception, and exception to exception, and reliance on elusively subtle distinctions. For those to whom intricate elegance is a virtue, this structure must be counted, with the verb forms in classical Greek, among the sublime creations of the human imagination. Needless to say, this part of German law is *Professorenrecht*, a matter for specialists. The complexity of the field is what recommends it as a test for the student's mastery of legal technique.

Success in resolving the German hypothetical requires a thorough knowledge of the remedial scheme and a comprehensive and systematic examination of the relevance of the various remedial provisions to the facts at hand. If the claimant in the hypothetical has several potential opponents, the claims against each must be discussed separately. If the claimant has more than one type of claim (*Anspruch*) against a particular party, the claims must be examined in the appropriate order. Much of German academic discussion focuses on questions of organization, and there are competing views on these questions. In general, primary claims are to be reviewed before secondary claims (specific relief before damages, replevin or ejectment before contract claims) and the claimant's primary objective before a secondary one. For each type of claim, there may be more than one potentially relevant basis for the claim (*Anspruchsgrundlage*)—the specific provision in the code or a well-established principle from the case law that offers the particular remedy to the claimant. Each substantive discussion begins with a statement of the relevant *Anspruchsgrundlage*, and all of the conceivably relevant bases for the claim must be examined in order—special before general norms, contractual before extra-contractual provisions, property-based provisions before restitution. For each particular provision, there is also an established order for the review of the legal requirements (*Tatbestandsmerkmale*). In tort, for example, though there is debate about the appropriate scheme, and any one of two or three alternatives is acceptable, the discussion traditionally begins with the nature of the harm, and then proceeds through the type of right that was violated, the tortious act, causation between the tortious act and the violation of the right, causation between the violation of the right and the harm, breach of duty (*Rechtswidrigkeit*), and fault (*Verschulden*). (The technique of the *Fallösung* is described in Uwe Diederichsen, *Die BGB-Klausur* 80-88 (6th ed. 1984), and in Dieter Medicus, *Bürgerliches Recht* 1-14 (14th ed. 1989).)

In short, greater emphasis is placed on the framework for the analysis than on the result. What is essential for success in the state examination is that the student subsume the facts correctly under the elaborated system of remedies. Of course, policy arguments may be raised in the answer, but only if they are incorporated into the appropriate phase of the discussion. In any case, nothing is to be mentioned that is not directly relevant to the question at hand. At the same time, no logically necessary step may be omitted. A serious error in construction may lead to failure even if the theories and policies are adequately examined. Most importantly, no step may be taken and no argument advanced unless it finds authority in a code provision or a well-established case-law principle. Though there may be slightly more flexibility and openness to innovation outside of the private law, adherence to preconceived outlines is cherished throughout German legal education.

Exclusive focus on the logic of the *Anspruchsgrundlage* encourages the German student to develop extraordinary rigor and orderliness and to pay close attention to subtle distinctions between the various remedial provisions. This emphasis, however, is not without its limitations. It tends to avoid explicit and wide-ranging discussion of policy alternatives and leaves the skill of advocacy largely undeveloped. Moreover, by concentrating on the accepted view and the firmly established remedial provisions, and by emphasizing the virtues of predictability and certainty, the *Fallösung* acquires a somewhat conservative cast.

German legal education, as it analyzes and orders the remedial scheme, enunciates a moral and political understanding of the nature of justice and of freedom under law. It asserts that a people is free when it deliberates in a parliamentary manner and when the commands of the legislature are rigorously executed by the judiciary. The implication is that progress in the law should be left to the political process and fine-tuning to the highest courts. The role of the individual judge is not to provide a remedy merely because it may seem just to do so but rather to respect the will of the people as promulgated in legislative enactments. The common lawyer may experience the German method as somewhat inflexible in reaching a legal conclusion and inattentive to the constellation of possibilities offered by the law. Yet, at the same time, the vision implicit in German legal education expresses not only a belief or yearning that is widely shared both inside and outside of Germany, but also a thought that may represent an element of every complex legal system.

French legal education focuses on a different skill and embodies a distinct understanding of the nature of law. To begin with, the French law professor avoids the hypothetical as a teaching tool: French law students are virtually never asked to consider a complicated fact pattern, identify the issues, and resolve the dispute. Instead, the focus is on a particular kind of synthesis. French students are taught to develop an overview of a legal topic or of a court decision and to convey that overview not only convincingly but also in a specific form.

The keystone of the French synthetic method is the *plan*, the organizational structure for the *exposé* or presentation. French jurists have developed the *plan* into an art form, one they elaborate according to strict rules. One rule is the maxim of elegance: the topic headings of the *plan*, when taken together, must envelop the entire subject matter, and each element of the whole must in fact be subsumed under one of the topic headings. Second, the *exposé*, between its brief introduction and its even briefer conclusion, generally contains exactly two parts, each divided into exactly two subparts. (A *plan* may include three principal parts—in its classical form, virtually never more than that—only if it is impossible to subsume one of the three under one of the other two.) The role of the introduction is to present and justify the *plan*. It begins from a commonplace that a legally educated reader would surely accept and then presents the subject matter in such a manner that the structural divisions of the *plan* seem convincing, even obvious. Each of the two principal parts of the *exposé* must be of approximately equal length. Each of two corresponding subparts must also be of similar proportion. Parallel topic headings must be symmetrical in syntactic form. In sum, the successful *exposé* gains clarity and persuasiveness by following the canons of balance and harmony. (The technique of the *plan* is described in Jean-Pierre Gridel, *La dissertation et le cas pratique en droit privé* 21-45 (2d ed. 1986).) This rule of two parts and two subparts is followed rigorously by students in both oral presentations and written examinations, and with some variation, by doctoral candidates writing dissertations, by the authors of law-review articles, and even by specialists when drafting comprehensive treatises.

The binary structure of the *exposé* may seem somewhat arbitrary and rigid, but, as with the rhyme scheme of a sonnet or the number of syllables in a *haiku*, the appearance is deceptive. The *plan* is essential to the French understanding of the nature of law. The insight underlying the French conception of the *plan* is that legal topics are best presented from the point of view of a fundamental tension or contradiction. Until a basic tension is discovered and the subject examined from that standpoint, any understanding is unsatisfying: the details will seem to have outflanked the author and the subject matter still to lie beyond the grasp. It is important to note that the French understanding does not represent a camouflaged metaphysical assertion about a supposed dialectical structure implicit in the law. There is nothing absolute or objective about the *plan* as the French conceive it. For any one subject, there could be as many *plans* as—or even more *plans* than—there are jurists.

The French conception of the *plan* is intoxicating to the point of addiction. No one who has successfully apprenticed in the French system deems a presentation successful, whether written or oral, unless it has been harmoniously organized into two parts, each with two subparts. From this perspective, any other organization of a legal discussion suggests only that the author has not yet fully mastered the material. The *plan* renders it uncommonly easy to see and retain the structure of the law and is capable of displaying the relationship among even the most far-flung topics. In the end, a persuasive *plan* is about as satisfying as intellectual things can be.

The single-minded French concentration on synthesis necessarily neglects much of what is otherwise interesting in the law. For example, French legal education fails to develop in its students a sensitivity to the facts or an understanding of the art of advocacy. It also produces an overly harmonious and unified vision of the law. It places the law student outside the law, at the point of synthesis, and removes all but the most accomplished jurists from active participation in legal change.

The vision implicit in French legal education is that the law is the organizing force in a society wrought with tension and contradiction. To organize contradiction, of course, does not mean to deny it. The law's task is to recognize the tension, to perceive how every legal question is divided against itself, to evaluate the contradictory views and present them in a balanced manner, and to offer, if only temporarily, an elegant and satisfying reconciliation of opposites. Law, in this perspective, both guarantees the realm of freedom and creates social unity and cohesiveness. It squares the circle, imposes order upon chaos. It is the center that holds against centrifugal force.

American legal education offers yet a different understanding. As are many other systems, it is principally the study of decided cases. But cases are not studied in America as they are studied elsewhere. In many other systems in which cases are read, the case serves almost exclusively to demonstrate to the law student how to apply the law to the facts, how to evaluate the comportment of individual parties by recourse to the norms available in the legal order. The object is to understand which party acted appropriately and which did not. In America, the study of cases may often fulfill a similar function, but the power of the case method lies elsewhere.

For one, cases are not generally taught alone. They are taught in pairs, triplets, or even entire series. The coupled cases may seem at first glance to provide differing solutions to the same set of facts. The task is then to reconcile the cases, to distinguish their facts in a convincing manner so that it becomes clear why each deserves the result the common law judge accorded to it. The challenge is to discover the perspective from which seemingly identical cases appear to be opposites.

In addition, the facts in reported cases are frequently used in American legal education as a challenge. The aspiration in many classrooms is for students to use the case to reconstruct the legal system. Legal norms are then not used to decide which of the two opposing parties acted properly. The answer to *that* question—this is one lesson from legal realism—is not an exclusively legal matter. Instead, American law teaching often uses a particular case as an occasion to evaluate the appropriateness of the legal rules. The object of such class discussion is to determine how the legal order should be structured so that it would resolve the case before the court in a satisfactory manner. The student learns to stand up in class and argue that, despite statute, regulation, and precedent, a rule is not what it ought to be. The goal is not merely for students to learn to spot the difficult issues, but also for them to learn that the difficulties must be resolved in a socially and politically responsible manner. For this reason, the case law method is neither rigorous nor formal. It is an impressionistic attempt to integrate statutory provisions, case law, policy considerations, jurisprudential theories, and notions of fairness and justice. What counts is what works, what convinces the socially and politically concerned listener.

The beauty—and the limitation—of American legal education is that it does so much with the rather limited resource of the appellate court opinion. Probably more than any other system of legal education, it encourages and develops the skill at drawing fine distinctions between the facts of similar cases and turning those distinctions into convincing legal arguments. It also teaches students not only to spot issues—to create them, really—but, at least to some extent, to advocate and achieve change. The case method can expand a student's imagination and creative potential in a way that may best be described as psychedelic. Of course, by concentrating on these skills very much to the exclusion of others, American law students often fail to achieve technical proficiency at manipulating code provisions and rarely gain a comprehensive overview of the relationship between the diverse fields of the law.

American law schools aspire to reorganize the past and prepare the future. The understanding of the law implicit in such a system is that the judge, the lawyer, and the individual litigant each has a role to play not only in vindicating, but in fact in creating individual rights. It is a vision of decentralized decision making, of a state in which every individual has direct access to a rule maker. It is the conception of the courtroom as a forum for democracy.

Of Legal Education and Cultural Projects

The diversity of meaning articulated in the various languages and systems of legal education suggests that every cultural tradition is distinct. Each pursues a particular goal, which it might be useful here to call a *cultural project*. The project is present in the language that is spoken, in the method of legal education, in the manner in which bread is baked—in short, in every aspect of life in a particular tradition.

Everyone who has lived abroad is aware of this. Yet, because it smacks of stereotyping, it seems slightly immoral to recognize it. One of the reasons stereotyping is such a serious sin is that the admission of global distinction may suggest grounds for prejudice and discrimination. For this reason, comparativists of all kinds usually attempt to demonstrate that, contrary to appearances, everything is really the same everywhere. Whatever the reason, little attention has been paid to the particularities of cultural projects. But the lesson of Babel is difficult to grasp until an effort is made to understand the peculiarities—and the potential contributions—of each of the various cultural traditions. What follows is a preliminary and subjective speculation about how language is related to the law in the three cultural traditions whose methods of legal education were examined above.

One particular feature of the German language is the manner in which abstraction is generated. It is part of the genius of the language that abstraction never loses touch with the concrete. In German, abstractions are living metaphors. They almost universally consist of two or more easily recognizable elementary words that have been yoked together. The basic, concrete meanings are generally active and present. The word *aufheben* is a good example. It consists of a prepositional prefix (*auf* = *up*) and a basic verb (*heben* = *to lift*). Its primary meaning is simply *to lift* or *to pick up* (to pick up a pencil from the floor) and the word is used in daily conversation in that sense. When used more abstractly, as is also common, the verb gains two virtually contradictory meanings. It can mean *to preserve* (to put something away in order to save it) as well as *to cancel* or *to set aside* (to abrogate or repeal a statutory restriction). Hegel employed the word philosophically to incorporate all of these meanings at once. To him it signified the process of transcending a stage of development by preserving it at a higher level.

The poetic and philosophical quality of the German language derives to a considerable extent from this constant resonance of the concrete in the abstract. For example, Hegel and Heidegger repeatedly interrogated the individual elements of composite words to discern their contribution to the resulting abstract concept. Both used the hyphen as the surgical tool for their investigation. Hegel, for example, on the last page of the *Phenomenology*, discovered in *Er-Innerung* (remembrance/internalization) not only an indication of Spirit's reimmersion into itself, but also the suggestion that history is the result of Spirit's own internal development. Heidegger transposed the technique mythopoeically to classical Greek, interpreting *Existenz* (existence) from the perspective of *Ek-sistenz* (to cause to stand and be exposed to), and *aletheia* (truth) as *a-letheia* (recovered from forgetfulness). Thus, one of the German language's central preoccupations is to assure that the individual element has been carefully and meaningfully integrated into the whole. Even basic words, when properly arranged with other words, gain metaphysical significance. The implication is that the individual not only gains meaning through, but to a large extent is identified with, its role in the complex whole.

Of course, this is not to say that this feature is unique to the German language. English, for example, occasionally employs the technique as well (*overcome, headhunter*), though English characteristically distinguishes between abstractions, which have Latin roots, and words for the concrete, which are derived from Anglo-Saxon. (Of course, *trans-late* too is a composite, both to those who know Latin and to English speakers who are aware of other *trans-* words (*transgress*) and other *-late* words (*elated*), but the elements are much less apparent than they are in the corresponding German compounds.) Moreover, the generation of abstraction is only one of the German language's central linguistic features. Another peculiarity, for example, is the delay of the verb until the end of the sentence, which requires a discipline in speaker and listener and an ability to anticipate and postpone gratification. Only after these and other elements have been illuminated can the nature of the German project become entirely clear.

This preoccupation with the role of the part in the whole, though only one of its elements, is constitutive of the German cultural project as well. The individual, though of course respected in its own right, is largely identified by its particular role in the community. It is a trait of Germanic languages, shared to some extent by English, that common proper names suggest the identification of the individual with its social role—*Schmidt* (smith), *Müller* (miller), *Wagner* (wainwright), *Krämer* (shopkeeper), *Bauer* (peasant farmer). The intensity of the German concern with these issues is what makes it so difficult to translate a sentence such as *Unserem Packmeister sind . . . Bedenken gekommen*. The suggestion of expertise implicit in the notion of the *Packmeister* or master packer emphasizes the importance of the development of a socially relevant skill to the identity of the individual. Moreover, by referring to the *Packmeister* as *unser* (our), the shipping firm both confirmed that the packer was in its employ and suggested that the master packer is a cultural resource, the polity's master packer, a person specially skilled in the craft and therefore deserving of job security and social insurance, a craftsperson of whom the entire nation might be proud. Furthermore, as the sentence suggests, master packers themselves are, in the end, only conduits for the tradition. The second thoughts arose from the practice of the craft over centuries, and merely came to rest in the person of the master packer. And, of course, the master packers' awareness of their role in the tradition redefines in turn how they conceive of themselves.

At the same time, there can be little doubt that the thoroughness with which the German project is organized generates a highly energized tension with individual rights and a heightened concern for the individual. That concern—which is also implicit in the Hegelian and Heideggerian hyphen—helps explain the focus in German philosophy on the status and nature of human freedom.

The German focus on the role of the part in the whole, though only one of its contradictory moments, is of great consequence to German legal education. The focus suggests the importance to the individual of a reliable social division of labor, both because of the security it affords and the opportunity it provides for the cultivation of craft and the mastery of technique. German legal education is simply a further expression of the same understanding. One of the hallmarks of a stable division of labor is a careful delimitation of the various social roles. The legislature makes the laws, while the lawyer and judge assure technical proficiency in their application. It seems, therefore, that central features of German legal education run parallel to the fundaments of the German language.

One of the exquisite qualities of spoken and written French lies in the distinction and alternation between the indicative and subjunctive moods of its verbs. Verbs in the indicative mood often end with syllables pronounced as open (despite the orthography), while those of the subjunctive are usually and emphatically closed (*vient/vienne*). The French subjunctive appears chiefly in subordinate clauses, generally after principal verbs expressing personal feeling, such as desire, joy, and sadness. Thus, as a simple proposition, *she is coming* (*elle vient*) is in the indicative, but is placed in French in the subjunctive following statements such as *I wish that . . .* (*je veux qu'elle vienne*). The subjunctive may also appear in relative clauses that indirectly express similar emotions, and even in principal clauses, namely in a few fixed idioms expressing a great personal commitment or excitement that coincides with a socially recognized injunction (*Vive la France! Sauve qui peut!* Run for your life!). Much of the concern in teaching French and the joy in learning it revolves around the mastery of the forms and distinctions involved in the use of the subjunctive. The poetic quality of the French language also derives in part from the interplay between the two moods. (*Vienne la nuit sonne l'heure/Les jours s'en vont je demeure*).

The French indicative describes the objective, the verifiable, the repeatable. The subjunctive invokes the subjective, the personal, the desired. To delimit the appropriate sphere for the pursuit of individual desire within the structure of social cohesion is the central concern. The opposition between the two moods legitimates a role for individual exuberance within the framework of social convention. From this perspective, the French project attempts to maintain sufficient room for the expression of individuality while maintaining a cohesive centralized order. Once again, legal education seems to be structured like the language, for this of course is also the object of the *plan*. The *plan* both recognizes the tension that may result from the assertion of individual interest and demonstrates the necessity of the law as the structure for social organization.

Of course, the alternation between indicative and subjunctive is not unique to French—in fact it is shared with the other Romance languages. Moreover, French has other characteristic features, such as the double negative (*ne . . . pas*, *ne . . .rien*), that must be explored before the French project can be thoroughly understood.

It would be useful to include here a short discussion of American English and of the American cultural project. A sense of the particularity of American English, however, is largely barred to me. One of the most direct lessons of the story of Babel, as Paul de Man has noted, is that the most alienated and uncomprehending relationship one can have with a language is usually the one native speakers have with their own. However, those I have consulted who speak English as a foreign language usually tend to note the same peculiarities. Spelling does not coincide with pronunciation (tough/though/through, read/read). Prepositions are employed in an apparently idiosyncratic manner (the alarm went *off*, to study *under*). Word formation often ignores etymology (hamburger/cheeseburger) (sandwich/fishwich). There are some rules that few master (the distinction between *that* and *which*, the proper use of the comma), other rules that tend to be honored chiefly in their breach (the prohibitions against the split infinitive and against ending a phrase with a preposition), elaborate rules that are seldom used (much about the various past tenses), and vast stretches with no enunciated rule and nothing to assist the foreigner who has not yet acquired a sense of the underlying enterprise. The stated rules seem to be of little importance, while the effective rules seem to be unstatable. In fact, idiomatic expressions are so prevalent that it is possible to master all the rules and still not speak the language fluently. The consensus is that it is a language of infinite imagination but little discipline, a restless language in constant innovation. ("We got the repeat," San Francisco 49ers running back

Roger Craig announced to the press after his team won the Super Bowl for the second year in a row, "now we want the *three*-peat.")

Needless to say, there is much in common here with American legal education, especially its impromptu and unsystematic character, the joy with which principles and theories are created, employed, and forgotten. The pragmatic American mode of politics, the role of individual initiative, and all the rest seem intimately bound up in all of this. But it can only be seen clearly by someone who takes it up from the perspective of another tradition. (Indeed, what I suggest above about the particular understanding implicit in American legal education is not my own insight but comes rather from Michel Pêcheux, who mentioned the idea in conversation shortly before his death.).

One lesson is that each system of legal education, like the language in which it is formulated, constitutes a part of a larger cultural project and represents a particular articulation of meaning. The even more far-reaching lesson from the story of Babel is that diversity deserves to be recognized, preserved, cultivated, and developed. The political and theoretical implications of this lesson are perhaps best observed from the point of view of postmodernity.

First, the story of Babel seems to confirm much of what postmodernity has to say about the implication of madness in understanding. The idea is that understanding is fundamentally constituted by the desire to escape from chaos. (The idea is discussed by William Corlett in *Community without Unity* (1989).) In the hope of domesticating chaos, understanding constructs polar oppositions and forces every element of existence to adhere to one or the other of two poles—male and female, white and black, right and left, sick and healthy, individual and collectivity. Understanding thus not only bears the trace of fear in its constitution, but is itself a kind of derangement.

This, in fact, is what the story of Babel is all about. The confusion of language resulted directly from the seemingly unavoidable tendency to think in terms of polar opposition. Certainly each of the cultural projects examined here, including their systems of legal education and their languages, attempt to conquer chaos in this manner. German legal education emphasizes the obedience of the judge to the will of the legislature in a way that reflects the concerns of the German cultural project about the importance of integrating the individual into the collectivity. French legal education emphasizes that the opposition between individual desire and legal order is to be expounded by binary opposition, and thereby mirrors the oppositions found in its language between subjunctive and indicative, subjective and objective, individual and collective. American legal education emphasizes the conflicting demands of judicial creativity and precedent—another version of the tension between individual and collectivity, which parallels the opposition in American English between idiomatic expressions and traditional rules.

Each cultural project and each system of legal education seems to attempt to escape from chaos by constructing its own set of polar oppositions, oppositions that can be ordered on many axes, including the relationship between individual and collectivity. The deconstructionists are justly worried about the power of these oppositions and are correct in suggesting that we try to defuse them. In this sense, *HaShem* was the original deconstructionist, for that was also *HaShem*'s concern. What *HaShem* noticed upon descending to Babel was that humankind recoiled in fright from the unknown, and that it was quick to try to protect itself by articulating meaning in terms of oppositions—Heaven and earth, life and death, unity and dispersion, naming and chaos. *HaShem* thereupon confused language and sent humankind out into the unknown that it most feared. By creating a multitude of languages, *HaShem* hoped to melt the dichotomies into diversity and to assist humanity in overcoming its reduction of meaning.

In sum, the understanding present in any one language or cultural project is plagued with the structure of opposition that deconstruction has taught us to notice and reject. Each of these understandings is therefore not only particular and limited, but in fact suffused with fear and madness, or rather constitutes one kind of madness in order to escape from another. That is why translation can be not only frustrating but literally maddening: it tends to lead the translator beyond the habitual bulwarks against insanity. Hölderlin's translations of Sophocles were some of the last lines he composed before he plunged into almost forty years of crazed silence.

A second concern of postmodernism is the problem of the unitary origin. As I understand it, one of the goals of postmodern politics is to demonstrate the importance of differential plurality and to create a society that takes advantage of the potential synergism of all types of difference. In this perspective, the postmodern philosophies of difference attempt to demonstrate that differences cannot be confined within an original unity or totality in which they might, in the end, be reconciled. Difference, we are told, is *anoriginal*. (The term is from Andrew Benjamin, who summarizes the argument in *Translation and the Nature of Philosophy* (1989).) The danger that postmodernity thereby seeks to avoid is the single totalizing structure that may be imposed upon, and thereby destroy, diversity.

Yet not all stories of origins have this problem. Accounts of origins are problematic only when they imply that it would be beneficial to reduce diversity to unity or to return to an original golden age. An example is the extraordinarily conservative and nostalgically romantic myth of return that inhabits Marx's thought and that seems to have led Heidegger to Nazism. But there is not the least suggestion in the story of Babel that humanity would be better off returning to the Noachian condition. Moreover, as the story makes clear, there was never any meaningful unity at the origin. The original language must have teemed with an incredible multitude of patterns and ideas. Otherwise its confusion could never have produced ten thousand human languages. What led to calamity was rather the human insistence on reducing that incredible wealth to one set of simple oppositions. Furthermore, it is clear that there is no way, starting from the natural languages that survive today, to piece together the original language. Language is and will remain for us always already disarticulated into difference. Any unity that might once have existed can never be resynthesized. Since the remaining languages can never be reduced to a single meaning, all that results from piecing them together is the understanding of how each represents the kind of intentionality that Walter Benjamin referred to as pure language (*die reine Sprache*). Thus, the story of Babel is not so much the story of an origin as the indication of a trace.

One last theoretical issue raised by the story of Babel concerns the status of diversity. This is a problem that is never really resolved in the garden variety philosophies of difference. These theories attempt to demonstrate the plausibility of a way of thinking that conceives of difference as primary. But the mere existence—or even the primacy—of difference cannot alone convince us that difference is good. Instead of a normative argument demonstrating the value of diversity, the philosophies of difference offer only a clutter of difference, what might better be called *indifference*. Though these philosophies may be read to imply that we should respect those who hold views that differ from our own, there is nothing in them to encourage us to devote our energy to examining with care articulations of meaning that we initially find unconvincing or strange. Theirs is a position at which one might arrive just as easily by indolence as by conviction.

It is in this sense that the story of Babel demonstrates how much more there is to diversity than the philosophers of difference have perceived. For the message of the story is not simply that difference is an unavoidable fact of life. It is rather that diversity expands the limits of intelligibility. The reason is as follows. Language does not simply take the world as it is, but rather constitutes intelligibility as it communicates. There is no intelligibility outside of language. This thought, which Heidegger took from Stefan George—No thing can be where the word is wanting (*Kein ding sei wo das wort gebricht*)—suggests that every language, and every tradition, is entitled to profound respect. However limited and deranged, the understandings in the surviving natural languages are the sum total of intelligibility. If each language constitutes a different fragment, then each is a treasure. We are the shepherds and not the masters of language.

The potential wealth of diversity is at least threefold. First, since the articulations of meaning present in the particular languages and traditions are each limited, each will find much that is evidently and practically useful in the other cultural projects. And this is true whether or not there was ever a single original language of which the surviving languages may be fragments. Second, the interplay between diverse traditions offers one of the few opportunities for the creation of truly new ideas, ideas that arise outside the scope of any one tradition's particular experience. Finally, diversity is a prerequisite to serious self-reflection. Without the existence of diverse traditions, it would become literally impossible to assess the peculiar characteristics of any particular understanding. Human beings who know only one language have little alternative but to consider the articulation of meaning within that language to be absolute. There is little they can do to step outside that understanding in order to relativize it. The articulation of meaning in their language will permeate everything they think or write and render it difficult to avoid totalizing reductionism. Should they become aware that other and different perspectives exist, they are of course capable of tolerance. But wisdom is not simply tolerance, never merely a recognition *of* diversity, no matter how generous and humanitarian. Wisdom rather is a vision *from* diversity, an understanding constituted in fragmentation. The multiplicity of languages is its irreducible condition. It is a blessing and not a curse.

Of Blessings

Blessings are opportunities. They are no less so because their realization requires effort and often suffering. The study of a foreign language and the initiation into a foreign culture can be intriguing and delightful, but they also involve mindless memorization, incessant repetition, and a painful reorientation of thought. When pursued seriously, they may result in a throbbing loneliness, the constant companion of foreigners who isolate themselves from their compatriots long enough to master the essentials of a foreign language. And apprenticeship in a foreign legal system can be even more disorienting and disturbing than learning the foreign language in the first place.

No one who succeeds at the enterprise does so without a good reason. Some have had their lives shattered in their homelands, been scattered into exile, and have been subjected involuntarily to the destructive force of diversity. They are thankful for the hospitality their hosts show them, but equally frustrated by the incomprehension they encounter. They survive the experience chiefly by clinging to the possibility of return. For others, diversity is a constant reminder of incompleteness, of the wound left in the soul by the dismemberment that occurred at Babel. Their awareness of the impoverished character of any single articulation of understanding requires them to reach out to embrace foreign cultures. But even for them, diversity is no more than a scar over a wound that can never heal.

There is no perspective from which the disastrous consequences of the confusion of language can be denied. But a blessing is not distinguished from a curse by the intensity of pain thereby avoided or by the quality of comfort it affords. What makes of Babel a blessing is that it offers, though at terrible cost, the otherwise unavailable challenge of possibility.

(I am deeply indebted to Susan Bender, Rabbi David Bleich, David Carlson, Mary Coombs, Michael Fischl, Christoph Grigoleit, Pat Gudridge, Arthur Jacobson, Dennis Patterson, Robert Rosen, Simon Schneebalg, Nicolo Trocker, Elisabeth Weber, and Steven Winter. And thanks to Nora de la Garza for helping me find the books.)

[3]

Law as Rhetoric, Rhetoric as Law: The Arts of Cultural and Communal Life

James Boyd White†

In this paper I shall suggest that law is most usefully seen not, as it usually is by academics and philosophers, as a system of rules, but as a branch of rhetoric; and that the kind of rhetoric of which law is a species is most usefully seen not, as rhetoric usually is, either as a failed science or as the ignoble art of persuasion, but as the central art by which community and culture are established, maintained, and transformed. So regarded, rhetoric is continuous with law, and like it, has justice as its ultimate subject.

I do not mean to say that these are the only ways to understand law or rhetoric. There is a place in the world for institutional and policy studies, for taxonomies of persuasive devices, and for analyses of statistical patterns and distributive effects. But I think that all these activities will themselves be performed and criticized more intelligently if it is recognized that they too are rhetorical. As for law and rhetoric themselves, I think that to see them in the way I suggest is to make sense of them in a more nearly complete way, especially from the point of view of the individual speaker, the individual hearer, and the individual judge.

I

Let us begin with the idea that the law is a branch of rhetoric. Who, you may ask, could ever have thought it was anything else? The ancient rhetorician Gorgias (in Plato's dialogue of that name) defined rhetoric as the art of persuading the people about matters of justice and injustice in the public places of the state,[1] and one could hardly imagine a more compendious statement of the art of

---

† Professor of Law and Professor of English Language and Literature, University of Michigan. I am grateful for helpful comments by Alton Becker, Lee Bollinger, Stanley Fish, Bruce Gronbeck, L.H. LaRue, Richard Lempert, Sallyanne Payton, Terrance Sandalow, Frederick Schauer, Stephen Shiffrin, Philip Soper, Cass Sunstein, Joseph Vining, and Christina Whitman. This article is a version of a chapter in my forthcoming book, HERACLES' BOW: ESSAYS ON THE RHETORIC AND POETICS OF THE LAW.

[1] PLATO, GORGIAS 452e, 454b. For further discussion, see my article, *The Ethics of Argument: Plato's* Gorgias *and the Modern Lawyer*, 50 U. CHI. L. REV. 849 (1983).

the lawyer than that. A modern law school is, among other things, a school in those arts of persuasion about justice that are peculiar to, and peculiarly effective in, our legal culture. And the commitment of the rhetorician to the cause of his client presents him, in the ancient and the modern world alike, with serious (and similar) problems of intellectual and personal integrity. How can it be that law was ever regarded as anything but rhetoric?

The answer lies, I think, in two traditions—one old, the other new—which I can summarize this way. The older (primarily Judaic and Christian) tradition saw the law as a set of authoritative commands, entitled to respect partly from their antiquity, partly from their concordance with the law of nature and of God. In this view law is not rhetoric but authority. The newer tradition is that of institutional sociology, the object of which is to describe and analyze the structure and function of various social institutions, so far as possible, from the point of view of "value-free" social science. These institutions may of course have certain kinds of political authority internal to the culture in which they are found, but they are normally not seen as sources of true moral authority, as law once was. With the apparent death of the first tradition in most Western European (but not Islamic!) countries, we are left with the second, and tend to view law as a system of institutionally established and managed rules. Actually, as this conception has worked itself out in practice it has led to a kind of substantive neutrality (or emptiness) that makes it natural once again to see a connection between modern law and ancient rhetoric, and to face—as Plato did in the *Gorgias*—the great question of what talk about justice can mean in a world as relativistic, adversarial, competitive, and uncertain as ours is and Plato's was.

As a result, the law is at present usually spoken of (by academics at least) as if it were a body of more or less determinate rules, or rules and principles, that are more or less perfectly intelligible to the trained reader. Law is in this sense objectified and made a structure. The question "What is law?" is answered by defining what its rules are, or by analyzing the kinds of rules that characterize it. The law is thus abstracted and conceptualized: H.L.A. Hart's major book on jurisprudence was appropriately entitled *The Concept of Law.*[2] Sophisticated analysis of law from this point of view distinguishes among various kinds of legal rules and among different sets or subsets of legal rules: substantive rules are

[2] H.L.A. HART, THE CONCEPT OF LAW (1961).

distinguished from procedural or remedial rules, or primary rules from secondary rules, or legal rules from more general principles.

This idea of law and legal science fits with, and is perhaps derived from, the contemporary conception of our public political world as a set of bureaucratic entities, which can be defined in Weberian terms as rationalized institutions functioning according to ends-means rationality. These institutions have goals, purposes, or aims, which they achieve more or less perfectly as they are structured and managed more or less well.

In this way, the government (of which the law is a part) and in fact the entire bureaucratic system, private as well as public, tends to be regarded, especially by lawyers, managers, and other policy-makers, as a machine acting on the rest of the world. This naturally reduces the rest of the world to the object upon which the machine acts. Human actors outside the governmental world are made the objects of manipulation through a series of incentives or disincentives. Actors within the legal-bureaucratic structure either are "will-servers" (whose obligation is to obey the will of a political superior) or are "choice-makers" (who are in a position of political superiority charged with the responsibility of making choices, usually thought of as "policy choices," that affect the lives of others). The choices themselves are likewise objectified: the items of choice are broken out of the flux of experience and the context of life so that they can be talked about in the bureaucratic-legal mode. This commits the system to what is thought to be measurable (especially to what is measurable in material ways) to short-term goals, and to a process of thought by calculation. The premises of cost-benefit analysis are thus integral to the bureaucracy as we normally imagine it. Whatever cannot be talked about in these bureaucratic ways is simply not talked about. Of course all systems of discourse have domains and boundaries, principles of exclusion and inclusion, but this kind of bureaucratic talk is largely unself-conscious about what it excludes. The world it sees is its whole world.

Law then becomes reducible to two features: policy choices and techniques of their implementation. Our questions are "What do we want?" and "How do we get it?" In this way the conception of law as a set of rules merges with the conception of law as a set of institutions and processes. The overriding metaphor is that of the machine; the overriding value is that of efficiency, conceived of as the attainment of certain ends with the smallest possible costs.

This is a necessarily crude sketch of certain ways in which law is commonly thought of. Later in this paper, I will propose a different way of conceiving of law, which I think can be both more true to its actual nature as practiced and more valuable to us as critics.

II

But I turn first to the meaning of "rhetoric." This term is in great flux, and what I say must be somewhat less dogmatic than my discussion of "law." It is my impression that rhetoric is at present usually talked about in either of two modes. The first of these is by comparison with science. The main claim of science is that it contributes to knowledge by informing us of what is knowable in the sense that it can be demonstrated. This is true both of deductive sciences, which establish propositions by demonstrating their entailment in certain premises, and of inductive sciences, which establish, but with less certainty, propositions that can be regarded as the most complete and economical accounts of the evidence available to us, and hence as presumptively true. From this point of view, rhetoric is thought of as what we do when science doesn't work. Instead of dealing with what is "known," it deals with what is probably the case. Thus in Aristotle the enthymeme is defined as a syllogism based upon propositions that are themselves not necessarily true but probable.[3] So regarded, rhetoric is the art of establishing the probable by arguing from our sense of the probable. It is always open to replacement by science when the truth or falsity of what is now merely probable is finally established.

The other heading under which rhetoric is frequently discussed is explicitly pejorative: rhetoric is defined as the ignoble art of persuasion. As I suggested above, this tradition has a history at least as old as the Platonic dialogues, in which rhetoric is attacked as a false art; it is also as contemporary as the standard modern condemnations of government propaganda and of the kind of advertising practiced by the wizards of Madison Avenue.

To the extent that law is today regarded as a kind of rhetoric, these two traditions establish the terms of analysis. In the courtroom the truth is never known, and each of the lawyers tries to persuade the jury not of the truth, but that his (or her) view is more probable than the other one (or that the other side has not attained some requisite degree of probability). In doing so, each lawyer employs untrustworthy arts of persuasion by which he seeks to make his own case, even if it is the weaker one, appear the stronger. Rhetoric, in short, is thought of either as a second-rate

[3] Aristotle, Rhetoric 1357a23-33.

way of dealing with facts that cannot really be properly known or as a way of dealing with people instrumentally or manipulatively, in an attempt to get them to do something you want them to do.

The tendency to think of rhetoric as failed science is especially powerful in the present age, in which determined attempts have been made to elevate, or to reduce, virtually every discipline to the status of true science. The idea of science as perfect knowledge has of course recently been subjected to considerable criticism, both internal and external. It is now a commonplace that scientific creativity is imaginative, almost poetic; that scientific knowledge is only presumptive, not certain; and that science is a culture that transforms itself by principles that are not themselves scientific. Yet the effort to make the language and conventions of science the ruling model of our age, our popular religion, lives on in the language and expectations of many people, especially of those who are in fact not true scientists. Much of economic discourse, for example, is deformed by the false claims of the discipline to the status of perfect science, which leads to the embarrassing situation in which economic speakers representing different political attitudes couch their differences in scientific terms, each claiming that the other is no true economist. This not only confuses the observer but renders the field of economics less intelligible than it should be, even to its participants, and it reduces important political differences, which might be the topic of real conversation, to the status of primary assumptions.

III

I shall sketch out a somewhat different way of conceiving of law, and indeed of governmental processes generally: not as a bureaucratic but as a rhetorical process. In doing this, I shall also be suggesting a way to think about rhetoric, especially that kind of rhetoric—I call it "constitutive rhetoric"—of which law can I think be seen as a species.

I want to start by thinking of law not as an objective reality in an imagined social world, not as a part of a constructed cosmology, but from the point of view of those who actually engage in its processes, as something we do and something we teach. This is a way of looking at law as an activity, and in particular as a rhetorical activity.

I want to direct attention to three related aspects of the lawyer's work. The first is the fact that the lawyer, like any rhetorician, must always start by speaking the language of his or her audience, whatever it may be. This is just a version of the general truth that to persuade anybody you must in the first instance speak a language that he or she regards as valid and intelligible. If you are a lawyer, this means that you must speak either the technical language of the law—the rules, cases, statutes, maxims, and so forth, that constitute the domain of your professional talk—or, if you are speaking to jurors or clients or the public at large, some version of the ordinary English of your time and place. Law is in this sense always culture-specific. It always starts with an external, empirically discoverable set of cultural resources into which it is an intervention.

This suggests that one (somewhat circular) definition of the law might be the particular set of resources made available by a culture for speech and argument on those occasions, and by those speakers, we think of as legal. These resources include rules, statutes, and judicial opinions, of course, but much more as well: maxims, general understandings, conventional wisdom, and all the other resources, technical and nontechnical, that a lawyer might use in defining his or her position and urging another to accept it.[4] To define "the law" in this way, as a set of resources for thought and argument, is an application of Aristotle's traditional definition of rhetoric, for the law in this sense is one set of those "means of persuasion" that he said it is the art of rhetoric to discover.[5]

In the law (and I believe elsewhere as well), these means of persuasion can be described with some degree of accuracy and completeness, so that most lawyers would agree that such-and-such a case or statute or principle is relevant, and another is not. But the agreement is always imperfect: one lawyer will see an analogy that another will deny, for example. And when attention shifts to the value or weight that different parts of the material should have, disagreement becomes widespread and deep. Ultimately, then, the identity, the meaning, and the authority of the materials are always arguable, always uncertain. There is a sense in which

[4] In light of the current view of law as a set of rules, it is worth stressing that while much legal argument naturally takes the form of interpreting rules, or redefining them, and while some rules are obviously of greater authority than others, the material as a whole is not structured as a set of rules with a hierarchical or other order, nor is it reducible to a set of rules. The rule is often the subject as well as the source of argument, with respect to its form, its content, and its relation to other rules. Perhaps the best way to understand what a rule is, as it works in the legal world, is to think of it not as a command that is obeyed or disobeyed but as the topic of thought and argument—as one of many resources brought to bear by the lawyer and others both to define a question and to establish a way to approach it.

[5] Aristotle, Rhetoric 1355b26-27.

the materials can be regarded in the first instance as objective, external to the self; but they are always remade in argument. Their discovery is, in a sense, an empirical process, their reformulation and use an inventive or creative one.

This suggests that the lawyer's work has a second essential element, the creative process to which I have just alluded. For in speaking the language of the law, the lawyer must always be ready to try to change it: to add or to drop a distinction, to admit a new voice, to claim a new source of authority, and so on. One's performance is in this sense always argumentative, not only about the result one seeks to obtain but also about the version of the legal discourse that one uses—that one creates—in one's speech and writing. That is, the lawyer is always saying not only, "Here is how this case should be decided," but also, "Here—in this language—is the way this case and similar cases should be talked about. The language I am speaking is the proper language of justice in our culture." The legal speaker always acts upon the language that he or she uses, to modify or rearrange it; in this sense legal rhetoric is always argumentatively constitutive of the language it employs.

The third aspect of legal rhetoric is what might be called its ethical or communal character, or its socially constitutive nature. Every time one speaks as a lawyer, one establishes for the moment a character—an ethical identity, or what the Greeks called an *ethos*—for oneself, for one's audience, and for those one talks about, and in addition one proposes a relation among the characters one defines. One creates, or proposes to create, a community of people, talking to and about each other. The lawyer's speech is thus always implicitly argumentative not only about the result—how should the case be decided?—and about the language—in what terms should it be defined and talked about?—but also about the rhetorical community of which one is at that moment a part. The lawyer is always establishing in performance a response to the questions, "What kind of community should we, who are talking the language of the law, establish with each other, with our clients, and with the rest of the world? What kind of conversation should the law constitute, should constitute the law?"

Each of the three aspects of the lawyer's rhetorical life can be analyzed and criticized: the discourse one is given by one's culture to speak; the argumentative reconstitution of it; and the argumentative constitution of a rhetorical community in one's speech or writing. The study of this process—of constitutive rhetoric—is the study of the ways we constitute ourselves as individuals, as communities, and as cultures, whenever we speak. To put this another way, the fact that the law can be understood as a comprehensibly organized method of argument, or what I call a rhetoric, means that it is at once a social activity—a way of acting with others—and a cultural activity—a way of acting with a certain set of materials found in the culture. It is always communal, both in the sense that it always takes place in a social context and in the sense that it is always constitutive of the community by which it works. Both the lawyer and the lawyer's audience live in a world in which their language and community are not fixed and certain but fluid, constantly remade, as their possibilities and limits are tested. The law is an art of persuasion that creates the objects of its persuasion, for it constitutes both the community and the culture it commends.

This means that the process of law is at once creative and educative. Those who use this language are perpetually learning what can and cannot be done with it as they try—and fail or succeed—to reach new formulations of their positions. It also means that both the identity of the speakers and their wants are in perpetual transformation. If this is right, the law cannot be a technique, as the bureaucratic model assumes, by which "we" get what we "want," for both "we" and our "wants" are constantly remade in the rhetorical process. The idea of the legal actor as one who is either making policy choices himself (or herself) or obeying the choices made by others is inadequate, for he is a participant in the perpetual remaking of the language and culture that determines who he is and who we are. The law is not merely a bureaucracy or a set of rules, but a community of speakers of a certain kind: a culture of argument, perpetually remade by its participants.

All three of these aspects of the lawyer's work flow from the fact that the law is what I have called culture-specific, that is, that it always takes place in a cultural context into which it is always an intervention. But it is in a similar way socially specific: it always takes place in a particular social context, into which it is also an intervention. By this I mean nothing grand but simply that the lawyer responds to the felt needs of others, who come to him or her for assistance with an actual difficulty or problem. (These felt needs may of course be partly the product of the law itself, and the very "intervention" of the law can create new possibilities for meaning, for motive, and for aspiration.) From this point of view, the law can be seen, as it is experienced, not as a wholly independent system of meaning, but as a way of talking about real events and actual people in the world. It is a way of telling a story about what has happened in the world and claiming a meaning for it by writing an ending to it. The lawyer is repeatedly saying, or imagining himself or herself saying: "Here is 'what happened,' here is 'what it means,' and here is 'why it means what I claim.'" The process is at heart a narrative one because there cannot be a legal case without a real story about real people actually located in time and space and culture. Some actual person must go to a lawyer with an account of the experience upon which he or she wants the law to act, and that account will always be a narrative. The client's narrative is not simply accepted by the lawyer but subjected to questioning and elaboration, as the lawyer sees first one set of legal relevances, then another. In the formal legal process, that story is then retold, over and over, by the lawyer and by the client and by others, in developing and competing versions, until by judgment or agreement an authoritative version is achieved. This story will in the first instance be told in the language of its actors. That is where the law begins; in a sense that is also where it ends, for its object is to provide an ending to that story that will work in the world. And since the story both begins and ends in ordinary language and experience, the heart of the law is the process of translation by which it must work, from ordinary language to legal language and back again.

The language that the lawyer uses and remakes is a language of meaning in the fullest sense. It is a language in which our perceptions of the natural universe are constructed and related, in which our values and motives are defined, and in which our methods of reasoning are elaborated and enacted. By defining roles and actors, and by establishing expectations as to the propriety of speech and conduct, it gives us the terms for constructing a social universe. Law always operates through speakers located in particular times and places speaking to actual audiences about real people; its language is continuous with ordinary language; it always operates by narrative; it is not conceptual in its structure; it is perpetually reaffirmed or rejected in a social process; and it contains a system of internal translation by which it can reach a range of hearers. All these things mark it as a rhetorical system.

IV

What I have said means something, I think, about what we can mean by "rhetoric" as well as what we mean by "law." What I have been describing is not merely an art of estimating probabilities or an art of persuasion, but an art of constituting culture and community. It is of this kind of rhetoric that I think the law is a branch.

Let me approach what I mean about rhetoric with a primitive example, meant to suggest that what I call "constitutive rhetoric" is actually the set of practices that most fully distinguish humans from other animals. Imagine a bear fishing for salmon in a river of the great Northwest. What is it doing? "Fishing," we say. Now imagine a man fishing in the same river for the same fish. What is he doing? "Fishing," we say; but this time the answer has a different meaning and a new dimension, for it is now a question, as it was not before, what the fishing means to the actor himself. If a person does it, it has a meaning of a kind it cannot otherwise have. Today the meaning may well be that of sentimental escape to the wilderness by one sportily clad in his L.L. Bean outfit, demonstrating his place in a certain social class; but once—for a Native American say—it might have been a religious meaning.

Whenever two people come together to fish (or hunt, or anything else), they necessarily share the question of the meaning of what they do. Their views may differ, and their differences may reach the meaning of their relationship as well as that of their common activity. There is, for example, the question of dominance or equality. Is one following the other, or are they in some real sense together? Do their views of the meaning of what they do coincide, and, if so, how do they know? Or is there tension or disharmony between them, and, if so, what is to be done about that? How long will the terms upon which they are proceeding remain stable? The establishment of comprehensible relations and shared meanings, the making of the kind of community that enables people to say "we" about what they do and to claim consistent meanings for it—all this at the deepest level involves persuasion as well as education, and is the province of what I call constitutive rhetoric.

Let me expand my example a bit. Think of the kind of opposition that begins the *Iliad,* the opposition between two male human beings quarreling over a female. From one point of view, this is just like two other male mammals doing the same thing, say two male bears or dogs. But from another point of view there is a completely new dimension added to the dispute: the question of what it means from each point of view, including that of the woman. It is from such a dispute, and from the claims of competing meanings for the events involved, that arose both the Trojan War (at least in Greek myth) and—much more importantly—from our point of view the *Iliad* itself. Agamemnon and Achilles are engaged in a struggle. At some level, the struggle is an animal one, with will opposed to will. It is also a human struggle, a struggle over what ought to be done, and why, and this is a struggle over meaning: what it means for Agamemnon to be deprived of a prize, or of this woman, or for Achilles to be deprived of a prize, or of this woman. (At moments in this poem, attention is directed to what such struggles mean from the point of view of the women themselves, for example in the cases of Helen and Andromache.[6])

Once the quarrel has begun and Achilles has separated himself from the other Achaeans, the question shifts to what *that* means, and, as time goes on, to how the quarrel might be made up. "Making up" a quarrel is a process in which the parties gradually, and often with great difficulty, come to share a common language for the description of their common past, present, and future, including an agreement as to what will be passed over in silence. In this process, they reestablish themselves as a community with a culture of their own. In the *Iliad,* Agamemnon's attempts to make up the quarrel fail; the community between the two antagonists is never reestablished, even when Achilles returns to the battle (because this happens for a different reason, the death of Patroclus).

Or think of another great literary moment, the beginning of *Paradise Lost,* when Satan and the other rebellious angels try to establish a community of their own in Hell, based upon a new language of value and meaning. Their incredible attempts at self-creation and self-assertion have won them the admiration of many readers from Shelley onwards; some even see Satan as the unacknowledged hero of the poem. ("The mind is its own place, and in it self / Can make a Heav'n of Hell, a Hell of Heav'n."[7]) But the poem shows that no community can be built upon the language that they use, a language of selfishness and hatred—a language that in fact made a "Hell of Heav'n"—even by figures with such enormous capacities of imagination and will as Milton represents the angels to have. Compare with this the efforts of the participants at our own Constitutional Convention in the summer of 1787, who were also trying to find or make a language, and a set of relations, upon which a new community could be made and upon which a new life could proceed. Their arguments can be read as the gradual attempt to make a language of shared factual assumptions, shared values, shared senses of what need and what need not be said—of what could be said ambiguously, of what they could not resolve at all—resulting in a text that they could offer to others as the terms on which a new community might begin its tentative life.

---

[6] HOMER, ILIAD bk. III, ll. 121-244; bk. VI, ll. 342-58, 404-39.

[7] JOHN MILTON, PARADISE LOST bk. I, ll. 255-56 (1st ed. London 1667).

What kind of community shall it be? How will it work? In what language shall it be formed? These are the great questions of rhetorical analysis. It thus always has justice and ethics—and politics, in the best sense of that term—as its ultimate subjects.

The domain of constitutive rhetoric, as I think of it, thus includes *all* language activity that goes into the constitution of actual human cultures and communities. Even the kind of persuasion Plato called dialectic, in which the speaker is himself willing, even eager, to be refuted, is in this sense a form of rhetoric, for it is the establishment of community and culture in language.

V

Like law, rhetoric invents; and, like law, it invents out of something rather than out of nothing. It always starts in a particular culture and among particular people. There is always one speaker addressing others in a particular situation, about concerns that are real and important to somebody, and speaking a particular language. Rhetoric always takes place with given materials. One cannot idealize rhetoric and say, "Here is how it should go on in general." As Aristotle saw—for his *Rhetoric* is, for the most part, a map of claims that are persuasive in his Greek world—rhetoric is always specific to its material. There is no Archimedean point from which rhetoric can be viewed or practiced.

This means that the rhetorician—that is, each of us when we speak to persuade or to establish community in other ways—must accept the double fact that there are real and important differences among cultures and that each person is to a substantial degree the product of his or her own culture. The rhetorician, like the lawyer, is engaged in a process of meaning-making and community-building of which he or she is in part the subject. To do this requires him or her to face and to accept the condition of radical uncertainty in which we live: uncertainty as to the meaning of words, uncertainty as to their effect on others, uncertainty as to our own character and motivations. The knowledge out of which the rhetorician ultimately functions will not be scientific or theoretical but practical, experiential—the sense that one knows how to do things with language and with others. This is, in fact, our earliest social and intellectual knowledge, the knowledge we acquire as we first begin to move and act in our social universe and learn to speak and understand. It is the knowledge by which language and social relations are made.

The rhetorician thus begins not with the imagined individual in imagined isolation (as Hobbes[8] or Locke[9] does), and not with the self, isolated from all of its experience except that of cogitation (as Descartes does[10]), but where Wittgenstein tells us to begin, with our abilities of language, gesture, and meaning.[11] This knowledge is itself not reducible to rules or subject to expression in rules, though many analysts wish that it were; rather it is the knowledge by which we learn to manage, evade, disappoint, surprise, and please each other, as we understand the expectations that others bring to what we say. This knowledge is not provable in the scientific sense, nor is it logically rigorous. For these reasons, it is unsettling to the modern scientific and academic mind. But we cannot go beyond it, and it is a mistake to try. In this fluid world without turf or ground, we cannot walk but we can swim. And we need not be afraid to do this—to engage in the rhetorical process of life—for all of us, despite our radical uncertainties, already know how to do it. By attending to our own experience, and that of others, we can learn to do it better if we try.

VI

What would be the effects of thinking of law in this literary and rhetorical way? If, as I think, it is more true to the experiences of those engaged in the activity of law than the standard conceptual accounts, it should in the first place lead to a richer and more accurate understanding of and control over what we do. The law is something that lawyers themselves make all the time, whenever they act as lawyers, not something that is made by a political sovereign. From this point of view, the law can be defined as the culture that we remake whenever we speak as lawyers. To look at law this way is to direct one's attention to places that are normally passed over: to the way in which we create new meanings, new possibilities for meaning, in what we say; to the way in which our literature can be regarded as a literature of value and motive and sentiment; to the way in which our enterprise is a radically ethical one, by which self and community are perpetually reconstituted; and to the limits that our nature and our culture, our circumstances and our imagination, place on our powers to remake our languages and communities in new forms.

To see law this way may also lead to a different way of reading

---

[8] THOMAS HOBBES, LEVIATHAN ch. 13 (London 1651).

[9] JOHN LOCKE, SECOND TREATISE OF GOVERNMENT bk. II, chs. 1-3 (London 1690).

[10] RENÉ DESCARTES, DISCOURS DE LA MÉTHODE pt. 4 (Leiden 1637).

[11] LUDWIG WITTGENSTEIN, PHILOSOPHICAL INVESTIGATIONS *passim* (1953).

and writing it. As I suggested above, the United States Constitution can be regarded as a rhetorical text: one that establishes a set of speakers, roles, topics, and occasions for speech. So understood, many of its ambiguities and uncertainties become more comprehensible, for we can see the text as attempting to establish a conversation of a certain kind and its ambiguities as ways of at once defining and leaving open the topics of the conversation.[12] A statute can be read similarly, not as a set of orders or directions or commands, but as establishing a set of topics, a set of terms in which those topics can be discussed, and some general directions as to the process of thought and argument by which the statute is to be applied. Similarly, the judicial opinion, often thought to be the paradigmatic form of legal expression, might be far more accurately and richly understood if it were seen not as a bureaucratic expression of ends-means rationality but as a statement by an individual mind or a group of individual minds exercising their responsibility to decide a case as well as they can and to determine what it shall mean in the language of the culture. And the view of law as constitutive rhetoric should define the lawyer's own work as far less manipulative, selfish, or goal-oriented than the usual models, and as far more creative, communal, and intellectually challenging.

From the point of view of the nonlawyer, this way of regarding law as rhetoric invites a certain kind of reading and of criticism, for it invites you to test the law in part by asking whether your own story, or the story of another in whom you have an interest, is properly told by these speakers and in this language. The basic idea of the legal hearing is that two stories will be told in opposition or competition and a choice made between them. On the rhetorical view of law suggested here, you are entitled to have your story told in your own language (or translated into it), or the law is failing. It is the role of the jury to insist upon the ultimate translatability of law into the common language of the culture. To ask, "What place is there for me in this language, this text, this story?," and to feel that you have a right to an answer, is a very different way of evaluating law from thinking of it as a mechanism for distributing social goods. The central idea is not that of goods, but of voices and relations: what voices does the law allow to be heard, what relations does it establish among them? With what voice, or voices, does the law itself speak? These are the questions with

[12] For further discussion, see my WHEN WORDS LOSE THEIR MEANING ch. 9 (1984) and THE LEGAL IMAGINATION 215-40 (1983).

which rhetorical criticism would begin.

At a more global level, we can see that the current habit of regarding law as the instrument by which "we" effectuate "our policies" and get what "we want" is wholly inadequate. It is the true nature of law to constitute a "we" and to establish a conversation by which that "we" can determine what our "wants" are and should be. Our motives and values are not, in this view, to be taken as exogenous to the system (as they are taken to be exogenous to an economic system) but are in fact its subject. The law should take as its most central question what kind of community we should be, with what values, motives, and aims. It is a process by which we make ourselves by making our language.

This means that one question constantly before us as lawyers is what kind of culture we shall have, as well as what kind of community we shall be. What will be our language of approval and disapproval, praise and blame, admiration and contempt? What shall be the terms by which we identify and refine—by which we create—our motives and combine them into coherent wholes? This way of conceiving of law invites us to include in our zone of attention and field of discourse what others, operating under present suppositions, cut out, including both the radical uncertainty of most forms of knowledge and the fact that we, and our resources, are constantly remade by our own collective activities. The pressure of bureaucratic discourse is always to think in terms of ends and means; but in practice ends-means rationality is likely to undergo a reversal by which only those things can count as ends for which means of a certain kind exist. This often results in a reduction of the human to the material and the measurable, as though a good or just society were a function of the rate of individual consumption, not a set of shared relations, attitudes, and meanings. To view law as rhetoric might help us to attend to the spiritual or meaningful side of our collective life.

As one example of what I mean by the difference between the material and the meaningful, consider the question of the invasion of privacy by officials. One way to try to compare different regimes would be to inquire how frequently police officers stopped individuals on the street, asked for their identification, and subjected them to pat-downs or searches. That would be a material mode of determining "how much" privacy existed in a particular culture. But far more important than that is the meaning of the described activities of the officers both to them and to the citizens. There are circumstances, war perhaps being the most obvious, in which almost everyone would agree that this kind of policing was important and valuable, and citizens would by and large not feel that their privacy was invaded, because they would feel that the officer was acting as their fellow worker in a common enterprise.

Such a conception of law as I describe would lead to a rather different method of teaching it as well. It would at first require a rather old-fashioned training in the intellectual practices that are the things that lawyers do, from reading cases to drafting statutes and contracts. The rhetorician must always start with the materials of his or her language and culture, and we should continue to train our students to understand these materials, their resources and limits, and to learn to put them to work in the activities of narrative and analysis and argument that make up their professional lives. The rhetorician must first of all master the starting points from which he or she is to proceed, then the methods by which he or she can move, in one direction or another, from the point so established.

But the lawyer's activities of speech and argument should not merely be learned as crafts to be performed as efficiently as possible; they should be contrasted with other ways of doing similar things, drawn both from ordinary life and from other disciplines. For example, learning how to argue in the law about the meaning of rules, or about fairness, or about blame, can be informed by attending to the ways in which we already know how to do these things in ordinary life, and by learning how they are done elsewhere. One focus would accordingly be upon the connection between legal language and ordinary language, legal life and ordinary life, as rhetoric connects them. A related focus would be upon other formal intellectual practices, in an interdisciplinary curriculum rather different from current models: not law *and* sociology or history or economics or literature, but law *as* each of these things. What kind of sociology or history or anthropology are we implicitly practicing in this legal rule, in that legal action or argument, in this judicial opinion? What can be said for and against our implied choices?

But the largest difference would be a shift in the conception of the triadic relation between the student, the teacher, and the subject. The law we teach would not be regarded as a set of institutions that "we" manipulate either to achieve "our policies," as governors, nor "our interests," as lawyers, but rather as a language and a community—a world, made partly by others and partly by ourselves, in which we and others shall live, and which will be tested less by its distributive effects than by the resources of meaning it creates and the community it constitutes: who we become to ourselves and to one another when we converse.[13] And our central question could become how to understand and to judge those things.

VII

By this kind of conjunction with the law, rhetoric itself might perhaps be seen in a somewhat different light. No longer a substitute for science when science does not work, it might be seen as a science itself, at least in the eighteenth-century meaning of that term as an organized form of knowledge. It is the knowledge of who we make ourselves, as individuals and as communities, through the ways we speak to each other. Rhetorical knowledge is allied with artistic knowledge in that it is tacitly creative and in that it acknowledges both its limits and the conditions of uncertainty under which it functions. Rhetorical analysis provides a way of addressing the central questions of collective existence in an organized and consistent, but not rule-bound, way. It directs our attention to the most significant questions of shared existence, which are wholly outside the self-determined bounds of science. Justice and ethics are its natural subject, art its natural method.

Rhetoric might also provide a set of questions and attitudes that could enable us to move from one academic and social field to another and, in doing so, to unite them. For at least tentative judgments of the kind that rhetoric calls for can be made about the work of experts—in history or psychology, for example—without one's having to be oneself an expert in the professional sense. Not that one has not always something to learn—of course one has—but one can never know everything and ought not be barred from making important observations and judgments of one kind by a want of competence at making others. We can say a great deal about the kind of history written by Gibbon,[14] for example—about the sort of community he establishes with us, about his language of value and judgment—without being able to make professional

---

[13] I do not mean that distributive effects are irrelevant but that the context in which they are relevant, and from which they derive their meaning, is social and ethical. What does it mean about us that power and wealth are divided this way, or that? Or, more precisely—since power and wealth are at bottom social and cultural—what does it mean about us that we create these powers, these wealths, in this way? Without a social and ethical context, one has after all nothing but brute material that has of itself no meaning at all, as wealth, power, or symbol.

[14] Edward Gibbon, The History of the Decline and Fall of the Roman Empire (London 1776-1788) (discussed in chapter 7 of my forthcoming book Heracles' Bow: Essays on the Rhetoric and Poetics of the Law).

judgments about his use of certain inscriptions as evidence on a certain point.

Rhetoric, in the highly expanded sense in which I speak of it, might indeed become the central discipline for which we have been looking for so long—which "science" has proven not to be—by which the others can be defined and organized and judged. One reason rhetoric might be able to perform this role is its continuity with ordinary discourse and hence with real communities, real values, and real politics. It is at least contiguous to a ground that is common to us all. Rhetoric must deal with ordinary language because it is the art of speaking to people who already have a language, and to reach and to persuade them one must speak their language.

One result of the affirmation of ordinary language is that it provides a ground for challenge and change, a place to stand from which to reformulate any more specialized language. Another result of this affirmation is that it confirms our right and capacity to say what we think is really good about what is good in our world and what is really terrible about what is terrible. Rhetorical analysis invites us to talk about our conceptions of ourselves as individuals and as communities, and to define our values in living rather than conceptual ways. For example, consider what is good about America. Our present public rhetoric seems for the most part to assume that what is good about it is its material productivity. But that is often wasteful, self-destructive, and ugly. I think what is really good about this country is its fundamental culture of self-government, independence, and generosity, and these qualities are obscured or denied by the way in which we habitually talk about our government and law.

How does rhetoric enable us to talk about these matters? It does so by giving us a set of very simple but fundamental questions to ask when someone speaks either to us or on our behalf, or when we ourselves speak, such as the following:[15]

> 1. *The inherited language*. What is the language or culture with which this speaker works? How does it represent natural and social facts, constitute human motives and values, and define those persuasive motions of the mind that we call reason? What does it leave out or deny? What does it overspecify? What is its actual or imagined relation to other sys-

[15] These questions focus on the three aspects of the lawyer's rhetorical situation that I identified *supra* p. 688-91.

tems of discourse?

2. *The art of the text.* How, by what art and with what effect, is this language remade by this speaker or writer? Is this text internally coherent, and if so, by what standards of coherence? Is it externally coherent (that is, does it establish intelligible relations with its background), and if so, by what standards of coherence? How, that is, does this text reconstitute its discourse?

3. *The rhetorical community.* What kind of person is speaking here, and to what kind of person does he speak? What is the voice here and what kind of response does it invite, or allow? What place is there for me, and for others, in the universe defined by this discourse, in the community created by this text? What world does it assume? What world does it create?

Such questions are only the beginning of an ethical and cultural criticism but they may enable us to approach a set of texts as they are actually made, in widely varying cultures, languages, and human relations, and to establish connections among them, across their contexts and above or behind their particularities. To ask them is of course not to answer them, but it may direct our attention to the proper place for thought to begin, and suggest, by implication, appropriate modes of inquiry and of judgment.

Part II
Law and Literature: Finding Meaning

[4]

Linguistic Indeterminacy

TIMOTHY A. O. ENDICOTT*

> No person shall take or possess, in the County of Lanark or the Regional Municipality of Ottawa-Carleton, any bullfrog unless the tibia thereof is five centimetres or more in length.[1]

We can think of cases in which liability for catching bullfrogs under this regulation is indeterminate—cases in which we know what facts a court will find, and do not know how the court will decide a case. What if a bullfrog has one tibia longer than 5 cm and one shorter? What if the length of a tibia is pushed over 5 cm by a rare growth? What of a bullfrog with a curved tibia that is 4 cm long when laid beside a ruler, but measures 6 cm with a tape?

Countless indeterminacies appear in linguistic formulations of legal rules: lexical ambiguities (does 'person' include a company?), syntactical ambiguities (does the person have to be in Ottawa? does the bullfrog?), uncertainty as to whether the seemingly redundant 'take' adds anything to 'possess', and so on.

Bullfrog hunters and their lawyers might face further legal indeterminacies that do not arise from the language of the regulation: if there is an unresolved conflict between the bullfrog regulation and another rule, or if the power to make the regulation or the procedures by which it was promulgated or enforced are suspect, or if it is unclear whether proof of some mental state is required for conviction, or whether principals are liable when agents take bullfrogs, or whether the regulation may be inapplicable on equitable grounds (suppose someone took a bullfrog from a busy road to keep it safe). And the lawyers and the bullfrog hunters may face further uncertainties that are neither linguistic nor legal, such as whether the authorities will exercise their discretion to prosecute, whether a witness will make it to court, and so on.

Those non-linguistic indeterminacies and uncertainties arise because life and legal systems are complicated. But people can choose their words, and it would be reassuring to think that linguistic indeterminacy, at least, could be eradicated by careful use of language. Perhaps the drafters of the bullfrog regulation set out to do this by avoiding vague terms like 'mature bullfrog' or 'large bullfrog'. What does their failure to eliminate linguistic indeterminacy show about law and language? Indeterminacy seems pervasive and obdurate.

* St Catherine's College, Oxford.

[1] Regulation under the Ontario Game and Fish Act, O Reg 694/81.

 Oxford Journal of Legal Studies Vol 16, No 4

This article addresses the claim that language (and therefore law) is *radically* indeterminate: that no question of the meaning or application of a linguistic expression has a single right answer. I conclude not only that the claim is wrong, but that, in spite of appearances, no one actually makes it. Those two conclusions raise the more important question of what to make of the allegations that legal sceptics of various types do make about linguistic indeterminacy. To get to that question, we need to start by identifying what legal theorists are talking about when they talk about indeterminacy.

The twilight zone

A metaphor popular in twentieth-century legal theory pictures linguistic indeterminacy as a penumbra, a shadowy purlieu between the clear applicability of an expression and its clear inapplicability. The metaphor is traditionally credited to H. L. A. Hart.[2] But Benjamin Cardozo had written in 1921 of 'the borderland, the penumbra, where controversy begins',[3] and Glanville Williams used the metaphor in an encyclopaedic review of legal problems about the meaning of words, written in 1945–6: 'Since the law has to be expressed in words, and words have a penumbra of uncertainty, marginal cases are bound to occur.'[4] Cardozo implicitly and Williams expressly presaged Hart's claim that the judge has a law-making role in penumbral cases.[5]

Since Hart popularized the metaphor of core and penumbra,[6] many legal theorists have insisted that the notion falsely attributes to words some kind of certainty, or absoluteness, or independence of context, or immunity to change, and that indeterminacy is more than a fringe or margin. They have questioned not the notion of a penumbra, but the notion of a core.

Is meaning like a partial eclipse of the sun—all penumbra? What can be made of claims that the meaning or application of words is entirely indeterminate? One response would be to reject those claims as obviously wrong: everyone knows

[2] Eg by Ken Kress, 'Legal Indeterminacy' (1989) 77 *Cal LR* 283, 287, and by Margaret Jane Radin (at 285–6), David Lyons (at 221), Frederick Schauer (at 434), all in Frederick Schauer, ed, *Law and Language* (Aldershot: Dartmouth 1993). *Law and Language* is a very useful collection of legal journal articles in which linguistic indeterminacy is a predominant concern; I will refer to several of the articles reproduced in *Law and Language*, using *LL* plus page number, with the author's name where necessary.

[3] Benjamin N. Cardozo, *The Nature of the Judicial Process* (New Haven: Yale UP, 1921) 130.

[4] *LL* 139. Hart acknowledged Williams' use of the notion: *The Concept of Law*, 2nd ed (Oxford: Clarendon Press 1994) 278. Also in the 1940s, Karl Llewellyn taught his students as follows in a versified theory of statutory interpretation:

A text lays out, the *text you see*,
unyielding, all perimeters;
though slight penumbra there must be
you'll find in force and quantity
sharp, given verbal limiters.

Quoted in William Twining, *Karl Llewellyn and the Realist Movement* (Norman: University of Oklahoma Press 1973) 240. How much of this is tongue-in-cheek is one of the puzzles in understanding Llewellyn.

[5] *LL* 140.

[6] 'We may call the problems which arise outside the hard core of standard instances or settled meaning "problems of the penumbra" . . .', 'Positivism and the Separation of Law and Morals' (1958) 71 *Harv LR* 593 at 607. Cf the discussion in *The Concept of Law* of 'a core of certainty and a penumbra of doubt' in the application of the general terms used in formulating legal rules (above n 4 at 123).

that there are cases in which words apply without any doubt or disagreement, just as there are situations in which it is unclear whether they apply. Another response would be to reject such claims as nonsensical—they declare themselves to be not exactly altogether true.

But one of the first lessons of jurisprudence is not to dismiss obviously wrong or nonsensical claims (eg 'what the officials do *is* the law' said by a legal realist, or 'an unjust law is not a law' said by a natural lawyer). Instead, it is worth asking what new emphasis or neglected insight a theorist is embellishing with absurdity. Nonsense in legal theory deserves the same tolerance that we apply when we ask if it's raining and someone says, 'yes and no'.

Tolerance recommends interpreting radical indeterminacy theses as hyperbolic objections to immodest claims (or to inarticulate assumptions) of determinacy. And indeed, intriguing and crazy claims of indeterminacy tend to crumble into sensible and less intriguing positions. In fact, the sensible positions typically accompany the crazy claims, as express concessions. I will argue that, when the concessions to determinacy are accounted for, every claim about indeterminacy that we will see is consistent with what Hart said about language: '[t]here will indeed be plain cases . . . to which general expressions are clearly applicable . . . but there will also be cases where it is not clear whether they apply or not'.[7] Then the debate is over whether determinacy is vast and typical (as Hart occasionally suggested),[8] or scarce, and likely to delude unimaginative theorists.

What is indeterminacy?

Legal theorists talk of 'legal indeterminacy' when a legal question has no single right answer.[9] I will use 'linguistic indeterminacy' to refer to unclarity in the meaning of linguistic expressions that could lead to legal indeterminacy. Concerning the application of the language in which laws are formulated, legal theorists make claims of *practical* indeterminacy and claims of *theoretical* indeterminacy. Practical indeterminacy arises in language when competence in the language is not enough to know whether an expression applies in a situation, and in law when legal competence is not enough to know the legal consequences of a situation. A *radical* indeterminacy claim would allege that competent speakers of a language can never know whether an expression applies, and that competent lawyers can never know what to tell a client. Theoretical indeterminacy claims do not outrage naive notions in that way. They allege that the meaning or correct application of words is not determined in the way that people might have thought, but in some manner so different that it is misleading even to call them determinate. Some theorists argue that the current debate about indeterminacy is entirely

[7] *The Concept of Law*, above n 4 at 126.

[8] Ibid, 124, 134, 154.

[9] See, eg, Kress, above n 2 at 283; Brian Bix, *Law, Language and Legal Determinacy* (Oxford: Clarendon Press 1993) 1. See also Laurence Solum, 'On the Indeterminacy Crisis' (1987) 54 *U Chic LR* 462.

about what I call theoretical indeterminacy.[10] Such theorists will not necessarily find any more practical indeterminacy in a legal system than, eg H. L. A. Hart did; this sort of theoretical indeterminacy thesis does not represent a claim about the extent of legal uncertainty, but the pursuit of a philosophical agenda.[11] I do not mean to assess theoretical indeterminacy claims. That job would require a fully-fledged theory of meaning, and no one has ever come up with enough feathers to fledge a theory of meaning.

There is a further limitation on the scope of this survey: because the topic is indeterminacy in the application to particular cases of the language in which the law is formulated, some recent discussions of indeterminacy are not addressed. An example is Charles Yablon's deconstruction of legal forms:

> A summons is a routine legal form. It is also an instrument of power and pain. That is the indeterminacy that gives it meaning.[12]

Here, 'indeterminacy' seems to mean capacity for symbolic force, or significance, or potential for use as a metaphor—which raise no question as to whether a particular document is, eg, a summons, or as to the legal effect of any form.

I cannot over-emphasize that the purpose of the survey is not to analyse the sophisticated theories of language that back the indeterminacy theses that will be encountered. There is no room here to do them sufficient justice to rebut them. It will be obvious that I basically agree with Hart's view that the application of linguistic expressions is sometimes determinate and sometimes indeterminate. But my aim is not to argue that Hart is right and radical indeterminacy theorists are wrong; it is to argue that there are no radical indeterminacy theorists, and that everyone basically agrees with Hart's view. So the purpose of the survey is to point out features of some prominent indeterminacy theories which support the interesting claim that, in spite of appearances, no one actually maintains a radical indeterminacy thesis. The fact that such a thesis would refute itself does not in itself explain this fact, as the legal deconstructionist David Gray Carlson has shown: 'That deconstruction is self-refuting—a fact it fully grasps, emphasizes, and even exploits—by no means proves that deconstruction is wrong about meaning.'[13] Carlson is right that self-refutation does not show that deconstruction is wrong about meaning; instead, it shows that deconstruction *says nothing* about meaning, so that it calls for the tolerance I proposed above.

The survey will start by discussing three variously related schools of doctrine: (1) the current consensus on the nature of interpretation, (2) deconstruction, and (3) semiotics. The discussions will show that radical indeterminacy theses

[10] See, eg, Robert Justin Lipkin, 'Indeterminacy, Justification and Truth in Constitutional Theory' (1992) 60 *Fordham LR* 595, 611: 'But the indeterminacy issue, as I understand it, challenges the *source*, not the fact, of one right answer existing in any given case. To be a proponent of determinacy, you must believe that a constitutional question has one right answer, *and* that the answer derives solely from the meaning of the law, independent of our purposes, needs, aspirations, and context'.

[11] In Lipkin's case, to 'rid ourselves of the notion of truth'. Ibid, 609 n 56.

[12] 'Forms' in D. Cornell, M. Rosenfeld, D. G. Carlson (eds), *Deconstruction and the Possibility of Justice* (New York: Routledge 1992) [hereafter, '*Deconstruction*'] 258 at 262.

[13] David Gray Carlson, 'Liberal Philosophy's Troubled Relation to the Rule of Law' (1993) 43 *UTLJ* 257, 278.

that issue from those theoretical perspectives tend to degenerate into concessions of determinacy. What is left after radical indeterminacy claims are discounted by the concessions? Often, a claim that meaning depends on *context*, or that meaning is *changeable*. So sections (4) and (5) will discuss context and change. Section (6) will review the case of Ludwig Wittgenstein, whose work on rules has been used to generate some extraordinary indeterminacy claims. A popular non-sceptical interpretation of Wittgenstein's remarks seeks to pour cold water on those claims. If that non-sceptical view is right, it devastates both radical and theoretical indeterminacy claims.

1. *The New Interpretive Orthodoxy and the Critical Predicament*

A new consensus has emerged about interpretation and, specifically, about its role in law: that understanding *is* interpretation and, specifically, that every application of the law is an interpretation of the law. This notion, which Dennis Patterson has called 'the current interpretive orthodoxy',[14] is particularly associated with Stanley Fish. He thinks that *everything* that people do with other people's utterances is interpretation:

> . . . in my argument, interpretation *is* conventional understanding.[15]

> . . . communications of every kind are characterized by exactly the same conditions—the necessity of interpretive work, the unavoidability of perspective, and the construction by acts of interpretation of that which supposedly grounds interpretation, intentions, characteristics and pieces of the world.[16]

Some people disagree with Fish about most of the latter claim, but agree on 'the necessity of interpretive work' to understanding and applying linguistic expressions and the law. The striking range of theorists who hold similar views establishes an interpretivist party line:

> Owen Fiss: 'Adjudication is interpretation: Adjudication is the process by which a judge comes to understand and express the meaning of an authoritative legal text and the values embodied in that text.'[17]

> Frederick Schauer: '. . . ordinary talk appears to reserve the word "interpretation" for those cases in which there seems to be a problem. In this respect, common

[14] 'The Poverty of Interpretive Universalism: Toward the Reconstruction of Legal Theory' (1993) 72 *Texas LR* 1. Patterson uses Wittgenstein's remarks on rules to attack the notion's manifestations in Ronald Dworkin and Stanley Fish, and discusses the general philosophical context of the notion. Martin Stone discusses 'the contemporary recourse to interpretation', and he too uses Wittgenstein to oppose it: 'Focusing the Law: What Legal Interpretation is Not' in Andrei Marmor (ed), *Law and Interpretation* (Oxford: Clarendon Press 1995) 31 at 36. Marmor has mounted the same Wittgensteinian attack on the notion that understanding presupposes interpretation, in *Interpretation and Legal Theory* (Oxford: Clarendon Press 1992) 146–54.

[15] 'How Come You Do Me Like You Do? A Reply to Dennis Patterson' (1993) 72 *Texas LR* 57, 62.

[16] *Doing What Comes Naturally* (Durham: Duke University Press 1989) 43–4.

[17] Owen Fiss, 'Objectivity and Interpretation' (1982) 34 *Stanford LR* 739, 739.

linguistic usage is potentially misleading, for *every* application of a rule is also an interpretation.'[18]

Margaret Jane Radin: '... every application of them [rules] is a reinterpretation.'[19]

Allan Hutchinson and Derek Morgan: 'Meaning is the product of interpretation....'[20]

Ronald Dworkin: 'So I am drawn to the interpretive answer to the question: what makes a proposition of law true? Even in easy cases, that is, even when it goes without saying what the law is, ... we do better to explain that phenomenon by speaking of a convergence on a single interpretation....'[21]

Michael Moore: 'I do not intend by the word ["interpretation"] to distinguish between finding the meaning of a law, and applying that law to the facts of some case.... Whatever I must do to connect the law to the facts in the manner earlier sketched is what I mean by "interpretation".'[22]

Drucilla Cornell: '... the rule itself is always in the process of reinterpretation as it is applied. It is interpretation that gives us the rule, not the other way around.'

Jacques Derrida: 'Each case ... requires an absolutely unique interpretation.'[23]

This is a bizarre consensus among people who agree on nothing else. It is a consensus that survives their different views on how to interpret, on whether an interpretation can intelligibly be called right or wrong, on the nature of truth and meaning, and so on. They all think that no legal question can be answered except by an interpretation.

The consensus itself shows that the new interpretive orthodoxy, and fascination with interpretation in general, do not compel any particular view on indeterminacy. Ronald Dworkin, for instance, seems to view law as more determinate than anyone else does.[24] And we should even hesitate to attribute any sort of indeterminacy thesis to Stanley Fish. In a reply to Patterson called 'How Come You Do Me Like You Do?' he seems hurt by the imputation.

In the world I describe, readers are situated (not by choice, but by histories that have befallen them) in communities whose traditions are constraints in the strongest way; ... they structure the individual consciousness, providing it with a limited set of

[18] *Playing by the Rules* (Oxford: Clarendon Press 1991) 207.

[19] *LL* 311.

[20] *LL* 478.

[21] 'On Gaps in the Law', in Neil MacCormick and Paul Amselek (eds), *Controversies about Law's Ontology* (Edinburgh: Edinburgh University Press 1991) 84 at 88. And see *Law's Empire* (Cambridge: Harvard University Press 1986) 87: 'Law is an interpretive concept ...'. Dworkin argues that a judge must use the same interpretive method to decide *any* case (*Law's Empire* 265–6, 353–4). Cf also *A Matter of Principle* (Oxford: Clarendon Press 1986) Part II: 'Law as Interpretation'. John Finnis has argued cogently against Dworkin's interpretive universalism in 'On Reason and Authority in *Law's Empire*' (1987) 6 *Law and Philosophy* 357 at 358–63.

[22] 'A Natural Law Theory of Interpretation' (1985) 58 *S Cal LR* 277, 284–5. But Moore's interpretivism is 'modest'—see Moore, 'Interpreting Interpretation', in Marmor (ed), *Law and Interpretation* (above, n 14) 1.

[23] 'Force of Law: The "Mystical Foundation of Authority"', in *Deconstruction*, above n 12, 3 at 23.

[24] See, eg, Dworkin, 'On Gaps in the Law', above n 21.

meanings and routes of interpretive action.... This is about as far as one could get (short of an out-and-out determinism) from a condition in which 'everything is permitted ...'.[25]

The interpretive consensus is logically neutral as to indeterminacy, because it claims that interpretation is needed when the application of language seems quite determinate—in situations where, if we are interpreting, there is only one correct interpretation. It claims that when you drive up to a stop sign, you cannot respond to the sign without interpreting.

The consensus seems to stretch the notion of interpretation over instances of understanding that are not interpretive at all. 'Interpretation' seems useful (and is generally used) as a term for making choices as to the meaning of an expression or a text. And while there are choices to be made when you drive up to a stop sign (eg, whether to stop), there are none to be made about its meaning. On this use of the term 'interpretation', we interpret when we can reformulate a rule in a way that clarifies its meaning. We do not interpret stop signs.[26]

But no one wants to argue about labels: we could say that there is only one admissible interpretation in some cases, and that determinacy is the inadmissibility of all other interpretations. Or we could describe such a case in terms of understanding, and keep the word 'interpretation' for cases in which something can or must be made of the object in question. People are free to use 'interpretation' as a synonym for 'understanding', or for a creative process of making choices. But interesting things happen when they use it for both at once. It is precisely because the use of the word 'interpretation' to describe a creative process is common and attractive, that the interpretive consensus lends itself to indeterminacy theses. If you think that every application of the law is an interpretation, and if you can simultaneously hold in your head the idea that interpretation is a matter of making choices among open alternatives, the result is indeterminacy. Thus, Sanford Levinson constructs an indeterminacy thesis by invoking Richard Rorty's pragmatist philosophy. Rorty thinks that an interpreter 'simply beats the text into a shape which will serve his own purpose',[27] and he insists that there is no distinction between that activity and understanding a text.[28]

Levinson joins a band of critical theorists who 'reject the very search for finality of interpretation',[29] and concludes that one can never say that a constitutional case 'was "wrongly" decided, for that use of language presupposes belief in the knowability of constitutional essence'.[30] And although he would like to criticize

[25] (1993) 72 *Texas LR* 57, 61–2.

[26] For further discussion of these claims see Timothy A. O. Endicott, 'Putting Interpretation in its Place' (1994) 13 *Law and Philosophy* 451.

[27] Rorty quoted by Levinson at *LL* 355.

[28] Cf Rorty, 'The Pragmatist's Progress', in Stefan Collini (ed), Umberto Eco, *Interpretation and Overinterpretation* (Cambridge: Cambridge University Press 1992) 89: 'On our view, all anybody ever does with anything is use it. Interpreting something, knowing it, penetrating to its essence, and so on are all just various ways of describing some process of putting it to work.' (at 93).

[29] *LL* 354.

[30] *LL* 356.

some of John Marshall's work as dishonest, he considers such criticisms 'irrelevant', because they assume 'the existence of a privileged discourse that allows me to dismiss Marshall as "untruthful" rather than merely different'.[31] Levinson stops short of asking what privileged discourse enables him to say that Marshall is 'different', or to say anything at all.

To be unable to say that a case was wrongly decided (or, of course, rightly) is an appalling predicament for a lawyer to land in, and Levinson occasionally voices despair about it.[32] Ironically, it is a characteristic predicament of theories that set out to be critical. By touting indeterminacy, legal theorists squander the possibility of saying anything.

There are various techniques for coping with this critical predicament, besides Levinson's despair. A standard response is to cleave to the belief that challenging the *status quo* is good in itself, even if the form of the challenge makes it absurd to propose a change.[33] This approach relies on the rhetorical potential of nonsense.

Pragmatists like Rorty make a more subtle response: they try to distinguish 'between knowing what you want to get out of a person or thing or text in advance and hoping that the person or thing or text will help you want something different—that he or she or it will help you to change your purposes, and thus to change your life'.[34] But a stop sign, for example, cannot help you to change your purposes, if all you ever do with a stop sign is to beat it into shape *for* your purpose.[35] The resolution of this tension in Rorty's work has to be some sort of interplay between text and purpose, which is only possible if some texts resist being beaten into some shapes. That resolution would be a concession of determinacy.

The critical predicament is more agonizing in legal theory than in literary theory, because the urge to say that an interpretation of a constitution is right or wrong is generally more pressing than the urge to say that an interpretation of a poem is right or wrong. And in spite of Levinson's intermittent despair, even he takes to the most common recourse of legal indeterminacy theorists: concessions of determinacy.

> ... I cannot be the arch-indeterminist that I sometimes appear to be. ... I will quickly concede that courts and other constitutional interpreters operate within constraints.[36]

> To be sure, none of the radical critics defend the position that any interpretation is just as good as any other.[37]

The second of these two concessions contradicts Levinson's denial that he can

[31] *LL* 359.
[32] *LL* 371–3.
[33] For an argument against using indeterminacy arguments tactically to free up people's thinking see Kress, above n 2, at 336.
[34] Above n 28 at 106.
[35] Stefan Collini points out this 'tantalizing' aspect of Rorty's philosophy: 'Introduction: Interpretation Terminable and Interminable' in *Interpretation and Overinterpretation*, above n 28, 1 at 12.
[36] *LL* 352, n 33.
[37] *LL* 354.

criticize John Marshall: to do so he would only have to give reasons why Marshall's interpretations are not as good as the alternatives. Levinson's indeterminacy thesis turns out not to be as radical as it seems.

We can say the same of interpretivist indeterminacy theorists generally. A *radical* interpretivist indeterminacy thesis would have to say that all applications of linguistic expressions are interpretations, and that no interpretation is ever better or worse than any other interpretation. No doubt it would be possible to make both claims, but it is hard to find anyone who does. If examples are to be found at all, we might seek them in the exotic reaches of interpretivism: deconstruction and semiotics.

2. *Deconstruction*

Deconstruction inverts whatever anything seems to mean, by reversing the 'privileging' of one interpretation over another. That is the technique of the guru, Jacques Derrida; 'deconstruction' is also occasionally used in a wider sense as more or less equivalent to what is sometimes called 'poststructuralism', or 'critical theory', or even just 'theory'.[38] Perhaps deconstruction is a sophisticated intellectual apparatus for disclosing ironies that pervade thought and language and experience. Perhaps it is bravura. Deconstructionists themselves do not differentiate:

> . . . explanations of deconstruction necessarily involve a modification of it. (J. M. Balkin)[39]
>
> No conception of deconstruction can be advanced with confidence, as every such conception is subject to further deconstruction. (Michel Rosenfeld)[40]
>
> All sentences of the type 'deconstruction is X' or 'deconstruction is not X', *a priori,* miss the point, which is to say that they are at least false. (Jacques Derrida)[41]

Derrida's own reflections on justice allege radical indeterminacy—at least in the application of the word 'just'. The result is newspeak:

> one cannot . . . say 'this is just' and even less 'I am just', without immediately betraying justice . . .[42]
>
> Justice in itself, if such a thing exists, outside or beyond law, is not deconstructible. No more than deconstruction itself, if such a thing exists. Deconstruction is justice.[43]

[38] For a thoughtful critique of indeterminacy claims in the work of Derrida and Drucilla Cornell see Stone, above n 14, esp 'Appendix: A Note on Deconstruction'.

[39] *LL* 402, n 54, Balkin.

[40] Michel Rosenfeld, 'Deconstruction and Legal Interpretation: Conflict, Indeterminacy and the Temptations of the New Legal Formalism' in *Deconstruction*, above n 12, 152 at 199, n 22.

[41] Jacques Derrida, commenting on how the word 'deconstruction' might be translated into Japanese, in 'Letter to a Japanese Friend', in David Wood and Robert Bernasconi (eds), *Derrida and Difference* (Coventry: Parousia Press 1985) at 7.

[42] Derrida, above n 23 at 10.

[43] Ibid, 14–15.

Derrida's insistence on the impossibility of calling anything 'just' arises from a paradox he creates: to be just, a decision must be responsible, and also free. So it must 'be both regulated and without regulation: it must conserve the law and also destroy it or suspend it . . .'.[44] The attractive way to take Derrida's paradox is as a recommendation of modesty in making claims of justice, and as a warning against hypocrisy and moral blindness. But the same deconstructionist principle that applies to 'just' also applies to 'unjust', either (i) by parity of deconstruction, or (ii) in virtue of the fact that if *no* decision can be just, no decision can be distinguished as unjust. 'Unjust' becomes either applicable to no decision, or meaninglessly applicable to every decision (it could not be used, eg, to distinguish the conviction of a prisoner who has been framed from the acquittal of a prisoner who has been framed). There is no attractive way to take the proposition that no one can ever say 'this is unjust' without betraying justice.

Warnings against moral blindness should not be ignored. In some cases no just decision may be possible: suppose that an accused is manifestly guilty on admissible evidence of serious criminal charges properly brought, and suppose that the penal system is abusive. It might be unjust to acquit, and unjust to convict, and a juror cannot make things better by assuming that the less bad option (if there is one) is just. But Derrida's paradox claims to prove more than that there may be no just decision on offer: it claims to prove that it is a betrayal of justice to say that any decision is just.

Curiously, Derrida's argument coincides with a concession of determinacy in *law*:

> . . . every time that we placidly apply a good rule to a particular case, to a correctly subsumed example, according to a determinant judgment, we can be sure that law (*droit*) may find itself accounted for, but certainly not justice.[45]

If examples can be subsumed correctly, if rules can be applied to particular cases, linguistic determinacy is conceded. If law finds itself accounted for as a result, legal determinacy is conceded. If legal determinacy is conceded, it is more straightforward to say that justice lies in rightly deciding whether to apply the law, than to say that justice must both conserve the law and destroy the law. But is rightly deciding whether to obey the law *the same thing* as destroying the law? Of course not. You do not destroy the law by making the right decision whether to obey it, any more than you will destroy your promise or a friend's request or your mother's demand if you make the right decision whether to follow them. This account of justice is not only more straightforward, it also explains the sound, undeconstructible burden of Derrida's argument, which is that it is not necessarily just to follow a rule—that 'Law (*droit*) is not justice'.[46]

[44] Ibid, 23.
[45] Ibid, 16. He even allows that a rule may guarantee a decision 'in no uncertain terms, so that the judge is a calculating machine . . .' (Ibid, 23).
[46] Ibid, 16.

But perhaps the concessions of determinacy are, in deconstructionist argot, erasable. Perhaps Derrida was only saying that his claim about justice would hold *even if* any legal judgment *were* certain. If talk of subsumption and correctness is erasable, we should be able to find concession-free assertions of indeterminacy in deconstruction if anywhere. And deconstructionists do make very gratifying claims of radical indeterminacy:

> . . . a text is always threatening to overflow into an indefinite number of different significations. (J. M. Balkin)[47]

> . . . all meaning depends on a future rewriting of past writings as rewritten in the present writing which confronts the interpreter. . . . the meaning of a text could possibly be anything except that which it presently appears to be. (Michel Rosenfeld)[48]

> If I may write under erasure, the so-called radical indeterminacy thesis is clearly correct. (David Gray Carlson)[49]

Yet even deconstructionists flinch:

> Deconstruction is not licentiousness or promiscuity at all . . . Nor does deconstruction deny the phenomenon of successful communication. Without question, every day provides examples of spoken sentences understood by listeners in the way the speaker would have them understood. But there is no guaranty of the successful arrival of the message, because language has a life in context that is beyond the control of the speaker. (David Gray Carlson)[50]

> The purpose of the deconstruction is not to establish that any interpretation of a text is acceptable, but that the yearning for originary meaning in the simple theory of interpretation [eg, the theory that interpretation is the identification of what the author intended to be done in such a case] is incomplete and cannot serve as a foundation for interpretation. (J. M. Balkin)[51]

It seems that nobody will say that anything goes. Deconstructionists take pains to escape the critical predicament: along with the concessions of determinacy, they rely on the value of an open mind.

> Deconstruction awakes us from our dogmatic slumber, and reminds us that our 'truth' is only an interpretation. . . . Deconstruction is not a denial of the legitimacy of rules and principles; it is an affirmation of human possibilities that have been overlooked or forgotten in the privileging of particular legal ideas. (J. M. Balkin)[52]

> . . . inversions of hierarchical oppositions expose to debate the institutional arrangements that rely on the hierarchies and thus open possibilities of change . . . (Jonathan Culler)[53]

[47] *LL* 423.
[48] Above n 40 at 157–8.
[49] Above n 13 at 282. But note that Carlson seems to use 'radical indeterminacy thesis' as I use 'theoretical indeterminacy thesis'—ibid, 278 n 51.
[50] Ibid, 282–3.
[51] *LL* 426.
[52] *LL* 405.
[53] Quoted by Balkin, *LL* 418.

Deconstruction exposes law to debate, but not to argument. It suggests new possibilities of change, but allows no claim that the reasons in favour of a particular change are better than the reasons against it. It points out the privileging of ideas, but it cannot say what ideas, if any, *should be* privileged. In favour of this approach, it can be said that it gives underprivileged ideas (and therefore, presumably, the people whose ideas they are) a kind of equality with the privileged. But the way in which it makes ideas equal is indiscriminate: its inversions lead only to further inversions.

Balkin responds with panache to this version of the critical predicament: he compares deconstruction to psychotherapy. When does psychotherapy end? When patient and therapist decide that 'the patient has been sufficiently enlightened and emancipated from the burdens of repressed material'.[54] At the analogous point in deconstruction, 'when the insights provided by deconstruction have produced sufficient enlightenment', the theorist makes 'a political and moral choice'.[55] In doing so, the theorist is 'strictly speaking, no longer a deconstructionist'.[56] Deconstruction itself has nothing to say about what choices people should make.

Derrida shares the concern for the critical predicament, and the open-mind response. He insists that deconstruction is not 'a quasi-nihilistic abdication before the ethico-politico-juridical question of justice and before the opposition between just and unjust . . .',[57] and claims that 'constantly to maintain an interrogation of the origin, grounds and limits of our conceptual, theoretical or normative apparatus surrounding justice is on deconstruction's part anything but a neutralization of interest in justice, an insensitivity towards injustice'.[58] How does deconstruction's interest in justice and sensitivity towards injustice express itself? In the denial that any decision is just. Here Derrida sees a solution to the critical predicament that is more positive and more radical than mere concessions of determinacy: he thinks that there is 'nothing more just than what I today call deconstruction'.[59] His claim seems to be that deconstruction has such paradoxically high standards that it rates nothing as just. But if deconstruction cannot say that any decision is *unjust*, it also has paradoxically low standards. As a technique for deciding what to do, it would be like a mad Robin Hood who gives the booty to the poor, and returns in the night to steal it back again.

3. *Semiotics*

In various versions, semiotics has melded the ideas of philosophers, linguists anthropologists, and literary critics into a collage of doctrines that share the

[54] *LL* 408.
[55] Ibid.
[56] Ibid.
[57] Derrida, above n 23 at 19.
[58] Ibid at 20.
[59] Ibid at 21.

attitude that the *sign* is the fundamental category for explanation of human culture (or of everything). Like the new interpretive orthodoxy, the study of signs and systems of signs is not tied to any particular indeterminacy thesis. Bernard Jackson's legal semiotics, for example, does not view semantic indeterminacy as a necessary part of 'the idea of meaning as a function of relationships' among signs.[60] He adopts a notion of a 'semic core' and a penumbra of doubt, which seems to translate Hart's view of indeterminacy into the vocabulary of semiotics. But the traditions of semiotics make radical and theoretical indeterminacy theses naturally attractive to semioticians.

From the nineteenth-century Swiss linguist Ferdinand de Saussure, semioticians take the structuralist ideas that meaning is a relation between signifier and signified, that the meaning relation is arbitrary, and that the meaning relation is constituted by relations within a system of signs. From the American pragmatist philosopher Charles Peirce, they take the idea that an 'interpretant' mediates between sign and object, and that the interpretant is itself a sign.[61]

The general view emerges that words are signs that are related to what they stand for by signs. And what do they stand for? Signs. That is what William of Baskerville, the hero of Umberto Eco's novel, *The Name of the Rose*, taught his protégé, Adso: 'A book is made up of signs that speak of other signs, which in their turn speak of things.'[62] In William's teaching, *things* are also signs:

omnis mundi creatura
quasi liber et pictura
nobis est in speculum.[63]

Every thing is a sign, and every sign stands for another sign. Things are books, books are made up of signs, signs speak of other signs which speak of things, things are books, ... This is a view that assimilates language to everything (or else vice versa). Everything is *code*. The result is the apotheosis of semiosis: a sign is that which stands for a sign, and the relation of standing-for is a matter of mediation by a sign.

The legal semiotician who makes the strongest claim of indeterminacy is Robert Benson. He includes Wittgenstein, along with Eco, Peirce, Fish, and Derrida, among his influences.[64] But his central semiotic claim is at odds with the core of Wittgenstein's later philosophy. Benson says,

> The something that has meaning— ... anything that stands for something else—can be called a sign.[65]

[60] Bernard S. Jackson, *Semiotics and Legal Theory* (London: Routledge and Kegan Paul 1985) 43. And see Jackson, 'On Scholarly Developments in Legal Semiotics' (1990) 3 *Ratio Juris* 415.

[61] See, in particular, 'Logic as Semiotic: The Theory of Signs', ch 7 in Justus Buchler (ed), *The Philosophy of Peirce: Selected Writings* (London: Kegan Paul, Trench, Trubner & Co 1940). And cf: 'The three terms of the relation are the sign itself, the object of the sign, and the interpretant, which is itself a sign and thus stands in the same triadic relation to a further interpretant!' Christopher Hookway, *Peirce* (London: Routledge and Kegan Paul 1985) 121.

[62] Umberto Eco, *The Name of the Rose*, trans William Weaver (London: Secker & Warburg 1983) 396.

[63] Ibid at 23, quoting the philosopher Alanus de Insulis.

[64] *LL* 496–8.

[65] *LL* 498.

Wittgenstein's *Philosophical Investigations* were directed against the idea that 'Every word has a meaning. This meaning is correlated with the word. It is the object for which the word stands.'[66] Benson's semiotic doctrine is a poststructuralist variant of that idea, in which the object for which a word stands is another sign.[67] Benson's poststructuralism reinterprets Saussure's basic opposition signifier—signified by counting the signified as itself a sign, so that meaning becomes a relation between signs, and not just a relation that derives its content from relations among signs. This doctrine leads Benson to diagram a 'web of signs',[68] in which 'the reader produces the meaning of a sign by travelling the connections of the web, linking a series of signs until losing interest in the process'.[69] He applies the web to the 1987 dispute between the Reagan Administration and Congress over the US–USSR Anti-Ballistic Missile Treaty, and concludes that 'texts don't possess meaning',[70] that readers make meaning,[71] and that 'the traditional myth of the "rule of law"'[72] helped to hide US state terrorism.

Even Benson makes a tacit concession of linguistic determinacy, when he concludes that readers have power 'to make meaning, even by openly disregarding a text'.[73] Disregarding a text would not be an option available to a reader, if texts did not possess meanings. The implication that there is something that can be disregarded is a concession of determinacy. But at least Benson makes no *express* concessions to determinacy. He does not even acknowledge the critical predicament. The process of travelling around the semiotic web 'ends only when the reader loses interest'.[74] As a result, the purity of Benson's theory purely undermines his critical purpose. By saying that meaning is what readers produce when they get tired of moving around a semiotic web, he disqualifies himself from saying that the ABM Treaty (or any text—that is, anything) means anything. Benson seems to view his theoretical claims as a particularly cutting way of undermining the Administration's arguments, and to rely on the sympathy of his audience to support the feeling that the Administration's actions were terrorist actions. But he has no argument that the Administration was wrong. He can give no reason why anyone *should* stop at the node in the semiotic web from which the US government's actions look like terrorism.

The US Government's attempts to evade its treaty exemplify the fact that when people don't want to do what they should, they have an interest in

66 *Philosophical Investigations*, trans G. E. M. Anscombe (Oxford: Basil Blackwell 1958) section 1.

67 One of several intersections between semiotics and deconstruction is that they share this principle: cf 'Every signified is actually a signifier in disguise . . . a sign can only represent still another sign'. (Balkin, *LL* 402); '. . . in the context of deconstruction, all texts (whether oral or written) are writings that refer to other writings.' Rosenfeld, above n 40 at 153.

68 *LL* 498.

69 Ibid.

70 *LL* 505.

71 *LL* 512. At this point Benson parts company with Eco, who thinks that 'in the course of the last decades, the rights of the interpreters have been overstressed'. 'Interpretation and History', in Eco, above n 28 at 23.

72 *LL* 513.

73 *LL* 512.

74 *LL* 498.

presenting what they want to do as an interpretation of their duty. Benson's doctrine has the consequence that they are right. Whatever they want to say *is* an interpretation. On this doctrine, no one can break a treaty, or a promise, or deny a constitutional right. The lies of the powerful become interpretations.

4. *Context*

When indeterminacy theorists make concessions to determinacy, they often retreat to assertions that the indeterminacy claim was actually a reminder of the context-dependence of meaning:[75]

> There are still rules. But there are no rules that can be understood apart from the context . . . (Margaret Jane Radin)[76]

> . . . if the meaning of a signifier is context bound, context is boundless—that is, there are always new contexts that will serve to increase the different meanings of a signifier. (J. M. Balkin)[77]

> Deconstruction . . . stresses that meaning is context bound—a function of relations within or between texts—but that context itself is boundless: there will always be new contextual possibilities that can be adduced, so that the one thing we *cannot* do is to set limits. (Jonathan Culler)[78]

To some extent, the boundlessness of context is irrelevant to questions of the application of rules. That boundlessness has a role in interpreting Dante's *Divine Comedy*, for instance, that it does not have in deciding whether goods are of satisfactory quality for the purposes of the Sale of Goods Act. We might call the first sort of interpretation 'generalizing interpretation'. It means giving a general account of the *Divine Comedy*, though it can be more general (if it claims to interpret the whole) or less (if it accounts for a part of the poem or an aspect of the poem). The complexity of that text and of the rest of the world make for endless possible interpretive statements about the *Divine Comedy*.[79] Of course, there could be generalizing interpretations of legal texts, as if someone asked for an interpretation of the Sale of Goods Act without giving a case to which the Act is to be applied.

The second sort of interpretation (which we might call 'applicative' interpretation) is different. It needs to meet some of the same standards (of

[75] The use of context in this connection has a distinguished pedigree: in his argument against Hart's claim that a rule like 'no vehicles in the park' has standard cases, Lon Fuller *first* embroidered Hart's claim by adding as one of the 'tacit assumptions' he ascribed to Hart, the rider 'whatever the context in which the word may appear', and *then* attacked it. L. L. Fuller, 'Positivism and Fidelity to Law: A Reply to Professor Hart' (1958) 71 *Harv LR* 630, 662; cf also 'regardless of context', 'in all ordinary contexts', and 'in all contexts' in Fuller's other formulations of Hart's claim, at 662–3.

[76] *LL* 309.

[77] *LL* 423.

[78] Jonathan Culler, 'In Defence of Overinterpretation', in Eco, above n 28, 109 at 121. See also the quotation from David Gray Carlson, in the text at n 50, above.

[79] You can agree to this even if you think that one interpretation of *The Divine Comedy* can be better than another.

plausibility, explanatory power, ...) as generalizing interpretation, but it faces the additional standard of relevance to the application of the linguistic expression in question to the situation in question. If an account of the text needs to be given in order to reach the applicative decision, the possibilities are restricted by the particularizing purpose of the interpretation: nothing about the statute or the world is *relevant* to the decision that is not *required* for the decision. Of course, there could be applicative interpretations in literary contexts, as if someone asked whether *The Divine Comedy* belongs to a particular genre.

It might be thought the boundlessness of context has similar implications in both generalizing interpretation and applicative interpretation: in the former there is an unlimited range of aspects of the world and of the *Divine Comedy* which an interpretation might address; in the latter there is an unlimited variety of cases to which, eg, the Sale of Goods Act might be applied. *This* similarity is misleading, because applicative interpretation *addresses* a case—and willy nilly the boundlessness of the variety of possible cases evaporates. But then the world that came up with the statute remains a complicated place, with complex needs and purposes and presuppositions and intentions which affect decisions about how to apply its words to a case. The need to give an account of the Act that puts it in its legal and commercial and cultural context is restricted, but is not eliminated. Moreover, while no applicative interpretation needs to cope with the boundlessness of context in the way that generalizing interpretation does, an applicative interpretation may have to deal with *any one* of a boundless range of possible cases.

So the relative limitability of context in applicative interpretation does not answer claims that context-dependence is a form of indeterminacy. Legal questions tend to be less subtle and ramified than literary questions, but they are not necessarily so; a question of application of the Sale of Goods Act might require a sensitive (and controversial) understanding both of the context of the case, and of the context of the Act.

A general response to claims that the meaning of language is indeterminate because it depends on context would need to show, (1) that meaning is not radically dependent on context, or (2) that context-dependence does not typically lead to indeterminacy. I propose that we should reject (1), and accept (2).

4.1 *Is meaning acontextual?*

Frederick Schauer has developed this response to indeterminacy claims. Schauer writes that 'ruleness' (a rule's capacity to demand different behaviour from the behaviour required by the rule's justification)[80] requires 'the possibility that a form of decision-making could conceivably be guided by the meaning of the formulated generalization rather than by the optimal particularized application of the justification behind that formulation'.[81] He argues that this possibility

[80] Frederick Schauer, *Playing by the Rules*, above n 18, at 102.
[81] Ibid, 61–2.

depends on 'semantic autonomy', which is the possession of 'acontextual' meaning. So Schauer's account of rules includes a claim that they can be applied without knowledge of context.

It seems obvious that the meaning of an utterance is not merely a function of the single event in which it occurs. Yet the various ways in which Schauer elaborates on the idea seem to run into trouble. Perhaps the difficulty is that it is impossible to describe what is relevant and important about an event (what could give meaning to an utterance) without describing, among other things, the conventions of a community in which the event takes place. But then in describing an event we would describe the rules of language, and whatever it is that Schauer is describing as 'autonomous' becomes part of the description of a single event. In other words, one problem with the notion of semantic autonomy is that the meaning of words is a *feature* of contexts in which they are used. Then, perhaps the question Schauer is addressing is how meaning differs from other features of contexts.

He calls semantic autonomy

> the ability of symbols—words, phrases, sentences, paragraphs—to carry meaning independent of the communicative goals on particular occasions of the users of those symbols.[82]

What is an ability to carry meaning? Any combination of letters, or even the position of a coat on a chair, is *able to carry* meaning, and Schauer wants to claim something more for the symbols of a language. He must mean that the signs used in a language *carry* meaning, not simply that they are *able* to carry meaning. That is very close to saying that they mean something. They do mean something, of course—but do they do so autonomously?

No one can use symbols to carry meaning independently of particular goals and occasions. But Schauer says that the waves of the ocean could do so:

> Suppose I go to the ocean and while there notice a group of shells washed up on the beach in a pattern that looks something like C-A-T. I will think then of small furry house pets and not of zeppelins or zebras, despite the fact that in this case there is no user of language whatsoever. My ability to think cat when I see 'C-A-T', and the fact that all speakers of English would have a rather closely grouped array of reactions to that same shell pattern, demonstrates the phenomenon I call semantic autonomy, the way in which language carries something by itself, independent of those who use it on particular occasions.[83]

In fact there *is* a user of language on the beach. Schauer has not demonstrated semantic autonomy of language, because he is one of 'those who use it on particular occasions'. And note that Schauer does not say that he *understands* the shells. He says that he thinks of cats when he sees the shells. Meaning and

[82] Ibid, 55.
[83] Ibid, 56.

understanding are not equivalent to any mental experiences or processes.[84] A multitude of experiences could be associated with seeing or hearing words, but none of them is 'the experience of understanding'. When someone uses the word 'cat' and we understand what they say, we may think of small furry animals. But that experience is not understanding. We could understand the word 'cat' without thinking of small furry animals, and the thought of small furry animals could go through our minds without our understanding the word 'cat'.

But there is obviously a truth in Schauer's discussion of cats: the word 'cat' does refer *to cats*, and no one can understand the word without knowing that it does. While you do not need to think about cats to understand the word 'cat', you *do* need to be able to do various things such as distinguish a cat from a dog, explain the word's meaning by pointing to a cat or by describing a cat. . . . But for meaning to be autonomous from context, it seems that it would have to be autonomous from facts about cats and dogs, so that we could know the meaning of the word without knowing anything about cats. Thus, in another formulation of the idea of semantic autonomy, Schauer says that

> there is at least something, call it what you will, shared by all speakers of a language that enables one speaker of that language to be understood by another speaker of that language even in circumstances in which the speaker and understander share nothing in common but their mutual language.[85]

In fact, there is no such something, call it what you will, because there are no such circumstances. The circumstances Schauer pictures are contradictory: a speaker and an 'understander' cannot share a language, and share nothing else—just as no one can know the English language, and know nothing else. The people Schauer imagines would not share *any* knowledge about cats, or about rain, or sleep, or food, . . ., and yet they would know the meaning of the words 'cat', 'rain', 'sleep', 'food'. . . . In fact, people who share a knowledge of the meaning of those words also share a lot of knowledge about cats, rain, sleep, food. . . .

But Schauer concedes that fact, when he says that communication is based on 'numerous contextual understandings', of which a sufficient number 'are similarly understood by both speaker and listener just because they inhabit the same planet and speak the same language'.[86] Another concession is a guarded description of the idea of acontextual meaning:

> In referring to this aspect of language as its acontextuality, I emphasize the way in which meaning is larger than the context of a particular utterance. The description of this characteristic as 'acontextual', however, cannot be taken too literally. To identify the phenomenon of acontextual meaning is not to deny that contextual factors are

[84] Wittgenstein harped on this point: 'The meaning of a word is not the experience one has in hearing or saying it, and the sense of a sentence is not a complex of such experiences.' *Philosophical Investigations*, above n 66 at 181. Cf also *Philosophical Investigations* sections 159–61.

[85] *Playing by the Rules*, above n 18 at 55–6.

[86] Ibid, 57.

presupposed in attributing even the barest amount of meaning to an utterance.[87]

It seems inconsistent to say that meaning is partly acontextual, but an utterance cannot have any meaning without a context. This tension is only resolved by the unclear metaphorical claim that meaning is 'larger' than context. The concessions against the idea of acontextual meaning multiply:

> The identification of acontextual meaning involves not the denial of the necessity of context, but the recognition that a large number of contextual understandings will be assumed by all speakers of a language.[88]

That is a sensible concession, and it makes 'acontextual' into a misnomer.

4.2 *Is context-dependence indeterminacy?*

We have to try to reconcile the plausibility of Schauer's reminder that the meaning of a word on an occasion of its use is not particular to that occasion, with the problems that arise in attempts to express the notions of semantic autonomy and acontextual meaning. It is worth remembering that children learn the meaning of a word from its use in particular situations, and learn to use it in similar situations. Then the meaning of a word may be thought of as its potential for use in particular situations. That potential could be called contextual (because words can only be used *in a context*), or acontextual (because they can be used in *various* contexts that are different as well as similar); but it can be misleading to call it either. Children often use words in surprising contexts that they see as similar enough to justify using the word. But context-dependence cannot be a form of radical indeterminacy: even children can grasp some relevant similarities among contexts, and learning a language involves learning to do so more effectively.

But these reflections on the nature of meaning are unsatisfying in a discussion of context. It seems paradoxical to talk in general terms about 'context', which is just whatever could help us to understand an utterance. The fact that there is a word 'context' for all that should not mislead us into thinking that we can generalize in a helpful way about it. Nevertheless, there is a general response to claims that context-dependence means indeterminacy: the context can and characteristically does answer questions of (ie determine) the application of words. The application of the word 'large' is radically context-dependent: if we are given the dimensions of an object, we are in no position to say whether 'large' applies to the object unless we know what sort of object it is. And we cannot say whether, eg, a house of a particular size is large unless we know a lot of facts about, eg, its location, the way of life of people in its community, the houses it might be compared with, and so on. But radical context-dependence does not make the meaning of 'large' radically indeterminate. In context we can say whether a particular house is large or not, except in borderline cases that fit

[87] Ibid, 56.
[88] Ibid, 57.

Hart's model. The word 'tomorrow' is radically context-dependent: it has a different reference every day! But its meaning is not radically indeterminate.[89]

This is an argument that the resort to context is a retreat from radical indeterminacy, and it needs to be weighed against the insistence of indeterminacy theorists that, if meaning varies with context, it can't be trusted:

> Because 'meaning is context-bound, but context is boundless', natural law's facticity is invaded by subjective interpretation, and liberalism loses its status as a philosophy.[90]

Context-dependence does not necessarily lead to 'subjective interpretation', because the context may give objective reasons for applying or not applying an expression to something. Suppose that a boat owner asks you to recommend 'a good painter'.[91] On the one hand, just knowing the meaning of 'good' and 'painter' will not allow you to help them out. On the other hand, the context will typically determine whether they need an artist, or a decorator, or a rope for a boat. It may be perfectly clear that the boat does not need painting, that it does need a rope, and that the owner is not interested in art. Then there are objective reasons for taking the boat owner to be asking about a rope.

Far from amounting to a source of indeterminacy, it can be tempting to think that the context always determines whether anything is 'a good painter', since it can determine both (i) what sort of painter is in question, and (ii) what is needed, in the case in question, from that sort of painter (ie, what is a 'good' painter). In fact, context may not be as determinative as that. It may make various incommensurable standards relevant (a rope's strength and its weight . . .). Indeed, the context may not even make it clear whether someone wants a decorator or a rope. Then you are faced with a genuine uncertainty arising from linguistic indeterminacy. But context-dependence would make the application of linguistic expressions radically indeterminate only (1) if people were typically ignorant of the relevant and important features of the context in which an expression was used, or (2) if those features typically left facts such as whether someone needs an artist, a decorator, or a rope, unclear. Since neither (1) nor (2) is the case, indeterminacy theses that merely point out the context-dependence of meaning are not radical. Two contexts do not have to be identical before an expression can apply in the same way in each; they need only be similar enough to present the same reasons for applying it. It does not matter if an indefinite range of different contexts could be imagined for a particular use of a word, as long as there are reasons for choosing what contextual factors are relevant to applying the expression.

So, even though it is risky to generalize about contexts, we should not underrate the extent to which they make meaning clear—just think how, if someone asks the meaning of an odd word, we instinctively ask for the sentence in which it

[89] And this is not to make any radical *determinacy* claim about the application of 'tomorrow'—an indeterminacy could arise in a particular use. If you tell me, 'she said she would do it tomorrow', it may not be clear whether 'tomorrow' means the day after she spoke, or the day after today.

[90] Carlson, above n 13 at 282.

[91] An example used by Mark Sainsbury in *Logical Forms* (Oxford: Basil Blackwell 1991) 35.

was used. A context can even determine when somebody means something other than what they said. Here is an example, ironically, from the papers of C. S. Peirce, one of the founders of the philosophy of indeterminacy:

> ... no sign can be absolutely and completely indeterminate ...*
>
> *Though the writing is unmistakable this should be 'determinate'. [Editors' note][92]

Peirce's editors were *right*: the context in which the sentence appears makes it *determinate* that he meant that no sign can be 'determinate'.

5. *Change*

Some concessions of determinacy retreat to assertions that the meaning of language changes:

> ... meaning although never permanently fixed does not thereby become purely arbitrary. (Michel Rosenfeld)[93]

> ... nor are there rules that can be understood as fixed in time. (Margaret Jane Radin)[94]

> I will quickly concede that courts and other constitutional interpreters operate within constraints ... but the point is that whatever constraints exist are not constant over time. (Sanford Levinson)[95]

The meaning of words does change, sometimes surprisingly. Levinson gives the example of the word 'sentimental', which used to be a term of praise and became a term of reproach.[96] There are many such examples: 'knave' once meant 'boy'; 'villain' comes from a word for 'serf'; 'nice' meant 'ignorant', then 'particular, hard-to-please', then 'pleasant', and now it hardly means anything.

But it should be obvious just how non-radical the indeterminacies are that arise from changes of that kind.[97] First, change in linguistic meaning is slow. Schauer puts it that arguing from change of meaning to indeterminacy is 'comparable to taking the ponderous progress of a glacier as indicating that it will move if we put our shoulders against it and push'.[98] The metaphor is apt, except that it suggests uniform motion. In fact, not only is linguistic change slow, it is episodic and unorganized. What makes 'nice' and 'sentimental' interesting is the way they have changed in meaning during periods in which much of the vocabulary of English has not. And the meaning of some words can be constant over vast ages. The n- in no, never, neither, etc appears in

[92] *Collected Papers of Charles S. Peirce*, Charles Hartshorne and Paul Weiss (eds) (Cambridge: Harvard University Press 1934) section 5.506.
[93] Michel Rosenfeld, above n 40 at 159.
[94] *LL* 309.
[95] *LL* 352 n 33.
[96] *LL* 346.
[97] As Levinson seems to point out: *LL* 347.
[98] *LL* 444.

Russian, Irish, French, German and Sanskrit, always with the same meaning that it had in their ancestor language, 'Proto Indo-European'. Linguists reconstructing that language, which was spoken more than 3000 years ago, conclude that the word 'three' was *trey-, the word 'two' was *dwo, the word 'cow' was *gwo-, the word 'mother' was *miter- ... So some words change slowly, and some change very, very slowly.

Secondly, when meanings of words change, no indeterminacy results unless it is unclear which of two or more meanings is to be used. When that *is* unclear, there will be indeterminacy. This is not radical indeterminacy: not only is it rare, it is contingent on something that can be described, as Levinson describes the change in the meaning of 'sentimental'.

Most claims about change in meaning are more radical: they are allegations that meaning is unstable—that it could change at any time, so that any particular judicial decision could apply a new meaning. These claims are very similar to indeterminacy claims based on context-dependence: they insist that every time an expression is used, it is used in a new context that gives it a changed meaning. Allan Hutchinson and Derek Morgan write, 'A sentence will never mean exactly the same thing to any two different people or even the same thing to one person on different occasions.'[99] In one sense this is true: every time you say, 'pass the pickles', you are asking for different pickles to be moved from a different location to a different destination, at a different time. ... But it is false in the only relevant sense, which has to do with what counts as pickles, and what counts as passing them.

The notion that the meaning of expressions changes every time they are used is part of poststructuralist theory,[100] but in legal theory it is considerably older. Edward Levi introduced his *Introduction to Legal Reasoning* by saying,

> In an important sense legal rules are never clear. ... The rules change as the rules are applied.[101]

Perhaps Levi was making a remark about judicial behaviour: that judges are always changing the rules. That would be an empirical claim. It might be true or false, but it would make sense only if it is possible for things to be otherwise—for rules to be applied, at least in some cases, without being changed. If Levi was making a remark on the *nature* of rules, it would amount to a radical indeterminacy claim which refutes itself in a new way. The concept of change presupposes an original: *something* transformed into *something else*. If there were radical indeterminacy, there would be no change.

* St Catherine's College, Oxford.

[99] *LL* 481. Cf Levinson: '... contemporary theory [makes] an attack on the stability of meaning ... at *any* given moment'. *LL* 347.

[100] See Collini, above n 35 at 7, concerning the 'instability of all meaning in writing'.

[101] Levi, *Introduction to Legal Reasoning* (Chicago: University of Chicago Press 1949) 1–3.

6. *Wittgenstein*

A spate of work on Wittgenstein and law has followed the recent debate in philosophy of language between Saul Kripke, who interpreted Wittgenstein's remarks on following rules as posing a sceptical paradox, and various antisceptical objectors. Proponents of legal indeterminacy have adopted the sceptical interpretation;[102] their opponents argue that they have been confused by a misleading philosophical question, and that Wittgenstein, far from answering that question sceptically, wanted to stop asking it.[103] Frederick Schauer, meanwhile, gives an idiosyncratic argument to the effect that Wittgenstein's remarks show that formulated rules are not radically indeterminate, but unformulated rules are.[104]

The scenario that leads to all this perplexity is simple: suppose that you are teaching a pupil who has learned to count, and is now learning to recite the even numbers. Everything goes smoothly as far as 1000, after which the pupil says '1004, 1008, 1012'. You find yourself at a loss, because all the examples of adding 2 which you had given (and which the pupil had mastered) seem unable by themselves to determine that 1002 comes after 1000. You meant them to be examples of 'add 2', but they could just as well have been examples of 'add 2 as far as 1000, and then add 4'. It seems that something extra is needed to connect a rule like 'add 2' with instances of its application. What can that something extra be?

This philosophical question—what connects a rule with its applications?—has consequences for the indeterminacy debate. On the sceptical interpretation, Wittgenstein is pointing out that, because there is no extra something, there is an unbridgeable gap between a rule and its applications. That is to say that there is no such thing as rules:

> There can be no such thing as meaning anything by any word. Each new application we make is a leap in the dark; any present intention could be interpreted so as to accord with anything we may choose to do.[105]

The sceptics deal with this paradoxical situation by saying that the consensus

[102] See Charles M. Yablon, 'Law and Metaphysics' (1987) 96 *Yale LJ* 613, Sanford Levinson, 'What Do Lawyers Know (And What Do They Do with their Knowledge)? Comments on Schauer and Moore' (1985) 58 *S Cal LR* 441 at 447–8, Margaret Jane Radin, 'Reconsidering the Rule of Law' (1989) in *LL*, Christopher L. Kutz, 'Just Disagreement: Indeterminacy and Rationality in the Rule of Law' (1994) 103 *Yale LJ* 997.

[103] See Brian Langille, 'Revolution Without Foundation: The Grammar of Scepticism and Law' (1988) 33 *McGill LJ* 451, Scott Landers, 'Wittgenstein, Realism and CLS: Undermining Rule Scepticism' (1990) 9 *Law and Philosophy* 177, Brian Bix, *Law, Language and Legal Determinacy* (Oxford: Clarendon Press 1993) at 38–41, Andrei Marmor, above n 14 at 146–54; Christian Zapf and Eben Moglen, 'Linguistic Indeterminacy and the Rule of Law: On the Perils of Misunderstanding Wittgenstein' (1996) 84 *Georgetown LJ* 485. These legal theorists draw on the non-sceptical response to Kripke developed by G. P. Baker and P. M. S. Hacker in *Scepticism, Rules and Language* (Oxford: Basil Blackwell 1984) and *Wittgenstein: Rules, Grammar and Necessity* (Oxford: Basil Blackwell 1985). For discussion of Marmor's version of the non-sceptical argument see Endicott, above n 26 at 460–6. Martin Stone makes an original argument in favour of the non-sceptical view, in a critique of Drucilla Cornell's *The Philosophy of the Limit* (New York: Routledge and Kegan Paul 1992): above, n 14.

[104] *Playing by the Rules*, above n 18 at 64–8.

[105] Saul Kripke, *Wittgenstein on Rules and Private Language: An Elementary Exposition* (Oxford: Basil Blackwell 1982) 55.

of a community licenses us to talk as if a rule existed: 'following a rule' is another way of saying 'doing what other members of the community say is following a rule'.

The non-sceptical interpretation claims that Wittgenstein was trying to dissolve a philosophical muddle rather than to generate one. On this view, he was not arguing that nothing bridges a gap between rule and application, but that there is no gap to be bridged. In philosophers' jargon, knowing that 1002 follows 1000 is internally related to understanding the rule 'add 2'.[106] They are not identical, since you could understand 'add 2' and yet not be able to count to 1000, or know that '1000, 1002' is an application of the rule (because the teacher has told you so) without understanding the rule. But they are necessarily related, and they need nothing to connect them: you cannot know how to count to 1002, and understand the rule 'add 2', without knowing that '1000, 1002' is a correct application of the rule. So learning a rule is neither finding something to bridge the gap, nor merely happening to do the same thing as other people, but grasping a way of using the examples the teacher gives.

Understanding this debate is basic to understanding the problems of law and language, because the philosophical question about what connects a rule with its applications amounts to the question of what connects a word with its applications, as both Kripke and the non-sceptical Wittgensteinians recognize. We have a *rule* of calling bullfrogs 'bullfrogs'—a general norm. It is not just a habit: we tell children that that is the right thing to call them. If a child calls a hamster a 'bullfrog', we do not just think 'that's unusual', we *correct* the child. The debate over Wittgenstein's remarks on rules is a debate about what makes it wrong to call a hamster a 'bullfrog', just as it is a debate about what makes '1000, 1004' wrong when you are counting by twos.

If the non-sceptical view is correct, Wittgenstein cleared away the misconception that something other than the rule determines what counts as an application, but he did not suppose that if nothing other than the rule determines its applications, its applications are indeterminate. He cleared away the misconception that philosophers have the job of looking for something to mediate between the word 'bullfrog' and bullfrogs. This has consequences for some of the views that we have surveyed:

1. The new interpretive orthodoxy, for all the consensus, is mistaken: as Wittgenstein put it, 'there is a way of grasping a rule which is *not* an *interpretation*'.[107] That remark is an obstacle, which no one has cleared away, to the use of Wittgenstein's remarks to support scepticism about rules.
2. Sceptical claims that nothing *guarantees* that a decision has followed a rule

[106] Cf Baker and Hacker: '. . . we define the series "+2", for example, in terms of the sequence "...998, 1000, 1002, 1004". The rule and its application are internally related, for we define the concept "following this rule" by reference to this result.' Wittgenstein, *Rules, Grammar and Necessity*, above n 103 at 148.

[107] *Philosophical Investigations*, above n 66 at section 201.

are simply put to rest.[108] They are claims that there is no bridge, where in fact there is no gap.

3. The critical predicament evaporates. In some circumstances, particular actions can and should be criticized for failing to follow a rule (if the rule ought to have been followed)—or, equally, for following a rule (if the rule ought not to have been followed).

It seems that the non-sceptical view, if it is right, defeats not just radical indeterminacy theses, but also theoretical indeterminacy theses. But if the sceptical view is right, Wittgenstein's argument *is* a theoretical indeterminacy thesis: he has shown that there could only be rules if there were some unimagined connection. There is none, but we are licensed to talk as if there were rules when there is something *like* a connection—the consensus of a community. Rule following is essentially social.

It is easy to see the attraction of the social view for people interested in law and language. Languages are social practices, and law is a social practice, and so their rules must be social practices. A rule is not a legal rule if it has no role in the practices of a society. The only mistake is to jump from those propositions to a view about the connection between a rule and its applications. That is, it is tempting to jump *from* questions such as whether there is a rule, what it is, who made it, who follows it, and so on (which are questions of social fact) *to* the question of what connects a rule with its applications (which is a philosophical question), and to conclude that the philosophical question is a question of social fact. Note that Wittgenstein's discussion is not about whether the rule that the pupil was supposed to apply was 'add 2', nor is it about whether 1002 comes after 1000 when that rule is applied. Wittgenstein's discussion takes it for granted that the answer to both those questions is 'yes'. The question is more basic: what *connects* '1000, 1002' with the rule 'add 2'? Wittgenstein's technique in such a situation was to *reject* the philosophical question.[109] The sceptical view is that the philosophical question has no answer, and needs to be changed into a question of social fact; the non-sceptical view is that the question should not be asked.

Margaret Jane Radin makes the jump from the social nature of law and language to the social view of rule following. She characterizes Wittgenstein as a rule sceptic[110] who thought that rule following is 'an essentially social phenomenon'.[111] She does not mean simply that social rules (such as the rules of law and of language) are social practices, but that there is no such thing as a rule unless people agree that there is a rule: 'Rule-following can only be understood to occur where there is reiterated human action both in responding to directives and in observing others respond.'[112] This seems to say that no action

108 Eg Carlson, in text above at n 50.
109 *Philosophical Investigations*, above n 66 at section 47.
110 *LL* 290.
111 *LL* 291.
112 Ibid.

can follow a rule unless there is a community that says that it does. That sceptical view of the social nature of rules cannot be right: if you live alone with a cat and call her 'Grimalkin', you are following a rule even if no one else ever finds out. There is no community consensus. Even if you and Grimalkin form a community, you don't need Grimalkin's agreement to follow a rule of calling her that. What if we say that you form a community of one, or that a hypothetical community of people like you would (counterfactually) agree on what is an application of the rule? Then we dissolve the notion of a community, and admit that an action can follow a rule, or fail to do so, without any consensus.

In your practice of calling your cat 'Grimalkin', it is true that there are all sorts of manifestations of what you have learned from your community—the notion of names, the notion that cats can be given names, the name itself (though *not* the fact that it is *your* cat's name), and so on. We learn what rules are and how to follow them from being part of a real community; but that doesn't mean that following *a* rule is doing what the community says. Perhaps some who take the social view of rules simply mean to point out that we learn the *general* practice of following rules from a community—that we acquire the concept from a community. Or they might argue, more strongly, that that is the *only* way it is possible to learn how to follow rules. To reduce the social view to either claim would change it significantly from the sceptical Wittgensteinian view. If the social view of rules were simply pointing out that you learned to follow rules from your community, or even if it were arguing that that is the *only* way to learn to follow rules, it would no longer be a distinct view about what rules are. It would become consistent with the non-sceptical view that the question of what connects a rule with its applications is not unanswerable, but misconceived.

Radin herself, it seems, does not need to adopt the sceptical view on rules. Her position on Wittgenstein can be seen as much weaker than the sceptical view, because she only uses the discussion to refute 'traditional formalism'[113] about rules. The formalism that Radin opposes claims that rules can be applied by *deduction*, at least in core cases.[114] No one appears to hold that view, which would be absurd. If I ask you for an apple, and you pick out an apple from the fruit bowl, you follow a rule. But you do not make a deduction. Deductions need premises, and here you only have an apple. 'This is an apple' could itself state a premise in a deduction, but it is not a deduction. Could a traditional formalist, if there were one, say that 'this is an apple' is necessarily the *conclusion* of a deduction, in which the premises are propositions such as 'every object that has such and such characteristics is an apple', and 'this object has such and such characteristics'? No, because an absurd regress would result: the judgments that this is an object, and that it has any particular characteristic, would become conclusions of other deductions premised on the conclusions of other

[113] *LL* 284.
[114] *LL* 285.

deductions. . . . As Hart wrote, 'Logic is silent on how to classify particulars'.[115] If formalism is the view that classifying particulars is a process of deduction, Radin does not need Wittgenstein to attack it.

Though Radin embraces the sceptical view on rules, her concerns are different from the concerns that debate addresses: she talks about what connects a rule with its applications only because she wants to make a point about what judges should do. So the social view of rules that she calls 'Wittgensteinian' ends up as the view that judges should be 'conscious of their obligation to act as independent moral choosers for the good of a society'.[116] That claim is consistent with the non-sceptical view of rules. If there are rules, then judges should be conscious that their obligations to society (and not just to society!) concern the exercise of what powers they have to deal with the rules (powers to apply them, change them, ignore them, interpret them in one way or another, restrict them or extend them, invalidate them . . .). Judges do not need to believe that there is no such thing as rules before they can be conscious of their obligations. Sometimes they blind themselves to their obligations by taking it for granted that there is only one thing to do with a rule. When they do that, they do not need someone to persuade them that 'following a rule' is a paraphrase for 'doing what people say is following a rule'. They need someone to persuade them that they are responsible for what they do with rules.

Since Radin is concerned with the rule of law, perhaps the best explanation for her approach is that she is concerned not with the conceptual possibility of following a rule (which Wittgenstein's discussion is about), but with the practical possibility of government by rules that are sufficiently clear to citizens to provide guidance, and sufficiently clear to officials that they can constrain the use of power, and with the practical possibility that officials might actually abide by the rules, and with the practical danger that rules can be followed unthinkingly. Perhaps she is trying to say that, when judges apply the words of a formulation of the law, they cannot act as calculating machines and should not pretend that they can. They act for reasons in which the community is interested and for which they should be responsible to the community. None of that requires rule scepticism.

The social view of rule following is not a radical indeterminacy thesis, but a theoretical indeterminacy thesis.[117] In the social view, a community could have a firm consensus. Like Stanley Fish, a sceptical interpreter of Wittgenstein could think that community consensus governs what can be called 'following a rule'

[115] *Essays in Jurisprudence and Philosophy* (Oxford: Clarendon Press 1983) 67. In the same essay, Hart wrote that in the penumbra of application of a legal rule, 'men cannot live by deduction alone' (at 64), seeming to suggest that men *can* 'live by deduction alone' in the core of application of a rule. That suggestion is simply misleading, as the rest of Hart's essay shows.

[116] *LL* 309.

[117] Thus Radin says: 'Although the Wittgensteinian view thus certainly admits that there can be action determined by a rule, it is not the kind of determined-ness required by . . . the traditional formalist conception of the nature of rules.' Ibid, 292. Jules Coleman and Brian Leiter present the sceptical view as a harmless theoretical indeterminacy thesis: 'Determinacy, Objectivity and Authority' in Marmor (ed), *Interpretation and Legal Theory*, above n 14, 203 at 219–23.

very strongly. The fact that the theoretically sceptical social view of rule following can lead to just as much practical determinacy as the non-sceptical view becomes important in Frederick Schauer's approach to the debate. His conclusion is that something is needed to bridge the gap between rule and application, but since everyone agrees that there are actions in accord with a rule, it *must* be there. And it does not matter what it is. This approach has a sensible ring: it relies on the difference between practical indeterminacy and theoretical indeterminacy, and postulates that the latter doesn't matter. But Schauer's approach runs into some bewildering problems.

Schauer emphasizes, and attributes to Wittgenstein, the claim that there is no unique correct answer to the question 'What number comes next in the series 1000, 1002, 1004, 1006, ____?'[118] The answer could be 1008, or 1019, or anything. Schauer says that the point is that 'something other than the prior numbers in the series makes 1008 correct and 1019 incorrect',[119] and that the debate over rule following is about what that 'something other' is. So, like the sceptics, he thinks that something *must* tie a rule to its applications, if there are to be rules.

But Schauer is not a sceptic. He says that if the series is accompanied by the 'verbally formulated instruction, "always add 2"', then '1008 becomes the right answer, and 1019 is simply wrong'.[120] He admits that this gambit seems to miss Wittgenstein's point, and that we might ask why 'always' could not mean, '... but if n > 1004, add 13'. His response is that any reason will do:

> The reason it couldn't, of course, is again the topic of the debate about what it is that supplies the benchmark for following or breaking a rule *of language*, where the very characterization of that bedrock question makes it circular and question-begging to answer the question in terms of the existence of rules of language.[121]

This response is actually a cryptic tautology: The topic of a debate about X *is* X. So Schauer is only saying that *the reason why a particular application is in accord with a rule* is '*what it is that supplies the benchmark for following or breaking a rule* ...'. This is a significant tautology, because it is important to Schauer's approach that he does not need to specify a reason. The reason can be 'community practices or agreement, to refer (without endorsement) to just one possible answer'.[122] But there *must* be something that makes 'always' mean always, and once it has done so, rules of language can be the foundation for legal rules.

There are three interconnected difficulties with Schauer's argument:

(1) 'Always add 2' is exactly as vulnerable to a sceptic as is 'give the next number in the series 0, 2, 4, 6, ..., 1000, 1002, 1004, 1006, ...'. The point of Wittgenstein's discussion is that we could not explain the meaning of 'always

[118] Schauer uses as an example a pupil who has got a little further than Wittgenstein's pupil, and knows the steps '1002, 1004, 1006'. *Playing by the Rules*, above n 18 at 65.
[119] Ibid, 65.
[120] Ibid, 66.
[121] Ibid.
[122] Ibid.

add 2' any better than by giving examples and saying 'and so on'. So 'always add 2' cannot 'entrench' the rule if 'give the next number in the series 0, 2, 4, 6, . . ., 1000, 1002, 1004, 1006, . . .' did not. This is the fact that Schauer was alluding to when he admitted that his argument seemed to miss Wittgenstein's point. His response is just to imply that it does not matter.

(2) Schauer sees the 'verbally formulated instruction' (or 'linguistically formulated direction', or 'specific instruction in language')[123] 'always add 2' as *entrenching* the rule that is expressed by 'something other than the prior numbers'. But 'give the next number in the series 0, 2, 4, 6, . . . 1000, 1002, 1004, 1006, . . .' is verbally formulated, is linguistically formulated, is in language, is an instruction, is a direction, and is specific.

(3) A contradiction emerges: 'there is no uniquely correct answer' to 'what comes next in the series 1000, 1002, 1004, 1006, . . .?', so 'something other than the prior numbers in the series makes 1008 correct and 1019 incorrect'.[124] If something *makes* 1008 correct, it is not the case that there is no uniquely correct answer. Of course, the right choice is to say that 1008 *is* (uniquely) correct—and this seems to be the alternative Schauer would choose. In a footnote he says that in '1000, 1002, 1004, ___?' 'there *is* a rule—. . . "add 2"', though the rule does not 'emerge uniquely from the series itself'.

Evidently, applications of a rule may be correct in the absence of an entrenching formulation. Schauer says that 'The divergence between rule and justification, a divergence I take to be crucial to understanding the idea of a rule, is possible only if formulated generalizations can have meanings differing from the result that a direct application of the justification behind a rule would generate on a particular occasion.'[125] That seems to be true—but it would be a different matter to show that *only* a formulated rule can have a different result than the direct application of its underlying justification. And Schauer does not do so; by characterizing Wittgenstein's discussion as having to do with formulations, he concludes that unformulated rules are left unexplained. In Schauer's view, the message of Wittgenstein's discussion is that

> The ability to explain the constraints *of an unformulated or unformulatable rule* is a difficult task, and one quite different from the task of explaining the potential constraint of a formulated rule.[126]

Schauer himself goes on to show that there is nothing particularly difficult about explaining constraint by unformulated rules.[127] He says, eg, that an unformulated customary rule reflected in the normative practices of a community can exist 'in the same way for that community as does a rule that actually has

[123] Ibid, 67.
[124] Ibid.
[125] Ibid, 61.
[126] Ibid, 67. (I do not know what an unformulatable rule is; I will only talk about unformulated rules.)
[127] Ibid, 68–71.

a canonical inscription'.[128] And he develops a theory of precedent that demystifies the constraint of unformulated rules.[129] After repeating the claim that Wittgenstein showed that constraint by non-formulated rules is mysterious,[130] Schauer shows that, even if the generalizing characterizations (ie, purported rule-formulations) of the precedent-setting court have no effect on the law, precedents can constrain: some generalizations are 'more possible than others'.[131] A precedent can be characterized as an instance of an indefinite variety of different rules, but subsequent decision-makers may have compelling reasons for taking it to be an instance of one rule rather than another. Schauer uses the example of *Donoghue* v *Stevenson*, which imposed liability on a manufacturer of ginger beer for harm to a consumer. It would be wrong for a subsequent court to take that decision as an instance of a rule that imposes liability only on manufacturers of ginger beer, and it would be wrong to take it as an instance of a rule that imposes liability on everyone who causes harm to another. Schauer concludes that 'nothing about precedent-based constraint uniquely differentiates it from rule-based constraint'.[132] This gives a quietus to the claim that the constraint of unformulated rules is difficult to explain and different from the constraint of formulated rules. In fact, it seems that there is no basis even for saying that common law rules are necessarily more indeterminate than rules with a canonical formulation: with all its indeterminacies, the rule that the defendant shall be liable when the facts are similar to those in *Donoghue* v *Stevenson* is as determinate as many provisions in written constitutions.

7. *Conclusion*

There are no radical indeterminacy theses. Not only do radical indeterminacy claims implicitly contradict themselves; people who make them regularly contradict them expressly, and turn them into theoretical indeterminacy claims. Theoretical indeterminacy claims are consistent with the sort of thoroughgoing practical determinacy that, eg, Stanley Fish asserts. And conversely, Hart's distinction between core and penumbra is consistent with widespread linguistic indeterminacy and legal indeterminacy.

All this makes it hard to grasp the real debate about indeterminacy: if the debate is about *how much* indeterminacy there is, it concerns a quantity that cannot be quantified. If the debate is about *how important* indeterminacy is, it turns on criteria of importance which would presumably be controversial, but which no one has ever articulated.

In favour of emphasizing determinacy is the fact that lawyers and law teachers can easily think of cases which illustrate the application of linguistically formulated

[128] Ibid, 71.

[129] Ibid, 181–7.

[130] '. . . the ability to identify the rule-based constraint in a series without a formulated generalization is deeply problematic'. Ibid, 185.

[131] Ibid, 186.

[132] Ibid, 187. Cf Ken Kress's discussion of Karl Llewellyn's theory of precedent, above n 2 at 297–301.

rules for clients and students—and very often clients and students don't need examples. Anyone who has read the bullfrog regulation and knows how to catch bullfrogs can come up with an example of a bullfrog that is protected by the regulation. Moreover, if it is complied with, the bullfrog regulation may accomplish its aim *completely*, in spite of its linguistic indeterminacies.

In favour of emphasizing indeterminacy is the practice of sensible lawyers who never give unqualified opinions, except for consumption of the other side, even on a question of bullfrog hunting in Ottawa.

In favour of over-emphasizing neither determinacy nor indeterminacy is the difference between income tax law and the law of spousal maintenance. If income tax statutes used the same sort of language as family law statutes, and made income tax depend on 'financial needs, obligations and responsibilities', there would be dramatic indeterminacies in income tax law that do not actually exist. Much of the law could be much more indeterminate than it is. But a regime of spousal maintenance law expressed in such words really does have dramatic indeterminacies, unless courts have imposed specific requirements for its application.

Can we draw any more general conclusions from a survey of indeterminacy claims? All we have established is that everyone more or less agrees, sometimes in spite of themselves, with H. L. A. Hart's platitude that there are clear cases and unclear cases of the application of linguistic expressions. The very great theoretical differences over the nature of clarity have not been resolved, and it is unclear how much is clear.

We can still learn some important lessons. First, judges and theorists should be modest in making claims of determinacy. Judges in particular should not take refuge in claims that the plain meaning of words compels a decision. But by the same token, if they do not want to do what, eg, a statute says to do, they should say so, and they should not take refuge in claims of indeterminacy (claims that they are interpreting the words of the statute).

Theorists should face the facts of linguistic determinacy and indeterminacy, whatever they say about their nature. They should also be precise about the *importance* of linguistic determinacy. It is possible to know that the linguistic formulation of a legal rule applies to the facts of some cases, but that mundane knowledge does not tell a judge what to do. Knowing whether the case fits the formulation of a rule does not even tell the judge what the law requires: the judge also needs to know whether the law requires that the rule be applied. And knowing *that*, in turn, does not tell the judge whether the word 'just' applies to the result. Linguistic determinacy should not mislead judges into thinking that it will even be possible to make a just decision in every case. Though 'just' and 'unjust', too, have some clear cases.

[5]

Texas Law Review

Volume 60, Number 3, March 1982

Law as Literature

Sanford Levinson*

I

> [T]he process of reading is not a half-sleep, but, in highest sense, an exercise, a gymnast's struggle; . . . the reader is to do something for himself, must be on the alert, must himself or herself construct indeed the poem, argument, history, metaphysical essay—the text furnishing the hints, the clue, the start or framework. Not the book needs so much to be the complete thing, but the reader of the book does. That were to make a nation of supple and athletic minds, well-train'd, intuitive, used to depend on themselves, and not on a few coteries of writers.
>
> Walt Whitman, *Democratic Vistas*[1]

> Ultimately, man finds in things nothing but what he himself has imported into them: the finding is called science. . .
> Is meaning not necessarily relative meaning and perspective? All meaning is will to power (all relative meaning resolves itself into it).
>
> Friedrich Nietzsche, *The Will to Power*[2]

"Law," said Christopher Columbus Langdell, "considered as a science, consists of certain principles or doctrines. To have such a mastery of these as to be able to apply them with constant facility and certainty to the ever-tangled skein of human affairs is what constitutes a true lawyer."[3] Langdell's argument was two-fold; his conceptualiza-

* Professor of Law, The University of Texas. A.B. 1962, Duke University; Ph.D. 1969, Harvard University; J.D. 1973, Stanford University. This essay is dedicated to the memory of Arthur Leff.

1. W. WHITMAN, *Democratic Vistas*, in WALT WHITMAN: POETRY AND PROSE 992-93 (Library of America ed. 1982).

2. F. NIETZSCHE, THE WILL TO POWER 327, 323 (W. Kaufmann & R. Hollingdale trans., W. Kaufmann ed. 1967).

3. C. LANGDELL, A SELECTION OF CASES ON THE LAW OF CONTRACTS vii (2d ed. 1879), *quoted in* Stevens, *Two Cheers for 1870: The American Law School*, in 5 PERSPECTIVES IN AMERICAN HISTORY 435-36 (1971).

tion of law as a science was only the first. The other was his assertion that "all of the available materials of that science are contained in printed books."[4] Both of these principles are crucial to his approach to law. For Langdell law was essentially a literary enterprise, a science of extracting meaning from words that would enable one to believe in law as a process of submission to the commands of authoritative texts (the rule of law) rather than as the creation of willful interpreters (with submission concomitantly producing the rule of men).

To an extent never sufficiently acknowledged by his many detractors, Langdell was altogether correct in linking the legitimacy of the law to the mastery of texts, whether of cases, statutes, or the Constitution. However much legal positivism justifiably emphasizes the origins of law in social facts,[5] the ordinary language of all developed legal systems includes constant recourse to texts that authorize specific conduct. One does not have to accept the entire Langdellian system (indeed, I most certainly do not) in order to recognize the centrality of textuality to the lawyer's enterprise.

Perhaps the easiest way to confirm this point is simply to note that most controversial decisions of the past three decades, especially those of the United States Supreme Court, rest on purported interpretations of the United States Constitution. And the authority of the written Constitution is a prominent theme in American political thought. John Marshall, after noting the "reverence" with which Americans viewed written constitutions, went on to label such creations the "greatest improvement on political institutions" made by the citizenry of the new country.[6] And Marshall deftly asserted the power of the "obvious meaning" of the constitutional text to undergird his claim for the primacy of judicial review. "The powers of the legislature are defined, and limited; and *that those limits may not be mistaken*, or forgotten, the constitution is written."[7]

4. Address by Christopher Langdell, Harvard Law School Association Meeting (Nov. 5, 1886), *quoted in* Stevens, *supra* note 3, at 436 n.50.

5. *See* H.L.A. HART, THE CONCEPT OF LAW (1961).

6. Marbury v. Madison, 5 U.S. (1 Cranch) 137, 178 (1803).

7. *Id.* at 175-76 (emphasis added). Marshall goes on to say, "To what purpose are powers limited, and to what purpose is that limitation committed to writing, if these limits may, at any time, be passed by those intended to be restrained?" *Id.* Marshall, however, undercut (dare one say "deconstructed"?) his argument in *Marbury* when he decided McCulloch v. Maryland, 17 U.S. (4 Wheat.) 316 (1819). So far are words from having obvious meanings that Marshall reminds us that "Such is the character of human language, that no word conveys to the mind, in all situations, one single definite idea; and nothing is more common than to use words in a figurative sense." *Id.* at 414. And the "writtenness" of the Constitution becomes a far more complicated issue once one supplements the textualism of *Marbury* with the "texturalism" of *McCulloch*: "There is no express provision for the case, but the claim has been sustained on a principle which so entirely pervades the constitution, is so intermixed with the materials which compose it, so interwoven

Law as Literature

No sense can be made of even present-day American political discourse without recognizing the power of constitutional writtenness within our language. Thus Senator Dale Bumpers of Arkansas attacked a bill pending before the Senate, which would have stripped the federal courts of their power to order busing as a remedy for unconstitutional segregation, by calling it part of a "continuing, sinister, devious attack" on the Constitution. "We will today begin the erosion," announced Senator Bumpers, "of *the only document* that stands between the people and tyranny."[8] Anyone familiar with English political discourse, on the other hand, knows that it is almost impossible to imagine similar language there; debate in England centers on the right or wrong of a particular bill, not on its fidelity to a presumptively authoritative text that stands above parliamentary activity.[9]

Citizens of the United States, however, retain within their active political language the purported commands of an allegedly comprehensible Constitution.[10] Comprehensibility is nothing peculiar to constitutions, however, for its possibility arises from the presumed attributes of writtenness. "The physical presentation of a text," the literary theorist Jonathan Culler points out, "gives it a stability . . . . Writing has something of the character of an inscription, a mark offered to the world and promising, by its solidity and apparent autonomy, meaning which is momentarily deferred."[11] In a more ominous vein, the late French critic Roland Barthes described writing as "a hardened language." Writing, he went on to say, "manifests an essence and holds the threat of a secret."[12]

with its web, so blended with its texture, as to be incapable of being separated from it without rendering it into shreds." *Id.* at 426. *See* Levinson, *Judicial Review and the Problem of the Comprehensible Constitution* (Book Review), 59 TEXAS L. REV. 395, 397-98 (1981). Indeed, the very multiplicity (if not promiscuity) of Marshall's approaches to constitutional interpretation, *see* P. BREST & S. LEVINSON, PROCESSES OF CONSTITUTIONAL DECISIONMAKING 35, 114 (2d ed. 1982), calls into question whether interpretation for Marshall (or for anyone else) ever transcended a desire to achieve specific political results.

8. N.Y. Times, Mar. 3, 1982, at A18, col. 4 (emphasis added); *see also* Broder, *Assault on Constitution*, Dallas Times Herald, Mar. 17, 1982, at A29.

9. I became especially aware of this difference in modes of discourse during a sojourn in Great Britain in the fall of 1979, when the Thatcher government put before Parliament several bills regarding rights of non-native-born Englishpersons that struck me (and many others) as racist in the extreme. Many letter writers pointed out the evils of the bills, but none claimed that the proposals violated the English constitution, since, of course, that notion—in its *Marbury* sense—makes no sense within the English language. The description of Great Britain and the United States as two countries separated by a common language never seemed more apt, for the two countries speak two entirely different constitutional languages, even if the words used sometimes seem deceptively similar.

10. *See* Levinson, *supra* note 7, at 418.

11. J. CULLER, STRUCTURALIST POETICS 131, 134 (1975).

12. R. BARTHES, WRITING DEGREE ZERO 19-20 (A. Lavers & C. Smith trans. 1978).

Constitutions, of the written variety especially, are usefully viewed as a means of freezing time by controlling the future through the "hardness" of language encoded in a monumental document, which is then left for later interpreters to decipher. The purpose of such control is to preserve the particular vision held by constitutional founders and to prevent its overthrow by future generations. The very existence of written constitutions with substantive limitations on future conduct is evidence of skepticism, if not outright pessimism, about the moral caliber of future citizens; else why not simply enjoin them to "be good" or "do what you think best"? Writers of constitutions must have a very high confidence in the ability of language both to "harden" and to control.

One form of "hardness" that any reader of written texts quickly becomes aware of, paradoxically, arises from the propensity of language to change, so that understanding past speech recorded in texts requires a "historical" dictionary. Consider, for example, the vicissitudes of the description of a person as "sentimental." The *Oxford English Dictionary* tells us: "Of persons, their dispositions and actions; characterized by sentiment. Originally in favourable sense: Characterized by or exhibiting refined and elevated feeling. In later use: Addicted to indulgence in superficial emotion; apt to be swayed by sentiment."[13] What had been a term of praise became one of mild reproach. What would be the task of a lawyer, then, if asked to construe a trust instrument written in 1720 establishing scholarships for "sentimental" youths?

Any writer, including a framer of constitutions, presumably imagines the following relationship between text and reader: "The reader sets himself to make out what the author has designed and signified through putting into play a linguistic and literary expertise that he shares with the author. By approximating what the author undertook to signify the reader understands what the language of the work means."[14] And, of course, in the case of those particular texts called legal, by understanding the meaning the conscientious adjudicator-reader becomes authorized to enforce it.

The remark just quoted comes from an essay vigorously attacking certain strains of contemporary literary criticism that Abrams finds in-

13. 2 OXFORD ENGLISH DICTIONARY 2730 (compact ed. 1971).

14. Abrams, *How to Do Things with Texts*, 46 PARTISAN REV. 566 (1979). I owe my familiarity with this comment to Richard Rorty. *See* R. RORTY, *Nineteenth-Century Idealism and Twentieth-Century Textualism*, in CONSEQUENCES OF PRAGMATISM 139 (1982), *reprinted from* 64 MONIST 155 (1981).

sufficiently respectful of determinate meanings allegedly generated by disciplined study of texts. The disputes currently raging through literary criticism precisely mirror some of the central problems facing anyone who would take law seriously; the basis of this parallelism is the centrality to law of textual analysis.[15] If we consider law as literature, then we might better understand the malaise that afflicts all contemporary legal analysis, nowhere more severely than in constitutional theory.

II

The example given above regarding "sentimental" presents no shattering difficulty, for it rests on the notion that the word has a determinate meaning at a specific historical moment. But the emphasis of much contemporary theory is an attack on the stability of meaning (or, concomitantly, on the possibility of establishing techniques by which to retrieve meaning) at *any* given moment. Moreover, our increasing propensity to view all social activity as embedded within linguistic codes has universalized the scope of the inquiry regarding the difficulties of reading texts, whether formally written or not. Indeed, much contemporary writing and painting is explicitly self-referential in its demand that the reader-viewer confront the extent to which language and image are unavoidably ambiguous, and its assertion that any given ascription of narrative line or meaning is the product of an interchange between object and viewer rather than an attribute of the object itself.

There is less of a gap between contemporary legal theory and literature than we might suppose, for many practitioners of each are united by a pervasive anxiety generated by what has been well described as "the loss of the sense of doing and speaking in the name of someone or something recognizable and unquestionably valid."[16] This loss undercuts the confidence in one's ability to ground description or analysis in a purported reality beyond the descriptions or analyses themselves.

15. The best short treatment of these disputes is Culler, *Issues in Contemporary American Critical Debate*, in AMERICAN CRITICISM IN THE POSTSTRUCTURALIST AGE 1-18 (I. Konigsberg ed. 1981). A very illuminating book-length study is F. LENTRICCHIA, AFTER THE NEW CRITICISM (1980). The commonality of some of the problems of law and literary analysis are touched on in Abraham, *Three Fallacies of Interpretation: A Comment on Precedent and Judicial Decision*, 23 ARIZ. L. REV. 771 (1981); Abraham, *Statutory Interpretation and Literary Theory: Some Common Concerns of an Unlikely Pair*, 32 RUTGERS L. REV. 676 (1980); Michaels, *Against Formalism: The Autonomous Text in Legal and Literary Interpretation*, 1 POETICS TODAY 23 (1979), *reprinted with minor changes as* Michaels, *Against Formalism: Chickens and Rocks*, in THE STATE OF THE LANGUAGE 410 (1980); and Yeazell, *Convention, Fiction, and Law*, 13 NEW LITERARY HIST. 89 (1981).

16. M. Robertson, Language as Hero in Post-Modern Formalist Fiction 180 (1979) (unpublished Ph.D. dissertation, Department of English, University of Wisconsin). I am greatly indebted to this thesis (and its author) for many of the ideas contained in this essay.

For American lawyers the primary example, as already suggested, is constitutional law and its relationship to (something recognizable as) the Constitution. Paul Brest has recently noted that little contemporary constitutional doctrine explicitly relies on "originalist sources," i.e., on close analysis of the text or of the presumed intentions of the framers. Instead what is increasingly important is "the elaboration of the Court's own precedents." So far as the documentary Constitution is concerned, "It is rather like having a remote ancestor who came over on the Mayflower."[17] Brest's image brilliantly conveys the sense of a distant Constitution which can be seen, if at all, only "through a glass darkly." To view it as a genuine source of guidance is naive, however heartbreaking this realization might be.

Two classic approaches to understanding a written constitution involve emphasizing either the allegedly plain words of the text or the certain meaning to be given those words through historical reconstruction. I think it fair to say that these particular approaches are increasingly without defenders, at least in the academic legal community.[18]

17. Brest, *The Misconceived Quest for the Original Understanding*, 60 B.U.L. REV. 204, 234 (1980).

Brest, of course, is not unique in his perception. *See, e.g.*, Sandalow, *Judicial Protection of Minorities*, 75 MICH. L. REV. 1162, 1183 (1977) ("[T]he evolving content of constitutional law is not controlled, or even significantly guided, by the Constitution, understood as an historical document."). And Michael Perry emphasizes that "[v]irtually all of modern constitutional decisionmaking by the [Supreme] Court—at least that part of it pertaining to questions of 'human rights,' [i.e. the rights individuals have, or ought to have, against government] . . . must be understood as a species of policymaking, in which the Court decides, ultimately without reference to any value judgment constitutionalized by the framers, which values among competing values shall prevail and how those values shall be implemented." M. PERRY, THE CONSTITUTION, THE COURTS, AND HUMAN RIGHTS 2 (1982). Perry tries to defend this policymaking role in his book.

18. One certainly does not have to be an academic in order to repudiate one or another of these approaches. See, for example, Justice Traynor's opinion in Pacific Gas & Elec. Co. v. G.W. Thomas Drayage & Ry. Co., 442 P.2d 641 (1968), concerning the application of the parol evidence rule. Traynor dismisses "a judicial belief in the possibility of perfect verbal expression" as "a remnant of a primitive faith in the inherent potency and inherent meaning of words." *Id.* at 643-44.

> If words had absolute and constant references, it might be possible to discover contractual intention in the words themselves and in the manner in which they were arranged. Words, however, do not have absolute and constant referents . . . . The meaning of particular words or groups of words varies with the ". . . verbal context and surrounding circumstances and purposes in view of the linguistic education and experience of their users and their hearers or readers (not excluding judges) . . . . A word has no meaning apart from these factors; much less does it have an objective meaning, one true meaning."

Id. at 644-45, *quoting* Corbin, *The Interpretation of Words and the Parol Evidence Rule*, 50 CORNELL L.Q. 161, 187 (1965). It is clear that the parol evidence rule is philosophically indefensible. *See also* Michaels, *supra* note 15.

Traynor does, however, seem to retain faith in the ability to ascertain satisfactorily the context of any given speech act. As we become ever more aware, though, of the myriad difficulties standing in the way of contextual understanding, *see, e.g.*, C. GEERTZ, THE INTERPRETATION OF CULTURES (1973), the threat of chaos looms ever larger. See the remarkable review by Gordon Wood, *Star-Spangled History*, THE NEW YORK REVIEW OF BOOKS, Aug. 12, 1982, at 4-9, for a

Even so capable an analyst as Professor Monaghan, who is eager to return to the confines of a knowable "originalist" Constitution, admits that he has no way of handling the authority of judicial precedents that (he argues) violate initial understandings.[19]

There is not time in this essay to canvass the problems of originalism. Suffice it to say that the plain meaning approach inevitably breaks down in the face of the reality of disagreement among equally competent speakers of the native language. Intentionality arguments, on the other hand, face not only the problem of explaining why intentions of long-dead people from a different social world should influence us,[20] but also, perhaps more importantly, the problem of extracting intentions from the collectivity of individuals and institutions necessary to give legal validity to the Constitution.[21] Even literary critics most committed to the existence of objective meaning through recovery of authorial intent, like E.D. Hirsch, admit that their approach applies only to individually authored works, and therefore cannot be used to analyze a document like the Constitution.[22]

As Richard Rorty has pointed out, however, there are at least two options open to critics who reject the two approaches outlined above but who, nonetheless, remain interested in interpreting the relevant texts. The first option involves the use of an allegedly more sophisticated method to extract the true meaning of the text. Thus Rorty refers to "the kind of textualist who claims to have gotten the secret of the

thoroughgoing attack on the possibility of continuing to write traditional narrative history, which relies for its cogency on the ability to embed events (and words) within a specific linear story. To the extent that cases are themselves narrative structures, there is disturbing relevance to the dilemma sketched by Wood. *See also infra* note 58.

It is not surprising that judges are ultimately limited in their skepticisms, at least so long as they continue to engage in their responsible tasks of judging. Academics, being irresponsible (and often socially marginal), are freer to follow ideas out to their most destructive limits.

19. Monaghan, *Our Perfect Constitution*, 56 N.Y.U. L. REV. 353, 382 (1981). Like Raoul Berger, *see* R. BERGER, GOVERNMENT BY JUDICIARY 412-13 (1977), Monaghan does not really counsel turning back the clock by instantly overruling all putatively misdecided cases. Both offer what might uncharitably be regarded as an "adverse possession" approach to constitutional interpretation, whereby precedents that should at one time have been properly overruled (as wrongly decided) become entitled to recognition as authoritative after the passage of enough time and after the citizenry has come to rely on them. Neither offers the slightest guidance for recognizing the terms of such possession. To be fair, no other theorist of precedent does any better. Perhaps the central difference between law and literature is the lack in the latter of the notion of stare decisis.

20. *See* Cover, Book Review, NEW REPUBLIC, Jan. 14, 1978, at 26 (reviewing R. BERGER, GOVERNMENT BY JUDICIARY (1977)). *See also* M. PERRY, *supra* note 17, at 75 ("I prefer to let the framers sleep. Just as the framers, in their day, judged by their lights, so must we, in our day, judge by ours.").

21. *See* Brest, *supra* note 17, at 214-15.

22. *See* E. HIRSCH, VALIDITY IN INTERPRETATION 123 & n.53 (1967); *see also* E. HIRSCH, THE AIMS OF INTERPRETATION 1-13 (1976).

text, to have broken its code," as a "weak" textualist,[23] where the term is seemingly a metaphor for the power of the individual critic. Whatever pyrotechnics might come from a critic who "prides himself on not being distracted by anything which the text might previously have been thought to be about or anything its author says about it,"[24] there remains the infatuation—110 years after Langdell—with the possibility of a science of criticism. A "weak" textualist "is just doing his best to imitate science—he wants a *method* of criticism and he wants everybody to agree that he has cracked the code. He wants all the comforts of consensus, even if only the consensus of readers of the literary quarterlies" (or law reviews).[25]

Perhaps the best current example of such a "weak" textualist is John Hart Ely, whose *Democracy and Distrust*,[26] however radical some of its criticisms of so-called "interpretivism" purport to be, is merely the latest effort to crack the code of the United States Constitution and discover its true essence. As James E. Fleming pointed out in a recent review, Ely is engaged in a "quest for the ultimate constitutional interpretivism" which would in effect foreclose further debate about the genuine meaning of the Constitution.[27]

Like Charles Black,[28] Ely is savagely critical of those who seek constitutional meaning in the isolated words of the clauses themselves. And, like Black, Ely looks instead to the overall structure of the Constitution for guidance. If the lines themselves are no longer a plausible source of meaning, there is still a Constitution to be discovered "between the lines," as it were, in the interplay of conceptual structures—states, nation, citizens, republican government—that are undoubtedly present in the constitutional text. Consequently, Ely's structuralism is no less addicted to a search for the "one-and-only truth" about the Constitution than are its discredited competitors. He continues to presuppose what Rorty calls a "*privileged vocabulary*, the vocabulary which gets to the essence of the object" and "expresses the properties which it has in itself as opposed to those we read into it."[29]

No one can read Ely and miss his anger at those who merely read their own views into the Constitution. Indeed, most of Ely's reviewers

23. R. RORTY, *supra* note 14, at 152.
24. *Id.* at 151-52.
25. *Id.* at 152 (emphasis in original).
26. See Levinson, *supra* note 7, for an extended review of J. ELY, DEMOCRACY AND DISTRUST (1980).
27. Fleming, *A Critique of John Hart Ely's Quest for the Ultimate Constitutional Interpretivism of Representative Democracy* (Book Review), 80 MICH. L. REV. 634 (1982).
28. *See* C. BLACK, STRUCTURE AND RELATIONSHIP IN CONSTITUTIONAL LAW (1969).
29. R. RORTY, *supra* note 14, at 152 (emphasis in original).

Law as Literature

agree with him at least on this last point, even as they criticize him for reading *his* preferred views into the Constitution. What unites Ely and most of his critics, though, is the continued belief that there is something "in" the Constitution that can be extracted if only we can figure out the best method to mine its meaning.

Against such weak textualists—the decoders, whatever the fanciness of their methods of decoding—Rorty posits "strong" textualists, who reject the whole notion of questing for the essential meanings of a text. "Strong," it should be emphasized, refers to the power of the critic, not the power of the text (or of its author). According to Stanley Fish, one of the leading proponents of this approach, "Interpretation is not the art of construing but the art of constructing. Interpreters do not decode poems; they make them."[30] Fish has argued that "[t]he objectivity of the text is an illusion and, moreover, a dangerous illusion, because it is so physically convincing. The illusion is one of self-sufficiency and completeness. A line of print or a page is so obviously *there* . . . that it seems to be the sole repository of whatever value and meaning we associate with it."[31]

Instead Fish emphasizes the reader's active role and concomitant inability to measure any given interpretation against the "actual" text. He correctly insists that the debate about what it means to read a text is of more than academic interest:

> [D]ifferent notions of what it is to read . . . are finally different notions of what it is to be human. In [one] view, the world, or the world of the text, is already ordered and filled with significances and what the reader is required to do is get them out (hence the question, "What did you get out of that?"). In short, the reader's job is to extract the meanings that formal patterns possess prior to, and independently of, his activities. In my view [on the other hand], these same activities are constitutive of a structure of concerns which is necessarily prior to any examination of meaningful patterns because it is itself the occasion of their coming into being.[32]

30. S. Fish, Is There a Text in This Class? 327 (1980); *cf.* Marcel Duchamp's statement, "It is the Observers who make the pictures," *quoted in* M. Caws, The Eye in the Text: Essays on Perception, Mannerist to Modern 135 (1981). *See generally* the valuable anthologies Reader-Response Criticism: From Formalism to Post-Structuralism (J. Thompkins ed. 1980); The Reader in the Text: Essays on Audience and Interpretation (S. Suleiman & I. Crosman ed. 1980). An excellent recent study is S. Mailloux, Interpretive Conventions: The Reader in the Study of American Fiction (1982).

31. S. Fish, *supra* note 30, at 43. For vigorous criticism of Fish and other radical literary critics, see Crews, *Criticism Without Constraint*, Commentary, Jan. 1982, at 65.

32. S. Fish, *supra* note 30, at 94. Professor Graff argues that the depiction of the controversy itself has ideological implications. Fish's statement might well be assessed against what Graff calls a "rhetorical scorecard":

Texas Law Review Vol. 60:373, 1982

As Fish notes, "The difference in the two views is enormous." The first one regards "human beings as passive and disinterested comprehenders of a knowledge external to them (that is, of an *objective* knowledge)."[33]

Bad	Good
representation	creation
text as determinate object	text as open, indeterminate "invitation"
boundaries and constraints	voyages into the unforeseen
docility, habit	risk
truth as correspondence	truth as invention, fiction
meaning as "product"	meaning as "process"

G. GRAFF, LITERATURE AGAINST ITSELF: LITERARY IDEAS IN MODERN SOCIETY 23 (1979).

33. S. FISH, *supra* note 30, at 94. It occurs to me, as I dutifully footnote Fish's statement, that the act of footnoting is itself a bow toward the notion of objective knowledge, for I am purporting, even as I describe Fish's reader-response theories, to be giving you (the reader) an "accurate" rendition of those theories. Indeed, the point of footnotes, especially if "cite-checked" by law review editors, is to suggest that the proof of my accuracy is that you would arrive at the same conclusions by reading the same material.

This generates an obvious, albeit important, paradox, one only made worse because I of course also expect you to grasp "my" argument and to be able to state it correctly (as Graff basically does), even if you (like Graff) reject it. I suppose, therefore, that I can be accused of being one of those "newreaders" who introduce their "own interpretive strategy when reading someone else's text, but tacitly relying on communal norms when undertaking to communicate the methods and results of [their] interpretations to [their] own readers." *Id.* at 303 (*quoting* Abrams, *supra* note 14, at 587). A similar point is made in Hirsch's review of H. GADAMER, WAHRHEIT UND METHODE (1960), *reprinted in* E. HIRSCH, VALIDITY IN INTERPRETATION 245 (1967); *see also* Graff, *Politics, Language, Deconstruction, Lies, and the Reflexive Fallacy: A Rejoinder to W.J.T. Mitchell*, SALMAGUNDI, Winter-Spring 1980, at 78.

Professor Graff is correct in his own contribution to this Symposium when he notes that I do on occasion use the word "correct" to refer to an interpretation, *see* Graff, *"Keep off the Grass," "Drop Dead," and Other Indeterminacies: A Response to Sanford Levinson*, 60 TEXAS L. REV. 405, 412 (1982), so that I cannot be the arch-indeterminist that I sometimes appear to be. I am not sure how far apart he and I actually are, for there is relatively little in his response that I genuinely disagree with. I do agree, as does Fish for that matter, that our ordinary speech acts are full of meanings instantly grasped by listeners, given the standard contexts in which they occur. I would further agree that the Constitution is not entirely incomprehensible, that, e.g., the President must take office on January 20. U.S. CONST. amend. XX, § 1. There are circumstances in which this might be problematic (what if Congress changed the calendar year), but it would be perverse to say that the ordinary reader would not be expected to give a single response to the question, "When does a newly elected President take office?" (Nor do I disagree with the Fifth Circuit that it was "quite incredible" to argue that ".82165" is not the equivalent of "82.165%." Oil & Gas Futures, Inc. of Texas v. Andrus, 610 F.2d 287, 288 (5th Cir. 1980), *reversing* [!] an unreported decision by the Honorable Finis E. Cowan of the United States District Court for the Southern District of Texas. Yet (presumably) competent lawyers and a (presumably) competent judge did not find even this proposition compelling.)

The problem, of course, is that constitutional litigation almost never concerns such clauses. Professor Graff recognizes the multiplicity of ambiguity that *can*, even if not *must*, be present in literary or legal texts. He seems to chide me for emphasizing power, rather than authority, in resolving conflicting interpretations, but this seems to be the principal explanation for why one legal result, rather than its equally plausible (indeed, on occasion more plausible) alternative, is imposed on the parties. Even here, I will quickly concede that courts and other constitutional interpreters operate within constraints. That is the importance of Fish's own distinction between "on-the-wall" and "off-the-wall" arguments; but the point is that whatever constraints exist are not constant over time.

Finally, I agree with Professor Graff that the alternative to determinacy (certainty) is not an anything-goes indeterminacy. However, especially from the perspective of the losers in a necessarily coercive legal system, a court decision that remains even within the ambit of "on-the-

Law as Literature

It is worth noting, I believe, that Felix Frankfurter's favorite single word was "disinterested,"[34] and that the ideology of the Harvard Law School, from Langdell's time to the days of Hart and Sacks and afterward, can be regarded as centered around the search for a "disinterested," impersonal approach to legal analysis.

The view endorsed by Fish regards "human beings as at every moment creating the experiential spaces into which a personal knowledge flows."[35] Meaning is created rather than discovered, though the source of creative energy is the particular community within which one finds him- or herself. Critics more Emersonian in their inspiration, like Harold Bloom, are willing to credit individual acts of creativity, though Bloom's emphasis on the ubiquity of "misreadings," rather than "truthful" renderings of what is inside texts, links him to Rorty's "strong" textualists.[36] All such readers could well join the Whitmanian anthem, where all readings, whether of life or of texts, become songs of oneself.

The patron saint of all strong textualists is Nietzsche:

> [W]hatever exists, having somehow come into being, is again and again reinterpreted to new ends, taken over, transformed, and redirected by some power superior to it; all events in the organic world are a subduing, a *becoming master*, and all subduing and becoming master involves a fresh interpretation, an adaptation through which any previous "meaning" and "purpose" are necessarily obscured or even obliterated.[37]

And the argument of Fish, Bloom, and other strong textualists, whether American or continental, is *not* that they prefer to do their thing as an alternative to the more banal work of "truthseekers" like Abrams or Hirsch, but rather that the project of ultimate truth-seeking is based on philosophical error. At the very least it presumes a privileged foundation for measuring the attainment of truth, and it is precisely this foundation that Nietzsche and most of the more radical literary theorists

wall" arguments may appear to be arbitrary (though not "whimsical"), given the presence of other available arguments that would have generated more palatable results.

34. *See* Levinson, *The Democratic Faith of Felix Frankfurter*, 25 STAN. L. REV. 430, 434 (1972) (author's student Note). No single citation, of course, can support the assertion that "disinterested" was Frankfurter's favorite word, but I challenge any reader of Frankfurter's prose to name a more oft-used and emotionally charged word in his vocabulary. (Proper nouns like Holmes or the Harvard Law School do not count.)

35. S. FISH, *supra* note 30, at 94. "Personal," incidentally, is a tricky word in this context, for Fish, like most structuralists and post-structuralists, rejects the meaningfulness of genuinely individualistic idiosyncracies, and instead emphasizes the inevitable membership of such "individuals" in communities of shared discourses which, indeed, ultimately supply any person's own sense of self. *See id.* at 338-55.

36. *See, e.g.*, H. BLOOM, A MAP OF MISREADING (1975).

37. F. NIETZSCHE, ON THE GENEOLOGY OF MORALS 77 (W. Kaufmann trans. 1967) (emphasis in original).

deny. Like Rorty, they do not substitute a new candidate for a winning method of how to recognize literary truth when one sees it; rather, they reject the very search for finality of interpretation.

To be sure, none of the radical critics defend the position that any interpretation is just as good as any other. Stanley Fish, for example, notes that he genuinely believes in the validity of any given view that he happens to hold, and he can present reasons for rejecting the views of his opponents on the interpretation of a given text.[38] In this regard Fish seems similar to Ronald Dworkin, who views judging as including the phenomenological experience of feeling oneself to have achieved the uniquely correct solution even to a hard case.[39] But Fish, more candid than Dworkin on this point, admits that his own conviction of rightness will provide no answer at all to anyone who happens to disagree with him, and that there is no way to resolve the dispute. It is at this point that he retreats to his Kuhnian[40] emphasis on communities of understanding and shared conventions. It may be true that these communities will share, at any given moment, a sense of what distinguishes "on the wall" from "off the wall" arguments,[41] but Fish is acutely aware of the contingency of such judgments. They describe only our own temporal sense of what is currently acceptable, rather than anything genuinely mirroring the essential characteristics of the texts being discussed.[42]

III

Presumably only those professionally interested in literature are forced to wrestle with the issues presented by Abrams, Culler, and Fish regarding poetics or the interpretation of fiction. But if law is, in some meaningful sense, a branch of literature, then the problems discussed above take on new and bothersome implications. And nowhere is this more true within our own culture than in constitutional interpretation and its emphasis on writtenness.

The role of our Constitution is not only to enable us to pretend that past linguistic acts can control future action. It is also presumably to prevent the rise of Nietzschean "masters." Nietzsche seems to sug-

38. S. FISH, *supra* note 30, at 338-71.

39. *See* R. DWORKIN, TAKING RIGHTS SERIOUSLY 279-90 (1977); Levinson, *Taking Law Seriously: Reflections on "Thinking Like a Lawyer"* (Book Review), 30 STAN. L. REV. 1071 (1978) (reviewing Dworkin).

40. *See* T. KUHN, THE STRUCTURE OF SCIENTIFIC REVOLUTIONS (2d ed. 1970).

41. S. FISH, *supra* note 30, at 356-57.

42. For the importance of the "mirroring" image, see R. RORTY, PHILOSOPHY AND THE MIRROR OF NATURE (1979). Rorty's basic mission is the criticism of the possibility of mirroring.

gest, however, that a massive exercise in social deception is necessary if we are not to recognize the way that "interpretation" inevitably implies a struggle for mastery in the formation of political consciousness. For a Nietzschean reader of constitutions, there is no point in searching for a code that will produce "truthful" or "correct" interpretations; instead, the interpreter, in Rorty's words, "simply beats the text into a shape which will serve his own purpose."[43]

E.D. Hirsch, perhaps the most consistent opponent of the radical critics, notes that, "With a numinous document like the Constitution or the Bible, the principles and methods of correct interpretation are as important as they are problematical."[44] If one takes seriously the views articulated by Nietzsche, Rorty, and Fish (among others), one must give up the search for principles and methods of constitutional interpretation. Instead, one assesses the results of an interpretive effort by something other than the criterion of adherence to an inner essence of the text being interpreted. Indeed, Robert Cover addresses this point directly in his remarkable review of Raoul Berger's *Government by Judiciary*, in which Berger vigorously attacks judges for allegedly straying from the original meaning (which is equated with the true meaning) of the Constitution. Cover himself quotes Nietzsche's comment that "[t]he knowledge of the past is desired only for the service of the future and the present"[45] and emphasizes that it is up to us, the living, to decide for our own reasons what we wish the Constitution to mean.

To put it mildly, there is something disconcerting about accepting the Nietzschean interpreter into the house of constitutional analysts, but I increasingly find it impossible to imagine any other way of making sense of our own constitutional universe. For some years I have organized my own courses in constitutional interpretation around the central question, "But did the Court get it right?", as if one could grade any given opinion by whether or not it measured up to the genuine command of the Constitution. Answering such a question, of course, requires the development of a full set of "principles and methods of correct interpretation," and my courses have involved a search for such principles and methods.

I still spend a great deal of time examining various approaches, ranging from the linguistic to the historical, from the structural to what my colleague Philip Bobbitt calls the "ethical,"[46] but I have less and

43. R. Rorty, *supra* note 14, at 151.
44. E. Hirsch, The Aims of Interpretation 20 (1976).
45. Cover, *supra* note 20, at 27.
46. See P. Bobbitt, Constitutional Fate (1982), for an extraordinarily subtle survey of

less confidence that this is a sensible enterprise. At the very least there is no reason to believe that the community of persons interested in constitutional interpretation will coalesce around one or another of these approaches. Moreover, insofar as one accepts the plausibility of an analysis like Rorty's, there is no reason to regret this, for it is the result of a genuine plurality of ways of seeing the world, rather than of the obdurate recalcitrance of those who refuse to bend to superior argument.

Yet there are obvious difficulties in adopting Rorty's metaphor of the conversation (rather than the argument),[47] for the principal social reality of law is its coercive force vis-à-vis those who prefer to behave other than as the law "requires." As Chairman Mao pointed out, a revolution is not a tea party, and the massive disruption in lives that can be triggered by a legal case is not a conversation. The legal system presents a conversation from which there may be no exit, and there are certainly those who would define hell as the vision of their least favorite constitutional interpreter, whether the Court or a benighted law professor.

What does one do, then, when studying opinions, if one gives up the enterprise of determining whether or not they are "correct"? Are cases simply historical fragments which should be studied for insight into the ideology of the time?[48] One no longer would say, for example, that *Dred Scott*[49] or *Lochner v. New York*,[50] or any other case, was "wrongly" decided, for that use of language presupposes belief in the knowability of constitutional essence. One *can* obviously show that constitutional tastes and styles shift over time, but this retreat into historicism has nothing to do with the legal science so desperately sought by Langdell and his successors.

A study of shifts in legal styles, moreover, may force us to come to grips with the fact that there may be no guiding criteria to enable us to state with confidence that any given piece of writing is "legal" writing, as opposed to writing about a subject of interest to the legal system.

various modes of constitutional argumentation. A shorter version of the book was published as Bobbitt, *Constitutional Fate*, 58 TEXAS L. REV. 695 (1981).

47. See R. RORTY, *supra* note 42, at 389.

48. This seems to be the approach taken by some of the most fruitful practitioners of "critical legal studies." *See, e.g.*, M. HORWITZ, THE TRANSFORMATION OF AMERICAN LAW, 1780-1860 (1977); M. TUSHNET, THE AMERICAN LAW OF SLAVERY 1810-1860 (1981).

49. Dred Scott v. Sandford, 60 U.S. (19 How.) 393 (1856).

50. 198 U.S. 45 (1905). There is obviously not space here to consider in depth the complexity of our responses to these two cases. One might begin, though, by asking whether Taney's or Peckham's arguments in the two cases are really "off-the-wall" in terms of the conventions of American legal discourse; it seems clear that the answer is no.

Law as Literature

Jonathan Culler has studied the ways in which readers use conventions to constitute something as a poem or a short story and to give it meaning.[51] It would be interesting to see what, besides identification of a particular piece of writing as emanating from a court, allows one with confidence to label it as peculiarly "legal."[52] Fish, as one might imagine, insists that poetry is anything we conventionally posit as such.[53] Is

51. J. CULLER, *supra* note 11, at 113-238.

52. Indeed, it is not even clear that material emanating from a court can, except by stipulation, be described as "legal writing." *See, e.g.,* Flood v. Kuhn, 407 U.S. 258, 260-64 (1972) (Justice Blackmun's ode to baseball).

53. S. FISH, *supra* note 30, at 322. One notes again the linkage between Fish and Duchamp, one of whose most famous artistic achievements was the transformation of a urinal into art by the mere act of placing it in a museum. We might have our individual favorite candidates for transforming dubious arguments into law through the aegis of placing them in a judicial opinion.

Indeed, yet further theoretical questions are suggested by the text of the paragraph to which this footnote is addressed. Consider, for example, the problem of parody, an extraordinarily sophisticated literary construction which depends for its force on the competence of the reader to know the "proper" or "conventional" style that serves as the background to the foreground of the parody itself. *See* J. CULLER, *supra* note 11, at 152-54; Culler, *Convention and Meaning: Derrida and Austin*, 13 NEW LITERARY HIST. 15, 22 (1981). The May 15, 1978, issue of the *New Yorker* featured, among its offerings, "Supreme Court Roundup," one example of which is the report of a first amendment decision in which "the Court ruled unanimously in favor of a twelve-year-old plaintiff who sought damages on account of being denied the chance to audition" for a movie. "The Court's opinion, written by Chief Justice Happ, argued that exclusion of the little girl was 'rotten, beastly, a crying shame—really makes the Court sick.' The case was not decided, as had been expected, on the ground of sex discrimination; rather, the Justices invoked the First Amendment's guarantee of freedom of expression. The Court thus affirmed for the first time the constitutional right to a screen test." Geng, *Supreme Court Roundup*, NEW YORKER, May 15, 1978, at 31. This is clearly parody, right? But then what is the genre of, say, Justice Douglas' opinion for the majority in Griswold v. Connecticut, 381 U.S. 479 (1965) ("the specific guarantees in the Bill of Rights have penumbras, formed by emanations from those guarantees that help give them life and substance"), or of Justice Brennan's description of "the give-and-take negotiation common in plea bargaining between the prosecution and the defense, which arguably possess relatively equal bargaining power," Parker v. North Carolina, 397 U.S. 790, 809 (1970), *quoted approvingly in* Bordenkircher v. Hayes, 434 U.S. 357, 362 (1978). And consider Justice Stevens' remark in Young v. American Mini Theatres, 427 U.S. 50 (1976), that "few of us would march our sons and daughters off to war to preserve the citizen's right to see 'Specified Sexual Activities' exhibited in the theaters of our choice." *Id.* at 70. Justice Stevens' "marching-off-to-war" standard garnered only three additional votes; perhaps the replacement of the dissenting Justice Stewart by Justice O'Connor will enable it to receive the fifth vote necessary to enshrine it in our constitutional litany as a certifiably serious approach to constitutional analysis.

One of the general problems facing so-called "post-modernist" writers is the impossibility of satirizing patterns of ordinary life and talk which themselves are bizarre. *See, e.g.,* the work of Donald Barthelme. Or, as Calvin Trillin has put it, "Someone who writes what has been officially labeled a 'humor column' about the American scene lives in constant danger of being blindsided by the truth." C. TRILLIN, UNCIVIL LIBERTIES 2 (1982). One sometimes wonders about the genre status not only of certain judicial opinions, but also of scholarly articles purporting to analyze them. *See, e.g.,* Michelman, *States' Rights and States' Roles: Permutations of "Sovereignty" in* National League of Cities v. Usery, 86 YALE L.J. 1165 (1977) (arguing that Justice Rehnquist's majority opinion requires states to provide essential services to their citizens); Tribe, *Unraveling* National League of Cities, 90 HARV. L. REV. 1065 (1977). For general reviews of the status of so-called constitutional scholarship, see Tushnet, *Legal Scholarship: Its Causes and Cures*, 90 YALE L.J. 1205 (1981); *Tushnet, Truth, Justice, and the American Way: An Interpretation of Public Law Scholarship in the Seventies*, 57 TEXAS L. REV. 1307 (1979).

Perhaps the best response to the issues raised in this footnote is to say that one should have a

the same thing true of legal writing?[54]

These remarks have obvious implications for legal education. Here, too, there are parallels to literary education. Some of Culler's most convoluted paragraphs are spent defending the enterprise of specialized undergraduate and graduate education in literature in the face of the attack by radical critics on the very notion of a science of criticism.[55] It is tempting to paraphrase Dostoyevski by saying that if there is no science, there is no truth, and if there is no truth, then anything is permitted. How does one describe education in such a climate of skepticism? As already indicated, Culler's major project is identifying the structured conventions by which readers supply meaning to texts; his own reference to only "*apparent* autonomy" in the remarks quoted earlier[56] indicates the limit of the extent to which he rejects reliance on the independent status of the language. It is we who establish what the monuments mean by ascribing content to them.

Insofar as Culler seeks the conventions that differentiate "competent" readers from incompetent ones, he faces the difficulty of establishing as well how one distinguishes "off-the-wall" readings that are the product of genuine incompetence from those that are simply brilliantly ahead of their time and in cadence with the next paradigm coming down the pike. Legal education too could devote itself more formally to studying the conventions of reading law and legal opinions, though such a move would face great hostility not only from students but from most present faculty members as well. I note the debate that raged in England over the appointment of Colin MacCabe to the English faculty at Cambridge.[57] MacCabe, with his interests in contemporary structuralism and post-structuralism, is fundamentally antagonistic to the view that the only task of students is to read set texts, without ever systematically reflecting on the notion of "reading" itself. Indeed, most constitutional law courses avoid discussing the as-

good sense of humor if teaching constitutional law these days, but this response works, of course, only if one has attained enough ironic distance so as not to care about the implications for living beings of the material analyzed.

54. Indeed, is *this* essay legal writing? If it is not, then why is it being published in the *Texas Law Review*?

55. *See, e.g.*, J. CULLER, *supra* note 11, at 258; *see also* J. CULLER, THE PURSUIT OF SIGNS: SEMIOTICS, LITERATURE, DECONSTRUCTION 210 (1981) ("Literary Theory in the Graduate Program").

56. *See* text accompanying note 11.

57. For descriptions of the MacCabe controversy, see *Unquiet Flow the Dons*, NEWSWEEK, Feb. 16, 1981, at 95-96; *Controversy at Cambridge*, TIMES LITERARY SUPPLEMENT, Jan. 30, 1981, at 112. The *TLS* also published an interesting symposium sparked by the MacCabe flap, *Modern Literary Theory: Its Place in Teaching*, TIMES LITERARY SUPPLEMENT, Feb. 6, 1981, at 135, with contributions by George Steiner, John Bayley, Denis Donoghue, C.J.E. Ball, L.C. Knights, Malcolm Bowie, Malcolm Bradbury, and Roger Scruton.

sumptions not only that there are standard cases that must be read, but also that the act of reading itself is, when all is (un)said and done, unproblematic.[58]

Consider also the way we treat the innovative judges of our legal tradition, particularly as they appear in law school courses. Do we really wish to argue that John Marshall or Earl Warren (or the most recent dynamic innovator, William Rehnquist)[59] got the essence right in their interpretations of the Constitution, or do we recognize instead the extent to which we have been subdued by their political visions?

Perhaps the most significant example of this dilemma is John Marshall himself, or rather I should say our response to Marshall. I have little trouble stating that I consider his major opinions to run the gamut from the intellectually dishonest[60] to the majestically visionary,[61] and rarely to contain the only (or even the most) plausible rendering of the Constitution. Yet there is also a profound irrelevance to such a criticism. Not only does it assume the existence of a privileged discourse that allows me to dismiss Marshall as "untruthful" rather than merely different, it also ignores the fundamental fact that John Marshall is as much a "founder" of the American legal system as those who wrote the Constitution he purported to interpret. He is, perhaps, the great Nietzschean judge of our tradition.

Indeed, Marshall is a worthy successor to the founders of 1787, for they too were aware of the awesome role they played as visionary leaders. When it was pointed out to the Philadelphia Convention that it was without authority to "revise" the Articles of Confederation by obliterating them, the response was candid and to the point. "There are great seasons when persons with limited powers are justified in exceeding them, and a person would be contemptible not to risk it."[62] So spoke Edmund Randolph, later the Attorney General in the Washington administration. Even James Madison, who gamely insisted that the

58. For all of the alleged emphasis on cases in American legal education, there is little systematic attention paid to what, beyond agreement with the teacher's own emphasis, constitutes "legal competence." Perhaps the most notorious example of the lack of reflection concerning case-reading is the bland assumption transmitted to generations of law students that cases can be "briefed." Exactly how it is that one distills "essence of case" from the full opinion, or why it was that the writer thought it necessary to write as fully as he or she did, is not usually brought to the student's attention.

59. *See* Fiss & Krauthammer, *The Rehnquist Court*, NEW REPUBLIC, Mar. 10, 1982, at 14.

60. *See* Marbury v. Madison, 5 U.S. (1 Cranch) 137 (1803) (presentation and construction of § 13 of the Judiciary Act of 1789).

61. *See* McCulloch v. Maryland, 17 U.S. (4 Wheat.) 316 (1819) (invocation of American nationalism).

62. M. FARRAND, 1 RECORDS OF THE FEDERAL CONVENTION 262 (1937) (speech of June 16, 1787, Yates transcription).

Convention was behaving properly, was reduced to arguing, in *The Federalist No. 40*, that the Philadelphia delegates "must have borne in mind, that as the plan to be framed and proposed, was to be submitted *to the people themselves* . . . its approbation [would] blot out all antecedent errors and irregularities."[63]

Madison's argument is significant, to be sure, and it serves to distinguish the Founders from twentieth-century authoritarians unconcerned with popular ratification of their acts. Nonetheless it establishes a powerful precedent for the general proposition that the people themselves can give their approval to what was arguably illegal conduct by visionary leaders, including judges who break the bonds of confining legal conventions and ultimately transform our vision of ourselves as a nation. Under this theory the difference between hero and villain is found not in fidelity to preexisting legal norms and adherence to their "correct" meaning, but in the ability of a hero-founder to impress the new understanding of the political order on the popular consciousness. And, in our particular culture we graft these new understandings, particularly if found in judicial opinions, on to something called "the Constitution" and pretend that the leader-judge has merely seen more deeply into its essence, rather than bent it to a new vision.

63. THE FEDERALIST No. 40, 265-66 (J. Madison) (J. Cooke ed. 1961) (emphasis in original). Compare Madison's argument with Lincoln's defense of his policy of military arrests and suspension of habeas corpus:

> The constitution contemplates the question as likely to occur for decision, but it does not expressly declare who is to decide it. By necessary implication, when Rebellion or Invasion comes, the decision is to be made, from time to time; and I think the man whom, for the time, the people have, under the constitution, made the commander-in-chief, of their Army and Navy, is the man who holds the power, and bears the responsibility of making it. If he uses the power justly, the same people will probably justify him; if he abuses it, he is in their hands, to be dealt with by all the modes they have reserved to themselves in the constitution.

THE POLITICAL THOUGHT OF ABRAHAM LINCOLN 262 (R. Current ed. 1967).

There is a similarity between these arguments and the one made by Richard Nixon in his interview with David Frost:

> *Mr. Frost:* So what in a sense you're saying is that there are certain situations . . . where the President can decide that it's in the best interests of the nation or something, and do something illegal.
>
> *Mr. Nixon:* Well, when the President does it, that means that it is not illegal.
>
> *Mr. Frost:* By definition.
>
> *Mr. Nixon:* Exactly. Exactly. If the President, for example, approves something because of the national security, or in this case because of a threat to internal peace and order of significant magnitude, then the President's decision in that instance is one that enables those who carry it out, to carry it out without violating a law. Otherwise they're in an impossible position.

Transcript of Frost-Nixon Interview, N.Y. Times, May 20, 1977, at A16, col. 5.

Paradoxically, it may be that what most differentiates Nixon from the founders and Lincoln, beyond obvious differences in their breadth of vision, is his unwillingness to submit his deeds to the populace for their approbation. There is a public quality to the acts of Marshall and the others that is wholly lacking in those of Nixon, as revealed by the very term "cover up."

Law as Literature

This description, of course, works only when a "strong" judge, like one of Harold Bloom's "strong" poets, successfully misreads the past to establish his or her own vision of reality as one for the writer's own time. But an age without such judges, or with contending candidates, can recognize only the existence of the competing visions themselves, with no recourse to the foundation document—the Constitution—being genuinely possible. It would obviously be nice to believe that *my* Constitution is the true one and, therefore, that my opponents' versions are fraudulent, but that is precisely the belief that becomes steadily harder to maintain. They are simply *different* Constitutions. There are as many plausible readings of the United States Constitution as there are versions of *Hamlet*,[64] even though each interpreter, like each director, might genuinely believe that he or she has stumbled onto the one best answer to the conundrums of the texts. That we cannot walk out of

64. Since writing the statement in the text, I have benefitted from an important article by Knapp and Michaels, *Against Theory*, 8 CRITICAL INQUIRY 723 (1982), which attacks similar arguments in S. FISH, *supra* note 30, at 367-69. Briefly, the authors argue that a statement like "There are as many plausible readings of the United States Constitution as there are versions of *Hamlet*" implies knowledge about the underlying nature of reality, whereas the general argument of Fish (and of this essay) is that we can never have confidence that we have such knowledge. Furthermore, they note that neither Fish nor any other critic, whether literary or legal, could actually live by such a view, since stands are constantly taken in the confidence, merited or not, that one's own views are indeed better than the alternatives. *See* Knapp & Michaels, *supra*, at 738-41. Indeed, I have written that Buckley v. Valeo, 424 U.S. 1 (1976), is "perhaps the worst decision . . . in the past forty years." Levinson, *supra* note 7, at 415. Such an assertion clearly entails at least a momentary rejection of the view that all constitutional approaches are equal, though I remain troubled as to how one could ever genuinely establish the superiority of any given constitutional theory.

Professor Fish himself, in his reply to this essay, emphasizes the degree to which we make judgments regardless of (some of) the implications of the anti-Realist philosophy he endorses, though I do not know if he would concede the legitimacy of Knapp and Michaels' general argument. In any event, *Against Theory* promises to provoke an important debate among literary theorists which will have obvious relevance for legal analysts. *See also infra* note 87. (I am grateful to Gerald Graff and Steven Mailloux for calling my attention to the Knapp and Michaels essay and for emphasizing its implications for the argument of this essay.)

Professor Bobbitt's inquiry, CONSTITUTIONAL FATE, *supra* note 46, is also highly relevant to the question of the intersection of theory and practice, since he finds our theories *in* our practices, rather than *underlying* them as a foundation.

One might, incidentally, be tempted to avoid the whole set of dilemmas raised in this Article by taking refuge in a simple "the Constitution is what the Court says it is" argument. Putting aside the usual responses to this argument (who or what authorizes the Court to say what the Constitution is?), there is an equally fundamental problem in relying on judicial precedent. Even if we ignore the fact that the Court itself does not feel bound by its own precedents, so that it regularly overturns them, there remains the question of how one figures out what a precedent means, and that of course brings us quickly back to the central problem of this Article. See, for example, Deutsch, *Harvard's View of the Supreme Court: A Response*, 57 TEXAS L. REV. 1445 (1979), which emphasizes "that our society is forced to live with an awareness of the *essentially uncertain nature* of the precedent contained in a judicial opinion." *Id.* at 1454 (emphasis added). Thus Deutsch argues that "[t]he reading of a holding as not only unintended, but as something contrary to the intent of the opinion's author, is a permissible one, since a later Court might so construe the earlier holding, and the meaning of a precedent is what is held by that later Court." *Id.* at 1453.

offending productions of our national epic poem, the Constitution, may often be anguishing, but that may be our true constitutional fate.

IV

Professor Owen Fiss has recently directed several arguments against the views expressed in an earlier version of the present essay.[65] Fiss forthrightly labels these views as "nihilism." He concludes his article by identifying what is at stake in the debate: "[T]his nihilism calls into question the very point of constitutional adjudication; it threatens our social existence and the nature of public life as we know it in America; and it demeans our lives." It is no surprise, then, that he goes on to state, "It must be combated and can be, but perhaps only by affirming the truth of that which is being denied—the idea that the Constitution embodies a public morality and that a public life founded on that morality can be rich and inspiring."[66]

In this section I shall first lay out what I perceive as the view of constitutional adjudication defended by Fiss. I shall then consider his response to those critics, like myself, who are unable to share it. I should emphasize at the outset that I share both Fiss' basic social and political values, even if not his theory of the Constitution, and his unhappiness about the implications of "nihilism." But a desire, however understandable, to combat it does not equal the ability to do so.

Professor Fiss first elaborated his views in a *Harvard Law Review* "Foreword."[67] For the purposes of this essay, the key paragraph is as follows:

> The rightful place of courts in our political system turns on the existence of public values and on the promise of those institutions—because they are independent and because they must engage in a special dialogue—to articulate and elaborate the true meaning of those values. The task [is] discovering the meaning of constitutional values such as equality, liberty, due process, or property . . . .[68]

A concomitant of "the meaning-giving enterprise implicit in constitutionalism itself"[69] is the judge's duty to be concerned with designing effective remedies. "The desire to be efficacious need not be seen as an assertion of will, but as a willingness of the judge to assume re-

65. Fiss, *Objectivity and Interpretation*, 34 STAN. L. REV. 739 (1982).

66. *Id.* at 763.

67. Fiss, *The Supreme Court, 1978 Term—Foreword: The Forms of Justice*, 93 HARV. L. REV. 1 (1979).

68. *Id.* at 51.

69. *Id.* at 57.

sponsibility for practical reality and its consonance with the Constitution." Indeed, "[t]he judge might be seen as forever straddling two worlds, the world of the ideal and the world of the practical, the world of the public value and the world of subjective preference, the world of the Constitution and the world of politics." It is the judge among all officials of government who "is in the best position to discover the *true meaning* of our constitutional values."[70]

Fiss more recently has spoken of the judicial duty to interpret legal texts; in doing so the judge "gives meaning and expression to the values embodied in that text."[71] Like Ronald Dworkin,[72] Fiss seems to assert the existence of uniquely valid ("true") solutions to the conundrums about the implications of our "public values," assuming in the first place that such values exist and can be ascertained. Moreover, like Dworkin's, Fiss' Constitution turns out to contain only the good, the true, and the beautiful.

Fiss takes pains to distinguish himself from that "arid and artificial conception of interpretation" which some label " 'interpretivism,' but [is] more properly called 'textual determinism.' "[73] He links this conception with that form of legal positivism that emphasizes "the 'written constitution' and stresses factors like the use of particular words or the intent or beliefs of the framers, all of which have little or no moral relevance."[74] The problem with this mode of interpretation goes well beyond any theoretical difficulty in ascertaining the true meaning of the text or the intentions of its authors.[75] As Fiss notes, even if one assumes the theoretical coherence of positivism, there remains the problem that "[a] too rigid insistence on positivism will inevitably bring into question the ultimate moral authority of the legal text—the justness of the Constitution."[76] Thus he concedes that an all-too-comprehensible Constitution might well be read to have protected slavery, and this fact alone would justify raising the question as to why the Constitution is worthy of respect and obedience. Indeed, the mere presence of such a question indicates "[a] moment of crisis in the life of a constitution."[77]

A resolution to any such crisis is close at hand, however. A judge

70. *Id.* at 58 (emphasis added).
71. Fiss, *supra* note 65, at 755.
72. *See* Levinson, *supra* note 39.
73. Fiss, *supra* note 65, at 743.
74. *Id.* at 753. For an example of that form, see Monaghan, *supra* note 19.
75. *See* Brest, *supra* note 17.
76. Fiss, *supra* note 65, at 753.
77. *Id.* at 754.

must be willing "[t]o read the moral as well as the legal text. The judge quickly learns to read in a way that avoids crises."[78] Indeed, Fiss accords the judiciary a "[s]pecial competence to interpret a text such as the Constitution, and to render specific and concrete the public morality embodied in that text."[79]

This assignment of authority to the judiciary is, allegedly, not a blank check, i.e., not an invitation to become a Nietzschean creator of meaning. Instead the judicial interpreter "is disciplined by a set of rules that specify the relevance and weight to be assigned to the material (e.g., words, history, intention, consequence), as well as by those that define basic concepts and that established the procedural circumstances under which the interpretation must occur."[80] There is, to be sure, no uniformity of rules of interpretation. Not only are the rules for interpreting poems different from those for interpreting legal texts, but, "even within the law, there may be different rules depending on the text—those for contractual interpretation vary from statutory interpretation, and both vary from those used in constitutional interpretation."[81] But in no case is an "interpreter . . . free to assign any meaning he wishes to the text," for the rules discipline the interpreter and thus succeed in "transforming the interpretative process from a subjective to an objective one, and they furnish the standards by which the correctness of the interpretation can be judged."[82] The disciplining rules derive from "an interpretive community consisting of those who recognize the rules as authoritative."[83]

Fiss' notion, of course, is very close to Fish's emphasis on the importance of interpretive communities,[84] and both have been influenced by the work of Thomas Kuhn.[85] It is easy enough to see why Fish and I find Kuhn's notions attractive, rooted as they are in the tradition of the sociology of knowledge and its rejection of the correspondence between ideas believed to be true and the external world itself.[86] It is harder to understand Fiss' embrace of Kuhn, given that the key element in Fiss' program is his defense of the objective truthfulness of

78. *Id.*
79. *Id.* at 755.
80. *Id.* at 744.
81. *Id.*
82. *Id.* at 745.
83. *Id.*
84. Indeed, the full title of Fish's book is IS THERE A TEXT IN THIS CLASS? THE AUTHORITY OF INTERPRETIVE COMMUNITIES.
85. *See* T. KUHN, THE ESSENTIAL TENSION: SELECTED STUDIES IN SCIENTIFIC TRADITION AND CHANGE (1977); T. KUHN, *supra* note 40.
86. Rorty, too, draws on Kuhn as an ally in his attack on the meaningfulness of seeking conceptions that "mirror nature." *See* R. RORTY, *supra* note 42, at 322-42.

claims about public and constitutional values.[87] The notions of "truth according to the conventions of my community" and "objective knowledge as determined by my reference group" differ substantially from notions of unmodified "truth" or "objective knowledge." The former exist within the language of skepticism, including that most virulent form castigated as nihilism. It was Nietzsche, after all, who emphasized the reduction of "truth" to the views of one's own perspective (and who thus went on to assert the possibility of changing our world by adopting different perspectives).

Fiss is aware, of course, that legal adepts argue vigorously among themselves over the meaning of the Constitution; he does not seriously suggest that legal academicians are significantly more in agreement with one another than are professors of literature debating the meaning of a poem or a novel. His most interesting (and dubious) move, however, is to differentiate the lawyer from the literary critic by asserting the significance of the membership of the former in an interpretive community presided over by authoritative courts and judges. The legal system offers procedures that can resolve disputes through, "for example, pronouncements by the highest court and perhaps even legislation and constitutional amendments. The presence of such procedures and a hierarchy of authority resolving disputes that could potentially divide or destroy an interpretive community is one of the distinctive features of legal interpretation."[88] Ultimately, then, the judge is "a combination of literary critic and moral philosopher. But that is only part of the picture. The judge also speaks with the authority of the Pope."[89]

This last assertion is directly relevant to an earlier essay of mine, in which I posited the existence of "protestant" and "catholic" ap-

87. In fairness to Fiss, I should note that he does not specifically endorse a correspondence theory of truth and, indeed, he specifically recognizes the participation of a reader-judge in bestowing meaning upon textual materials. "The idea of objective interpretation accommodates *the creative role* of the reader." Fiss, *supra* note 65, at 744 (emphasis added). Yet Fiss' article is replete with the tension generated by the joint embrace of creativity and objectivity.

The implications of Kuhn's thought for resolution of this tension are themselves the subject of an important scholarly debate. To be a critic of Kuhn does not seem to require a commitment to a correspondence (or context-independent) notion of truth, nor, apparently, does being a supporter entail commitment to radical indeterminacy. *See, e.g.*, H. PUTNAM, REASON, TRUTH AND HISTORY 113-19 (1981) (presenting criticisms of Kuhn within the context of a larger argument criticizing correspondence theories). Nonetheless it is clear that Kuhn has been most warmly embraced by critics of the notion of objectivity (and, beyond that, even of rationality) and that any theory which emphasizes the relevance of interpretive communities must confront the difficult sociological tasks of accounting for their composition and relationship to one another. *See* Brest, *Interpretation and Interest*, 34 STAN. L. REV. 765 (1982) (comments on Fiss). See the Fall 1982 issue of *Critical Inquiry* dealing with the politics of interpretation. 9 CRITICAL INQUIRY 1 (1982).

88. Fiss, *supra* note 65, at 747.

89. *Id.* at 755.

proaches to the Constitution.[90] That Fiss embraces a "catholic" Constitution, in the senses of looking to unwritten norms and accepting the institutional authority of the judiciary, tells us a great deal about him but only a little about the interpretive community. Indeed, a recent article co-authored by Fiss, attacking Justice Rehnquist, manifests all too well the problems faced by those seeking to slay the nihilist dragon.[91]

V

The March 10, 1982 issue of *The New Republic* had as its cover story "The Rehnquist Court." The illustration of the cover is worth noting: A Sphinx-like head of Justice Rehnquist perches atop the "body" of the Supreme Court building. Reaching out on each side of the steps are the menacing paws of Sphinx-Rehnquist. The head, incidentally, is gazing with an ominous serenity into the distance. The phrase "Equal Justice Under Law" does not appear on the building. Finally, the magazine places the tag line ". . . and what it's doing to the Constitution" opposite the title. Fiss and his co-author, Charles Krauthammer, claim to have decoded the riddle of this particular sphinx, however, and it is the purpose of their article to bring the alarming news to the public. Whether or not the reader is convinced by the argument that the intellectual leader of the current Court is Justice Rehnquist, the specific way Rehnquist is described and criticized in the article gives great insight into the operation of Fiss' overall approach to legal analysis.

According to the article, Rehnquist's "opinions fall radically short of the ideals of the profession. He repudiates precedents frequently and openly, and if that is impossible (because the precedent represents a tradition that neither the Court nor society is prepared to abandon), then he distorts them."[92] The "failings of craft," however, pale before the real problem, which "is substance. Rehnquist has a constitutional program for the nation: he wants to free the states from the restrictions of the national Constitution, particularly those emanating from the

90. Levinson, *"The Constitution" in American Civil Religion*, 1979 SUP. CT. REV. 123, 132.

91. Fiss & Krauthammer, *supra* note 59.

92. *Id.* at 15. I confess myself mystified, incidentally, by what it means to say that "society" (rather than the Court) is or is not prepared to abandon a precedent, since the only relevant evidence we have is the Court's behavior. That behavior may indeed be based on its assessment of what society would tolerate, but it is also possible that a judge's attitude toward a precedent would be based on internal legal considerations, leading to a vote to overturn a (putatively mistaken) precedent even though society generally endorses the extra-constitutional decision.

Civil War Amendments and the Bill of Rights."[93] Thus Rehnquist rejects the incorporation doctrine as it has been used by the Court in the past two decades to "nationalize" the Bill of Rights.[94] Moreover, Rehnquist has led the way in questioning the extent to which Congress may legislate the behavior of the states.[95] And, the authors point out, Rehnquist has scarcely shown himself a textualist in his theory of constitutional interpretation, for he has proved skillful in adopting structural arguments to defend his particular theory of federalism.[96] Rehnquist "is no conservative, as that term is ordinarily understood in the law, but rather a revisionist of a particular ideological bent. He repudiates precedents; he shows no deference to the legislative branch; and he is unable to ground state autonomy in any textual provision of the Constitution."[97]

Yet the authors point out that Rehnquist claims more than his personal views as authority for his opinions. Indeed, he disparages those who emphasize contemporary social needs or morality as authorizing a "living Constitution";[98] instead Rehnquist is an "originalist,"[99] who sees the Court's task as enforcement of the goals of the framers themselves. Although Fiss and Krauthammer mention their doubts about the cogency of originalism,[100] they prefer to challenge Rehnquist on his own ground, for their argument is that he ignores the intent of the authors of the Civil War Amendments to diminish the state autonomy that concededly might have been the vision of at least some of the framers.[101] These amendments were not, they argue, "merely technical modifications to what Rehnquist claims to be the understanding at Philadelphia, corrections that assured all persons formal equality before the law. Rather, these amendments represent a second starting

93. *Id.* at 16.

94. *See, e.g.*, First Nat'l Bank v. Bellotti, 435 U.S. 765, 823 (1978) (Rehnquist, J., dissenting) (rejecting equal application of first amendment standards to state and national government).

95. Fiss and Krauthammer discuss Pennhurst State School v. Halderman, 457 U.S. 1 (1981), and National League of Cities v. Usery, 426 U.S. 833 (1976). They also mention Rizzo v. Goode, 423 U.S. 362 (1976), which severely limited the power of federal courts to impose effective remedies on state agencies. In *Rizzo* "a small percentage" of members of the Philadelphia police department had been found by a lower court to have systematically deprived people of their constitutional rights. Council of Organizations on Philadelphia Police Accountability and Responsibility v. Rizzo, 357 F. Supp. 1289, 1318 (E.D. Pa. 1973), *aff'd in part and rev'd in part sub nom.* Goode v. Rizzo, 506 F.2d 542 (3d Cir. 1974), *rev'd*, 423 U.S. 362 (1976).

96. *See* National League of Cities v. Usery, 426 U.S. 833, 845-52 (1976) (arguing that Congress cannot infringe on a state's sovereign power and that imposition of minimum wage laws on municipalities infringes on essential sovereign functions).

97. Fiss & Krauthammer, *supra* note 59, at 18, 20.

98. *See* Rehnquist, *The Notion of A Living Constitution*, 54 TEXAS L. REV. 693 (1976).

99. *See* Brest, *supra* note 17.

100. Fiss & Krauthammer, *supra* note 59, at 20.

101. *Id.*

point, a basic change in the postulates of our constitutional system. Any appeal to history which ignores that is a sham."[102]

I have no trouble agreeing that Rehnquist's jurisprudence is questionable in theory and pernicious in practice. But the terms of this attack, derived as they are from the allegedly internal professional norms of the legal interpretive community, present the occasion for embarrassment, if not incoherence. For, as the authors recognize, "the Marshall Court (in its affirmation of nationalism) and the Warren Court (in its affirmation of equality) also repudiated strict constructionism and practiced judicial activism."[103] Indeed, for Fiss and Krauthammer, "[t]he most plausible interpretation of *Brown*[104] is that it simply repudiated *Plessy*,[105] in an attempt to reflect a truer understanding of the fourteenth amendment. For the Warren Court, as for Rehnquist, precedent had less force than the framers' original understanding of the text they wrote."[106] It is clear from Fiss' earlier comments, though, that he would defend *Brown* even if he were convinced beyond a reasonable doubt that the framers of the fourteenth amendment did not understand that amendment to bar school segregation.[107]

If Rehnquist were simply a conservative law professor, like Robert Bork,[108] Ralph Winter,[109] or Richard Posner,[110] then it would be easy to dismiss his views by noting the extent to which they require the modification or abandonment of many of our "papal edicts" from the Warren Court. But the very point of the article, of course, is based on the proferred fact that Rehnquist is rapidly becoming the chief declarer of

102. *Id. But see* Benedict, *Preserving Federalism: Reconstruction and the Waite Court*, 1978 SUP. CT. REV. 39, 47-48 (footnotes omitted):

> Historians now recognize that every Reconstruction-era effort to protect the rights of citizens was tempered by the fundamental conviction that federalism required that the day-to-day protection of the citizen had to remain the duty of the States . . . . As to the permanent protections for Americans' rights, despite arguments to the contrary by those modern legal scholars who write in the tradition of a new nationalism, all the evidence of the congressional discussions, the ratification debates, and the public controversy indicates that Republicans intended the States to retain primary jurisdiction over citizens' rights. They attempted to write into the Constitution an obligation that antislavery theorists already believed incumbent on the States: the requirement that they protect all citizens equally in fundamental human rights. They did not intend the national government to replace the States in fulfilling that obligation.

Benedict builds on the important book by Harold Hyman, A MORE PERFECT UNION (1973).

103. Fiss & Krauthammer, *supra* note 59, at 20.

104. Brown v. Board of Educ., 347 U.S. 483 (1954).

105. Plessy v. Ferguson, 163 U.S. 537 (1896).

106. Fiss & Krauthammer, *supra* note 59, at 20 (footnotes added).

107. *See supra* text accompanying notes 73-79.

108. Now Judge Bork of the Court of Appeals for the District of Columbia.

109. Now Judge Winter of the Court of Appeals for the Second Circuit.

110. Now Judge Posner of the Court of Appeals for the Seventh Circuit.

what the Constitution requires, and that the Court-directed interpretive community will increasingly revolve around him.

It is hardly likely, of course, that Professor Fiss (or I) will start teaching students the (normative) Constitution according to Rehnquist, even as we make our students aware of the existence of the appalling Rehnquist *oeuvre*. But will Professor Fiss argue that the interpretive community has been taken over by a false pope, a usurper, against whom the truly faithful must rally? Moreover, given the willingness of the voting public to elect a President and a majority of the Senate who share many of Rehnquist's values, how will Fiss (or anyone else) show that they contravene the public values embodied in the Constitution, especially given the undoubted interest of our Constitution-writers in protecting at least some measure of both state autonomy and the rights of private property owners?

Fiss' approach to the Constitution, like that of Professor Dworkin, ultimately rests on the premise that there is no genuine conflict among the values that animate the different parts of the public.[111] But, as Bray Hammond put it in his analysis of the early dispute in our history about the power of Congress to charter the Bank of the United States, "The controversy demonstrated at the very outset that the Constitution had not displaced rival principles or reconciled them but had become their dialectical arena."[112] This last term may bring to mind either the

111. See Levinson, *supra* note 39, at 1083-84, for a critique of Dworkin on this point. See also J. ELY, DEMOCRACY AND DISTRUST 43-72 (1980), for a comprehensive attack on the "fundamental values" approach that Fiss in fact is defending.

112. B. HAMMOND, BANKS AND POLITICS IN AMERICA 120 (1957). See also Paul Bator's reminder that "the Constitution itself contains a multiplicity of various sorts of values, many in tension with each other: process values as well as substantive values, structural and institutional values as well as those embodying individual rights." Bator, *The State Courts and Federal Constitutional Litigation*, 22 WM. & MARY L. REV. 605, 633 (1981). Indeed, Professor Bator argues eloquently for the desirability of a role for state court participation in constitutional adjudication precisely in terms of the ability of state judges to recognize values that federal judges are prone to overlook. In contrast to an argument which assumes "that the Constitution contains only one or two *sorts* of values: typically, those which protect the individual from the power of the state, and those which assure the superiority of federal to state law," Bator presents a different view:

> But the Constitution contains other sorts of values as well. It gives the federal government powers, but also enacts limitations on those powers. *The limitations, too, count as setting forth constitutional values*. Will the federal judge be more sensitive than the state judge in insuring that these limitations are complied with? Whose institutional "set" is likely to make one more sensitive to the values underlying the tenth amendment? . . . Why don't these sorts of issues even seem to count?

Id. at 631-32 (emphasis in original). Though I suspect I share more of Fiss' political values than I do those of Professor Bator, I have little hesitation in saying that I think Bator presents a more plausible view of the Constitution. That view, however, offers no guidance as to the dilemmas generated by recognizing the multiplicity (and contradictions) of constitutional values.

Resolving the dialectical tension, of course, is a central dilemma. See, for example, Tushnet, *Darkness on the Edge of Town: The Contributions of John Hart Ely to Constitutional Theory*, 89 YALE L.J. 1037 (1980), for an argument that value conflict cannot be resolved within the frame-

controversy of the seminar table or warfare in which each side claims adherence to the "true" meaning of the disputed document. It is the latter mode of dispute resolution that is suggested by Justice Black's comment that "the fundamental issues over the extent of federal supremacy had been resolved by war."[113] But surely there is something peculiar about the assertion that fundamental ideological issues are "resolved" by war, even if we concede that political power indeed often comes from the barrels of guns, and even if it is possible to identify clearly the doctrinal position that won or lost a particular battle. Indeed, Fiss and Krauthammer may even be correct that Rehnquist's views, taken to an extreme, reopen the dilemmas that ultimately led to the outbreak of war. But if that be so, it is only because of the continuing tension in American values and the inability of either armed victory or judicial articulation to settle the dispute firmly one way or another. Perhaps Rehnquist is attempting to resolve what he sees as a genuine legal crisis by reasserting certain traditional moral and legal values. That he cannot achieve resolution says more about the pervasiveness of the fundamental conflicts than it does about his mistake in reading our fundamental values.

The American wish is that one can avoid having to answer the political question posed by a Harlan County labor song, "Which side are you on?", by responding that one stands by the Constitution and that, in turn, the Constitution itself stands for the proper values. The transformation of political questions into legal questions, first emphasized by de Tocqueville,[114] allows the "adjudication" of disputes. As Fiss notes, however, "The idea of adjudication requires that there exist constitutional values to interpret, just as much as it requires that there be constraints on the interpretive process. Lacking such a belief, adju-

work of traditional liberal constitutionalism. See also the remarkable article by Frank Easterbrook, *Ways of Criticizing the Court*, 95 HARV. L. REV. 802, 811-31 (1982), which demonstrates by the use of social choice theory the extreme unlikelihood (indeed, impossibility, given the most likely empirical conditions) of the existence of a procedure for legal decisionmaking adequate to generate "definitive" decisions over time by the Supreme Court (let alone by the community at large). Easterbrook's article is a major challenge to those who look to the Supreme Court for clear articulation of basic legal precepts, especially if one accepts the proposition that there are at least three values contending in Hammond's "dialectical arena." Whether or not Easterbrook is accurately described as a "nihilist," his conclusions are in their own way every bit as hopeless as any in Tushnet's writings or the instant essay.

113. Testa v. Katt, 330 U.S. 386, 390 (1947).

114. 1 A. DE TOCQUEVILLE, DEMOCRACY IN AMERICA 290 (Vintage ed. 1945). It should be noted that de Tocqueville specifically stressed the tendency of a political question to be "resolved, sooner or later, into a judicial question." *Id.* For the importance of the emphasis on the judiciary as institutional resolver, see Levinson, *Fidelity to Law and the Assessment of Political Activity*, 27 STAN. L. REV. 1185, 1190-91 (1975).

dication is not possible, only power."[115]

As he portrays the bleakness of a world that rejects belief in the possibility of principled adjudication, Fiss speaks with much of the same eloquence and vigor as does Gerald Graff. It is worth noting that Richard Rorty, whose work has much influenced me, has indicated his own empathy with the attacks of Graff and others on the new literary criticism. What is at stake is a conception of the possibility of a shared moral life. Rorty refers to "the view that, in the end, when all the intellectuals have done all their tricks, morality remains widely shared and available to reflection—something capable of being discovered rather than created, because already implicit in the common consciousness of everyone."[116] Critics with this view "want criticism to bring an antecedent morality to light, enlarge upon it and enrich it," and they consequently "resist the suggestion that there is no common vocabulary in terms of which critics can argue with one another about how well this task has been performed."[117] No one with a democratic sensibility can easily reject the vision of a common discourse described by Rorty and evoked by Fiss.

Empathy, however, does not equal agreement. It would be contradictory to say that the historicist pragmatism celebrated by Rorty is "true," or that philosophy has "disproved" the possibility of true and certain knowledge about the natural world, including its moral component. But those who do not already share Fiss' faith are unlikely, I suspect, to be persuaded by his attack on positions like the one articulated in the present essay. The inability of Fiss and his co-author to mount a persuasive attack on Justice Rehnquist in anything other than political terms reveals the parlous state of contemporary constitutional discourse. The united interpretive community that is necessary to Fiss' own argument simply does not exist.[118] What one does in the absence of such a community is, of course, a problem of more than merely theoretical import. The decreasing propensity of the body politic to accord

115. Fiss, *supra* note 65, at 763.

116. R. RORTY, *supra* note 14, at 157.

117. *Id.* Indeed, responding to an earlier version of the present essay, Rorty wrote,

> I confess that I tremble at the thought of Barthian readings in law schools . . . . I suspect that civilization reposes on a lot of people who take the normal practices of the discipline with full "realistic" seriousness. However, I should like to think that a pragmatist's understanding of knowledge and community would be, in the end, compatible with normal inquiry—the practitioners of such inquiry reserving their irony for after-hours.

Letter from Richard Rorty to author (Apr. 28, 1981) (copy on file with the *Texas Law Review*). It is not clear, then, what Rorty's stance would be to those who would attempt to make his own thought central to their regular daily work.

118. *See supra* text accompanying note 111.

the Supreme Court ultimate authority in constitutional interpretation may portend an ever deeper constitutional crisis, especially if any of the jurisdiction- and remedy-limiting bills now before Congress had passed and received presidential signature.[119]

VI

Even poets who emphasize the contingency of perception nevertheless continue to write their poems. "Even the linking of stars is a lie./ But for a while now let's be happy/ to believe the symbol. That's enough."[120] And so we who take the constitutional firmament seriously continue as well to write our articles and dispute with one another.[121] And, just as constellations are human attempts to link the separate stars, so are doctrinal analyses likely to serve as similar attempts to demonstrate that the cases themselves are meaningfully linked and intellectually patterned. All such writing (and reading) is a supreme act of faith. We can hope that some future conjunction of author and reader will provide a common language of constitutional

119. *See, e.g.,* S. 158, 97th Cong., 1st Sess. ("Human Life" bill) (1981); S. 481, 97th Cong., 1st Sess. (1981) (depriving federal courts of jurisdiction over cases regarding voluntary prayers in public schools). Although both of these bills were ultimately defeated in the Senate, conservative forces have indicated their intention to raise both issues again early in the next Congress. It is therefore unlikely that Congress has definitively resolved these conflicts. *See* N.Y. Times, Sept. 17, 1982, at A19, col. 1.

120. R. RILKE, DUINO ELEGIES AND THE SONNETS TO ORPHEUS 105 (A. Poulin trans. 1975) (Sonnets to Orpheus, First Series, No. 11).

121. Grant Gilmore has noted the existence in an earlier generation of "nihilist" individuals who were led by their own arguments to eschew writing itself. *See* G. GILMORE, THE AGES OF AMERICAN LAW 80-81 (1977) (discussing Wesley Sturges). Although the peculiar traditions of law schools in regard to tenure have meant that there have always been a relatively high number of nonwriters on law school faculties, *see* Ackerman, *The Marketplace of Ideas*, 90 YALE L.J. 1131, 1132-35 (1981), it may be that at least some of the failure to write is based on a conviction of having "nothing to say" in the profoundest sense of that term. It is not a coincidence, I suspect, that a substantial amount of the writing of scholars Fiss would be likely to view as "nihilists" is in the area of legal history and, more particularly, the ideological analysis of legal thought, whether expressed in cases, classic legal writings, or the work-product of scholars. In addition to the works cited *supra* note 48, see, e.g., Gordon, *Historicism in Legal Scholarship*, 90 YALE L.J. 1017 (1981); Katz, *Studies in Boundary Theory: Three Essays in Adjudication and Politics*, 28 BUFFALO L. REV. 383 (1979); D. Kennedy, The Rise and Fall of Classical Legal Thought 1850-1940 (1976) (unpublished manuscript); Kennedy, *The Structure of Blackstone's Commentaries*, 28 BUFFALO L. REV. 209 (1979); Schlegel, *American Legal Realism and Empirical Social Science: From the Yale Experience*, 28 BUFFALO L. REV. 459 (1979); Schlegel, *American Legal Realism and Empirical Social Science: The Singular Case of Underhill Moore*, 29 BUFFALO L. REV. 195 (1980). This (greatly truncated) list belies any genuine notion that persons alienated from a traditional stance of reverence (or even respect) for law have nothing to say. But it is fair to say that no one who defines his or her task as the search for "certain principles or doctrines," *see supra* text accompanying note 2, is prepared to listen. Few today would admit that they *are* engaged in such a search, for all of us portray ourselves as post-Realists, focusing on "policies" underlying the law. But see Gordon, Book Review, 1974 WIS. L. REV. 1216 (reviewing G. GILMORE, THE DEATH OF CONTRACT (1974)), for an analysis of the desiccated nature of the so-called policy analysis that occurs in American law schools.

discourse fit for "a nation of supple and athletic minds,"[122] but for now we can only await its coming and make do with the fractured and fragmented discourse available to us.[123]

122. W. WHITMAN, *supra* note 1, at 545.

123. *See* Leff, UNSPEAKABLE ETHICS, UNNATURAL LAW, 1979 DUKE L.J. 1229, 1249:

> All I can say is this: it looks as if we are all we have. Given what we know about ourselves and each other, this is an extraordinarily unappetizing prospect; looking around the world, it ap, ars that if all men are brothers, the ruling model is Cain and Abel. Neither reason, nor love, nor even terror, seems to have worked to make us "good," and worse than that, there is no reason why anything should. Only if ethics were something unspeakable by us, could law be unnatural, and therefore unchallengeable. As things now stand, everything is up for grabs.
>
> Nevertheless:
>
> Napalming babies is bad.
>
> Starving the poor is wicked.
>
> Buying and selling each other is depraved.
>
> Those who stood up to and died resisting Hitler, Stalin, Amin, and Pol Pot—and General Custer too—have earned salvation.
>
> Those who acquiesced deserve to be damned.
>
> There is in the world such a thing as evil.
>
> [All together now:] Sez who?
>
> God help us.

[6]

THE HERMENEUTICS FILE

THOMAS C. GREY*

> "Hermeneutics seems to me to be animated by this double motivation: willingness to suspect, willingness to listen; vow of rigor, vow of obėdience."
>
> —Paul Ricoeur[i]
>
> "If the poet says, 'Go and catch a falling star,' or whatever it may be, he doesn't seriously issue an order."
>
> —J.L. Austin[ii]

* * *

The following four memoranda, written by George McGarr in the immediate aftermath of Terence Conn's death, are here published for the first time. They cast new light on the papers of the late Professor Conn, papers which first came to public notice in Professor McGarr's article published soon after their discovery (The Legacy of Terence Conn, THE BULLETIN, *Vol. 53, No. 2; and also George McGarr,* Editing the Conn Papers, THE BULLETIN, *Vol. 54, No. 7). Professor Conn's "Draft #13 (Conning McGarr)" is reprinted after the first memorandum for the reader's convenience. The footnotes have been prepared by Marvin Subal, Esq., who wishes to acknowledge the indispensible assistance of Professor McGarr.*

I

To: Dean Peter Stutz
From: George McGarr
Re: Terry Conn's Papers

Peter, thanks for your help with the memorial service. I have been

---

* Professor of Law, Stanford University. B.A. 1963, Stanford University; B.A. 1965, Oxford; LL.B 1968, Yale University. My thanks to Barbara Babcock, Paul Brest, Lawrence Friedman, Bob Gordon, Mark Kelman, Herb Lindenberger, Diane Middlebrook, Ken Walton, and Ian Watt for reading and commenting on an earlier draft. Thanks as well, for education, to colleagues participating in the Stanford 'Interpretation Seminar' over the last several years; and, for help and incomparable ambience, to the Fellows and staff of the Stanford Humanities Center, where this was written.

i. P. RICOEUR, FREUD AND PHILOSOPHY 27 (1967).

ii. J. AUSTIN, PHILOSOPHICAL PAPERS 228 (1961).

virtually in shock during the whole business, and I couldn't have gotten through it without you. Your remarks were just perfect, in contrast to some others—and I don't exempt my own. I have been in such a swirl of confusion, sorrow, and resentment that I couldn't strike the right tone, or any consistent tone. But to the business at hand.

The immediate problem, as I understand it, is the status of Terry's papers. Let me review where we stand. You are effectively the custodian of them, since they were in his law school office at the time of his death. Janet asked you to go through them; though she and Terry were never formally divorced, in light of the estrangement she didn't think she was the one to deal with them. You agreed, and the two of you also agreed that I should help.

Early in our search of his office, I found, in a file-folder marked "Hermeneutics," a poem entitled "Draft #13 (Conning McGarr)" which was apparently addressed to me. The poem was handwritten on a single piece of paper, which had been crumpled and then smoothed out. From a photocopy of it I have had a version of the poem typed up, which I append here. It quite accurately represents the position on the original paper of the written matter which is (apparently) extraneous to the poem itself: namely, the date in the upper left-hand corner of the page; and the words "Cal. Prob. Code Ann. 53, 102 (1)" in the lower left-hand corner.[1] (I should also mention, though it seems clearly extraneous, that on the back of the piece of paper containing the poem appear the words "the red bird," also in Terry's hand, and written casually at an angle across the page.)

As you recall, I immediately showed you the poem after I had read it, with the remark that it was a joke characteristic of Terry's less attractive side, a somewhat malicious last shot at me in our longstanding debates about interpretation. It seemed obvious to me at the time, and as I recall you agreed, that the document could not actually be a legal will. It wasn't witnessed; it wasn't even signed. We went on with our search, and found nothing that looked like a will. You then went to look through the papers at Terry's apartment, and called me to tell me that there was no will there either. Terry had told me, and Janet con-

1. The poem is reprinted at the end of this memorandum as it appeared in Professor McGarr's original report in these pages (THE BULLETIN, Vol. 53, No. 2, at 17). In his editorial comment accompanying the original publication, Professor McGarr explained his decision to include the words "Draft #13" as part of the title, while excluding the date and legal research notes as extraneous; the reader's attention is drawn to his distinctions between "writing" and "text," and between "poem-text" and "will-text." We had wished to include a photographic reproduction of the original as part of this study, but this has not proved possible.

firmed, that he had no living relatives; thus it seemed clear that he had died intestate, and she as his wife would take his entire estate.

As much out of curiosity as caution, I looked up the Probate Code section referred to at the bottom of the poem. Section 53 turned out to be the provision dealing with "holographic wills." I don't know if you are as weak on trust and estate law as I am, but I had barely been aware that there are special rules governing wills written by hand. What I thought I did know was that wills have to be formal documents, signed on each page, with two or three witnesses attesting, and so forth. Imagine my feelings as I found, reading section 53 and the summaries of cases in the Code Annotated, that Terry's poem arguably met the formal requirements for a valid holographic will.[2] The poem was apparently written entirely in his hand, and was dated by him. A holographic will need not be witnessed, and the cases suggest that the phrase "I, Conn . . ." with which the poem begins might serve as an adequate signature.[3]

My immediate reaction was anger. What did Terry think he was doing, placing me in an ambiguous position, possibly as his executor, without even asking, in a document that was at the same time a tasteless joke at my expense? What should I ever make of his gnomic "instructions," which seemed designed to spread confusion rather than to communicate anything? The damned thing didn't even make the debater's point it seemed designed to make; when had I ever denied that a person who set out to write an uninterpretable (or, the same thing, infinitely interpretable) set of "instructions" could do just that? My point against Terry had always been that most legal instruments, like most utterances generally, are designed to convey a definite content, a meaning that can be rationally discerned by the process of interpretation. This is all I have ever said, and it always seemed to me that only

2. *See* CAL. PROB. CODE § 53 (West 1956):

> A holographic will is one that is entirely written, dated and signed by the hand of the testator himself. It is subject to no other form, and need not be witnessed. No address, date or other matter written, printed or stamped upon the document, which is not incorporated in the provisions which are in the handwriting of the decedent, shall be considered as any part of the will.

Section 53 was amended in 1982, after Professor McGarr's memorandum was written, but the substance of its requirements remains the same. CAL. PROB. CODE § 53 (West Supp. 1984).

3. *See, e.g.*, In re Bloch's Estate, 39 Cal. 2d 570, 248 P.2d 21 (1952) (name written anywhere in will qualifies as signature if testator wrote it there with intent of authenticating instrument); In re Button's Estate, 209 Cal. 325, 287 P. 964 (1930) (words "Love from 'Muddy' " near end of letter, propounded as will, from deceased to former husband to whom she was known by that name, was valid signature).

Terry's perversity led him to deny so obvious a common sense truism. But I digress.

My next discovery was that my anger was premature. The cases construing section 53 clearly establish—and (as "Code Ann." suggests) Terry surely knew this[4]—a principle that avoids the horror of making Terry's poem into a valid will. Even an instrument that has met the (undemanding) formal requirements for a holographic will is not accepted as such if it fails to manifest "testamentary intent," or "*animus testandi*." The courts have relied on this principle to reject a wide variety of dubious handwritten documents proferred as holographic wills.[5]

Now there surely can be no difficulty in concluding that Terry had no "testamentary intent" when he wrote this poem. First, of course, there are serious doubts whether it was even meant to be a final document: it is entitled a "draft"; it breaks off in mid-line and mid-sentence; and he had crumpled up the page. Further, the scrawled legal research at the bottom of the page and the evidently unrelated note on its reverse side are not the sort of thing a testator would be likely to write on a final version of a will.

But, overriding these considerations, surely it is clear from the basic content that Terry was not attempting to make a will at all. He was writing a poem, for my eyes, a poem that took the form of a will: a pseudo-will, a fictional will. Who writes an obscure poem to dispose of one's estate—including in Terry's case one's voluminous unpublished life's work? Who vaguely orders his property distributed to "friends" in "reasonable shares"?[6] Terry had been a good lawyer, and he was always a master of language; he knew what he was doing, and what he was doing was writing an ironic poem, not a will. The point is confirmed by his leaving the poem in a file marked "Hermeneutics"—the topic of our many debates. In the same filing cabinet were file-folders marked "Personal-Miscellaneous" and "Personal-Financial" that con-

---

4. The annotated code contains summaries of the case law construing the statutory provision as well as the text itself; the statute itself could have been cited, and normally would be, without the explicit reference to the annotation.

5. *See, e.g.*, In re Henning's Estate, 186 Cal. 307, 199 P. 39 (1921) (handwritten letter not a will because written in contemplation of matrimony not death); In re Kenyon's Estate, 42 Cal. App. 2d, 109 P.2d 38 (1941) (handwritten letter discussing politics and weather was not a will because it contained no evidence that decedent intended it to be such).

6. The intention of testator to make a testamentary disposition of his property . . . must be expressed in such terms that the court can determine his intention or wish without resort to conjecture. Both the thing given and the persons to whom it is given must . . . be set forth with such certainty that the court can give effect to such gift when the estate is to be distributed.

1 Bowe-Parker, Page on Wills 187-88 (1960).

tained practical documents among which a will might naturally have been lodged. Finally, the decisive point is the parenthesized title, in which I take some wry comfort; it says straight out that the document is meant only as a last poke at me.

I conclude, then, that we are not in possession of a will of Terry Conn's. I have told Janet this. She has asked me if I would sort out the papers in Terry's office. She wants them disposed of, one way or another, without her having to deal with them. I have told her, what I am sure you will approve, that the Law School will retain custody of them in Terry's locked office (to which I now have a key) for the time being.

* * *

Draft #13 (Conning McGarr)

I, Conn, sound as age allows,
Bequeath to friends in reasonable shares
My money and my goods. As for the rest,
My hoard (imagined, literary *res*)
Shall be arranged with care, substance preserved,
And put out in due time, plain as can be.

All this shall be done by George McGarr,
My colleague, friend, conscience of afternoons,
Who also shall respect this final wish:
That my inchoacies may never come,
My Scottish breadman, to harsh scrutiny,
Those of my writings that are incomplete,
Destroy.

The stacks of pages wait for you;
Do not see in them matter wanting form,
Pebbles for a Japanese gardener's hand,
But mind's fixed intercept of lexicon.
You said, through all our restless afternoons,
"To interpret is to find intent in words;"
Now, exegete, now that the words are mine,
Now, grave George, draw from them what I mean —
Who knows my currents better than the shore
Against whose sea-wall they have spent their surge?

If you can judge which of my works are done
Not seeking shape where I let fracture be
(Old seconder of motions to adjourn!)
Nor forcing me unfinished into view

(The literate insist, and what's to hide?)
Nor claiming bold emender's privilege
(Conn says to mean, so mean away his say)
Then can your last word close our long jaw-jaw
Conformant to your sober principles.
But take care. Traps are here. Words mean.
I mean. You, reading, want

II

To: Peter
From: George
Re: Terry's Papers

I have spent the last five days reading the papers in Terry's office—with an eagerness that goes beyond any duty to you or Janet. Terry and I talked two or three times a week for years about his ideas, and yet I had never seen a word he wrote, apart from those summaries of contract and evidence law he handed out to his students. Eventually I will make a complete inventory of his writings, but for now I thought I should at least fill you in.

Also, I want to respond to your suggestion about the handling of the poem. You raise the point that perhaps if it arguably meets the formal requirements for a valid will, we should at least file it with the Superior Court, pursuant to the Probate Code.[7] I don't read you as disagreeing with my conclusion that there is no "testamentary intent" here, but you think that in our respective positions, yours as temporary custodian of the papers (and the "will"), and mine as putative executor or whatever, we should in all caution leave it to the court to determine the intent question. I see the point, but I don't agree. Let me postpone saying why until after I tell you something about Terry's papers.

There really is a "hoard" in there. First, Terry left behind a fair amount of regular legal scholarship. We know about the contracts and evidence summaries. There are earlier versions of them in piles of old class materials for those courses. In his files are exchanges of letters with the publishers to whom you, Jack Goldberg, and I showed our pirated version of the summaries, hoping they could pry these manu-

7. Section 320 of the California Probate Code provides:

The custodian of a will, within 30 days after being informed that the maker thereof is dead, must deliver the same to the clerk of the superior court having jurisdiction of the estate, or to the executor named therein. Failure to do so makes such person responsible for all damages sustained by any one injured thereby.

scripts out of his obsessive grip and publish them. This was Terry's response:

> How did you vultures get a copy of my Evidence summary? Please send all copies in your possession to me at once. I write these summaries only so that I can tell my students to stop bothering me with their complaints about not learning doctrine in my classes. I have not authorized their use for any other purpose, and I regard you as in possession, now knowing possession, of stolen property.

(I remember telling Terry how helpful I thought those summaries would be if published, lucid doctrinal statements that they were, and his saying to me, in his coldest way, that when they were ready for publication I would be the first to know.)

Terry also left behind what I take to be the two article-drafts he showed his then colleagues when he induced them to give him tenure about fifteen years ago. They seem to me clear and intelligent doctrinal pieces, well above the norm of such work, though not otherwise remarkable. (One of them deals with the parol evidence rule and documentary interpretation; "hermeneutics" surfaced in Terry's mind long ago.)[8] These pieces seem to me finished works, but the typescripts are marked "draft"—as is every single bit of Terry's writing I have come upon. There is also a long fragment of an article on the hearsay rule, written after the first two doctrinal pieces. Then there follows a gap of more than seven years for which there are no writings, except the earliest versions of the contracts and evidence summaries.

Then, about seven years ago, begins the "imagined, literary *res*." There are quite a few poems; how good they are I'm certainly not qualified to say. There are a lot of short stories of a "fable" sort, Borges-like or Kafka-esque—or like law school exam questions. (I'm not much more confident in making any judgment of quality here either, but I do find some of them very intriguing.) There is a long, curious essay comparing the lawyer's distinction between fact and law with the distinction between perception and imagination made by various poets and novelists—Coleridge, Shelley, Proust, and Wallace Stevens.[9]

There is another quite long essay that I read more intently because it is on the very topic ("interpretation") that was our favorite subject of

8. Professor McGarr hopes that these essays, entitled "When do Words Speak for Themselves?" and "Nondisclosure as Deceit," will eventually be published in a volume that collects a number of Terence Conn's miscellaneous shorter writings.

9. This essay, entitled "Until Now I Never Knew," will be published, as will a selection from Conn's poems and stories, in the projected volume referred to *supra* note 8.

discussion in our afternoon walks around the campus. Terry examines the theories of several of the philosophers he got me to learn a little about, especially Wittgenstein and Derrida. He makes the curious remark about these two (both Jewish I think) that Derrida is a "Protestant" while Wittgenstein was a "good Catholic," a believer in tradition; Terry used to ascribe our differences to my Scottish Protestant and his Irish Catholic background, mixing hermeneutic theory with vulgar ethnic jokes. The piece breaks off without a conclusion. Reading it leaves me remembering Terry most vividly.[10]

There is a 200-page typescript of a murder story. The murder is at a law school, and the suspects are various members of the faculty, an assemblage of actual well-known law teachers from different schools, thinly disguised and more or less subtly defamed (you and I are not included). There are two competing detectives, whose efforts are chronicled in alternating chapters. Seamus is a private eye turned law student late in life; he follows intuitions, breaks into apartments and offices, gets hit on the head, and drinks too much, all told a la Raymond Chandler. Jane Muffett is a young lady philosopher from Oxford, visiting the faculty; she has tea with colleagues, examines rare old books in the library, and ratiocinates in her office—told as if by Dorothy Sayers. The two avoid and loathe each other, but then are thrown together in a confrontation in which there is a kind of courtship by exchanged insults, as in a Hepburn-Tracy movie. The book ends (breaks off?) with them going off for a drink together, the murder left unsolved, clues dangling, erotic tension high. Is the murder story a kind of allegory of the love story? (He will make me into a literary critic yet!)[11]

There is also a stack of notebooks written by Terry over the last six years, filled with quotes from his reading, aphorisms, short sketches (germs of stories and poems in several cases) and ideas for articles. These are especially interesting to me, echoing as they do so many of the things he said in our talks. (I myself intermittently kept a notebook recording things Terry said to me, frustrated as I was at never being able to see what he was writing.)

Finally, the longest typescript is a 603-page autobiography (all the typescripts are unprofessionally typed, presumably by Terry himself;

10. This essay, entitled "Rough Ground and Abyss," will likewise be published in the projected book referred to *supra* note 8.

11. For Professor McGarr's account of the controversy over publication of this work, see McGarr, *Editing the Conn Papers*, THE BULLETIN, Vol. 54, No. 7.

his secretary tells me she never saw this material). The thing is titled, facetiously, in a handscrawled cover page, "The Tao of Derry."[12] I have read every word of it. To me, this work best reveals Terry's powers. There is a lot of direct narrative of the events in his life (many of them I had never known about), and this is intertwined in the most absorbing way with his reflections, which are often expressed in imaginary colloquy with two interlocutors, addressed as "my saint" and "my sinner"—evidently Augustine and Rousseau. I know the device sounds impossibly grandiose, and I may have been carried away by my fascination with Terry, but I truly think this is an astonishing work.

I have described Terry's "hoard" in this much detail partly because you deserve to know right away what we have here. You stuck by Terry when many people wanted you to pressure him to resign. I recall with gratitude your stiff response when Grimmett said Terry didn't belong here "because he isn't publishing anything and whatever he's teaching, it isn't law."

But in addition, some sense of the material does seem relevant to the question whether we should file the poem with the court and leave it to the judge to decide if Terry intended it to be his will. It seems relevant in this sense—what if some damn-fool judge *did* decide the poem was a will? We would be stuck with Terry's crazy "instructions" (which of course are really only mock-instructions) to destroy all the writings that are "incomplete." The chances are, I assume, strongly against a judge making any such idiotic ruling, but why take the chance?

I am not suggesting that we evade the letter or spirit of the law. If we had found a real will that gave such instructions, we would of course have to file it, and face up to the grim possibilities. But clear as we are that this poem is not a will, we are under no legal or moral obligation to take the risk. The Code section that imposes an obligation to file the "will" of a deceased within 30 days after death[13] simply doesn't apply to us; we have no "will," only a poem in the form of a will, a pretend-will, something completely outside the scope of the statutory requirement.

Nor are we putting ourselves or the University at any practical risk of liability by not filing. The only sanction for noncompliance with the

12. This work is now scheduled to appear under the title CONN'S WAY (Multiversity Press, forthcoming).

13. *See supra* note 7.

statutory duty to file seems to be liability for damages to any person injuried by the failure to file.[14] Here, even if this were a will, no one would be injured by its suppression. Where there is no harm that can come from not filing, a long-shot risk of harm if we do file, and we are clear in our own minds that no will exists, I say we should not file.

III

To: Peter
From: George
Re: Terry's Will

When I said that there was no one who could be injured by suppression of the will, you were right that I had not considered Terry's "friends" who would get his (nonliterary) property in "reasonable shares" under his instructions. In my defense, I could not accept this as a serious disposition of property. Also, Terry seems to have had practically no money or goods. But all this becomes irrelevant, I believe; as you know, a much more momentous injury, in all but the legal sense, is now threatened if Terry's estate passes to Janet by intestacy.

After I sent the last memo to you, I met with Janet to tell her what was in Terry's office. When I mentioned the autobiography, she immediately asked whether it said anything about her. Well, it does indeed; there are many pages that deal with Terry's marriage and breakup with Janet. Since these events coincided with Terry's intellectual rebirth, the story and the ideas are closely intertwined here; and these are among the most important and, to me, among the best parts of the book. I don't know why I had not thought before of the possibility that Janet might object to these passages; perhaps because in them Terry seems to be hard on himself and understanding of her.

When I told Janet she was in the book, she wanted to see it right away, and (as I told you) I gave her the key to the office, thinking that I could hardly deny her access to what we had agreed were *her* papers. In no more than twenty minutes, she came back, very angry, and told me that she wanted all his papers destroyed! There was no arguing with her in that state of mind, so I called to warn you, and resolved to wait until she had cooled down. As I recall it, you were to tell her that any final disposition of the papers had to wait at least until the university counsel ruled on whether we had to submit the "will" to the court.

14. *Id.* This is inaccurate, however. Professor McGarr was apparently unaware that Probate Code section 321 permits a judge to order the possessor of a will to produce it. One failing to comply with such an order may be incarcerated.

In the meantime, I went back to Terry's office to think, and I write this having been at his desk ever since; many hours now. As I turned over in my mind what I might say to Janet to dissuade her, I could not escape the possibility that she might remain implacable. She is quite capable of taking an extreme position and passionately holding to it. After all, that is what she did with Terry. When she was splitting up with him, I once tried to suggest that he wasn't so bad, that his new line of work sounded interesting, and so on. She responded in perfect, complete sentences with a denunciation of him so total that I wrote it down at the time: "He will never do anything worthwhile. His talk about new work is dilettante bullshit. He will not do anything in literature or philosophy for the same reason he did not do anything in law: he is a drunk and a liar; and he drinks and lies because he is a coward." Perhaps to be expected when someone is going through a painful breakup. The startling thing is that when I spoke with her just after we had learned of Terry's death, and said something vague and soothing about him again, she gave me the same speech; it might have been word for word. No *de mortuis.*

Let me give another example (these are not the digressions they may seem, as Janet's character is a central point in all this). While she and Terry were breaking up, we were good friends and I spent considerable time with her as a kind of sounding board (a role which, curiously, Susan played more with Terry; even then, before her illness, Susan had a febrile quality that matched Terry's temperament). After the breakup, Janet and I talked almost every day here in my office, sometimes for hours. After about a month, all at once, she stopped coming by, and then very suddenly (perhaps you'll recall) arranged to take a year's leave away. During that year, I took up my talks with Terry again. After she returned, and I know it was because of those talks, she would scarcely speak to me at all, and, to my great regret, she has not been more than civil to me for all these years—implacable Janet.

Having said all that, let me repeat what I said on the phone. While her reaction is extreme and wrong, it is understandable. Terry did put her through hell. I think many of our colleagues, and sometimes even you, Peter, have missed what a fine person Janet is; she can be difficult and rigid, but she is absolutely straight, dependably honest, and a generous friend. Like anyone, she closes herself off when she feels disliked, and she has had every reason to feel disliked around here. I only hope she will now listen to reason and back off from this awful resolve of hers.

But it *is* an awful resolve, and with that in mind I have made myself reread Terry's will. In fact, I have really read it seriously for the first time. Because what I am going to say comes in the shadow of Janet's threat to destroy the papers, believe me that I am aware of the ironies that hedge me round on all sides. I have little hope of convincing the larger world of this, Peter, but I do want to convince you: while the desire to save Terry's work has made me look hard at his will, it has not dictated what I find there.

This rereading—this first careful reading—has led me to see "Conning McGarr" as Terry's intended will. Let me try to set down for you (and for myself) what seem to me the main considerations supporting this.

First, read the actual words of the poem itself, putting in the background, for a moment, the contextual aspects—its verse form, its title, the crumpled page, the other writing on the paper, the file Terry left it in, and its apparent inconsistency with Terry's own often-asserted views on interpretation. I will come back to each of these features to show how none of them negates his testamentary intent. But look at the words first; as Terry wrote, "Words mean."

While there are some obscurities in the poem, careful reading reveals a serious, coherent statement of Terry's wishes about the disposal of his legacy. Of course, some instructions are vague; particularly "friends" and "reasonable shares," but I think it fair to conclude that Terry did not much care what was done with his very limited property. Further, the most crucial instructions, those on which writings to publish and which to destroy, leave room for much interpretation: I am to destroy writings that are "incomplete" or "unfinished," yet I must judge the completeness of each work not by my own relatively classical sense of "shape," but with due regard for Terry's modernist tendency to leave deliberately frayed ends—to "let fracture be."

Yes, these are vague instructions, but as we tell our law students, or at least as we should, vagueness (unlike irony or ambiguity) has its legitimate and indeed essential uses in serious legal drafting; vague words, like those of the United States Constitution, can grant the people subject to them flexibility to deal intelligently with new and unforeseen situations. Terry did not want to tie my hands with mechanically precise instructions about his manuscripts; he did not know what state his papers would be in when he died, and he trusted me to make reasonable judgments subject to the basic considerations he set down. These were certainly not contentless. Indeed, I am not happy about his instructions, for I would like to publish even those works that by Terry's own standards *are* incomplete. But the instructions are intelligible, coherent, and manageable—my calling them "crazy" in the earlier memo to you was a result of my failure, shocked and upset as I was, to read carefully and think clearly.

Now let me turn to the features of the will, including the more contextual ones, that might be thought to undercut testamentary intent. First, Terry put it in a file marked "Hermeneutics," kept with other subject-matter files, rather than among his business and financial records. I think the placement of the will in such a file, especially as the only item in the file, was simply Terry's way of emphasizing to me that he wanted me to interpret the will in the light of our debates about interpretation, or "hermeneutics."

The fact that the paper had been crumpled does suggest that Terry may have doubted at one time whether to preserve this as a final version (we found no preliminary drafts).[15] In the end, though, he carefully smoothed out the paper and preserved it; surely it is understandable that he did not take the trouble of recopying the whole document in the uncharacteristically small, neat handwriting that would be required to fit it on a legal-size sheet of paper. (I place no significance on the words "the red bird" written on the reverse side of the paper. Perhaps he mistakenly used the page as a piece of scrap paper when it was lying face down.)

The marginal note at the bottom, referring to the holographic will section of the California Probate Code, is an obvious signal that Terry knew the poem had the legal form of a valid will. (Incidentally, section 102, to which Terry also refers in the same note, provides in pertinent part: "Of two modes of interpreting a will, that is to be preferred which will prevent a total intestacy.")[16]

What about the use of the word "Draft" in the title? The fact is that this term is appended to *every single one* of Terry's writings that I have found. Unless we are to assume that he meant them all to be

15. Professor McGarr did not raise the question of whether Conn's crumpling of the holograph might have constituted a revocation under § 74 of the California Probate Code, which provides that a will is revoked if is "burnt, torn, canceled, defaced, obliterated or destroyed, with the intent and for the purpose of revoking the same." CAL. PROB. CODE § 74 (West 1956).

16. CAL. PROB. CODE § 102 (West 1956). *See infra* note 27 for the text of the entire section.

considered incomplete, and thus to be destroyed—a conclusion his instructions negate by presuming that distinctions are to be drawn among his works—that word cannot be said to show a lack of intent to endorse the document as his final statement. His use of the word "Draft" is consistent with his admonition to me that writings of his that were left in what might strike me as open, unfinished form, may nevertheless be finished, as finished as they can be, by his standards—"let fracture be." As various remarks in his notebooks indicate, Terry was drawn to the view, apparently common among contemporary French writers, that the "work" (finished, closed, classical) should be replaced by the "text" (open, infinitely interpretable, fluid).[17] "Draft" may sometimes be a good word for "text" in this sense.

Now let me deal with the two things that at first quickly led me to conclude that this poem could not possibly have been meant as a will. First, of course, is the verse form itself; let me put off discussing that until I deal with the second feature, the apparently ironic sense of the thing. The most striking indication of this to me was the title, "Conning McGarr"; but ironic intent seems equally obvious from the poem's express challenge to me to try and carry out the principles of interpretation I had supported in my debates with Terry over the years. The message seemed to be the mocking one that if I tried to meet this challenge, I would inevitably fail, thus giving final, posthumous victory to Terry. The only other reading would be that Terry had somehow come to believe that I was right, that objective interpretation was a realistic possibility, a matter of finding "intent in words," and that he was conceding this to me and asking me to do, on his behalf, what he had always insisted couldn't be done.

The second reading seemed to me an impossible one. The poem is dated several months before Terry's sudden death, and in our discussions after that date there had been no indication of any change in Terry's position, or any slackening in the vigor with which he opposed me. Thus, the indication in the poem that this was my best chance to implement my theory, and that if I did so I would close our debate "conformant to" my "sober principles," seemed to be meant as a jab at me, one presupposing the impossibility of the task.

But I now see how the ironic reading ignores the language of the poem. The instructions are entirely serious in tone. There is no indication of irony (apart from the affectionate irony of line 25, and the ironi-

17. Professor McGarr informs me that the Conn notebooks refer to R. BARTHES, *From Work to Text*, in IMAGE-MUSIC-TEXT 155 (1977).

cally casual disposition of Terry's largely nonexistent material wealth, in lines 2-3). Read it: is its tone not one of challenge and serious entreaty? I should not have needed the jolt of Janet's threat to see this; I only needed to read, carefully, with open mind and heart. Consider what was at stake here from Terry's point of view. He could be a funny man, sometimes oddly and inappropriately so (as in the silly title he jokingly gave his autobiography), but he was deadly serious about his ideas and his writing. Think of the long hours he slaved to build this "hoard." He and Janet never began divorce proceedings; he knew she was legally his wife and might still be when he died. He knew how she felt about him, and about his later work. Is it likely that he meant to leave the disposition of his papers to her unguided mercies? And who is more suited than I to be the natural editor of his work—no self-praise intended, only the reminder that he talked about his ideas more with me than with everyone else put together?

To accept this reading, must I assume that in his will Terry is somehow recanting his long held position about interpretation? The last several hours of reading and recollection have brought me to a kind of revelation on this point. As I read the long precatory part of the poem, it was as if I could hear myself talking, but in Terry's voice. The views are recognizably mine. He distinguishes (lines 13-16) between regarding texts as mere raw material for the interpreter's untrammeled creativity, and seeing them as the determinate expression of the author's intent through the public conventions of language—"mind's fixed intercept of lexicon." He then attributes the latter position to me in my own plainer speech (lines 17-18), and illustrates a point I often made in argument with him: that theories of the impossibility of objective interpretation (such as I have always attributed to Terry) are likely to have their genesis in the fact that in many interesting cases (Terry's will and his papers providing one) correct reading is very difficult. But these cases in which interpretation is difficult are to be contrasted with the easy ones—as when someone says "pass the salt" in an ordinary dinner table situation—by the presence of various identifiable factors. I was never able to summarize these factors quite as concisely as Terry has in the last lines of the poem: "Words mean. I mean. You, reading, want . . . ." To put it prosaically, there is, first, the problem of possible conflict between meaning as determined by public conventions of language, and meaning as determined by speaker's intent; and there is, second, the problem of distortions introduced by the interests of the reader or interpreter. Yet these are sources of difficulty—"traps"—not guarantors of impossibility.

How is this restatement of my views to be explained, if not as irony on the one hand, or (implausibly) as surrender on Terry's part to me on the other? The answer has come to me in reflection upon one strand of Terry's position, a strand he constantly reiterated to me, but which I have never before really come to terms with. Terry always resisted my describing our debate as one between an "objective" and a "subjective" theory of interpretation. He would say that these terms were familiar ways of talking about our differences, but they brought along a lot of metaphysical freight he didn't want to carry. (He would then quickly get too deep for me.)

More illuminating to me now is what Terry would say when I raised my favorite argument, which I got from the literary theorist Hirsch. People who deny that utterances have an objective meaning that is "in" them to be discovered by the interpreter are just as vehement as anyone else about condemning their critics for "misreading" or "misinterpreting" their writings—thus contradicting themselves.[18] When I made this argument, Terry would say "there you go, misinterpreting me again"—and when I asked for something more than this cute paradox, he said things I never understood. Or when I understood him, as when he talked of words as counters and of statements as moves in a game, it seemed to me he was just talking about the need to take context into account in determining the speaker's or author's intent—something I had never denied. He got me to read Derrida on "inhabiting the structures we deconstruct."[19] But to me, all of that was just sophism designed to allow the half-hearted skeptic to say something and then hedge: "I don't really mean what I say." Terry denied this, saying Derrida was not a "giggler" (his word for people who take skeptical positions, giggle in self-congratulation, and go on as before). Well, if these words were not meant simply as a hedge, were they not then just dressed-up public relations advice—to get the swing voters you have to speak their lingo? In a way that was true, Terry once said,

18. E.D. Hirsch, The Aims of Interpretation 6, 91 (1976).

19. "The movements of deconstruction do not destroy structures from the outside. They are not possible and effective, nor can they take accurate aim, except by inhabiting those structures. Inhabiting them *in a certain way*, because one always inhabits, and all the more when one does not suspect it. Operating necessarily from the inside, borrowing all the strategic and economic resources of subversion from the old structure, borrowing them structurally, that is to say without being able to isolate their elements and atoms, the enterprise of deconstruction always in a certain way falls prey to its own work. This is what the person who has begun the same work in another area of the same habitation does not hesitate to point out with zeal. No exercise is more widespread today and one should be able to formalize its rules."

J. Derrida, Of Grammatology 24 (1976) (emphasis in original).

but he added "we have met the swing voters and they are us." More cleverness without real answers, from my perspective.

Another aid he called in to try to explain things to me was Borges' story "Pierre Menard."[20] He said: "when you say someone is misinterpreting, you speak as Cervantes; when I say it, I speak as Pierre Menard." I read the story, thought it clever but baffling, and still didn't grasp his point; it seemed that Borges, too, was talking about saying something in scare-quotes, and anyway, wasn't Pierre Menard an ironist?[21] Yet Terry and his fellow subjectivists could complain angrily and quite without irony that they were being misinterpreted.

Now, just in the last few hours, I believe that I finally understand what Terry meant. He could protest against misinterpretation, seriously and angrily—of course he could; I have heard him do it many times. How could anyone live in our world, constituted of language as it is, and *not* talk in these terms? In just the same way, he could ask me, seriously and sincerely, to interpret his words accurately, regarding them as "mind's fixed intercept of lexicon."

At the same time, he could protest against my views, which I always phrased in terms of the possibility of this very kind of interpretation. What he was arguing to me through our long afternoon debates was that these rhetorical structures, of "objective interpretation" or whatever, were by now wholly problematical, that I could no longer just assume their viability. On the other hand, he would not claim that these very rhetorical structures—the same ones that he used in his will—no longer existed, or could simply be bypassed or ignored. Queer dying anachronistic structures that they were, they remained the only ones around. He hoped some day they would be replaced, but that would be a historical and collective achievement, not the gesture or act of some individual like himself. He always resisted the notion that individuals could just opt out of cultural forms, imagining themselves to exist as individuals apart from their culture—he used to say that that was the great Protestant fallacy.

20. J. BORGES, *Pierre Menard, Author of the* Quixote, in LABYRINTHS 36 (D. Yates & J. Irby eds. 1964). Borges' fable tells of Pierre Menard, an early twentieth century French Symbolist who made it his project to write *Don Quixote*: "not . . . another *Quixote*—which is easy—but *the* Quixote *itself*. Needless to say, he never contemplated a mechanical transcription of the original . . . ." *Id.* at 39 (emphasis in original).

21. The narrator of Borges' story speaks of Menard's "resigned or ironical habit of propagating ideas which were the strict reverse of those he preferred." *Id.* at 42.

I remember him telling me that he and Janet had been married by an Anglo-Catholic Episcopal minister in a religious ceremony, though he was a renegade Catholic and she was an unbelieving Jew. None of the available forms really fitted their case; they thought the purely civil forms conveyed the wrong sense of marriage. He said he still thought of it more as a sacrament than as a legal status or contract. Of course he would have argued against all the minister's religious doctrines, just as he argued with what I said about interpretation. I think I am his minister in this case, and he is an unbeliever asking me to serve him in God's name. There are many ironies in such an invocation, but not the kind of self-contradiction that cancels the message and renders the whole thing a mockery.[22]

Peter, reading back over these paragraphs I despair at how opaque they must seem. Terry, a master of language, had years to make this point to me, an intent listener, and yet I never got it until now. I will have to struggle hard in the days and years to come to make myself clearer. Terry could accept pretty insouciantly that being understood is not a matter of effort, good will, or skill in explaining; people either get points or they don't. I can't accept that; what can be said can be said clearly—that is the Tao of George. But I see that I cannot now clearly explain "McGarr's epiphany" to you—what will I ever do if I have to explain this to a judge?

But I must continue and finish. What about the title "Conning McGarr"? What can that mean except that Terry is putting one over on me? The answer is not difficult to find, especially when I read a passage by the poet Yvor Winters that Terry copied into one of his notebooks: "Poetry is a medium by means of which one mind may to a greater or lesser extent take possession of another, almost in the sense in which the term *possession* is used in demonology."[23] Terry wanted to use the poem to get his view across to me finally and forcibly, so that I could truly understand him in order to act for him; thus, "Conning McGarr." Argument alone had not worked; maybe poetry could do the job. And there, too, is the answer to the last interpretive objection: Why would he use verse to make a final disposition of his legacy? The answer is that he wanted to possess me, as I suppose every testator who gives other than mechanical instructions would like to possess his executor, and he thought verse the medium best suited to the task.

22. Professor McGarr later learned that Terence Conn and Janet Berg were in fact married by a judge.

23. Y. WINTERS, IN DEFENSE OF REASON 600 (1947).

In truth, Terry's poem could not do what he wanted it to do, not on its own. I'm not an experienced reader of poetry, but I imagine those who are will find it somewhat prosaic, somewhat lacking in possessory magic. It does speak very clearly to me now, but only after the shock administered by Janet's threat. As a poem, it probably is a bit too lawyerly, a little professorial; but on the other hand, why not—one law professor talking to another?

IV

Dear Peter,

Thank you truly for the heartfelt words of thanks; they mean a lot to me. Thank you too for the words of concern. I *have* been working long hours on this business. But it has never seemed a chore, only a fascinating challenge. As you know, I've always worked long hours, and especially so in recent months with Benjamin at college and Susan away in the hospital. It's good therapy, among its other rewards.

Peter, thank you too for your forebearance in the face of "McGarr's epiphany." When you say that you respect and accept what I decide though you do not fully understand what I say, your honesty makes your thoughtfulness all the more welcome. I do remain convinced that Terry meant the poem to be his last will and testament. It is true that the exalted feeling of revelation I recorded in writing to you during that long night in his office has faded a little in the light of common day—as I suppose is inevitable. I guess I would describe its residue as a subtle change in my attitude, a difference of degree in the way I look at the questions Terry and I debated: a more pragmatic view of language, a stronger sense of its rhetorical dimension, an enhanced suspicion of Platonic meanings, a feeling that talk about finding "intent in words" states a dilemma rather than a goal in many cases. But these theoretical matters should be reserved for more extensive treatment in calmer times.

Let me proceed in our now-established mode: me writing, for our future reference, some things you already know. When I first told Janet I had decided that it *was* Terry's will—the first morning after my "tower experience"—she was angry and incredulous.[24] "He really did con you." She insisted that she would go to court, contest the will; the money wouldn't matter to her even if there were any, but she would

24. After his famous "tower experience," Martin Luther wrote that "a totally other face of the entire Scripture showed itself to me." MARTIN LUTHER: SELECTIONS FROM HIS WRITINGS 11 (J. Dillenberger ed. 1961). Professor McGarr informs me that he and Terence Conn had read together and discussed the Reformation debates on Biblical hermeneutics.

fight to have "that self-indulgent garbage" destroyed. She would also pursue her community property claims on the papers.

My inspiration at this point was to urge her to read something of Terry's other than the painful chapters in the autobiography. At first she just raged: when she wanted to read literature or philosophy she knew where to go for it, and it wasn't to a dilettante law professor fleeing from his mid-life crisis. Terry was—the same litany—a liar and a coward. None of us knew him as she did. And so on.

But when I narrowed my urgings to get her to read his legal writings, to my surprise she agreed. It turned out the two draft articles had been a sore point with her; he had always refused to show them to her claiming they "weren't him." I had photocopies made for her to take home, so she wouldn't have to stay in his office to read.

The next day, she had changed her tone considerably. She thought the articles were good; they reminded her of a Terry she had forgotten. She conceded that, if she had the papers in her charge, she would want the legal writings published, if possible, to let people know that there had once been a "real Terry Conn." It turns out that she had even come to doubt that he had ever written *anything*; she wasn't here when he got tenure. She thinks of him as a dreadful liar, and tended to distrust anything he said.

I gave her my familiar (to you) pitch on the "lying." In my experience, Terry never lied to get a concrete benefit for himself, never made up things that put him in a better light. I call him a confabulator; he would imagine a story to illustrate a point of his or challenge someone else's, but would lose control over its origin in his imagination, and would claim it really happened.[25] When I put that to Janet, she admitted that was usually how it was, but said that he also lied about his drinking, "like all drinkers." She said a further interesting thing: the drinking had been worse before he started his new line of work seven years ago, though (as you and I know) it by no means stopped afterwards.

Janet and I talked a long time that day, not just about the papers but about Terry generally. We broke off with her still talking about having the "literary" writing destroyed, but saying it with much less conviction. The next night we went out to dinner and had another long talk, the upshot of which was that she would not object to publication

25. Professor McGarr indicates that Conn often repeated Nietzsche's aphorism, "There are no facts, only interpretations."

of anything Terry wrote except the passages mentioning her in what she calls "his memoirs"; she did not want these published in her lifetime. If she could get a binding agreement to this effect, she would not contest the will.

I tried to press her further, pointing out that the passages put her basically in a good light, but she said she would feel violated if that material came out in print. It was hard enough for her to agree to their being preserved and possibly published after she died. But she had decided that it was superstitious to concern herself with what happened then; even if she ever had any children, she wouldn't object if they saw it—she just could not stand it for herself. In any case, she thinks I greatly overrate the likely interest in the "memoirs," and doesn't suppose there is any likelihood that there will be readers or a publisher for them after she dies, even if there is now—which she also doubts.

Peter, how can I insist on more than this from Janet? She has been honest and fair, and she has been much more openminded than I expected. (It has been hard for us to be in the position of bargaining adversaries, rather than as—what I feel we are—old friends renewing a relationship that had lapsed by an unhappy accident.)

What I propose to offer her is this agreement: She will promise not to oppose the will, and I will give her a veto over publication of the passages mentioning her, during her lifetime. The problem with this, of course, is the possible conflict with Terry's instructions. To me, there are two alternatives; keep the whole autobiography suppressed as long as she exercises her veto, or edit it to excise, temporarily, the passages mentioning her, for publication now. My own inclination would be to do the latter, on the grounds that now is "due time." On the other hand, I recognize the will's strictures against publication of any but complete works; and I would never argue that the autobiography minus the Janet passages was "complete." In a sense, what it comes down to is a choice of interpretive presumptions. Does the will absolutely prohibit publication of any but complete works? Or is this a principle to be accommodated with the principle of timely publication, at least in the special case of a work that one day will be available in complete form?

Of course I realize that these are not the only two alternatives. I *could* simply try to get the will probated and take Janet on, and if I won, the whole autobiography could be published now. (I should say I am inclined to think that though the book in a sense "breaks off," this is a case of "fracture" rather than one of "incompleteness" in the terms of the will.)

If I pressed the fight with Janet, I might win, but I could easily lose; I have not forgotten that my own first reaction was that it was crazy to think this poem could be a will. I see now that I was wrong, and maybe I could convince a judge (or a jury?), but maybe I couldn't. If I lost, the whole corpus would pass to Janet by intestacy. I do believe that in that case she would publish the legal writings, but after the bitterness of litigation, who knows what attitude she would take toward the literary writings? Her destroying or completely suppressing them is not out of the question.

Whether I can properly accept a compromise really turns on what the dominant intent of the will is: is it to get at least some of Terry's work out into the world, or is it to make sure that only finished work is seen? And I cannot put aside, even from the point of view of Terry's intent, the gruesome picture of Janet and me snarling over his remains in court.

There is one further consideration that cuts in favor of entering into a compromise with Janet now. If she has the security of a legal veto over the passages that bother her, I believe she might eventually come to see that publishing them would do her no harm. As long as she and I are talking to one another, there is a decent chance that her thoughts will keep moving in this direction; once we are adversaries in litigation though, that is unlikely. If I can involve Janet to some degree as a collaborator in the work of editing Terry's papers, perhaps her sense of him as only a source of pain will lessen; perhaps she will even come to care that he be presented to the world in his best light.[26]

I mention this because, in a way, this process has already begun in the course of our talks. To get off the painful subject of the autobiography, I described to her some of my general problems in applying the will to the papers. What should I do with the fact that all of them are marked "draft"; and that none of them have clear-cut endings in the usual sense? I cannot simply mechanically invoke "let fracture be" to publish everything Terry wrote; *he* obviously thought there were choices to be made between finished and unfinished works. I am not to be cowed by "the insistent literate" to push works he would have regarded as "unfinished" into the world. Obviously I need (what I have

26. For Professor McGarr's account of his unfolding resolution of this dilemma, see McGarr, *supra* note 11.

already mentioned) an overall presumption in favor of publication on the one hand or suppression on the other.

During this conversation, Janet pointed out to me something that I had not noticed. You recall the scribbled note below the poem: "Cal. Prob. Code Ann. 53, 102(1)." In researching that note, I had paid little attention to section 102, startled as I was by section 53. Later I made some reference to section 102, which does state a presumption in favor of "that mode of interpretation which will prevent a total intestacy." Janet, the careful tax lawyer, asked me about the reference of the parenthesized "(1)": did the section have subsections?

This got me to take another look at section 102. There are no numbered subsections in it; it is made up of a single sentence, with two clauses divided by a semicolon, the *second* of which is the presumption against intestacy I quoted earlier. Perhaps "102(1)" was meant to refer specifically to the *first* clause, which reads: "The words of a will are to receive an interpretation which will give to every expression some effect, rather than one which will render any of the expressions inoperative."[27]

What could Terry have meant by stressing this boilerplate interpretive maxim? It is certainly a principle of literary criticism that in a poem every word is supposed to count. So I went back over the text again, focusing on phrases I had passed over as obscure, or as mere rhetorical or rhythmic filler. There are a number of phrases whose full import escape me; for example, "plain as can be" in line 6. But the one phrase that had struck me before and still struck me as completely enigmatic was the address to me as "my Scottish breadman" in line 11. "Scottish," sure, but what is "breadman" about?

In our next talk, I described to Janet the line of thought her suggestion had triggered. Did she make anything of the "breadman" reference? We batted it around for a few minutes, but couldn't come up with much beyond an implication of homely simplicity in "bread." Then we got back to what by then we were calling our "settlement conference." Only a few minutes of that had gone by when she suddenly interrupted me to ask, "Max Brod?" When I asked her what she meant, she said, "The baker. Brod sounds like German for bread. He

27. The entire text of § 102 reads: "The words of a will are to receive an interpretation which will give to every expression some effect, rather than one which will render any of the expressions inoperative; and of two modes of interpreting a will, that is to be preferred which will prevent a total intestacy." CAL. PROB. CODE § 102 (West 1956).

is calling you his Scottish Max Brod. Didn't Kafka leave his writings with Brod, and tell him to destroy them, but he didn't?"[28]

Well, it is a little far-fetched, but I haven't been able to give a better sense to the word "breadman." Terry was a great reader of Kafka, and I would guess he knew the Max Brod story. It's the only plausible reading I've got for "breadman," and Terry has told me to find a reading for every word. If he did have Brod in mind, I would read the phrase as suggesting to me the same basic presumption in favor of publication that Brod exercised. Terry might have obliquely suggested such a presumption rather than explicitly stating it to create some doubt in my mind, and prevent me from running wild with it. After all, a reference to Brod *could* be a caution rather than a license, though the placement and tone suggest otherwise.

Janet says I am being much too finicky about this. She sees Terry as having been driven by two contradictory urges: One, a terrible fear of facing judgment (possibly augmented by some neurotic association between finishing work, publishing, and dying), which prevented him from submitting anything for publication during his lifetime; but second, a powerful egotism that could only be satisfied by the conspicuous publication of every word he ever uttered. She sees the poem, and to her it is just a poem, as the completely ambivalent expression of these incompatible urges, not as a rational scheme for mediating or compromising them.

She puts great weight on the appeal he makes to *my* interests in lines 23-31. Terry there recognized that he would be dead and gone when the poem was read, and Janet sees him as surrendering the final word to me—me not as his literal legal executor, but as the personification of his readership. This means that I should use his writings for my own purposes, in the way readers always have the last word in their dialogues with writers. Together with the earlier reference to Max

28. *See* Brod, *Postscript to the First Edition*, in F. KAFKA, THE TRIAL 326 (W. Muir & E. Muir trans. 1937). Brod says "I wrested from Kafka nearly everything he published by persuasion or guile." *Id.* at 326. Kafka applied "the highest religious standard to his art," a standard that was "too high." *Id.* at 327. This was the background against which Brod read a note to him written in Kafka's hand, found on his desk at his death: "Dearest Max, my last request: Everything I leave behind me . . . [is] to be burned unread." *Id.* at 328. Brod said he had "good and sufficient reasons" for violating these instructions. *Id.* at 329. Among other things, Kafka had earlier told Brod that destruction of his manuscripts would be his last wish, and Brod had replied that he would never do such a thing. "The whole conversation was conducted in the jesting tone we generally used together, but with the underlying seriousness each of us took for granted in the other." *Id.* at 330. Finally, Brod admits that he would never have destroyed the unpublished writings, which included THE TRIAL and THE CASTLE, however unequivocal he thought his friend's last wishes. *Id.* at 332.

Brod, she thinks that that passage expresses, consciously or unconsciously, the side of him that gives himself into the hands of his future readers hoping that they will make him into another Kafka, whose every surviving word will be read—while he can retain the fastidious modesty of a writer who never submitted a word for publication.

I can't see it that way myself. Perhaps if it were just a poem, that would be the most interesting reading, and for that reason, in some sense, the right reading. As a poet, Terry meant to be interesting. But to me, it is more than a poem; it is Terry's will. We owe him something more than the most interesting reading.[29] I can't "mean away" his "say" in the name of intriguing and admittedly plausible suspicions about his unconscious wishes, or projections from his sense of aesthetic value. I have to stick closer to the words.[30]

The only way to treat the will as a consistent set of instructions is to see it as creating a complex agency relation, McGarr Conned. Terry was addressing *me*, George McGarr, "grave George," the man of the "sober principles," the somewhat overconscientious "conscience of [his] afternoons." At the same time, he did want me to grasp his way of seeing things better than I had while he was alive; that was why he tried to possess me; that is the point of the title "Conning McGarr." But he didn't want me to *become* him (Pierre Menard decided not to *become* Cervantes[31]). If I were to identify fully with him and his intentions, it would necessarily be with his limitations; then, neurotically paralyzed like him, I would never publish any of his work. He wanted me to "fuse my horizons" with his, not to narrow my own.[32]

Even if Terry was in some sense the contradictory mess of a modern man Janet says he was, he wanted to be treated as better and more coherent, and he had a right to be so treated. I think the California

29. In connection with this statement, Professor McGarr draws my attention to E.D. Hirsch's dictum: "All understanding of verbal meaning is necessarily genre-bound." E.D. HIRSCH, VALIDITY IN INTERPRETATION 76 (1967).

30. Section 105 of the California Probate Code provides: "[W]hen an uncertainty arises upon the face of a will, as to the application of any of its provisions, the testator's intention is to be ascertained *from the words of the will*." CAL. PROB. CODE § 105 (West 1956) (emphasis added).

31. Borges' narrator tells us that Pierre Menard rejected, after some preliminary experiment, the method of trying, by historical reconstruction, to "*be* Miguel de Cervantes."

> To be, in the twentieth century, a popular novelist of the seventeenth, seemed to him a diminution. To be, in some way, Cervantes and reach the QUIXOTE seemed less arduous—and, consequently, less interesting—than to go on being Pierre Menard and reach the *Quixote* through the experiences of Pierre Menard.

J. Borges, *supra* note 20, at 39.

32. The reference is to Hans-Georg Gadamer's theory of text interpretation; for "horizon-fusion" see H. GADAMER, TRUTH AND METHOD 267-74 (1975).

Probate Code gives me my marching orders, in a provision Terry didn't cite, section 103—a profound moral statement, if its word "will" is expanded beyond its technical legal sense: "All the parts of a will are to be construed in relation to each other, and so as, if possible, to form one consistent whole. . . ."[33]

What do you think of all this?

George

33. Section 103 reads in full:

> Where the meaning of any part of a will is ambiguous or doubtful, it may be explained by any reference thereto, or recital thereof, in another part of the will. All the parts of a will are to be construed in relation to each other, and so as, if possible, to form one consistent whole; but where several parts are absolutely irreconcilable, the latter must prevail.

CAL. PROB. CODE § 103 (West 1956).

[7]

INTERPRETING THE LAW: HERMENEUTICAL AND POSTSTRUCTURALIST PERSPECTIVES

DAVID COUZENS HOY*

I. HERMENEUTICS AND JUDICIAL REVIEW

Hermeneutics is the field of philosophy most concerned with investigating the nature of understanding and interpretation. Hermeneutic philosophers usually engage in constructing theories that will be sufficiently general to account for all kinds of interpretation, and thus of understanding as a single phenomenon, just as epistemologists aim at giving an account of knowledge per se. Unlike epistemology, however, hermeneutics cannot assume from the start that different kinds of interpretation will have any more than the vaguest family resemblance to one another. Ever since Kant, epistemologists have taken one particular area of knowledge, the natural sciences, as paradigmatic of all other areas of knowledge, so that accounting for the possibility of scientific knowledge is the major part of the epistemological task. Hermeneutics, in contrast, has been more preoccupied with procedures for understanding and interpreting in the historical or human sciences than in the physical sciences. Since the various historical and humanistic disciplines appear to differ from one another as much as they differ from the natural sciences, a central question is whether these disciplines share a common conception of understanding and interpretation. A further question is whether the procedures they use for understanding and interpretation are rigorous enough to be called scientific, or whether normative (moral, aesthetic, or political) commitments relativize the conclusions reached with these procedures.

The best tack for hermeneutical philosophy, then, is not to start, as epistemology does, by legislating *a priori* a method that any discipline must follow if it is to count as rigorous science. Instead, hermeneutics must take seriously the self-understanding of practitioners of various disciplines, and scrutinize those particular disciplines to see how under-

* Professor of Philosophy, Department of Philosophy, University of California, Santa Cruz. B.A. 1965, Ph.D. 1972, Yale University.

standing and interpretation really work. As a result, hermeneutics must be modest about what it can do for the practical disciplines themselves. It will not be able to "lay foundations" to help disciplines overcome methodological crises as, for instance, Husserl hoped transcendental phenomenology would be able to do for all the sciences. Unlike epistemology, hermeneutics cannot decide in advance what interpretation is and then tell interpreters what they are doing, whatever the interpreters may think they are doing. Taking the interpreters' self-understanding seriously does not mean, however, that hermeneutics cannot find inconsistencies in that self-understanding. Most of the historical sciences are divided by conflicting accounts of what the best methods are. Philosophical hermeneutics may try to clarify these debates about method, but it should not expect to lead to a total change in the empirical practices of the discipline.

I have noticed that the word "interpretation" is used in recent literature on judicial review in a way that runs contrary to hermeneutical theory, particularly Hans-Georg Gadamer's. Hermeneutics is usually opposed to epistemological, although not necessarily to legal, positivism, and claims against the latter that a sharp distinction cannot be drawn between understanding the text in its own terms and reading the interpreter's concerns into it. Some hermeneutical theorists, such as the Italian jurisprudent Emilio Betti or the American literary critic E.D. Hirsch, follow an older tradition by distinguishing a first operation, the cognitive act of understanding or explicating a text's meaning, from a second, the normative interpretation of a text's significance. The second operation is then distinguished in turn from a third, the reproductive application of that sense to a specific situation, one that is similar in some respects but different in others. These theorists insist that these operations are distinct from one another and maintain that any attempt to conflate them will undermine the objectivity of understanding and lead to relativism or nihilism. To underscore the objectivity of understanding they need to specify, of course, what the object of understanding is in the first operation. They think there must be, in principle, only one right reading of any given text, and they specify that what makes a reading the right one is whether it captures the intention of the author or authors.

In contrast, Gadamer does not rely on a theory of meaning that equates textual meaning with speaker's intention. Since what a person really says is often different from what the person intended, Gadamer's theory takes the process of understanding what a text means to be different from the way Hirsch and Betti construe it. To understand is to grasp the relevant context that determines the possible parameters of the sentence or expression. Unlike the intentionalist theory that bases objectivity on the possibility of determining the intention, this theory links objectivity with determining the appropriate context.[1] Intentionalists object to Gadamer's theory, arguing that whether a context is appropriate depends too much on the purposes of the interpreter, and is thus too variable and relative. Gadamer's line of reply is twofold. First, he agrees that the objectivity of interpretation will be undermined if determining the context depends on the arbitrary, conscious volitions or decisions of the reader. Although recent reader-based or "reception" theories owe much to Gadamer, they are more psychological than his, at least as I interpret his work.[2] Theories stressing the reader's intentions rather than the author's seem to imply that the reader can consciously decide textual meaning by arbitrarily altering the context. Gadamer's reply depends instead on a second and deeper claim: that the context itself conditions the reader's grasp of the text, not the other way around. Furthermore, the context is historical in that it changes over time with changes in the conditions influencing various readings. This insistence on historical variation in interpretation is not in the least subjectivistic or voluntaristic. On the contrary, the position entails that the reader is not completely free to decide the meaning of the text. The text is already determinate enough, for instance, to narrow the range of possible contexts. Thus, the text must seem to the reader to resist willful misreading, or on rereading, to correct initial misunderstandings. Moreover, if the reader knows earlier interpretations of the text, the text will itself seem to be correcting what now

1. The difference here is illustrated by some advice to historians from Thomas Kuhn, who attributes his sudden break from standard historiography of science to his "discovery of hermeneutics":

> When reading the works of an important thinker, look first for the apparent absurdities in the text and ask yourself how a sensible person could have written them. When you find an answer, . . . when those passages make sense, then you may find that more central passages, ones you previously thought you understood, have changed their meaning.

T. KUHN, THE ESSENTIAL TENSION: SELECTED STUDIES IN SCIENTIFIC TRADITION AND CHANGE xii (1977).

2. See my discussion of some reception theories of literary interpretation in D. HOY, THE CRITICAL CIRCLE: LITERATURE, HISTORY, AND PHILOSOPHICAL HERMENEUTICS (1978). In this book I argue in detail that Gadamer's theory is not relativistic and that Hirsch's criticisms of Gadamer are mistaken. Since there I attack Hirsch's intentionalism, here I take legal hermeneutics in a different direction than does Simeon C.R. McIntosh, who defends intentionalism in McIntosh, *Legal Hermeneutics: A Philosophical Critique*, 35 OKLA. L. REV. 1 (1982).

clearly appear to be misreadings, even though they did not appear to be so at the time.

Because of the historical character of understanding, then, there can be no sharp separation between the three operations identified by the intentionalist theorists. Understanding is always already interpretation, Gadamer maintains, and interpretation is always already application. If legal scholars currently debating judicial review are right, however, legal adjudication does not fit into Gadamer's theory. The debates suggest that judges often go "beyond interpretation" and make their decisions on the basis of value judgments not contained in the statutes.[3] Condoning this practice tends to make one a noninterpretivist, while condemning it pushes one into interpretivism. Many of those who disagree about the legitimacy of this practice seem to agree nevertheless that going beyond interpretation is an observable feature of judicial review, and that the distinction between interpretive and noninterpretive review is a distinction in kind and not simply one of degree. On Gadamer's theory, if there is an observable distinction at all, it should be merely one of degree. A deliberate, conscious break with tradition or precedent could (or at least should) occur only when the precedent appears to be a clearly mistaken reading (perhaps for historically explainable reasons) of the original language.

The question I will pursue in the first Part of this Article, then, is whether Gadamer is wrong about what judges really do (which may be different from what they say they do). Alternatively, are theorists like Betti and Hirsch right to think that three distinct operations are usually discernible in the interpretation of the law, and thus that the objective correctness of the first operation (the understanding and exegesis) can be assessed independently of the appropriateness and legitimacy of the others? In the second Part of the Article I will move from the question of how interpretation is possible to that of whether conflicts of interpretation can be rationally adjudicated. Gadamer's hermeneutical theory has the consequence that interpretation inevitably involves normative questions. Legal interpretation, for instance, would always be permeated by political commitments and social philosophy. Do these commitments mean, then, that disagreements will not be resolved, or even rationally discussed? The answer depends on how "rationality" is con-

3. I take the phrase "beyond interpretation" from Grey, *Do We Have an Unwritten Constitution?*, 27 STAN. L. REV. 703, 715 (1975). Michael Perry's definition of interpretive and noninterpretive judicial review sets up a distinction in kind and not merely in degree. M. PERRY, THE CONSTITUTION, THE COURTS, AND HUMAN RIGHTS 11 (1982).

ceived, and I will argue that there are better and worse conceptions of the rationality required by a theory of understanding.

A. The Gadamer-Betti Debate

The exchange between Gadamer and Betti includes points similar to those arising among American constitutional theorists on the issue of noninterpretive review. I would like to consider that exchange to explain not only why, on Gadamer's theory, the distinction between interpretive and noninterpretive review cannot be clear-cut, but also why there are limits on what can count as legitimate interpretation. I recognize, of course, that some legal theorists think the distinction is not so clear, and that how the distinction is drawn depends on the theorist's commitment. I find the books by John Hart Ely and Michael Perry especially instructive.[4] In *Democracy and Distrust*, Professor Ely suggests that his own view could be located somewhere between interpretivism and noninterpretivism since both these theories are inadequate.[5] If I understand the exchange correctly, Perry defends noninterpretivism by first defending interpretivism against Ely's charge that if interpretivism applies itself to the Constitution it turns out not to be what the Constitution requires. Perry thinks interpretivism is not "hoist by its own petard," as Ely claims,[6] but wrong for other reasons, and he then classifies Ely as an interpretivist (which Ely allows is possible, although he prefers the "between" position). Generalizing from this use of the labels for the differing perspectives, I suspect that noninterpretivists will see Gadamer's theory, with its emphasis on the tradition-bound character of understanding, as interpretivist, whereas interpretivists will see it as noninterpretivist because of its insistence on the continual need for new interpretations.

Finally, neither label will neatly fit the hermeneutical discussion since the issue there is less about how interpreters should proceed than about what interpretation is like for any interpreter, taking into account the fact that different interpreters will disagree about substantive doctrine. Gadamer thinks Betti misdescribes the phenomenon of legal interpretation when Betti asserts a distinction in kind between the interests of the judge and those of the legal historian. This distinction depends on the claim that the legal historian can entirely forget the

4. J. Ely, Democracy and Distrust: A Theory of Judicial Review (1980). M. Perry, *supra* note 3.

5. J. Ely, *supra* note 4, at 12.

6. *Id.* at 43.

present when researching laws still in force and reconstitute the original meaning of the legal formula, preferably by ascertaining the intentions of the legislators. Betti thus has an "objectivist" picture of the historian's enterprise. In contrast to the historian, the judge starts with a current case and asks what the law requires now, in what is a new and probably unforeseen situation. What the judge does is to take the historical account and then in a separate conceptual operation apply it to the present. But this act of application is not arbitrary or relative. The judge's judgment about the meaning of the law now is valid or correct because it is based on an equally correct understanding of the original meaning of the law. Betti's objectivist account of historical interpretation is thus complemented by an objectivist account of legal interpretation. Since I do not wish to do Betti's detailed theory an injustice, I will refer simply to a broadly objectivist picture and not to his view. As described so far, this picture should be clear enough to debate while at the same time sufficiently general to include a variety of positions (for instance, legal positivism, but also recent nonpositivistic variants of interpretivism).

Gadamer disagrees with the objectivist pictures of both the legal historian and the judge. The historical changes between the original and the present contexts mediate the historian's perception, so that the historian cannot feign ignorance of the kinds of cases arising in the meantime. Why the task of looking back to the original context is significant is conditioned by present needs. In contrast to Betti, who takes the historian's activity as paradigmatic by making the judge's objectivity depend on the historian's objectivity, Gadamer sees the judge's activity as paradigmatic since the historian's understanding is not disinterested, but conditioned by present needs. But neither judges nor historians are simply free to read whatever they want into their perceptions of the present or the past. On the contrary, both present needs and the history of legal interpretation condition and delimit their interpretation in ways that they do not consider arbitrary. In sum, for Gadamer, understanding always presupposes a tradition.[7]

B. The Interpretivist-Noninterpretivist Debate

While this disagreement between Gadamer and Betti is not the same as that between American interpretivists and noninterpretivists, I think there are common issues. I cannot say whether noninterpretive review ought to be acknowledged as a procedure legitimated by the

7. H. Gadamer, Truth and Method 293-94 (1975).

Constitution. Instead, I am interested in asking whether interpretive review is not itself always conditioned by the needs and interests of the present. In other words, if the interpreter can never draw a sharp line between where strict exegesis ends and the interpreter's own interests enter, then there is no sharp line between, on the one hand, a reading of the statutes that is absolutely certain no extrinsic factors have been interpolated, and on the other, one that believes itself to be a correct interpolation even if underdetermined by the evidence.

Why do I say "underdetermined"? Hermeneutical philosophers are much impressed by the argument that no reading of a text with any complexity is completely determined by all the available evidence.[8] At the same time, readings are overdetermined in that factors not explicitly stated in the text inevitably condition the reading in ways that nevertheless cannot be eliminated without substantial loss. That such factors do condition the reading will cause debates about whether they are intrinsic or extrinsic to the text. But this conflict between interpreters does not entail that a purely intrinsic reading is possible. Reader *A* can accuse reader *B* of forcing an obviously extrinsic factor into the reading without believing at the same time that *A*'s own interpretation is a purely internal reconstruction of the text. Reader *A* may simply believe that there is no good reason to suspect *A*'s reading of distorting the text in implausible ways while there is now good reason to suspect that *B*'s reading does distort it in a specifiable way. We may believe in general that our own interpretations involve factors unique to us, without knowing exactly what those factors are. Until someone can specify these factors, and presents an alternative reading, we can still believe that our own particular readings are the right ones. Moreover, we may have to believe that they are correct if we lack plausible alternatives.

The intrinsic-extrinsic distinction cannot be stipulated *a priori.* Since the special concern in this paper is with written texts and not with ordinary speech acts, the author's intention, or "utterance meaning," is not determinative of what counts as intrinsic. Constitutional interpretation has a special kinship with the interpretation of literary works since there is no direct access to the author's or framers' intention. The interpreter wants to understand what the *text* means, and this "textual meaning," as I shall call it, is not necessarily equivalent to the psychological intentions of the author.[9] The author of a literary work has no

8. For a similar discussion of underdetermination, see Schauer, *An Essay on Constitutional Language*, 29 UCLA L. REV. 797 (1982).

9. In Munzer & Nickel, *Does the Constitution Mean What It Always Meant?*, 77 COLUM. L.

more privileged access to the textual meaning than any reader, and the author's self-interpretations do not define the boundaries of intrinsic interpretation. The textual meanings and the author's psychological intentions are not immediate givens; both are something the interpreter must reconstruct. The former meanings are those which really should concern the interpretation of literature. I am also persuaded by constitutional theorists who argue that intention is not determinative of the meaning of constitutional phrases or statutes because it is the textual meaning that is voted on and ratified, not the psychological intentions of the writers.[10] Writers are themselves readers of their texts, and that they rewrite various drafts shows that they recognize the potential autonomy of the written text. Of course, a fundamental hermeneutical tenet is that there is no such thing as the "text-in-itself," independent of any particular reading or interpretation. As a result, hermeneutics does not have the same problem as epistemology with the question whether there are mind-independent "things-in-themselves." A text only comes to be in a reading, that is, in an act of understanding and interpretation.

The difficulty that arises in interpreting written language is that the range of possibilities for textual meaning is greater than for speaker's meaning. However, a point I will be arguing later but wish to stress now is that the range should not be exaggerated. Some poststructuralist, deconstructionist theorists imply that the range is infinite. In practice, though, an interpreter will consider only a small number of different possible interpretations; two, three, or four is more likely. Of course, facing two conflicting interpretations is problematic enough. Someone could argue that hermeneutical theory cannot explain cases such as those where, for instance, a judge, somewhat like King Solo-

---

REV. 1029 (1977), Stephen R. Munzer and James W. Nickel use a distinction between utterance meaning, or the sense a statement has when uttered by a particular speaker on a particular occasion, and language meaning, the senses a statement could have in a given language. What I am calling "textual meaning" is closer to language meaning, except that "textual meaning" includes only those senses a statement could have in the context allowed by the complete text and the history of its reception. I am contrasting textual meaning with the psychological intention of the speaker or writer, not necessarily with what speech act theorists refer to with their technical, linguistic term "intention." Like Munzer and Nickel, I would not equate "constitutional meaning" with "utterance meaning."

10. *See id.*; *see also* Dworkin, *How to Read the Civil Rights Act* (Book Review), THE NEW YORK REVIEW OF BOOKS 37 (December 20, 1979). In Fiss, *The Varieties of Positivism*, 90 YALE L.J. 1007, 1012 (1981), Owen M. Fiss argues more generally against John Austin's equation of law and will (the will being that which has an intention), and for thinking of law as answering to reason rather than to the will of the sovereign. Perry's argument that we should forget the framers goes too far. *See* M. PERRY, *supra* note 3, at 75. We should not forget the history of interpretation, which includes the framers' interpretation among others, and which forms and therefore should inform our present interpretations.

mon, is confronted with at least two equally compelling alternatives and must choose between them. I hope this model is rarely if ever true. If it is, then interpretation becomes simply an arbitrary, capricious decision. Both this model of interpretation and the type that would base a decision procedure on an algorithm or a regulative ideal like the author's intention seem equally mistaken as phenomenological descriptions of the process of understanding and interpreting. Understanding is not adequately construed if involving only a set of beliefs and some formulatable rules for combining and applying these beliefs. Understanding includes some nonpropositional content that is more properly described as an ability than as a rule. Skills are one such aspect of understanding, but there are also cognitive abilities such as recognizing violations of rules in different situations. These abilities cannot themselves be reduced to rules, but involve practical capacities, the lack of which would be called a lack of understanding.[11] In contrast to the voluntaristic, decisionistic model of understanding, what really happens in the process of interpretation is that, first, there seems to be no obvious algorithm or decision procedure; second, there are competing factors that need to be taken into account; but, third, a line of interpretation finally emerges that convinces the interpreter that that interpretation weighs the competing factors as equitably as possible and, therefore, is the best explanation possible of how competing claims are to be understood and evaluated.

The objectivistic objection to this hermeneutic line is that in no discipline is the "best explanation" necessarily the *right* or *true* interpretation. An interpreter could give what seemed at the time the best explanation, but when new data challenged the adequacy of the explanation, the interpreter would have to admit there was a genuine question as to whether the initial interpretation was the correct one. This admission would be at the same time an acknowledgment that "right" interpretation means more than "best explanation."

There are several lines of rebuttal to this objection that the best we can do does not necessarily give us the true account. One should note that explanation is not prediction, so the best explanation of a given set of data is not necessarily at the same time a prediction of what will be entailed by new data.[12] There may be an expectation that a similar

11. For further analysis of this point in the philosophical literature, see Hoy, *Hermeneutics*, 47 Soc. Research 649, 663 (1980).

12. Here I diverge from Gadamer, who claims that, in principle, correct legal reasoning predicts the judge's decision. H. Gadamer, *supra* note 7, at 294. Cases of explanation in science show the difference between explanation and prediction. As my colleague Richard Otte reminds

explanation will be able to account for that data too. Given the vagueness of the word "similar," it is often possible to extend the explanation in this way, although doing so may encumber the interpreters so much that they will look for another line of explanation.

The objection can be pressed that there are cases where the explanation says the fact of the matter is one way and it turns out to be different. Solomon's decision did not necessarily show who was the natural mother of the disputed child. This objection assumes, however, that there is only one possible question involved in such a case, so that the proffered explanation is the only possible answer. If the question in Solomon's case was who was the best mother (recognizing a normative and not just a biological sense of the term), then the outcome seems appropriate. Interpretations are not simply answers to given and agreed-on questions, but depend on formulating a complex of questions in such a way that it first becomes possible to see what the best answers are.

Finally, to the objection that even given all the data the interpreter is likely to get, there could be several contenders for "best explanation," so that there would still be a question of which one was "right," the hermeneutic reply is that "right" used in this way is vacuous. The thought that the best explanation under ideal circumstances is not necessarily the right account holds on to the objectivist assumptions that are at issue, and thus begs the question. In fact, the thought that our best confirmed theories may not correspond to the way things really are, may not be intelligible, since how the phrase "the way things really are" could be referring to anything is not clear.[13] The objection thus fails to force hermeneutic theorists to assume an objectivist conception of correct interpretation. But it does remind us of the possibility, given the underdetermination of theories by evidence, that there may be more than one explanation. What counts as "best" depends on the purposes of the interpretation, and even with the same purposes, the possibility of equally good explanations cannot be ruled out in advance. Again, however, until an alternative explanation is given, it cannot be

me, good predictions are not always good explanations, since from the length of a flagpole's shadow we could predict its height, but that would not explain its height. Also, we can explain events of low probability when they occur, but precisely because of their low probability we could not have predicted them reliably. That good explanations will always be good predictions is thus debatable. I am not using a hypothetical-deductive model of explanation, but a broader conception of best explanation as that inferential account of a phenomenon that maintains maximum coherence among my beliefs and practices.

13. *See* H. PUTNAM, REASON, TRUTH, AND HISTORY 1-21 (1981).

judged, so that in the absence of a genuine alternative there is sufficient reason to accept the available interpretation as the right one.

What happens, however, when a legal historian tells us that there is a conflict between the original meaning and the way later judges decided? Suppose we assume that Michael Perry is right that most current constitutional doctrine about freedom of expression, equal protection, freedom of religion, and the right to vote is the result of noninterpretive review, or at least of something more than strict and narrow reading.[14] To describe such a meaning change as "noninterpretive" implies that at some point judges willfully and arbitrarily added to the constitutional doctrine. Of course, if the judges know that their interpretations go beyond both the statutes and the precedents, then I suppose they should be candid. But the historical fact of meaning change does not necessarily entail noninterpretivism unless an exaggerated conception of rationality is assumed. To say that judges should have been more candid about their setting policy and not simply interpreting the text alleges in addition something akin to intellectual self-deception or dishonesty. Since noninterpretivists do not generally offer historical substantiations of this allegation, however, noninterpretivism remains incomplete as an account of the complexity of meaning change in interpretatons, and an alternative account is called for.

Hermeneutical theory makes such change more understandable and less reprehensible, although at the cost of blurring the distinction between interpretive and noninterpretive review. Since the judges' normative viewpoints are not sheerly volitional, but historically conditioned, it is not surprising if they fail to notice where the text stops and their own perspective takes over. Candor might not show what Perry thinks. Judges could be equally candid if they admitted that they lacked the self-knowledge necessary to be certain that their decisions were entirely noninterpretive. Acknowledgment that their solutions were not immediately evident from the text alone would not entail confessions of forcing the reading or inventing doctrine. To expect admis-

14. Perry's claim may depend, though, on an objectivist conception of the historian's task. If the historian's perception is itself conditioned by present interests, it is not a neutral fact-finding operation. Perry's claim that later constitutional doctrine "cannot plausibly be explained or defended in terms of the value judgments embodied by the framers," M. PERRY, *supra* note 3, at 92, is contested by David A.J. Richards' thesis that there is a continuity between the values of the framers and contemporary contractarian theorists such as himself and John Rawls. Historical spadework alone, however, will probably not resolve their conflict of interpretation. *See* Richards, *Human Rights as the Unwritten Constitution: The Problem of Change and Stability in Constitutional Interpretation*, 4 U. DAYTON L. REV. 295 (1979).

sions of noninterpretivism would be to ask for more than is rationally required.[15]

Central to hermeneutical theory, but most susceptible to the charge of historical relativism, is the thesis that the interpretation of a work is invariably conditioned by the prior history of the effects of that work. Any prior interpretation will count as part of that history, but other effects will also be influencing factors. It follows from this theory, for instance, that subsequent poets could not write the way they did unless previous poets had written in a certain way. Our perception of an earlier poet will therefore be conditioned by having read later poets as well. The history of the interpretation of poetry will thus evolve as the history of poetry itself evolves. (What counts as "the history" of either of these will also change, since that too is a historically-conditioned interpretation.) This history of the effects and reception of works and their interpretations is what Gadamer labels *Wirkungsgeschichte*, and the awareness of the earlier interpretations and their importance for the present interpretation is called *wirkungsgeschichtliches Bewusstsein* (a phrase I shall translate hereafter as "hermeneutical awareness").[16] Gadamer's view is that any interpretation is conditioned by a *Wirkungsgeschichte*, no matter how aware the interpreter is of this history (and Harold Bloom says the same for the poets themselves[17]). But the interpreter is better off knowing more about the conditioning effects than not knowing about them, so the more highly developed a hermeneutical awareness an interpreter has, the better.

C. Gadamer and Dworkin on Law and Literature

Increased hermeneutical awareness will lead to more attention to theoretical and normative commitments. These commitments may be the same in both the text and the interpretation, but they may also be different. I will discuss some problems about the rational adjudication of conflicts in the second Part of this Article, but for now I want to focus on the question whether interpretation is relativized by its own theoretical and normative commitments. Ronald Dworkin has argued

15. Perry himself remarks that a noninterpretivist judge can still candidly say that an action violated the Constitution. The judge thereby is presumably saying more than simply that the action violates the judge's personal values. On Perry's theory, what the judge means is that the action "contravenes the Court's developing equal protection doctrine." M. Perry, *supra* note 3, at 144 n. The emphasis here on the constitutive role of tradition, on the development of the doctrine in a continuous line, is compatible with the hermeneutical theory of understanding as conditioned by the history of intervening interpretations.

16. *See* H. Gadamer, *supra* note 7, at 267-74.

17. H. Bloom, The Anxiety of Influence: A Theory of Poetry (1973).

that legal interpretation is inevitably imbued with political commitments, and the interpretive procedures (such as looking or not looking for the framers' intentions) are politically laden.[18] He argues, as hermeneutical theorists also do, that there are significant analogies between legal and literary interpretation.

To bring out how I think that the relation of the interpretation to its normative commitments should be conceived, I should like to note a similarity and a difference between Gadamer's account of the interpretation of artworks and Ronald Dworkin's. Like Gadamer, Dworkin does not think that the theory of interpretation should say *a priori* what makes an interpretation true or false, sound or unsound, objective or subjective. In fact, whether the theory can ever say this at all is problematic, and will depend on the answer to the prior question, namely, what an interpreter must believe about the interpretation (and about interpretation in general) to believe it to be the best (or most plausible) interpretation.[19]

Dworkin and Gadamer thus agree on the phenomenology of interpretation, and on the role that criteria play within any interpretation. One thing that the interpreter will have to believe is that the interpretation is an interpretation and not a misinterpretation. To believe this, the interpreter must have some understanding of how to distinguish interpretation from misinterpretation (or interpretation from invention, or reading from "reading into," or finding from forcing), and must be aiming at the former rather than the latter. A minimal condition for something to count as an interpretation is that it rely on a way of making that distinction. *How* the interpreter makes this distinction can be criticized, of course, since the standards used to draw it may be too easy, vague, or slipshod. Some interpretations are therefore better than others, even if there is no general way to draw the distinction so that it will hold nontrivially for all possible interpretations.

Where Dworkin diverges from hermeneutics, and I think from the phenomenology of interpretation that he himself depicts, is in his claim about how aesthetic interpretation works. He states:

> My apparently banal suggestion (which I shall call the "aesthetic hypothesis") is this: an interpretation of a piece of literature attempts to show which way of reading (or speaking or directing or acting) the

18. *See* Dworkin, *Law as Interpretation*, in THE POLITICS OF INTERPRETATION 249 (W. Mitchell ed. 1983).

19. Dworkin, *My Reply to Stanley Fish (and Walter Benn Michaels): Please Don't Talk about Objectivity Any More*, in THE POLITICS OF INTERPRETATION 287, 289-90 (W. Mitchell ed. 1983).

> text reveals it as the best work of art. Different theories or schools or traditions of interpretation disagree, on this hypothesis, because they assume significantly different normative theories about what literature is and what it is for and about what makes one work of literature better than another.[20]

The striking fact about this assertion is that it states what literary interpretations do when one rarely finds interpretations that *say* they are interpreting the work to reveal it as the best artwork.[21] If Dworkin finds it significant that judges think of themselves as interpreting rather than inventing, then it would also be significant whether literary critics think of themselves as showing which reading reveals a text as the best artwork. Few if any critics spend much time arguing for a conception of the best artwork, or arguing that their interpretation makes the work the best artwork so conceived. Some critics might say simply that they leave this task to philosophers, but I suspect that they really think philosophical disputes about the nature of art and aesthetics are irrelevant to their enterprise.

Of course, Dworkin says only that critics "assume" such conceptions, so they need not be explicitly conscious of their particular conception. Nevertheless, I think Dworkin's aesthetic hypothesis misses a step. His hypothesis is misleading if it implies that the interpreter reads an aesthetic theory into the text, whether or not the text allows that aesthetic. By "allows" I mean that there may be respects in which the text excludes the interpreter's own aesthetic, perhaps by embodying a different one because of temporal or cultural distance. So the interpreter must first inquire into the work's own conception of itself as an artwork. Dworkin's aesthetic hypothesis is an important but different and further question, namely, whether when read in this way the work is the best artwork it can be. (There is yet a further question, as he is aware, about how good the work then is.) While there is some connection between the questions whether a reading is plausible and whether it maximizes the aesthetic value of the work (either on the work's own terms or on ours as well), these are distinguishable questions, with the first being prior to the second.

---

20. Dworkin, *supra* note 18, at 253.

21. I am making an empirical assertion here that could be disproved, hoping thereby to make Dworkin's suggestion less banal than he himself says it might seem. In support of my assertion I can cite Barbara Herrnstein Smith's opening statement in Smith, *Contigencies of Value*, 10 CRITICAL INQUIRY 1 (Sept. 1983), about the "exile of evaluation" from literary studies during the past fifty years: "I refer here to the fact not merely that the study of literary evaluation has been, as we might say, 'neglected,' but that the entire problematic of value and evaluation has been evaded and explicitly exiled by the literary academy."

Furthermore, although the fact that a particular reading maximizes the aesthetic value of the work might be a reason for preferring that reading over others, accepting it as the best reading has certain costs. If these costs are high enough, one might reject the maximally aesthetic reading in favor of other methodological criteria or normative commitments. These could be as trivial or as diverse as faithfulness to the maximal amount of detail; historical differences between aesthetic tastes; psychological or sociological or political doctrine; or a postmodern, deconstructionist theory that the ideal of the best artwork is to be abandoned altogether. Revealing the best artwork is only one factor in the interpretation of a text. Contrary to Dworkin's thesis, the aesthetic hypothesis is not always the decisive factor in practice, and in some interpretations where other normative considerations are more operative it may play little, if any, role.

Dworkin advances his hypothesis to show that politics forms a normative background for legal interpretation, just as aesthetics does for literary interpretation. He wants to model legal on literary interpretation, whereas Gadamer prefers to model literary on legal interpretation. Finally, there may be little disagreement here since the result is that there is no such thing as pure interpretation that is not shot through with normative and evaluative components.[22] As these components develop or change, so will the interpretation.

The advantage of Gadamer's preference for the legal paradigm over Dworkin's preference for an aesthetic one is that Gadamer's theory makes clearer why the value preferences preserved (whether implicitly or explicitly) in the interpretation are not optional or volitional. For Gadamer, literary interpretation is itself not purely aesthetic, since on his account there is always some real content at stake in the literary work. The interpreter's understanding of that content may be the same as the work's, the work's may deepen the interpreter's, or the inter-

22. Dworkin himself notices that there is no reason to think that the aesthetic theory is held prior to the theory of interpretation. The relation could be the reverse: "The point is so banal that it might as well be put the other way around: different theories of art are generated by different theories of interpretation." Dworkin, *supra* note 18, at 256. Gadamer's theory would prefer this ordering of the relation of hermeneutics and aesthetics since it sees aesthetic understanding as only one form of the more general phenomenon of understanding. *See* H. GADAMER, *supra* note 7, at 146. Furthermore, Dworkin also thinks evaluation is always implicated in interpretation:

> There is no longer a flat distinction between interpretation, conceived as discovering the real meaning of a work of art, and criticism, conceived as evaluating its success or importance. Of course some distinction remains because there is always a difference between saying how good a particular work can be made to be and saying how good it is. But evaluative beliefs about art figure in both these judgments.

Dworkin, *supra* note 18, at 256.

preter may profoundly disagree with the work. But for the hermeneutic theory there is a dimension of truth or meaningfulness in the literary work. In the history of aesthetics since Kant, what Dworkin calls the aesthetic hypothesis has led theorists to ignore or deny that dimension. That is why Gadamer takes legal hermeneutics as paradigmatic, since in this domain commitment to the ideal of a right (in the sense of either "true" or "just") outcome cannot be waived in the name of, for instance, poetic license. Gadamer does not think there is a unique kind of aesthetic experience that is detached, disengaged, subjective, and thus unlike other areas of experience more directly concerned with the world.

This strategy of taking the law rather than art as the paradigm of interpretation is seriously threatened, however, if judges are freer than literary critics to impose their own values on the texts. But if judges are not going beyond interpretation when they decide hard cases and if all cases are in some sense hard cases because there is never one that is exactly covered by the language of a particular law or rule,[23] then there is no point to saying legal interpretation is a matter of imposing values on texts.

In this respect, hermeneutic theory would agree with John Hart Ely's charge that Alexander Bickel's question about which values the court should vindicate is misconceived.[24] Ely's reasons depend on features of constitutional theory, but in general the process of interpretation is misdescribed if it is construed as a secondary imposition of values on a primary set of facts. Seeing the case as one to which the law applies at all is a matter of discerning the relevant features that are *objectively* involved and attempting to distinguish these from those that might be subjectively imposed. The "relevant features" cannot be broken down into objective facts on the one hand and subjective values on the other, so the fact-value distinction is not apt or useful in describing the process of interpretation at this level. Furthermore, hermeneutic theory would make it impossible to say that literary interpretations are more "subjective" or legal interpretations more "objective." To think of the text and its meaning as objective and the interpretation of that meaning as subjective is to presuppose an artificial cognitive-normative

23. Concerning what Gadamer calls the "concretisation of law," he suggests that all cases are special cases. Something like good taste is called for not only in aesthetic judgment, but also in moral and legal judgment. In such judgments, a particular case must be understood in its individuality and thus as more than simply a typical instance of a universal rule. *See* H. GADAMER, *supra* note 7, at 36-37.

24. *See* J. ELY, *supra* note 4, at 43-72.

distinction and to distort the phenomenon of understanding. Since the text comes to be only in an act of understanding, the distinction between the way it is "in itself" before being read and the way it appears in an interpretation is a false reification of the process of understanding.[25]

The normative dimension of interpretation becomes problematic in cases in which conflicting normative commitments produce conflicting readings. If theorists share the same interpretive practices and similar aesthetic or political views, rational arbitration of their differences seems possible. They could reasonably believe that a resolution could be rationally ascertained. When political, aesthetic, or philosophical differences enter, however, it becomes more difficult to prove that there is a right answer, and that conflicts can be decided rationally. Dworkin believes in the possibility of getting the correct answer in conflicts, even though he believes that the interpretations depend on political or aesthetic theories. He holds out the possibility of there being a correct answer because he further believes that aesthetic and political theories depend on underlying epistemological theories. I assume he then infers that since epistemological theories generally depend on the belief that there can be only one correct epistemology, all of these theoretical differences presuppose, at least in principle, the possibility of a correct answer to theoretical conflicts. Conflicts would thus be rationally resolvable.

Hermeneutical theory might well accept this conclusion, but not the reasoning behind it. Unlike epistemology, hermeneutics does not presuppose that there is always only one right interpretation, or that there is always a single correct answer to interpretive disputes. Nevertheless, hermeneutical theory maintains that interpretation is a rational procedure, and that interpretive problems can be rationally resolved. The nature of rationality is thus a crucial issue, and in the next Part of the Article I will discuss some aspects of that issue raised in some recent literature on the role of social theory in interpretation.

II. CRITICAL THEORY AND POSTSTRUCTURALISM

Since 1960, when Gadamer published *Truth and Method*,[26] hermeneutics has been criticized and taken in different directions. These developments have implications for legal interpretation, and the current

25. *See* H. GADAMER, *supra* note 7, at 276-77.
26. H. GADAMER, *supra* note 7.

task is to spell them out. I will discuss two ways of going beyond the hermeneutical theory I have sketched so far, and try to show the critical consequences for some related trends in the literature on judicial review. The first development is Jürgen Habermas' attempt to avoid the threat of relativism by giving hermeneutics a "transcendental" turn. The second development is French poststructuralism, which is critical of both Gadamer's and Habermas' theories. Some poststructuralists who offer a radically different account of textual interpretation are Derrida, Foucault, Deleuze, Blanchot, and Barthes, but for present purposes I will refer mainly to Derrida since his work has been so influential for American literary theorists of deconstruction. I think there are important parallels in Anglo-American jurisprudence between the poststructuralists and the Critical Legal Studies Movement, but first I will discuss the disagreement between Habermas and Gadamer.

A. The Habermas-Gadamer Debate

1. *Gadamer on Tradition*

Despite Gadamer's disclaimers, his theory is generally conceived as conservative. Although his view is that a text is always understood differently by different people, and thus that there will always be a need to criticize and revise previous interpretations, his critics find his account lacking in two important respects. First, given Gadamer's stress on the historical change of understanding, there seems to be no ground on which to base criticism. The interpreter cannot simply say that the *text* disconfirms prior interpretations and confirms the present one, since there is no text independent of some interpretation, and what counts as relevant in the text is dependent on the interpretation. (That is to say, there is no reading that is not already theory-laden.) Second, Gadamer's notion of the constitutive force of the *Wirkungsgeschichte* leads him to suggest that the *tradition* supplies the most important standard for criticism. Any reading is said to be conditioned by the prior history of related readings, and thus to stand in a tradition of interpretation. Gadamer is frequently misread as saying that an interpretation must stay in contact with that tradition and that "nontraditional" readings are therefore wrong. This interpretation of Gadamer mistakes a descriptive claim about the nature of understanding for a normative one about what an understanding ought to do. What Gadamer in fact maintains is that often an interpretation will correct the traditional way of reading a text. He can say this because what comes to be taken as traditional may be only a partial feature of what the tradition really involves when it is not obscured by overemphasizing a derivative part and thus distorting the whole. In other words, what counts as the tradition is itself a matter of interpretation, and one that any interpretation ought to address.

To illustrate Gadamer's point, consider the force of precedent in legal reasoning. The appeal to precedent is an excellent example of what Gadamer means by *Wirkungsgeschichte* and *wirkungsgeschichtliches Bewusstsein.* Legal interpretation is a clearer case than literary interpretation of the constitutive force that the history of a text's reception has for the formation of further interpretations. But the fact that precedents are sometimes declared mistaken and overruled also sharpens the question about the basis on which an intervening interpretation can be disconfirmed.

A passage from Raoul Berger cited by Michael Perry illustrates how an interpretation of the tradition established in a precedent can be challenged by claiming that interpretation to be a false perception of what the genuine tradition is. At the same time, this passage attests to the occurrence of the objectivist and intentionalist theory of interpretation to which hermeneutical theory is opposed.

> Why should "adherence to precedent" rise above effectuation of the framers' clearly expressed intention, which expresses the value choices of the sovereign people, not merely of judicial predecessors?
>
> . . . .
>
> I assert the right to look at the Constitution itself, stripped of judicial encrustations, as the index of the constitutional law and to affirm that the Supreme Court has no authority to substitute an "unwritten Constitution" for the written Constitution the Founders gave us and the people ratified.[27]

Perry cites a similar passage from Garry Wills' book *Inventing America*, arguing that to recreate the original world of the text "we must forget what we learned, or what occurred, in the interval between our time and the text's."[28]

According to hermeneutical theory, this forgetting would be neither possible nor desirable. Naturally we should avoid anachronism, but why should we posit the impossible methodological ideal of forgetting all we have learned? More problematically, although these

27. R. BERGER, GOVERNMENT BY JUDICIARY 300 (1977), *cited in* M. PERRY, *supra* note 3, at 68.

28. G. WILLS, INVENTING AMERICA: JEFFERSON'S DECLARATION OF INDEPENDENCE 259 (1978) *cited in* M. PERRY, *supra* note 3, at 62.

passages deny the force of tradition in one sense (namely, the history of precedents and "judicial encrustations"), they nevertheless appeal to tradition in another (the original tradition or context in which the document was adopted). So the force of tradition (whatever is taken as the real tradition) is not denied but instead confirmed by this objectivist theory which diverges from Gadamer's hermeneutical theory in every other respect. Hermeneutics wins out over objectivism here, since objectivism undermines its own argument against the constitutive force of the intervening history of interpretations (or *Wirkungsgeschichte*) by tacitly relying on a commitment to tradition. Or at least it can be said that the disagreement does not take place at the most basic philosophical level of the theory of understanding and interpretation (where Gadamer's theory is to be placed), but at a different level, closer to the details of particular practical interpretations and concerns about which aspects of tradition to emphasize and which to play down.

Even criticism of the intervening conceptions of the tradition can involve, then, an underlying normative commitment to continuity with the tradition. Criticism of what is commonly but superficially taken as "traditional" may be advanced for the sake of recovering lost aspects of the real tradition. There is another problem with the appeal to tradition, though, and that is the apparent emptiness of the notion of tradition as a standard for criticism. Two conflicting interpretations could both be based on an appeal to the tradition, but also on divergent understandings of the tradition. The appeal to continuity with tradition is not decisive. Professor Ely gives a concrete illustration of this problem[29] in terms of the *Regents of the University of California v. Bakke* case.[30] He maintains that there is more than one American tradition on the question whether racial majorities can aid minorities, and at best the traditions are ambiguous enough to lend support to both sides of the case. He also thinks that in addition to these practical difficulties there are theoretical ones. As a source of constitutional values, tradition's "overtly backward-looking character highlights its undemocratic nature: it is hard to square with the theory of our government the proposition that yesterday's majority, assuming it was a majority, should control today's."[31] Ely thinks that the appeal to tradition is not a primary criterion, but is derivative from what he calls "the most com-

29. J. ELY, *supra* note 4, at 60-63.
30. 438 U.S. 265 (1977).
31. J. ELY, *supra* note 4, at 62.

mon reference-in-chief, the genuine consensus of contemporary American thought."[32]

I will turn to the notion of consensus shortly, for that is precisely the notion Habermas substituted for Gadamer's concept of tradition. The practical problem about tradition that Ely raises is a variant of the more general criticism by Habermas and the poststructuralists of Gadamer's notion of the tradition-laden character of understanding. The question is why tradition should be valued so highly. Even if our understanding is conditioned by a tradition of interpretation, and even if the ideal of a complete break with past traditions is merely utopian (or dystopian), there may be more point to changing than to restoring tradition.

Gadamer's reply depends precisely on recognizing that to talk about change is to presuppose an understanding of the history that has led up to the need for change. This understanding must be assumed to be correct, and thus an element of the call for change will be the willingness to discuss the importance of this history for the present. Furthermore, to call for change is at the same time to have a view about how change is possible. In order for change to be practicable, and to avoid empty utopianism, it must be to some extent consistent with the tradition and the antecedent history out of which it grows.

Admittedly, Gadamer's theory is abstract and general, but its consequences are not such as to discourage or retard practical efforts at formulating new interpretations, whether these interpretations rely on precedent or whether they significantly revise precedent. The charge of emptiness is not directly relevant to Gadamer's theory, then, since by tradition he does not mean established conventions, privileges, or values. He simply tries to describe how the process of understanding and interpretation works, even when the interpretation radically alters previous understandings of the tradition. Of course, the attempt to revise precedent can be overturned. However, insofar as the arguments for doing so are based not on a denial of tradition, but on the hope of becoming part of tradition, Gadamer's model stands.[33] Gadamer's

32. *Id.* at 63.

33. Gadamer explicates his phrase "connection with the tradition" as follows:

> Changing the established forms is no less a kind of connection with the tradition than defending the established forms. Tradition exists only in constant alteration. "To gain a connection" with the tradition is a formulation intended to call attention to an experience whereby our plans and wishes are always in advance of reality, and are, so to speak, even without connection with reality. What then becomes important is to mediate between desirable anticipations and practicable possibilities, between sheer wishes and genuine intentions—that is, to imagine the anticipations in the substance of reality.

H. GADAMER, *Replik*, in HERMENEUTIK UND IDEOLOGIEKRITIK 307 (1971).

conception of the methodological role of the tradition in understanding is thus more descriptive than normative. The normative component becomes more explicit, however, when the interpretation tries to become conscious of how it is both enabled and limited by antecedent history, including traditional preconceptions not only about doctrine but also about method. That is, the interpretation may need to make explicit the intervening history (or *Wirkungsgeschichte*) that inevitably plays a role in the formation of the interpretation. Hermeneutical philosophy does not tell interpreters what to do, but it does imply that an understanding that tries to understand itself (including both its doctrinal and methodological commitments) is better than one that does not. For the issue of judicial review, this point suggests that in the making or appraising of judicial decisions, the theory of judicial review behind those decisions also ought to be made clear. Then if the theory can be challenged (for instance, by arguing for a hermeneutical conception of interpretation over the intentionalist, objectivist one stated by Berger and Wills[34]), that result will be a factor in appraising the substantive decision.

2. *Habermas on Consensus*

Professor Ely maintains that the appeal to tradition never stands alone, but always smuggles in the ideal of consensus. That is to say, the appeal to tradition will not by itself settle a dispute unless there is general agreement in the present that the traditional features in question ought to be preserved. Habermas makes much the same point against Gadamer's conception of the tradition-bound character of understanding, except that Habermas maintains further that all discursive understanding presupposes the ideal of consensus. Habermas thinks that the hermeneutic insistence on the context-bound character of understanding must be supplemented by some contextless (or quasi-"transcendental") conception of "reason"—that is, some universal standard for the rational discussion of conflicts of interpretation and for the adjudication of principles. Ely's analysis of the appeal to consensus in determining what the contemporary values are runs directly counter to Habermas' theory, however, since Ely thinks consensus does not in fact give any content to the "inherently contentless notions of 'reason' and 'principle.' "[35] Gadamer makes a similar charge against Habermas' attempt to take hermeneutics in a transcendental direction.

34. *See supra* notes 27-28 and accompanying text.

35. J. ELY, *supra* note 4, at 63.

I will summarize the disagreements between Habermas and Gadamer before returning to the ramifications for the issue of judicial review. I see Habermas' position as leading toward noninterpretivism and Gadamer's objections as holding back. But the issue is now a broader one than what judges can do within the confines of current legal practices. Habermas raises the larger question about how current practices could themselves become the object of criticism, or how they could be legitimated.[36] He does not call into question the whole idea of the "rule of law" as dramatically as the French poststructuralists do, but he sets up a framework in which the question of the legitimacy of the rule of law could be asked. He constructs, in Thomas McCarthy's words, "a theoretically grounded form of advocacy in situations of social conflict."[37] In doing so, he appears to go beyond Gadamer's theory, which seems to presuppose the rule of law, or at least does not specify how it could be genuinely challenged.

Habermas' basic worry about Gadamer's historicist hermeneutics is that not enough is said about how the interpreter can transcend and criticize the present context. Habermas thinks that there must be some ideal of truth which transcends the particular interpretation if the interpretation is believed to be not merely plausible, or the best we can do, but also right, and therefore binding on everybody. In a conflict of interpretations there could be no rational attempt to adjudicate the dispute unless the interpretations shared some standards for resolving disagreement. Any interpretation claiming to be correct would have to presuppose a notion of truth common to any other interpretation. In Habermas' terms, all rational discourse presupposes, at least counterfactually, the ideal of a speech situation in which the participants are not constrained by any interfering factors and can consider all the relevant information until the best argument wins unanimous consent. Such consensus is for Habermas presupposed by any claim to know what is true, and by appeals to the morally right as well.

Habermas thinks this notion of truth as consensus in an ideal speech situation is required to avoid the relativism he fears in Gadamer's theory.[38] Gadamer's objectivist critics accuse him of diminishing the status of the text by denying that the text has any standing

36. In Tushnet, *Legal Scholarship: Its Causes and Cure*, 90 YALE L.J. 1205, 1222 (1981), Mark Tushnet suggests Habermas' theory may be one cure for the reluctance of legal scholarship to question the liberal theory of law, and for its present "intellectual marginality."

37. T. MCCARTHY, THE CRITICAL THEORY OF JÜRGEN HABERMAS 332 (1978).

38. For a discussion of the early exchanges between Habermas and Gadamer, see D. HOY, *supra* note 2, at 117-28.

independent of an interpretation. In contrast, Habermas argues that Gadamer overemphasizes the text. In *Theorie des kommunikativen Handelns*,[39] Habermas maintains that Gadamer is overly influenced by the paradigm of the classical philologist and incorporates into the relation of the text and the interpreter an asymmetry in favor of the text.

The difficulty arose in Gadamer's earlier reply to Betti, where Gadamer had defended himself from the charge of relativism (and of underemphasizing the role of the text) by arguing that his objectivist critics failed to appreciate his insistence on what he called the *Vorgriff der Vollkommenheit* (the anticipation of the completeness or perfection of the text). For Gadamer interpretation does not involve simply understanding the text, but also the text's subject matter. That is, the interpreter should have an understanding of the issues or ideas gained independently from reading the text, or perhaps as the result of being motivated by the text to think independently about the subject matter. The interpreter who has no understanding of the issues and questions that the text addresses obviously does not understand what the text is about. Habermas thinks Gadamer is right to maintain that questions about what a text means cannot be completely separated from those about how to determine its validity or value. However, he believes Gadamer privileges the text too much. At times Gadamer, who is himself a scholar of Plato and Aristotle, implies that the best way to approach eminent texts is to assume that they are unlikely to be wrong, however difficult or alien they seem initially. The dialogue between text and interpreter would thus be asymmetrical, and weighted in favor of the text.

To show that Gadamer has not correctly analyzed the structure of all understanding, Habermas points to a different case of understanding where the superiority of the interpreted object over the interpreter is not assumed. Anthropologists, Habermas maintains, cannot always presuppose the superiority of their object; instead, they must reconstruct the learning processes that separate their beliefs from those of the tribe being studied, and that distinguish modern from mythical thinking. Because Gadamer's hermeneutics is based on the paradigm of the interpretation of eminent texts (for example, legal, sacred, and artistic ones), Habermas thinks that the account of understanding is too one-sided, and does not account for the need of the interpreter to criticize the object of interpretation. The backward-looking humanist is less likely than the present-oriented social scientist or the forward-looking

39. J. Habermas, 1 Theorie des Kommunikativen Handelns 194 (1981).

social critic to recognize the need for a conception of progress. Some account is required of why we can believe we know more than the past did, or why our society is better than it was, or why society's critics can believe it could be improved. Habermas does not find this critical dimension in Gadamer's theory. He thinks Gadamer's position abets the mistaken tendency of confusing *Verständnis* and *Einverständnis*, comprehension and consent. To understand something is not necessarily to believe it.

Gadamer's position does not entail, however, that understanding is believing. In response to Betti he had pointed out that his stress is as much on the *Vorgriff*, the anticipation, as on the *Vollkommenheit*, or perfection of the text. That is, the notion is not intended as a metaphysical claim about the sacrosanctity of the classics (or, I presume, the infallibility of the law). Instead, it is a heuristic recommendation to the interpreter, suggesting that it will be more useful to go along with the text as far as possible than to dismiss the text's truth claims as outdated or its arguments as primitive. Of course, Habermas is forcing the issue to make clearer why the interpreter must be able not only to understand that which is being interpreted (whether a text or a tribe), but also to *criticize* it. He sees Gadamer's argument that all thinking is conditioned by *Vorurteile* (prejudgments or prejudices) as presupposing a deeply conservative belief in the legitimate and inevitable authority of the tradition. Like Heidegger, Gadamer thinks that any of these prejudgments could be brought to thought—they are not ineffable or inarticulatable—but he denies that they could *all* be articulated at once. We could not end with a completely self-transparent thinking, with what Hegel called "Absolute Knowledge." Gadamer thinks that authority is inevitably involved in understanding insofar as it is always constrained in some respects by tradition and precedent, that is, by preunderstanding. Gadamer sees vestiges of this ideal of reason lurking in Habermas' conception of rationality, which appears utopian in its model of discourse unconstrained by authority or by unexamined assumptions.

Habermas' view is roughly that no authority is legitimate unless an enlightened discussion would result in consenting to it. Since agreements in the everyday world may not include all the relevant parties affected, or since constraints may force an agreement contrary to the participants' real interests, Habermas says the ideal speech situation may be only a counterfactual assumption. That is, discourse in the real world may generally fall short of the ideal, but nevertheless the discussants could not engage in anything that could be called rational discussion unless they presupposed the possibility of attaining an uncoerced consensus based on the best arguments. So although this ideal may be counterfactual, it is nevertheless a necessary presupposition of all real discourse (i.e., all language activity aiming at cognitive results). To believe their discourse rational, the participants must assume that in the ideal speech situation, reason (i.e., the best arguments) would prevail and the authority to be legitimated would no longer be functioning as *authority*.

Habermas' theory applies to normative as well as cognitive matters. In fact, there is a more natural tendency to think of ethical norms as being validated by consensus, however cognitive claims are validated. The rightness of a normative principle is certainly connected with its being acceptable to all who are affected by it. To extend his theory to ethics, Habermas first denies that the foundation of the binding character of norms is a monological reflection about whether any other agent ought to do what a particular agent is considering. Whereas in Kant's theory reflection on the universalizability of moral maxims is conducted monologically, Habermas thinks that the proper basis for a universalistic ethics is interpersonal dialogue aiming at unanimous agreement. He thus calls his theory "communicative ethics." This ethics is a cognitivist one, because norms are not simply noncognitive, subjective preferences, but the results of objective, public, and legitimate procedures. Ethics is as cognitive as science since the process for validating norms is the same as the process of determining truths. Both science and ethics presuppose the possibility of consensus as the source of the legitimacy of belief. Unlike Kant's moral philosophy, which separates morality and legality because only the former involves internal autonomy whereas the latter presuposes external authority, Habermas thinks that agreement is also the basis for both moral and legal norms:

> Only *communicative ethics* guarantees the generality of admissible norms and the autonomy of acting subjects solely through the discursive redeemability of the validity claims with which norms appear. That is, generality is guaranteed in that the only norms that may claim generality are those on which everyone affected agrees (or would agree) without constraint if they enter (or were to enter) a process of discursive will-formation. The question of which sectors should, if necessary, be regulated through compromise or formal norms of action can also be made the subject of discussion. Only communicative ethics is universal (and not, as is formalistic ethics,

> restricted to a domain of private morality separate from legal norms). . . .[40]

Again, however, the ideal and counterfactual status of such agreement makes the theory seem more applicable to a utopian world than to our own. Habermas admits that in an unjust world there will be conflicts between private morality and public mores. His argument is that merely to *conceive* of resolving these conflicts requires us to hypothesize an ideal speech situation in which norms would be discursively determined through consent. But he realizes that

> [t]his does not exclude the necessity for compelling norms, since no one can know (today) the degree to which aggressiveness can be curtailed and the voluntary recognition of discursive principles attained. Only at that stage, at present a mere construct, would morality become strictly universal. It would also cease to be "merely" moral in terms of the distinction made between law and morality. Internalization too would only be complete when the principle of the justification of possible principles (that is, the readiness to engage in discursive clarification of practical questions) was alone internalized, but in other respects the continuous interpretation of needs was given over to communication processes.[41]

To critics of this thesis of the "withering away" of morality who accuse him of utopianism, Habermas admits the utopian component of his theory, but stresses that it is only a formal one of procedure. His model does not specify anything about the actual make-up of the ideal society: "Ethical universalism does indeed have a utopian content, but it does not *sketch out* a utopia."[42] Habermas thinks this minimal utopian component is necessary if social theory is to be *critical* theory, and if we are to be able to transcend our historical conditions in the attempt to criticize our own or other societies.

The challenge I think both Gadamer and such French poststructuralists as Michel Foucault would raise here is why we need this utopian projection to criticize the present. Does this eternal, unhistorical, and supposedly impartial and impersonal ideal really have enough content to show that we have progressed over the past, and to help us decide what would constitute moral and social progress in the future? Habermas, however, clearly thinks his counterfactual, regulative ideal does have real critical bite. Although there is no appeal to a speculative philosophy of history in the notion of the ideal speech situation,

40. J. HABERMAS, LEGITIMATION CRISIS 89 (1975) (emphasis in original).

41. *Id.* at 87.

42. J. HABERMAS, *A Reply to My Critics*, in HABERMAS: CRITICAL DEBATES 251 (J. Thompson & D. Held eds. 1982) (emphasis in original).

Habermas says this notion is both (1) a necessary condition of all real communication, and (2) a political ideal we must try to achieve, and that can be more or less achieved in real societies. We will criticize ourselves and others according to the degree the procedural ideal is approached. The critical theorist attempts a counterfactually projected reconstruction of social institutions guided by the question:

> How would the members of a social system, at a given stage in the development of productive forces, have collectively and bindingly interpreted their needs (and which norms would they have accepted as justified) if they could and would have decided on the organization of social intercourse through discursive will-formation, with adequate knowledge of the limiting conditions and functional imperatives of their society?[43]

Gadamer's response to Habermas' notion of the ideal speech situation is to say that this idealization is too formal and empty to have any bearing on practice. He could supplement his argument by pointing to the practical problems Ely sees, namely, that there is not likely to be a consensus on the questions that come up for adjudication in a forum like the courts, or that consensus could not be reliably discoverable, at least by responsible social agencies like the courts.[44]

These practical objections to consensus as a legitimation of interpretations will not apply to a minimal (but then uncontroversial and trivial) version of Habermas' transcendental claim. If Gadamer is right that the ideal is a purely formal one, then he could equally well accept as reject it. Gadamer could agree without undermining his own theory that when particular prejudices do become conscious, we can test them with counterfactual reasoning procedures of the sort Habermas (and Rawls) describe. The intuitions at stake here are not mutually exclusive. Habermas thinks correctly that any rational participant in a dialogue would ideally want to articulate a consistent set of beliefs. Those who are on Gadamer's side are equally right to insist that whatever holds under ideal circumstances, we ordinary agents need not believe that all our beliefs are consistent. We could believe they are not, though we do not yet know in what respects, and still believe in our rationality and the rationality of our practices. To think we are irrational so long as all our beliefs are not explicitly examined and con-

43. *Id.* at 113.

44. J. ELY, *supra* note 4, at 64. That Habermas' notion of consensus cannot be used effectively in the theory of legal interpretation may be suggested by the fact that Ely's noninterpretivist opponent Michael Perry, who in early writings had been a consensus theorist, has come to accept Ely's criticism of consensus. *See* M. PERRY, *supra* note 3, at 94.

sciously formed into an error-free, coherent set condemns us to irrationality permanently.

However, this argument that rationality is better modeled on everyday rather than ideal circumstances does not invalidate Habermas' account of how we could go about deciding whether particular beliefs are rational and coherent with our other beliefs. Habermas can be understood as making a *procedural* point that is legitimate and potentially useful, as hermeneutic theorists could acknowledge. They may think too much is claimed for this procedure and that there are other, equally legitimate procedures, such as appeal to continuity with tradition. The case for each such procedure can be made independently of the others, though, and the only real disagreement will be about whether the ideal of "rationality" requires that there be only one supreme procedure. Hermeneutic theorists who do not think interpretation requires a transcendental foundation can resist the ideal of such a supreme procedure because it will be too thin to be of use in practical criticism, which can legitimately take many forms and which is not helped by the philosophical construction of a transcendental theory of truth. This point could be made another way by arguing that the procedure of agreement, as one procedure among others, will have independent appeal and does not have to be grounded in something more basic, such as the nature of discursive communication.[45] Habermas may think that his ethical theory has more force if it is transcendentally grounded in a necessary presupposition of the use of language. But if the concept of agreement has more intuitive connection with moral rightness than with truth, the case for the ethical theory should be kept separate from that for the theory of truth.

B. Deconstruction and the Critical Legal Studies Movement

1. *"New Nihilism"?*

With the discussion of Habermas, the question of interpreting the law has moved from the limited problem of how to interpret the law without at the same time challenging its legitimacy, to the larger issue of the legitimacy of both particular laws and the legal organization of society. This larger question is no longer one about interpreting the law in the sense of reading particular statutes and applying them to hard cases. Instead, it is about interpreting "the law" as such; that is, it

45. I owe this point to Harvard philosopher Thomas Scanlon, who made it in a discussion of the differences between his own contractualist moral philosophy and Habermas' theory.

is about justifying or rectifying the political and social organization that the code of laws and the judiciary serve and perpetuate. Since the object of interpretation is different at this level, the discussion might seem to be safely beyond the questions involved in the dispute about interpretivism versus noninterpretivism in judicial review. The larger questions seem more like ones for political theorists than for judges or constitutional theorists. However that may be, in the theory of interpretation there is now a tendency to push beyond the hermeneutical position I have sketched so far, in a way that would undermine even legal interpretation's minimal claim to rationality (let alone to objectivity or correctness).

Professor Fiss has labeled this tendency as "a new nihilism, one that doubts the legitimacy of adjudication" and that has begun "a romance with politics."[46] I do not know for certain whom he would include among the new nihilists. Both Ronald Dworkin and Roberto Unger, for instance, argue that interpretivism is closely bound up with politics, but as I will show, they have different conceptions of politics as well as of the interconnection between law and politics. Whether all noninterpretivists would be nihilists is also not clear, but I assume that many representatives of the Critical Legal Studies Movement would be. Fiss mentions deconstruction under this rubric,[47] so I assume a French poststructuralist like Derrida is to be included, as well as some American critics. Fiss identifies a basic premise of this trend toward nihilism in the theory of interpretation as follows: "for any text there are any number of possible meanings and the interpreter creates a meaning by choosing one."[48] He says that he accepts this premise, but thinks that the interpreter's freedom is "constrained by rules that derive their authority from an interpretive community that is itself held together by the commitment to the rule of law."[49]

Given Fiss' intention, I think there are several reasons why he should not grant the premise at all. First, as I have argued, the theoretical model that says an interpreter creates a meaning by choosing one misdescribes what interpreters must believe about their interpretations. Second, when textual meaning is distinguished from utterance meaning, it does not follow that the textual meaning can be interpreted arbitrarily. Context will still constrain the possible alternatives, and

46. Fiss, *Objectivity and Interpretation*, 34 STAN. L. REV. 739, 740 (1982).

47. *Id.* at 741 & n.9.

48. *Id.*

49. *Id.* at 762.

variations or shifts between possible contexts will be constrained by factors such as suitability, purpose, and plausibility. Third, I think a hermeneutic theory should be cautious about making the consensus of an existent interpretive community the sole source of interpretive authority. Whether Habermas is right about the necessity of presupposing an ideal speech situation, he is right that real speech situations are imperfect and frequently distorted by the inadequate self-understanding of the discussants. Before deciding whether a hermeneutical line of defense against the new nihilism is needed, however, I should first state how I understand this tendency that Fiss deplores.

Pushed to its limits, this new nihilism would show that all interpretation, even the "interpretivist" attempt to stick to the statutes, is "noninterpretive" in the sense of imposing the interests of the interpreter and deliberately distorting the language of the law. What this position holds in common with noninterpretivism is the view that (1) the language of the law (the textual meaning) is not identical to the psychological intentions of the authors of the law, and (2) the interpreter may candidly manipulate the language to serve other purposes. Procedurally, then, this new tendency and noninterpretivism seem equivalent. Where they diverge is in political doctrine. But noninterpretivism is vulnerable in that its theory of interpretation is a slippery slope that may not be able to stop the slide toward a political outcome that it would find undesirable. Although noninterpretivists discount the author's or framers' intentions, they continue to assume that the language of the law has a coherence and unity, and is in principle capable of being in harmony with the moral and social order, which is also assumed to be coherent and unified. The new nihilists' conception of meaning and interpretation sees the language as either incoherent or else a disguised attempt to impose the interests of the dominant social group. The interpreters (for instance, the judges), who invariably belong to the dominant social group, overlook the contradictions either within the law or between their legal-moral ideals and the existent social structure. Whereas the interpreters may think of themselves as finding the inner harmony between the rationale of the law and the social order, in actuality they are reinforcing their own social power by imposing their illusory social and moral vision on everybody else.

The difficulty here is a general one for "institutional" theorists of interpretation. Any theory suggesting that the standards for adjudicating conflicts of interpretations are simply internal to different (actual, not counterfactual) social groups or institutions seems to have no satisfactory answer to the charge that interpretation is nothing more than an institutionalized way of reinforcing unequal social power relations. Most literary critics fail to take this problem seriously, for two reasons. First, they do not perceive themselves as exercising social power directly the way a judge does (or theologians used to do). Second, literature and art (unlike the law now, and formerly, Scripture) do not seem to be powerful social institutions. Literary theorists can therefore espouse and practice interpretive techniques more or less harmlessly, while interpreters in spheres such as law and theology cannot. The sacrosanctity of religious texts, for instance, would not survive deconstructive readings, and an interpreter holding a text sacred could hardly attempt its deconstruction.

Are there examples of deconstructive legal readings, and what would their political consequences be? Duncan Kennedy's reading of Blackstone[50] comes to mind as a possible case, although it could not count as purely syntactical, Derridean deconstruction since it rests on a political commitment and a substantial doctrine. Could the same be done for the Constitution? For Kennedy, Blackstone's *Commentaries* are a self-deceptive attempt to see servitude as freedom and chaos as rational order. Kennedy thinks all legal thinking is contradictory in a similar way, for it attempts both to find the utopian conditions of social justice and at the same time to deny the disturbing truth about the existent social arrangement. He reads Blackstone's *Commentaries* as "an instrument of apology—an attempt to mystify both dominators and dominated by convincing them of the 'naturalness,' the 'freedom' and the 'rationality' of a condition of bondage."[51]

Like Hegel's owl of Minerva, deconstruction would seem to emerge only when a text no longer had an unquestionable authority, or in a culture in which no text was in principle sacrosanct.[52] As used by Derrida on philosophical texts, deconstruction does not take apart a text that is working, but instead it shows why something (for instance,

50. Kennedy, *The Structure of Blackstone's Commentaries*, 28 BUFFALO L. REV. 209 (1979).

51. *Id.* at 210.

52. Stanley Cavell argues that a distinguishing feature between European and American intellectual life is that the American "has no sacred intellectual texts, none whose authority the intellectual community at large is anxious to preserve at all costs—no Marxian texts, no Freudian, no Hegelian, no Deweyan, and so forth." Cavell, *A Reply to Gayatri Spivak*, in THE POLITICS OF INTERPRETATION 367, 370 (W. Mitchell ed. 1983). Then in parenthesis he adds, "I am not considering the Declaration of Independence as a candidate for such a text." *Id.* Why not? He could hardly mean that it and the Constitution are not "intellectual" enough. Perhaps he means that they are so much more than intellectual texts. In any case, his caveat shows the special status of these legal texts and their interpretation.

either a central philosophical metaphor or an entire metaphysics) that seemed to work, never really did work.[53] The deconstructive textual analysis then shows how the illusion is perpetrated by syntactical and rhetorical devices in the text.

Does deconstructionist theory really threaten legal interpretation and adjudication? One might think so, given that one of its central tenets is that the referents and truth-values of discursive language are "undecidable."[54] This notion of undecidability has some kinship with hermeneutics, particularly with the insistence that interpretation is not a voluntaristic, fully conscious act, and should not be represented as an algorithmic decision procedure. Derrida means much more than this, however, since he holds up the undecidability of specific texts in the history of philosophy and literature as a sign of the inevitable failure of the hermeneutic attempt to find an interpretation that will integrate the elements of a text into a maximally coherent account. The hermeneutic search for the meaning of the literary, philosophical, or historical text, or the judge's attempt to interpret the legal text and to decide the case, would always be self-deceptive if all texts were in principle shot through with undecidability.

As a theory of poetry and literature this idea of undecidability may have a certain applicability since fictional and figurative discourse can reasonably be said to block attempts at decipherment.

As a theory of philosophical discourse, at least in the history of philosophy, it could also apply since no one will deny that metaphysical constructions often rely on literary devices. Thus, questions about whether there really are forms, monads, sense-data, and other such posits no longer seem genuine. In other words, there is no longer a viable vocabulary or research program in which anyone would try to decide whether assertions using these notions were genuinely referential. However, what it would be like for our own vocabulary to be similarly a dead language is impossible for us to say, and it still seems

53. Marjorie Grene succinctly expresses Derrida's theory of philosophical language as follows: "Derrida . . . is looking not at a working machine too simply understood, but at a dream of language, an alleged machine that has never existed and never worked at all. True, it is a dream we cannot escape. The hope of presence is incurable"; M. GRENE, *Life, Death, and Language: Some Thoughts on Wittgenstein and Derrida*, in PHILOSOPHY IN AND OUT OF EUROPE 142, 144 (1976); "Language is our *hamartia*, our missing of the mark. The moment we speak we introduce not a well-oiled machinery, but a species-specific neurosis. . . . We are always saying never quite what we mean; we always mean never quite what we say." *Id.* at 148.

54. *See* Hoy, *Deciding Derrida*, 4 LONDON REVIEW OF BOOKS 3 (February 18 to March 3, 1982); Hoy, *Derrida*, in THE RETURN OF GRAND THEORY IN THE HUMAN SCIENCES (Q. Skinner ed. 1985).

reasonable and important to us to decide what we mean by crucial terms such as rationality, rights, obligation, justice, and fairness. In principle, we cannot accept the thought that these terms are undecidable, or that they do not have a genuine use, however difficult it is in practice to work out exactly how the terms are best used.

On my hermeneutical view, deconstruction exaggerates the theory of interpretation in two respects. First, from its destruction of the ideal of determining from the author's intention the one and only appropriate reading of the text, it tends to conclude too quickly that the text could mean anything to any number of different readers. This inference is mistaken, however, since from the fact that any particular context for making sense of a text can be called into question it does not follow that no context is reasonable or justifiable. Deconstruction infers from the collapse of the ideal of absolute justification that no justification is possible. Alternatively one may say that justification is misdescribed in the first place if it is thought that some belief or theory is justified only if all the possible evidence and arguments have been examined and accounted for.

The second exaggeration is to take what is only one moment of the process of interpretation as the inevitable outcome of all interpretation. This one-sidedness distorts interpretation, and would make it an incoherent and unrecognizable practice. Any interpretation should try to avoid reading into the text only what is already familiar. Deconstruction is a reasonable procedure as the practical attempt first to find the rhetorical devices that function to give the text the appearance of coherence, and then to show that since they are *rhetorical* devices there are other elements that disrupt this coherence. But to disrupt the apparent unity or sense of a text there must be another, hermeneutical moment of finding unity in the textual complexity, of making sense of difficult figurative devices. Deconstruction (or "dissemination," as Derrida calls it) goes as far as it can with the thought that the text might be infinitely complex, and allow infinitely many readings. This thought may be well-intended in its desire to insure that the potential complexity of the text is not underestimated, but projecting it as a fundamental principle of understanding and interpretation is philosophical overkill.

The hermeneutical moment is also required since we cannot really contemplate an infinity of meanings and still claim to be understanding the text. Understanding necessarily involves the hermeneutical moment of making sense of the text, of eliminating some possible readings, and therefore of not overestimating the textual possibilities.

Hermeneutics denies that the interpreter can read anything and everything into the text and still claim to be understanding the text. I prefer to think of understanding as a matter of balancing two factors that are rarely in equipoise, namely, complexity and sense.[55] A reading is precisely an attempt to gain a reflective equilibrium in which the two appear as balanced as possible. The equilibrium is a reflective one since intuition alone will not settle all the questions. However, reflection is not the same as consciously choosing or creating a meaning.

The thought that the interpreter is completely free to vary the context and thus the meaning of the language to be interpreted is wrong for at least two reasons. First, only some of the logical or syntactical possibilities are real ones, and the interpreter does not understand at all if this difference does not make a difference. Second, the lack of equipoise must be found by the interpreter to be a problem in itself. The interpreter does not simply choose arbitrarily and disinterestedly between possibilities, but finds interpretation difficult because it puts prior commitments up for reassessment. As John Rawls describes reflective equilibrium in moral interpretation, it is a matter of confronting our intuitions with our principles, such that we may have to revise either in terms of the other.[56] This description is not simply a better phenomenological characterization of moral reasoning, but also a corrective to a rigid philosophical picture of rationality. Similarly, the notion of reflective equilibrium I have sketched generates a different philosophical picture of interpretation and justification than the absolutist one the deconstructionist successfully attacks. On this hermeneutical model there is no privileged starting point for the interpretation, and no self-evident data. Furthermore, there is no ideal final resting place in the search for equilibrium, no point at which we would have examined *all* the relevant observations and arguments. The ideal is not implicated even counterfactually, for what sense we could make of such an ideal is not apparent. New cases will always call on us to reconsider our assumptions and weightings, so that the ideal of a final

55. The "hermeneutic circle" is the claim that understanding the text as a whole depends on understanding its parts, but that the parts cannot be understood independently of the whole. Using the metaphor of the circle then forces hermeneutic theorists to argue lamely that this circle is not a logically vicious one, but simply an unavoidable feature of all understanding. The metaphor of the circle thus creates its own problems, which can be obviated by changing the metaphor to that of weighing or balancing. Besides, the metaphor of balancing seems more natural in the context of legal interpretation, given the classical image of the scales of justice. In either case, the point is that reading must account for *both* (1) the complexity of the parts of the text, and (2) the sense of the text as a whole.

56. *See* J. RAWLS, A THEORY OF JUSTICE 20-21, 48-51 (1971); Hoy, *supra* note 11, at 666.

consensus determining a correct and unchangeable outcome is inappropriate.

The theory behind deconstruction thus starts from the implausibility of a rigid and absolutist model of what understanding and interpretation are, as well as what is involved in the justification of interpretations or the adjudication of conflicts of interpretation. Although it is correct in this regard, it mistakenly infers from the failure of the absolutist model that no understanding is justified and that no attempt at adjudication of conflicts can claim to be correct or rational. What should instead be inferred is that a more plausible account of understanding and rational justification is required. The account should not make it seem impossible to decide how a text applies in different circumstances, but should show that a reasonable interpreter can legitimately claim to be understanding the text and not simply to be articulating extratextual values. A theory of interpretation concluding that undecidability is inevitable is by *reductio* shown to be wrong. Since it could not decide the truth-values of its own claims, it could not exclude contradictory principles, and thus refutes itself.

2. *Unger and Dworkin on Politics*

Professor Unger's manifesto for the Critical Legal Studies movement is not paradoxical in the same way, but it too argues from the collapse of an overly demanding theory of interpretation to one that risks a "paradoxical voluntarism."[57] Unger begins by distinguishing the procedural belief in value-neutral methods of legal interpretation from the substantive belief in the morality and justice of the laws, however *ad hoc* the process of legislation seems. He calls the former belief "formalism" and defines it as "a commitment to . . . a method of legal justification that can be clearly contrasted to open-ended disputes about the basic terms of social life, disputes that people call ideological, philosophical, or visionary."[58] The latter is called "objectivism" and is defined as the belief that the "authoritative legal materials" ("the system of statutes, cases, and accepted legal ideas") are "not merely the outcome of contingent power struggles or of practical pressures lacking in rightful authority"; instead, the laws are thought to "embody and sustain a defensible scheme of human association" and to "display,

57. For a reply to this objection, see Unger, *The Critical Legal Studies Movement*, 96 HARV. L. REV. 563, 586 (1983).

58. *Id.* at 564.

though always imperfectly, an intelligible moral order."[59] Formalism is said to presuppose a qualified objectivism since either the moral order would be completely extrinsic to the laws or it could coincide with the laws by "a sheer miracle."[60]

The rhetorical stage is already set with these definitions, however, since if the internal rationale of the legal system, "the intelligible moral order," cannot be specified in detail, then the only alternative appears to be that the legal system is not a system at all, that the laws have only an instrumental rationality and are simply the result of *ad hoc* power plays. On Unger's initial presentation of the situation of legal interpretation, there now seem to be only two possible accounts of interpretation. Either the legal interpreter has a "single cohesive theory" explaining how "the many conflicts of interest and vision that lawmaking involves, fought out by countless minds and wills working at cross-purposes, would have to be the vehicle of an immanent moral rationality," or legal reasoning becomes "a game of easy analogies" in which every thoughtful lawyer can argue "too well or too easily for too many conflicting solutions."[61]

Even Hegel would have balked at this characterization of the alternatives. Hegel did write a philosophy of right trying to show the rationale for the existent social order,[62] but he did not try to show that it fit the contemporary laws precisely. Presumably one purpose of a general philosophy of right would be to criticize some of the existent statutes and practices as inconsistent with other, more important ones. The interpreter has alternatives other than to assume that there is either a miraculous "preestablished harmony" between the laws and a complete theory of right, or the laws are merely *ad hoc*. If we give up the idea that justification is possible only through a complete and consistent set of verified beliefs, it does not follow that we are condemned to believe our interpretations are unjustifiable and arbitrary. A conception of rationality which humans could not live up to absent a miracle should be rejected as irrational.

If we think of interpretation not in this ultra-rationalistic fashion, but as the hermeneutical process of balancing the principles implied in the legal language with the exigencies of particular cases, then we need not think of the laws as either miraculously rational or merely ad hoc.

59. *Id.* at 565.
60. *Id.* at 566.
61. *Id.* at 570-71.
62. *See* G. HEGEL, PHILOSOPHY OF RIGHT 1-36 (1952).

They are not *ad hoc* if some reasoning about principles and policies is involved at their inception, and they can be rationally and justifiably understood and applied if similar reasoning is used. Exactly the same reasoning both at the inception and at the later interpretation is not required, though, since the circumstances will be different; it will be sufficient if the later interpretation is a continuation and development of the earlier instances, given that how we understand principles and policies depends on what we learn from our attempts to act on them.

What I have said should not be taken as a defense of formalism and objectivism, as Unger defines them, but simply as a reaction to starting from what seems like a false dilemma. Unger is correct in objecting to the claim that lawmaking and law application "differ fundamentally" in "both how they work and how their results may properly be justified."[63] I have also not mentioned anything about the substantive theses of the Critical Legal Studies Movement. A claim to the effect that the law and society are in an antagonistic relationship is not one that could be challenged *a priori.* It can be considered only in terms of a detailed, empirical interpretation. Furthermore, an ideal such as the "cumulative loosening of the fixed order of society"[64] is not objectionable, even if one thinks, as Hegel did, that any society will have some fixed order. A cumulative loosening is still a form of *Wirkungsgeschichte* and still involves some connection or continuity with tradition.

Calling his position a "superliberalism,"[65] Unger insists he is best understood as pushing liberal premises about freedom to their limits and trying "to remake social life in the image of liberal politics" (although doing so requires changing the liberal conception and practice of politics). A hermeneutical theory of interpretation cannot object to the thought that legal intepretation always involves, whether implicitly or explicitly, political commitments arising from continuity with a tradition. This thought is itself one way of illustrating the notion of the *wirkungsgeschichtliches Bewusstsein*, or hermeneutical awareness of the interpretive context.

The claim that legal interpretation always involves, and ought to involve, *politics*, however, can mean different things. While Professors Unger and Dworkin both make this claim, I question whether either could agree with the other's meaning. Roughly, the difference between

63. Unger, *supra* note 57, at 565.
64. *Id.* at 584.
65. *Id.* at 602.

what they mean by "politics" is the difference between political action and political theory. Dworkin thinks, for instance, that how the equal protection clause is interpreted necessarily presupposes "some theory about what political equality is and how far equality is required by justice."[66] Theory is not simply political theory either, for as I mentioned,[67] he thinks it would be possible to trace different political theories back to distinctive epistemological theories, and perhaps also to work out from these toward matching aesthetic theories: "politics, art, and law are united, somehow, in philosophy."[68]

In contrast, Unger thinks of politics more in terms of instrumental calculation and strategies of domination—in short, power relations. He accuses the "rights and principles school" of legal interpretation of being a "watered-down version" of nineteenth-century legal science, itself merely a "diluted version" of the conservative social doctrines that served to justify and perpetuate a stratified society before the emergence of the rights-orientation of modern social theory.[69] He thinks that both liberal and conservative political theory rest on a prior political choice that results from the perceived dilemma: "either resign yourself to some established version of social order, or face the war of all against all."[70]

Thus, Dworkin argues against conservative lawyers who appeal to an author's intention style of interpretation, that this style itself represents a political theory, and that therefore these lawyers undermine themselves in believing political theory to be a corruption of interpretation. Political theory for him is "part of what interpretation means."[71] But whereas Dworkin sees the practice of interpretation as grounded in political theory, Unger sees political theory as grounded in a self-deceptive attempt to preserve the political *status quo* through the practice of legal interpretation. For Dworkin, the theory can be masked by an interpretive practice that refuses to think itself through, and thus that lacks hermeneutical awareness. The better interpretations would be aware of the interconnection of political theory and interpretive practice, although this awareness is clearly not the same thing as simply imposing one's own values on the text. For Unger, in contrast, what is masked by both the theory and the interpretive practice is the political

66. Dworkin, *supra* note 18, at 269.
67. *See supra* text following note 25.
68. Dworkin, *supra* note 18, at 270.
69. Unger, *supra* note 57, at 576.
70. *Id.* at 577.
71. Dworkin, *supra* note 18, at 269.

struggle for power, the interpretation being an *ad hoc* element of the power play. Better interpretation for him is that which does not try to avoid seeing the social conflicts that produce the interpretive conflicts. Instead of trying to discover an inherent harmony, the better interpretation recognizes the lack of congruence between the available social ideals and their flawed institutional actualizations. Unger thus calls for a self-reflective rationality or "internal development" model that will try either to revise the ideals or to transform the actualization. For this more modest conception of rationality I should think the reflective equilibrium model would be equally appropriate.

There should be a sharp contrast in style between the ways a rights-and-principles theorist and a Critical Legal Studies theorist read the legal material. The former searches for the unity and coherence in the law by specifying the systematic interconnection of politics, morality, and legality, holding out the possibility of finding the right interpretations of hard cases and apparent conflicts. The latter tries instead "to recognize and develop the disharmonies of the law: the conflicts between principles and counterprinciples that can be found in any body of law."[72] These disharmonies within the legal materials suggest that there is not a single vision of human association operant in them, but several alternatives in addition to the dominant one. For this reason, I think it is appropriate to consider the style of interpretation used by the Critical Legal Studies Movement as deconstructive, as opposed to Dworkin's reconstructive style.

It would be facile to conclude, however, that both can legitimately claim to be equally correct understandings of different aspects of the texts. There is clearly a conflict here, and much will depend on how strong a case each can make for its own readings. Of course, neither side thinks there is a neutral way to adjudicate the conflicting readings, so how good the case appears to be will depend on the political commitments of the observer. What I wish to stress, however, is that as radical a conflict of interpretations as this is, it is better described by the hermeneutical model of interpretation than by either the objectivist picture I discussed earlier or the noninterpretivist model. Both parties deny a nonpartisan way of adjudicating their conflicting interpretations. Yet if I understand them correctly, both claim to be articulating what is really going on in the text, or what is the best explanation of how the text applies to a given situation. To recognize that in all candor each would have to believe its understanding of the text was not

72. Unger, *supra* note 57, at 578.

simply invented, one would have to recognize that interpreting is not the same as inventing. However, there are inventive interpretations, that is to say, original interpretations that make us find in the text or the situation points and possibilities we would otherwise not have seen. I do not believe a philosophical theory of interpretation could say in advance how to distinguish novel strategies of reading from arbitrary impositions on the text. In this Article I have argued against the conception of philosophical theory expecting philosophical theories to be capable of drawing this line. I conclude with the hope that the arena of interpretation is encompassing enough for adjudication and criticism not only of conflicting interpretations, but also of conflicting philosophies of interpretation.

[8]

TRANSCENDENTAL DECONSTRUCTION, TRANSCENDENT JUSTICE

*J.M. Balkin**

INTRODUCTION

A meaningful encounter between two parties does not change only the weaker or the stronger party, but both at once. We should expect the same from any encounter between deconstruction and justice. It might be tempting for advocates of deconstruction to hope that deconstruction would offer new insights into problems of justice, or, more boldly, to assert that "the question of justice" can never be the same after the assimilation of deconstructive insights. But, as a deconstructionist myself, I am naturally skeptical of all such blanket pronouncements, even — or perhaps especially — pronouncements about the necessary utility and goodness of deconstructive practice. Instead, in true deconstructive fashion, I would rather examine how deconstructionists' claims of what they are doing — which are often refused the name of "theory" or "method" — are uncannily altered by their encounter with questions of justice. In fact, as I hope to show, when deconstruction focuses on specific and concrete questions of justice, we will discover that deconstruction has always been something quite different from what most people thought it to be.

When I first began to write about deconstruction and law, I faced the task of translating deconstructive arguments in philosophy and literature to the concerns of law and justice. In the process, I proposed an understanding of deconstruction that enabled it to be employed in a critical theory of law. I fully recognized then that, in translating the insights of deconstructionists to the study of law, I was also working a transformation — for to translate is to iterate, and iterability alters.[1] Not surprisingly, I was subsequently accused of misunderstanding both Derrida and deconstruction, and of emphasizing a logocentric version of deconstruction that misinterpreted Derrida's texts and subverted and undermined "true" or "proper" deconstruc-

---

* Charles Tilford McCormick Professor of Law, University of Texas. — Ed. My thanks to Guyora Binder, David Gray Carlson, Sandy Levinson, Jay Mootz, and Tom Seung for their comments on previous drafts of this essay.

1. *See* J.M. Balkin, *Deconstructive Practice and Legal Theory*, 96 YALE L.J. 743, 745 & n.8, 761 n.56 (1987) (comparing the account of legal deconstruction to a translation or alteration of it, and offering it as a dangerous supplement to Derridean deconstruction).

tive practice.[2]

There is a certain irony to this accusation — the subversion of a putatively "orthodox" or properly performed deconstruction by a closet logocentrist. Yet it must be true, mustn't it, that there is a better and a worse way to engage in deconstructive argument? After all, deconstructive arguments are studied in departments of philosophy and comparative literature, and tests are given, and Ph.D. theses written, and degrees awarded, on the basis of this assumption. Aren't these tests graded as better or worse, and aren't these theses subjected to examination and sent back for revisions? How could one make sense of what deconstructionists do if there were not a better and a worse way to understand and perform deconstructive arguments? Surely it cannot be the case that "everything goes," where the determination of what is or is not a better use or understanding of deconstruction is concerned.

Nevertheless, I shall short-circuit this deconstructive quandary, which is potentially interminable. I plead guilty to the charge. If one is to adapt deconstruction to the critical study of law, the practice of deconstruction must, in fact, be altered, changed, modified, and, I would even say, improved. Certain features of Derrida's texts, for example, must be emphasized and others deemphasized and regarded as mistaken. Only in this way can deconstructive argument be made a useful tool of critical analysis. Only in this way can it escape the many criticisms of nihilism that have been leveled at it.

How logocentric of me.

So, I freely confess, I am a traitor to deconstruction. Yet, as we know, "traitor" and "tradition" come from the same root: The traditionalist hands down, while the traitor hands over. In both cases there is a passing off, a changing. (Yet the ambiguities continue: one can pass off a baton, as in a relay race, or pass off counterfeit money or goods.) The traitor-traditionalist distinction, with all of its accompanying uncertainties, is surely one of the most interesting for a deconstructionist.[3] There is an important sense in which I am continuing in the tradition of deconstructive argument even as I am insufficiently deconstructive by the standards of a purportedly "pure," "orthodox," "properly performed" deconstruction. If every traditionalist is also, in

2. *See* Pierre Schlag, *The Problem of the Subject*, 69 TEXAS L. REV. 1627, 1695 (1991) ("[T]his is not Derrida, and it is not deconstruction."); *see also* Pierre Schlag, *"Le Hors de Texte, C'est Moi": The Politics of Form and the Domestication of Deconstruction*, 11 CARDOZO L. REV. 1631, 1641-42 (1990).

3. For a discussion, see J.M. Balkin, *Tradition, Betrayal, and the Politics of Deconstruction*, 11 CARDOZO L. REV. 1613, 1619-20 (1990).

some sense, a traitor to what she preserves in the name of tradition — by altering it, freezing it in time, sucking the life out of it, and substituting the dry husk of unthinking imitation — might not every traitor also be, in some sense yet to be determined, a traditionalist of the first order?

As a traitor, however, I have an even greater satisfaction. As time has passed, Derrida himself has followed my perfidy. He has left the ranks of his apostles and joined the ranks of the apostates. His encounter with justice has brought him to many of the same conclusions about the meaning and use of deconstruction I have offered. So perhaps I was following him all along, in following the direction in which he later followed me. Perhaps I agreed with him all along, in agreeing with that with which he would later agree. Who is the traitor, and who the traditionalist now?

A key deconstructive idea is that iterability, or the capacity to be repeated in new contexts, results in change. Nevertheless, in examining how repetition is linked to change, we must always keep in mind two possible explanations, two different paths of explanation. The first claims that what we understand later really is different from the original and is consequently an improvement or a falling away. The second claims that this repeated thing has really always been the same; the new context has merely altered our understanding of it, with a consequent improvement or falling away of that understanding. Often it is very difficult to tell which claim we are making. It is often unclear whether we are traditionalists, who preserve the old in new guises and new understandings, or betrayers, who offer only an altered, imperfect substitute. After all, everyone is familiar with sectarian disputes between competing groups of believers — whether religious, political, or academic — who offer competing interpretations concerning the common object of their belief, branding their opponents as traitors while describing themselves as keepers of the faith.

It is this type of perfidy (which is at the same time a form of faithfulness), this alteration of deconstruction (which is at the same time not an alteration) that I would like to discuss here.

Of course, a deconstructionist must have texts to work with, texts to make her argument with. I take as my texts three writings by Jacques Derrida. The first is a lecture he gave in 1989 at a conference at the Cardozo Law School on "Deconstruction and the Possibility of Justice." This talk was later published under the title *Force of Law: "The Mystical Foundation of Authority"*.[4] In this address, he an-

4. Jacques Derrida, *Force of Law: The "Mystical Foundation of Authority,"* 11 CARDOZO L.

swered critics who accused deconstruction of nihilism or (perhaps worse) political quietism and complete irrelevance to questions of justice. Derrida replied that, far from failing to address the question of justice, deconstruction had addressed little else.[5] As evidence he listed a series of recent articles he had written that, in his opinion, concerned questions of justice.[6]

Of course, from a deconstructionist's standpoint, what might be most interesting about this list are the articles that Derrida did not choose to mention. One might think that these articles were withheld because they were wholly irrelevant to questions of justice. After all, in several of the writings that Derrida does mention, it takes quite a stretch to see them as directly addressing the question of justice.[7] A fortiori, the articles not mentioned must be even more divorced from these issues. Yet no deconstructionist worth her salt would accept such an obvious attempt at marginalization so readily; it would be like waving a red flag in front of a bull. Let us look, then, at the discarded, irrelevant parts of the Derridean corpus. Among them we find two substantial pieces on the controversy surrounding Paul de Man's wartime journalism.[8]

The basic story surrounding this scandal is by now well known.[9] Paul de Man, Sterling Professor of Comparative Literature at Yale University, was a close friend of Jacques Derrida and one of the central figures in the development of literary deconstruction. He died in 1983, a beloved and respected teacher and scholar. In 1987, a young graduate student doing research for a thesis on de Man discovered articles de Man had written between 1940 and 1942 for the Belgian newspaper *Le Soir.* During the Nazi occupation of Belgium, *Le Soir* was seized by pro-German forces and used as a mouthpiece for pro-Nazi propaganda and antisemitic statements.[10] De Man wrote for *Le Soir* during that period. He was still in his early twenties. Some of his

REV. 919 (1990) (Mary Quaintance trans.). A slightly different version of this essay appears in DECONSTRUCTION AND THE POSSIBILITY OF JUSTICE 3 (Drucilla Cornell et al. eds., 1992).

5. Derrida, *supra* note 4, at 935.

6. *Id.* at 929 (listing various writings on Levinas, Hegel, Freud, Kafka, Nelson Mandela, and the Declaration of Independence).

7. See, for example, JACQUES DERRIDA, GLAS (1974), whose subject matter has never precisely been determined.

8. Jacques Derrida, *Biodegradables: Seven Diary Fragments,* 15 CRITICAL INQUIRY 812 (1989) (Peggy Kamuf trans.) [hereinafter Derrida, *Biodegradables*]; Jacques Derrida, *Like the Sound of the Sea Deep Within a Shell: Paul de Man's War,* 14 CRITICAL INQUIRY 590 (1988) (Peggy Kamuf trans.) [hereinafter Derrida, *Paul de Man's War*].

9. For various accounts, see DAVID LEHMAN, SIGNS OF THE TIMES: DECONSTRUCTION AND THE FALL OF PAUL DE MAN (1991); RESPONSES: ON PAUL DE MAN'S WARTIME JOURNALISM (Werner Hamacher et al. eds., 1989) [hereinafter RESPONSES].

10. *See* Werner Hamacher et al., *Paul de Man, a Chronology, 1919-49 in* RESPONSES, *supra*

articles were exclusively literary, while others were in various degrees concerned with politics. Moreover, as Derrida himself puts it, the "massive, immediate, and dominant effect" of de Man's political articles conformed to the "official rhetoric . . . of the occupation forces."[11] And one article in particular, *The Jews in Contemporary Literature,*[12] is overtly antisemitic.

The revelation of these writings created a furor in the academy over de Man's posthumous reputation, the relation of his past writings to his later academic work, and the possible relationship between de Man's wartime activities and the normative claims — or lack of normative claims — of deconstruction. Many silly and intemperate accusations were leveled on all sides of this dispute. In the midst of this controversy, Derrida wrote two substantial articles. In the first, *The Sound of the Deep Sea Within a Shell: Paul de Man's War,*[13] he defends his old friend — and deconstruction itself — from what he regards as unjust accusation, and he tries to place de Man's life and works in their proper perspective. In the second, *Biodegradables: Six Literary Fragments,*[14] he responds to six critics of the previous essay. Here he defends not only de Man and deconstruction, but also himself, from what he regards as unjust treatment and unfair criticism.

One can agree or disagree with Derrida's particular stance on these issues. Nevertheless, it is hard to argue that these articles do not raise, on every line of every page, issues of justice, responsibility, and fair treatment. Their major concerns are how one should judge de Man, deconstruction, and Derrida himself, and how various critics have fairly or unfairly treated them. The question of responsibility overhangs the entire discussion — responsibility for the Holocaust, responsibility for collaboration, responsibility for one's silence about collaboration, responsibility in reading the work of another person, and responsibility in judging another's life and works.

Posed in the often byzantine setting of academic disputes and academic reputations, these articles concern the most concrete questions of justice and raise the most impassioned prose from Derrida. Indeed, the second article borders on the polemical. They stand in marked contrast to the relatively abstract pronouncements on justice and re-

---

note 9, at xiii. Members of the Belgian public derisively referred to the captured institution as *Le Soir volé* ("The Stolen Evening"). *Id.*

11. Derrida, *Paul de Man's War, supra* note 8, at 607 (emphasis omitted). Derrida offers the same formula in Derrida, *Biodegradables, supra* note 8, at 822, as proof that he was not underplaying the malignancy of de Man's writings.

12. Paul de Man, *Les Juifs dans la Littérature Actuelle*, LE SOIR, Mar. 4, 1941, at 1.

13. Derrida, *Paul de Man's War, supra* note 8.

14. Derrida, *Biodegradables, supra* note 8.

sponsibility Derrida offers in his Cardozo Law School address, *Force of Law: The Mystical Foundation of Authority.*

Thus, it is all the more puzzling that Derrida did not think to list these essays in his catalogue of examples of deconstruction's encounter with justice. Derrida could hardly have forgotten them, for they had only recently been published when he gave his address at Cardozo. Nor could he have expected that his audience would not know about them, for they were published in a well-known literary journal; indeed the first article had attracted considerable controversy and led to a symposium of critiques in which the second appeared as a response.[15] Nor can one object that these two articles do not discuss deconstruction or employ deconstructive techniques. In fact, both possess interesting and sustained discussions of deconstruction and its place in the academy, as well as many passages explicitly offering and rejecting possible connections between deconstruction and justice, or between deconstruction on the one hand and fascism or totalitarianism on the other.

Perhaps one might think that these articles are not worthy of mention precisely because they are so concerned with a particular event, and therefore lack universalizability. Yet, as Derrida himself reminds us in his Cardozo address, justice is always addressed to events and persons in all of their singularity.[16] What better way, one might think, to discover what Derrida really thinks about justice than to study his remarks concerning an issue about which he feels the most deeply, which gets him, as the saying goes, "where he lives"? We often witness people speaking abstractly, in high sounding phrases, about what is just and what is good. Yet, one might believe, we only see what they really think about these matters when they are faced with a concrete question of justice that truly affects them. So I read these three texts together — the abstract disposition on justice with the more concrete discussions of the de Man controversy. The first is sedate, the others brimming with anger and anguish. The relationship of deconstruction to justice lies somewhere in the conversation between them.

Of course, there is a sense, too, in which even the more abstract Cardozo Law School address, which nowhere explicitly mentions de Man, is motivated by and concerns the de Man controversy. For by the late 1980s this scandal had raised anew accusations that deconstruction was the easy refuge of nihilists or those without values or conscience, that a doctrine that found complications of meaning in all

15. *See* Symposium, *On Jacques Derrida's "Paul de Man's War,"* 15 CRITICAL INQUIRY 765 (1989).

16. Derrida, *supra* note 4, at 949.

texts was tailor-made for collaborationists with evil, unscrupulous opportunists, or simply weak-willed souls unable to commit to a just course of action when faced with obstacles or uncertainties. Thus, when Derrida rose to address the audience at the Cardozo Law School in the fall of 1989 — which was also the fall of the 1980s — it was all the more important to establish that deconstruction was not, nor had it ever been, nihilistic, opposed to justice, or even (God forbid) unconcerned with justice, but that it was, quite the contrary, fully committed to the critique of injustice and the creation of a more just world. Deconstruction, Derrida hoped to convince his audience, could properly be used for beneficial purposes of social and cultural critique, and indeed, it was perhaps most correctly used for such purposes.

Yet, in rising to respond to these critics, just as he had previously responded to the critics of de Man, Derrida offered examples of deconstructive argument that were not wholly consistent with all of his previous deconstructive writings. They are, however, consistent with the practice of deconstruction that I have advocated. This is Derrida's perfidy, his betrayal of deconstruction. Yet it is a betrayal that I heartily endorse.

In these essays, Derrida offers four different statements of the possible connection between deconstruction and justice. First, deconstruction can call into question the boundaries that determine who is a proper subject of justice — that is, to whom justice is owed. Second, deconstruction demands "a responsibility without limits."[17] Third, deconstruction requires one to address the Other in the language of the Other. Fourth, deconstruction is opposed to all intellectual forms of totalitarianism, and hence, by analogy, to political totalitarianism as well.

Like Derrida, I am also concerned with deconstruction's possible relationship to justice. In this essay, I offer an extended critique of Derrida's views in order to make two basic points about the relationship between justice and deconstruction. First, Derrida offers deconstructive arguments that cut both ways: Although one can use deconstructive arguments to further what Derrida believes is just, one can also deconstruct in a different way to reach conclusions he would probably find very unjust. One can also question his careful choice of targets of deconstruction: One could just as easily have chosen different targets and, by deconstructing them, reach conclusions that he would find abhorrent. Thus, in each case, what makes Derrida's deconstructive argument an argument for justice is not its use of

17. *Id.* at 953.

deconstruction, but the selection of the particular text or concept to deconstruct and the way in which the particular deconstructive argument is wielded. I shall argue that Derrida's encounter with justice really shows that deconstructive argument is a species of rhetoric, which can be used for different purposes depending upon the moral and political commitments of the deconstructor.

Second, and equally important, Derrida's use of deconstructive argument to critique existing arrangements as unjust presumes belief in an idea of justice that may be indeterminate but is not reducible to any conventional notion of justice. Derrida's arguments simply make no sense unless he is relying on a transcendental idea of justice, which human law only imperfectly articulates. Moreover, I shall argue, he admits this, albeit only tentatively and haltingly, in his more recent writings on deconstruction.

Derrida's resistance to such a recognition is altogether understandable. A postulation of transcendent human values brings us a long way from the philosophical conception Derrida offered in *Of Grammatology.*[18] There he argued against the very existence of a "transcendental signified" and made his famous statement that "[t]here is nothing outside of the text."[19] Nevertheless, I believe that a transformation of deconstruction becomes inevitable when deconstructionists begin to confront real questions of justice and injustice. If deconstruction can have salutary effects for the study of legal theory, there are equally salutary effects that law can have for deconstruction. So, I argue, when we try to make sense of Derrida's arguments about law and justice and read them charitably to avoid confusing and self-contradictory interpretations, we arrive at an important variant of deconstructive practice, which relies on the existence of human values that transcend any given culture. For want of a better name, I shall call this type of deconstruction *transcendental deconstruction.* It is the form of deconstruction I have advocated in my own work.

A belief in transcendental values is often associated with the tradition of Platonism. However, the view I am concerned with is not the Platonism of the *Republic.*[20] It does not assert the existence of eternal and unchanging Ideas that exist in a Platonic Heaven. It does not postulate normative standards of determinate content. Rather, it is

---

18. JACQUES DERRIDA, OF GRAMMATOLOGY (Gayatri C. Spivak trans., Johns Hopkins Univ. Press 1976) (1967).

19. *Id.* at 158 (emphasis omitted).

20. PLATO, *Republic, in* THE COLLECTED DIALOGUES OF PLATO 575 (Edith Hamilton & Huntington Cairns eds., Bollingen Foundation 1961) [hereinafter COLLECTED DIALOGUES] (Paul Shorey trans., 1930).

concerned with those indeterminate values or urges located in the human soul, which human beings articulate through positive morality and cultural conventions, and which nevertheless always escape this articulation.

Surprisingly enough, the origins of this nonplatonic transcendentalism also lie in Plato's work. Plato came to a similar view after he had written the *Republic,* in later dialogues like the *Statesman,*[21] *Sophist,*[22] and particularly the *Laws.*[23] He abandoned his earlier dreams of political perfection for a more democratic, skeptical vision.[24] By the time of the *Laws,* Plato realized that our idea of justice is inchoate and indeterminate. It is a mere skeleton; it must be fleshed out in the world of culture. For this reason, we must *construct* a conception of justice using our human values and intuitions. T.K. Seung has called this approach "platonic constructivism"; he argues that it is a substantial modification of the more familiar Platonism we recall from the *Republic.*[25] But Seung's constructivism has a curious consequence: The articulation of our values in human culture, law, and convention makes these concrete articulations different from the inchoate values they articulate. It is this gap or discrepancy that deconstructive argument seizes upon as the basis for its critique. The essence of what I am calling *transcendental* deconstruction, then, is to note the interval between the human capacity for judgment and evaluation that inevitably and necessarily transcends the creations of culture, and the prescriptions and evaluations of that culture, which in turn articulate and exemplify human values like justice. It is in this sense that transcendental deconstruction depends, as Platonism itself does, on a conception of values that "go beyond" the positive norms of culture and convention. But these transcendent values do not come to us in a fully determinate form; they need culture to turn their inchoate sense into an articulated conception. And these transcendent values do not exist in an imaginary Platonic Heaven; they exist rather in the wellsprings of the human soul.

The idea of values that "transcend" culture might suggest that when human beings evaluate they do so from a place outside culture.

21. PLATO, *Statesman, in* COLLECTED DIALOGUES, *supra* note 20, at 1018 (J.B. Skemp trans., 1952).

22. PLATO, *Sophist, in* COLLECTED DIALOGUES, *supra* note 20, at 957 (Francis M. Cornford trans., 1935).

23. PLATO, *Laws, in* COLLECTED DIALOGUES, *supra* note 20, at 1225 (A.E. Taylor trans., 1934).

24. Here I draw on the excellent discussion in T.K. SEUNG, INTUITION AND CONSTRUCTION: THE FOUNDATION OF NORMATIVE THEORY 175-211 (1993).

25. T.K. SEUNG, KANT'S PLATONIC REVOLUTION (forthcoming 1994).

But it is difficult to make sense of this claim, because culture helps constitute us as individuals. Thus, standing outside of culture would be like standing outside of ourselves. We can only express our values through their articulations in culture. How, then, is it possible to speak of transcendent human values when the ways we express our values must always be immanent in culture? How can values be both immanent and transcendent?

To understand how values can be transcendent, we must recognize that *value* is properly a verb, not a noun. People do not "have" values as if they were objects that could be kept in their pockets. Rather, they possess an inexhaustible drive to evaluate — to name the beautiful and the ugly, the better and the worse. This feature of human evaluation is poorly captured by our standard metaphors of value. These are metaphors of determinate measurement: Values work like scales or rulers, and to evaluate is to measure. These metaphors have two important conceptual entailments: The first is that a value provides a fixed standard of measurement; the second is that there is a necessary separation between the value that measures and the thing measured. If a value is a standard of measure, it must be determinate just as a ruler is of a determinate length. Moreover, it must exist separately from the thing it measures. One cannot use a ruler to measure itself any more than one can use a balance to weigh itself. Hence, the metaphor of measurement leads us to assume that values can be transcendent only if they somehow exist as determinate standards apart from the culture that they measure. This leads to Plato's ontology, and, I submit, to Plato's error.

Instead we must consider a contrasting metaphor of value — that of an indeterminate urge or demand. Instead of viewing values as determinate standards of measurement, we should understand them as a sort of insatiable and inchoate drive to evaluate. Because they are inchoate they can never be made fully determinate; because they are insatiable they can never be fully satisfied. Our values are like an inexhaustible yearning for something that cannot clearly and fully be described; hence our values always demand more of us than we can ever satisfy, despite our best efforts.

Thus, we have two metaphorical accounts of value: one of determinate measurement, and one of indeterminate longing. Each is helpful in its own way, but neither can be usefully employed in all contexts and circumstances. To understand the phenomenon of transcendence we must recognize the metaphor of measurement as a metaphor, and exchange it for a different one.

The metaphor of value as an insatiable urge or demand offers a more plausible account of how our values are transcendent and why our articulations of them are imperfect. Under the metaphor of measurement, our institutions fail to be just because they are imperfect representations of a determinate standard of justice; this standard is transcendent because it exists separate and apart from culture. Thus, virtue is a matter of copying, and the virtuous person is a good copyist. Under the contrasting metaphor, values are inchoate yearnings that we attempt to articulate through our cultural constructions. To be just we must construct examples of justice using the indeterminate urge for justice as our goad rather than as our guide. This means that the virtuous person is not a good copyist but a good architect. She attempts to satisfy her sense of justice by constructing just institutions. Nevertheless, she responds to an indefinite and indeterminate value. This has two consequences. First, there will be many different ways of constructing a just institution, depending upon the situation in which she finds herself and the resources she has available to her. Second, her constructed example of justice will never exhaust the insatiable longings of human value. Thus, human cultural creations will always fail to be perfectly just, but not because they are defective copies of a determinate standard. Their imperfection arises from the necessary inadequation that must exist between an indeterminate and inexhaustible urge and any concrete and determinate articulation of justice. This relationship of inadequacy between culture and value is what we mean by "transcendence." The goal of transcendental deconstruction is to rediscover this transcendence where it has been forgotten.

Some people have thought that deconstruction is aimless; that it has no goal or purpose. Others have argued that at best its goal is the mindless destruction and annihilation of all conceptual distinctions. Neither charge applies to the form of deconstructive practice I advocate here. Transcendental deconstruction has a goal; its goal is not destruction but rectification.[26] The deconstructor critiques for the purpose of betterment; she seeks out unjust or inappropriate conceptual hierarchies in order to assert a better ordering.[27] Hence, her argument is always premised on the possibility of an alternative to existing norms that is not simply different, but also more just, even if the results of this deconstruction are imperfect and subject to further deconstruction. Such a deconstruction assumes that it is possible to speak meaningfully of the more or the less just; it decidedly rejects the claim

26. I borrow this expression from T.K. Seung. *Id.*

27. For a defense of this normative approach to deconstruction, see J.M. Balkin, *Understanding Legal Understanding: The Legal Subject and the Problem of Legal Coherence*, 103 YALE L.J. 105, 124-27 (1993).

that nothing is more just than anything else, or that all things are equally just. Rather than effacing the distinction between the just and unjust, it attempts to reveal the mistaken identification of justice with an inadequate articulation of justice in human culture and law.

If this analysis is sound, deconstructive argument becomes something quite different from what most of its critics (and even some of its adherents) have imagined. Now deconstructive argument is premised on the assumption of transcendent yet only imperfectly realizable values of justice and truth. The practice of deconstructive argument may be skeptical about the perfection of any and every particular example of justice, but it is decidedly not nihilistic. Indeed, it is a deconstruction founded on faith — faith in human values which, although only articulable through culture, surpass and hence act as a perpetual admonition to culture. This is the type of deconstructive practice I have advocated, and the one that makes the most sense when applied to law and political theory.

Jacques Derrida, I shall argue, has gradually come around to a similar view, although he would not perhaps use the term *transcendental* to describe it. Yet it is an inevitable consequence of the connections he now wishes to draw between deconstruction and justice. Moreover, he has begun to insist that something like this is what he always had in mind by deconstruction.[28] Is this an adequate description of his project or a specious substitution? Is this tradition or betrayal? That is for the reader to judge.

I. Deconstruction and the Subjects of Justice

The first connection between justice and deconstruction that Derrida hopes to demonstrate concerns the definition of who is a subject of justice, that is, who can be treated justly or unjustly. Throughout Western civilization, Derrida argues, the category of subjects of justice has been limited.[29] Deconstruction furthers justice, he insists, because it calls these limitations into question.[30]

Derrida argues that Western civilization has traditionally considered justice and injustice to be concepts that apply only to persons, in particular to persons who possess the capability of language.[31] These are persons whom one can speak to — and hence reason with. "[O]ne

28. Here one must be sensitive to the possibility that my assessment of Derrida applies with equal force to me: Repetition of older arguments in new contexts may have produced changes in views that I claim always to have held.

29. Derrida, *supra* note 4, at 951-53.

30. *Id.* at 953-55.

31. *Id.* at 951.

would not speak of injustice or violence toward an animal, even less toward a vegetable or a stone."[32] For example, "[a]n animal can be made to suffer, but we would never say, in a sense considered proper, that it is a wronged subject, the victim of a crime . . . and this is true *a fortiori,* we think, for what we call vegetable or mineral or intermediate species like the sponge."[33] Indeed, Derrida continues, throughout human history "[t]here have been, there still are many 'subjects' among mankind who are not yet recognized as subjects and who receive this animal treatment . . . ."[34] To treat a person as an animal — that is, one who is incapable of being addressed in language — is to consider that person's treatment not to be a question of justice or injustice. This argument reminds one of Chief Justice Taney's famous assertion in *Dred Scott v. Sandford*[35] that blacks "had no rights which the white man was bound to respect."[36] Derrida even suggests that the primitive tradition of animal sacrifice confirmed and supported the notion of a separation between human subjects — who can speak and are the subjects and objects of just and unjust treatment — and "animals" who, by the logic of this opposition, are not capable of being treated unjustly.[37]

The boundaries of justice, in other words, are determined by the boundaries of who is "human" as opposed to who is merely an "animal" — that is, one without language or, alternatively, without a recognized right to speak. Yet these boundaries and the justifications for these boundaries can be deconstructed, even to the point, as some animal rights activists would maintain, of calling into question the exclusion of animal life from questions of justice. At this point the distinction between "human" and "animal" would no longer serve to distinguish subjects of justice from nonsubjects; we would have to invent a new distinction.

Thus, Derrida argues, the opposition "subject of justice" versus "nonsubject of justice" is unstable. Because of its instability, it may continually be questioned, and the criteria that separate the subjects of justice from those nonsubjects — earlier identified by the distinction between "humans" and "animals" — must continually be revised. Hence, Derrida wants to insist, deconstruction is relevant to justice because we can deconstruct the boundaries of who is considered a

32. *Id.*
33. *Id.*
34. *Id.*
35. 60 U.S. (19 How.) 393 (1857).
36. 60 U.S. (19 How.) at 407.
37. Derrida, *supra* note 4, at 951.

"person" or, more generally, a proper subject of justice. By challenging these boundaries, we can move from a world in which the conception of a subject of justice is wrongfully limited to one in which it receives a just expansion.[38]

In this way, Derrida insists, the use of deconstruction might not lead to nihilism or injustice. Instead deconstruction would form part of a progressive project that sought increasingly to expand political rights to those other than white male European human beings by deconstructing the boundaries of who are and are not the proper subjects of justice. As he says, in a slightly different context, "[n]othing seems to me less outdated than the classical emancipatory ideal."[39]

These egalitarian sentiments are surely to be applauded. Yet Derrida has not shown a necessary connection between deconstruction and justice. He has merely pointed out that one might deconstruct certain oppositions in a way that produces increasingly egalitarian conclusions. He has not shown that these are the only oppositions one might deconstruct. Nor has he shown that one can only deconstruct these oppositions in a way that produces increasingly egalitarian results.

Derrida might have chosen to deconstruct or problematize the distinction between justice and injustice, between liberty and slavery, or between tolerance and bigotry. He does not do so. But nothing in deconstructive theory — if such a thing exists — directs him or forbids him from doing so. Deconstructive argument does not cease to operate when the conclusions one might draw from it are inegalitarian, although it is hardly surprising that Jacques Derrida sees egalitarian consequences flowing from his use of deconstruction. Indeed, this possibility is admitted by his very claim that deconstruction "does not *necessarily* lead to injustice . . . but *may* . . . lead to a reinterpretation" that is more just.[40] Derrida, like every good deconstructor, picks his targets carefully.

Moreover, even given the targets of his deconstruction — the historically enforced oppositions between the subjects and nonsubjects of justice — Derrida has not shown that the only way in which these

38. As Derrida puts it:

> [A] deconstructionist approach to the boundaries that institute the human subject (preferably and paradigmatically the adult male, rather than the woman, child or animal) as the measure of the just and the unjust, does not necessarily lead to injustice, nor to the effacement of an opposition between just and unjust but may, in the name of a demand more insatiable than justice, lead to a reinterpretation of the whole apparatus of boundaries within which a history and a culture have been able to confine their criteriology.

Id. at 953.

39. *Id.* at 971.

40. *Cf. id.* at 953 (emphasis added).

oppositions might be deconstructed leads to increasingly just results. If deconstruction calls into question the boundaries of subjects of justice, it does not follow that the only way to question these boundaries is to advocate their expansion. They may well be unstable, as Derrida insists. Yet their instability might be evidence that they are about to implode, rather than expand. Furthermore, even if there must be an expansion, one can expand the boundary in two opposite directions — by expanding the scope of what is assigned to the "human," who is a subject of justice, or by expanding the scope of what is assigned to the "nonhuman," which is not a proper subject of justice. In this way, the instability of these boundaries might well be used, as it has in the past, to show that blacks, or Asians, or women are not fully human beings, or that the distinction between women and animals, for example, is so unstable that it cannot fully be maintained.

Indeed, one can understand the history of bigotry as the continuous deconstruction of an imagined unity of humankind. It is the perpetual claim that the unity of humankind is a pious fiction, a papered-over discontinuity and heterogeneity, and that the Other within this imagined unity must be located and understood in all of its difference and inferiority. The egalitarian claims to rediscover the true similarity of the subjects of justice by reclaiming those who were wrongly grouped with nonsubjects; the bigot claims to rediscover the true similarity of nonsubjects of justice by rejecting those who were wrongly grouped with the subjects of justice. Both deconstruct boundaries and categories, and the act of deconstruction does not decide between them.

One might also use deconstruction to show that the boundaries of who may possess certain civil and political rights are unstable. Thus, early American feminists argued that the expansion of political rights to black males required the expansion of political rights to women. However, a similar criticism applies here. The claim that the current limitations of political rights — like the franchise or the right to life — are unstable and that the justifications for these boundaries are self-deconstructing may argue in favor of further restricting the scope of these rights rather than expanding them. If the extension of antidiscrimination laws to disabled persons cannot be squared with the denial of such rights to homosexuals, then perhaps this result counsels in the direction of shrinking the rights of the disabled rather than expanding the rights of homosexuals. The strongly egalitarian bias of the academy makes this an unthinkable position, but it is not made unthinkable by any feature of "deconstructive theory." It is made unthinkable by the preexisting moral commitments of those who make the deconstructive argument.

If one begins with an egalitarian ideology, one can easily be misled into thinking that the "emancipatory ideal" that Derrida endorses is the same as deconstruction. But this assumption is based on an implicit opposition or conceptual homology — namely, that deconstruction is to logocentrism as emancipation is to slavery, or as expansion of the subjects of justice is to contraction of the subjects of justice. Of course, one of the most important deconstructive techniques is the demonstration that the homology "*A* is to *B* as *C* is to *D*" is reversible; one deconstructs ideologies by subverting the conceptual homologies upon which they rest. My point is that this technique can be performed as easily with the present set of conceptual oppositions as with the opposition between speech and writing in *Of Grammatology*.

Furthermore, even if one accepted that deconstruction necessarily led to an increased domain of subjects of justice, Derrida's argument rests on the additional assumption that increasing the number of subjects of justice increases justice. But it does not. The second half of the nineteenth century saw two great expansions of the domain of subjects of justice in the United States. The first was the emancipation of the slaves and the bestowal of civil and political rights upon them through the Thirteenth, Fourteenth, and Fifteenth Amendments. The second came twenty years later in *Santa Clara County v. Southern Pacific Railroad*,[41] in which the U.S. Supreme Court held that corporations were persons for purposes of the civil and political rights guaranteed by the Fourteenth Amendment. In Derrida's terms, corporations too became subjects of justice, and indeed, through the same constitutional amendment that granted civil rights to blacks. The result of this decision was that corporations had contract and property rights against other individuals that the courts were constitutionally bound to enforce, and they did so with a vengeance during America's Gilded Age, with results that today make most economic egalitarians shudder.[42] The legacy of *Santa Clara* continues to this

41. 116 U.S. 394 (1886).

42. I want to emphasize here that the granting of "personhood" and even "citizenship" to corporations was originally designed to protect the property interests of individuals who owned shares in a corporation. To this extent, the expansion of corporate rights seems a perfectly justifiable protection of individual property rights — assuming always that the theorist in question believes that the basic structure of economic rights is justified. It therefore furthers, rather than detracts from, the "emancipatory ideal." However, one might protect these individual property rights in ways other than by creating a new legal subject with constitutional rights. The egalitarian critique, as I understand it, is that the choice of this strategy has had unexpected consequences that cannot all be explained as necessary to protect the (just) rights of shareholders. To some degree the fiction of the corporation as a person has taken on a life of its own and has been used to work injustices and denials of individual rights. *See, e.g.*, Connecticut Gen. Life Ins. Co.

day: The Supreme Court has held that corporations as constitutional "persons" have First Amendment speech rights like those of private citizens.[43] This holding seems unexceptional but for the fact that corporations usually have considerably more money and therefore can exercise their speech rights more effectively than the average citizen, through donations to political campaigns, purchase of time and space on broadcast and print media, and so on. The recognition and protection of corporate civil and political rights has enabled corporations to convert huge concentrations of property rights into concentrations of political power and thereby exercise considerable control over the American political process. Not surprisingly, some scholars on the left find these results to be perverse and to represent a net loss of individual liberty.[44]

In recent times, one of the most pressing questions before the American public has been the scope of the right to abortion. Antiabortion activists have been on the forefront of expanding the boundaries of personhood. One might almost believe that they were taking their cue from Derrida, for their arguments are nothing if not deconstructive: *Effacing* the distinction between fetus and child, they have argued that fetuses are "babies" and doctors who perform abortions are "baby killers." Insisting on the *undecideability* of any boundaries (such as viability) between the person and the nonperson, they have characterized the current law of the United States as the most violent act of mass murder since the Holocaust. If, as Derrida points out, justice and injustice have been reserved in Western culture to the possessors of language, and if this reservation is itself in need of destabilizing and deconstructing — in the case of animals, for example — the contemporary antiabortion advocate can hardly be faulted for seeing in this claim an argument for the protection of defenseless fetuses, who lack the power of speech and are routinely slaughtered by

v. Johnson, 303 U.S. 77, 87-90 (1938) (Black, J., dissenting) (arguing that *Santa Clara* should be overruled); C. EDWIN BAKER, HUMAN LIBERTY AND FREEDOM OF SPEECH 220-21 (1991). For an examination of some of the alternative ways the issue might have been conceptualized and the consequences of the *Santa Clara* decision, see Morton J. Horwitz, Santa Clara *Revisited: The Development of Corporate Theory*, 88 W. VA. L. REV. 173 (1985).

43. *See* First Natl. Bank v. Bellotti, 435 U.S. 765 (1978) (striking down limitations on corporate spending designed to influence voters).

44. *See, e.g.*, Mark Tushnet, *Corporations and Free Speech*, *in* THE POLITICS OF LAW 253 (David Kairys ed., 1982); *cf.* Owen M. Fiss, *Why the State?*, 100 HARV. L. REV. 781, 787-91 (1987) (describing the media's control of public debate and business's control of the political process). Indeed, the U.S. Supreme Court has itself been somewhat equivocal on the question of whether the scope of this First Amendment right should be equal in all respects to the right enjoyed by natural persons. *See* Austin v. Michigan Chamber of Commerce, 494 U.S. 652 (1990). The question for Derrida, of course, is whether further deconstruction of the boundary that excludes corporations from full membership as "subjects of justice" would be a good thing or a bad thing.

those who possess this power. Everything that Derrida says about the exclusion of animals from the domain of justice, they might argue, could be said on behalf of the human fetus: If a cat or a chimpanzee should be protected from torture or vivisection, how much more so should the human fetus who likewise lacks the power of speech, and who likewise is slaughtered for the benefit of those whom the state has already recognized as subjects of justice — women?

Needless to say, many women's groups and commentators on the left (including, one assumes — although one does not know this for certain — Derrida himself) would find such an argument abhorrent. But is the argument abhorrent because it is not deconstructive or rather because it *is* deconstructive — because nothing in "deconstruction" prevents such an argument? Is the reason that a feminist who employs deconstruction would not make such an argument because deconstruction forbids it or because it conflicts with her deeply held moral and political commitments — her sense of the just and the unjust? In other words, isn't she really *using* deconstructive argument to make sense of her existing commitments, to articulate her values?

In the examples of corporate speech, or the pros and cons of abortion, we witness what I call "ideological drift" at work.[45] An argument or principle that appears on its face to have determinate political consequences turns out to bear a very different political valence when it is inserted into new and unexpected contexts. Yet because, as deconstruction itself reminds us, one cannot fully control the contexts into which an argument or a claim can be inserted, one cannot fully control its political valence in future situations. The notion of ideological drift follows from the basic deconstructive point that iterability alters. We have merely applied this point to the practice of deconstructive argument itself. *If* the practices of deconstruction by human beings are themselves subject to the insights of deconstruction, this alteration seems inevitably to follow. The practice of deconstruction by human beings must also be subject to ideological drift. So is Derrida then hoisted on his own petard? *If* what is called "deconstruction" is a rhetorical practice, a series of arguments, a set of approaches that can be taught, repeated, iterated, used again and again in different contexts, places, and times, all this would seem to follow. Deconstruction, or more correctly deconstructive arguments made by human beings, must be iterable in ways that lead to both just and unjust results.

45. *See* J.M. Balkin, *Ideological Drift and the Struggle Over Meaning*, 25 CONN. L. REV. 869 (1993).

What, then, of this "if"? We are not prepared to answer this question. At least not yet.

II. A Responsibility Without Limits

A. *The Infinite and the Indefinite*

Let us continue. Derrida posits a second possible relation between deconstruction and justice — it is "[t]he sense of a responsibility without limits."[46] This responsibility is "necessarily excessive, incalculable, before memory."[47] Deconstruction leads to justice because it reveals the limitlessness of our responsibility.

Nevertheless, a responsibility without limits is not the same thing as justice. We do not necessarily increase justice by increasing responsibility. Suppose a plaintiff is injured in a traffic accident. The plaintiff picks a name at random from the phone directory and sues this person as a defendant. We do not necessarily increase justice by holding this person liable for the accident. Justice is increased by eliminating her responsibility.

Nor do we necessarily increase justice by increasing the responsibility of all persons. Suppose that a defendant strikes a plaintiff because the plaintiff is homosexual and the defendant hates homosexuals. We can justly hold the defendant responsible for this brutality. Suppose, however, that the defendant argues as follows: His parents are also responsible because they abused him as a child. The bystanders on the street are responsible because they did not intervene on the plaintiff's behalf. The police are responsible because they did not prevent the injury from occurring. The state's mental health agencies are responsible because they did not offer the defendant free counseling to deal with his aggression and his hatred of homosexuals, and so on.

The difficulty is that to increase the responsibility of one person is often to decrease the responsibility of another. Here the defendant attempts to decrease his responsibility by shifting it to third parties. There is no problem in increasing the responsibility of all persons as long as we insist that the defendant also remains fully responsible. Indeed, this may be a more adequate description of the situation. The difficulty arises anew, however, when we determine the appropriate remedy for an injustice. How are we to divide up the responsibility when the plaintiff demands compensation? The more persons who are held responsible, the less each will have to pay, all other things being

46. Derrida, *supra* note 4, at 953.

47. *Id.*

equal. We might try to avoid this dilemma by allowing the plaintiff full recovery from each person held responsible, but surely this solution creates its own form of injustice.[48]

The demand for an increase of justice is not necessarily the demand for increased responsibility. It is rather the demand for an *appropriate apportionment* of responsibility. That is what "just" means — neither too much nor too little, but just the right amount of responsibility for each person. The very notion of apportionment implies the possibility that the responsibility of some persons will be decreased, if not eliminated. Justice involves the recognition that people are simply not responsible for some of the things for which others would like to hold them responsible. Furthermore, the demand for an appropriate apportionment of responsibility presupposes that there is a notion of appropriateness — that not every assertion of responsibility is as valid as any other. If the deconstructive argument is to make sense, it must assume that one's responsibility goes as far as it should, but no further, whether or not this can be known for certain.

In this light, Derrida's essays on Paul de Man offer a useful counterweight to his more abstract formulation. In these essays, Derrida does not assert that either he, or de Man, have limitless responsibility. Rather, he attempts to put de Man's responsibility in its proper perspective. He attempts to offer a just apportionment of responsibility, blame, and innocence regarding de Man, himself, and his critics.

First, Derrida argues, de Man is not responsible for all of the many evils of Nazism or for the Holocaust. To compare him to Mengele, as one writer did, is unjust.[49] Second, it is unjust to read de Man's later writings as an admission of guilt or responsibility — or as an attempt to deny responsibility — for what he did during World War II.[50] Third, although de Man wrote a series of articles expressing the ideology of the occupation forces and one article which is blatantly antisemitic, it is unjust to judge his whole life based on that one episode in his youth.[51] Fourth — and this is the most controversial point in his argument — Derrida suggests that de Man's articles are not as

48. Increasing responsibility, moreover, always comes at a cost. The more things for which people are held responsible, the less time and money they have for their own pursuits. Responsibility to others comes at the price of one's freedom of action as well as one's security. An infinite protection of security for all will result in an infinite responsibility for all, which will paradoxically abolish the liberty of all, and with it the security of all. The demand for infinite responsibility is like the paradoxical predicament of the pantheist who finds she must remain motionless because she fears that any movement on her part will inadvertently destroy a bug or a microorganism. Whatever she does, she is responsible. Yet her failure to act makes her doubly responsible.

49. *See* Derrida, *Biodegradables, supra* note 8, at 821.

50. Derrida, *Paul de Man's War, supra* note 8, at 640-51.

51. *Id.* at 650-51.

damning as one might be led to expect when they are read in the appropriate context. According to Derrida, the explicit antisemitism of the worst article is equivocal, and it is hardly as bad as many other articles in *Le Soir.*[52]

In the same way, Derrida responds to the critics who attacked his discussion of de Man by arguing that his responsibility and that of the institution they call "Deconstruction" is less than they imply or contend. They are unjust to Derrida, a Jew who was a teenager during the Second World War: "I . . . who have *nothing whatever to do* with everything that happened; I who, at the time, was rather on the side of the victims."[53] They are unjust as well to the practitioners of deconstruction, "which at the time was at year minus twenty-five of its calendar!"[54]

These remarks suggest that Derrida cannot mean by "a responsibility without limits" a limitless responsibility. Otherwise, he, de Man, and indeed all of us are responsible without limits for the Holocaust and many other horrible crimes, both past and present. But this would not be just: The demand of justice is often the demand that we are *not* responsible, even though we have been unjustly accused.

Instead, we must offer an alternative account of "a responsibility without limits" that saves it from these difficulties. This account inevitably leads us to the transcendental conception of deconstruction. A limitless responsibility could be an infinite responsibility, or it could be a responsibility whose full contours cannot be defined in advance. This is the distinction between the *infinite* and the *indefinite.* We can say, both in the case of the infinite and the indefinite, that one cannot draw determinate and clear boundaries, so that in both cases we are, in a sense, "without limits." The meaning of "without limits," however, is different in each case. The infinite cannot be bounded because it is infinite. The indefinite has no clear boundaries because its scope is so heavily dependent on context, and not all possible future contexts can be prescribed in advance. The indefinite has boundaries, but we do not know precisely where they are. The infinite has no boundaries, and we know this for certain.

Thus, the indefinite is unlimited, but not in the way that the infinite is. It makes perfect sense to say that an individual's responsibility is "without limits" because it is always indefinite — that is, because

52. *Id.* at 621-32. In fact, Derrida asserts that, because de Man specifically distances himself from so-called "vulgar" antisemitism, one can even read his article as implicitly rebuking the more virulent examples of antisemitism in the pages of *Le Soir. Id.* at 625-26.

53. Derrida, *Biodegradables, supra* note 8, at 820.

54. *Id.*

the full contours of this responsibility can never be completely articulated — but it is nevertheless limited in another sense because it is not infinite. Paul de Man's responsibility for his wartime journalism is without limits because its scope cannot be fully demarcated: His actions will have had effects on individuals that he could not have foreseen. Moreover, his actions will continue to have effects about which modern day judges of his responsibility do not and cannot know. In this sense, Paul de Man indeed has a responsibility without limits. But it is not an infinite responsibility. He is not responsible for the Holocaust, or the Lockerbie plane bombing, or the French Revolution.

We can also apply the distinction between the infinite and the indefinite to the meanings of texts. People often associate deconstruction with the claim that the meaning of texts is indeterminate. Yet there are two ways to claim that meaning is indeterminate: One can say that a text's meaning is infinite — that is, that it means everything — or one can say that its meaning is indefinite. If the meaning of every text is infinite, then all texts mean the same thing, because all texts have every meaning. But if one says that the meaning of every text is indefinite, we mean that the contexts in which the text will take its meaning cannot be specified in advance, and therefore the text will always have an excess of meaning over that which we expect (or intend) it to have when it is let loose upon the world. The first view of texts is consistent with a nihilistic account of deconstruction; the second is consistent with the type of deconstruction I advocate.

The choice between these two approaches also corresponds to two different explanations of how one deconstructs a conceptual opposition. The strategy of the nihilistic view is one of *total effacement* — all conceptual distinctions are imaginary because the meanings of each side of the opposition are infinite. Therefore both sides mean the same thing. The strategy of transcendental deconstruction is one of *nested opposition.* A nested opposition is an opposition in which the two sides "contain" each other — that is, they possess a ground of commonality as well as difference.[55] In this case, the deconstruction argues that the two sides are alike in some contexts and different in others; the logocentric mistake has been to assert categorically that they were simply identical or simply different. Because the two sides form a nested opposition, their similarity and their difference rely on context, but because context cannot be fully determined in advance, the scope of their similarity and difference is indefinite. In this way the transcendental conception of deconstruction preserves the possibility of

55. For a fuller discussion, see J.M. Balkin, *Nested Oppositions*, 99 YALE L.J. 1669 (1990) (book review).

conceptual distinctions, while the nihilistic version does not.[56]

The distinction between transcendental deconstruction and its unworkable alternative rests upon the distinction between the indefinite and the infinite. However, since one can deconstruct any distinction, one should also be able to deconstruct the distinction between the indefinite and the infinite. Even here, however, we need to ask what conception of deconstruction we should use to critique the theory — the transcendental or the nihilistic. If we use a nihilistic conception, we would be effacing this distinction. We would say that there is no difference between the indefinite and the infinite in any circumstance or situation. So, for example, we would be saying that everything with indefinite boundaries is infinite in extension. It would follow that each day is infinite in length because the boundary between day and night is indefinite. Thus, the use of nihilistic deconstruction leads to an untenable position, just as it leads to the destruction of many other useful distinctions. But this is a reason to think that the nihilistic conception of deconstruction is seriously flawed.

Instead, we might deconstruct the distinction between the indefinite and the infinite using the technique of transcendental deconstruction. To deconstruct a conceptual opposition is to show that the conceptual opposition is a nested opposition — in other words, that the two concepts bear relations of mutual dependence as well as mutual differentiation.[57] For example, we might discover that they have elements in common, which become salient in some contexts, but that in other contexts we note very important differences between them, so that they are not the same in all respects. In fact, we would note that the meaning of each depends in part on our ability to distinguish it from the other in some contexts.

Thus, transcendental deconstruction, which relies on the indefi-

---

56. Note that even when deconstructive arguments *are* employed to efface a particular distinction, they do not necessarily efface the distinction in all contexts. Thus they should be distinguished from a strategy of total effacement. Take for example the distinction between writing and speech discussed in DERRIDA, *supra* note 18. Derrida argues that speech and writing are special cases of a more general form of "writing." He claims that people often assume that speech is closer to truth or true meaning than writing, but this assumption is not necessarily justified. Both possess the same features of signification, which are simply more obvious in the case of writing. Derrida's argument uses deconstruction for purposes of rectification; it argues that this new conception is a better — that is, truer — way of viewing things than the received wisdom. It is not a strategy of total effacement because his argument does not in fact efface the distinction between writing and speech in all contexts; it does so only with respect to the issue of semiotic function. Writing is still written, and speech is still spoken; hence even after the deconstruction we cannot say that writing and speech are identical in all contexts of judgment. This is a deconstructive argument of rectification; it shows not that speech and writing are identical, but that there is a nested opposition between the two concepts. *See* Balkin, *supra* note 55, at 1689-93.

57. *Id.* at 1676.

niteness rather than the effacement of all conceptual boundaries, would insist that although we can offer relatively clear examples of bounded but indefinite concepts — for example, between day and night — we cannot demarcate in advance every example of the indefinite from every example of the infinite. Some of the things that we currently think are indefinite may turn out, in a different context of judgment, to be infinite and vice versa. We cannot know for sure because this distinction, like all others, is context dependent. Nevertheless, the very fact that this distinction is so heavily dependent upon context means that we cannot say that the distinction is meaningless, or that the terms collapse into each other.[58]

B. *Deconstruction and Reconstruction*

We have seen that, if Derrida's arguments about responsibility are to make sense, he must be committed to a transcendental conception of deconstruction, whether or not he specifically recognizes this fact. Moreover, the concept of an indefinite, rather than an infinite, responsibility better corresponds to the very important relationship of mutual differentiation and dependence that must always exist between law and justice. Laws apportion the comparative responsibility of parties. But laws can never perform this apportionment perfectly. They can never determine and assign completely the full responsibility of each and every person, living or dead, in exactly the right amount. First, laws must limit their concern to certain features of a situation and to certain effects that have already happened (or that can be proved in a court of law to have happened). Second, laws can extend their reach only to some parties, but not to all who might, in some larger sense, be responsible — for example, those who escape judgment because they are dead, out of the relevant jurisdiction, or bankrupt. Third, laws must speak in general terms that must be applied to many different

58. I have argued that transcendental deconstruction is premised on the assumption of transcendent values, and that this assumption inevitably leads to a logic of indefinite rather than infinite meanings. We might be tempted to identify transcendent values with the infinite rather than the indefinite because people sometimes think of the transcendent as that which surpasses all others. However, the question of transcendent values really concerns the relationship between general normative concepts like justice or beauty and their particular instantiations in the real world. Our notion of justice is transcendent because no particular example of justice in the world is perfectly just; it is indefinite because it cannot be reduced to any determinate formula. These are two ways of describing the same phenomenon.

Nevertheless, our idea of justice is not infinite; it does not lack boundaries, even if these are not fully determined. For example, the value of justice is not the same thing as the value of beauty. If general normative concepts really had no limits, they would all be identical because there would be no way to distinguish them from each other. So, although our transcendent notion of justice is not specific enough to match any determinate example of justice or any determinate formula of justice, it is specific enough to be distinguished from other normative concepts. That is why it is indefinite but not infinite.

factual contexts and therefore at best can fit each of these contexts like a mass-produced suit fits a body — perhaps well enough in some circumstances to be presentable, but certainly not perfect in all respects. Because responsibility is so deeply tied to context — both the contexts which have already emerged and those which in the fullness of time will emerge — human law must always, even in its best moments, be merely a heuristic, a catch-as-catch-can solution to the problem of responsibility rather than a fully adequate solution. Thus, to speak of the indefiniteness of human responsibility, and to speak of its failure to be fully measured, apportioned, and captured by human laws and human conventions, are really two ways of saying the same thing.

At the same time, our notion of justice can only be articulated and enforced through human laws and conventions. We may have an idea of justice that always escapes law and convention, but the only tools we have to express and enforce our idea are human laws and human conventions. In this sense our conception of the just relies for its articulation and enforcement on the imperfect law from which it must always be distinguished.

In sum, law is never perfectly just, but justice needs law to be articulated and enforced. This argument is exemplary of a transcendental approach to deconstruction, the only approach that can rescue deconstruction from the nihilistic abyss of infinite meaning. It assumes that human values like justice transcend the positive norms of human culture, even as they depend upon these norms for their articulation and expression. Human values like justice are always indeterminate; they must be constructed and articulated through culture, law, and convention. Yet any articulation of human value never fully exhausts the scope of human evaluation. We may offer a theory of what is just, and this theory may assist our judgments of what is just, but it does not ever fully displace our sense of justice. We always retain the ability to understand that our conventions, laws, and theories of justice fall short of our value of justice. Thus, our indeterminate values continue to demand more from us than our articulations of them can ever give; our urge to evaluate serves as a perpetual reminder of the gap between our values and their articulations in law or convention.

Equally important, my argument assumes that it makes sense to speak of the more just and the less just in a given context, even though our sense of justice is always indeterminate and indefinite. It denies that every conceptual articulation of justice is as good as any other, or that every solution to the problem of justice is as good as any other. If I claim that a human law only imperfectly captures the responsibility of individuals, I must assume that there is another accounting of responsibility that would be more just, even if I cannot describe a perfectly just solution. If I do not assume this, then my argument has no critical import. If there is no more just solution, then either the solution which I criticize is the best possible solution — in which case I have no reason to criticize it — or this solution is as good as any other solution I might offer as an alternative — in which case there is no reason to choose between them.

Thus, the transcendental conception of deconstruction is premised on the possibility of an alternative *reconstruction* that is superior to the given target of deconstruction. In this sense, deconstruction always depends on reconstruction, even though this reconstruction may be subject to further deconstructive critique. At the same time, theoretical (re)construction always depends on the tools of deconstruction. If we wish to construct a just account of moral or legal responsibility, we must be able to choose between competing alternatives and discard those that prove unsatisfactory. However, to critique the various possibilities, and discover their hidden incoherences, we need the critical tools of deconstruction.[59]

A deconstructionist, Derrida included, can hardly avoid this analysis. Does he accept it? In his later writings, he seems to move toward it. Deconstruction, he argues, demands that we "constantly . . . maintain an interrogation of the origin, grounds and limits of our conceptual . . . apparatus surrounding justice."[60] This demand does not "neutraliz[e an] interest in justice" but "[o]n the contrary . . . hyperbolically raises the stakes of exacting justice."[61] Deconstruction requires a "sensitivity to a sort of essential disproportion" between existing law or custom and justice.[62] The deconstructive attitude "strives to denounce not only theoretical limits but also concrete injustices, with the most palpable effects, in the good conscience that dogmatically stops before any inherited determination of justice."[63] Hence, Derrida connects the notion of limitless responsibility with deconstruction's "engage[ment]" by an "infinite demand . . . for justice."[64]

Yet the claim of an essential disproportion between law and justice simply restates the point that there is an idea or value of justice that

59. For a fuller discussion of the relationship between deconstruction and reconstruction, see Balkin, *supra* note 27, at 124-27.

60. Derrida, *supra* note 4, at 955.

61. *Id.*

62. *Id.*

63. *Id.*

64. *Id.*

transcends any specific example of justice, whether embodied in law, custom, or convention. Indeed, as Derrida later notes, "the deconstruction of all presumption of a determinant certitude of a present justice itself operates on the basis of an infinite 'idea of justice.' "[65] This is perhaps the closest Derrida comes to the transcendental conception. He hesitates at this point because he does not wish "to assimilate too quickly this 'idea of justice' to a regulative idea (in the Kantian sense), to a messianic promise or to other horizons *of the same type.*"[66] Nevertheless, Derrida's hesitation is unnecessary, for the deconstructive approach I advocate is not based on a fixed and determinate Idea of justice, but an indeterminate and indefinite human value. This value is the very sort of "demand" that Derrida identifies with justice: an insatiable urge that is never fully realized in the products of human law, culture, and convention.

III. Speaking in the Language of the Other

Derrida's third formulation of the relation between deconstruction and justice notes the etymological connections between justice and answering. To be just is to have responsibility, which is to respond to or to answer for something. Thus, Derrida speaks of justice as an "infinite demand."[67] However, not any answer will do. Justice, Derrida insists, requires one to address oneself to the Other in the language of the Other: It requires us to forswear our own way of thinking, talking, and looking at things in order to understand the Other in all of her singularity and uniqueness.[68] This requirement is ultimately impossible to attain, and hence the infinite demand of justice can never fully be satisfied.

Because justice demands that we address ourselves in the language of the Other, the law can never be fully just. The problem for law, Derrida argues, is threefold. First, law must speak in general terms, and therefore it must simplify and falsify the situation at hand.[69] Legal understanding never allows us to understand situations or the

---

65. *Id.* at 965.

66. *Id.* By a "regulative idea," Kant meant an idea that we must postulate or employ as a heuristic, in order to assist our use of reason. The self, the world, and God are examples of regulative ideas. *See* IMMANUEL KANT, THE CRITIQUE OF PURE REASON 549-60 (Norman K. Smith trans., London, MacMillan 1929) (1781).

67. Derrida, *supra* note 4, at 955. In discussing Derrida's arguments concerning justice I shall follow his practice of speaking about the "demand" of justice, or about what justice "demands," to describe what is just or unjust. Nevertheless, I should note at the outset that this familiar locution has the twin rhetorical effects of anthropomorphizing justice and downplaying human subjectivity, as I describe more fully below. *See infra* text accompanying notes 136-37.

68. *See* Derrida, *supra* note 4, at 949.

69. *See id.*

persons affected in all of their uniqueness. We must understand them instead filtered through a set of legal categories, or classes of situations, that lump them together with many other equally heterogenous and unique circumstances. The enforcement of the law according to these categories is a form of simplification and falsification, and this simplification and falsification are sources of injustice.[70]

Second, as James Boyd White has recently noted, the problem of justice is inherently a problem of translation.[71] For judges or other parties to speak in the language of another, they must translate the Other's language into their own. But translations are always imperfect. They never fully convey the sense of the original. Hence the very necessity of translation renders it impossible fully to speak in the language of the Other.[72]

Third, the requirement that law be impartial demands that we not speak in the language of a particular party, but in a language that is neutral and fair.[73] To speak in the language of only one of the parties risks the danger of undue partiality toward that person, for the situation will be completely described in terms of her experience and her concerns. This result is unfair because it may give short shrift to the experience and concerns of other parties. Hence, law, which requires fairness to all parties, must proceed in the language of neither one party nor the other, but in a third language that attempts — even if it does not always succeed — to be fair to both sides. Legal justice strives for an impartiality that is also impersonal. Yet this solution creates its own set of problems, for the neutral language of a third party fails to speak in the language of either party, and hence it doubly falsifies the situation by denying or obscuring the uniqueness and singularity of each side.[74]

Derrida's ethics of Otherness contains two separate imperatives. The first demands that we see a situation in all of its singularity. The second demands that we attempt to see things from the Other's point of view, using her vocabulary and her way of understanding the world. To deal justly with each of these two points, we must not conflate them, but rather deal with each separately — that is, respecting the singularity and difference of each.

---

70. *See id.*

71. *See* JAMES B. WHITE, JUSTICE AS TRANSLATION 257-69 (1990).

72. *See* Derrida, *supra* note 4, at 949. This idea is related to a theme that Derrida borrows from Heidegger and Levinas — the Other, because it is an Other, always remains ultimately unreachable and unfathomable.

73. *See id.*

74. *See id.*; WHITE, *supra* note 71, at 262-63.

A. *Justice as the Recognition of Singularity*

Derrida's demand that we see each situation in all its singularity is ambiguous. We could interpret it either as a claim of absolute difference among situations or only as one of relative difference. A claim of absolute difference means that we must see each situation as completely different from every other. A claim of relative difference means that we must see each situation as different from any other in some respects but not in others. Each situation is both different from and similar to every other situation; its uniqueness consists in the fact that this *combination* of similarity and difference manifests itself in different ways for each situation to which it is compared. Thus, *A* and *B* are both similar to and different from *C;* but *A* and *B* are unique because they are similar to and different from *C* in different ways.

We may state this distinction in another way. Consider three situations *A, B,* and *C.* They are all different. But are two of them more alike than the third? There are two positions we can take. One argues that all of them are absolutely different; consequently, no situation is any more like another than any other situation. The alternative position would insist that we cannot answer this question until we know what context the questioner has in mind. Given a particular context of decision, it will often be possible to say that two situations are more like each other than either is to a third; but this judgment may shift radically if the context of judgment is sufficiently altered. If we are concerned only with the question of weight, an elephant and a truck are more alike than either is to an amoeba. Yet if the context of judgment is shifted to the question of animate versus inanimate, the elephant and the amoeba are more alike than either is to the truck. This alternative position asserts the relative similarity and difference of all situations.

Does Derrida mean to suggest a theory of absolute difference or a theory of relative difference? If justice is an "infinite demand," perhaps we must keep trying to view a situation as different from any other in every respect. That would presume a theory of infinite difference. Yet, if Derrida means that justice requires us to assert the absolute difference of every situation, his claim is incoherent. It will be impossible to decide any case, because no case can be compared to any other. Because each case is completely different from all others, no case is a better point of comparison than any other. We cannot apply any consistent principle to different cases; hence, our judgment is merely one of fiat, for no decision is any more principled or unprincipled than any other. Conversely, we might also say that all decisions are equally principled. Because there are no relative degrees of comparison, any judgment is as good an exemplar of our principles as any other.

If Derrida's claim is based on a notion of relative difference, however, it accurately describes the predicament of just decisionmaking.[75] Each case is both similar to and different from every other, depending on how we look at it. The difficulty of just decisionmaking lies precisely in deciding what is the appropriate context of judgment. The question of principled consistency is the question of which cases our case is most like and which cases it is least like, given the appropriate context of judgment.

Consider the recent example of a seventeen-year-old high school student who was sentenced by a judge in Thomaston, Georgia to three years in prison for stealing an ice cream bar from the school cafeteria.[76] The judge defended his decision on the grounds that the case was a burglary, and the penalty for burglary was three years. He argued that the appropriate context of judgment involved the definition of burglary, the legislature's decision to fix the age of majority at seventeen, and his county's practice of uniform punishments for all violators of the same crime. His judgment was criticized on two grounds, each of which offered a competing context of judgment. First, what the student did was more like a schoolboy prank than a professional breaking and entering. Second, on the same day the student was sentenced to three years, the judge gave suspended sentences and fines to several people convicted of drug possession and drunk driving.[77]

We can only criticize the judge's decision if we assume the relative difference of situations — that is, only if we argue that this situation is both different from *and* similar to others. In order to differentiate this case from an "ordinary" case of burglary, we must be able to say that this defendant was a student like other students, that his action was a prank like other schoolyard pranks. In order to argue that it is unfair that drug users and drunk drivers should receive a lesser penalty, we must be able to assess comparative degrees of responsibility and harm between situations. Yet this means that we must already be able to see these situations as similar in some respects; this similarity is necessary for them to be comparable or commensurable according to some com-

75. This interpretation seems most consistent with his criticisms of Levinas. *See, e.g.*, DRUCILLA CORNELL, THE PHILOSOPHY OF THE LIMIT 53-55, 68-72, 83-85 (1992); JACQUES DERRIDA, WRITING AND DIFFERENCE 126-28 (Alan Bass trans., Univ. of Chicago Press 1978) (1967); Guyora Binder, *Representing Nazism: Advocacy and Identity at the Trial of Klaus Barbie*, 98 YALE L.J. 1321, 1376 (1989).

76. Christopher Sullivan, *Small Town Ponders Prison for Snickers Theft*, AUSTIN AM. STATESMAN, Sept. 19, 1993, at A10.

77. *Id.*

mon metric. We cannot compare these situations if we assume that each is unique in the sense of absolutely different. We can only make such a judgment if we see each situation as relatively different. Thus, justice may require that we understand each situation in its uniqueness, but, ironically, this requires that we treat it like the situations that are most similar to it in the appropriate context of judgment. To recognize its uniqueness, we must also recognize its similarity to other situations.

The same criterion of relative difference applies when we seek a just understanding of persons who are different from us. It is important to try to understand and respect people who are different from us. To understand and respect their difference, however, we must first understand their similarity to us. We must try to see how their concerns and values are really similar to our concerns and our values, and thus, how the situation they find themselves in and their reactions to that situation make sense. At the same time, to grasp this similarity, to put ourselves in other people's shoes, we must recognize how our lives and theirs are different. That is why every attempt at understanding is a simultaneous assertion of commonality with and difference from the Other. If we unthinkingly assume that the Other is too much like us, we will never understand her actions when they diverge from our own; if we insist on our absolute difference from her, she will never be able to understand us.

The competing interpretations of absolute and relative difference offer two different accounts of the predicament of judging. The theory of absolute difference suggests that just judging is impossible because no situation is really like any other. All principled decisionmaking is completely indeterminate because we have no way of comparing situations when each is absolutely different. On the other hand, the theory of relative difference argues that doing justice is difficult because there are so many ways to see situations as similar as well as different. The problem is not that no two situations are ever similar; it is that there are too many ways in which situations are similar to each other, and we must try to parse out the right ways to assess this similarity. In other words, the secret of judging lies in determining the appropriate context of judgment. However, we can never fully determine the present context, and we can never fully know of the presence or absence of other events that might significantly alter the context of our judgment when we decide a case. Therefore we are always uncertain — at least to some degree — about the justice of our decision.

Note that the dependence of justice on context is much like the dependence of meaning on context. The indeterminacy of meaning and the uncertainty of judgment are both based on the indefiniteness of context. This view is consistent with the transcendental approach to deconstruction. In contrast, an approach that asserts the infinite difference of each situation is just the flip side of an approach that asserts that meaning is infinite. The former asserts the absolute difference of all situations and all people, while the latter asserts the absolute identity of all meanings. Both approaches lead to normative nihilism and a failure of understanding. As before, Derrida's arguments only make sense if his is a transcendental account of deconstruction.

B. *Justice as Understanding the Other's Point of View*

Derrida's ethics of Otherness has a second component: It employs a different sense of individuality and uniqueness. Under this view, justice requires one to speak in the language of the Other by trying to see things from the Other's point of view.[78] This conception of justice seems most attractive when we are the injurer or the stronger party in a relationship, or when we are in the position of a judge who is attempting to arbitrate between competing claims. For example, suppose that we are the State, the stronger party, the oppressor, or the injurer, or suppose that we are contemplating an action that might put us in such a position. It seems only just that we should try to understand how we have injured or oppressed the Other (or might be in a position to injure or oppress). We can only do this if we try to see the problem from the Other's perspective and understand her pain and her predicament in all of its uniqueness. The duty we owe to the Other is the duty to see how our actions may affect or have affected the Other; to fulfill this duty we must put away our own preconceptions and vocabulary and try to see things from her point of view. Similarly, if we are a judge in a case attempting to arbitrate between the parties, the ethics of Otherness demands that we try to understand how our decision will affect the two parties, and this will require us to see the matter from their perspective.

Suppose, however, that we are not the injurer, but the victim; not the State, but the individual; not the strong, but the weak; not the oppressor, but the oppressed. Does justice require that we speak in the language of the person we believe is injuring or oppressing us? Must a rape victim attempt to understand her violation from the rapist's point of view? Does justice demand that she attempt to speak to the rapist in his own language — one which has treated her as less than human?

78. *See* Derrida, *supra* note 4, at 949.

Must a concentration camp survivor address her former captor in the language of his worldview of Aryan supremacy? We might wonder whether this is what justice really requires, especially if the injustice we complain of is precisely that the Other failed to recognize us as a person, refused to speak in our language, and declined to consider our uniqueness and authenticity.

When we move from Derrida's grand pronouncements on the ethics of the Other to the place "where he lives," to his writings on Paul de Man, we see this pleasant formula properly deconstructed. Derrida both adopts and rejects the formula in different contexts. For example, Derrida applies the formula when he demands that his critics read both him and de Man fairly. His first rule of just interpretation is "respect for the other, that is, for his right to difference, in his relation to others but also in his relation to himself."[79] To judge de Man fairly, one must speak to de Man in his own language and read him in the proper context.

Thus, Derrida insists that we evaluate de Man through the ethics of the Other. But what is the proper attitude to take toward de Man's critics? Derrida argues that he faces a serious problem: These critics cannot or will not read what he and de Man say; he describes them through the neologism *ne pveulent pas lire* — they can't/won't read.[80] These critics have failed the call of justice; they have not been open to the Other — de Man and Derrida.[81] What does justice demand of Derrida in defense of de Man? Here Derrida's practice deconstructs his theory: The essay *Biodegradables* cannot be described as anything other than a polemic. Derrida is perfectly aware of this but considers it unavoidable:

> I have never in my life taken the initiative of a polemic. Three or four times, and *always in response, and always because I was invited to do so,* I have simply tried to confront some manipulations that were too serious to ignore. . . .
>
> Of those who might regret the harshness or the high-handedness of certain of my remarks, right here, I ask — isn't it only fair? — to reread

79. Derrida, *Paul de Man's War, supra* note 8, at 644.

80. Derrida, *Biodegradables, supra* note 8, at 823. Derrida combines the "p" in *pouvoir* (can) and the "v" in vouloir (want) to create the expression "*je ne pveux pas lire* (I can/will not read)." *Id.* at 828; *see also id.* at 827, 843.

81. Indeed, so egregious is their practice of reading that at one point Derrida wonders whether they can even be considered to be morally responsible for their actions. *Id.* at 823. Because the category of *ne pveut pas lire* "displaces the category of responsibility," Derrida insists that he is not passing judgment on his critics: "Moreover, I bear these five no ill will; I have nothing against them; I would even like (if only in order to avoid this spectacle) to help them free themselves from this frightened, painful, and truly excessive hatred." *Id.* However, given the tone of the rest of the article, one might be pardoned if one were tempted to take these protestations of good will at less than face value.

> one more time the critical responses. Then they will have a better measure of the aggression — its violence and its mediocrity — that has me as its victim . . . . It is not possible for me to respond on that level. And it is my duty not to accept it. One does not always decide by oneself on a high-handed tone.[82]

Justice, it seems, does not always demand that one speak in the language of the Other, especially when the Other is not playing by the same rules.[83] Jesus might have advised his followers to turn the other cheek and to love their enemies, but this approach is not necessarily what justice requires or a particularly good strategy for achieving a just result. Not all encounters with an Other will involve willing participants in an open dialogue. Nevertheless, justice demands that the oppressor answer for her wrong, whether or not she admits her fault. Even if she makes no answer *to* her victim, she must answer *for* her crime. Justice demands satisfaction, even (and especially) if the miscreant is unwilling to provide satisfaction. The answer that an oppressive Other must provide to an oppressed Other — for example, a prison sentence or a money judgment — is not necessarily addressed to the victim in her language. It is not necessarily even understood by the injurer as an answer to the victim, or as an attempt to understand the victim in all of her singularity. Sometimes justice makes its demand precisely when people will not understand each other, when they will not treat others as equals.

Thus, perhaps unsurprisingly, justice demands that we deal with people and things not in a self-abnegating manner, but in the manner appropriate to the situation before us. Centuries ago, Confucius argued that the virtuous man is one who knows both how to love people to the extent they are deserving of love, and to hate people to the extent that they are deserving of hate.[84] Justice demands that we speak in the language of the Other to the extent that it is appropriate to do so because this would further justice, but it equally demands that we not do so when it would increase injustice.

---

82. *Id.* at 872.

83. Indeed, Derrida insists, one does not even have to respond at all to accusations that are fundamentally unfair or disrespectful:

> Is it necessary to respond to every interpellation. to everyone no matter who, to every question, and especially to every public attack? The answer is "yes," it seems, when time and energy permit, to the extent to which the response keeps open, in spite of everything, a space of discussion. Without such a space no democracy and no community deserving of the name would survive. But the answer is "no" if the said interpellations fail to respect certain elementary rules, if they so lack decency or interest that the response risks shoring them up with a guarantee, confirming in some way a perversion of the said democratic discussion. Yet, in that case, it would be necessary that the nonresponse be appropriately interpreted as a sign of respect for certain principles and not as contempt for the questioner.

Id. at 837.

84. CONFUCIUS, THE ANALECTS 4:3 (D.C. Lau trans., Chinese Univ. Press 1983) (1979).

We may connect this point to our earlier criticism of the notion of a "responsibility without limits." Derrida has argued that the ethics of Otherness imposes upon us a responsibility to speak in the language of the Other. However, because justice is a responsibility without limits, we might ask as before whether this responsibility to the Other is an infinite responsibility or merely an indefinite one.

Thus, there are two different interpretations of the ethics of Otherness. The first imposes an infinite duty; the second imposes only an indefinite duty. The first corresponds to a nihilistic conception of deconstruction; the second to the transcendental conception. The requirement of an infinite duty means that we must in every case use all the available means at our disposal to speak in the language of the Other; the requirement of an indefinite duty means we must make some attempt to speak in the language of the Other, and that the boundaries of our duty are uncertain and contextually driven. In the first case, the demand of justice is never satisfied because this demand is infinite; in the second case, we can never be certain that the demand of justice is satisfied because the duty it imposes is indefinite.

All of the difficulties with the ethics of Otherness arise from the assumption that our responsibility to speak in the language of the Other is infinite. We can restate the difficulty by relating it to a similar problem in understanding the views of another. This is the problem of hermeneutic charity. When we try to understand what another person means, we usually do so by trying to envision how what they are saying makes sense. As Hans-Georg Gadamer has argued, we must make an "anticipation of completion" that what another is saying is coherent and has a claim to truth.[85] A stance of openness and interpretive charity is actually essential to the process of understanding. If we do not take this stance, we cannot be sure that our discovery of incoherence or falsity in another's position is due to a defect in their argument or our inability to understand it fully.[86]

In other words, when attempting to understand another person, especially a person with a different world view from our own, we must be open to the possibility that the truth is more on their side than ours, that what they are saying is really true and valid — indeed, more true and valid than our own beliefs. Thus, we must be open to the possibility that our encounter with the Other will change our own views about what is true and good.[87] Understanding, then, is a kind of vulnerabil-

85. HANS-GEORG GADAMER, TRUTH AND METHOD 261-62 (Garrett Barden & John Cumming eds. & Sheed & Ward Ltd. trans., Seabury Press 1975) (1960).

86. *See id.* at 263.

87. *Cf. id.* at 262.

ity or openness to the truth that the Other may have to express.[88] It always requires the possibility that our beliefs will be changed through our encounter with the Other. Indeed, Gadamer argues, if we do not come to our encounter with this hermeneutic openness, we can never achieve real understanding; at most we achieve a halfway measure, in which we withhold ourselves from true understanding because we withhold ourselves from the necessary hermeneutic vulnerability.[89]

The duty of hermeneutic charity in Gadamer's theory of interpretation strongly resembles Derrida's version of the ethics of Otherness. Given the common influence of Heidegger on both thinkers, this commonality should not be surprising. Yet Gadamer's duty of interpretive charity and openness to the object of interpretation raises a serious difficulty. If this duty is endless, it is hard to distinguish this duty from a duty to reach an agreement with the person we are trying to understand. We do not know, in other words, at what point we should cease our efforts to see the truth in the views of the other party and simply recognize that they are wrong or that their argument is incoherent. If we go too far, we risk the danger of what I call *hermeneutic cooptation.*[90] By repeatedly blaming the incoherence or wrongness of the argument of another solely on our insufficient failure to understand it, we place all the responsibility for intellectual change upon ourselves. There is the danger that our drive to understand the truth in the other person's views will lead us to be coopted by those views and brought into agreement with things we should not agree with, because they are false, misleading, or unjust.[91]

There is a further difficulty. If the Other's views treat us as objects or as persons who deserve no respect, the requirement of continual hermeneutic charity will require us to adopt ways of thinking and talking that are unjust to ourselves. That is why we hesitate to think that justice requires that a political prisoner strive to speak in the language of her former torturers, or that a Holocaust survivor attempt to understand her own situation in the language of Aryan supremacy. To require this sort of understanding is to require these people to injure themselves psychically through the duty of understanding. For want of a better name, let us call this the requirement of *hermeneutic masochism.* True justice toward another should never involve hermeneutic cooptation, and it should never require hermeneutic masochism.

An infinite responsibility to speak in the language of the Other cre-

88. *See id.* at 262.

89. *Id.* at 270.

90. *See* Balkin, *supra* note 27, at 163.

91. *Id.* at 160-61, 167-69.

ates the perpetual danger of hermeneutic cooptation and hermeneutic masochism. It leads to the ridiculous spectacle of the rape victim being asked to understand that, in the eyes of her attacker, she was really just an object for subordination and conquest. It leads to the conclusion that blacks should be more understanding when white police officers automatically assume that they are likely to be criminals.[92] An infinite responsibility to speak in the language of the Other can easily lead to perpetual justification of the Other, no matter how unreasonable their position. This is not what justice requires.

The postulation of an infinite duty is untenable. Yet we might still make sense of the ethics of Otherness by viewing the duty to understand as indefinite rather than infinite. We have some duty to speak in the language of the Other, but our duty is not infinite. Instead, justice demands that we make just the right amount of effort to understand the Other. Beyond that point, it is not only appropriate but necessary for us to recognize that the Other's views are incoherent or unjustified, and that our own position is more reasonable. We have a duty to be open to and absorb that part of the Other's point of view which furthers justice while disagreeing with the rest.

But if we have this responsibility, how will we know when to cease our efforts at understanding? How will we know when we have done all that justice requires? We cannot know the full contours of our responsibility in advance of our encounter with the Other. Each situation will be different, and our responsibility in each situation will depend heavily on the context of the encounter. Hence our responsibility to the Other, while not infinite, is nevertheless indefinite.

There is a further reason why our duty to the Other must be indefinite. It has to do with the symmetrical nature of Otherness.[93] We are always an Other to the person who is an Other to us. The ethics of Otherness seems most appealing when we sympathize with the Other because the Other is the oppressed, the victim, or a potential object of injustice. However, we cannot state as a general rule that only the oppressor needs to speak in the language of the oppressed, or the injurer in the language of the victim. An additional problem of indefiniteness arises because these categories are not always clearly defined. In different contexts, and from different perspectives, different people appear to be strong or weak, injurer or victim, oppressor or oppressed, judge or judged.

First, the roles of the two parties may shift radically depending on

92. *See* Patricia J. Williams, The Alchemy of Race and Rights 46, 58-79 (1991).

93. *See* Cornell, *supra* note 75, at 54; Derrida, *supra* note 75, at 128.

how one describes the situation. Consider two neighbors who make conflicting uses of their property. Suppose that Neighbor One needs to operate machinery to run her business while Neighbor Two needs peace and quiet for her health. The second neighbor regards the first neighbor as an injurer; Neighbor One should try to understand how important it is for Neighbor Two to have peace and quiet. But Neighbor One has a symmetrical complaint. If she has to stop operating her machine, she will go out of business. Neighbor Two's demand is unreasonable under the circumstances, and justice requires that Neighbor Two understand the significant costs her request will impose on Neighbor One.[94] In this situation each party is an Other to the other, and each is an Other to the judge who must decide the case. Thus there are at least four different potential duties to respond. Both neighbors must make some effort to understand the position of the Other, but the roles of oppressor and oppressed, victim and injurer, are not determined in advance. Similarly, the judge must attempt to understand the situation of each neighbor from each neighbor's perspective, but the extent of this duty depends on which neighbor is acting unjustly toward the other, and this is the very question that the judge must decide.

Thus, the scope of the duty owed to speak in the language of the Other depends on our definition of the roles of the parties — as victim or injurer, strong or weak — but this definition will in turn be affected by the scope of the duty to speak in the language of the Other. For example, the more we try to see things from Neighbor One's perspective, the clearer it may become that Neighbor Two is being unreasonable, oppressive, and playing the role of the potential injurer. Yet the opposite conclusion might follow if we attempt to see the situation from Neighbor Two's perspective. The scope of our duty to speak in the language of the Other does not exist before we decide what their respective roles are, but the roles each plays cannot fully be determined before we fix the scope of the duty; each feature of the situation provides the proper context in which the other feature is to be judged. Because of the mutual dependence and differentiation of these contexts, the scope of the duty toward the Other is indefinite. It is neither infinite nor nonexistent, but dependent on facts and circumstances that are never fully clear, and whose precise contours we cannot fully determine in advance. Thus, the duty to speak in the language of the Other becomes a duty without limits, but it is by no means an infinite duty as Derrida suggests.

94. This example draws on the familiar Coasean point that both parties are causal factors in their conflicting use. R.H. Coase, *The Problem of Social Cost*, 3 J.L. & ECON. 1, 2 (1960).

The difficulty that produces indefiniteness may be subdivided into two problems: Let us call them the problem of certainty and the problem of proportion or degree. The problem of certainty arises when we cannot be sure whether a person is in fact an oppressor or an oppressed person. Justice may require us to *decide* this question, rather than use it as a basis for determining just action. Suppose a criminal defendant is accused of rape. If he really raped the victim, he is an oppressor. Justice demands that he recognize how he has harmed his victim and answer for his crime. If he is innocent, however, he will be oppressed if the State fails to do justice to him. The State must therefore ensure that it hears his story and understands the situation from his point of view; it must make sure that it does not convict him based on false evidence or unreasoning stereotypes. At the same time, it must not unthinkingly accept every piece of exculpatory evidence and every exculpatory account the defendant might offer, for that might create an equal and opposite injustice. In a criminal case we cannot determine in advance whether a person is guilty or innocent; that is precisely the purpose of a criminal trial. Given this situation, does justice demand that we speak to the defendant in his language or that he speak to us in our own? Our uncertainty in this regard leads to the indefiniteness of the duty.

The problem of degree arises because a person may at one and the same time be an injurer or oppressor to some degree and a victim or an oppressed person to another degree. Suppose that we are quite sure that a criminal defendant is guilty of rape. He nevertheless deserves to be treated with some respect; for example, the State should not be permitted to torture him to extract a confession, and it must give him an opportunity to defend himself in court. His crime may be less bad than other crimes of the same sort; if so, justice requires that he be given a chance to produce exculpatory evidence, and the State has a duty to consider it and lessen his sentence to the appropriate extent. If the State fails to protect the defendant's rights, he may be in the position of an oppressed party, despite his horrible crime. Thus, the State has a duty to speak in his language with respect to some features of the situation, but not with respect to others. These complications also produce an indefinite duty.

The case of Paul de Man is a perfect example of the indefiniteness of our duty toward the Other. The entire debate surrounding de Man concerns what role he should be assigned. Is de Man a victim of unjust accusation or a person who unjustly accused others (Jews)? Was he a collaborator, an ambitious man without a moral compass who sought to forget his sordid past, or was he an immature youth who made an early mistake yet matured into a respected scholar? The question of his status is inextricable from the question of what it means to be fair to him. Moreover, even if de Man willingly wrote antisemitic literature, justice requires that he be condemned only to the extent that he is responsible, but not to the extent that he is not responsible. In order to be fair to de Man, we must try to understand what he did and wrote, and this endeavor may require us to understand how he understood his actions and his writings. Nevertheless, we do not have to accept everything he said or did at face value or interpret every one of his writings or actions so as to exculpate him, just as we should not deliberately interpret his life in its worst possible light. Our duty of fairness is indefinite, but not infinite in either direction — toward exculpation or inculpation. We can be unjust either by refusing to speak in the language of the Other or by exclusively adopting that tongue.

Note that we cannot avoid these difficulties by insisting that all parties, whether victim or injurer, oppressor or oppressed, have an equal and infinite duty to speak in the language of the Other. An equal and infinite duty on all sides leads to either incoherence or injustice. It means that the rapist and the rape victim have equal duties to understand each other in terms of each other's conception of each other, and this requirement permits neither a determinable decision nor a just one. Justice demands that each "speak in the language of the Other" to the proper amount, to the proper degree, and in the proper circumstances. This duty is without limits not because it is infinite but because it is indefinite — because the question of duty to the Other is bound up with the very description of the situation which the duty concerns.

An indefinite duty, like an indefinite responsibility, is "without limits" because its contours are context bound and because this context cannot be fully determined in advance. What would an indefinite duty toward the Other mean? It would be a duty that can never fully be satisfied. However, it cannot be satisfied because we are uncertain about its scope, not because the demand is infinite.[95]

95. We should not confuse the question whether our responsibility to the Other is infinite or indefinite with still another reason why the demand of justice may remain unsatisfied in a particular case: the impossibility of a commensurable remedy. Often subsequent reparations for an injury never seem adequate to compensate for a previous loss. But this impossibility is not because either the loss or the responsibility for the loss is infinite, in the sense of having a limitless magnitude. Rather, the problem is one of incommensurability between the loss and any remedy we could offer. This incommensurability arises from the fact that our lives change in response to the events that happen to us. Our situation after an injury cannot be made fully commensurable with the situation before because both we and the world around us have changed as a result and can never be the same again. The past, precisely because it is past, can never fully be redeemed.

Previously we identified the concept of an infinite responsibility with normative nihilism. The notion of an infinite duty to speak in the language of the Other — which is a total abandonment of ourselves to the language of the Other — also leads to a kind of nihilism. Hoping to efface the distinction between self and Other, we succeed only in effacing the self and its language, just as the effacement of all distinctions leads to the destruction of meaning. This endeavor leads to a "nihilism of the self." The preservation of the self is the preservation of its Otherness from the Other, which is also the preservation of its partial similarity to the Other, and a source of the indefiniteness of its duty toward the Other. When we understand deconstruction to require an indefinite obligation, we preserve the self and make sense of the demand of justice; but when we understand deconstruction to require an infinite demand, it must lead to effacement or nihilism.

IV. Deconstruction as an "Antitotalitarian" Form of Analysis

Derrida's final suggestion connects deconstruction to an opposition to totalitarianism in thought. Derrida insists that what he has always practiced under the name of deconstruction "has always seemed to me favorable, indeed destined (it is no doubt my principal motivation) to the analysis of . . . totalitarianism in all its forms, which cannot always be reduced to names of regimes."[96] He finds examples of totalitarian thinking in criticisms of Paul de Man; since these critics are so concerned with denouncing political totalitarianism, he argues, they should avoid reproducing the logic of totalitarianism in their judgments and readings.[97] In fact, deconstructive analysis, which they attack, is the best way to avoid totalitarian logic: "[D]econstructions have always represented . . . the at least necessary condition for identifying and combating the totalitarian risk" in discourse.[98]

What is a "totalitarian" logic of discourse or a "totalitarian" ges-

---

The nature and direction of our lives have been irrevocably altered by previous actions and events; we become different people because of what has happened to us.

Thus, if the defendant accidentally breaks the plaintiff's leg, she may be deeply sorry for what she has done. Yet her action has affected the lives of others in a way that cannot fully be repaired, no matter what good deeds she later performs, and no matter how much assistance she offers to the victim and the victim's family. In such circumstances, the reason why the injurer's responsibility can never be fully satisfied is not because it is infinite in magnitude. The problem is that any remedy we could offer will be of the wrong kind, because we cannot relive the past. Thus, the fact that we live our lives in unidirectional time by itself can make subsequent remedies for finite harms incommensurable and hence essentially and perpetually inadequate.

96. Derrida, *Paul de Man's War, supra* note 8, at 648.

97. *Id.* at 645.

98. *Id.* at 647.

ture in discourse? Derrida seems to identify it with various forms of oversimplification, falsification, or rushing to judgment. His examples describe features that he finds objectionable in various critical readings of de Man's work:

> purification, purge, totalization, reappropriation, homogenization, rapid objectification, good conscience, stereotyping and nonreading, *immediate* politicization or depoliticization (the two always go together), *immediate* historicization or dehistoricization (it is always the same thing), immediate ideologizing moralization (immorality itself) of all the texts and all the problems, expedited trial, condemnations, or acquittals, summary executions or sublimations. This is what must be deconstructed.[99]

All of these sins of reading and understanding share an inattention — whether willful or innocent — to problems of context. They oversimplify by failing to spend the time or effort to see the multifaceted and complicated textures of meaning that attend any text or any event.[100] The totalitarian gesture, then, is oversimplification and inattention to complexity and context; the antitotalitarian gesture, which is just, is a corresponding attention to these features of texts.

Of course, a judgment whether one is being insufficiently sensitive to context is itself a contextual judgment. For example, in some contexts, dismissing another's arguments, making categorical distinctions, and even rushing to judgment may not be an entirely bad practice.[101] Derrida denies that "we have access to a complete formalization of this [totalitarian] logic" or can be absolutely exterior to it.[102] There is no "systematic set of themes, concepts, philosophemes, forms of utterance, axioms, evaluations, hierarchies which, forming a closed and identifiable coherence of what we call totalitarianism, fascism, nazism, racism, antisemitism, never appear outside these formations and especially never on the opposite side."[103] Indeed, there is no "systematic coherence proper to each of them, since one must not confuse them too quickly with each other."[104] Conversely, there is no discursive act which is completely antitotalitarian, for there is no "property so closed and so pure that one may not find any element of these systems in discourses that are commonly opposed to them."[105]

Derrida's identification of deconstructive argument with antitotal-

99. *Id.* at 646.

100. *Id.* at 645.

101. For example, Derrida himself thinks it important to condemn Nazism and political totalitarianism in all of their forms. *See id.*

102. *Id.*

103. *Id.*

104. *Id.*

105. *Id.*

itarianism is really a special case of his critique of logocentrism. The problem of logocentrism is the problem of categorical judgment. Categorical judgments are judgments that employ categories; whenever we predicate a property of an object, we place it in a category. We say that it is this way rather than that, that it goes into this box rather than another. In fact, categorical judgments are necessary to our thought; they are the basis of all judgments of similarity and difference. Of course the term *categorical* has another meaning as well — insensitivity to context. Categorical obligations are unconditional; to state something categorically is to assert it without regard to (at least some types of) context. Thus, categorical judgments, because they are categorical, are to some degree acontextual. They must lump some things together as similar and exclude others as different, without attending to the similarities across, or the differences within, the boundaries that they establish. Hence every categorical judgment is a sort of falsification or oversimplification of the situation. Of course that is precisely why categories are useful. In a world of infinite diversity, change, and differentiation, categories gather things together and treat them as similar so that the human mind can understand the world before it. One might think of categories, then, as heuristics that aid understanding through partial simplification.[106]

What is most remarkable about categorical judgment, then, is that it is simultaneously useful, adequate, and empowering in some contexts and deficient, inadequate, and misleading in others. We cannot do without categorical judgments of some type, yet if we do not pay sufficient attention to the context in which we make them, they may lead us away from what is true and what is just. Deconstruction helps us to recognize the discrepancy between the categorical judgments we make and the context our judgment overlooks. A perfectly just treatment of a situation would require us to understand the situation in all of its contextual richness.[107] Nevertheless, we must make categorical judgments of some type to articulate the very context we seek to uncover. Context itself must be describable in terms that are unavoidably categorical. Hence the process of deconstructive analysis, while

106. Although this sort of argument is generally associated with conceptual relativism, we should note that it is perfectly consistent with a realist ontology. One might believe that linguistic categories lump together objects that are really similar in some respects, although different in others, and that the grounds of this similarity and difference are not simply a matter of human convention.

107. Thus, Derrida insists, "one must analyze as far as possible this process of formalization and its program so as to uncover the statements, the philosophical, ideological, or political behaviors that derive from it and wherever they may be found." Derrida, *Paul de Man's War*, *supra* note 8, at 646.

"urgent," is also "interminable."[108] Deconstruction becomes "the tireless analysis (both theoretical and practical) of . . . adherences"[109] to the totalitarian discourses that remain lodged even in one's own ways of thinking and which one is trying to combat.

Indeed, in articulating his point, Derrida falls prey to the very danger he warns against. Derrida labels all the various forms of oversimplification and acontextual judgment as "totalitarian."[110] But this comparison is itself a gross overstatement and highly misleading. To be sure, totalitarian regimes may make use of simplistic slogans and lump various persons together into categories of undesirables, but it hardly follows that every oversimplification deserves the name "totalitarian," especially given the powerful connotations that usually accompany this word. In Derrida's terms this comparison is in itself an oversimplification, a "totalitarian" move that provides Derrida's attack on de Man's critics with much more rhetorical force than it really deserves. It would be more appropriate — and more just — to argue that these critics do not read de Man in the proper context and with the proper degree of charity; but this accusation, even if true, in no way justifies the claim that, in misreading de Man, they are reproducing the logic of totalitarian discourse.

In fact, when we strip away its more obfuscating elements, Derrida's identification of deconstruction with antitotalitarianism is really better expressed in terms of deconstruction's continual allegiance to transcendental human values, which law, language, and convention never fully serve and always partially obscure. We deconstruct categorical judgments because they take us further away from truth; we deconstruct legal categories because they deviate from what is just. Nevertheless, a deconstruction in the service of justice is always premised on the possibility of reconstruction — that is, on the hope of some categorical scheme that would better articulate the appropriate context of judgment. If we do not believe that there is a better description, there is no point in deconstructing in the first place. We are simply substituting one description for another, without any assertion that one is better than another.

Does this practice in fact presuppose a transcendental norm of justice? We might deconstruct only in order to show that a categorical judgment fails to live up to the norms of our particular culture or legal

108. *Id.*

109. *Id.* at 648.

110. *See id.* at 645 ("Such a formalizing, saturating totalization seems to me to be precisely the essential character of this logic whose project, at least, and whose ethico-political consequence can be terrifying.").

system. In that case the ultimate ground of our deconstruction is to obtain increasing fidelity to positive norms. However, such a practice places the positive norms beyond criticism because they are the basis of deconstructive critique. Yet one can easily imagine cases in which this very refusal to critique positive norms would itself be totalitarian.

However, to say that positive norms are inadequate — and hence in order to deconstruct them — we must refer to values that lie beyond the norms we are critiquing and that serve as the source of our criticism, even if we believe that the values we wish to uphold are to some extent realized in our culture. Suppose that we denied that we need concern ourselves with transcendental values: Suppose we assert that we are only interested in engaging in an "immanent" critique. In other words, we say that we are using one aspect of our cultural norms to critique other aspects, and therefore we need make no reference to anything beyond the positive norms of our culture. For example, we might use the commitment to equality expressed in the Civil Rights Act of 1964[111] to criticize the lack of civil rights for homosexuals in the United States. The question remains, however, why we saw a particular aspect of our cultural practices as a worthy basis for our critique and another aspect as unworthy. Since both are equally aspects of our culture, culture by itself cannot serve as a norm to decide between them.

We might say that one is a more central feature of our cultural norms than the other, but this leads to two different interpretations. If something is central because it is more prevalent, we refer only to a positive norm. Yet mere prevalence does not guarantee the worth of a cultural practice, unless our only goal is to reinforce positive norms for their own sake. For example, racial inequality may be central to a regime of Jim Crow or apartheid, but this fact does not make it a worthy basis for a critique of egalitarian norms that might exist elsewhere in the culture. Indeed, by reinforcing the most prevalent practices of a culture, we may reinforce its most deeply unfair elements. On the other hand, by "central" we could mean "more valuable" or "more just." In that case our judgment must also refer to a transcendent conception of value or justice that informs our notion of centrality. Thus, whenever we speak of the proper continuation of positive norms or about deciding between alternative interpretations of positive norms, we must eventually make use of transcendental norms of justice. Although we may find these norms partially realized in portions

111. Pub. L. No. 88-352, 78 Stat. 241 (codified as amended principally at 42 U.S.C. §§ 2000a to 2000h-6 (1988)).

of our own culture, these inadequate articulations do not exhaust their meaning for us.

V. Deconstruction as a Normative Chasm

I want to conclude this essay by juxtaposing two different claims. I began this essay by noting that the normative import of any particular deconstructive argument depends largely upon what the deconstructor chooses to deconstruct, and the values and commitments that she brings to her act of deconstruction. As we have seen,[112] Derrida tends to pick targets for deconstruction that correspond to the injustices he perceives. He deconstructs inegalitarian conceptions, but not egalitarian ones; he deconstructs the cultural practice of apartheid and Western practices that support it, but not arguments against apartheid; he deconstructs unfair accusations of Paul de Man, but not those assessments which he believes to be fair. At the same time, I have argued for a transcendental version of deconstruction: When we employ deconstruction to discuss questions of justice, we always refer to the discrepancy between human law, culture, and convention, and the human values which they articulate.

When we put these two claims together, we arrive at a curious problem. If deconstruction makes reference to transcendental values, why should the results of deconstructive argument turn on the target of our deconstruction? How is it possible that deconstructive arguments can be wielded for contrary purposes? Why isn't deconstructive argument always a force for good?

In the three essays I have discussed, Derrida does not deal adequately with the many difficult questions concerning the ethics of deconstructive argument. He is preoccupied with showing that deconstruction is not *necessarily* nihilistic.[113] Nevertheless, he never offers much of an argument for why deconstructive argument cannot lead to contradictory normative positions or even be used to promote injustice. In *Biodegradables,* he does little more than scoff at the notion that one can use deconstruction to promote both good and evil political regimes; he demands proof that deconstruction could ever be used

112. *See supra* notes 9, 15, 31-40 and accompanying text.

113. For example, he insists that deconstruction does not "correspond (though certain people have an interest in spreading this confusion) to a quasi-nihilistic abdication before the ethico-politico-juridical question of justice and before the opposition between just and unjust." Derrida, *supra* note 4, at 953. But this failure of correspondence may mean either that deconstruction — properly employed and understood — need not lead to injustice, or that it cannot do so. Even if people do not use deconstructive arguments to efface the distinction between the just and the unjust, they might still use deconstructive arguments to argue for what is unjust through sophistical means.

for a bad purpose.[114] This burden is easily met, however: As the first part of this essay shows, it takes very little effort to produce numerous examples of deconstructive arguments that point in opposite directions.[115] In his Cardozo Law School address, Derrida tries a different tack. He seems to suggest that any example of deconstruction that leads to injustice is not really deconstructive, just as no example of law is ever fully just. In his view, both deconstruction and justice are impossible. Thus, deconstruction itself can never be unjust; in fact, Derrida asserts, "Deconstruction is justice."[116] In these passages, Derrida simply offers a mystical equation between justice and deconstruction; he strings together provocative metaphysical formulas but does not begin to offer a convincing argument for them.

Nevertheless, it is possible to make sense of deconstruction's proper relationship to justice, and, in the process, to offer a more charitable interpretation of Derrida's rather obscure discussion. To solve this quandary, let us distinguish between deconstructive *arguments* made by human beings, which we might call the *rhetorical practice* of deconstruction, and the relationship of mutual dependence and differentiation that exists between human values and human language, convention, and culture. In this relationship, human conventions articulate human values but never fully capture them. Let us call this relationship of simultaneous inadequacy and dependence the *normative chasm* between inchoate human values and their cultural articulations.[117]

What is the relationship of the rhetorical practice of deconstructive argument to this normative chasm? When people make deconstructive arguments about justice, they make use of this chasm in two ways. First, their arguments implicitly rely on values which, to some indefinite degree, transcend human conventions. Second, their critiques partially describe the discrepancy between law, convention, and culture and the human values of justice and truth. Yet deconstructive arguments that make use of this normative chasm are not themselves identical to this chasm, nor do they ever articulate it completely. In-

114. *See, e.g.*, Derrida, *Biodegradables*, *supra* note 8, at 827 (rejecting the claim of a critic that deconstruction can be used for either "fascist" or "liberal" purposes and demanding "some proof, please, some arguments, some examples, at least one example!").

115. *See supra* text accompanying notes 40-45; *see also* Balkin, *supra* note 3, at 1613-25 (offering competing readings of a U.S. Supreme Court opinion on parental rights).

116. Derrida, *supra* note 4, at 945.

117. Perhaps unsurprisingly, Plato was among the first philosophers to stress this relationship; it is a principal motivation for his theory of Forms. *Cf.* SEUNG, *supra* note 24, at 209-10. Nevertheless, one does not have to accept the entire ontological baggage of the Forms to acknowledge Plato's genius in recognizing this fundamental inadequacy between our indeterminate values and their articulations in the world of culture.

deed, because human values are inchoate and indeterminate and human conventions are indefinite in their reach and scope, the relationship between the two is doubly problematic. It may even be misleading to think of this normative gap as a single, homogenous thing that any mind could ever grasp or describe as a totality. Thus, there are two things that human law, language, and convention fail adequately to capture: The first are the human values on the other side of the normative chasm; the second is the chasm itself.

The human practice of deconstructive argument always involves a limited use of the normative gap between value and articulation. It is limited in two senses. First, a deconstructive argument must always begin somewhere, at a certain place or with a certain target. Each deconstructive argument shows the instability of the distinctions with which it starts, and the mutual dependence and differentiation of the conceptual oppositions it targets. Yet these deconstructive arguments themselves must rely on distinctions and conceptual oppositions, otherwise they could not be expressed in language and understood by others. Furthermore, no deconstructive argument destabilizes all of the conceptual structures in language or culture at once; for every distinction it contests, it leaves unexamined thousands more. Thus, every deconstructive argument fails ultimately to offer an adequate account of the normative chasm; instead it examines and articulates only a little part of this phenomenon, using conceptual tools that are already symptoms and effects of this chasm.

Second, each deconstructive argument must come to an end. It generally ends with a conclusion that a particular distinction or set of distinctions is effaced, undecidable, or more complicated than one had first imagined. It ends when the deconstructor believes that she has reached an appropriate degree of enlightenment from the process of deconstructive argument.[118] For example, Derrida ends his essay on de Man by showing that de Man's situation is more complicated than his critics thought. So deconstruction as practiced by human beings always arrives at a conclusion in two senses of the word — both an end and a result of reasoning. Yet the decision to stop and assess the conclusions of one's argument, to state them as conclusions — in both senses of that word — leaves unspoken the many further steps that could be taken. These additional steps could lead to a partial or even a complete transformation of the conclusions just arrived at. Thus, from another perspective, the conclusion of a deconstructive argument is a conclusion in neither sense of the word: for it does not end the

118. *See* Balkin, *supra* note 1, at 766.

possible lines of deconstructive argument, nor does it lead to a fixed and determinate result.

We thus obtain the curious result that the discrepancy between value and articulation that makes each human practice of deconstruction possible is itself indescribable through the finite rhetorical practice of deconstruction. One might try to imagine a God's-eye point of view from which all the mutual differentiations and dependences, all the uncanny reversals and undoings of human conceptual structures, could be understood and appreciated. But such a view is not possible for any human intelligence. Thus, the rhetorical practice of deconstructive argument is always inadequate to express the predicament of human culture that makes this sort of argument possible.

It is possible that, when Derrida speaks of "Deconstruction" in his more mystical pronouncements, he has in mind something like this normative chasm, this essential inadequation between transcendent human values and human culture. If so, then no human practice of deconstructive argument is "Deconstruction," because no argument ever fully describes the relationship between value and articulation. Indeed, such a complete description would be impossible. It would not follow, however, that "Deconstruction" itself was impossible, only a fully adequate account of it. So Derrida's equation between Deconstruction and justice is flawed. Justice is "impossible" only in the sense that one never finds a fully and categorically just act in this world. Yet "Deconstruction" is not impossible, even though one never finds a fully deconstructive argument. The relationship of mutual dependence and differentiation that exists between culture and value is not impossible; it is the case. Moreover, it is simply not true, as Derrida asserts, that Deconstruction is justice. This assertion is a confusion of the normative chasm between culture and value with a particular inchoate and indefinite human value. Derrida's mystical formula simply obscures a valuable insight.[119]

119. In other words, if Derrida were correct that Deconstruction is justice because both are impossible of attainment, then Deconstruction would not only be justice, but also beauty, wisdom, and temperance, as none of these virtues is perfectly realized in this world. A more appropriate view would be Derrida's assertion that "deconstruction takes place *in the interval that separates* the undeconstructibility of justice from the deconstructibility of *droit* (authority, legitimacy, and so on)." Derrida, *supra* note 4, at 945 (first emphasis added). In other words, Deconstruction is the gap itself, rather than one side or another of this gap.

If by Deconstruction Derrida means this normative gap, Deconstruction would not even be an activity of human beings. Instead Deconstruction would simply be *the case that* there is a fundamental inadequation. Thus, elsewhere Derrida suggests that "[d]econstruction takes place, it is an event that does not await the deliberation, consciousness, or organization of a subject, or even of modernity. *It deconstructs it-self.*" Letter from Jacques Derrida to a Japanese Friend 4, *reprinted in* DERRIDA AND *DIFFÉRANCE* 1-5 (David Wood & Robert Bernasconi eds., 1988) [hereinafter Letter from Derrida]. This "it," Derrida insists, "is not . . . an impersonal thing that is opposed to some egological subjectivity." *Id.* It is not the result of a subject applying a force

This account of Deconstruction also explains two other puzzling Derridean statements. The first is Derrida's insistence that Deconstruction is not a method or a technique.[120] The second is his assertion that Deconstruction itself, like justice, is not deconstructible.[121]

Derrida's repeated denial that deconstruction is a method or a practice — and therefore, unlike these denials, not repeatable — has struck many as strange and possibly a clever way of dodging criticism: if deconstruction is not a method, then only a certain elect — presumably Jacques Derrida and his followers — can tell whether a given argument is truly deconstructive or not. They can thus disown all examples that put their practices in a bad light. Whether or not Derrida has sought to shield himself from criticism through obfuscation, there is another, more charitable way of accounting for his statements. Derrida's insistence on separating deconstruction from "method" is consistent with a view of Deconstruction as a normative chasm that cannot adequately be captured by any human rhetorical practice of deconstructive argument. This chasm is not part of any conventional practice of deconstruction; rather, it is what these conventions imperfectly articulate. The human practices of deconstructive argument are conventional, repeatable, transmissible, and hence deconstructible. In contrast, Deconstruction — which is the case that there is an indescribable inadequacy between human values and their articulations — is not a convention, and hence it is not deconstructible.[122]

Nevertheless, it follows that deconstructive *arguments* are surely part of a practice or convention of deconstructive rhetoric. This claim has two consequences. First, the practice of deconstructive argument is as deconstructible as any other set of conventional understandings and practices. This resolves the question left unanswered earlier in this essay. We noted that if deconstruction argument were a repeatable rhetorical practice, expressible through repeatable linguistic signs and conventions, it would be subject to "ideological drift": The insertion of deconstructive arguments into new and different contexts would result in arguments with widely varying political and moral valences. This would mean both (1) that deconstructive arguments

to an object. It would perhaps be better to say simply that "Deconstruction happens," or "There is Deconstruction".

120. *See* Letter from Derrida, *supra* note 119, at 3.

121. Derrida, *supra* note 4, at 945.

122. A similar argument would apply to justice. Only human culture, law, and convention are deconstructible because, and to the extent that, they depend upon but vary from inchoate human values. A human value like justice would not be deconstructible, although any particular articulation of it would be, just as the normative gap — Deconstruction itself — would not be deconstructible, although any particular articulation of it would be.

could be used for a variety of different political purposes, depending on the context in which they were offered; and (2) that any normative uses of deconstruction would themselves be subject to further deconstructive critique.

These conclusions are fully warranted. Deconstructive argument, like all other forms of rhetoric, is a communal practice existing in various human institutions. It can be — and is — learned and taught, copied and parodied, understood and misunderstood. It can be — and is — the subject of countless Ph.D. theses and books. It is repeatable and transmissible, like all other features of human life existing in and articulated through human language and human social conventions. It is therefore subject to the vagaries of iterability and ideological drift. It is deconstructible.[123]

Furthermore, because deconstructive argument is a practice of rhetoric, it is hardly surprising that it can be used for good or for ill. Like all rhetoric, deconstructive argument is a form of persuasive advocacy. As Aristotle pointed out, the advocate always takes large portions of her audience's beliefs for granted and does not try to contest them.[124] Instead, she focuses on specific questions and makes use of beliefs and attitudes that she and her audience hold in common.[125] Some of these beliefs may be only partially correct; others may even be the result of unthinking acceptance of community norms. Nevertheless, the advocate refrains from attacking them because they actually assist her in making her argument.

In this regard the human practice of deconstructive argument is much the same as other forms of persuasive rhetoric. It begins somewhere and ends somewhere. It takes certain features of culture and

---

123. It might seem strange for me to note the obvious — that people learn to deconstruct in departments of comparative literature, that theses on deconstruction that repeatedly apply deconstructive arguments are produced in great numbers, that these theses are criticized or applauded as good and bad examples, that people can apply the varieties of deconstructive arguments they find in certain texts to later problems, and that other members of the relevant interpretive community of deconstructive scholars agree that these later applications are also deconstructive. I emphasize these features — the repeatability and the communal nature of deconstructive practice — precisely because Jacques Derrida has always been so uncomfortable with such statements, leading as they do to the conclusion that there is, after all, a deconstructive method, that can be taught, practiced, and repeatedly applied in new situations. At the same time, Derrida has been quick to point out that certain arguments are misstatements of deconstruction, that others are poorly performed versions of deconstruction, and that particular deconstructive readings are themselves subject to further deconstruction. My theory of Deconstruction as a normative chasm shows how one might consistently hold these positions; nevertheless it commits Derrida — and other deconstructionists — to something like a transcendental account of deconstruction.

124. *See* ARISTOTLE, THE "ART" OF RHETORIC, Book I, § 1.12 (John H. Freese trans., Loeb Classical Library 1982).

125. *See id.*

convention for granted and uses them to deconstruct others. Thus, people can use deconstructive argument for different purposes because they can begin their critiques with different texts or different features of the same text. Because the normative chasm between value and articulation applies to all aspects of human culture and convention, there will always be some discrepancy or instability to deconstruct in every conceptual structure and in every normative position. Thus, depending upon where one starts and where one ends, one can put into question different distinctions and conceptual oppositions that support or justify different interpretations or different actions.

If deconstructive argument is a form of rhetorical practice, then the ethical status of deconstruction is very much like the question of the relationship of rhetoric to ethics. The latter question has been the focus of a great historical debate. Quintilian, the great Roman theorist of rhetoric, claimed that good oratory is a good person speaking well.[126] This statement might be read to suggest that well-done oratory must also serve a just objective and, conversely, that arguments motivated by an unjust purpose or a bad character will always manifest poor rhetorical style.[127] Although this position has had its adherents throughout history,[128] many people consider it wishful thinking.[129] A more common position on the ethics of rhetoric is that of Plato, who compared rhetoric to cosmetics, flattery, and the baking of pastries.[130] Plato argued that rhetoric misleads people by giving certain positions an artificial appeal, just as a pastry chef gives food an artificial appeal that is undeserved given its lack of nutritional value.[131] Thus, far from always serving just ends, rhetoric was a device inherently designed to falsify and obfuscate.

Aristotle struck a middle position between these two extremes. He emphasized that rhetoric is a useful and important feature of public

126. 4 QUINTILIAN, INSTITUTIO ORATORIA, Book XII, § 1.1 (H.E. Butler trans., Loeb Classical Library 1961).

127. *See id.*, §§ 1.3-.13.

128. A recent example is RICHARD WEISBERG, POETHICS 5-15 (1992), which argues that unjust judicial opinions usually display rhetorical flaws.

129. Quintilian himself recognized that "common opinion is practically unanimous in [rejecting] this view." QUINTILIAN, *supra* note 126, § 1.14. His claim is all the more puzzling given that he was involved in the training of lawyers, who are taught to argue both sides of a case with equal ability. However, Quintilian's position was motivated by a much more plausible one: He believed that the proper use of rhetoric could only be guaranteed by a rigorous moral education that produced a good character; hence he felt that rhetorical and moral education must occur together. *See id.*, §§ 2.1-.2.

130. PLATO, *Gorgias*, *in* COLLECTED DIALOGUES, *supra* note 20, at 229 (W.D. Woodhead trans., 1953).

131. *Id.* at 245-57.

life.[132] But its publicity means that it can be used for many different purposes.[133] It is surely wrong to employ rhetoric for evil ends; nevertheless, it is worthwhile to be able to argue both sides of a case precisely so that one can better respond to the unjust use of rhetoric when one encounters it.[134] Although one can use rhetoric for good or for ill, the same can be said of many useful things, like strength, health, wealth, and strategic expertise.[135] Rhetoric's ability to be employed for both good and wicked purposes should lead us to recognize the responsibility that each of us has for the arguments that he or she makes. Each of us — Derrida and de Man included — may become skillful at persuasion. Yet with this skill comes responsibility. Like all other kinds of rhetoric, we must use the practice of deconstruction responsibly, because the practice itself will not guarantee the purity of our motives or the goodness of our actions.

CONCLUSION

The encounter between deconstruction and justice has changed both parties; yet, of the two, deconstruction appears to be the more transformed. If deconstructive practice is to be of any use to the question of justice, it must become a transcendental deconstruction. It must exchange the logic of the infinite for that of the indefinite. It must act in the service of human values that go beyond culture, convention, and law. It must recognize the chasm that differentiates human value from articulated conceptions of it, and it must identify Deconstruction with that chasm. Finally, one must understand deconstructive practice as a rhetorical practice that employs Deconstruction but is not identical to it. Because deconstructive practice is a practice, it is repeatable, teachable, and alterable like any other human convention. Because it is rhetorical, it can be used for good or for ill.

There is one more transformation yet to come. Understanding the subject of justice must lead us to reunderstand the subject. Derrida speaks repeatedly of the "infinite demand" of justice. But his metaphor obscures a central point: Justice does not demand anything, for justice is not a person that could demand. Justice is a human value. It

132. *Cf.* ARISTOTLE, *supra* note 124, Book I, § 1.10 (offering arguments for the utility of rhetoric).

133. As George Kennedy reminds us, "Aristotle was the first person to recognize clearly that rhetoric as an art of communication was morally neutral, that it could be used either for good or ill." George A. Kennedy, *Introduction* to ARISTOTLE ON RHETORIC ix (George A. Kennedy trans., Oxford Univ. Press 1991).

134. ARISTOTLE, *supra* note 124, Book I, § 1.12.

135. *See id.*, § 1.13.

is a value lodged in the hearts of human beings. It is people who demand justice, and who demand it of one another.

Derrida's placement of justice in the role of the grammatical subject — the subject who demands justice — obscures the fact that the real subject of justice is, and always has been, not a concept, not a grammatical subject, but a person. This subject of justice is someone who can experience justice and injustice, who can feel wronged or vindicated, harmed or helped, who can understand that she or someone else has been treated justly or unjustly.

There is something uncannily appropriate in Derrida's way of expressing himself, replacing the individual subject with a grand abstraction. Deconstruction first came to public attention in the wake of structuralism, an intellectual movement that effaced the human subject and sought to explain it as an effect or byproduct of language and culture. These attempts to dissolve the human subject were in turn part of a larger tendency in French thought toward antihumanism.[136] Derrida broke with structuralism in several respects, but not in this one. He adopted the largely antihumanist assumptions then reigning in French intellectual life, as well as the unfortunate tendency in Continental philosophy to make grammatical subjects out of philosophical predicates.

In fact, there has always been the temptation in Derrida's work to do without the individual human subject, to speak of Deconstruction, but not of deconstructors; of signs, but not those who signify; of meanings, but not those who mean; of justice, but not of people who value the just. Especially in his early works, one sometimes finds the suggestion that there are simply signs pointing to each other, without the necessary support of any human intelligence.[137]

Nevertheless, this raises a serious difficulty. How can there be signs without subjects to understand them? After all, as Charles Sanders Pierce defined it, a sign is something that stands for something else *to somebody* in some relation or context.[138] Without the "somebody" to make or understand the sign, signification becomes impossible, and Derrida's philosophical project falls apart. Thus, although antihumanism and semiotics are often identified with each other, in fact they are mutually incompatible.

---

136. On French antihumanism, see KATE SOPER, HUMANISM AND ANTI-HUMANISM (1986).

137. *See, e.g.*, DERRIDA, *supra* note 75, at 25 ("[T]he meaning of meaning . . . is infinite implication, the indefinite referral of signifier to signifier.").

138. 2 COLLECTED PAPERS OF CHARLES SANDERS PIERCE ¶ 228 (Charles Hartshorne & Paul Weiss eds., 1960).

One way out of this difficulty is to postulate a Transcendental Subject who does all of the work of meaning and understanding all signs. This is the Hegelian solution; it projects human intelligence onto a single great Mind. The second solution, which Derrida has occasionally toyed with over the years, is semiotic materialism.[139] It argues that signs are material traces or are formed from the juxtapositions of material elements. Thus, a sign does not need to be understood by anyone in order to exist as a sign; its semiotic character is ensured by its relationship to other signs without the mediation of a consciousness. Moreover, instead of explaining signs in terms of consciousness, as Pierce did, we explain consciousness in terms of signs. So the self becomes an "effect" or "determination" of a system of differentiated signs.[140] Neither of these solutions is completely satisfactory. A third and better solution is simply to abandon antihumanism and to reemphasize the importance of individual subjects in the creation of a culture that in turn creates them.

Deconstruction's confrontation with questions of justice presses this third alternative upon us; confronting the question of justice raises the problem of the subject with renewed urgency. Derrida wants to speak of responsibility and choice; he wants to say that de Man's critics are unfair and that de Man was a good and generous person. He wants to assert that each of us has an infinite responsibility to the Other. Yet, in order to speak in this way, he needs subjects who are response-able — who can make choices and can be praised or blamed, rewarded or held responsible for them. His arguments about justice become incoherent unless he assumes the existence of individuals who are more than the products of cultural writing, and who can bear a responsibility to others, whether this responsibility is infinite or indefinite.

Thus, the antihumanist vocabulary that has for so long been associated with deconstruction must be abandoned when deconstruction confronts questions of justice in the real world. Once again, it is interesting to look at the treatment of the subject in Derrida's essays about Paul de Man. In these essays, Derrida jettisons the antihumanist rhetoric of his earlier writings. He speaks of individual actions, individual

139. *Cf.* RICHARD HARLAND, SUPERSTRUCTURALISM: THE PHILOSOPHY OF STRUCTURALISM AND POST-STRUCTURALISM 146-54 (1987); T.K. SEUNG, STRUCTURALISM AND HERMENEUTICS 256-57 (1982).

140. *See* JACQUES DERRIDA, SPEECH AND PHENOMENA 147 (David B. Allison trans., Northwestern Univ. Press 1973) (1967-1968). Of course, the words "effect" and "determination" must be put in quotes because the very notions of "cause" and "effect" become inadequate in Derrida's approach. *Id.*

meanings, and individual responsibilities.[141] Indeed, when Derrida discusses the ethical responsibilities of de Man and his critics in these writings, one could easily be forgiven for mistaking his discourse with familiar liberal notions of autonomy and free will.

The subject who emerges from deconstruction's encounter with justice may not be in all respects the relatively autonomous subject of traditional political theory; nevertheless, she is a person who can choose and hence bear the responsibility for her choices.[142] Deconstruction's encounter with justice shows how urgently the concept of a socially constructed subject needs revision. The challenge is to integrate deconstructive insights about language and meaning with the reality of individual subjects and the claims of individual responsibility. The transcendental conception of deconstruction can prove helpful in this endeavor. It argues that human beings articulate their values through culture and conventions. But this articulation is by no means uniformly limiting. To the contrary, the articulation of human values through language and culture simultaneously empowers individuals. Although the cultural articulation of human values fails fully to capture these values, at the same time it opens up possibilities for action and hence for responsibility. It creates degrees of moral and practical freedom.[143] Thus, contrary to antihumanist assumptions, culture and language do not efface human autonomy but are the conditions of its very possibility.

In one sense, it was inevitable that deconstructionists would have to rethink deconstruction's relationship to the subject the moment they became concerned with questions of justice. The notion of responsibility toward others presupposes people who can be responsible. The idea of an indefinite demand presupposes people to whom this demand can be addressed. The attempt to deconstruct systems of law or legal doctrines presupposes concern about the people unjustly affected by them. Finally, the transcendental conception of deconstruction inevitably leads us back to the individual subject. For this conception locates justice not as a determinate, unchanging Idea in Heaven but as a value or urge within the human soul; hence the importance of paying attention to the person possessing that soul.

141. *See, e.g.*, Derrida, *Biodegradables*, *supra* note 8, at 825-28.

142. Drucilla Cornell reaches a similar conclusion in her study of the ethics of deconstruction. *See* CORNELL, *supra* note 75, at 149; *cf.* Binder, *supra* note 75, at 1383 ("There can be no right of self-determination if there is no self.").

143. These arguments are further elaborated in J.M. Balkin, *Cultural Software*, 15 CARDOZO L. REV. (forthcoming 1994).

[9]

Washington and Lee Law Review

Volume 45 | Summer 1988 | Number 3

THE ANNUAL JOHN RANDOLPH TUCKER LECTURE

FORCE

Stanley E. Fish*

In the opening chapters of his magisterial study, *The Concept of Law,* H. L. A. Hart emphatically rejects John Austin's view that the essence of the law is a "situation where one person gives another an order backed by threats" and thereby "obliges him to comply."[1] Hart objects that this view fails to distinguish the law and its operations from the action of a gunman who "orders his victim to hand over his purse, and threatens to shoot him if he refuses."[2] It is simply counter-intuitive, he contends, to assimilate law to this reductive paradigm, and indeed, "Mere temporary ascendancy of one person over another is naturally thought of as the polar opposite of law, with its relatively enduring and settled characters." "In most legal systems," he adds, "to exercise such short term coercive power as the gunman has would constitute a criminal offense."[3] "Coercive power" is the key phrase here for it identifies what is for Hart the important distinction between what the law is and what the gunman does. Rather than coercing individuals by the exercise of mere force, the law binds members of society to a rule or set of rules that has the character of being general and impartial, that is, no respecter of persons. Without "the idea of a rule," Hart declares, "we cannot hope to elucidate even the most elementary forms of law."[4] Of course, as Hart himself sees, the notion of a rule does not entirely eliminate coercion, since where there is a rule of law there is necessarily some form of constraint in relation to which "human conduct is made in

---

* Professor of English and Law, Duke University. This article was prepared in connection with Professor Fish's presentation of the 40th Annual John Randolph Tucker Lecture, October 13, 1988, at the Washington and Lee University School of Law.

1. H.L.A. Hart, The Concept of Law 6 (1961).
2. *Id.*
3. *Id.* at 24.
4. *Id.* at 78.

some sense nonoptional or obligatory."[5] The phrase "in some sense" identifies the difference Hart would like to establish between legal obligation and the model of the gunman; while the individual under the law is not wholly free—such freedom would be incompatible with the very idea of law—the obligations to which he is subject are not merely the effect of arbitrary power but of a power that is enabled by an independent and authoritative source. That source is the rule of law which, Hart says, operates by "conferring powers . . . on persons qualified in certain ways to legislate by complying with a certain procedure."[6] Notice how much distance there is in this account between the source of power and the object of its exercise. In the gunman scenario, the coercion is direct and discrete; in the world of rule the coercing agent stands at the end of a long and articulated chain, beginning with the rule itself. The rule mandates not an act but a procedure which itself can only be put in motion by persons who meet prestipulated and abstract qualifications (age, education, skills, etc.), and these persons authorize still other persons who must themselves satisfy additional formal requirements. It is from this chain and not from any temporarily ascendant outlaw that the pressure of obligation issues, and the obedience that then follows, if it follows, will be the result not of force and violence, but of a principled process.

Or so it might seem. Could it not be said that procedure rather than doing away with force merely masks it by attenuating it, by placing it behind a screen or series of screens? After all, the crucial question, which returns the original problem to center stage, still has to be asked: Who gets to make the rules? And once that question is answered, another question (it is really the same) waits behind it: Who gets to say who gets to make the rules? If the answer to these questions turns out to be something like "whoever seizes the opportunity and makes it stick," then there is finally little to distinguish the rule centered legal system from the actions of the gunman; this gunman is merely better camouflaged. It is precisely such a danger that Hart spies when, later in the book, he identifies and considers another and more subtle form of imposition and coercion, that exercised by a court when, under the cover of its responsibility to interpret law, it instead *makes* law, and thereby demonstrates the truth of Bishop Hoadley's famous observation: "whoever hath an absolute authority to interpret any written or spoken laws, it is he who is the lawgiver to all intents and purposes and not the person who first wrote or spake them."[7] As Hart notes, this is simply an older version of what is to us a familiar claim: "The law (or the constitution) is what the courts say it is."[8] If this is indeed the case, then the rule of law or, more precisely, the law of rule, becomes an illusion, for the rule as a constraint, as a safeguard against casual

5. *Id.* at 80.
6. *Id.* at 75.
7. *Id.* at 137.
8. *Id.* at 138.

violence, falls to the daily acts of violence committed by judges who call the tune as they happen to see (and desire) it. Here is a "temporary" ascendancy of one person not only over another, but over many; here is a forceful capture even more sinister than that performed by the gunman because it wears the face of legitimate authority.

The great merit of Hart's analysis is that it makes clear the close relationship—a relationship so close as to be one of identity—between the threat posed to law by force and the threat posed to law by interpretation. If it is the business of law to protect the individual from coercion that is random, unpredictable, and arbitrary, then the individual is no less at risk when he is at the mercy of an interpreting court than when he is at the mercy of an armed assailant. In both cases he is nakedly exposed to an agent who has seized authority and is in the accidental circumstance of being able to get away with it. Of course, there is the difference that in one case a legislature (sometimes democratically elected) intervenes between the would-be coercer and his victim, but that is cold comfort if Bishop Hoadley is right and the interpreter "is he who is the lawgiver to all intents and purposes." If the gunman is the paradigmatic instance of force outside the law, interpretation is the force that resides within the law, and like the gunman it must be regulated and policed lest it subvert the law's claim to enact the dictates of general principles of justice and equity. It is crucial that the law not issue from anyone in particular—even from a justice of the Supreme Court—but from an impersonal source that resists the encroaching desires of particular (interpretive) wills. *The Concept of Law* is an extended search for such a point of resistance, and after having failed to discover it in the writings of his predecessors, Hart announces that he has found it in "the idea of a rule,"[9] and more particularly in the idea of a "determinate rule" in which, he says, "the life of the law consists."[10] Determinate rules, in contrast to vague or general rules that allow "the applications of variable standards, do *not* require from officials and individuals a fresh judgment from case to case."[11] Indeed, it would be more accurate to say that determinate rules (assuming for the moment that such exist) do not *permit* a fresh judgment from case to case because they are so directing as to leave no room in which the judgment might operate. Determinate, in short, means settled, complete in and of itself, and therefore in no need of further elaboration or addition. Determinate rules perform as barriers or walls on which is written "beyond this point interpretation cannot go."

Given that in Hart's view Law is all that stands between us and "the free use of violence,"[12] and given too that for him Law is thinkable only in terms of determinate rules, it is hardly surprising that he equates the

9. *Id.* at 78.
10. *Id.* at 132.
11. *Id.* (emphasis in original).
12. *Id.* at 167.

absence of such rules with the advent of chaos. "If it were not possible to communicate general standards of conduct, which multitudes of individuals could understand, without further direction, as requiring from them certain conduct when occasion arose, nothing that we now recognize as law could exist."[13] This single sentence is at once a compendium and an explication of the fears and desires that inform the tradition in which Hart writes; there must be a mode of communication that is general, not tied to the linguistic system of any particular community. Once produced, these general communications must be understandable by anyone, no matter what his individual educational or cultural experience. Indeed this understanding must be so immediate as not to be in need of any further elaboration; in fact its self-sufficiency shall be so perfect that elaboration or direction—otherwise known as interpretation—will constitute an impiety. The content of this unavoidable and self-sufficient understanding will be a set of matching orders. The hearer or reader will be "required" that is, compelled, left without choice, deprived of any opportunity to exercise his creative ingenuity. Unless all of this is the case, unless the framing of such general standards in a fail-safe interpretation-proof mode is a possible achievement, there will be no law.

The point is made even more dramatically by the court in *Cargill Commission Co. v. Swartwood*[14] when it refuses to take into consideration a prior oral agreement entered into by parties who subsequently executed a written contract. In the course of its decision the court invokes the so called "parol evidence rule" which states that when a written instrument is the complete and final expression of the contracting parties, it cannot be varied or contradicted by oral testimony. Obviously the intention of the rule is to keep the writing—the palpable evidence of a binding agreement— authoritative by declaring it off-bounds to interpretation. The alternative is so dreadful that the *Cargill* court can only contemplate it in the act of dismissing it:

> Were it otherwise, written contracts would be enforced not according to the plain effect of their language, but pursuant to the story of their negotiations as told by the litigant having at the time being the greater power of persuading the trier of fact. So far as contracts are concerned the rule of law would give way to the mere notions of man at to who should win law suits. . . . Without [the parol evidence] rule there would be no assurance of the enforceability of a written contract. If such assurance were removed today from our law, general disaster would result. . . .[15]

It takes one hundred and forty pages for Hart to move from the rejection of force to the identification of force, and its potentially disastrous

---

13. *Id.* at 121
14. 159 Minn. 1, 198 N.W. 536 (1924).
15. Cargill Comm'n Co. v. Swartwood, 159 Minn 1, ____, 198 N.W. 536, 538 (1924).

consequences, with interpretation. The court in *Cargill* does it in only four sentences, and in steps that can serve as a paradigm for the formalist argument. The "plain effect" of contractual language is opposed to the shifting and variable effects produced by stories powerfully—that is, forcefully—told. On the one hand, we have a stable and fixed (authoritative) shape; on the other, we have the many shapes brought into being by the exercise of verbal ingenuity. On the one side, we have the independent power of self-construing language; on the other, we have the power generated by the artful distortions of interested agents. If the power of interest is allowed to obscure matters of fact, if the determination of fact turns into a contest of persuasive styles, then the notion of a contract—of an agreement sealed by its verbal representation—goes by the boards; and if that happens, general disaster—the wholesale breakdown of communicative certainty and trust—cannot be far behind.

What the *Cargill* opinion makes clear is that in the court's view, as in Hart's, the foundations of Law are linguistic. The safeguards the law erects in order to repel the depredations of force are made of language, and if they are to perform *as* safeguards, they must be made of a certain kind of language, language that is capable of making what Hart calls an "authoritative mark."[16] An authoritative mark is a mark that commands the field in which it operates; it is a mark so complete and self-sufficient in its declaration that no one could mistake it or misread it. An authoritative mark is a determinate mark, and because it is possible to produce such a mark, it is possible to fashion determinate rules, and finally to elaborate a genuine system of law. So long as determinate rules embodied in authoritative marks are available as something to which we can have recourse in the event of disputes, we have "in embryonic form the idea of a legal system," "the germ of the idea of legal validity."[17]

Some of you will have recognized in the vocabulary of "authoritative marks" and "determinate rules" a familiar theory of language. In that theory communication is anchored by something variously called literal language, neutral language, objective language, explicit language, etc. By any name what is referred to is a level of language immune from contextual variation and therefore resistant to interpretation. The problem with this theory is well known: it seems undermined by the variety that is so obviously a feature of interpretive performance; nothing is more common than disputes concerning the meaning of supposedly plain or literal language. In the face of these disputes, in what sense could anything made of language be "determinate"? Hart answers this question by dividing language into two zones; there is at its center a "core of settled meaning" and at its outer edges or "penumbra" a realm of uncertainty and doubt. Disagreements arise in tha area of the penumbra where a certain looseness and vagueness results in that he calls "open texture,"[18] but disagreements must themselves

16. HART, *supra* note 1, at 93.
17. *Id.*
18. *Id.* at 120.

have a point of reference—something one is disagreeing *about—and* that point of reference is given by the settled core which determines the parameters of any dispute that might occur. Interpreters are thus constrained by the core even as they move with (relative) freedom in the area of the penumbra, and it is because of this "duality of a core of certainty and a penumbra of doubt"[19] that communication is able to occur. "If we are to communicate with each other at all . . . then the . . . words we use . . . must have some standard instance in which no doubts are felt about its application."[20] For then, "when we . . . frame some general rule . . . the language . . . fixes necessary conditions which anything must satisfy it if is to be within its scope, and certain clear examples of what is certainly within its scope may be present to our minds."[21]

The passage then is from words with a core of settled meaning to rules with a core of settled meaning, and later, as we shall see to historical bodies of material (decisions, statutes) whose significance is no less settled. Hart acknowledged that at every level variety and difference exist at the fringe—"nothing can eliminate this. . .penumbra of doubt"—but he insists that the variety is finally controlled and contained by a stability at the center, by the "core," the "germ," the "embryon." By using these words to characterize that which stands between us and the advance of unconstrained interpretation, Hart (inadvertently) alerts us to its fragility. In each of these spatial metaphors, the still unmoving point (core, center, germ, embryon) is surrounded by a much larger area (of fringe, penumbra, open texture), and the impression is of an insurgent force always on the verge of overrunning the fortress at the center, of blurring the line that demarcates the variable from the constant, of erasing (by writing over) the authoritative mark. It is Hart's strategy repeatedly to assure us (and himself) that the encroachment of interpretative will can be resisted if only we cling to the "core," but it is a strategy of desperation, and at times Hart himself seems more than half aware that it has already failed.

The sequence is always the same: he offers a candidate that will fill the position of "authoritative mark"—of something so self-sufficiently clear that it compels agreement and precludes interpretation—but then he so qualifies the status of the "mark" that its authority is put seriously in question. We see this first in his discussion of what he calls "primary rules of obligation" (where primary, of course, is another world like center, embryon, core), rules that place "restrictions on the free use of violence, theft, and deception to which human beings are tempted but which they must, in general, repress, if they are to coexist in close proximity with one another."[22] As they first emerge, these rules are "unofficial"; that is, they

19. *Id.* at 119.

20. Hart, *Positivism and the Separation of Law and Morals,* 71 HARV. L. REV., 593, 607 (1958).

21. HART, *supra* note 1, at 125.

22. *Id.* at 89.

stem from a shared desire for peace and security rather than from any developed and codified legal apparatus. But even as they are introduced, the primary rules are found to be inadequate, for it is only in a "small community closely knit by ties of kinship, common sentiment and belief" that they could function successfully. As soon as numbers increase and beliefs diverge—one suspect that the trouble begins when the number reaches two—there will arise "doubts. . .as to what the rules are or as to the precise scope of some given rule." In the absence of an "authoritative text" or of "an official whose declarations. . .are authoritative" there "will be no procedure for settling. . .doubt."[23] At a very early stage then a regime of primary rules will be characterized by "uncertainty" and when that happens the rules "will require supplementation."

But if the rules are uncertain and require supplementation, how can they be rules? Hart's project would seem to be compromised even before it gets under way. The entire *point* of rules, after all, is to stand alone and provide a center (core, germ, embryon) to which all parties can turn in the event of disputes. If the rules are incomplete, if one cannot know even what they are without the aid of some supplementary elaboration, then rather than constraining interpretation, the rules—so called—provoke it. Hart, however, is not without resources, and he moves to anticipate just such an objection by introducing a new line of defense in the form of a set of "secondary rules," which, he says, will provide a "remedy" for the "defects" of the primary rules. Chief among these is the "rule of recognition," a "rule for conclusive identification of the primary rules," a rule that will provide an "affirmative indication" as to whether or not a primary rule put forward by some interest is, in fact, "a rule of the group."[24] In order to perform this function, a rule of recognition must be of "a different kind"[25] than other rules of the system, and much of Hart's discussion is an attempt to specify the difference. He finds it first in the fact that this rule is "inscribed, written down in a list" or "carved on some public monument," but he realizes at once that the fact of the inscription will not be sufficiently distinguishing, since writings can proliferate just as easily as oral sayings or undeclared beliefs. The "crucial step," he declares, is "the acknowledgment of reference to the writing or inscription as *authoritative,*"[26] and this happens when the rule of recognition has been "accepted."[27] But the notions of "acknowledgment" and "acceptance" are obviously and fatally at odds with the requirement that the rule be "ultimate" and "supreme,"[28] for a rule that depends on the acknowledgment and acceptance of those who are to be bound by it can fail in both respects. It could remain unacknowledged—go *unrecognized—and* it could be refused, perhaps

23. *Id.* at 90.
24. *Id.* at 92.
25. *Id.*
26. *Id.* (emphasis in original).
27. *Id.* at 97, 105.
28. *Id.* at 102, 103.

in favor of other candidates. In order to be a rule of recognition in the strong sense—and that is the only sense that will do the job—the rule must be capable of recognizing or announcing itself and it must *compel* rather than await acceptance. How can a rule be "a supreme criterion of validity"[29] if its own validity can either go unnoticed or become a matter of dispute?

The same difficulty attends Hart's second attempt to claim for the rule of recognition a special, privileged status. Here the claim is that the rule exists "on a different level"[30] from the other rules and from the system whose center or core it is. It is in the nature of the rule, says Hart, that when confronted by it, "we are brought to a stop in inquiries concerning validity: for we have reached a rule which. . .provided criteria for the assessment of the validity of other rules; but it is also unlike them in that there is no rule providing criteria for the assessment of its own legal validity."[31] Where other rules must "satisfy criteria" in order to be validated, "no such question can arise as to the validity of the very rule. . .which provides the criteria."[32] But the question has already arisen as soon as acknowledgment and acceptance have been made the criteria for identifying the rule of recognition; for these criteria bring with them precisely what the rule of recognition supposedly eliminates, an area of choice, and choice in turn brings with it the spectres of dispute, doubt and uncertainty, earlier named as the defects of the primary rules, defects which were to have been remedied by the rule of recognition. If that rule can itself go unrecognized or be refused, it is not the end, but the beginning of inquiry and we are no better off than we were before.

Throughout this section of his argument Hart knows that he must firmly demarcate the rule of recognition from the field it must regulate; it cannot, in other words, be a mere item in that field, but must precede it. Indeed, says Hart, "Even if it were enacted by statute, this would not reduce it to the level of statute; for the legal status of such an enactment necessarily would depend on the fact that the rule existed antecedently to and independently of the enactment."[33] The very "assertion that it exists can only be an external matter of fact."[34] That is, its existence is not a matter of inference or interpretation; it is, and must be, self-evident, immediately perspicuous. It "escapes the conventional categories used for describing a legal system, though these are often taken to be exhaustive."[35] But even as he asserts the independence and perspicuity of the rule, Hart gives a disturbing answer to the question of how it is to be identified. Given what is required of this rule, it is a question that should not even be asked, for to ask it is to deprive the rule of the adjectives "supreme" and "ultimate"

29. *Id.* at 103.
30. *Id.* at 94.
31. *Id.* at 104.
32. *Id.* at 105.
33. *Id.* at 108.
34. *Id.* at 107.
35. *Id.*

and to yield the supremacy to the agency contained in the answer. In this case the answer is, to say the least, surprising. If the identification of the rule or recognition "were doubted" (and even to admit this possibility is to lose the game), "it could be established," Hart says, "by reference to actual practice: to the way in which courts identify what is to count as law. . . ."[36] But surely this is to put the cart before the horse: Hart's entire argument depends on a rule that stands *apart from* the field of practice, a rule to which practitioners can turn when they are in doubt as to what to do, and a rule to which arbitrators can turn when different practitioners want to do different things. If, however, one can know the rule only by extrapolating from practice, then practice rather than being generated or tested by the rule is the source of the rule; and insofar as practice is itself unsettled—not at all points uniform and stable—there will not one but many rules and no *independent* mechanism for deciding between them. Once the rule of recognition recedes into practice it becomes not a matter of fact, but of interpretation, and the way is open to exactly the situation Hart hopes to avoid, the situation in which the law is what the courts say it is. For if one locates the rule by looking "to the way in which courts identify" it, then the actions of the court come first and rule second. In short, the rule of recognition is secondary in a sense much stronger than Hart intends; it is belated in relation to the activity it purports to govern, and that activity, rather than being constrained by the rule, makes and unmakes it in response to the opportunities afforded by power and occasion.

By "that activity" I mean, of course, interpretation, and the failure of the rule of recognition prompts me to formulate a rule of my own: Whatever is invoked as a constraint on interpretation will turn out upon further examination to have been the product of interpretation, or to put it in Hart's terms, although it is always possible to distinguish a settled core form the area of open texture that surrounds it, that core has itself been formed by the very forces it supposedly repels. While the distinction between core and penumbra can always be made at a particular moment, at another moment the *interpretive* conditions within which the distinction is perspicuous can be challenged and dislodged; if that happens the distinction will not so much disappear as it will take on a new *historical* form, one that is no less precariously in place than its predecessor. The point is one Hart makes himself when he observes that "canons of interpretation"—verbal directions designed to restrict interpretation's scope—"make use of general terms which themselves require interpretation;"[37] and once one sees this, one sees too that attaching canons to the canons—putting restrictions on the formulation of restrictions—will not remedy but merely extend the difficulty. No matter how many or what kinds of rules one promulgates, the scope of interpretation will not have been the least whit diminished; for each new attempt to control it will be the occasion for its exercise.

36. *Id.* at 105.
37. *Id.* at 123.

Although Hart both sees and says this, he cannot quite grasp its implications, for he continues to believe that the inability of rules to constrain is only partial and that at the very least they serve to narrow the area in which interpretation can operate. Hart's argument is that a rule framed in the appropriately general terms (e.g., "vehicles are prevented from entering the park") will pick out "standard instances" of its application, and that these instances will constitute a set of "central" or "plain cases" in relation to which other, less clear, cases, can be classified. Thus someone "faced with the question whether the rule prohibiting the use of vehicles in the park is applicable to some combination of circumstances in which it appears indeterminate," can proceed by considering "as one does who makes use of a precedent, whether the present case resembles the plain case "sufficiently" in "relevant respects."[38] The words "sufficiently" and "relevant" indicate Hart's awareness that the agent's discretion remains wide, but still it is a bounded area, marked off by a plain case that at once gives interpretation a direction and holds it in check.

As an account of what people do (line up present cases with clear, paradigm cases) this is impeccable, but as I read it, it is an account not of interpretation subdued, but of interpretation triumphant. The question is not whether there are in fact plain cases—there surely are—but, rather, of what is their plainness a condition and a property? Hart's answer must be that a plain case is inherently plain, plain in and of itself, plain independently of the interpretive activities it can then be said to direct. But it takes only a little reflection to see that the truth is exactly the reverse. A plain case is a case that was once *argued;* that is, its configurations were once in dispute; at a certain point one characterization of its meaning and significance—of its *rule—was* found to be more persuasive than its rivals. At *that* point the case became settled, became perspicuous, became undoubted, became plain. Plainness, in short, is not a property of the case itself—there is no case itself—but of an interpretive history in the course of which one interpretive agenda—complete with stipulative definitions, assumed distinctions, canons of evidence, etc.—has subdued another. That history is then closed, but it can always be reopened. That is, on some later occasion, the settled assumptions within which the case acquired its plain meaning can become unsettled, can become the object of debate rather than the in place background in the context of which debate occurs; and when that happens, contending arguments or interpretive agendas will once again vie in the field until one of them is regnant and the case acquires a new settled and plain meaning. So that while there will always be paradigmatically plain cases—Hart is absolutely right to put them at the center of the adjudicative process—far from providing a stay against the force of interpretation, they will be precisely the result of interpretation's force, for they will have been written and rewritten by interpretive efforts.

38. *Id.* at 124.

Another name for this process is precedent. Hart thinks of precedent as a means of controlling an indeterminate present by reference to an already determined (and therefore determining) past. To quote again the key sentence, the agent who must decide considers "whether the present case resembles the plain case 'sufficiently' in 'relevant' respects." The question that is here elided is what does the plain case resemble; what is *it* like? Hart's answer, which he gives by not giving it, is that the plain case resembles itself, establishes its own configurations in relation to which later cases are either like or unlike it. But resemblance and its opposite—that is, sameness and difference—are not immanent in the object but emerge from the perspective of the differential criteria that inform perception. If I see two poems or two cases as similar, it will be because of the categories (of size, or period, or theme. . .) within which I search; were I to search within different categories (of sameness and difference), the relationship between the two poems or cases would be seen differently. Moreover, since each is known *in terms* of the relationship between them, the poems and cases would be different depending on the different categories of difference within which they are seen. What this means is that resemblance (or difference) is always a constructed *(i.e. interpretive)* phenomenon and therefore it can always be constructed again. In fact, that is what happens in the citing of precedents; the so-called plain case doesn't sit still, silently measuring the distance or closeness between it and the present case. Indeed the demands are made from either direction, for it is the interests and concerns of the present case that generate the pressure for comparison and dictate its terms; and it is in the light of the interests and concerns flowing from the present case that the "plain case" will then be constituted.

As a result, when the plainness of the settled case is characterized, the very terms of the characterization will have been set by the case that has yet to be settled; rather than the past controlling the present, the present controls the past by providing the perspective from which the two must be brought into line. The truth about precedent then is the opposite of the story we tell about it; precedent is the process by which the past gets produced by the present so that it can then be cited as the producer of the present. It is in this way that the law achieves what Ronald Dworkin calls "articulate consistency,"[39] a way of thinking and talking about itself which creates and re-creates the continuity that is so crucial to its largest claim, the claim to have an unchanging center that founds its authority. Articulate consistency is not a fact, but an achievement, something that is forever being wrested out of diverse materials which are then retroactively declared always to have had its shape. The court in *Cargill* fears that if the parol evidence rule is disregarded, the rule of law would give way to the power of those who are able to tell the most persuasive story; but that is already the *whole* of the law, whose collective story is continually being made up and then told both to the lay public and to the agents in the legal system,

39. R. Dworkin, *Hard Cases*, in Taking Rights Seriously 88 (1977).

i.e., to the tellers. Again Hart himself admits as much when he discusses the ways in which courts can slip out of the net of precedent; the chief way is to "distinguish" the earlier case, to find that the scope of its rule is narrower than the concerns of the present case which can then be decided independently of it. All you have to do, Hart explains, is to think up "some legally relevant difference" between the two cases, and moreover, he adds, "the class of such differences can never be exhaustively determined." That is to say, the finding of difference is for all intents and purposes an unconstrained activity, an activity which once know no natural stopping point, an activity that cannot be stopped. Yet even though Hart makes this point he fails to see how fatal it is to his general project, and continues blithely on, asserting that "not withstanding these. . .forms of legislative activity"[40] courts are bound by a "vast number"[41] of determinate rules. But his own analysis tells us that the rules are determinate only to the extent that interpreters desire them to be; if the desires of interpreters change, they will always be able to give those rules a new shape and then to declare them determinate even as they are in the process of determining them.

At one point Hart comes very close to saying as much. He is discussing those situations in which it appears that courts are "exercising creative powers which settle the ultimate criteria by which the validity of the very laws, which confer upon them jurisdiction as judges, must itself be tested."[42] That is, at times courts seem to be themselves constituting the authority (the rule of recognition) they subsequently cite as legitimizing their actions. (Just this account has often been given of the American practice of judicial review.) It may be the case, says Hart, that "when courts settle previously unenvisaged questions concerning the most fundamental constitutional rules, they *get* their authority to decide them accepted after the questions have arisen and the decision has been given."[43] In short, it may be, as I put it at the beginning of this chapter, that authority rests with whoever seizes an opportunity to act and then makes the action stick, that, as Hart observes, "all succeeds is success."[44] This is a remarkable statement which is perfectly congruent with my argument not for the denial of "cores" and "centers" and "authoritative marks," but for their status as historical constructions that are in place only so long as a more powerful construction has not yet dislodged them. But even as he moves toward this position Hart pushes it away by once again invoking the distinction between the settled core and the fringe area of doubt as if it were unproblematical. "[N]ot every rule," Hart points out (correctly), "is open to doubt on all points," and, he adds, "[T]he possibility of courts having authority at any given time to decide

40. Hart, *supra* note 1, at 131.
41. *Id.* at 132.
42. *Id.* at 148.
43. *Id.* at 149 (emphasis in orginal).
44. *Id.*

these limiting questions concerning the ultimate criteria of validity, depends merely on the fact that, at that time, the application of those criteria to a vast area of law, including the rules which confer that authority, raises no doubt. . .''[45] Hart misses what is almost, and should be, his own point: while it is true that at any one time there are vast areas free of doubt which constitute a core of certainty, that core has been established by the very forces that it now (but *temporarily)* holds in bounds. It is still the case that what succeeds is success; it is just that one of the things success brings (for a time) are vast areas free of doubt. What must be remembered is that those areas rest on a foundation that is itself doubtful, *i.e. subject* to challenge, and therefore are in no sense (except the local sense of their ascendancy) determinate.

I could go on with this reading of *The Concept of Law,* but it would only reveal further variations on the pattern we have repeatedly seen: a mechanism is proposed with the claim that it will keep force—whether in the form of the gunman or the interpreter—at bay; and in each instance force turns out to be the content of the mechanism designed to control it. No matter how many layers of rules, plain cases, cores of settled meanings, precedents one puts in place, the bottom line remains the ascendancy of one person—or of one set of interests aggressively pursued—over another, and the dream of general rules ''judicially applied''[46] remains just that, a dream. It would seem that Richard Rorty is right when he characterizes interpretation as an operation in which the agent— be he a judge or a literary critic—''simply beats the text into a shape which will serve his own purpose'' and ''makes the text refer to whatever is relevant to that purpose.''[47]

Rorty's casually brutal language names the fear in response to which Hart and so many others mount their projects, the fear, first that nothing stands between the exercise of power and its victims, and, second, that the activities we engage in are finally meaningless. The point has been succinctly put by Wayne Booth: If disagreements are settled by ''the most forceful means of persuasion,'' we are condemned ''to a sense of ultimate futility in what we do,'' and we become successively and perpetually bound ''to whichever suitor woos most winningly.''[48] The alternative is, of course, to find a stay against the workings of persuasive power, and for most of those who have thought about the questions, that stay is some form of rationality, whether is be a logic, a special kind of language, a determinate rule, a monumental text, a neutral procedure. E. D. Hirsch sums up an entire tradition (which begins at least with Plato) when he declares it is ''essential to distinguish hypotheses and evidence from the rhetoric used to convey them.''[49] It is essential because rhetoric is by definition the forceful pres-

45. *Id.*
46. *Id.* at 202.
47. R. Rorty, The Consequences of Pragmatism 151 (1982).
48. W. Booth, A Rhetoric of Irony 195 (1974).
49. E. Hirsch, The Aims of Interpretation 154 (1976).

entation of an interested argument—rhetoric is another word for force—and what is desired is a way of neutralizing interest so that the decisions generated by the system will not be the product of any partial or partisan point of view.

It is just such a way that Hart seeks, but even if he were to find it (in some rule or precedent) he would only have done half the job, for the neutralization of interest is an interior as well as an exterior task. The success rhetoric may have in turning the mind away from purely rational considerations is a function as much of tendencies in the mind as it is of pressuring forces external to the mind; an illegitimate appeal can hardly have an effect if there is nothing to appeal to. (Remember, primary rules are necessary because of the human susceptibility to base actions). If genuine evidence is to be disentangled from partisan posturing, a corresponding separation must occur in the mind, lest the genuine go unrecognized. As part of its program to protect the individual from force, the law must also control, by neutralizing, the forces that live within the individual, the forces that, if left unchecked, would prompt him to the subversion of the very rules that offer him a world of security and stability. That is why those who, like Hart, argue for a neutral space in the world must also argue for a neutral space in the mind, one free of biases, prejudices and presuppositions. Thus Stephen Toulmin urges us to "discount" any "biases and prejudices" we may have to that we might act "in a disinterested way,"[50] and in a similar vein, Wayne Booth advises that we "develop a habit of great skepticism about one's own hypothesis"[51] and "[exercise] a healthy tentativeness about oneself and one's responses."[52] The advice seems sound until one thinks about acting on it. Just how does one distance oneself from oneself? With what part of oneself can one be tentative about oneself? The answer lies in the assumption by Toulmin and Booth of a *psychological* core that is the equivalent of the cores Hart finds in determinate rules, settled meanings, centrally clear cases, etc.; it is this core of rationality inside us that protects us from the pressure of our own convictions and predispositions. The danger represented by the predispositions, the danger of surrendering to illegitimate appeals, is exactly like the danger represented by the gunman in Hart's scenario. The only difference is that this gunman is in our heads, but that is finally no difference at all as Terry Eagleton makes clear when he equates being "forced mindlessly" into an action by an "ideological obsession" with the pressure of somebody "holding a gun to my head."[53] It is one thing, Eagleton adds, to be "convinced by the arguments and evidence," and quite another to hold convictions "because they are convenient. . .or fashionably eccentric." In the first case one is

50. Toulmin, *The Construal of Realty,* in THE POLITICS OF INTERPRETATION, 107 (W. Mitchell ed. 1982).

51. BOOTH, *supra* note 48, at 225.

52. *Id.* at 226.

53. Eagleton, *Ineluctable Opinions,* in THE POLITICS OF INTERPRETATION 376 (W. Mitchell ed. 1982).

"able to weigh the arguments" and become convinced in a way that is "'freer'"; in the second one is the victim of "a spontaneous ideological prejudice."[54] Of course, the source of that prejudice is oneself, and therefore one is, in a curious way, self-victimized. It follows then that in order to cease being a victim one must cease being oneself. That at least is the implication of Eagleton's odd phrase "forced mindlessly"; since what you are being forced by in his scenario are the beliefs and predispositions what now fill your mind, in order not to be so forced you would have to empty your mind of everything it contains, so that in Wallace Stevens' words, you would "have a mind of winter."

The problem with this strategy is simply that it is not possible to follow it; and, moreover, even if we could somehow follow it, the condition of being free from ideological control would be wholly disabling because there would be nothing either to be free *with* or *for*. *There* would be nothing to be free *with* because were every preconception, acquired belief, assumed point of view, opinion, bias and prejudice removed from the mind, there would be nothing left with which to calculate, determine and decide. There is nothing to be free *for*, because a mind divested of all direction—a mind not already oriented toward this or that purpose or plan or agenda—could not recognize any reason for going in one direction rather than another or, for that matter, for going in any direction at all. It is often claimed that reason itself is what is left when belief, preconception and prejudice have been set aside or discounted, but reason cannot operate independently of some content—of some proposition or propositions whose content is definitions, distinctions, and criteria already assumed—and that content will reflect some belief or attitude that will inform whatever outcome reason dictates. (This is to say, once again, that the "core" is always and already invaded by the penumbra.) I am aware that in so arguing I am asserting the identity of two entities that are often distinguished and even opposed, reason and belief. Indeed, it is not too much to say that the quest for a way of quarantining the process of law from force depends on that opposition; for if one defines knowledge as that which exists independently of any particular perspective, belief—which is another name for perspective—becomes a bar to its achievement. In this view beliefs are the property of partisan agendas and if one is to resist their appeal, an appeal that amounts to nothing less than coercion, one must distance oneself from them and neutralize their force. It is my contention that this is precisely what one cannot possibly do, and still remain a "one," a being with a capacity for action. In short, you can never get away from your beliefs which means that you can never get away from force, from the pressure exerted by a partial, nonneutral, nonauthoritative, ungrounded point of view.

We see then that the two strategies by which force is to be held in check fail in the same way. On the other hand there is the attempt to erect an *external* barrier—sometimes a determinate rule, or a plain case or a

---

54. *Id.*

settled meaning—but in every ins ance the barrier turns out to be indistinguishable from that which it would hold back; force is already inside the gate because it *is* the gate. On the other hand there is the attempt to perform an *internal* housecleaning, to remove from the mind the tendencies that correspond to force's appeal; but this turns out to be at once impossible and in a very literal sense *self-defeating,* since a mind so cleansed would have nothing inside it. The ideal of a mind that is insulated from pressure is as unattainable as the ideal of a rule that will be a stay against the assault of interpretive desires. The mind, insofar as it is anything, *is* a structure of pressures, of purposes, urgencies, interests already in place; and the rule, insofar as it is intelligible, is an extension of some interested agenda that cannot be kept out because it is already in. To the extent that the law is compelling, it is compelling in relation to the very prejudices and biases it supposedly neutralizes; the reasons for which we do something or refrain from doing something *are* reasons only by virtue of the preconceptions and predispositions we already have.

The conclusion is inescapable and it is the one I have repeatedly reached: The force of the law is always and already indistinguishable from the forces it would oppose. Or to put the matter another way: there is always a gun at your head. Sometimes the gun is, in literal fact, a gun. Sometimes it is a reason, an assertion whose weight is inseparable from some already assumed purpose. Sometimes it is a desire, the urging of a state of affairs to which you are already predisposed. Sometimes it is a need you already feel. Sometimes it is a name—country, justice, honor, love, God—whose power you have already internalized. Whatever it is, it will always be a form of coercion, of an imperative whose source is an interest which speaks to the interest in you. And this leads me to a second aphorism: not only is there always a gun at your head; the gun at your head *is* your head; the interests that seek to compel you are appealing and therefore pressuring only to the extent they already live within you, and indeed *are* you. In the end we are always self-compelled, coerced by forces—beliefs, convictions, reasons, desires—from which we cannot move one inch away.

Another way to put this is to say that while there are constraints on the will and therefore on interpretation, those constraints are *internal* to the will and do not provide a point of reference independent of it. By "internal" I mean something directly opposite to what Hart means when he distinguishes between the internal and the external "points of view" with respect to the imperatives of a legal system. In his analysis, one operates from the external point of view when one notes, in the manner of an anthropological observer, that "a social group accepts [certain] rules;"[55] one operates from the internal point of view when one "uses" those rules in determining one's everyday obligations. The internal agent need not, and characteristically does not, state the rules by which he is guided; his knowledge of them is more integral than that of the mere observer and is

55. Hart, *supra* note 1, at 99.

expressed in the way he applies them from moment to moment. To this I would object that neither of these "points of view" is genuinely internal. To be sure, they are different: in one the agent specifies the rules without being committed to them, while in the other, the agent is committed to the rules but does not (characteristically) specify them. Both agents, however, are in the same relation of *distance* to the rules in the sense that they could be held at arms length and examined; it is just that for one the examination or nothing of the rules is the end point of the activity; while the other goes on to use or apply them. The very words "use" and "apply" make my point, that the rules in Hart's picture are separate from a self that is free to employ them or not. The words "use" and "apply" signify instrumentality in relation to an independent actor; but what I have been arguing is that the actor is never is such a relation and that the imperatives to which he responds cannot be held at arm's length—cannot, in Eagleton's terms, be "weighed"—because they are constitutive of the actor's every gesture, including the gesture of weighing.

This is the only internal perspective worth the name (and indeed the only perspective there is: even the "external" observer does his observing from a vantage point he could not observe because it grounds him; his conclusions are no less internal than the conclusions of a community member) and it is the perspective Hart cannot endorse or even acknowledge because it leaves no room for a "core" or "center" to which the agent's prejudices and desires can be referred for judgment. It is in relation to that core and to the possibility of disinterestedly identifying it that Hart imagines a superior group of citizens who, unlike their less reflective fellows, do not obey the laws out of fear or habit, but "appraise" them "critically"[56] and obey them in a more self-consciously rational way. It is this self-consciousness that marks the Hartian internal point of view which is in fact the point of view achieved when the agent has purged himself of whatever is inside him in favor of a standard he prefers to his own. That is to say, Hart's internal point of view is an external point of view in disguise and, moreover, as I have repeatedly demonstrated, it is one that cannot be occupied.

In so saying I may seem to confirm Hart's fear of a world without order or principle, wholly given over to force in the form either of gunmen or of judges unconstrained in their actions or of wills unchecked by any core of rationality. But in fact the implication of my argument is that this fear is unrealizable and is based on an incorrect understanding of what force is and is not. What force is not is "mere" force, force unconnected with any agenda or program. Force is simply a (pejorative) name for the thrust or assertion of some point of view, and in a world where the urging of points of view cannot be referred for adjudication to some independent tribunal, force is just another name for what follows naturally from conviction. That is to say, force wears the aspect of anarchy only if one regards it as an empty blind urge, but if one identifies it as *interest aggressively*

---

56. *Id.* at 113.

pursued, force acquires a content and that content is a complex of goals and purposes, underwritten by a vision, and put into operation by a detailed agenda complete with steps, stages, and directions. Force, in short, is already a repository of everything it supposedly threatens—norms, standards, reasons, and yes, even rules. One could, of course, object (or complain) that such rules, standards and reasons are merely local and partisan and provide no mechanism for principled adjudication. But this would be to reinvoke the dream of a principle that was neutral— of a rule of recognition, or a centrally plain case or a core of settled meaning—and in response I could only offer once again the analyses of the preceding pages in which that neutrality is shown to be unavailable, both in its material and psychological forms. What I am trying to show now is that this state of affairs is in no way disastrous or even disabling; it appears to be disabling only if the alternative to neutrality is principled force—and it is my argument that there is no other kind—then the unavailability of neutrality simply does not have and *could not have* the consequences Hart fears. The absence of external or independent constraints only means that the constraints inherent in the condition of belief—the condition of having been persuaded to some vision, the condition of not seeking, but already occupying a position—are always and inescapably in force. The facts that you can never move one inch away from your beliefs means too that you can never move one inch away from norms and principles.

To be sure, this does not solve our practical problems, since we still are faced with the difficulty of adjudicating between beliefs in the absence of a calculus that is not itself a function or extension of belief. It is a difficulty that cannot be removed, but the fact that it cannot be removed does not condemn us to uncertainty and paralysis, but to conflict, to acts of persuasion in which one party attempts to alter the beliefs of another by putting forward arguments that are weighty only in relation to still other beliefs. By definition the career of persuasion is unpredictable and theoretically interminable; there is no guarantee that either party will be victorious although in some social structures—and the law is certainly one of them—victory is mandated in the form of the obligation to render a decision. But when victory occurs, whether by the surrender of one party to the party of which he now becomes a member or by jurisdictional fiat, it is always provisional; for since it has emerged from argument, from forceful urging of some partisan point of view, it is always provisional; for since it has emerged from argument, from forceful urging of some partisan point of view, it is always possible, and indeed likely, that what has apparently been settled will become unsettled, and argument will begin again.

Once again we reach a conclusion that seems to realize one of Hart's worst fears, in this case the fear of a legal (?) structure marked by the "mere temporary ascendancy of one person over another."[57] The burden of Hart's complaint falls on "temporary," for which we might substitute,

57. *Id.* at 24.

occasional, local, transitory, ad hoc, etc. It is not difficult to see why words like these are distressing; they run contrary to the assumption, so powerful in our legal culture, that what courts and judges do is extend into the present abiding principles of law and morality. This is the content, for example, of Ronald Dworkin's notion of "law as integrity" and of his distinction between principle and policy.[58] There are all kinds of good reasons why that assumption continues to inform the story the law tells about itself even as its history enacts quite another story. After all, the law could hardly advertise itself as resting on force (given that word's bad press) and still be accepted as law. Hart is right when he insists that it is the very essence of law to distinguish itself from force; and, moreover, that distinction is *real* insofar as it refers to a society's understanding of its foundational moorings in relation to the energies that would threaten to dissolve them. My point is that such an understanding, necessary as it is to the constitution of any society or community, is itself an artifact of time, a "mere temporary ascendancy" of one vision or agenda over its rivals, and that when that temporary ascendancy has been succeeded by another, the distinction between law and force will still be in force, but the content and distribution of its terms will be different. It is that succession of differences that makes up the law's history, a history that includes a claim of continuity that is belied by its own events.

Are legal actors then living out a lie, asserting as absolute what they should acknowledge as fragile and transitory? Not at all. Legal actors, like everyone else, live *within* the temporary ascendancies they at once affirm and undo (by endlessly modifying the givens that make action possible) and no analysis of their situation, even the analysis offered here, will remove them from it. That is to say, the acknowledgment that from the long run point of view law is inseparable from force is itself without force, since no one inhabits the long run point of view, and in the succession of short runs that make up our lives, the distinction between law and force is unassailable, although one can always assail the form it has presently assumed.

I say this to ward off a conclusion often reached on the left: That a recognition of the temporally contingent nature of our "fundamental" assumptions would lessen their force and make us less likely to surrender to them. But the conclusion is possible only if one makes the mistake (which I have called "antifoundationalist theory hope") of turning the recognition of contingency into a way of avoiding contingency, as if contingency acknowledged were contingency transcended. You may know *in general* that the structure of your convictions is an historical artifact but that knowledge does not transport you to a place where those convictions are no longer in force. We remain embedded in history even when we know that it is history we are embedded in, and while that knowledge may be satisfying in relation to alternative stories about our convictions (for example that they correspond or should correspond to the unchanging nature of

58. *See generally*, R. Dworkin, Law's Empire (1986); R. Dworkin, *supra* note 39.

things), in relation to the particular convictions (including itself) by which we are not grasped and constituted, it is of no force whatsoever.[59]

59. This essay was completed before the publication of Robert N. Moles' *Definition and Rule in Legal Theory*. Professor Moles' emphasis differs from mine—he is interested in rehabilitating John Austin—but many of the points we make are complementary. For instance, Moles writes, "Hart's mistake is. . .to suggest that ways of thinking have some autonomous existence independent of the will and device of their human authors." R. MOLES, DEFINITION AND RULE IN LEGAL THEORY 103 (1987). Moles also writes, "If the. . .core elements. . .are merely an extrapolation from the practice of the courts, then they are too vague to be helpful." *Id.* at 119. Moles further writes, "The distinction between a 'literal' and a purposive approach presents us with a false dichotomy." *Id.* at 156. Finally, Moles writes,"'Distortion' is an inevitable feature of knowledge and cannot therefore have the perjorative connotations which may initally be suggested by the use of this word." *Id.* at 183.

Part III
The Law of Language

[10]

COLUMBIA LAW REVIEW

Vol. 63 MARCH 1963 No. 3

MORALS AND THE CONSTITUTION: THE SIN OF OBSCENITY†

LOUIS HENKIN*

The several cases[1] in which the Supreme Court of the United States has examined obscenity legislation under the light of the Constitution have unloosed a torrent of writing—official, legal, psychological, and lay. The many words have reflected and evoked passion; they have not brought clarity, to the constitutional questions or to the social questions. They have not spoken to a common effect; they have not joined issue. The Supreme Court itself has split and splintered in variegated opinions and doctrines. Students of the Court's work have cast stones at some Justices, or at all of them. Those who make the obscenity laws and those who enforce them, and others who vigilantly support their hands, have welcomed the Court's decisions with a spate of metaphor about the poison of obscenity and its fearful consequences for man and child. "Libertarians" have deplored another breach in the constitutional bulwark against repression.

At risk of adding yet another tongue to Babel, I venture a few pages with modest purpose. I wish to focus on a small point, but one of constitutional consequence. To me it seems that the unusual confusion—more prevalent than in discussions of other attempts of government to regulate forms of expression—is due in large measure to misapprehension of the concern and the interest that inspire government to regulate obscenity. Specifically, I believe, despite common assumptions and occasional rationalizations, that obscenity laws are not principally motivated by any conviction that obscene materials inspire sexual offenses. Obscenity laws, rather, are based on traditional notions, rooted in this country's religious antecedents, of governmental responsibility for communal and individual "decency" and "morality."

If I am correct about the origins and purposes of obscenity legislation, much of the constitutional discussion about the control of obscenity seems out

† When this Article was conceived, my friend Professor Louis B. Schwartz offered to write a companion piece on "Morals Offenses and the Model Penal Code." Because the *Columbia Law Review* is dedicating its April issue to comments on the Model Penal Code, Professor Schwartz's companion article will appear in that issue.

* Professor of Law and of International Law and Diplomacy, Columbia University.

1. See, *e.g.*, Manual Enterprises, Inc. v. Day, 370 U.S. 478 (1962); Times Film Corp. v. City of Chicago, 365 U.S. 43 (1961); Kingsley Int'l Pictures Corp. v. Regents of the Univ. of the State of N.Y., 360 U.S. 684 (1959); Roth v. United States, 354 U.S. 476 (1957); Kingsley Books, Inc. v. Brown, 354 U.S. 436 (1957); Butler v. Michigan, 352 U.S. 380 (1957).

of focus. Concentration on whether obscenity may—or may not—incite to unlawful acts aims beside the mark. The question, rather, is whether the state may suppress expression it deems immoral, may protect adults as well as children from voluntary exposure to that which may "corrupt" them, may preserve the community from public, rampant "immorality." This different question may receive the same or a different answer; clearly, the path and the guide posts, the facts sought, the issues considered, and the doctrine applied may be very different. Indeed, this inquiry might today command attention even to a question that must have appeared insubstantial earlier in the history of the Constitution: the authority of government under the Constitution to adopt "morals legislation," to suppress private, individual indulgence which does no harm to others, in the name of traditional notions of morality.

The proper issues of obscenity regulation, I believe, do not lead constitutional lawyers deep into the penumbra in which speech moves toward unlawful action; they demand, rather, forthright and sophisticated exploration of the claims of "unsophisticated" morality and of the community's authority to maintain standards of "decency" and to prevent the corruption of individual character and morals. We may glance at *Schenck*[2] and *Dennis*.[3] More relevantly, we might look instead at innumerable unquestioned assertions in cases like *Stone v. Mississippi*[4] and *Mugler v. Kansas*.[5]

I. The Purposes of Obscenity Regulation

One cannot, of course, demonstrate beyond doubt a single aim of obscenity regulation. Motives and purposes for legislation are notoriously elusive, ambiguous, and multifarious. The fear that obscenity may induce crime is one occasional reason or rationalization for regulation. Perhaps some legislators enacting or re-enacting traditional laws against obscenity have this reason in mind. At bottom, there are other, authentic motives for obscenity laws.

Clearly, "obscenity," and other concepts to which it is frequently joined in legislation, include at least some expressions that do not relate at all to "incitement" to illegal action. For one instance—too often concealed by the emphasis on sex in discussions of obscenity—the accepted definition of obscenity includes not only the sexual but the scatological.[6] Surely the latter does not lead to any unlawful act: it may be emetic; it is not aphrodisiac.[7]

2. Schenck v. United States, 249 U.S. 47 (1919).
3. Dennis v. United States, 341 U.S. 494 (1951).
4. 101 U.S. 814, 818 (1880).
5. 123 U.S. 623, 662 (1887).
6. See, *e.g.*, Model Penal Code § 251.4(1) (1962): "Material is obscene if, considered as a whole, its predominant appeal is to prurient interest, that is, a shameful or morbid interest, in nudity, sex or *excretion* . . . ." (Emphasis added.)
7. I owe the phrase to Judge Woolsey's felicity. See United States v. One Book Called "Ulysses," 5 F. Supp. 182, 185 (S.D.N.Y. 1933), *aff'd*, 72 F.2d 705 (2d Cir. 1934).

"Sexual obscenity," too, is regulated for purposes unrelated to fear that it may lead to "sex crimes." Obscenity—sexual or scatological—is forbidden, in large part, not because it incites but because it offends. A state forbids obscenity—and nudity, "indecent exposure," graffiti—as it forbids public fornication and public excretion, because it is offensive to others. The state seeks to suppress or abate these noxious emanations on grounds akin to traditional notions of "nuisance." While "nuisance" may here be a metaphor—and metaphor has tended to obscure rather than clarify constitutional analysis—this kind of obscenity legislation has a social purpose to protect others from the impact of acts or expressions offensive to them.[8]

Let it be admitted immediately that control of scatological obscenity or of sexual "nuisance" obscenity does not raise the difficult questions. Socially, as well as constitutionally, troublesome issues derive from a large and important area of regulation aimed at sexual materials addressed to willing adults who would not be subject to this "obscenity" if they did not wish to be and who, if they stumbled upon it innocently, might quickly and effectively avoid it. The forms of regulation, too, are not designed and limited to protect the unwitting and unwilling, or to render obscenity private. Regulation frequently aims to prevent even the eager from obtaining the materials or from regarding them, however clandestinely; government seeks to destroy the materials and to prevent and to deter their production.

No doubt many who support such regulation of private voluntary indulgence in obscenity have said or felt that this obscenity may incite the person exposed to it to unlawful sexual action. Today, psychologists are examining and debating whether some obscenity may inspire "psycho-sexual" tension possibly harmful to mental health. They strive to determine, too, whether different kinds of "obscenity" in different circumstances might influence behavior: whether it may sublimate and deflect from sexual activity, or whether, in some cases at least, obscenity may incite an "abnormal" person to commit unlawful sexual acts. Greater psychological knowledge may some day provide an intelligent basis for evaluating the impact of obscenity on behavior. Even then, but surely now, conclusions as to whether such materials incite to unlawful action may not determine the constitutionality of laws regulating obscenity. For, it seems clear, obscenity legislation has had other purposes and motivations. The accepted definition of obscenity, as that which "appeal[s] . . . to prurient interest,"[9] makes no assumption that it will incite to any action. The history of obscenity legislation points, rather, to origins in aspirations to holiness and propriety. Laws against obscenity have ap-

8. I am not suggesting that the state may always, under the Constitution, prefer the sensibilities of others to the freedom of the actor. Surely, it cannot bar expression of ideas that may be intellectually "offensive," or even infuriating. See note 61 *infra*.

9. This is the definition of the MODEL PENAL CODE § 207.10(2) (Tent. Draft No. 6, 1957), identical in relevant part to the 1962 official draft, see note 6 *supra*, adopted by the Supreme Court in Roth v. United States, 354 U.S. 476, 487 (1957). See note 45 *infra*.

peared conjoined and cognate to laws against sacrilege and blasphemy, suggesting concern for the spiritual welfare of the person exposed to it and for the moral well-being of the community.[10] Metaphors of "poison" and "filth" also emphasize concern for the welfare of the one exposed and for the atmosphere of the community. A "decent" community does not tolerate obscenity. A "decent" man does not indulge himself with obscene materials.

The moral concern of the community may consist of several different strands frequently entangled beyond separation. Obscenity is immoral, an individual should not indulge it, and the community should not tolerate it. In addition, obscenity, like other immoral acts and expressions, has a deleterious effect on the individual from which the community should protect him. Obscenity is bad for a man, and the concern is not for his "psyche," his mental health. Obscenity is bad for character. It "corrupts" morals, it corrupts character. Character, of course, bears on behavior, but the corruption feared, it should be emphasized, has a very unclear, very remote, and problematic relation to a likelihood that he will commit any particular unlawful act or indeed any unlawful act at all, immediately or in the future.

This concern of the state for the "character" and "morals" of the person exposed is particularly evident in the plethora of laws designed to prevent the "corruption of youth." Among other evil influences, obscenity, it is assumed, may "corrupt" a child. The state assists parents who seek to prevent this corruption, or may even act in loco of those parents who are remiss in protecting their own children. The Supreme Court built constitutional doctrine on these assumptions when it held that Michigan could not "reduce the adult population of Michigan to reading only what is fit for children."[11] Again, the corruption of youth by obscenity is deemed to have some immeasurable effect on character and personality; it is not believed to "incite" to any particular actions now or in the future. While in regard to youth it has always been assumed that government has special responsibility and authority,[12] laws adopted for their protection reflect assumptions and attitudes about obscenity not inapplicable to the regulation of obscenity for adults.

Society intervenes because it is immoral for a person to indulge in obscenity and because obscenity corrupts morals and character of man or child. Either purpose is aimed at saving the "user" from his own indulgence, however private and discreet. But if indulgence in obscenity is prevalent, the prevalence becomes notorious, and the immoral activity takes on a public

10. See, for example, the statutes cited by the Supreme Court in *Roth*. 354 U.S. at 482-83 & nn.12-13.

These statutes may also reflect concern for the sensibilities of those who would be shocked by these expressions, and who might even react violently, creating disorder. See note 61 *infra*. But violent reaction seems an unlikely consequence of obscenity, particularly if exhibited privately.

11. Butler v. Michigan, 352 U.S. 380, 383 (1957). See also Prince v. Massachusetts, 321 U.S. 158, 168 (1943).

12. See note 11 *supra*. Recall the crimes of Socrates in ancient Athens.

character and offends "public order."[13] The state may seek to eradicate even isolated, clandestine obscenity; it is concerned in particular to suppress commercial exploitation in order to reduce the public disorder, as well as to protect individuals from their own moral weakness by preventing the spread of the moral infection.[14]

Communities believe, and act on the belief, that obscenity is immoral, is wrong for the individual, and has no place in a decent society. They believe, too, that adults as well as children are corruptible in morals and character, and that obscenity is a source of corruption that should be eliminated. Obscenity is not suppressed primarily for the protection of others. Much of it is suppressed for the purity of the community and for the salvation and welfare of the "consumer." Obscenity, at bottom, is not crime. Obscenity is sin.

II. Obscenity Regulation: The Relevant Constitutional Inquiry

If obscenity laws are seen primarily as "morals legislation," if a principal purpose of these laws is to protect, from himself, the person who wishes to indulge, and to maintain the moral "tone" of a community,[15] constitutional discussion of such laws would seem to deserve emphasis different from that which has preoccupied the judges and the writers.

Immediately, we would move aside discussion based on the assumption that "unlawful action" incited by obscene materials is the "evil" at which obscenity laws are directed. These writings[16] bear the mark of the particular time in the history of constitutional adjudication when the obscenity cases made their way up to the Supreme Court. For the principal cases raising the issue of freedom of communication in recent years have involved "speech" found to be part of a pattern of subversive action believed to endanger the

---

13. This is a different concern from that reflected in laws aimed at what was described above as "nuisance" obscenity, wherein the state seeks to protect members of the public from being unwillingly exposed to obscenity that is offensive to them.

14. As with other "morals" crimes (*e.g.*, gambling, prostitution), commercial exploitation of obscenity is a particular focus of regulation because it lends itself to the evils of the underworld of organized crime, because commercial exploitation of individual vices and weakness is deemed particularly abhorrent, and because suppression of commerce in obscenity is considered essential to the control of obscenity. Of course, these reasons for suppressing commercial exploitation reflect the community's attitudes that obscenity itself is undesirable and should be suppressed.

15. Most obscenity laws hit equally at nuisance obscenity, at commercial exploitation, at notorious indulgence, and at private obscenity privately indulged. This tends to confirm, of course, that these laws are morals legislation aimed ultimately at suppressing indulgence by the individual in what is deemed immoral. Perhaps a statute with limited focus could avoid some difficult constitutional questions, see note 68 *infra*, but the opinions upholding obscenity legislation would support equally laws aimed at the most private indulgence in obscene matter.

16. *Cf.*, *e.g.*, Kingsley Int'l Pictures Corp. v. Regents of the Univ. of the State of N.Y., 360 U.S. 684 (1959); Kalven, *The Metaphysics of the Law of Obscenity*, 1960 Supreme Court Rev. 1; Rogge, *State Power Over Sedition, Obscenity and Picketing*, 34 N.Y.U.L. Rev. 817 (1959); Note, 71 Harv. L. Rev. 326 (1957).

safety of the nation.[17] In this context, the Supreme Court struggled to establish lines between theoretical speech and "incitement" to unlawful action. It accepted a test akin to "clear and present danger" (though somewhat diluted) to distinguish immune speech from that which was linked to unlawful action.[18] The Court's opinions emphasized that speech may blend into and become action, and may then be controlled or suppressed to avoid the violent overthrow of government—a clearly evil consequence that government could clearly prevent.

As was perhaps inevitable, this preoccupation with the relation between speech, and action, and undeniably unlawful consequences, led lawyers as well as Justices carelessly to impose this context upon the problem of obscenity when it finally forced itself upon the Supreme Court's attention. If in fact the state's concern with obscenity has little to do with incitement to action, constitutional discussion based on the link between obscenity and unlawful action seems far beside the point. If unlawful action is not the evil at which the state aims, whether obscenity creates a "clear and present" danger of an unlawful action is not the relevant concern. The evils at which the state aims are not unlawful action, but indecency and corruption of morals.[19] Of these evils, the dangers assumed are clear and immediate. The impact of "nuisance" obscenity on others is indubitable and immediate. The immorality of indulgence even in private obscenity, the state may believe, is clear; the consequences of widespread indulgence and commercial exploitation on prevailing "decency" are present and certain.

Clear and present danger of unlawful action is a relevant inquiry on only one view—that the state cannot suppress obscene materials for the "moral" purposes we have suggested, that it can regulate forms of expression, including those falling within the definition of the obscene, only if they are "brigaded with action," only if they incite, say, to rape or other violence, or perhaps to adultery or fornication.[20] This seems to be the view of Mr. Justice

17. See, *e.g.*, Yates v. United States, 354 U.S. 298 (1957); Dennis v. United States, 341 U.S. 494 (1951).

18. See cases cited in note 17 *supra*.

19. The "test" suggested by Mr. Justice Holmes is commonly misread or mistaken. Holmes did not say that speech may be suppressed only if it creates a clear and present danger of unlawful action; it may be suppressed if it creates a clear and present danger of any undesirable consequence at which the state might aim. "The question in every case is whether the words used are used in such circumstances and are of such a nature as to create a clear and present danger *that they will bring about the substantive evils that Congress has a right to prevent.*" Schenck v. United States, 249 U.S. 47, 52 (1919). (Emphasis added.) The gloss upon that test by Judge Learned Hand, adopted by several Justices of the Supreme Court, also says nothing about unlawful acts, and retains the emphasis on "evils that Congress has a right to prevent": "In each case [courts] . . . must ask whether the gravity of the 'evil' discounted by its improbability, justifies such invasion of free speech as is necessary to avoid the danger." United States v. Dennis, 183 F.2d 201, 212 (2d Cir. 1950), *aff'd*, 341 U.S. 494 (1951).

20. To those who take this view, what is meant by "incitement," and what constitutes "incitement," would presumably present, *mutatis mutandis*, the same kinds of questions of degree, and perhaps the same inquiries into scienter, purpose, immediacy, probability, and gravity, with which the Court struggled in *Dennis* and *Yates*.

Black, and others have supported him. It is constitutional doctrine at which one may arrive; surely one cannot begin—and end—there. One cannot dismiss, without consideration, what appears to be the principal basis of obscenity laws. One cannot assume, without consideration, that the Constitution forbids society to hold the view societies have held and continue to hold—that obscenity is immoral, that it corrupts morals and character of the persons exposed and the moral tone of a community, and should be suppressed to prevent such corruption.

If minority views have mistaken the moral purposes of obscenity legislation, or dismissed them, without consideration, as constitutionally impermissible, prevailing views too have failed to attend to moral foundations of obscenity laws in framing issues and building doctrine. To the majority of the Supreme Court in *Roth v. United States*,[21] the purpose of the legislation was apparently irrelevant. The Court asserted that "obscenity is not within the area of constitutionally protected speech or press."[22] It seemed to reach that conclusion by reading "freedom of speech" in the first amendment as having an important qualification: the speech protected by the Constitution is only that which has some "redeeming social importance." Obscenity, the Court said, has none. The Court supported this reading of the Constitution by reference to history: obscenity was not intended to be included in the freedom of speech protected by the first amendment and in the liberty which the states could not deny without due process of law. Since the constitutional language does not protect obscenity, and was not intended to protect obscenity, there is no need to ask what is the purpose of obscenity legislation or whether it has any purpose at all. "Clear and present" danger, of unlawful action or of some other evil consequence, is also irrelevant. So is, presumably, any consideration of "preferred" freedom, or the weight to be given to the interest of the speaker, or the interest of society in his freedom to speak or in his particular speech.

That the Supreme Court's approach leaves too much to be desired has been suggested by others, beginning with the Justices who did not join the Court's opinion. Critics have questioned the Court's reading of constitutional

---

On this view, obscenity legislation—except perhaps that which is designed to protect the sensibilities of others—has little to support it. For there has appeared little scientific evidence that "obscene" materials do clearly and presently—even as now defined—lead to undesirable action. Surely there is little evidence that they "incite" to such action in the sense in which incitement is deemed to be required by *Yates* in the case of "subversive" political activity. While state legislatures and civic groups may "feel" that these materials do incite to undesirable action, surely this feeling, this right of the state to experiment and be mistaken, is no longer lightly tolerated against the "preferred" freedom of expression. If an occasional scientist might testify that such materials may immediately excite an occasional "abnormal" person to unlawful action, one may still ask whether the state can limit "normal" people to only those expressions that are fit for the abnormal. *Cf.* Butler v. Michigan, 352 U.S. 380, 383 (1957), quoted in text accompanying note 11 *supra*.

21. 354 U.S. 476 (1957).

22. *Id.* at 485.

language and of history. They have thought to trace circles in the Court's reasoning, and to identify questions that it seemed to beg. Some of the criticism might be met by reducing the reference to "redeeming social importance" from doctrine to rationalization, from a constitutional standard to an explanation of a historical exception. *Roth*, then, does not limit the protection of the first amendment to speech having social importance; *Roth* asserts simply that as a matter of historic interpretation the general phrases of the first and fourteenth amendments did not purpose to deny to government the authority to suppress that which is obscene. Those to whom history is not a whole answer may support the decision by suggesting that it reflects the attitude of a majority of the Court in other "speech cases"; the Court, invoking history, is asserting that expression is not ipso facto immune to regulation for social ends, that obscenity is a proper object of social regulation, that in the balance of freedom and authority under the scrutiny of the Constitution the public's interest in suppressing obscenity outweighs the exponent's freedom of expression.

These restatements of the *Roth* doctrine may provide more respectable doctrine; they do not justify disregard of the special character of obscenity laws as "morals legislation." The claims of history, generally, are subject to the caveat that laws and practices accepted as valid when a constitutional provision was adopted may yet be found invalid in the light of later readings of an organic, creative Constitution.[23] In regard to "morals laws," in particular, one may ask that the Court consider whether moral assumptions and assertions of a past day necessarily survive as exceptions to freedom today. The Court accepts "appeal to prurient interest" as the test for permissible limitations of obscene materials under the Constitution. If this is asserted as the traditional meaning of obscenity, the Court does not appear to reexamine its continuing validity as a constitutional standard. If it is a new test, the Court does not distinguish it from past notions of obscenity and justify it as presently valid to effect purposes presently permissible to the community.[24] Should not the Court ask why may the state today outlaw obscenity? What governmental purposes, valid today, are these laws designed to effectuate? Are the means proper to these purposes? History, surely, does not foreclose argument that in new light old laws reveal no reasonable foundations, or are based on irrational or false assumptions.

If, history apart, we are to balance conflicting claims of liberty and authority, the balances of 1789 ought not to be determinative; one might urge that a court consider that not all of an ancient morality remains equally

23. Recently, the Court has, again, scrutinized laws of old vintage that have been with us since and before constitutional provisions. See the "Blue Law" cases discussed at text accompanying note 53 *infra*.

24. See note 45 *infra*; *cf.* L. Schwartz, *Criminal Obscenity Law: Portents From Recent Supreme Court Decisions and Proposals of the American Law Institute in the Model Penal Code*, 29 PA. B.A.Q. 8 (1957).

vital, that changing values may have dissipated notions once deemed fundamental to morality, and that countervailing values of freedom, growing in potency, may now outweigh these values in the constitutional scale. In *Roth*, the Court, again, does not examine the nature of the public interest in regulation, and the relation to this interest of the means used, to determine the weight to be given to authority. Since the Court—like most statutes—does not distinguish between proscription of the most private indulgence in obscenity and social attack on public obscenity or organized commercial exploitation, the claims of authority appear to rest strictly on the historic concern for private morality. The nonrational, nonutilitarian aims of "morals legislation," like obscenity laws, might well have weight quite different from other historically accepted regulations of speech that have a social, utilitarian purpose, *e.g.*, libel laws.[25] On the other balance, the Court dismisses obscenity as utterly without "redeeming social importance." It does not consider that there may be "social importance" to expressions or words even if they do appeal predominantly to prurient interest.[26] It does not ask: whether regulation of obscenity may have a deterrent and limiting effect on other expressions not themselves obscene; whether there are social values in leaving all individuals free to express, others free to receive, without external limitations and without the shadow of the censor and the vigil of the heirs of Comstock; whether, like other attempts to regulate "the morals" of adults and to save them from themselves (*e.g.*, Prohibition), efforts to deal with obscenity by law may produce greater evils, and may even aggravate the very evils at which these laws are directed.[27]

The need for facing the questions here suggested may be emphasized by reference to a unanimous decision of the Supreme Court that does not deal with obscenity at all. In *Kingsley Int'l Pictures Corp. v. Regents of the Univ. of the State of N.Y.*,[28] the state had refused to license the film "Lady Chatterley's Lover" on the ground that it was "immoral," or "of such a character that its exhibition would tend to corrupt morals." The legislature had defined these terms to apply to any film "which portrays acts of sexual immorality . . . or which . . . presents such acts as desirable, acceptable or proper patterns of behavior."[29] The New York courts affirmed the denial of a license for the

25. See Beauharnais v. Illinois, 343 U.S. 250 (1952).

26. This appears to be Mr. Justice Harlan's view, reiterated in his opinion, in which Mr. Justice Stewart joined, in Manual Enterprises, Inc. v. Day, 370 U.S. 478, 487 (1962). He stresses that the obscenity that may be constitutionally suppressed is that which in addition to appealing to prurient interest is also foul and offensive. Apparently, Justices Harlan and Stewart, at least, would permit suppression only of "hard-core pornography." *Accord*, People v. Richmond County News, Inc., 9 N.Y.2d 578, 586, 589, 175 N.E.2d 681, 685, 687, 216 N.Y.S.2d 369, 375, 378 (1961).

27. While such considerations may ordinarily be primarily for the legislature, the Supreme Court cannot wholly avoid them when it balances communal interests against individual freedom.

28. 360 U.S. 684 (1959).

29. N.Y. EDUC. LAW § 122-a.

film "because its subject matter is adultery presented as being right and desirable for certain people under certain circumstances."[30]

The Supreme Court of the United States was agreed in reversing the state's judgment below, though hardly in the reasons for doing so. The majority recognized—as some writers have not—that this was not an obscenity case, that there was nothing in the film that appealed to prurient interests, that the case could not be decided on the basis of some special exception to the freedom of speech enjoyed by "obscenity laws." Yet the Court's opinion, too, did not wrestle with what, I believe, is the real issue. It did not consider that while this was not an obscenity case, it was a "morals" case. The Court stated that New York was censoring the advocacy of an idea, whereas the Constitution, the opinion said, guarantees freedom to advocate ideas. "It protects advocacy of the opinion that adultery may sometimes be proper, no less than advocacy of socialism or the single tax."[31] But ideas promoting adultery—unlike those urging the single tax—impinge on traditional morality. The state, indeed, did not claim that the film incited to adultery; it found the film to be immoral and tending to corrupt morals. Incitement to action, one might urge, is as irrelevant here as it is to obscenity cases in which, in effect, the state bars the obscene because it is immoral and tends to corrupt morals.

Recognition that laws against "obscenity" and laws against "immorality" are equally "morals" legislation would have required a very different opinion from the Court, if not a different result. The Court would have had to recognize that legislation against the "immoral" had historical credentials similar to, if not better than, obscenity laws, that the common obscenity statute indeed also forbade the "immoral"; legislation against the "immoral," then, might have as good a claim as obscenity legislation to historical exception from the freedom of speech. The result in the case could have been reached only by distinguishing, in some relevant way, this "morals legislation" from obscenity laws. An acceptable distinction does not readily appear. Somehow, the Court seemed to be denying to the state the assumption that ideas can be immoral or can corrupt morals, even though it had permitted to the state, in effect, the assumption that obscenity is immoral or can corrupt morals. (Would the Court hold that a child also is deprived of his liberty without due process of law if the state keeps from him materials expressing ideas that may "corrupt morals" without inciting to action?) Or did the Court silently measure and conclude that freedom for "ideas," any ideas, inevitably outweighs the state's interest in preventing "immorality by idea" or corruption of morals by ideas?[32]

30. Kingsley Int'l Pictures Corp. v. Regents of the Univ. of the State of N.Y., 4 N.Y.2d 349, 369, 151 N.E.2d 197, 208, 175 N.Y.S.2d 39, 55 (1958) (concurring opinion).
31. 360 U.S. at 689.
32. If so, might the Court look differently on matter that, while it appeals to prurient interest, also contains ideas? See note 26 *supra*.

The confusion remains. Nothing we have said suggests that any of the obscenity cases before the Court was wrongly decided, or that the dissenters, pursuing the analysis urged, could not again find themselves in dissent. The questions suggested may well reconfirm a majority in the conclusion that "obscenity is not within the area of constitutionally protected speech or press." Dissenting Justices may yet conclude that although a state may legislate against certain acts on the ground that they are immoral, it cannot constitutionally suppress expression on the ground that it is immoral or that it corrupts morals. On any view, the recognition of the moral foundations of obscenity laws may suggest that proper differentiation might bring different constitutional results in different cases. It may be that the Constitution regards state concern with private morality privately indulged differently from state protection of the sensibilities of others against offensive public display, or state prohibition of commercial exploitation and promotion of obscenity. It may be that however much one questions the authority of the state to impose morals, even on children, our society recognizes the authority of parents to educate their children, and the state may protect and support the right of parents to impose their morality on their children.

Courts and lawyers, it seems to me, must face the problem of obscenity on the terms in which society has framed it. Laws against obscenity are rooted in traditional notions of morality and decency; the moral foundations of these laws cannot be disregarded in re-assessing their constitutional validity today. It should not be assumed, without re-examination, that the morality of another day remains between the lines of the Constitution. Nor should it be assumed, without re-examination, that the morality of an older day remains a legitimate aim of government with social import outweighing growing claims of individual freedom.

III. The Constitutional Claims of Private "Immoralities"

It has been suggested that the Supreme Court has read obscenity out of the protection for expression in the first and fourteenth amendments without asking whether the "moral" character of obscenity laws continues to justify that historical exception today, or whether the moral aims of these laws may properly outweigh the freedoms suppressed. I venture now to suggest that the moral purpose and motive of obscenity legislation—and of other prevalent laws aimed at private indulgence in "immoral" activity—may invite inquiry of yet a different, fundamental order.

We lay aside now claims of freedom to communicate, even the obscene: we are concerned, instead, with claims of the "consumer" to freedom and privacy to indulge in what others may deem immoral.[33] The authority of the

33. The freedom of speech and expression discussed in the previous section may include also a correlative freedom in the would-be listener or reader to receive com-

state, under the Constitution, to enact "morals legislation"—laws reflecting some traditional morality having no authentic social purpose to protect other persons or property—has always been assumed; it has deep roots, and it has seemed obvious and beyond question. It may now be respectable to ask whether indeed the state may adopt any "morals legislation." And if it be concluded that morals legislation is not ipso facto beyond the state's power, can one avoid asking: what morality the state may enforce; what limitations there are on what the state may deem immoral; how these limitations are to be determined?

In doctrinal terms, one may present these as several constitutional questions, not wholly discrete. For the sake of clarity, I declare them as hypotheses to be examined:

First: even if the "freedom of speech" protected by the first and fourteenth amendments does not include a freedom to communicate obscene speech, suppression of obscenity is still a deprivation of liberty or property—of the person who would indulge in it, at least—which requires due process of law. Due process of law demands that legislation have a proper public purpose; only an apparent, rational, utilitarian social purpose satisfies due process. A state may not legislate merely to preserve some traditional or prevailing view of private morality.

Second: due process requires, as well, that means be reasonably related to proper public ends. Legislation cannot be based on unfounded hypotheses and assumptions about character and its corruption.

Third: morals legislation is a relic in the law of our religious heritage; the Constitution forbids such establishment of religion.

The inquiry urged can only be suggested here. I would attempt to state the principal issues. I would underscore the complexity of the questions involved. I would urge, too, that the questions suggested are not clearly insubstantial.

A. *Morals as a Legislative Concern—The Requirements of Due Process*

The relation of law to morals has been a favored preoccupation of legal philosophers for a thousand years; in the history of American law the relevance of that relation to constitutional limitations has lain unexamined behind discussions of the scope and the limits of government. That morals were the concern of government was assumed, not explored, in discussions of the reaches of the "police power" limited by substantive "due process of law."

May the state, under our Constitution, legislate in support of "morals"? The question may take us back to another: What are the purposes for which

munication. Here I do not deal at all with the freedom to give or receive communication. I focus on the freedom of private activity not affecting others. None of the cases which reached the Supreme Court involved conviction for private possession of or indulgence in obscene materials. Commercial exploitation, public indulgence, "corruption" of children, raise additional questions. See notes 15 *supra* & 68 *infra*.

the state may legislate under the Constitution? That question, in other contexts, once deeply troubled the Supreme Court. Not too many years ago the Court seemed to assume that by the law of nature and by social contract government was given limited powers for limited purposes.[34] Freedom was the rule; government had to justify itself, and the justifications had to satisfy the Constitution. The state could, of course, legislate to protect one from his neighbor. Perhaps the whole function of government was to assure that, in regard to one's liberty as well as one's property, *sic utere tuo ut alienum non laedas*.[35] But government also had other purposes, among them the regulation of morality. "Whatever differences of opinion may exist as to the extent and boundaries of the police power, and however difficult it may be to render a satisfactory definition of it, there seems to be no doubt that it does extend to . . . the preservation of good order and the public morals."[36] Even when *laissez faire* had the strongest constitutional credentials, the Supreme Court agreed that the police power of the states might deal with matters that "relate to the . . . morals . . . of the public."[37] Later definitions, abandoning prejudgments against governmental "interference," and recognizing new goals of "general welfare" which the state might pursue, accepted that the police powers "are nothing more or less than the powers of government . . . ."[38] But the newer doctrine was recognizing additional purposes for which government might legislate; it did not, of course, deny the traditional concerns of government, among them "morality."

No one seemed disposed to doubt that the legitimate purposes of government included the preservation of morals, public or private.[39] All law indeed may have appeared as an implementation of accepted morality; no one seriously suggested that laws for the preservation of "morals" might not have the clear justification which is obvious in laws having a social purpose of protecting the person or property of others. Morals legislation, like social legislation, might have appeared equally rooted in "the law of nature," which had respectable credentials in the history of American law. It was obvious that the state could forbid persons to enter into a usurious contract, to gamble, to drink intoxicating liquors, to be a prostitute, to visit a prostitute, to commit fornication or adultery with another willing adult, to enter into a polygamous

34. See, *e.g.*, Citizens' Sav. & Loan Ass'n v. Topeka, 87 U.S. (20 Wall.) 655, 663 (1875).

35. See, *e.g.*, Munn v. Illinois, 94 U.S. 113, 136, 145-47 (1877) (Field, J., dissenting). Justice Field was speaking primarily of the regulation of property. The majority expressed similar ideas. *Id.* at 124-25.

36. Boston Beer Co. v. Massachusetts, 97 U.S. 25, 33 (1878).

37. Lochner v. New York, 198 U.S. 45, 53 (1905).

38. The phrase, by Chief Justice Taney in the License Cases, 46 U.S. (5 How.) 504, 583 (1847), was resurrected and adopted by the Court in Nebbia v. New York, 291 U.S. 502, 524 (1934).

39. The cases speak of "morals" and "public morals" interchangeably. There is no intimation that "private" morals were something different and not subject to governmental control. "Public morals," as used, was not limited to concern for that which was overt, nor to that which impinged obviously on others.

marriage, to utter obscenity, profanity, immorality in act or word. Clearly, too, the state could declare the morality that determined "public policy," relied on in various contexts to frustrate consensual arrangements.

If the challenge had been seriously pressed, some utilitarian reason for these laws might have been found.[40] But they would have been rationalizations and might have been recognized as such. In truth, the legislation reflected traditional morality, and the preservation of this morality was an unquestionable and unquestioned purpose of government. If the Supreme Court glanced at the authority of the state to enact such legislation, it blended moral and utilitarian bases for the legislation in indisputable justification.[41]

Today, a court would probably not begin with the assumption that government has defined purposes and corresponding "inherent," "natural" limitations. The only limitations on the state, a court might say, are the prohibitions of the Constitution—specific, like those few in the original Constitution, or more general, like those in the Civil War amendments. If one would today examine embedded assumptions about morals legislation, the question, then, is not whether legislation for decency and morality is within the accepted powers of government; we must ask, rather, whether such legislation deprives one to whom it applies of "liberty or property" without due process of law. But if that question looks very different from the one that might have been asked in the nineteenth century, it may be less different than it looks. For some of the "inherent" limitations on the police power may still be with us in notions that the state may legislate only for a "public purpose."[42] And "due process" still requires some link in reason between purpose and the means selected by the legislature to achieve that purpose. We may state the question, then, as whether morality legislation deprives one of liberty or property without due process of law. The subsidiary questions may still be: Is the state's purpose in "morality legislation" a proper public purpose? Are the means used to achieve it "reasonable"?[43]

Emphasis on "public purpose" has usually been intended to exclude legislation for the special interest of some private person or group. Morals

40. See notes 58-59 *infra*.

41. See, *e.g.*, L'Hote v. New Orleans, 177 U.S. 587, 596 (1900) (prostitution); Mugler v. Kansas, 123 U.S. 623, 662 (1887) (liquor); Phalen v. Virginia, 49 U.S. (8 How.) 162, 168 (1850) (gambling). See also note 58 *infra*, discussing the polygamy cases.

42. Last Term, in Goldblatt v. Hempstead, 369 U.S. 590, 594-95 (1962), the Court said: "The classic statement of the rule in Lawton v. Steele, 152 U.S. 133, 137 (1894), is still valid today: 'To justify the state in . . . interposing its authority in behalf of the public, it must appear, first, that the interests of the public . . . require such interference; and, second, that the means are reasonably necessary for the accomplishment of the purpose, and not unduly oppressive upon individuals.'" However, the Court was emphasizing the need of a public rather than some private purpose; it was not concerned with whether some public purpose was proper. See Thompson v. Consolidated Gas Util. Corp., 300 U.S. 55, 69, 77-80 (1937); Citizens' Sav. & Loan Ass'n v. Topeka, 87 U.S. (20 Wall.) 655 (1875). See also Everson v. Board of Educ., 330 U.S. 1, 6 (1947).

43. A further, and different question, particularly in speech cases, is whether the public purpose, and means to achieve it, outweigh the liberty suppressed.

legislation presumably does not serve a strictly "private purpose," even if some groups seem more concerned about morals legislation than is the community at large. The beneficiaries of this legislation, it is assumed, are each citizen and the whole community. But is every "nonprivate" purpose a proper public purpose of government? Can the state legislate, not to protect the person or property of others or to promote general economic or social welfare, but to protect and promote "morals," particularly morals reflected—or violated—in private activity?

Perhaps the question can have no provable answer. Supporters of legislation like obscenity laws may urge that government has always legislated in support of accepted morality, and may challenge those who would deny the authority of government to find anything in the Constitution that would take it away.[44] But supporters of the past do not have the only word. Others will stress that the due process clause has intervened, and that it requires government to be reasonable, in purpose as well as in means to achieve the purpose. One may even accept the right of the state to impose restrictions on the individual for his own good—by preventing his suicide, or forcing medical aid, or compelling education; in the context of society, these are "rational" ends, reasonably achieved. But how can "morals," a nonutilitarian, nonrational purpose, be "reasonable"? Could government conjure up some new (or old), nonsocial principle of morality and impose it by law? Could a state forbid me to go to an astrologer—or require me to go to one or abide by his conclusions? And if history is invoked, does the fact that some behavior has been deemed "immoral" in the past—by some, even a violation of "natural law"—render it forever a proper object of legislative prohibition?[45] Is it sufficient to justify legislation that such acts continue to be regarded as "immoral," "sinful," "offensive" by large segments of the community?[46] Or

44. See, *e.g.*, Poe v. Ullman, 367 U.S. 497, 545-46 (1961) (Harlan, J., dissenting)

> Yet the very inclusion of the category of morality among state concerns indicates that society is not limited in its objects only to the physical well-being of the community, but has traditionally concerned itself with the moral soundness of its people as well. Indeed to attempt a line between public behavior and that which is purely consensual or solitary would be to withdraw from community concern a range of subjects with which every society in civilized times has found it necessary to deal. The laws regarding marriage which provide both when the sexual powers may be used and the legal and societal context in which children are born and brought up, as well as laws forbidding adultery, fornication and homosexual practices which express the negative of the proposition, confining sexuality to lawful marriage, form a pattern so deeply pressed into the substance of our social life that any Constitutional doctrine in this area must build upon that basis. Compare McGowan v. Maryland, 366 U.S. 420.

45. The definition of obscenity as that which appeals to prurient interest is itself one which seems to entail limitations on state regulation not recognized half a century ago. Much that was then considered obscene or indecent would now be held not within the definition and therefore not subject to regulation. Increasing "sophistication" may also, of course, render some things not obscene because they are accepted and no longer appeal to prurient interest.

46. And how clear, indeed, is it that the community—even some particular community—regards as immoral some actions that violate the criminal law? Even if the moral and immoral be determined only by what a society preaches, is gambling today immoral? Or fornication? Or even private homosexuality? Or obscenity?

does the due process clause, in this context too, serve to protect individuals from the irrationalities of the majority and of its representatives?

One may ask, it is suggested, whether any nonutilitarian morality can be a reasonable public purpose of legislation. But purpose aside, due process requires also that the means to achieve that purpose be not unreasonable.[47] Of course, means and purposes are not discrete categories, and purposes may themselves be means to other purposes. But assuming that the preservation of private morals continues to be a proper purpose of government, obscenity legislation, in particular, raises the further question whether suppression of obscenity is reasonably related to the morality that the state seeks to preserve.

The question may be clarified if one compares obscenity laws to other morals legislation, *e.g.*, laws against incest. Incestual relations have indubitably been deemed "immoral," at least since Biblical times. If the state may suppress what is immoral, there can be no doubt about the validity of laws against incest. Exposure to obscenity, on the other hand, is at most a derivative, secondary "immorality." In itself, it has no ancient roots; presumably, it would have been condemned, or frowned on, as inconsistent with admonitions to be holy and to avoid pagan abominations.[48] In modern times, obscenity has been condemned in large part because it corrupts morals or character. Since, I have said, corruption of morals or character has no clear relation to any unlawful acts, or even acts that could be made unlawful, what evidence is required of the state, or what assumptions permitted to it, to support the conclusion that obscenity corrupts morals? What are these "morals" and this "character," and what does their corruption mean? And if we accept the concept of "morals" as well as their corruption, how does one decide whether the state is reasonable in its conclusion that indulgence in obscenity does or does not effect this "corruption" of these "morals"?[49]

The Constitution does not enact legal positivism; it does not enact natural law. Due process, I hypothesize, requires that the state deal with the area of the reasonable and deal with it reasonably. It is proper to ask whether the preservation of a nonsocial morality is within the realm of the reasonable, whether concepts like "private morality" and its corruption are subject to logic and proof inherent in reasonableness and rationality. These, of course, are not merely technical requirements of constitutional jurisprudence. They suggest that the Constitution renders unto government the rational governance of the affairs of man in relation to his neighbor; only if government is kept within this domain can it be limited government, subject to constitutional requirements of rational, reasonable action administered by an impartial judiciary. It is only by confining government to what is reason-

47. See note 42 *supra*.
48. See *Leviticus* 18:26, 27, 30; 19:2; 20:23.
49. One may ask, too, how one can tell whether there be clear and present danger of such corruption? See note 19 *supra*.

able that the Constitution and the courts can protect the individual against the unreasonable. Private "morals," and their "corruption," and what "corrupts" them, as differently conceived, have profound significance in the life of a nation and of its citizens. But they are not in the realm of reason and cannot be judged by standards of reasonableness; they ought not, perhaps, to be in the domain of government.

Civilized societies, including ours, have increased the area of government responsibility to protect one against his neighbor. The authority of government to protect us from ourselves is less clearly recognized today, except when injury to ourselves may in turn have undesirable social consequences; although, we have suggested, one may justify—within the limits of the "rational"—governmental efforts to prevent suicide, or compel health measures, "for the individual's own good." When we deal not with physical injury to ourselves but with "sin," respectable and authoritative voices are increasingly heard that there exists "a realm of private morality and immorality which is, in brief and crude terms, not the law's business."[50] Should not the Supreme Court today, or tomorrow, consider whether under the Constitution some morality, at least, may be not the law's business and not appropriate support for legislation consistent with due process of law?

B. *The Religious Origins of Morals Legislation*

I have suggested the need to examine, in the light of the due process clause, the power of the state to deprive a person of liberty or property for the purpose of preserving "morality" serving no social, utilitarian purpose. Contemporary constitutional doctrine may suggest yet another, related difficulty about obscenity and other morality laws. For the morality that these laws would protect can trace a discernible path back to origins in religious authority. Can government, which may not establish religion, or interfere with the free exercise of religion and non-religion, enforce a morality rooted in religion? Is legislation, the sole or chief purpose of which is the preservation of a quasi-religious morality, consistent with the separation of Church and State now recognized as the law of the Constitution?

Here, history may again appear to claim constitutional immunity for old laws, but here the Supreme Court has already made it clear that history does not say the last word. The prohibitions of the first amendment in regard to religion have only in recent decades been declared applicable to the states

50. See Comm. on Homosexual Offenses & Prostitution (Wolfenden Committee), *Report*, CMD. No. 247, at 24 (1957). See also Commonwealth v. Gordon, 661 Pa. D. & C. 101, 154 (Ct. Quarter Sess. 1949) (Bok, J.), *aff'd per curiam sub nom.* Commonwealth v. Feigenbaum, 166 Pa. Super. 120, 70 A.2d 389 (1950). *But cf.* Poe v. Ullman, 367 U.S. 497, 545-46 (1961) (Harlan, J., dissenting), quoted in note 44 *supra*. See also text accompanying notes 69-71 *infra*.

by the fourteenth amendment.[51] And for both state and federal government, careful separation of Church from State is doctrine not long articulated and applied.[52] These doctrines have been applied not only to new practices but also to laws that have been with us since before the Constitution. In 1961, for a major example, the Supreme Court re-examined, carefully and at length, the Sunday Blue Laws dating from colonial days. These laws, in origin, were designed to foster and promote religious observance; they were also "morals" legislation, reflecting the attitude that work on the Sabbath was immoral, sinful. The Court upheld the laws,[53] despite rather than because of their history. The Court seemed unanimous that such laws reflecting religious doctrine and serving a religious function would be a forbidden establishment of religion. They could be upheld only because, the majority concluded, the laws had shed their religious origins and purposes and now served primarily an independent, secular, utilitarian, social function.

The Court's opinion in the "Blue Laws" cases is highly relevant to the inquiry we suggest into the validity of "morals legislation" rooted in religion. Immediately, it helps put the inquiry into narrower focus. Of course, the Justices recognized, some morality underlies all law and our morality and our laws can be followed back to roots in the Bible.[54] Surely, the fact that the mass of our traditional laws reflects a morality rooted in religion, or once identified with religon, raises no constitutional question either serious or substantial. The growth of the secular state—even on Erastian principles—and notions of strict separation of Church and State could not have signified any general rejection of this traditional morality. The morality reflected in most of our common laws, moreover, has lost its religious origins and shares with the law of the mass of organized mankind a modern, utilitarian social basis.[55] Laws punishing homicide or theft, though they, too, may have religious roots by way of notions of "natural law" and the Bible (we still refer to them as *malum in se*), are obviously within the power of the most secular state, subject to the most rigorous constitutional limitations, living by strictest doctrines of limited government.

The constitutional issue begins to stir when we deal with legislation reflecting our particular morality—when the religious origins are more apparent and persistent, when the law is not common to all civilized nations, when it has no clear utilitarian basis. Some crimes I have mentioned—

51. See Murdock v. Pennsylvania, 319 U.S. 105 (1943); Cantwell v. Connecticut, 310 U.S. 296 (1940); Gitlow v. New York, 268 U.S. 652, 666 (1925). See also Everson v. Board of Educ., 330 U.S. 1 (1947).

52. Jefferson's wall of separation, cited in Reynolds v. United States, 98 U.S. 145, 164 (1879), was given new recognition in *Everson*. 330 U.S. at 16. It was not in fact given application until McCollum v. Board of Educ., 333 U.S. 203 (1948), and again recently in Engel v. Vitale, 370 U.S. 421 (1962).

53. McGowan v. Maryland, 366 U.S. 420 (1961).

54. See *id.* at 442 (Court's opinion), quoted in note 58 *infra; id.* at 462 (Frankfurter, J., concurring).

55. A kind of *ius gentium*, to which divine origins are not necessarily attributed.

polygamy and incest, adultery and fornication, gambling, intoxication, usury —find their origin in notions of morality rooted in our particular history, the values of the American nation inevitably derived from ancestral voices raised on the moral teachings of the Bible.[56] These laws clearly embody ancient religious attitudes not yet dissipated or diluted although now wearing secular garb. Is it a form of establishment of religion for the state to impose this nonsocial religious morality? Is it, perhaps, an interference with the free exercise of nonreligion by those who do not accept the religious principles and religious authority from which this morality emanates?

The argument need not be taken too far. As to many laws that originate in Biblical morality, it may be urged that, like the Blue Laws, they too have shed their religious origins. The morals of a people are a present reality regardless of their sources.[57] Whatever their roots, whatever their erstwhile function or context in religious observance, laws against incest or polygamy, for example, now reflect mores and institutions—in particular, the family—that are the fabric of our society.[58] Moreover, many morals crimes rooted

56. For the prohibitions on incest, sodomy, and adultery see particularly *Leviticus*, chs. 18 & 20. See also *Leviticus* 19:29, *Deuteronomy* 23:17 (prostitution). The prohibition on polygamy is also of old standing and has religious sanction although it is post-biblical. *But see* 1 *Timothy* 3:2. Since polygamy was not forbidden, the original biblical prohibition of adultery applied only to extramarital cohabitation by a married woman, not by a married man. In the King James translation, the word "adultery" appears sometimes to be used for any forbidden sexual act. *Cf., e.g., Exodus* 20:14. For the prohibitions on usury see *Exodus* 22:25, *Leviticus* 25:35-37, *Deuteronomy* 23:19-20. (Compare, for example, an old usury statute, 13 Eliz. c. 8, which included: "all usury, being forbidden by the law of God, is sin and detestable . . . .") The use of intoxicating liquors was forbidden to one who took the Nazirite vows, see *Numbers* 6:3-4, and to the priests in service. *Leviticus* 10:9.

Also relevant, as sources of religious authority for other prohibitions on "immorality," are general exhortations and commandments, *e.g.*, "Ye shall be holy." *Leviticus* 19:2.

57. Compare Poe v. Ullman, 367 U.S. 497, 545-46 (Harlan, J., dissenting), quoted in note 44 *supra*.

The "moral" standards of a community discussed here are not to be confused with the "conscience of mankind" and society's notions of "ordered liberty" which are now found in the due process clause. See Adamson v. California, 332 U.S. 46 (1947); Palko v. Connecticut, 302 U.S. 319, 323, 325 (1937). In the latter concept, the "morality" common to civilized men is invoked to determine whether procedures meet a minimum of fairness to the individual; fairness is, of course, a social value subject to examination in the light of standards of reasonableness. The standard is designed to protect the individual from unreasonable action by the community. In "morals legislation," on the other hand, we face notions, more or less widely accepted, as to what is proper individual action in circumstances in which such action does not impinge on anyone else. Surely, for constitutional purposes, it is one thing to invoke the "morals of a people" (as in its sense of fairness) as a limitation on government; it is quite another thing to invoke them to justify limitations on individual freedom.

58. When the Supreme Court upheld the application of antipolygamy laws to the Mormons, it saw no question about the power of Congress to enact such laws and to apply them generally. The only issue the Court dealt with was the claim that these laws invaded the religious freedom of the Mormons. In that context it justified these laws as clearly proper because polygamy has always been "odious" to the nations of Western Europe, and because of its social consequences. See Reynolds v. United States, 98 U.S. 145, 164-66 (1879). Blending social and moral objections, the Court also found polygamy "to shock the moral judgment of the Community," and referred to "acts, recognized by the general consent of the Christian world in modern times as proper matters for prohibitory legislation." Davis v. Beason, 133 U.S. 333, 341, 343 (1889); *cf.* Cleveland v. United States, 329 U.S. 14, 18-19 (1946). *But cf.* Musser v. Utah, 333 U.S. 95 (1948).

in the Bible—incest, polygamy, usury, perhaps also adultery—may find some secular rationalization or justification, some valid governmental purpose even in a secular state, some concern defined in terms of categorical imperative, of avoiding injury to others, of achieving some social aim.[59] That other morals crimes, however, retain heavy traces of their religious origin is evidenced, in part, by the fact that they are not universally punished as crimes and cannot be credibly rationalized. What secular purpose based on injury to others, or to the group, can justify laws against private homosexuality between willing adults? Against other forms of private sodomy? Against various practices of the conjugal bed, including contraception?[60] Against "profanity," "sacrilege," "immorality," "obscenity"?[61] In these cases, one may argue, the religious elements are clear and predominant. Most would accept that it would be a forbidden establishment of religion, or interference with freedom of religion, if the state sought to prohibit taking the name of the Lord in vain or making graven images;[62] why may the state

---

In McGowan v. Maryland, 366 U.S. 420, 442 (1961), the Court said:

> However, it is equally true that the "Establishment" Clause does not ban federal or state regulation of conduct whose reason or effect merely happens to coincide or harmonize with the tenets of some or all religions. In many instances, the Congress or state legislatures conclude that the general welfare of society, wholly apart from any religious considerations, demands such regulation. Thus, for temporal purposes, murder is illegal. And the fact that this agrees with the dictates of the Judeo-Christian religions while it may disagree with others does not invalidate the regulation. So too with the questions of adultery and polygamy.

59. Note that for the Blue Laws, the Court did not consider that Sunday "rest" was now part of present secular morality. It struggled to find a social, utilitarian purpose.

Some other morals laws may find, at least, some secular rationalization. Laws against incest, against marriage between persons in certain degrees of relationship, may have justification in concern for genetic welfare, for the psychiatric health of the participants, and for the protection of the family. Laws against adultery, fornication, prostitution may be justified by a need to prevent illegitimacy, to protect the family, to curb the spread of disease. Laws against the use of intoxicants may serve to prevent the injuries to others to which intoxication may lead. Gambling may dissipate the earnings of the poor, creating hunger and need, and adding to the public charge. Even usury laws may reflect recognition of economic duress as vitiating consent to inequitable arrangements.

It is less easy, however, to find a sufficient secular basis when legislation insists on its religious origins. Compare, for example, the Rhode Island incest law which excepts from the prohibitions against marrying kindred "any marriage which shall be solemnized among the Jews, within the degrees of affinity or consanguinity allowed by their religion." R.I. GEN. LAWS ANN. § 15-1-4 (1956).

60. For what appears to be the first allusion to these constitutional questions in the pages of the Supreme Court see Poe v. Ullman, 367 U.S. 497, 545-46 (1961) (Harlan, J., dissenting), quoted in note 44 *supra*. See also *id.* at 509, 515 (Douglas, J., dissenting). *But cf.* Sanitary Vendors, Inc. v. Byrne, 72 N.J. Super. 276, 178 A.2d 259 (Super. Ct. 1962).

61. See note 63 *infra*. That blasphemy and sacrilege might offend the sensibilities of others would seem no greater justification for laws forbidding these, than would laws against violating the Sabbath (if the Supreme Court had found no secular justification for them). It is a different question whether acts offensive to the religious sensibilities of others might be barred in circumstances in which such acts might lead to disorder. *Compare* Feiner v. New York, 340 U.S. 315, 320-21 (1949), *with* Garner v. Louisiana, 368 U.S. 157, 170-73, 193-96 (1962) (Court and concurring opinions), *and* McGowan v. Maryland, 366 U.S. 420, 561, 563-64 (1961) (Douglas, J., dissenting).

62. *Cf. Exodus* 20:4, 7.

constitutionally forbid homosexuality? The state could not, probably, prohibit private blasphemy or sacrilege;[63] why may it prohibit obscenity?

Different elements in traditional morality may retain different residues of religious origin. That no credible secular rationalization has grown up to support an ancient morality, that the morality is not shared alike by other societies, by all religions, by religious and nonreligious, may be some evidence of abiding nonrational content identified with particular religious conceptions. Different laws may also retain, in different degrees, a present religious function in support of present religious practice or Church interest.[64] In those instances, links between religion and morality, between religion and morality-legislation, are not wholly and clearly broken. In regard to morality laws, too, the separation of Church and State may require the drawing of constitutional lines and the measuring of constitutional degrees.

Perhaps the objection that some morals legislation imposes a religious morality is a facet of the earlier argument that morals legislation cannot be rationally supported. For in substantial part the effect, if not the purpose, of constitutional provisions forbidding religious establishment and guaranteeing the free exercise of religion is also to bar the interference of government in the realm of the nonrational, the sacred precincts of personal belief, the personal "Answer," even personal idiosyncrasy. The domain of government, it is suggested, is that in which social problems are resolved by rational social processes, in which men can reason together, can examine problems and propose solutions capable of objective proof or persuasion, subject to objective scrutiny by courts and electors. I ask whether legislation that is based on a particular religion, even on what is common to many religions, on what is supported by history only, on what is not capable of reasoned consideration and solution, is rendered unto government by the Constitution.

IV. Conclusion

Laws against obscenity reflect values of morality, decency, and modesty inherited from an earlier age and from religious ancestors. These laws reflect, too, assumptions about the nature of character and morals; they assume a concept of "corruption of morals" and assume that obscene material has such a corrupting effect. The roots, the purposes, and the assumptions must be taken into account in any considerations of the constitutionality of obscenity laws. These are relevant in regard to the freedom of communication affected by obscenity laws. They must be considered, too, in relation to the freedom

63. See Joseph Burstyn, Inc. v. Wilson, 343 U.S. 495, 505 (1952); *id.* at 518 (Frankfurter, J., concurring). See also McGowan v. Maryland, 366 U.S. 420, 563-64 (1961) (Douglas, J., dissenting).

64. This may make a stronger case for barring laws against blasphemy or sacrilege. See note 61 *supra.* Perhaps, too, laws against contraception are more subject to this objection. See note 60 *supra.* That the Blue Laws are a present aid to particular religions was one of the arguments invoked in McGowan v. Maryland, 366 U.S. 420 (1961).

of the individual to obtain and indulge—at least privately—even in what others may consider obscene. I have asked whether the morality that is the concern of obscenity laws, and of other morals legislation, is still the law's business and so a valid purpose for legislation under the due process clause. I have asked whether the perpetuation by government of a morality religious in origin and having no present social purpose is a form of establishment of religion, and interference with the free exercise of "nonreligion," forbidden to both state and federal governments. I have suggested that perhaps the Constitution denies to government and to majorities the domain of the non-rational, leaving private morality to Church, and Home, and Conscience. I suggest that perhaps, at least, legislatures might be required to re-examine old laws based on moral and religious views of an earlier day, to identify motives and purposes for regulation presently acceptable, and to determine anew whether and which regulation is now called for.

That the "morals" character of obscenity laws should have been considered in determining their validity as exceptions to the freedom of communication seems obvious; the further hypothesis that at least when applied to private indulgence obscenity laws may raise serious questions of liberty and privacy is perhaps novel.[65] What is suggested implies that in the generalities of "due process of law" may lie unexplored limitations on government to regulate individual action in the name of "morals," and that when the morals protected are rooted in particular religious dogma and reflect no utilitarian social purpose there is substantial question whether the separation of Church and State has been breached. Of course, any such limitations would further increase the claim of liberty against the claims of representative democracy. But that appears to be the direction of the Constitution.[66] While substantive due process long ago ceased to imply limits on government regulation for general economic and social welfare, it has increasingly provided doctrine to support individual freedom of action or expression, frequently even against regulations claiming some utilitarian, social purpose. Substantive due process has, in particular, provided protection for liberties and privacies claimed by one who would be let alone, who does not seek freedom to impinge on others. Clearly the Constitution, both in the first and fourteenth amendments, has been read liberally to limit government when it interferes with freedom of religion, including freedom from religion.[67] But if the doctrine is novel, its consequences need not be revolutionary. It aims particularly at the

65. That morals legislation may raise constitutional questions has been suggested previously, for example, by the draftsmen of the Model Penal Code. See MODEL PENAL CODE § 207.1, comments, at 207 (Tent. Draft No. 4, 1955). *But cf.* Poe v. Ullman, 367 U.S. 497, 545-46 (1961) (Harlan, J., dissenting), quoted in note 44 *supra*.

66. See, *e.g.*, Henkin, *Some Reflections on Current Constitutional Controversy*, 109 U. PA. L. REV. 637, 638-42 (1961).

67. See, *e.g.*, Torcaso v. Watkins, 367 U.S. 488 (1961); note 52 *supra; cf.* Engel v. Vitale, 370 U.S. 421 (1962).

intrusion of law into private indulgence by adults in acts that are not apparently antisocial. Public activity, commercial exploitation, the "morals" of children, involve additional questions that may suggest differences of degree and the drawing of lines.[68]

Of course, it should be clear, I have asserted hypotheses for further consideration. That the government may act only for social purpose, for the protection of persons and property, is doctrine easy to state, and perhaps no more difficult to apply than some other constitutional doctrine. But the right of the state to legislate in the field of morals, to deprive the citizen of liberty or property for the sake of accepted notions of morality, is deeply part of our law; some will argue that it is beyond question or need for justification. It asks much of the Supreme Court to tell legislators, and communal groups behind them, that what has long been deemed the law's business is no longer, that even large majorities or a "general consensus" cannot have their morality written into official law. And a reluctant Court can find support in history, and some among the philosophers.

The philosophers are not irrelevant. I have attempted, it will have been observed, to set forth the constitutional arguments against laws that govern private morals without injecting the differences which regularly agitate the universe of political philosophy. One must yet note the current controversy, across the seas from our Constitution, where Lord Devlin and Professor Hart have provided a contemporary version of nineteenth century debate:[69] whether it is proper, justified, desirable, even necessary, for government to enforce by law the common nonutilitarian morality. By my hypotheses, the United States would be a polity nearer the heart of Professor Hart, and of John Stuart Mill. To their philosophical arguments, we have added the special concerns of the American Constitution: that government shall be limited; that the limitations should be subject and susceptible to judicial scrutiny and enforcement; that legislatures shall therefore be limited to the

68. One should emphasize that, on any view, obscenity laws should not be treated without discrimination or differentiation. Laws designed primarily to protect sensibilities of others may require examination of the circumstances in which the "moral" sensibilities of others may invoke law to suppress acts and expressions offensive to them. See notes 15 & 61 *supra*. Different questions may be raised by laws responding to community objections to having overt, prominent obscenity "going on" in their midst, derogating from the moral tone of the community. Still different may be laws aimed exclusively at commercial exploitation. The hardest case—on which I have focused—involves the statute designed to forbid private indulgence in obscene materials in circumstances in which it need not impinge on others or even come to their attention.

One must consider also how much difference it makes if laws are designed to protect only the morals of a child. While many of the constitutional arguments against morals legislation apply equally to legislation protecting the morals of children, one can well distinguish laws which do not impose a morality on children, but which support the right of parents to deal with the morals of their children as they see fit. See text accompanying notes 11-12 *supra*.

69. *Compare* H. L. A. HART, LAW, LIBERTY, AND MORALITY (1963), *with* DEVLIN, THE ENFORCEMENT OF MORALS (1959). *Cf.* ROSTOW, THE SOVEREIGN PREROGATIVE 45-80 (1962).

rational and the reasonable; that, in addition—for reasons particular to our society—legislatures are debarred from enacting those nonrationalities of the majority which reflect its religions. Lord Devlin, of course, might dismiss us as, for these reasons, a special case. But Lord Devlin may find himself, instead, adopted by Supreme Court Justices reluctant to accept the hypotheses proposed. They may respond to his view that the enforcement by law of a people's morality is essential to the existence of a society,[70] and accept his deduction that therefore "the suppression of vice is as much the law's business as the suppression of subversive activities";[71] if so, they are not likely to find that the Constitution stands in the way. With Professor Hart, I might accept Lord Devlin's proposition that the preservation of a nation's "morality" is essential to its ultimate cohesiveness, but I could hardly agree that "morality" as there used includes every element of popular attitude which is called "morals," particularly those few and special attitudes to the private indulgences which are our subject. In any event, whether on grounds rooted in history or in philosophy, the Supreme Court might yet proclaim that even under our Constitution the morals of the people, whatever they are and in all respects, may be enforced by law. The Court will still have to justify this pronouncement under today's Constitution; it will have to struggle, in particular, to distinguish and divide between the people's morals and its religions, its superstitions, its prejudices.

What is important is that the underlying questions be recognized and considered, in the context of concrete cases, in the light of new facts, new insights, new views of morality, new readings of the Constitution. Obscenity laws, at least those directed at private adult acts done privately, provide the Supreme Court an occasion to recognize and wrestle with the problem of morals legislation under the Constitution. If the Court will not look afresh at obscenity laws, particularly in its private aspects, other morals legislation may soon afford the Court another occasion.[72] It is time to begin to examine —if only in order to justify—the right of constitutional government to legislate morality which has no secular, utilitarian, or social purpose. It is time to attempt to define and articulate the extent to which the religious antecedents of our values may continue to motivate our governments in the enactment and enforcement of law. The Court, one may hope, will begin to attempt to disentangle and separate crime from sin in a secular country having warm feelings toward its religions and its religious ancestry, and having the strong conviction that the wall between Church and State is a good fence making good neighbors.[73]

70. Devlin, *op. cit. supra* note 69, at 14-15.
71. *Id.* at 15.
72. Perhaps the birth control cases will do so, if they again reach the Court, in another posture. See note 60 *supra*.
73. See McCollum v. Board of Educ., 333 U.S. 203, 232 (1948) (Frankfurter, J., concurring).

[11]

PORNOGRAPHY AS DEFAMATION AND DISCRIMINATION†

CATHARINE A. MACKINNON*

> What matters for a legal system is what words *do*, not what they *say* . . . .[1]

A few years back, during a referendum campaign in Cambridge, Massachusetts, on the civil rights ordinance against pornography that Andrea Dworkin and I conceived,[2] a xeroxed leaflet was placed on cars and telephone poles in several neighborhoods late one night. Over a large scrawled black swastika, it said: "Help stop commie kike lezzie cunts from telling us what we can read." This little triumph of economy of abuse referred, of course, to the supposed politics, religious heritage, sexuality, and gender of the ordinance's proponents, and made the further quaint assumption that consuming pornography is reading.

While we absorbed this and pondered what to do, to our astonishment the police decided that a crime had been committed and confiscated most of the leaflets before morning. We had forgotten that Massachusetts has a law against group defamation.[3] Freedom of speech in Massachusetts seems to

* Professor, University of Michigan Law School. This lecture was given in the Boston University School of Law Distinguished Lecturer Series on February 16, 1990. It was delivered in a different form at the Hofstra University Conference on Group Defamation & Freedom of Speech, April, 1988. The comments of Owen Fiss and Burke Marshall were especially helpful, as was the valuable research assistance of Carmela Castellano. The contributions of Andrea Dworkin, as always, were formative.

[1] Edward J. Bloustein, *Holmes: His First Amendment Theory and His Pragmatist Bent*, 40 RUTGERS L. REV. 283, 299 (1988) (discussing Oliver Wendell Holmes's approach to freedom of speech).

[2] The ordinance received 42% of the vote. *The Nation*, L.A. TIMES, Nov. 12, 1985, at 2 (reporting that 9,419 people voted for the measure and 13,031 against it, while 1,931 voters abstained).

[3]
> Whoever publishes any false written or printed material with intent to maliciously promote hatred of any group of persons in the commonwealth because of race, color or religion shall be guilty of libel and shall be punished by a fine of not more than one thousand dollars or by imprisonment for not more than one year, or both. The defendant may prove in defense that the publication was privileged or was not malicious. Prosecutions under this section shall be instituted only by the attorney general or by the district attorney for the district in which the alleged libel was published.

MASS. GEN. LAWS ANN. ch. 272, § 98C (West 1990).

have survived the existence of this law and this instance of its enforcement. The Cambridge ordinance there did not survive its detractors, however, who defended pornography in the name of a freedom of speech that would also have precluded this law.

In discussing this tiny masterpiece of vilification, I have encountered widely differing responses to its elements. Part of the reason, I have come to think, is that real atrocities provide the vocabulary of experience that animates the concept of group defamation, and some of the situations referred to are real to people, and some are not. Some are seen as threatening as well as offensive; others are regarded as perhaps insulting but comparatively harmless. The comparatively more real situations are the Holocaust against the Jews under Germany's Third Reich, the genocide of Native Americans, the slavery and segregation of Blacks in the United States and South Africa, and the internment and atomic bombing of the Japanese during World War II.[4] The verbal and visual terms of vilification and denigration that mark these peak episodes, when reiterated, keep their specific traumas alive as well as reinscribe and revivify a prejudice that did not begin or end with them. These experiences are not mere examples for application of the doctrine of group defamation. They are its life, its blood; it exists because they happened.

Typically, from discussions of these epithets to international instruments resolving to eradicate their doctrines,[5] their role in systematically reducing, violating, and killing people because of who they are is recognized. Even when a law against group defamation is rejected as censorship, the defamatory words, and the ideas and attitudes they animate and actualize, are conceded to have justified, legitimated, and potentiated the devastation. The words are understood to construct social reality. The epithets from the leaflet which refer to race, religion, and politics, and sometimes even those which refer to sexual orientation, are often granted to be not only offensive but also dangerous; the prejudices they express, mobilize, propagate, and imprint are seen as false and are condemned.

In the same discussions, one encounters the sense that the reality these terms represent is not happening here and now, at least not the way it was "there" and "then." These events, it seems, are regarded as essentially over,

---

[4] These examples were discussed at the Hofstra University Conference on Group Defamation & Freedom of Speech, April, 1988. The proceedings of that conference will appear in a forthcoming book edited by Monroe Freedman.

[5] *See, e.g.*, International Convention on the Elimination of All Forms of Racial Discrimination, *opened for signature* Mar. 7, 1966, 660 U.N.T.S. 195, 218-20, *reprinted in* 5 I.L.M. 352 (1966) (entered into force Jan. 4, 1969) ("State parties . . . shall declare an offence punishable by law all dissemination of ideas based on racial superiority or hatred . . . . "); *see also* POSITIVE MEASURES DESIGNED TO ERADICATE ALL INCITEMENT TO, OR ACTS OF, RACIAL DISCRIMINATION, IMPLEMENTATION OF THE INTERNATIONAL CONVENTION ON THE ELIMINATION OF ALL FORMS OF RACIAL DISCCRIMINATION, 1986, U.N. DOC. CERD/2, U.N. SALES NO. E.85.XIV.2 (1986).

lurking only in the isolated unpleasant or insensitive remark or in the occasional bizarre but largely impotent incident, like magic marker leaflets published at night by xerox. Nothing large or systematic or cumulative is happening. In the view of most of my interlocutors, the formative experiences of group libel live on in discourse principally as analogy or memory, at most casting a shadow across the future in a tenuous kind of causality. Yet always the question of explanation of the past is anguished over: how could these atrocities have been allowed to happen? What could people have been thinking? How could they have not known or have looked the other way? How could the law have become so perverted as to legalize them? Implicit here is that "we," here and now, would recognize these past outrages for what they were at the time. "We" would have seen through them, spoken out against them, stood up to them, done something to stop them.

Here and now, there is something virtually never included in the lexicon of group defamation. People are being callously dehumanized, horribly brutalized, and sometimes killed. Verbal, visual, and physical atrocities are committed, demeaning an entire group because of a condition of birth, targeting them for physical atrocities which *are being done*. This case is distinctive in a number of ways, including the fact that a lot of money is being made from the defamatory materials, and that the connections between the material and specific physical abuses are far better documented than in any other instance.[6] Yet the atrocity is not acknowledged but is widely denied. Its ideas are neither widely identified as false nor generally condemned. On the contrary, the materials are rather widely celebrated, alternately defended as freedom itself and as the price "we" must pay for freedom. Not only is this permitted to happen, it is defended by many as a measure of principle. I refer to the "cunts" of the leaflet: to pornography and the situation of women.

Part of the problem in this case is the lack of recognition, militant at times, that there is such a thing as the condition of women of which this body of materials could be a part. In reality, the status and treatment of women has certain regularities across time and space, making gender a group experience of inequality on the basis of sex. Traditionally, women have been disenfranchised, excluded from public life and denied an effective voice in public rules, denied even the use of their own names. Women are still commonly relegated to the least compensated and most degraded occu-

---

[6] Examples of its official documentation include FINAL REPORT OF THE ATTORNEY GENERAL'S COMMISSION ON PORNOGRAPHY (1986) (U.S.); PORNOGRAPHY AND PROSTITUTION IN CANADA: REPORT OF THE SPECIAL COMMITTEE ON PORNOGRAPHY AND PROSTITUTION (1985) (Can.); REPORT OF THE JOINT SELECT COMMITTEE ON VIDEO MATERIAL (1988) (Austl.); SEXUAL OFFENSES AGAINST CHILDREN: REPORT OF THE COMMITTEE ON SEXUAL OFFENCES AGAINST CHILDREN AND YOUTHS ch. 55 (1984) (Can.). For further analysis, see Diana E.H. Russell, *Pornography and Rape: A Causal Model*, 9 POL. PSYCHOL. 41 (1988) (demonstrating that pornography causes rape by undermining inhibitions to raping and facilitating its social acceptance).

pations. Their forced dependency is exploited and venerated as woman's role; their work is devalued because they are doing it, as women are devalued through devaluing the work they do. Women remain reproductively colonized, subjected to systematic physical and sexual insecurity and violation, and blamed for it. Women are commonly raped, battered, sexually harassed, sexually abused as children, forced into motherhood and prostitution, depersonalized, denigrated and objectified—and told this is just and equal by the left, and inevitable and natural by the right. Women's abilities and contributions continue to be suppressed, their achievements denied and marginalized and, when valued, appropriated, and their children stolen. Women are used, abused, bought, sold, and silenced.[7]

Little of this has changed to the present; some of it has gotten better, and some of it has gotten worse. The level of victimization of women varies within and across cultures; in the contemporary United States, for example, women of color are hardest hit.[8] But no woman is exempt from this condition from the moment of her birth to the moment of her death, in the eyes of the law, or in the memory of her children.

This condition is imposed by force. Some force comes in the more covert forms of socialization, pressure, and inculcation to passivity and femininity, some in the more overt forms of poverty and sexual violence. In the United States, the average woman does not yet have an income that is two-thirds that of the average man. Forty-four percent of American women report rape or attempted rape at least once in their lives. Thirty-eight percent report having been sexually abused as children. Between a quarter and a third are battered in their homes. Eighty-five percent have been, or will be, sexually harassed in the workplace, thirty-five percent of them physically. Most prostitutes are female.[9] Although these facts are uncontested and incontestible, neither are they really acknowledged or faced. Mostly this reality is elided because neither women nor men like thinking about it, and because men like living it, or at least benefit from it. So its victims go under without a trace. Life and letters are unchanged. Law and politics go on as usual. Virtually nothing is done about any of it, by anyone, anywhere.

Pornography has a central role in actualizing this system of subordination in the contemporary West, beginning with the conditions of its production. Women in pornography are bound, battered, tortured, harassed, raped, and sometimes killed; or, in the glossy men's entertainment magazines, "merely" humiliated, molested, objectified, and used. In all pornography, women are prostituted. This is done because it means sexual pleasure to pornography's consumers and profits to its providers, largely organized crime. But to those who are exploited, it means being bound, battered, tortured, harassed, raped,

---

[7] For citations from which this description is drawn, see CATHARINE A. MACKINNON, TOWARD A FEMINIST THEORY OF THE STATE 276 n.2 (1989).

[8] For sources, see Catharine A. MacKinnon, *Reflections on Sex Equality Under Law*, 100 Yale L.J. 1281, 1298 n.83, 1301 n.100 (1991).

[9] *See* MACKINNON, *supra* note 7, at 17.

and sometimes killed, or merely humiliated, molested, objectified, and used. It is done because someone who has more power than they do, someone who matters, someone with rights, a full human being and a full citizen, gets pleasure from seeing it, or doing it, or seeing it as a form of doing it.[10] In order to produce what the consumer wants to see, it must first be done to someone, usually a woman, a woman with few real choices. Because he wants to see it done, it is done to her.

To understand how pornography works, one must know what is there. In the hundreds and hundreds of magazines, pictures, films, videocassettes, and so-called books now available across America in outlets from adult stores to corner groceries, women's legs are splayed in postures of sexual submission, display, and access. We are named after men's insults to parts of our bodies and mated with animals. We are hung like meat. Children are presented as adult women; adult women are presented as children, fusing the vulnerability of a child with the sluttish eagerness to be fucked said to be natural to the female of every age. Racial hatred is sexualized; racial stereotypes are made into sexual fetishes. Asian women are presented so passive they cannot be said to be alive, bound so they are not recognizably human, hanging from trees and light fixtures and clothes hooks in closets. Black women are presented as animalistic bitches, bruised and bleeding, struggling against their bonds. Jewish women orgasm in reenactments of actual death camp tortures. In so-called lesbian pornography, women do what men imagine women do when men are not around, so men can watch. Pregnant women, nursing mothers, amputees, other disabled or ill women, and retarded girls, their conditions fetishized, are used for sexual excitement. In the pornography of sadism and masochism, better termed assault and battery, women are bound, burned, whipped, pierced, flayed, and tortured. In some pornography called "snuff," women or children are tortured to death, murdered to make a sex film. The material features incest, forced sex, sexual mutilation, humiliation, beatings, bondage, and sexual torture, in which the dominance and exploitation are directed primarily against women.[11]

Hearings held by the Minneapolis City Council when our pornography ordinance was introduced there documented the harms of pornography's

---

10 Andrea Dworkin and I discuss these issues, and those in the paragraphs following, in these terms in ANDREA DWORKIN & CATHARINE A. MACKINNON, PORNOGRAPHY AND CIVIL RIGHTS: A NEW DAY FOR WOMEN'S EQUALITY 25-26 (1988).

11 *See* Gloria Cowan et al., *Dominance and Inequality in X-Rated Videocassettes,* 12 PSYCHOL. WOMEN Q. 299, 306-07 (1988) (finding that pornography contains abuse and violence that is directed primarily against women); Park E. Dietz & Alan E. Sears, *Pornography and Obscenity Sold in Adult Bookstores: A Survey of 5132 Books, Magazines, and Films in Four American Cities,* 21 U. MICH. J.L. REF. 7, 38-43 (1987-88) (documenting violence, bondage, sado-masochism, and gender differences in pornography); Neil M. Malamuth & Barry Spinner, *A Longitudinal Content Analysis of Sexual Violence in the Best Selling Erotic Magazines,* 16 J. SEX RES. 226, 226-27 (1980) (documenting increases in violent sex in pornography).

making and use in proceedings a member of the city's Civil Rights Commission likened to the Nuremberg Trials.[12] The studies of researchers and clinicians documented the same reality women documented from life: pornography increases attitudes and behaviors of aggression and other discrimination by men against women. Women told how pornography was used to break their self-esteem, train them into sexual submission, season them to forced sex, intimidate them out of job opportunities, blackmail them into prostitution and keep them there, terrorize and humiliate them into sexual compliance, and silence their dissent. They told of being used to make pornography under coercion, of the force that gave them no choice about viewing the pornography or performing the sex. They told how pornography stimulates and condones rape, battery, sexual harassment, sexual abuse of children, and forced prostitution. Those not expressly coerced into pornography were there for the same reasons prostitutes are in prostitution: poverty, sexual abuse as children, homelessness, hopelessness, drug addiction, and desperation. Those who say women are in pornography by choice should explain why it is women who have the fewest choices who are in it most.

In the Minneapolis Hearings, women and men spoke in public about the devastating impact of pornography on their lives. Women spoke of being coerced into sex so that pornography could be made of it. They spoke of being raped in a way that was patterned on specific pornography that was read and referred to during the rape, or repeated like a mantra throughout the rape, of being turned over as the pages were turned over. They spoke of living or working in neighborhoods or job sites saturated with pornography. A young man spoke of growing up gay, learning from heterosexual pornography that to be loved by a man meant to accept his violence, and as a result accepting the destructive brutality of his first male lover. Another young man spoke of his struggle to reject the thrill of sexual dominance he had learned from pornography, and to find a way of loving a woman that was not part of it. A young woman spoke of her father using pornography on her mother, and to silence her protest against her mother's screams, threatening to enact the scenes on the daughter if she told anyone. Another young woman spoke of the escalating use of pornography in her marriage, unraveling her self-respect and belief in her future, destroying any possibility of intimacy, violating her physical integrity. She spoke of finding the strength to leave. Another young woman spoke of being gang-raped by hunters who looked up from their pornography at her and said it all: "There's a live one." Former prostitutes spoke of being made to watch pornography and then duplicate the acts exactly, usually starting when they were children. Many spoke of the self-revulsion, the erosion of intimacy, the unbearable

[12] All of the following accounts are contained in *Public Hearings on Ordinances to Add Pornography as Discrimination Against Women, Minneapolis City Council, Government Operations Committee* (Dec. 12 and 13, 1983) (on file with author). Andrea Dworkin and I discuss this in these terms at DWORKIN & MACKINNON, *supra* note 10, at 32-35.

indignity, the shattered self, and the shame, anger, anguish, outrage, and despair they felt at living in a country where their torture is enjoyed, and their screams are heard only as the "speech" of their abusers. They spoke of the silence, and out of the silence, that pornography had imposed on them.

For those who could not speak for themselves, therapists told of battered women tied in front of video sets and forced to watch, and then participate in, acts of sexual brutality. Psychologists who worked with survivors of incest spoke of the role of pornography in sexual tortures involving sex with dogs and electric shocks. One study documented more rapes in which pornography was specifically implicated than the total number of rapes reported at the time in the city in which the study was done. Another study showed correlations between increases in the rate of reported rape and increases in the consumption figures of an index of major men's entertainment magazines. Laboratory experiments showed that pornography that portrays sexual aggression as pleasurable for the victim—as so much pornography does—increases the acceptance of the use of coercion in sexual relations. They showed that this acceptance of coercive sexuality appears related to sexual aggression, and that exposure to violent pornography increases men's punishing behavior towards women in the laboratory.[13] Pornography increases men's perception that women want rape and are not injured by rape, that women are worthless, trivial, non-human, object-like, and unequal to men.

The testimony, taken as a whole, revealed that the more pornography men see, the more abusive and violent they want it to be. The more abusive and violent it becomes, the more they enjoy it and the more aroused they get. The more abusive and violent it becomes, the less harm they see in what they are seeing or doing.

Over time, the evidence on the harm of pornography has only become stronger. When explicit sex and express violence against women are combined, particularly when rape is portrayed as pleasurable or positive for the victim, the risk of violence against women increases as a result of exposure. It is uncontroversial that exposure to such materials increases aggression against women in laboratory settings, increases attitudes which are related to violence against women in the real world, and increases self-reported likelihood to rape. As a result of exposure, a significant percentage of men, many not otherwise predisposed, as well as the twenty-five to thirty-five percent who report some proclivity to rape a woman, come to believe that violence against women is acceptable.[14] Materials which combine sex with aggression

---

[13] *See* MICHAEL J. MCMANUS, INTRODUCTION TO FINAL REPORT OF ATTORNEY GENERAL'S COMMISSION ON PORNOGRAPHY xvi-xviii (1986) (discussing consensus among researchers).

[14] *See* James V.P. Check & Ted H. Guloien, *Reported Proclivity for Coercive Sex Following Repeated Exposure to Sexually Violent Pornography, Nonviolent Dehumanizing Pornography and Erotica, in* PORNOGRAPHY: RESEARCH ADVANCES AND POLICY CONSIDERATIONS 159, 171, 177 (Dolf Zillmann & Jennings Bryant eds., 1989); Edward

also have perceptual effects which desensitize consumers to rape trauma and to sexual violence. In one study, simulated juries who had been exposed to such material were less able than real juries to perceive that an account of a rape was an account of a rape, through which the victim was harmed.[15]

The most advanced research in this area studies the effects of materials which degrade and dehumanize women without showing violence, as that term is defined in the research.[16] Such material has been shown to lower inhibitions on aggression by men against women, increase acceptance of women's sexual servitude, increase sexual callousness toward women, decrease the desire of both sexes to have female children, increase reported willingness to rape, and increase the belief in male dominance in intimate relationships. For high-frequency consumers, these materials also increase self-reported sexually aggressive behavior.[17]

Men who use pornography often believe that they do not think or do these

Donnerstein, *Pornography: Its Effect on Violence Against Women, in* PORNOGRAPHY AND SEXUAL AGGRESSION 53, 78-79 (Neil M. Malamuth & Edward Donnerstein eds., 1984); Edward Donnerstein & Leonard Berkowitz, *Victim Reactions in Aggressive Erotic Films as a Factor in Violence Against Women*, 41 J. PERSONALITY & SOC. PSYCHOL. 710, 720-23 (1981); Neil M. Malamuth, *Predictors of Naturalistic Sexual Aggression*, 50 J. PERSONALITY & SOC. PSYCHOL. 953, 960 (1986); Neil M. Malamuth, *Factors Associated with Rape as Predictors of Laboratory Aggression Against Women*, 45 J. PERSONALITY & SOC. PSYCHOL. 432, 440-41 (1983); Neil M. Malamuth & James V.P. Check, *The Effects of Aggressive Pornography on Beliefs in Rape Myths: Individual Differences*, 19 J. RES. PERSONALITY 299, 313-14 (1985); Neil M. Malamuth & James V.P. Check, *The Effects of Mass Media Exposure on Acceptance of Violence Against Women: A Field Experiment*, 15 J. RES. PERSONALITY 436, 442-43 (1981).

[15] Daniel Linz et al., *The Effects of Multiple Exposures to Filmed Violence Against Women*, 34 J. COMM., Summer 1984, at 130, 142 (1984) (documenting that men exposed to filmed violence against women judged a rape victim to be less injured than did the control group); *see also* Neil M. Malamuth & James V.P. Check, *Penile Tumescence and Perceptual Responses to Rape as a Function of the Victim's Perceived Reactions*, 10 J. APPLIED SOC. PSYCHOL. 528, 542-43 (1980) (documenting that exposure to rape depictions affected future reactions to rape).

[16] Most of the researchers define sexual violence as requiring the appearance of the use of physical force. Pornography researchers commonly define the term to include rape when the materials expressly present sex they call rape, or when the women in the materials are shown to resist the sexual acts. *See* James V.P. Check & Neil M. Malamuth, *Pornography and Sexual Aggression: A Social Learning Theory Analysis*, 9 COMM. Y.B. 181, 189 (1986). The problem is that not all force is physical and that many women are coerced offstage.

[17] Check & Malamuth, *supra* note 16; Russell, *supra* note 6; Dolf Zillmann & Jennings Bryant, *Effects of Prolonged Consumption of Pornography on Family Values*, 9 J. FAM. ISSUES 518 (1988); Dolf Zillmann & Jennings Bryant, *Effects of Massive Exposure to Pornography, in* PORNOGRAPHY AND SEXUAL AGGRESSION, *supra* note 14, at 115, 130-31; Dolf Zillmann & James B. Weaver, *Pornography and Men's Sexual Callousness Toward Women, in* PORNOGRAPHY: RESEARCH ADVANCES AND POLICY CONSIDERATIONS, *supra* note 14, at 95; James G. Buchman, Effects of Nonviolent Adult

things. But the evidence shows that the use of pornography makes it impossible for men to tell when sex is forced, that women are human, and that rape is rape. Pornography makes men hostile and aggressive toward women, and it makes women silent.[18] While these effects are not invariant or always immediate, and do not affect all men to the same degree, there is no reason to think they are not acted upon and every reason and overwhelming evidence to think that they are—if not right then, then sometime, if not violently, then through some other kind of discrimination.

On the basis of this evidence and analysis, Andrea Dworkin and I designed a law—the ordinance whose advocates were libeled in the leaflet mentioned at the outset—that recognizes pornography as a practice of sex discrimination. Our law defines pornography as graphic sexually explicit pictures or words that subordinate women and also include one or more of a number of specified scenarios which typify pornography.[19] Four practices are actionable: coercion into pornography, forcing pornography on a person,

---

Erotica on Sexual Child Abuse Attitudes, Paper Presented at a Meeting of the American Psychological Association (Aug. 1990) (Boston, Mass.) (on file with author).

[18] The effect on women of consumption of pornography is just beginning to be studied systematically. The best work to date is Charlene Y. Senn, The Impact of Pornography in Women's Lives (1991) (unpublished Ph.D. dissertation, York University) (on file with author). Prior useful studies include Charlene Y. Senn and H. Lorraine Radtke, *Women's Evaluations of and Affective Reactions to Mainstream Violent Pornography, Nonviolent Pornography, and Erotica*, 5 VIOLENCE AND VICTIMS 143 (1990); Carol L. Krafka, Sexually Explicit, Sexually Violent, and Violent Media: Effects of Multiple Naturalistic Exposures and Debriefing on Female Viewers (1985) (unpublished Ph.D. dissertation, University of Wisconsin (Madison)) (on file with author); Charlene Y. Senn, Women's Reactions to Violent Pornography, Nonviolent Pornography and Erotica (1985) (unpublished Master's thesis, University of Calgary) (on file with author); Charlene Y. Senn and H. Lorraine Radtke, A Comparison of Women's Reactions to Violent Pornography, Nonviolent Pornography, and Erotica, Paper Presented at the Annual Convention of the Canadian Psychological Association (1986) (Toronto, Can.) (on file with author).

[19] The Model Ordinance defines "pornography" as

> the graphic sexually explicit subordination of women through pictures and/or words that also includes one or more of the following: a. women are presented dehumanized as sexual objects, things or commodities; or b. women are presented as sexual objects who enjoy humiliation or pain; or c. women are presented as sexual objects experiencing sexual pleasure in rape, incest, or other sexual assault; or d. women are presented as sexual objects tied up or cut up or mutilated or bruised or physically hurt; or e. women are presented in postures or positions of sexual submission, servility, or display; or f. women's body parts—including but not limited to vaginas, breasts, or buttocks—are exhibited such that women are reduced to those parts; or g. women are presented being penetrated by objects or animals; or h. women are presented in scenarios of degradation, humiliation, injury, torture, shown as filthy or inferior, bleeding, bruised or hurt in a context that makes these conditions sexual.

The use of "men, children, or transsexuals in the place of women" in this definition is also

assault due to specific pornography, and trafficking in pornography.[20] We did not claim that these atrocities never happen without pornography. We said that sometimes they do, but when it is proven to have happened because of pornography, it should be possible to do something about it. We did not claim that these atrocities are the only things that happen because of pornography. We said that no matter what else happens, this does. Pornography is thus not a prognostication or representation of second class citizenship acted out elsewhere, but an integral dynamic in it, and hence a civil rights violation.

In this light, pornography, through its production, is revealed as a traffic in sexual slavery. Through its consumption, it further institutionalizes a subhuman, victimized, second class status for women by conditioning men's orgasm to sexual inequality. When men use pornography, they experience in their bodies, not just their minds, that one-sided sex—sex between a person (them) and a thing (it)—is sex, that sexual use is sex, sexual abuse is sex, sexual domination is sex. This is the sexuality that they then demand, practice, purchase, and live out in their everyday social relations with others. Pornography works by making sexism sexy. As a primal experience of gender hierarchy, pornography is a major way in which sexism is enjoyed and practiced, as well as learned. It is one way that male supremacy is spread and made socially real. Through the use of pornography for masturbation—what the leaflet was pleased to call reading—power and powerlessness are experienced and inculcated as sexual excitement and release. Inequality between women and men is what is sexy about pornography—the more unequal the sexier. In other words, pornography makes sexuality into a key dynamic in gender inequality by viscerally defining gender through the experience of hierarchical sexuality. On the way, it exploits inequalities of race, class, age, religion, sexual identity, and disability by sexualizing them through gender.

Seen in this way, pornography is at once a concrete practice and an ideological statement. The concrete practices are discriminatory; the ideological statements are defamatory. Construed as defamation in the conventional sense, pornography says that women are a lower form of human life defined by their availability for sexual use. Women are dehumanized through the

---

pornography. Model Ordinance, *reprinted in* DWORKIN & MACKINNON, *supra* note 10, at 138-39.

The Cambridge ordinance contained a very similar definition. Bill to Amend § E, ch. 25, "Human Rights" of City of Cambridge, Mass., *reprinted in* DWORKIN & MACKINNON, *supra* note 10, at 134.

[20] Model Ordinance, *supra* note 19. In the Indianapolis ordinance, by contrast, the scenarios were limited so that only victims of coercion or assault could sue for materials that did not show violence. INDIANAPOLIS AND MARION COUNTY, IND., CODE ch. 16, § 16-3(g)(8) (1984). In the Bellingham version of the ordinance, defamation through pornography was also included as a cause of action. DWORKIN & MACKINNON, *supra* note 10.

conditioning of male sexuality to their use and abuse, which sexualizes, hence lowers, women across the culture, not only in express sexual interactions. Pornography makes women a public sexual spectacle and common sexual property, works to lower the public standard of their perception and treatment, terrorizes and humiliates women, and also at times offends their sensibilities. Like group libel's historic atrocities, pornography's effects are known but denied or blinked at while being acted out. The abusive acts are presumptively illegal but pervasively permitted, decried in public and savored in private.

When pornography's reality is examined against the terms of group defamation as a legal theory, some of the theory fits, but much of it does not. Pornography does purvey an ideology about all women; too, pornography of women and men of color sexualizes racism. It is in this sense defamatory. But its ideological impact, the prejudice it engenders, while very real, is only one of its effects and is not the one on which the civil rights approach centrally focuses. The deepest injury of pornography is not what it says, but what it does.

It is possible to say what pornography says without doing what it does. For example, the paragraphs above say what it says but do not do what it does. Its damage neither begins nor ends in its mental content. Although all discriminatory damage says something as well as does something, coercion is not an idea; force is not an argument; assault is not advocacy, nor is trafficking in human beings a discourse. On a deeper level, pornography provides direct sexual stimulation, the experience of which is one of sex, not just the idea of sex. There is no adequate analogy to this,[21] and no reply in kind exists. Its pleasure is a specific reinforcer for bigotry itself, not an argument about why bigotry is right, nor even a base appeal to bigoted interests. If you think an orgasm is an argument, try arguing with one some time.

The conditions of the production of pornography distinguish it further from the rest of group defamation. Nobody has to violate or use anybody to make most anti-Semitic propaganda. Nobody has to pose for a lynching, i.e. be lynched, to create most Klan hate literature. Most cities do not offer businesses where one can go and pay to abuse a Jew or a Black, unless she is a woman and the abuse is sex. When a live human being is not used, and the materials are not sex, it makes some sense to discuss the materials as representations or images and to focus on their consequences as the effects of ideas. Their idea content is a substantial vehicle for the harm they do. But, except in a realm of abstraction totally divorced from reality (where most academics seem to prefer to reside), it covers up reality to discuss pornography in these terms. Both pornography and hate literatures are hateful; both propagate invidious group stereotypes; both promote and often instigate violence; both dehumanize. But pornography, because it is also an industry,

---

[21] It may be that much of the pleasure of dominance enjoyed in racial defamation is also sex, but considerably more evidence and analysis would be required to sustain such an argument.

because its dynamic is sexual, and because the camera requires live fodder, not only springs from abuse and leads to abuse; it *is* abuse. It is not merely the groundwork or persuasive basis or impelling rationalization, however destructive or immediate, for consequent acts. It is an act.

This is the reason that pornography is most appropriately addressed as discrimination, not defamation. Defamation and discrimination emerge from distinct theoretical and political traditions. The idea of group defamation, like the idea of obscenity, is that group defamation *is* an idea about a group; discrimination, even when it expresses an attitude, as it always does, is always recognized as an act. Defamation is a tort addressing reputational harm to individuals; it is only derivatively applied to groups. Discrimination is first and always a group-based concept, even when applied to one person at a time. The law of defamation since *New York Times v. Sullivan*[22] has been explicitly circumscribed by First Amendment safeguards because state laws against individual libel, and with it group libel, have been thought potentially to compromise freedom of expression. But discrimination that takes a verbal form has never—not until pornography was challenged as sex discrimination—been regarded as protected by the First Amendment.[23]

Most common forms of discrimination are significantly accomplished through words: "you're fired," "it was essential that the understudy to my Administrative Assistant be a man,"[24] "whites only,"[25] "[m]ale help

[22] 376 U.S. 254 (1964).

[23] *But cf.* Doe v. University of Mich., 721 F. Supp. 852, 868 (E.D. Mich. 1989) (holding that the University of Michigan's policy against discriminatory harassment of students was invalid because it covered "verbal conduct" protected as speech under the First Amendment).

[24] Davis v. Passman, 442 U.S. 228, 230 (1971).

[25] Palmer v. Thompson, 403 U.S. 217 (1971) (holding that the closure by the city of Jackson, Mississippi, of public swimming pools formerly available to "whites only" did not violate Equal Protection Clause of the Fourteenth Amendment because both Blacks and whites were denied access); Jones v. Alfred H. Mayer Co., 392 U.S. 409 (1968) (prohibiting discriminatory sale or rental of property to "whites only"); Blow v. North Carolina, 379 U.S. 684 (1965) (holding that restaurant serving "whites only" violated Civil Rights Act of 1964); Watson v. Memphis, 373 U.S. 526 (1963) (holding that city's operation of large percentage of publicly owned recreational facilities for "whites only" due to delays in implementing desegregation violated the Fourteenth Amendment); *see also* Hazelwood Sch. Dist. v. United States, 433 U.S. 299, 302-05 (1977) (stating that, in employment discrimination claim against school district, plaintiffs alleged that district's newspaper advertisement for teacher applicants specified "white only"); Pierson v. Ray, 386 U.S. 547, 558 (1967) (holding that Black and white clergymen did not consent to their arrest by peacefully entering the "White Only" designated waiting area of bus terminal).

wanted,"[26] "did you get any over the weekend?"[27] "sleep with me and I'll give you an 'A'."[28] and "walk more femininely, talk more femininely, dress more femininely, wear makeup, have [your] hair styled, and wear jewelry."[29] Nearly every time a refusal to hire or promote or accommodate is based on a prohibited group ground, some verbal act either constitutes the discrimination or proves it. When words are not the discriminatory act itself, like sexually harassing comments are, for example,[30] they prove that the treatment is based on a prohibited group ground. In the discrimination context, verbal expressions are actionable per se or are evidence of actionable practices, not protected speech; they are smoking guns, not political opinion. No sexual harassment defendant to my knowledge has ever claimed his sexually harassing remarks were protected expression. Not yet.

Not even clearly symbolic conduct such as cross burning has been considered protected by the First Amendment,[31] even though, unlike pornography, it is pure expression. Cross burning inflicts its harm through its meaning as an act which promotes racial inequality through its message and impact, engendering terror and effectuating segregation.[32] Its damages to equality

[26] Pittsburgh Press Co. v. Pittsburgh Comm'n on Human Relations, 413 U.S. 376, 391 (1973) (holding that sex segregated job advertisements violate human rights laws and are not protected under the First Amendment).

[27] Morgan v. Hertz Corp., 542 F. Supp. 123, 128 (W.D. Tenn. 1981) (issuing injunction in sexual harassment case against making such statements), *aff'd*, 725 F.2d 1070 (6th Cir. 1984).

[28] In Alexander v. Yale University, 459 F. Supp. 1, 3-4 (D. Conn. 1977), *aff'd*, 631 F.2d 178 (2d Cir. 1980), "Plaintiff Pamela Price asserts that she received a poor grade . . . not due to any 'fair evaluation of her academic work', but as a consequence of her rejecting a professor's outright proposition 'to give her a grade of "A" . . . in exchange for her compliance with his sexual demands.' " Allegations that the university lacked a grievance procedure for sexual harassment complaints were found to state a cause of action for sex discrimination under Title IX.

[29] Price Waterhouse v. Hopkins, 490 U.S. 228, 235 (1989) (quoting statements as evidence of sex-discriminatory stereotyping in promotion evaluation).

[30] Meritor Sav. Bank v. Vinson, 477 U.S. 57, 65 (1986) (holding that unwelcome verbal conduct of a sexual nature constitutes sexual harassment creating a hostile working environment)

[31] Not until very recently was this possibility even raised. *See In re* R.A.V., 464 N.W.2d 507, 511 (Minn. 1991) (upholding conviction for burning cross under city ordinance which prohibits bias-motivated disorderly conduct on the ground that the ordinance could be interpreted to prohibit only expressive conduct which falls outside of First Amendment protection), *cert. granted sub nom.* R.A.V. v. St. Paul, 59 U.S.L.W. 3823 (U.S. June 10, 1991) (No. 90-7675); *see also* State v. Miller, 398 S.E.2d 547, 551-52 (Ga. 1990) (holding that wearing a Klan Hood is not protected expression).

[32] *See* United States v. Lee, 935 F.2d 952, 956 (8th Cir. 1991) (concluding that the act of crossburning is an overt act of intimidation which, because of its historical context, is often considered a precursor to violence, and thus invades the victim's privacy interests). In our amicus curiae brief for the National Black Women's Health Project in *R.A.V. v. St. Paul*, Burke Marshall and I make this argument, offering an equality defense for a

rights is not symbolic but real. Cross burning does not so much harm a group's reputation as it effectuates terror, intimidation, and harassment on a group basis. The First Amendment frame on the issue, taken as exclusive, sees what is said but not what is done. When the traditions of defamation and discrimination confront each other, the First Amendment questions how equality can exist without free expression, and the Fourteenth Amendment questions how expression (or anything else) can ever be free without equality.

Defamation and discrimination imagine their harms differently. Defamation addresses harm to group reputation, discrimination to group status and treatment. But to the degree status is a matter of reputation, and reputation a matter of status, they overlap.[33] Whether the treatment is verbal, symbolic, or physical, being treated as a second class citizen certainly furthers the second class reputation of the group of which one is a member. Segregated lunch counters or toilets or water fountains were not challenged as defamatory symbolic expression, nor defended because of what they said—that is, as symbolic speech or as expressions of political opinion—although they were arguably both expressive and political. Racial segregation in education was not regarded as protected speech to the extent it required verbal forms, such as laws and directives, to create and sustain it. Nor was it regarded as actionable defamation against African-Americans, although a substantial part of its harm was the message of inferiority it conveyed, as well as its negative impact on the self-concept of Black children.[34] Yet the harm of segregation and other racist practices is at least as much what it says as what it does. Just as with cross burning, what it says is indistinguishable from what it does. Considered this way, it can be said that pornography does substantial reputational damage to women, but the harm does not end

---

Minnesota statute prohibiting cross burning. Brief for the National Black Women's Health Project, R.A.V. v. St. Paul, 59 U.S.L.W. 3823 (U.S. June 10, 1991) (No. 90-7675) (on file with author).

[33] Convergence is implicit in the design of international instruments for the regulation of racist speech, which casts group defamation as a practice of discrimination, International Convention on the Elimination of All Forms of Racial Discrimination, *supra* note 5, and the extensive national legislation that parallels this Convention. *See, e.g.*, 1988 E.D.L.A. 114, leg. 23.592 (Arg.); Act of July 1, 1972, No. 72-546 (amending C. PÉN. art. 24, ¶ 5) (Fr.); Laws of October 13, 1975, art. 654 (ratifying Convention), Gazz. Uff. art. 337, Dec. 23, 1975, Parte I, 1976 Lex, p. 6, Law No. 654 art. 3(b) (Italy).

[34] *See* Brown v. Board of Educ., 347 U.S. 483, 494 (1954) ("To separate them from others of similar age and qualifications solely because of their race generates a feeling of inferiority as to their status in the community that may affect their hearts and minds in a way unlikely to ever be undone."). *Brown* thus did not decide that these children were offended by segregation, and that the harm was therefore subjective, and hence irrelevant or nonexistent. Rather, it decided that the children were harmed by it in their feelings and self-concept, hence in their ability to learn. *See also* Charles R. Lawrence III, *If He Hollers Let Him Go: Regulating Racist Speech on Campus*, 1990 DUKE L.J. 431, 438-40 (arguing that *Brown* may be read as regulating the content of racist speech).

there. The civil rights approach to pornography does not center on its defamatory aspects any more than the civil rights approach to segregation centered on its defamatory aspects, although they are there in both cases.

Pornography is propaganda, an expression of male ideology, a hate literature, an argument for sexual fascism. It conveys ideas like any systematic social practice does. It is also, like most group defamation, often immoral, tasteless, ugly, and boring. But none of this is what pornography distinctively is, how it works, or what is most harmful about it. Was the evil of the Holocaust what it *said* about Jews? If the tortures at Dachau had been required to make anti-Semitic propaganda, would its harm be considered ideological? Would it be subject to varying interpretation? If lampshades made of women's skin were sold beside the road, would the law examine the impact of this practice on women's self-image or public reputation? Perhaps this traffic would offend people, but would we reduce its harm to its offensiveness, as if that were all it was about?

The theory of group defamation does not adequately encompass the reality of pornography. One has to wonder whether it adequately encompasses the reality of group defamation either. For instance, building on the individual libel model, some laws of group defamation require that the statements be proven false or permit truth as a defense.[35] While much of what visual pornography says about women is a pack of lies, it actually has to happen to be made, and in that sense is empirically true. What it shows happened to the person it shows it happening to: what you see is what she got. Most group defamation contains a similar mix of lies with imposed realities. The stereotypes defamation presents begin false and remain largely false, but to the extent the stereotypes are imposed on a group, they will accurately describe at least some of its members sometimes. Success in forcing the world to correspond to a defamatory image, as in making the world a pornographic place, makes defamation both more true and arguably more damaging, not less, but it is, for that reason, legally regarded as *less* defamatory, or not illegal as defamation at all, where truth is a defense.[36] Also, do we really want hearings on comparative African-American penis size or whether Jews bathe?

As another example, the law of group libel generally restricts the promotion of hatred, or hatred and contempt.[37] Hatred is an extreme feeling of

---

[35] *See, e.g.*, R.S.C., ch. C-46, § 319(3)(a) (1985) (Can.) (providing under the Canadian Criminal Code that no one who wilfully promotes hatred against any identifiable group shall be convicted "if he establishes that the statements communicated were true").

[36] Whether the onus should be on the speaker to prove truth or on the victim to prove falsity, or whether truth is not relevant, is subject to various legal treatments worldwide. The Belgian penal code, for example, punishes statement of a malicious fact which injures a person's honor or exposes them to contempt without producing legal proof. Les Codes Larcier § 443, Code Penal Edition 1985 (Belg.).

[37] *See, e.g.*, ILL. REV. STAT. ch. 38, ¶ 471 (1949) (repealed 1961) (statute litigated in Beauharnais v. Illinois, 343 U.S. 250, 251 (1952), which outlawed publications which

negative animus which can express itself verbally or physically.[38] Discrimination begins with an assumption of human status and focuses on deviations in treatment from that standard. If a man chains his dog in his backyard, most people probably will not say that the dog's civil rights are violated. If a man chains a woman in his basement, maybe they will. It does not matter if he loves her or hates her. What matters is how he treats her and what that treatment and its permissibility say about what a woman socially is.[39] Perhaps, in terms of human rights, such treatment can be considered hateful regardless of his subjectivity. But the bottom line of discrimination, I think, is less do they hate and more will they kill. Hatred rationalizes and impels genocide, certainly, but so do some things far colder, like self-interest, sense of superiority, or fun, and something far more banal, like indifference or system. In the case of women and men, love deals at least as much death, and so does something hotter, like pleasure. The fact that pornography so often presents itself as love, indeed resembles much of what passes for it under male dominance, makes its construction as hate literature a challenging exercise in demystification, to say the least. The concept of discrimination aims not at what is felt by perpetrator or victim or what is said as such, but at what is done, including through words.

A related issue in the contrast between defamation and discrimination is the mental element of "wilfulness" or a least knowledge of falsity required in many group defamation statutes.[40] Sincere sex bigots, which the consumption of pornography creates, would presumably be exempt. Discrimination, on the other hand, need not always be intended or meant to be discriminatory.[41] Indeed, after dealing with unconscious bigots, it can be an improve-

---

expose "the citizens of any race, color, creed or religion to contempt"); R.S.C., ch. C-46, § 319(1) (1985) (Can.) (proscribing public communication which incites hatred against an identifiable group).

[38] The most illuminating discussion of the subject I have read is Patrick Lawlor, Group Defamation: Submissions to the Attorney General of Ontario (Mar. 1984) (on file with author).

[39] I recognize that some discussions of animal rights and defenses of sado-masochism would question this example, or use it to make other points.

[40] *See, e.g.*, R.S.C., ch. C-46, § 319(2) (1985) (Can.) (creating under the Canadian Criminal Code an offense for the wilful promotion or incitement of hatred against an identifiable group through statements other than in private conversation); § 130-31 *StGB* (1987) (Ger.).

[41] In the United States, violations of the Equal Protection Clause and disparate treatment violations of Title VII must be intentional to be discriminatory. Personnel Adm'r v. Feeney, 442 U.S. 256, 274 (1979); International Bhd. of Teamsters v. United States, 431 U.S. 324, 335-36 (1977); Washington v. Davis, 426 U.S. 229, 238-41 (1976). But disparate impact violations of Title VII need not be intentional. Griggs v. Duke Power, 401 U.S. 424, 431 (1971). Under international law, dissemination of ideas based on racial superiority and racial hatred is prohibited "despite lack of intention to commit an offense and irrespective of the consequences of the dissemination, whether they be grave or insignificant." POSITIVE MEASURES, *supra* note 5, ¶ 83.

ment to have one's humanity recognized enough to have it wilfully degraded. This is no less the case for the standard examples of group defamation than it is for pornography.

This analysis suggests that an equality theory may remedy some of the same inadequacies for group defamation that it has for pornography. A discrimination theory of defamation would center on its harm to subordinate groups.[42] Group libel is an equality issue when its promotion undermines the social equality of a target group that is traditionally and systematically disadvantaged. Group defamation promotes the disadvantage of disadvantaged groups. Group-based enmity, ill-will, intolerance, and prejudice are the attitudinal engines of the exclusion, denigration, and subordination that comprise social inequality. Without bigotry, social systems of enforced separation and apartheid would be unnecessary, impossible, and unthinkable. Stereotyping and stigmatization of historically disadvantaged groups through group hate propaganda shape their social image and reputation, arguably controlling the opportunities of individual members more powerfully than their individual abilities do.[43] It is impossible for an individual to receive equality of opportunity when surrounded by an atmosphere of group hatred or contempt.

In this light, group defamation can be seen as a specific kind of discriminatory practice, a verbal form inequality takes. Anti-Semitism promotes the inequality of Jews on the basis of religion and ethnicity. White supremacy promotes inequality on the basis of race, color, and sometimes ethnic origin. Group defamation in this sense is not the mere expression of anti-Semitic or white supremacist opinion but a practice of discrimination similar to sexual harassment and other discriminatory acts that take verbal form. It is arguably an integral link in systemic discrimination which keeps target groups in subordinated positions through the promotion of terror, intolerance, degradation, segregation, exclusion, vilification, violence, and genocide. The nature of the practice can be seen and proven from the damage it does, from

---

[42] The Women's Legal Education and Action Fund (LEAF), with my participation, made the argument outlined in the following paragraphs of the text in defense of the constitutionality of the hate propaganda provision of the Criminal Code of Canada under which the defendant had been convicted in R. v. Keegstra, [1991] 2 W.W.R. (Supreme Court) 1, 6 (Can.). In response to the argument that criminalizing hatemongering violated the defendant's constitutionally protected freedom of expression, LEAF argued that the provisions were protected under the constitutional equality provisions. Although found to be violations of the freedom of expression, the provisions were upheld by the Supreme Court of Canada as justified in a free and democratic society largely on an equality rationale.

[43] The Supreme Court in *Beauharnais v. Illinois* saw this clearly, upholding Illinois's libel statute outlawing publications which denigrate a class of citizens by virtue of their race or religion: "[A] man's job and his educational opportunities and the dignity accorded him may depend as much on the reputation of the racial and religious group to which he willy-nilly belongs, as on his own merits." Beauharnais v. Illinois, 343 U.S. 250, 263 (1952).

immediate psychic wounding to consequent physical aggression.[44] Where advocacy of genocide is part of group defamation,[45] an equality approach to its regulation would observe that to be liquidated because of the group you belong to is the ultimate inequality.

Thus, any nation that has a constitutional guarantee of equality can potentially defend a group defamation statute that is challenged as a violation of freedom of expression on equality grounds.[46] A law against group defamation promotes equality and opposes inequality. It would violate any constitutional equality provision in existence for a legislature to pass a law authorizing the promotion of hatred on the basis of sex, race, religion, and national origin. It follows that governmental action against promoting group hate is protected under constitutional equality provisions. Just as governmental action to promote group hatred would violate a constitutional equality provision, governmental action to prohibit group hatred promotes constitution-based equality.[47]

Once laws against group defamation can be supported as well as challenged on a constitutional level, the tension between equality and speech would be resolved by whatever standards constitutional conflicts are accommodated. Typically, the courts would decide whether the group libel provision burdened expression significantly or at all, and whether its regulation promoted equality as unintrusively as possible, and in a way a legislature could have found effective.[48] The balancing would be done however balancing is done, but it would be two constitutional rights in the balance, not just one constitutional right against a nice idea or good manners or political sen-

---

[44] *See* THEY DON'T ALL WEAR SHEETS: A CHRONOLOGY OF RACIST AND FAR RIGHT VIOLENCE—1980-86 (C. Lutz comp. 1987) (compiling data on incidents of racial, religious, and homophobic violence); Richard Delgado, *Words That Wound: A Tort Action for Racial Insults, Epithets, and Name-Calling*, 17 HARV. C.R.-C.L. L. REV. 133, 143-49 (1982) (discussing the emotional and psychological harms of racial insults); Mari Matsuda, *Public Response to Racist Speech: Considering the Victim's Story*, 87 MICH. L. REV. 2320, 2335-41 (1989) (detailing negative effects of racist hate messages).

[45] For example, as defined in the Canadian Criminal Code, R.S.C., ch. C-46, § 318(2)(a)-(b) (1985) (Can.).

[46] Of course, to succeed, this approach requires that constitutional equality mandates be interpreted properly. For an example of a standard conducive to protecting group libel laws, see the equality approach under the Canadian Charter of Rights and Freedoms in Andrews v. The Law Society, [1989] 1 S.C.R. 143, 171 (interpreting the purpose of § 15(1) of the Charter as ensuring equality in the formulation and application of the law, including promoting a society in which all of its members are recognized at law as equally deserving of concern, respect, and consideration), as applied in *Keegstra*, 2 W.W.R. 1.

[47] *See Keegstra*, 2 W.W.R. at 50 (quoting LEAF's factum to this effect).

[48] This generally describes the respective tests in the United States and Canada. In the United States, the two steps are collapsed into one: does the provision violate freedom of expression? *See, e.g.*, *Beauharnais*, 343 U.S. at 266-67. In Canada, whether freedom of expression is violated is one step; whether it can be justified as a limit on expression in a free and democratic society is determined separately. *See, e.g.*, *Keegstra*, 2 W.W.R. 1;

sitivity or standards of civility. Considered as defamation, the harms are comparatively trivialized, and the state interest is obscured, disabling the constitutional defense of such laws against First Amendment attack. When the equality interest is recognized, focusing on lived consequences rather than message content, practices like lynching, cross burning, and pornography are revealed as expressive forms inequality takes, and the constitutional balance shifts.

Analyzing group defamation in equality terms recasts many well-worn issues in free expression debate. Perhaps the most startling concerns the dogma that there is no such thing as a false idea for purposes of constitutional analysis of speech.[49] When equality is recognized as a constitutional value and mandate, the idea that some people are inferior to others on the basis of group membership is authoritatively rejected as the basis for public policy. This does not mean that ideas to the contrary cannot be expressed. It should mean, however, that social inferiority cannot be imposed through any means, including expression.[50] Because society is made of language, distinguishing talk about inferiority from verbal imposition of inferiority may be complicated at the edges but is nonetheless very clear in most instances.[51] At the very least, such practices would not be constitutionally insulated from regulation on the ground that the ideas they express cannot be regarded as false. And attempts to address such practices should not be considered inva-

---

Irwin Toy Ltd. v. Quebec [1989] 1 S.C.R. 927, 991-1001; R. v. Oakes, [1986] 1 S.C.R. 103, 139.

Germany also provides an instructive comparison. *See* Eric Stein, *History Against Free Speech: German Law in European and American Perspective, in* VERFASSUNGSRECHT UND VOLKERRECHT: GEDACHTNISSCHRIFT FUR WILHELM KARL GECK, WILFRIED FIEDLER UND GEORG RESS 855-56 (Hrsg.) (Carl Heymanns Verlag K.G.) (1989).

[49] Gertz v. Robert Welch, Inc., 418 U.S. 323, 339 (1974) ("Under the First Amendment there is no such thing as a false idea.").

[50] *Cf.* International Convention on the Elimination of All Forms of Racial Discrimination, *supra* note 5 (requiring state parties to criminalize "all dissemination of ideas based on racial superiority or hatred").

[51] This seems to be what is at stake in the discussion about campus hate speech codes, most of which, in essence, extend sexual harassment prohibitions to racial and ethnic slurs and insults, and some to sexual orientation as well. Some of the literature in this area includes Kent Greenawalt, *Insults and Epithets: Are They Protected Speech?*, 42 RUTGERS L. REV. 287 (1990) (considering legal claims against those who engage in harmful speech); Rodney Smolla, *Rethinking First Amendment Assumptions About Racist and Sexist Speech*, 47 WASH. & LEE L. REV. 171 (1990) (advocating narrowly drawn restrictions on racist and sexist speech); and especially the insightful Lawrence, *supra* note 34. I do not think that the discrimination rationale on which sexual harassment law is based, and the sexual nature of the harassment which makes it so act-like, can be so simply transposed into the racial and ethnic defamation context. It is equally clear, however, that what is harassment in the gender context does not suddenly become pure idea in the racial context and that an equality theory can support such codes when properly drawn.

lid because, in taking a position in favor of equality, they assume that the idea of human equality is true. There is no requirement that the state remain neutral when inequality is practiced—quite the contrary. Expressive means of practicing inequality have never been recognized as exceptions.[52]

In the United States, the receptivity of the law of free speech to an equality theory of group defamation can be partially assessed from courts' responses to the sex discrimination ordinance against pornography. The U.S. Court of Appeals for the Seventh Circuit in *American Booksellers Association v. Hudnut* found that the ordinance violated the First Amendment guarantee of freedom of speech.[53] The court reached this conclusion in spite of its agreement that pornography contributed materially to rape and other sexual violence, was a form of subordination in itself, and was partly responsible for second class citizenship in various forms, including economic ones.[54] In some passages, the court conceded that pornography is a practice.[55] Yet protecting the pornography was held to be more important than avoiding or remedying its harms. Indeed, the court held that pornography's importance as speech can be measured by its effectiveness in doing the harm that it does.[56]

The civil rights law against pornography was held to be a form of discrimination on the basis of "viewpoint" because it was not neutral on the subject of sex-based exploitation and abuse.[57] By this standard, every discriminatory practice and every anti-discriminatory law expresses a point of view. Acts express ideas, yet they are legally restricted and do not have to be proven expressionless first. Segregation expresses the view that Blacks are inferior to whites; rulings against segregation express the contrary view. Segregation is not therefore protected speech, nor are rulings against it considered "thought control."[58] Affirmative action plans and anti-discrimination policies are not regarded as discrimination on the basis of viewpoint, although they prohibit the view that Blacks are inferior to whites from being expressed by discriminating against them, including by telling them "you're fired" for the wrong reasons. This remains true even though deinstitutionalizing segregation does a great deal to undermine the point of view it

[52] *See* Norwood v. Harrison, 413 U.S. 455, 470 (1973) ("Invidious private discrimination may be characterized as a form of exercising freedom of association protected by the First Amendment, but it has never been accorded affirmative constitutional protection.").

[53] American Booksellers Ass'n v. Hudnut, 771 F.2d 323 (7th Cir. 1985), *aff'd mem.*, 475 U.S. 1001 (1986).

[54] *Hudnut*, 771 F.2d at 328-29.

[55] *Id.* at 329.

[56] *Id.*

[57] *Id.* at 328.

[58] In *Hudnut*, the court held that the ordinance prohibiting pornography, defined as "[s]peech that 'subordinates' women," "establishes an 'approved' view of women," and was thereby "thought control." *Id.* In so holding, the court missed that "subordinates" is a verb, an act, not a thought about an act.

expresses, just as making pornography actionable as sex discrimination would delegitimize the ideas the practice advances. Under the ordinance, misogynist attitudes toward women and sexuality can be expressed; they just cannot be practiced in certain ways, such as when verbal and visual subordination based on sex are trafficked. What the *Hudnut* court missed is both that acts speak and that speech acts.[59]

As an illustration of the convergence of expression with action, consider lynching.[60] Lynching has a vocabulary and a message. It is a vehicle for the communication of an ideology. It expresses a clear point of view about African-Americans, one that is difficult to express as effectively any other way. One point of lynching is that other Blacks see the body. The idea expressed by hanging the body in public is that all Blacks belong in a subordinate position and should stay there or they will be horribly brutalized, maimed, and murdered. Another point of lynching is that whites see the body. Its display teaches them that they are superior and deserve to live: this was done for them. Photographs have sometimes been taken of lynchings and made available for fifty cents apiece for those who missed seeing the real thing.[61] Compare such a photograph, or the photograph of Michael Donald hanging lynched from a tree sent out by Klanwatch in an envelope with a warning that the photograph within is highly disturbing,[62] with a 1984 *Penthouse* spread in which Asian women were bound, trussed, and hung from trees.[63] One cannot tell if they are dead or alive. In both cases, individuals are tied up and hung from trees, often with genitals displayed. In both cases, they are people of color. In both cases, sexual humiliation is involved. But when the victim is a man, the photograph is seen to document an atrocity against him and an entire people. I doubt many masturbate to it. Because the victim in *Penthouse* is a woman, the photograph is considered entertainment, experienced as sex, called speech, and protected as a constitutional right.

If Blacks were lynched in order to make photographs of lynchings on a ten-billion-dollar-a-year scale, would that make them protected speech? The issue here is not whether the acts of lynching are formally illegal or not. As with the acts surrounding pornography, on paper lynchings were illegal, while in reality they mostly were not, until a specific law—a civil rights law—was passed against them. The issue is also not whether lynchings or sexual atrocities can be visually documented, although it does matter how

---

[59] For a discussion of "the inseparability of the idea and the practice of racism," see Lawrence, *supra* note 34, at 443-44.

[60] Andrea Dworkin and I discuss this example in these terms in our book, see *supra* note 10, at 60-61.

[61] *See, e.g.*, JAMES R. MCGOVERN, ANATOMY OF A LYNCHING 84 (1982) (stating that "disappointed late-comers were willing to pay fifty cents for a photograph" of Claude Neal's lynching).

[62] MORRIS DEES, A SEASON FOR JUSTICE, photograph reproduced at page facing 181 (1991).

[63] 16 PENTHOUSE 118 (Dec. 1984).

they are presented. The issue is, rather, given the fact that someone must be lynched to make a picture of a lynching, what is more important, the picture or the person? If it takes a lynching to show a lynching, what is the social difference, really, between seeing a lynching and seeing a picture of one? What would it say about the seriousness with which society regards lynching if lynching were illegal, but pictures of lynchings were affirmatively protected and constituted a highly profitable, visible, and pervasive industry, defended as a form of freedom and a constitutional right? What would it say about the seriousness and effectiveness of laws against lynching if people paid good money to see one, and the law looked the other way, so long as it was mass-produced? What would it say about one's status in the community that society permits one to be hanged from trees and calls it entertainment—that is, protects its for those who enjoy it, rather than prohibits it for those who it harms? What would it mean if the courts held that because lynching effectively expresses a point of view about African-Americans, it is an "idea" whose mass expression, over and over and over again, thousands every year, is protected speech?

Actually, *Hudnut* does not rule on the Indianapolis ordinance at all, but on some imaginary group defamation ordinance directed toward what pornography says. By turning harmful practices into bad thoughts and acts into ideas about acts, *Hudnut* does rule on hate speech regulation, which, unlike the Indianapolis ordinance, *does* turn on point of view. Under anti-hate laws, love is not racially defamatory; hate is. After reducing discriminatory acts to defamatory ideas, the *Hudnut* court held that no amount of harm from group-based speech can justify legal action by its victims.[64] This is simply legally wrong. Courts are supposed to measure value against harm, not by harm. A doctrinally correct approach to the ordinance would have balanced the harms of such materials against their value, if any,[65] or might even have considered the value of the materials irrelevant so long as they are proven to do injury which states can legitimately regulate. The harm of pornography as made actionable by the ordinance is not done through viewpoint, or even through content as such. Pornography is identified in part

[64] *Hudnut*, 771 F.2d at 329. On February 27, 1992, the Supreme Court of Canada explicitly held to the contrary in Butler v. The Queen, No. 22191, 86 D.L.R.4th — (1992), adopting LEAF's argument that pornography damages social equality. The court ruled unanimously that pornography's harm to women justifies its criminal prohibition as obscenity. The court recognized the substantial body of opinion holding that pornography "results in harm, particularly to women and therefore to society as a whole," in concluding that harm to women violated community standards. In addition to applying to violent materials, the court's opinion found that "degrading and dehumanizing" materials can be prohibited because they "place women (and sometimes men) in positions of subordination, servile submission or humiliation. They run against the principles of equality and dignity of all human beings." Slip op. at 25 (Sopinka, J., majority opinion).

[65] *See* New York v. Ferber, 458 U.S. 747, 758 (1982) (holding that child pornography's harm outweighs its value as expression, if any).

through its content, but regulated through its acts, the acts the ordinance makes actionable. But it must be faced that the *Hudnut* approach is fatal for regulating racial defamation, no matter how much harm it does.

Just as courts have often protected the group defamation of the past,[66] when the Supreme Court summarily affirmed *Hudnut*, protecting and defending pornography became the official state position in the United States. An entire class of women can be discriminated against so that others can have what they call freedom of speech: freedom meaning free access to women's bodies, free use of women's lives; speech meaning women's bodies as a medium for expression. As African-Americans, men as well as women, once were white men's property under the Constitution, all women are now men's "speech" because our pain, humiliation, torture, use, and second class status is something they want to say. It does not matter that they cannot say it without doing it.

Now that the law has adopted the point of view of the pornographers on women's rights as its basis for state policy, holding that the pornography is more important than the women they know it harms, one might ask again the same questions that are asked of the classic experiences of group defamation. Why the silence? Why the complicity? How can "we" let this go on? How can it be officially permitted? How can the law be so twisted as to collaborate in it? What are people thinking? Don't they know? Don't they see? Don't they care? Perhaps the lack of explanation for the success of past campaigns of group defamation is connected with the lack of recognition of present ones. Why have most of you not heard all this before? Why have those who have seen the pornography not seen it in this way? Now that you know, why will most of you find satisfying reasons to do nothing about it?

---

[66] David Riesman, in *Democracy and Defamation: Control of Group Libel*, 42 COLUM. L. REV. 727 (1942), explains how German courts espoused a general doctrine that only an individual could be defamed, thereby protecting favored groups. *Id.* at 765-66. Riesman recounts the use of defamation and manipulation of the law against defamation as a major weapon in the Nazi rise to power, making it possible systematically to defame Jews in a way calculated to lower their public esteem and to lure them into ruinous lawsuits. *Id.* at 728-29. Also important, members of the government were exempt from legal responsibility for defamation. *See also* David Riesman, *Democracy and Defamation: Fair Game and Fair Comment II*, 42 COLUM. L. REV. 1282, 1310-11 (1942) (arguing that American courts of the period failed to use the law of defamation to "protect those weaker groups and weaker critics who cannot rely on wealth or power over public opinion as their safeguard").

The *Hudnut* court equates the role of Nazi propaganda in the Nazi rise to power with the role of pornography in the status of women as an argument for protecting pornography. *Hudnut*, 771 F.2d at 329.

[12]

Pornography and the First Amendment: A Reply to Professor MacKinnon

Thomas I. Emerson*

Professor Catharine MacKinnon, in a recent article in this journal, powerfully and perceptively developed her thesis that pornography is "[c]entral to the institutionalization of male dominance."[1] Pornography, she urges, is "a political practice" that "causes attitudes and behaviors of violence and discrimination which define the treatment and status of half of the population." I am not sure that I would draw the line between Eros and dehumanization at the same point as Professor MacKinnon appears to. Moreover, all the evidence is not yet in as to the actual impact of pornography, and Professor MacKinnon may overstate its role in the subordination of women.[2] Nevertheless, generally speaking, I accept Professor MacKinnon's basic position and proceed upon the premise that pornography plays a major part in establishing and maintaining male supremacy in our society.

My concern arises not from Professor MacKinnon's statement of the problem but from her proposals for a solution. Despite her opening remark that "pornography cannot be reformed or suppressed or banned," but "can only be changed," it is clear that Professor MacKinnon would deal with the problem by invoking the power of the government to suppress pornography. Her specific proposals are embodied in the Minneapolis and Indianapolis Ordinances, which she and Andrea Dworkin drafted and persuaded the city councils of those cities to adopt. The Minneapolis Ordinance was vetoed by the Mayor as a violation of the first amendment, but

* Augustus E. Lines Professor Emeritus of Law, Yale University. Professor Emerson is the author of TOWARD A GENERAL THEORY OF THE FIRST AMENDMENT (1966) and THE SYSTEM OF FREEDOM OF EXPRESSION (1970).

1. MacKinnon, *Not a Moral Issue*, 2 YALE L. & POL'Y REV. 321 (1984).

2. *See* Affidavit of Richard Green, American Booksellers Ass'n. Inc. v. Hudnut, Cause No. IP 84-791C, slip op., (S.D.Ind. 1984). This psychiatrist concludes: "The relationship between the availability of pornography to the public and the incidence of sex crimes does not support the view that pornography leads to sexual assault. Indeed, the data suggest the reverse effect." *Id.* at 5. *See also* PORNOGRAPHY AND CENSORSHIP (D. Copp & S. Wendell eds. 1983). This book contains essays from a number of social scientists who have attempted to ascertain whether the wide availability of pornography has produced harmful consequences. The editors conclude that "the question cannot yet be given a definitive answer." *Id.* at 12.

the Indianapolis ordinance was signed into law and is now the subject of litigation in the federal courts. I will take the Indianapolis Ordinance as showing, in concrete terms, what an attempted suppression of pornography by government mandate would entail.[3]

The Indianapolis Ordinance is based upon the theory that "pornography is a discriminatory practice based on sex which denies women equal opportunities in society." It creates administrative and judicial machinery empowering any woman to bring civil proceedings for a cease and desist order (that is, an injunction) to prohibit the "production, sale, exhibition, or distribution of pornography," and require the offender "to take further affirmative action as will effectuate the purposes" of the Ordinance.

The key provision of the Ordinance is the definition of pornography: "Pornography shall mean the graphic sexually explicit subordination of women, whether in pictures or in words," that also includes one or more ways in which "women are presented." The features that make material pornographic include not only presentations of women being subjected to violence, but also presentation of women as "sexual objects who enjoy pain or humiliation"; women as "sexual objects who experience sexual pleasure in being raped"; women "being penetrated by objects or animals"; women "in scenarios of degradation, injury, abasement, . . . shown as filthy or inferior, . . . or hurt in a context that makes these conditions sexual"; and women "presented as sexual objects for domination, conquest . . . exploitation, possession, or use, or through postures or positions of servility or submission or display."[4]

The sweep of the Indianapolis Ordinance is breathtaking. It would subject to governmental ban virtually all depictions of rape,

3. The proposed Minneapolis ordinance, amending MINNEAPOLIS, MINN., CODE OF ORDINANCES RELATING TO CIVIL RIGHTS, tit. 7, chs. 139, 141, was approved by the City Council on December 30, 1983, and subsequently vetoed by Mayor Donald Fraser. The measure was again introduced, passed and vetoed in 1984. The Indianapolis provisions are Indianapolis, Ind., Ordinance No. 24 (May 1, 1984) and Ordinance No. 35 (June 15, 1984), amending the INDIANAPOLIS AND MARION COUNTY, IND., CODE, ch. 16. These measures are collectively referred to as the "Indianapolis Ordinance." On November 19, 1984, a federal district court in Indianapolis declared the ordinance unconstitutional in American Booksellers Ass'n, Inc. v. Hudnut, Cause No. IP 84-791C, slip op., (S.D.Ind.). Judge Sarah Evans Barker held that "pornography," as defined and regulated by the Ordinance, "is constitutionally protected speech under the First Amendment." *Id.* at 46.

4. For an even broader definition of pornography, taken from the first Minneapolis Ordinance, see MacKinnon, *supra* note 1 at 321 n.1 (1984). "Pornography," as defined by Professor MacKinnon, encompasses a far wider range of material than does "obscenity," as defined by the Supreme Court. *See infra* text accompanying notes 7-8. Professor MacKinnon's definition of pornography is accepted for purposes of this article.

verbal or pictorial, and a substantial proportion of other presentations of sexual encounters. More specifically, it would outlaw such works of literature as the *Arabian Nights*, John Cleland's *Fanny Hill*, Henry Miller's *Tropic of Cancer*, William Faulkner's *Sanctuary*, and Norman Mailer's *Ancient Evenings*, to name but a few. The ban would extend from Greek mythology and Shakespeare to the millions of copies of "romance novels" now being sold in the supermarkets. It would embrace much of the world's art, from ancient carvings to Picasso, well-known films too numerous to mention, and a large amount of commercial advertising.

The scope of the Indianapolis Ordinance is not accidental. Nor could it be limited by more precise drafting without defeating the purpose of its authors. As Professor MacKinnon emphasizes, male domination has deep, pervasive and ancient roots in our society, so it is not surprising that our literature, art, entertainment and commercial practices are permeated by attitudes and behavior that create and reflect the inferior status of women. If the answer to the problem, as Professor MacKinnon describes it, is government suppression of sexual expression that contributes to female subordination, then the net of restraint has to be cast on a nearly limitless scale. Even narrowing the proscribed area to depictions of sexual activities involving violence would outlaw a large segment of the world's literature and art.

I. *The Ban on Pornography and Traditional First Amendment Doctrine*

If we test Professor MacKinnon's proposals against traditional first amendment doctrine, there is no way that her solution of the pornography problem can be sustained. Obviously, the founding fathers, whatever restrictions they might have found constitutionally permissible with respect to sexually explicit speech, could not have intended the first amendment to allow the government to prohibit all speech that supported male domination. On Professor MacKinnon's own analysis, the very idea could not have occurred to them as members of the dominant male hierarchy. Insofar as "original intention" is a guide to constitutional interpretation, then, it runs squarely counter to the position taken by the proponents of the Indianapolis Ordinance.

Nor can government suppression of pornography be justified under current first amendment doctrine. The core element in first amendment theory is that the impact of speech—whether considered good, bad or indifferent—cannot be invoked as a basis for government control of speech. Speech, or more generally expression, occupies a specially protected place in a democratic society. As Justice Holmes remarked long ago: "[I]f there is any principle of the Constitution that more imperatively calls for attachment than any other it is the principle of free thought—not free thought for those who agree with us but freedom for the thought that we hate."[5]

The reason for the supremacy of freedom of expression in our constitutional hierarchy is that it is essential to the operation of the democratic process. The values served by a system of free expression—individual self-fulfillment, advancement of knowledge, participation in self-government, and promotion of consensus by nonviolent means—form the bedrock of our democratic existence.[6]

It follows that, as a general proposition, speech cannot be prohibited, curtailed or interfered with by government authorities. The state must seek to achieve its social goals by methods other than the suppression of expression. Were it otherwise, the government could readily outlaw or regulate expression that hampered the effectiveness of government operations, urged basic reform in our society, opposed government policies abroad, or cast aspersions on fellow citizens. Clearly the suppression of pornographic speech, on the ground that it causes or reflects discrimination against women, would run afoul of this basic mandate of the first amendment.

The Supreme Court has, of course, made some exceptions to the constitutional protection afforded freedom of expression. But it has never countenanced any degree of control that would create as gaping a hole in our system of freedom of expression as would the attempted suppression of "pornography."

The exception that bears the closest resemblance to the proposed ban on pornography is found in the law concerning obscenity. In its obscenity decisions, the Supreme Court has ruled that the government may prohibit the dissemination of materials "which taken as a whole, appeal to the prurient interest in sex, which portray sexual

5. United States v. Schwimmer, 279 U.S. 644, 654-55 (1929).

6. It is for this reason that Ku Klux Klansmen may assemble peacefully to burn their crosses, that adherents of religious cults may prosletyze at public airports, and that members of the American Nazi Party may march through a predominantly Jewish community. *See* Brandenburg v. Ohio, 395 U.S. 444 (1969) (per curiam) (overturning conviction for speech made at Ku Klux Klan rally); Int'l Soc'y for Krishna Consciousness v. Rochford, 585 F.2d 263 (7th Cir. 1978) (invalidating restrictions on religious solicitation at airport); Nat'l Socialist Party v. Village of Skokie, 432 U.S. 43 (1977) (per curiam); Smith v. Collin, 578 F.2d 1197 (1978), *cert. denied* 436 U.S. 953 (1978); Village of Skokie v. Nat'l Socialist Party, 69 Ill. 2d 605, 373 N.E.2d 21 (1978) (thwarting attempts to interfere with Nazi demonstrations). For a more extensive exposition of first amendment theory, see EMERSON, THE SYSTEM OF FREEDOM OF EXPRESSION, ch. I (1970).

conduct in a patently offensive way, and which, taken as a whole, do not have serious literary, artistic, political, or scientific value."[7] The theory upon which the Supreme Court permits the suppression of obscenity, as thus defined, is the legal fiction that "obscenity is not within the area of constitutionally protected speech," in other words, that obscenity is not covered by the first amendment at all.[8]

Since obscenity law thus rests upon a totally irrational premise—that obscene materials are not speech—it is difficult to make a rational projection as to how far the obscenity exception extends. As a practical matter, however, it is inconceivable that the Supreme Court would hold that the far broader area of "pornography" is simply outside the scope of first amendment protection. More importantly, as Professor MacKinnon points out, the social goals sought by the obscenity laws are essentially moral in nature; they do not extend to what Professor MacKinnon describes as a political process—discrimination against the female sex. The likelihood that the Supreme Court would permit the government to embark upon a venture to control speech in this area of politics, free from the restraints of the first amendment, is most remote.[9]

A second exception to the general rule that expression is entitled to the full protection of the first amendment occurs in the case of expression by, or directed to, children. Thus in *New York v. Ferber*,[10] the Supreme Court upheld a New York statute that prohibited the use of children in "a sexual performance" and in aid of that provision prohibited dissemination of materials depicting sexual performances by children. The validity of such a measure rests upon the proposition that children are not and cannot be full participants in the system of freedom of expression. That system presupposes a maturity of understanding and judgment that children do not possess. As a result, the Supreme Court has consistently applied different rules, in the area of expression and elsewhere, to children than to adults.[11] It explicitly did so in the *Ferber* case, making it clear that

7. Miller v. California, 413 U.S. 15, 24 (1973).

8. Roth v. United States, 354 U.S. 476, 485 (1957).

9. For a more complete critique of the obscenity doctrine, see EMERSON *supra* note 6, at ch. XIII (1970).

10. 458 U.S. 747 (1982).

11. Cases that have applied a different first amendment standard to children than to adults include Ginsberg v. New York, 390 U.S. 629 (1968) (state could prohibit sales to minors of sexually explicit materials that were "not obscene for adults") and Prince v. Massachusetts, 321 U.S. 158 (1944) (state could prohibit use of children to distribute literature on streets). Cases that have applied a different constitutional standard outside the first amendment context include Schall v. Martin, 468 U.S. —, 104 S. Ct. 2403 (1984) (state could confine juveniles accused of criminal offenses under circumstances

the result would have been different were the statute not "limited to works that *visually* depict sexual conduct by children."[12] Moreover, the Supreme Court has made it plain that the special rules pertaining to children cannot operate to infringe the first amendment rights of adults.[13]

Other exceptions to full protection under the first amendment are based on doctrines pertaining to libel, clear and present danger, and regulation of the time, place and manner of expression. None of these theories justifies the relaxation of the traditional guarantees of the first amendment in the case of pornographic materials. Libel laws deal exclusively with the protection of reputation against false statements and are narrowly circumscribed.[14] The clear and present danger exception is applicable only to advocacy that is "directed to inciting or producing imminent lawless action and is likely to incite or produce such action."[15] Pornography is not "directed" toward producing "imminent lawless action," nor is there persuasive evidence that it is "likely" to do so, except possibly in a most aberrational case. Time, place and manner regulations are sanctioned primarily in situations where exercise of the right to freedom of expression creates a physical conflict with the exercise of other rights, such as the use of a public street for a demonstration in a way that interferes with normal traffic.[16] In any event, anti-pornography

where it could not confine adults), and McKeiver v. Pennsylvania, 403 U.S. 528 (1971) (plurality opinion) (state was not obligated to provide for jury trial in juvenile proceedings). *See also* Carey v. Population Services Int'l, 431 U.S. 678, 693 n.15 (1977) (observing in dictum that lesser scrutiny is appropriate in evaluating state restrictions on distribution of contraceptives to minors as opposed to adults "both because of the State's greater latitude to regulate the conduct of children and because . . . the law has generally regarded minors as having a lesser capability for making important decisions.") (citations omitted).

12. 458 U.S. at 764 (emphasis in original).

13. *See* Butler v. Michigan, 352 U.S. 380, 383 (1957) (overturning obscenity statute that, by prohibiting distribution to general public of materials "tending to the corruption of the morals of youth," would have "reduce[d] the adult population of Michigan to reading only what is fit for children").

14. *See* New York Times v. Sullivan, 376 U.S. 254, 279-80 (1964) (public official cannot recover damages for defamatory falsehood without proving statement was made "with knowledge that it was false or with reckless disregard of whether it was false or not"); Gertz v. Robert Welch, Inc., 418 U.S. 323 (1974) (states cannot impose liability without fault for defamatory falsehoods injurious to individuals who are neither public officials nor public figures).

15. Brandenburg v. Ohio, 395 U.S. 444, 447 (1969) (per curiam).

16. *See, e.g.*, Clark v. Community for Creative Non-Violence, 468 U.S. —, 104 S.Ct. 3065 (1984) (government did not violate first amendment by prohibiting groups from camping overnight in park near White House); Heffron v. Int'l Soc'y for Krishna Consciousness, 452 U.S. 640 (1981) (state could limit to fixed locations solicitation of visitors to state fair); Kovacs v. Cooper, 336 U.S. 77 (1949) (city could regulate use of sound trucks); Cox v. New Hampshire, 312 U.S. 569 (1941) (upholding narrowly drawn

measures are not concerned with time, place and manner but with content. In all these areas, first amendment theory requires that the exceptions be confined to narrow and concrete categories that have the least inhibiting effect upon the system of freedom of expression. Creation of a vast new exception that would remove from the protection of the first amendment all sexually explicit expression that tended to promote the subordination of women would, to the contrary, leave the system a shadow of its former self.

The nearest analogy to what is proposed in the Indianapolis Ordinance would be an official enactment prohibiting all expression that promoted or encouraged racism in our society. The laws, constitutional and statutory, that attempt to eradicate racism in our national life have never been carried to such a point. They deal with discriminatory acts, not the expression of discriminatory beliefs, opinions, ideas or attitudes. And it is hard to believe that the Supreme Court would permit their extension into such areas. One is not likely to find the Supreme Court enjoining performance of the *Merchant of Venice* or banning William B. Shockley from expounding his views on the inferiority of the Negro race. It is true that in *Beauharnais v. Illinois*,[17] decided in 1952 by a five to four vote, the Supreme Court upheld a group libel law. At that time, however, first amendment doctrine was in its infancy and received scant attention in the majority opinion. In any event the major premise of *Beauharnais*—that libel laws are not within the coverage of the first amendment—was overruled in *New York Times v. Sullivan*.[18] While *Beauharnais* was cited in Justice White's opinion in the *Ferber* case, somewhat ambiguously, the prevailing view is that group libel laws cannot be reconciled with modern first amendment doctrine.[19] Nor, in practice, have such measures come to be relied upon as a solution to the problems of racism.

The Indianapolis Ordinance's banning of pornography not only

parade-permit statute). *Cf.* Police Department of Chicago v. Mosley, 408 U.S. 92 (1972) (invalidating ordinance that prohibited demonstrations on streets abutting schools during class hours because, by excluding labor picketing from its proscription, the ordinance discriminated among classes of protected expression based on their subject matter).

17. 343 U.S. 250 (1952).

18. 376 U.S. 254 (1964).

19. *See, e.g.*, Collin v. Smith, 578 F.2d 1197 (7th Cir. 1979), *aff'g* 447 F. Supp. 676 (N.D. Ill. 1978), *cert. denied* 439 U.S. 916 (1979). The opinion of the Seventh Circuit questioned the continuing precedential vitality of *Beauharnais* in holding that the town could not prohibit a Nazi demonstration merely because it would portray or promote racial or religious hatred. For reference to the legal literature, see Note, *Group Vilification Reconsidered*, 89 YALE L.J. 308, 308-309 (1979).

fails to fit within any of the exceptions to protection under the first amendment, but also relies heavily upon the injunctive powers of the courts. This is a crippling form of "prior restraint" that seeks to suppress expression in advance of its publication or dissemination. As the Supreme Court has repeatedly held, "prior restraints on speech and publication are the most serious and least tolerable infringement on first amendment rights."[20] Few prior restraints have been upheld by the Supreme Court, and none on the scale contemplated by the Indianapolis Ordinance.[21]

Finally, it should be noted that the attempt to avoid first amendment difficulties in the Indianapolis Ordinance by asserting that pornography "is a discriminatory practice" cannot succeed. This device, which has been hailed as a new approach to the problem, is no more than a play on words. Pornography is speech or expression, as those terms are used in first amendment theory, and like most expression has an impact upon attitudes and behavior. The question is whether, because of this impact, pornography can be proscribed. It does not help to eliminate the intermediate step in the legal analysis and declare that pornography "is" discrimination.

II. *The Dynamics of Suppressing Pornography*

Professor MacKinnon argues the case for the suppression of pornography at a high level of abstraction. One must also take into account the dynamics at work in implementing a program such as she contemplates. The hazards to our system of freedom of expression are manifest.

Most important is the inhibiting atmosphere inevitably created by subjecting a broad area of expression to governmental intervention.

20. Nebraska Press Ass'n v. Stuart, 427 U.S. 539, 559 (1976) (judge could not prohibit publication of confession of accused murderer until jury had been impaneled in his trial).

21. *Compare* New York Times v. United States, 403 U.S. 713 (1971) (per curiam) (government could not enjoin publication of Pentagon Papers); Joseph Burstyn, Inc. v. Wilson, 343 U.S. 495 (1952) (overturning statute that prohibited unlicensed exhibition of motion pictures and authorized denial of license for films found to be sacrilegious). and Near v. Minnesota, 283 U.S. 697 (1931) (invalidating state law providing for judicial abatement as public nuisance of "malicious, scandalous and defamatory" publications), *with* Times Film Corp. v. City of Chicago, 365 U.S. 43 (1961) (city could require that films be submitted prior to commercial exhibition to local officials who could censor those found obscene or in violation of other specified criteria) and Kingsley Books, Inc. v. Brown, 354 U.S. 436 (1957) (state could authorize local authorities to seek temporary *ex parte* orders against distribution of obscene materials as well as orders for seizure and destruction of materials determined to be obscene in judicial proceedings). For a discussion of the rationale underlying the prior restraint doctrine, see Emerson, *The Doctrine of Prior Restraint*, 20 LAW & CONTEMP. PROBS. 648 (1955).

Persons engaging in any form of communication touching on sexual matters face the prospect of being haled before a censorship board, involved in prolonged litigation, saddled with back-breaking legal fees, compelled to justify their exercise of first amendment rights to government officials, threatened with damage awards and subjected to other forms of "affirmative action" such as confiscation of earnings—all of this occurring at countless locations scattered across the country. It is true that the Indianapolis Ordinance does not provide for criminal penalties, apart from the possibility of criminal contempt. There is nothing in the legal theory underlying the Ordinance, however, that would preclude the censorship of sexual materials through the apparatus of police investigations, criminal prosecutions and prison sentences. One can hardly expect a system of freedom of expression to flourish under these conditions.

Moreover, there is a strong likelihood that the powers conferred by the Indianapolis Ordinance would be diverted to reactionary political ends. It is often difficult to separate the pornographic elements of a communication from other ingredients. It is entirely possible that the more powerful interests in our society, possessing the requisite funds, could utilize the machinery of government censorship of pornography to harass or silence unwanted points of view. One can readily imagine the Moral Majority or similar groups invoking anti-pornography laws against feminist authors who seek to make male domination "graphic" and "sexually explicit." Such a development has taken place in the operation of the libel laws; more and more, the right to sue for libel has provided the basis for litigation designed to weaken or eliminate criticism from less powerful political opponents.[22] Thus, censorship of pornography, far from being a liberating force, could become a tool with which to harass feminist or other progressive movements.

Along the same lines, the suppression of pornography through governmental intervention encourages the intolerance syndrome throughout a society. Civil liberties are, as is often said, indivisible. The legal doctrines, governmental machinery and attitudes that suppress speech in one area also promote suppression in other areas. The censorship of pornography thus gives comfort to the forces of

22. *See* Glasser, *The Punitive Libel Trials*, N.Y. Times, Dec. 10, 1984, at A23, col. 1. This commentator observes, for example, that the mayor of a Texas town had brought a libel suit against THE NATION magazine because of allegations of police abuse and voter intimidation in an article on the rights of farmworkers. "The suit was preposterous, but the Nation could not afford to defend itself," writes Glasser. "The mayor, knowing that, sued, clearly to suppress public criticism of his performance as a public official."

reaction and advances the cause of those who seek a closed society. The movement for gender equality has little to gain from such a climate of opinion.

One additional, overriding consideration must be faced: The elimination of pornography by governmental censorship is simply not workable, at least by any democratic process. The area of prohibition is so vast, the machinery of civil litigation so cumbersome, the hope of changing attitudes by government decree so quixotic, that nothing positive is likely to be accomplished. Rather, the results, in terms of selective enforcement, underground circulation of "violative materials," encouragement of organized crime, and the general discrediting of law enforcement, would be entirely negative. In the ensuing confusion, the original problem would remain unsolved.

III. *The Rejection of Traditional First Amendment Theory*

Professor MacKinnon, as I read her, rests her case not primarily on traditional first amendment theory but rather on an attack upon first amendment theory. Her position is that "[t]he theory of the first amendment under which most pornography is protected from governmental restriction proceeds from liberal assumptions which do not apply to the situation of women." Indeed, she goes beyond this and argues that the traditional approach is "worse than useless." She would, in other words, discard the first amendment, at least until it was modified to reflect "non-liberal" assumptions. Since there is no chance the Supreme Court is going to reject traditional first amendment theory, this seems to leave Professor MacKinnon without any remedy short of constitutional amendment — or revolution. In my judgment, Professor MacKinnon seriously overstates the case against traditional first amendment doctrine and thereby grossly underestimates, in fact neglects altogether, the role that the system of freedom of expression can play in dealing with the issue of pornography and gender equality.

Professor MacKinnon's critique of the "liberal assumptions" underlying first amendment theory rests upon four propositions. The first is that the first amendment "presumes the validity of the distinction between public and private," the former being "the sphere of social power" and the latter "the area of private right." She contends that this distinction "does not cut the same for women as for men" because the exercise of male power that results in the subordination of women, as in the case of pornography, often takes place in the home, and that women may therefore need a higher degree of governmental, or social, intervention in the "private" than in the "public" sphere.

The private-public distinction is not one between governmental controls of conduct inside or outside the home, but one between individual right and collective power. The making of this distinction is a basic problem in any society, liberal or otherwise. The first amendment, generally speaking, places speech within the realm of individual right and action within the realm of collective power. This does preclude governmental control of pornographic speech, but it also leaves open a vast area of governmental control over male domination in the form of action. And this control can be directed against conduct inside the home as well as outside. Legislation imposing penalties for spousal rape, now being enacted in a number of states, illustrates that no liberal public-private assumptions foreclose such governmental attempts to achieve equality between the sexes.[23]

Professor MacKinnon's second criticism of liberal first amendment theory deals with the assumption that freedom of expression "helps discover truth," promotes "consensus," facilitates "progress," and "frees the mind to fulfill itself." She argues that, although securing these values may justify freedom of expression "in a non-hierarchial society," the theory is not adequate "in a society of gender inequality." In such a society, she urges, "the speech of the powerful impresses its view upon the world," providing "the appearance of consent" but making "protest inaudible as well as rare."

There can be little doubt that, in any society, the more powerful forces will engage in a greater volume of speech, on a more pervasive scale, and with a deeper impact than the less powerful groups. A fully balanced equality of speech among all groups and individuals is probably unattainable, at least without a degree of governmental intervention that would destroy the freedom of the system. What the system does guarantee is that the unorthodox, minority, dissenting and submerged elements of the society have a constitutional right to express their views and endeavor to gain adherents. The system is not designed only for a "non-hierarchal society," assuming such a social order exists. It is designed precisely to give a

23. *See New Laws Recognizing Marital Rape as a Crime*, N.Y. Times, Dec. 29, 1984, at A5, col. 1 (observing that 26 states had, by the end of 1984, enacted laws allowing prosecution of husbands for raping their wives).

subordinated group, such as women, a way out of their "powerlessness" by some method other than force.

It should be added that Professor MacKinnon has surely overdrawn the picture in contending that, under the first amendment today, protest against the status of women is "inaudible as well as rare." Her own work, and that of the whole feminist movement, can scarcely be so described.

Professor MacKinnon's third criticism of traditional first amendment doctrine is that it fails to recognize the harm that can be caused by speech. She asserts that first amendment logic "has difficulty grasping harm that is not linearly caused in the 'John hit Mary' sense," and that first amendment doctrine assumes that "words and pictures can only be harmful if they produce harm in a form that is considered action." This is not correct; first amendment theory does recognize that speech may cause harm, as well as good, and it is quite capable of recognizing the kind of harm that Professor MacKinnon describes. The theory rests upon the proposition, however, that the values served by freedom of expression are so essential to a free society that speech requires special, near absolute, protection against government interference regardless of any harm that may be caused. It also rests upon the premise, as noted above, that the government possesses sufficient powers to deal with such harms through means other than the suppression of speech. Thus, again, a vast area is open for government measures to promote gender equality. But the superficially easy out—passing a law to prohibit speech—is not available under first amendment theory.

It is admittedly difficult to draw the line between speech and action in some situations. But obviously the whole concept of the first amendment—that speech is entitled to special protection—requires that it be done. Of course, in the overwhelming proportion of cases, including pornography, the classification of the conduct involved as speech is not open to question.

Professor MacKinnon's fourth criticism, which is closely related to the second, challenges the first amendment assumption that "socially, speech is free," and that the problem is to prevent the government from constraining it. In actuality, she contends, "whole segments of the population" are "systematically silenced *socially*, prior to government action." "For women," she concludes, "the urgent issue of freedom of speech is not primarily the avoidance of state intervention as such, but finding an affirmative means to get access to speech for those to whom it has been denied."

Insofar as the argument is that the speech of the most powerful forces in society "impresses its view upon the world," the answer is the same as above: Freedom of speech does not protect individuals or groups from being persuaded, even against their own interests, but it does guarantee that every individual or group has a right to try to persuade others. Granted the right exists, the question of actually obtaining access to the means of communication becomes a crucial one. There is nothing in the first amendment, however, that precludes "finding an affirmative means to get access" for the less powerful, and indeed the failure to do so is one of the major weaknesses in our system of freedom of expression.[24] But that does not sanction government intervention to restrict the free speech rights of others or to take any similar form of action that would undermine the system as a whole. Nor can it be said, as a factual matter, that those who have wished to speak out for women's rights have been denied access to do so.

Taking all these factors into consideration, it would seem that proponents of equality for women in our society have more to gain from participating in the traditional system of freedom of expression than from abandoning it in favor of a form of relief that would destroy it.

IV. *Conclusion*

Any attempt to deal with the problem of pornography through governmental suppression would involve a dangerous evisceration of the first amendment. The damage to our system of free expression would extend far beyond the area of pornography. Moreover, such an effort would almost certainly prove unworkable.

This does not mean that nothing can be done to achieve gender equality. One course of action is to utilize the system of freedom of expression, as Professor MacKinnon has so eloquently done, and thereby raise the American level of consciousness. Another is to expand the right of access to the media of communication through measures that utilize the opportunities afforded by cable television, satellites, video-cassette recorders and other advances in the technology of communication. A third is to mobilize non-governmental economic power through organization, picketing, demonstrations, boycotts and other forms of pressure. Surely opponents of pornog-

24. For a discussion of the use of the first amendment as an affirmative force to promote the system of freedom of expression, see Emerson, *The Affirmative Side of the First Amendment*, 15 Geo. L. Rev. 795 (1981).

raphy would receive sympathy and support from broad sections of the public in such endeavors. Ultimately, as Professor MacKinnon has emphasized, the issue is one of increasing the economic, political and social power of women. There are many ways to do so—through enactment of anti-discrimination laws, litigation to assure pay equity, ratification of the Equal Rights Amendment, and numerous other measures that do not impair the operation of the first amendment.

The difficulties in turning around centuries of male supremacy are manifest. But progress has been made and, one hopes, will continue.

[13]

Cultural Heterogeneity and Law: Pornography, Blasphemy, and the First Amendment

Robert C. Post†

Feminists have recently sought the regulation of pornography on the grounds that pornography injures women as a group. This feminist challenge raises a vital constitutional question about the kinds of values the first amendment should protect. Professor Post here considers that question in light of three alternative means by which a legal order might be structured for a society made up of heterogenous groups: (1) assimilationism, which seeks social uniformity by imposing on all individuals the values of a dominant cultural group; (2) pluralism, which nurtures social diversity by protecting the values of competing cultural groups; and (3) individualism, which favors the choices of individuals over the values of any cultural group. He identifies the differences and connections among these perspectives by comparing the English and American laws against blasphemy. That comparison reveals the profoundly individualist character of American first amendment doctrine. Professor Post argues that the feminist challenge against pornography is controversial because it represents a pluralist challenge to our first amendment individualism, and he concludes that the success of the feminist challenge depends on its proponents' ability to offer a convincing vision of the first amendment that is consistent with pluralist values.

Twenty-five years ago legal academics viewed the law of obscenity as the regulation of sex. Laws prohibiting obscenity were understood to stem from "traditional notions, rooted in this country's religious antecedents, of governmental responsibility for communal and individual 'decency' and 'morality.' "[1] They protected our common cultural "environment."[2] The constitutional issue posed by such laws, therefore, was whether the first amendment permitted expression to be suppressed for the purpose of preserving "the purity of the community and . . . the

---

† Professor of Law, Boalt Hall School of Law, University of California, Berkeley. A.B. 1969, Harvard College; J.D. 1977, Yale Law School; Ph.D. 1980, Harvard University. This essay is based upon a paper originally delivered at a conference on the first amendment sponsored by the Faculty of Laws at the University of Tel Aviv. It has since been much improved by the comments of many good friends, for which I am very grateful.

1. Henkin, *Morals and the Constitution: The Sin of Obscenity*, 63 COLUM. L. REV. 391, 391 (1963).

2. A. BICKEL, THE MORALITY OF CONSENT 74 (1975); *see* Paris Adult Theatre I v. Slaton, 413 U.S. 49, 58-61 (1973).

salvation and welfare of the 'consumer.' "[3]

During the 1980's, however, this view of obscenity changed, in large measure because of the remarkable work of Catharine MacKinnon[4] and Andrea Dworkin.[5] For MacKinnon and Dworkin the issue is neither decency nor community morality, but rather the oppression of women. They use the term "pornography" to signify their concern with the sexually explicit subordination of women, and not with mere prurience.[6] Pornography is for them "an institution of gender inequality," which not only causes discrete acts of sexual violence against individual women, but, more fundamentally, which hurts "individuals, not *as* individuals in a one-at-a-time sense, but as members of the group 'women.' "[7] Women as a group are harmed because "pornography constructs the social reality of gender," and hence in a deep sense all women are "defined in pornographic terms" as sexually unequal.[8] The efforts of MacKinnon and Dworkin have posed an important constitutional question for the 1980's, which is whether the first amendment will permit expression to be suppressed for the purpose of preventing this assault on the "status"[9] of women as a group.[10]

---

3. Henkin, *supra* note 1, at 395.

4. *See* C. MACKINNON, FEMINISM UNMODIFIED: DISCOURSES ON LIFE AND LAW (1987).

5. *See* A. DWORKIN, PORNOGRAPHY: MEN POSSESSING WOMEN (1981).

6. Dworkin, *Against the Male Flood: Censorship, Pornography, and Equality*, 8 HARV. WOMEN'S L.J. 1, 15-17 (1985).

7. C. MACKINNON, *supra* note 4, at 148, 156 (emphasis in original).

8. *Id.* at 166; *see also id.* at 161: "[P]ornography *constructs* women and sex, defines what 'woman' means and what sexuality is, in terms of each other" (emphasis in original). The emphasis on the social construction of gender helps to explain why MacKinnon and Dworkin include in their definition of pornography " 'the use of men, children or transsexuals in the place of women.' " *Id.* at 146 n.1. Because MacKinnon and Dworkin are chiefly concerned with the nature of the female social role, they are relatively indifferent as to the question of whether that role is filled by men or transsexuals. Of course to the extent that the female role comes characteristically to be filled by persons other than women, the claim that the role is in fact that of the female gender becomes problematic.

9. *Id.* at 178.

10. *See, e.g.*, American Booksellers Ass'n v. Hudnut, 771 F.2d 323, 328-32 (7th Cir. 1985), *summarily aff'd*, 106 S. Ct. 1172 (1986); Branit, *Reconciling Free Speech and Equality: What Justifies Censorship?*, 9 HARV. J.L. & PUB. POL'Y 429 (1986); Brest & Vandenberg, *Politics, Feminism, and the Constitution: The Anti-Pornography Movement in Minneapolis*, 39 STAN. L. REV. 607, 659-60 (1987); Bryden, *Between Two Constitutions: Feminism and Pornography*, 2 CONST. COMMENTARY 147, 152-53 (1985); Chemerinsky & McGeady, *Outlawing Pornography: What We Gain, What We Lose*, 12 HUM. RTS. 24 (No. 3, Spring 1985); Emerson, *Pornography and the First Amendment: A Reply to Professor MacKinnon*, 3 YALE L. & POL'Y REV. 130 (1984); Jacobs, *Patterns of Violence: A Feminist Perspective on the Regulation of Pornography*, 7 HARV. WOMEN'S L.J. 5, 41-45 (1984); Lynn, *'Civil Rights' Ordinances and the Attorney General's Commission: New Developments in Pornography Regulation*, 21 HARV. C.R.-C.L. L. REV. 27 (1986); Stone, *Anti-Pornography Legislation as Viewpoint-Discrimination*, 9 HARV. J.L. & PUB. POL'Y 461 (1986); Sunstein, *Pornography and the First Amendment*, 1986 DUKE L.J. 589, 591-92.

For a summary of recent developments in England, which have followed a similar course, see A. SIMPSON, PORNOGRAPHY & POLITICS: A LOOK BACK TO THE WILLIAMS COMMITTEE 72 (1983):

This Article is meant to propose a tentative framework to assist in the analysis of that question. It is a question that implicates many of the same issues as those raised by government attempts to regulate speech that vilifies particular minorities or ethnic cultures.[11] At the most general level, it is a question that involves the obligations of a legal order in a heterogeneous society comprised of diverse and competitive groups. In this Article I shall suggest three different ways of understanding these obligations. I shall then explore the historical and sociological underpinnings of these perspectives by examining the crime of blasphemy in England and America. Finally, I shall bring these perspectives to bear on the constitutional challenge posed by the contemporary feminist critique of pornography.

I

We can begin by noting the outlines of a rather crude triptych. Consider the options available to a legal order in a society consisting of heterogeneous groups. The law can place the authority of legal sanctions behind the cultural perspectives of a dominant group; or it can foster a regime in which diverse groups can escape from such domination and maintain their distinctive values; or it can ignore group values and perspectives altogether and recognize only the claims of individuals. I shall call these three options, respectively, assimilationism, pluralism, and individualism.[12] Most legal orders, and certainly our own, contain elements of each of these three options, and are, for example, individualist with respect to one issue, but assimilationist with respect to another.

Assimilationist law places the force of the state behind the cultural perspective of a particular, dominant group. If a society is relatively homogeneous, so that the values of this group are representative of the society as a whole, assimilationist law can be said to be expressive of common community norms. But if the society is heterogeneous, assimi-

At a theoretical level however it is clear that whereas the Williams Committee saw pornography primarily as a public nuisance problem, the harm flowing from it consisting in the offence it caused, many feminists do not accept this. Pornography is seen as a political problem in that it is a mechanism for securing a certain distribution of power in society, one in which women lose out and is in itself an act of violence; the slogan "pornography is violence against women" rejects the notion that the harm produced by pornography is to be sought in the consequences of pornography, but not in the material itself.

11. For two recent discussions of these issues, see D. DOWNS, NAZIS IN SKOKIE: FREEDOM, COMMUNITY, AND THE FIRST AMENDMENT (1985); Delgado, *Words that Wound: A Tort Action for Racial Insults, Epithets, and Name-Calling*, 17 HARV. C.R.-C.L. L. REV. 133 (1982).

12. These three options do not, of course, exhaust the field. For example, a legal order may found its laws upon neither group values nor individual claims, but upon instrumental reason. On the relationship between instrumental reason and constitutional rights, see Post, *Between Governance and Management: The History and Theory of the Public Forum*, 34 UCLA L. REV. 1713 (1987). The question of pornography, however, does not raise technological issues of this kind.

lationist law can instead be understood as an attempt, which may be more or less hegemonic in character, to extend the values of a dominant group to the larger society.[13] An example of an assimilationist law is the federal anti-bigamy statute, which was upheld in *Reynolds v. United States*[14] on the grounds, inter alia, that "[p]olygamy has always been odious among the northern and western nations of Europe."[15] Another example is the requirement that school children salute the flag, which was upheld in *Minersville School District v. Gobitis*[16] on the grounds that a state can enforce "the traditions of a people" and hence "create that continuity of a treasured common life which constitutes a civilization."[17]

In each of these examples law was used to support the values of a dominant culture, notwithstanding the dissenting values of marginal or subordinate groups. From the perspective of these latter groups, assimilationist law can often appear based in "cultural chauvinism, social hypocrisy, and disdain for diversity."[18] Assimilationist values, however, have deep roots in American history.[19] With respect to newly arrived immigrants, for example, our "most prevalent ideology" has been the concept of "Anglo-conformity," which "demanded the complete renunciation of the immigrant's ancestral culture in favor of the behavior and values of the Anglo-Saxon core group."[20] Assimilationist values in this country are probably best exemplified by the "Americanization" move-

13. For an example of the interplay between expressive and hegemonic functions of assimilationist law in the area of defamation, see Post, *The Social Foundations of Defamation Law: Reputation and the Constitution*, 74 CALIF. L. REV. 691, 702-03 (1986).

14. 98 U.S. 145 (1878).

15. *Id.* at 164; *see* H.L.A. HART, LAW, LIBERTY & MORALITY 39-43 (1963).

16. 310 U.S. 586 (1940).

17. *Id.* at 597. Three years later the requirement was struck down in West Virginia State Bd. of Educ. v. Barnette, 319 U.S. 624 (1943).

18. Karenga, *The Problematic Aspects of Pluralism: Ideological and Political Dimensions*, in PLURALISM, RACISM, AND PUBLIC POLICY: THE SEARCH FOR EQUALITY 226 (E. Clausen & J. Bermingham eds. 1981); *see* Gusfield, *On Legislating Morals: The Symbolic Process of Designating Deviance*, 56 CALIF. L. REV. 54, 59 (1968). Assimilationist law can be particularly cruel when applied to immutable traits like race. In the South before World War II, for example, defamation law enforced the values of the dominant white culture, making it defamatory to say that a Caucasian was black, but not permitting blacks to sue for defamation upon being labeled white. This result followed from the fact that defamation law understood itself to be reflecting "the intrinsic difference between whites and blacks," a difference inhering in the fact that, "from a social standpoint, the negro race is in mind and morals inferior to the Caucasian." Wolfe v. Georgia Ry. & Elec. Co., 2 Ga. App. 499, 505-06, 58 S.E. 899, 901-02 (1907). In such extreme circumstances, where the dominant culture imposes an immutable hierarchy of caste, it is almost a misnomer to call the law "assimilationist," since subordinate groups are given no option to join the dominant culture. They are instead required to submit to that culture's impositions.

19. *See, e.g.*, L. FRIEDMAN, TOTAL JUSTICE 111-20 (1987).

20. M. GORDON, ASSIMILATION IN AMERICAN LIFE: THE ROLE OF RACE, RELIGION, AND NATIONAL ORIGINS 89, 85 (1964); *see* W. NEWMAN, AMERICAN PLURALISM: A STUDY OF MINORITY GROUPS AND SOCIAL THEORY 53-62 (1973).

ment that flourished during the early years of the 20th century.[21]

Opposed to assimilationist values are those of pluralism, which embrace, rather than reject, group heterogeneity. The concept of pluralism is now in rather bad repute among many legal scholars, for it has come to be associated with a vision of politics as a "struggle among self-interested groups for scarce social resources" in which any concept of the "common good" is "incoherent, potentially totalitarian, or both."[22] But pluralism has a prior and deeper meaning, one in which the affirmative value of diversity is explicitly acknowledged and celebrated.[23] In 1909, for example, William James used the term in this sense in his Hibbert Lectures, entitled *A Pluralistic Universe.*[24] Fifteen years later James' literary executor, Horace Kallen, coined the term "cultural pluralism" to express the importance of "manyness, variety, differentiation," as opposed to what Kallen viewed as the dead uniformity of Americanization.[25] For Kallen, "[d]emocracy involves, not the elimination of differences, but the perfection and conservation of differences. It aims, through Union, not at uniformity, but at variety . . . . It involves a give and take between radically different types, and a mutual respect and mutual cooperation based on mutual understanding."[26]

---

21. M. GORDON, *supra* note 20, at 98-101. For a brief overview of the "Americanization" movement, see Gleason, *American Identity and Americanization*, in W. PETERSEN, M. NOVAK, & P. GLEASON, CONCEPTS OF ETHNICITY 79-96 (1982).

22. Sunstein, *Interest Groups in American Public Law*, 38 STAN. L. REV. 29, 32 (1985); *see, e.g.*, W. ESKRIDGE & P. FRICKEY, CASES AND MATERIALS ON LEGISLATION 46-65 (1988); Farber & Frickey, *The Jurisprudence of Public Choice*, 65 TEX. L. REV. 873, 875 (1987).

23. *See* Bernstein, *The Varieties of Pluralism*, 5 CURRENT ISSUES EDUC. 1, 14-16 (1985). For the history of the term "pluralism," see Breitling, *The Concept of Pluralism*, in THREE FACES OF PLURALISM: POLITICAL, ETHNIC AND RELIGIOUS 1-19 (S. Ehrlich & G. Wootton eds. 1980). For illustrative examples of the variant usages of the term, see C. LARMORE, PATTERNS OF MORAL COMPLEXITY 23 (1987); D. NICHOLLS, THREE VARIETIES OF PLURALISM (1974); RELIGIOUS PLURALISM (L. Rouner ed. 1984); C. YOUNG, THE POLITICS OF CULTURAL PLURALISM (1976); Haug, *Social and Cultural Pluralism as a Concept in Social System Analysis*, 73 AM. J. SOC. 294 (1967).

24. W. JAMES, ESSAYS IN RADICAL EMPIRICISM AND A PLURALISTIC UNIVERSE (1971). James noted that "[t]he pluralistic world is thus more like a federal republic than like an empire or a kingdom." *Id.* at 274. Harold Laski would later cite this observation as a part of his attempt to define a "pluralist," as distinct from a "monist," theory of state sovereignty. H. LASKI, STUDIES IN THE PROBLEM OF SOVEREIGNTY 10, 23-25 (1917).

25. H. KALLEN, CULTURE AND DEMOCRACY 43 (1924); *see* Gleason, *supra* note 21, at 96-97.

26. *Id.* at 61. For further exposition of Kallen's thought, see H. KALLEN, CULTURAL PLURALISM AND THE AMERICAN IDEA (1956); Ratner, *Horace M. Kallen and Cultural Pluralism*, in THE LEGACY OF HORACE M. KALLEN (M. Konvitz ed. 1987). Kallen's work has proved deeply influential for American educators. *See, e.g.*, D. GOLLNICK & P. CHINN, MULTICULTURAL EDUCATION IN A PLURALISTIC SOCIETY 22-30 (1986); Castaneda, *Persisting Ideological Issues of Assimilation in America: Implications for Assessment Practices in Psychology and Education*, in CULTURAL PLURALISM 60-62 (E. Epps ed. 1974); Glazer, *Cultural Pluralism: The Social Aspect*, in PLURALISM IN A DEMOCRATIC SOCIETY 3-21 (M. Tumin & W. Plotch eds. 1977); Kopan, *Melting Pot: Myth or Reality?*, in CULTURAL PLURALISM 49-54 (E. Epps ed. 1974).

Sociologists and educators have introduced numerous variations into the concept of cultural

The values of pluralism, like those of assimilationism, also have deep roots in American history. They reach back beyond Walt Whitman's chants in praise of the United States as "the modern composite nation," the "Nation of many nations,"[27] to the very structure of our federalism, which seeks to the extent possible to preserve the heterogeneity inherent in local and regional differentiation.[28]

If assimilationist law attempts to unify society around the cultural values of a single dominant group, pluralist law attempts to create ground rules by which diverse and potentially competitive groups can retain their distinct identities and yet continue to coexist.[29] These ground rules can range from the requirement of state neutrality respecting conflicting religions, to the enforcement of norms of mutual respect, as exemplified by the group libel statute upheld in *Beauharnais v. Illinois.*[30] That statute imposed criminal penalties on any expression that exposed "citizens of any race, color, creed or religion to contempt, derision, or obloquy."[31] In *Beauharnais* the Court stressed that the need to foster "the manifold adjustments required for free, ordered life in a metropolitan, polyglot community" justified the legal provision of "[s]uch group-protection on behalf of the individual."[32]

Pluralist law rests on two premises: that diversity is to be safe-

---

pluralism. Michael Novak, for example, lists five different possible meanings for the concept. Novak, *Cultural Pluralism for Individuals: A Social Vision,* in PLURALISM IN A DEMOCRATIC SOCIETY, *supra* at 34-36; *see* W. NEWMAN, *supra* note 20, at 63-82. Cultural pluralism is most often contrasted with the notion of "amalgamation," *id.* at 63, or, as it is commonly called, the idea of the "melting pot." M. GORDON, *supra* note 20, at 115-31. The concept of amalgamation is that diverse cultural groups fuse and combine to form a new and distinctive cultural entity. From the point of view of the legal order, however, a given law would either reflect the perspective of this new entity, in which case the law would be assimilationist, or the law would view the new entity as simply one of a number of competing cultural groups, in which case the law would be pluralist.

27. W. WHITMAN, LEAVES OF GRASS AND SELECTED PROSE 37, 518 (1950). Whitman also noted, however, that "the fear of conflicting and irreconcilable interiors, and the lack of a common skeleton, knitting all close, continually haunts me." *Id.* at 466. His fear, one might say, is realized in the conception of value-free pluralism advanced by contemporary political scientists and legal academics. *See supra* note 22.

28. Harold Laski, for example, viewed American federalism as exemplifying pluralist values by effecting a "wide distribution of . . . sovereign powers" so as to protect a "variety of . . . group life." H. LASKI, *supra* note 24, at 275; *see* Rapaczynski, *From Sovereignty to Process: The Jurisprudence of Federalism after Garcia,* 1985 SUP. CT. REV. 341, 404-05. Kallen was aware of the analogy between his views and the principles of federalism, noting that "in effect the United States are in the process of becoming a federal state not merely as a union of geographical and administrative unities, but also as a cooperation of cultural diversities, as a federation or commonwealth of national culture." H. KALLEN, *supra* note 25, at 116.

29. Pluralism has been defined as aspiring toward "a plurality of cultures with their members seeking to live together in amity and mutual understanding and mutual cooperation, but maintaining separate cultures." R. HAVIGHURST, ANTHROPOLOGY AND CULTURAL PLURALISM: THREE CASE STUDIES, AUSTRALIA, NEW ZEALAND AND USA 3 (1974).

30. 343 U.S. 250 (1952).

31. *Id.* at 251 (quoting ILL. REV. STAT. ch. 38, para. 471 (1949) (repealed 1961)).

32. *Id.* at 259, 262.

guarded, and that diversity inheres in the various perspectives of differing groups. "In a multi-ethnic society," the historian John Higham has written, "the assimilationist stresses a unifying ideology, whereas the pluralist guards distinctive memory."[33] The pluralist guards his distinctive memory because for him "[i]ndividuals can realize themselves, and become whole, only through the group that nourishes their being."[34] Hence pluralism "stresses the rights of the ethnic group over the rights of the individual."[35] As Justice Black dryly noted in his dissent in *Beauharnais,* the Court had in effect held that the value of providing group protection was more important than that of safeguarding an "individual's choice" to speak.[36]

This focus on group rights, which is intrinsic to pluralist law, has always been controversial in America because it appears "to predetermine the individual's fate by his ethnic group membership."[37] Americans have traditionally attached great importance to the image of the independent individual capable of transcending his or her particular social or ethnic background; "we strongly assert the value of our self-reliance and autonomy."[38] Thus if pluralist law protects the ability of groups to maintain their distinctive identities, law based on the value of individualism focuses instead on the protection of individuals vis-á-vis groups. If pluralism celebrates the diversity of cultures, individualism acclaims instead the diversity of persons.

The distinction between the two forms of law is illustrated by the case of *Wisconsin v. Yoder,*[39] where the Supreme Court held that the free exercise clause of the first amendment prohibited the State of Wisconsin from requiring that Amish children attend public or private schools until the age of sixteen.[40] In his opinion for the Court, Chief Justice Burger noted that such a requirement would pose the "very real threat of undermining the Amish community and religious practice as they exist today," and would require the Amish to "either abandon belief and be assimi-

33. Higham, *Integration vs. Pluralism: Another American Dilemma,* THE CENTER MAGAZINE, July/Aug. 1974, at 68.

34. *Id.; see also* Garet, *Communality and Existence: The Rights of Groups,* 56 S. CAL. L. REV. 1001, 1065-75 (1983).

35. Banks, *Cultural Pluralism: Implications for Curriculum Reform,* in PLURALISM IN A DEMOCRATIC SOCIETY, *supra* note 26, at 228.

36. 343 U.S. at 270 (Black, J., dissenting).

37. M. GORDON, *supra* note 20, at 150; *see also* I. BERKSON, THEORIES OF AMERICANIZATION: A CRITICAL STUDY, WITH SPECIAL REFERENCE TO THE JEWISH GROUP 81-93 (1920).

38. R. BELLAH, R. MADSEN, W. SULLIVAN, A. SWIDLER, S. TIPTON, HABITS OF THE HEART: INDIVIDUALISM AND COMMITMENT IN AMERICAN LIFE 151 (1985); *see also* D. RIESMAN, THE LONELY CROWD 240-60 (1961).

39. 406 U.S. 205 (1972).

40. *Id.* at 207. The Amish refused to permit their children to attend school after they had completed the eighth grade. *Id.*

lated into society at large, or . . . to migrate to some other and more tolerant region."[41] Burger thus construed the first amendment as protecting the identity of the Amish community and as shielding that community from forced assimilation into the dominant culture.

Justice Douglas argued in dissent, however, that the Constitution safeguarded instead the rights of individual Amish children to choose whether or not to become part of the Amish community. Douglas viewed religion as "an individual experience," and hence interpreted the first amendment as guaranteeing the rights of children "to break from the Amish tradition."[42]

> It is the future of the student, not the future of the parents, that is imperiled by today's decision. If a parent keeps his child out of school beyond the grade school, then the child will be forever barred from entry into the new and amazing world of diversity that we have today. The child may decide that that is the preferred course, or he may rebel. It is the student's judgment, not his parents', that is essential if we are to give full meaning to what we have said about the Bill of Rights and of the right of students to be masters of their own destiny.[43]

For Burger the "amazing world of diversity" to be protected inhered in the continuing traditions of the Amish community; for Douglas that diversity was constituted instead by the decisions of individuals to embrace or reject those traditions. Burger's opinion rests on the values of pluralism; Douglas' on the values of individualism.[44]

The contrast between individualism and assimilationism can appear equally stark. The latter upholds the cultural values of the dominant group; the former protects the rights of individuals to dissent from those values. In *Gobitis* the Supreme Court supported the values of assimilationism by upholding the right of a majority to require dissenters to swear allegiance to the flag, and to the cultural perspective for which it stood.[45] But three years later the Court dramatically reversed itself, and in *West Virginia State Board of Education v. Barnette*[46] issued the classic defense of "intellectual individualism": "If there is any fixed star in our

41. *Id.* at 218.

42. *Id.* at 243-45 (Douglas, J., dissenting).

43. *Id.* at 245.

44. Of course there are many situations where the values of individualism and pluralism do not conflict. This was the case, for example, in the years immediately following Brown v. Board of Education, 347 U.S. 483 (1954), when the goal of desegregated education was consistent with both individualist and pluralist values. In later years, however, the question of affirmative action has separated those who view the antidiscrimination principle as grounded in the protection of individuals, from those who view it as founded in the protection of groups. *Compare, e.g.*, Wygant v. Jackson Bd. of Educ., 106 S. Ct. 1842, 1859 n.8 (1986) (Opinion of Powell, J.) *with id.* at 1860 (Marshall, J., dissenting).

45. Minersville School Dist. v. Gobitis, 310 U.S. 586 (1940). *See supra* text accompanying notes 16-17.

46. 319 U.S. 624 (1943).

constitutional constellation, it is that no official, high or petty, can prescribe what shall be orthodox in politics, nationalism, religion, or other matters of opinion . . . ."[47] *Barnette* rested squarely on the individual's "right to differ as to things that touch the heart of the existing order,"[48] a right that seems deeply incompatible with assimilationist law.

We are thus in a position to draw rough distinctions between three different kinds of law: assimilationist, pluralist, and individualist. Each postulates a different kind of relationship between cultural heterogeneity and the legal order. Assimilationist law strives toward social uniformity by imposing the values of a dominant cultural group; pluralist law safeguards diversity by enabling competing groups to maintain their distinct perspectives; individualist law rejects group values altogether in favor of the autonomous choices of individuals.[49]

It is tempting to view these three kinds of law as sharply distinct and mutually exclusive. But they are not. There are in fact subtle and fascinating connections between them. In the next section I shall explore these connections using the example of the crime of blasphemy, which in both England and America has been one legal response to the presence of religious diversity. By examining the complex interrelationships among individualist, pluralist, and assimilationist law, I hope to offer a theoretical structure that will assist in the analysis of the feminist critique of pornography.

II

In England, blasphemy was a common law crime. It was one of the four branches of criminal libel, the other three being obscenity, sedition, and defamation.[50] All four branches of libel sought to ensure that speech did not violate established norms of respect and propriety. The particular province of blasphemy was to prevent disrespect toward God, which according to Blackstone could be manifested "by denying his being or providence; or by contumelious reproaches of our Saviour Christ."[51]

---

47. *Id.* at 641-42.

48. *Id.*

49. Although these three alternatives are by no means exhaustive, see *supra* note 12, they do reflect a certain internal logic with respect to law that flows from the cultural values of its surrounding society. Pluralist law rests on the twin premises that diversity is valuable and that the value of diversity inheres in group, rather than individual, perspectives. Eliminate the first premise and law will become assimilationist; eliminate the second and law will become individualist.

50. *See* Spencer, *Criminal Libel—A Skeleton in the Cupboard (1)*, 1977 CRIM. L. REV. 383. English law sometimes recognizes a technical distinction between the crime of blasphemy, which is oral, and the crime of blasphemous libel, which is written. Nothing turns on this distinction, however, and I shall ignore it in this Article.

51. 4 BLACKSTONE, COMMENTARIES ON THE LAWS OF ENGLAND 59 (1769). Benjamin Norton Defoe defined blasphemy as "vile or opprobrious Language, tending to the Dishonour of God." B. DEFOE, A COMPLEAT ENGLISH DICTIONARY n.p. (1735). Samuel Johnson defined it as

A

Although blasphemy and obscenity originally shared a common concern with regulating the profane,[52] blasphemy was in its early years most closely allied to sedition, since attacks on God and religion were viewed as equivalent to attacks on the social order.[53] The classic statement in this regard was delivered by Sir Matthew Hale in *Taylor's Case*,[54] in which the defendant was accused of "uttering . . . divers blasphemous expressions, horrible to hear, (viz) that Jesus Christ was a bastard, a whoremaster, religion was a cheat; and that he neither feared God, the devil, or man."[55] Hale ruled

> that such kind of wicked blasphemous words were not only an offence to God and religion, but a crime against the laws, State and Government, and therefore punishable . . . . For to say, religion is a cheat, is to dissolve all those obligations whereby the civil societies are preserved, and that Christianity is parcel of the laws of England; and therefore to reproach the Christian religion is to speak in subversion of the law.[56]

Underlying *Taylor's Case* is "the plain principle that the public importance of the Christian religion is so great that no one is allowed to deny its truth."[57] Proceeding on this principle, the law of blasphemy was successfully used to prosecute individuals for publishing such works as Thomas Paine's *Age of Reason*,[58] Shelley's poem "Queen Mab,"[59] and the popular Discourses of an early Deist, a minister and Fellow of Sydney Sussex College at Cambridge, which urged that the miracles reported in the New Testament be interpreted allegorically, rather than literally.[60] In 1841 the English Commissioners on Criminal Law could report "that the common law of England punishes as an offence any general denial of

---

"an offering of some indignity unto God himself." S. JOHNSON, A DICTIONARY OF THE ENGLISH LANGUAGE n.p. (1756).

52. L. LEVY, TREASON AGAINST GOD: A HISTORY OF THE OFFENSE OF BLASPHEMY 306-07 (1981). For English observers, "the line between blasphemy and obscenity was at times thin." Note, *Blasphemy*, 70 COLUM. L. REV. 694, 701 (1970); *see also* F. SCHAUER, THE LAW OF OBSCENITY 1-18 (1976); Comment, *Blasphemy and Obscenity*, 5 BRIT. J.L. & SOC'Y. 89 (1978).

53. *See* THE LAW COMMISSION, WORKING PAPER NO. 79: OFFENCES AGAINST RELIGION AND PUBLIC WORSHIP 5-6 (1981) [hereinafter WORKING PAPER NO. 79]; L. LEVY, *supra* note 52, at 303-06; G. NOKES, A HISTORY OF THE CRIME OF BLASPHEMY 67 (1928).

54. 86 Eng. Rep. 189, 1 Vent. 293 (K.B. 1676).

55. *Id.*

56. *Id.* For discussions of *Taylor's Case*, see H. BONNER, PENALTIES UPON OPINION 28-32 (1934); L. LEVY, *supra* note 52, at 312-14; G. NOKES, *supra* note 53, at 46-61; Kenny, *The Evolution of the Law of Blasphemy*, 1 CAMBRIDGE L.J. 127, 129-31 (1922); Leigh, *Not To Judge But to Save: The Development of the Law of Blasphemy*, 8 CAMBRIAN L. REV. 56, 58-63 (1977).

57. 2 J. STEPHEN, A HISTORY OF THE CRIMINAL LAW OF ENGLAND 475 (1883).

58. *Id.* at 471-73; Rex v. Williams, 26 Howell's St. Tr. 653 (K.B. 1797); Rex v. Carlile (Richard), 1 St. Tr. N.S. 1387 (1819); *cf.* Rex v. Carlile (Mary), 1 St. Tr. N.S. 1033 (1921).

59. Regina v. Moxon, 4 St. Tr. N.S. 693 (1841).

60. Rex v. Woolston, 94 Eng. Rep. 112, 1 Barn. K.B. 162 (1729); *see* H. BONNER, *supra* note 56, at 34-35.

the truth of Christianity, without reference to the language or temper in which such denial is conveyed."[61]

Until quite recently, then, the crime of blasphemy was a paradigmatic example of assimilationist law. Christians were the dominant group in England, and blasphemy made Christian values "parcel of the laws" in England. Christian values rested on the asserted truth of certain theological and doctrinal propositions, and blasphemy prohibited those propositions from being controverted. As the Court of King's Bench was reported to have succinctly stated in *Rex v. Woolston:* "the Christian religion is established in this kingdom; and therefore [it] would not allow any books to be writ, which should tend to alter that establishment."[62] Not only did the law of blasphemy offer no protection to subordinate or minority religions,[63] but it seemed likely that even non-Anglican Christian denominations were "protected only to the extent that their fundamental beliefs [were] held in common with the established Church."[64]

About the middle of the 19th century, however, the crime of blasphemy began to change. One can detect the transformation in Lord Denman's charge to the jury in *Regina v. Hetherington:*

> [U]pon the question whether it is blasphemous or not I [make] this general observation . . . namely, that the question is not altogether a matter of opinion, but that it must be, in a great degree, a question as to the tone, and style, and spirit, in which such inquiries are conducted. Because, a difference of opinion may subsist, not only between different sects of Christians, but also with regard to the great doctrines of Christianity itself; and . . . even discussions upon that subject may be by no means a matter of criminal prosecution, but, if they be carried on in a sober and temperate and decent style, even those discussions may be tolerated, and may take place without criminality attaching to them; but that, if the tone and spirit is that of offence, and insult, and ridicule, which leaves the judgment really not free to act, and, therefore, cannot be truly called an appeal to the judgment, but an appeal to the wild and improper feelings of the human mind, more particularly in the younger part of the community, in that case the jury will hardly feel it possible to say that such opinions, so expressed, do not deserve the character [of blasphemy] affixed to them in this indictment.[65]

61. COMMISSIONERS ON CRIMINAL LAW, SIXTH REPORT 83 (1841); *see also* G. NOKES, *supra* note 53, at 70.

62. *Woolston,* 94 Eng. Rep. at 113, 1 Barn. K.B. at 163. As recently as 1867 the House of Lords held unenforceable a contract to rent a hall for giving lectures on "The Bible shewn to be no more Inspired than any other Book," on the grounds that the contract was for the criminal purpose of propagating blasphemy. Cowan v. Milbourn, 2 L.R.- Ex. 230, 235 (1867), *overruled,* Bowman v. Secular Society, Ltd., [1917] App. Cas. 406.

63. Regina v. Gathercole, 116 Eng. Rep. 1140, 1157, 2 Lewin 237, 254 (1838).

64. WORKING PAPER NO. 79, *supra* note 53, at 82. This parochialism remains true even of contemporary English blasphemy law. *Id.*

65. 4 St. Tr. N.S. 563, 590-91 (1841).

For Lord Denman the crime of blasphemy did not inhere so much in the substance of what was said, as in the style in which it was said. It was not blasphemous to deny "the great doctrines of Christianity," so long as that denial were advanced "in a sober and temperate and decent style." But if Christianity were attacked in a "tone and spirit . . . of offence, and insult, and ridicule," then the attack was blasphemous. Attacks that were not civil were irrational; they did not leave "the judgment really . . . free to act," and were instead appeals "to the wild and improper feelings of the human mind."

In 1883 Lord Coleridge made explicit this altered view of blasphemy. Whatever the "old cases" may have said, he explained, "the mere denial of the truth of Christianity is not enough to constitute the offence of blasphemy."[66] To be blasphemous, expression must instead be "calculated and intended to insult the feelings and the deepest religious convictions of the great majority of the persons amongst whom we live."[67] The point of blasphemy was thus to prevent "outrages to the general feeling of propriety among the persons amongst whom we live,"[68] and hence "if the decencies of controversy are observed, even the fundamentals of religion may be attacked without the writer being guilty of blasphemy."[69]

Today the crime of blasphemy in England is essentially a restatement of Coleridge's view of the law.[70] It is a view that has been attacked as resting on a highly vulnerable distinction between style and substance.[71] The concept of assimilationist law, however, is helpful in casting Coleridge's view in a more sympathetic light, for the concept invites us to focus on the nature of the social group that Coleridge's view was designed to protect. Coleridge had in effect altered the group whose val-

---

66. Regina v. Ramsay and Foote, 15 Cox C.C. 231, 236 (1883).

67. Regina v. Bradlaugh, 15 Cox C.C. 217, 230 (1883).

68. *Id.* at 231.

69. *Ramsay and Foote*, 15 Cox C.C. at 238.

70. WORKING PAPER NO. 79, *supra* note 53, at 14.

71. Peter Jones, for example, has perceptively observed that "Coleridge intended his ruling in 1883 to imply" the distinction "between matter and manner." Jones, *Blasphemy, Offensiveness and Law*, 10 BRIT. J. POL. SCI. 129, 141-42 (1980).

> The intention behind the distinction is plain. Granted that it is possible to distinguish manner from matter, a law restricting only forms of expression need not prevent the assertion of any substantive point of view. The usual conflict between freedom of opinion and prevention of offense is therefore largely avoided. . . .
>
> . . . .
>
> The failing of the matter-manner distinction is that it supposes that statements are capable of more or less offensive formulations which are nevertheless identical in meaning. The manner of an assertion is treated as though it were so much verbal wrapping paper whose features had no bearing upon the content of the parcel. In certain cases this assumption may not be unjustified. . . . More often, however, manner and matter are so integrally related that it is impossible to distinguish the offensive manner from the offensive matter of a statement.

Id. at 142-43.

ues were to be implemented by blasphemy law. That group was no longer Christians holding allegiance to certain theological and doctrinal propositions; it was instead Christians holding allegiance to "the decencies of controversy." The members of this latter group, whom Coleridge explicitly understood to comprise "the great majority of the persons amongst whom we live," were not offended by the mere fact of religious difference,[72] but were outraged when Christianity was not treated with the respect that they felt it deserved. They understood this respect to be coincident with the requirements of reason: blasphemy would permit attacks on Christianity if cast in the form of "an appeal to the judgment," but it would penalize such attacks if they constituted instead "an appeal to the wild and improper feelings of the human mind" that did not leave "the judgment really . . . free to act." [73]

To the modern eye, it is clear that the concept of reason underlying the reformulation of blasphemy law is not universal, but rather the product of the mores of a particular culture. It is perhaps more generally true that in matters of deep human meaning, like religion (or sex), what counts as reason, as an appeal to the judgment rather than to "the wild and improper feelings of the human mind," is ultimately determined by the proprieties of discourse.[74] That is why the purported style/substance distinction proposed by Coleridge cannot withstand close logical scrutiny: in the end the distinction rests not on logic at all, but instead on a specific cultural sense of "the decencies of controversy."

The particular group whose values these "decencies" were meant to reflect is in retrospect apparent enough. In 1930, during parliamentary debates on a proposed law to abolish the common law crime of blas-

---

72. Writing in 1883, James Fitzjames Stephen could observe:

> [T]he present generation is the first in which an avowed open denial of the fundamental doctrines of the Christian religion has been made by any considerable number of serious and respectable people. For many centuries the maintenance, or even the expression of opinions, suspected or supposed to involve a denial of the truth of religion in general, was regarded in the same kind of light as high treason in the temporal order of things. . . . A man who did not believe in Christ or God put himself out of the pale of human society; and a man who on important subjects thought differently from the Church, was on the high road to disbelief in Christ and in God, for belief in each depended ultimately upon belief in the testimony of the Church. In our own days the physical sanctions of the law are so much more frequently appealed to, and are so much more effective than its moral sanctions, that it is only by an effort that we can understand the horror with which our ancestors regarded a man who held opinions which, in their view, were inconsistent with a real hearty assent to the principles on which they believed all human society, whether spiritual or temporal, to repose.

J. STEPHEN, *supra* note 57, at 438.

73. *See supra* text accompanying note 65.

74. This would not be true of instrumental reason, the success or failure of which is determined, in a more or less universal fashion, by its ability to predict and control nature. For a succinct discussion of the distinction between instrumental reason and "communicative action," see J. HABERMAS, TOWARD A RATIONAL SOCIETY 91-94 (J. Shapiro trans. 1970). For a fuller discussion, see J. HABERMAS, KNOWLEDGE AND HUMAN INTERESTS (J. Shapiro trans. 1971).

phemy,[75] it was repeatedly observed that "[w]hat it really comes to is that, where opinions are strongly held by an educated man, those opinions will be expressed in a way which the law cannot touch, while those expressed by an uneducated man, simply because he is uneducated, will come under the penalties of the law."[76] After Coleridge, then, the crime of blasphemy reflected the values of educated and "respectable"[77] Christians.[78] Because the crime imposed these values on society as a whole, it remained deeply assimilationist in character and aspiration.

There were no successful prosecutions for blasphemy in England between the years 1922 and 1977.[79] In the 1970's, however, interest arose in the potential use of blasphemy to check cultural manifestations that were viewed as objectionable.[80] Ultimately this interest came to focus on a magazine entitled *Gay News,* which in 1976 published a poem by Professor James Kirkup entitled "The Love that Dares to Speak its Name." The poem described in explicit detail acts of sodomy and fellatio with the body of Christ immediately after his death, and ascribed to Christ during his lifetime promiscuous homosexual practices with the Apostles and with other men.[81] The poem was accompanied by a drawing of the Crucifixion featuring the body of Christ in the embrace of a Roman centurion.[82] In 1977 Mrs. Mary Whitehouse, an English moral crusader,[83] brought a private prosecution for blasphemy against Gay

75. The law was never passed. *See* WORKING PAPER NO. 79, *supra* note 53, at 29.

76. 234 PARL. DEB., H.C. (5th Ser.) 535 (1930) (remarks of Mr. Kingsley Griffith); *see also id.* at 499:

> We have writers to-day who can commit the offence of blasphemy with impunity, if the offence of blasphemy is an attack on the Christian religion. There are men like Sir Arthur Keith, Mr. H. G. Wells, Mr. Bertrand Russell, Mr. Aldous Huxley and others who are able to attack the Christian religion without any danger whatever of their being prosecuted, while poor men, expressing the same point of view more bluntly and crudely, expose themselves to fine and imprisonment. That is a thoroughly unsatisfactory state of the law. After all, if one concedes the right to attack religion . . . one has to concede to the people who care to do this thing the right to choose their style of doing it. Different styles are needed for different circumstances and different audiences. I do not suppose the kind of style that would go down in a select circle in the West End would be effective amongst the democracy of the East End.

(remarks of Mr. Thurtle); *see also id.* at 558 (remarks of Mr. Lansbury).

77. *Id.* at 565 (remarks of Mr. Scrymgeour).

78. The crime continued to protect the sensibilities of Christians, but not of Jews or Moslems, or other religious minorities. Outrageous assaults on Judaism or Islam were not blasphemous. *See supra* note 64.

79. WORKING PAPER NO. 79, *supra* note 53, at 17.

80. *Id.* at 17-18; *see* Jones, *supra* note 71, at 129.

81. Regina v. Lemon, 1979 App. Cas. 617, 632 (per Lord Diplock).

82. *Id.* at 660 (per Lord Scarman).

83. For a biographical study of Mary Whitehouse, who had previously been involved in anti-obscenity campaigns, see M. TRACEY & D. MORRISON, WHITEHOUSE (1979). Whitehouse stated that "When the [Kirkup] poem arrived on my desk, and I read it, I had one overwhelming feeling that this was the recrucifixion of Christ with 20th century weapons—with words, with obscenities, and if I sat there and did nothing I would be a traitor. It was just as simple as that." Anderson &

News Ltd., the publisher of *Gay News,* and against Denis Lemon, its editor. Lemon was convicted and sentenced to nine months imprisonment (suspended for eighteen months) and fined £ 500, and Gay News Ltd. was fined £ 1000.[84]

The case attracted widespread notice,[85] and eventually wound its way up to the House of Lords.[86] The actual grounds of the appeal turned on the rather technical question of whether the prosecution ought to have demonstrated a specific intent to blaspheme on the part of the defendants. But the real underlying issue was whether the crime of blasphemy in 1979 in England was an embarrassment that should be discouraged.[87] In 1979 the Law Lords, by a 3-2 vote, upheld the conviction.[88] The decisive and to American eyes most compelling opinion was by Lord Scarman. What makes his opinion particularly pertinent for this discussion, however, is its fascinating attempt to envision a law of blasphemy based on pluralist, rather than assimilationist, foundations.

Scarman was willing to assume that Lemon could establish "that he had no intention to shock Christian believers" and had published "the poem not to offend Christians but to comfort practising homosexuals by encouraging them to feel that there was room for them in the Christian religion."[89] But Scarman deemed Lemon's intent to be irrelevant, because the whole point of blasphemy law was "to protect religious feeling from outrage and insult."[90] Hence "[t]he character of the words pub-

---

Rose, *Who the Hell Does She Think She Is?,* 3 POLY L. REV. 13, 15 (1980) (interview with Mary Whitehouse).

84. *Lemon,* 1979 App. Cas. at 660. An account of the trial may be found in N. WALTER, BLASPHEMY IN BRITAIN: THE PRACTICE AND PUNISHMENT OF BLASPHEMY, AND THE TRIAL OF GAY NEWS (1977). The trial judge concluded his charge to the jury by telling the jurors

> to answer the following questions about the poem: "Did it shock you when you first read it? What was your immediate reaction? Would you be proud or ashamed to have written it? Would you read it aloud to a Christian audience, and if you did would you blush? What reaction would you expect from an audience of fellow Christians?"

Id. at 16. After the verdict the trial judge is reported to have "expressed his hope that, as a result of the case, the 'pendulum of public opinion would swing back towards a more healthy climate.' " Adam, *Protecting Our Lord,* NEW STATESMAN, July 15, 1977, at 74, col. 1.

85. *See, e.g.,* Buxton, *The Case of Blasphemous Libel,* 1978 CRIM. L. REV. 673.

86. Along the way the Court of Appeal upheld the fines but quashed the sentence on the grounds that "[w]e do not consider this an appropriate case for a prison sentence." 1979 Q.B. 10, 30.

87. For later assessments of this issue, see Spencer, *Blasphemy: The Law Commission's Working Paper,* 1981 CRIM. L. REV. 810; *Blasting Blasphemy,* 129 SOLIC. J. 489 (1985).

88. *Lemon,* 1979 App. Cas. at 617. The European Commission on Human Rights later found no inconsistency between the conviction and the European Convention on Human Rights and Fundamental Freedoms. *See* Gay News Ltd. v. United Kingdom, 5 Eur. Comm'n H.R. 123 (1982).

89. *Lemon,* 1979 App. Cas. at 660.

90. *Id.* at 658. Scarman rejected the notion that blasphemy was criminal because of its tendency to cause a breach of the peace. It is "a jejune exercise," he said, "to speculate whether an outraged Christian would feel provoked by the words and illustration in this case to commit a breach of peace. I hope, and happen to believe, that most, true to their Christian principles, would not allow themselves to be so provoked." *Id.* at 662.

lished matter; but not the motive of the author or publisher."[91] If in Kirkup's poem "the argument for acceptance and welcome of homosexuals within the loving fold of the Christian faith [had] been advanced 'in a sober and temperate . . . style,' . . . there could have been no criminal offence committed."[92] But for Scarman "the jury (with every justification) [had] rejected this view of the poem and drawing."[93]

Scarman's rejection of the requirement of intent flowed from his understanding of "legal policy in the society of today"; in his view, that policy should strive to find a "way forward for a successful plural society."[94] Although Scarman, as a judge, could not expand the common law crime of blasphemy to protect the religious feelings of non-Christians, he wanted to use the *Lemon* case as a platform to urge that the common law be changed by legislation to protect the sensibilities of all religious groups. His repudiation of the requirement of intent was integral to that ambition. He made this powerfully clear at the very outset of his opinion:

> My Lords, I do not subscribe to the view that the common law offence of blasphemous libel serves no useful purpose in the modern law. On the contrary, I think that there is a case for legislation extending it to protect the religious beliefs and feelings of non-Christians. . . . In an increasingly plural society such as that of modern Britain it is necessary not only to respect the differing religious beliefs, feelings and practices of all but also to protect them from scurrility, vilification, ridicule, and contempt. . . . When [in the 19th century] Lord Macaulay protested in Parliament against the way the blasphemy laws were then administered, he added (Speeches, p. 116): "If I were a judge in India, I should have no scruple about punishing a Christian who should pollute a mosque." . . . When Macaulay became a legislator in India, he saw to it that the law protected the religious feelings of all. In those days India was a plural society: today the United Kingdom is also. I have permitted myself these general observations at the outset of my opinion because, my Lords, they determine my approach to this appeal. I will not lend my voice to a view of the law relating to blasphemous libel which would render it a dead letter, or diminish its efficacy to protect religious feeling from outrage and insult. My criticism of the common law offence of blasphemy is not that it exists but that it is not sufficiently comprehensive. It is shackled by the

91. *Id.* at 665 (citation omitted).

92. *Id.* at 662 (citation omitted).

93. *Id.* The weakness of the style/substance distinction is starkly displayed in *Lemon*, for, as Jones rightly points out:

> when the expression of a view occurs in a literary work—as in the Gay News case—the mode of expression is essential to the enterprise. To say that Kirkup should have produced an academic speculation on Christ's attitude toward homosexuality after the manner of Bishop Montefiore would be to say that he should not have written a poem.

Jones, *supra* note 71, at 143.

94. *Lemon*, 1979 App. Cas. at 664-65.

chains of history.[95]

Scarman offers a compelling vision of blasphemy law transformed by statute into an instrument of pluralism. If at common law blasphemy protected only the hegemonic status of Christianity, Scarman wants the law altered to ensure that distinct and competing religious groups treat each other with sensitivity. He believes it imperative "[i]n an increasingly plural society" to use the law to enforce respect for the "religious beliefs, feelings and practices of all."[96] Reformulated in this way, the law of blasphemy would be part of a pluralist legal framework designed to maintain the integrity of diverse religious groups.[97]

Scarman's opinion represents a major and thoroughgoing effort to reestablish blasphemy on a pluralist, rather than assimilationist basis. What is most interesting about the opinion, however, are the intrinsic limitations of that effort. For Scarman's opinion necessarily rests on the crucial (and unobtrusive) assumption that all religious groups in a "plural society" can be measured by a common metric of "outrage and insult." As we have seen in our analysis of mid-19th-century blasphemy law, however, the metric used by Scarman itself reflects particular cultural values, and there is no reason to assume that in modern England diverse religious groups would in fact share this same sense of the "decencies of controversy." Scarman's opinion therefore implicitly presupposes that religious groups *should* tolerate disagreement if conducted in a temperate and sober style. Despite the purity of Scarman's pluralist intentions, his effort paradoxically rests on a quintessentially assimilationist value.

This conclusion suggests that assimilationism and pluralism may

---

95. *Id.* at 658.

96. *Id.* Scarman might have had in mind the Prevention of Incitement to Hatred Act which had been enacted in 1970 for Northern Ireland, and which provided:

> A person shall be guilty of an offence under this Act if, with intent to stir up hatred against, or arouse fear of, any section of the public in Northern Ireland—
>
> (a) he publishes or distributes written or other matter which is threatening, abusive or insulting; or
>
> (b) he uses in any public place or at any public meeting words which are threatening, abusive or insulting;
>
> being matter or words likely to stir up hatred against, or arouse fear of, any section of the public in Northern Ireland on grounds of religious belief, colour, race or ethnic or national origins.

N. Ir. Pub. Gen. Acts ch. 24, § 1 (1970). The background of the statute is discussed in Leopold, *Incitement to Hatred—The History of a Controversial Criminal Offence,* 1977 PUB. LAW 389, 399-402. For a brief international survey of blasphemy statutes, some of which have the form suggested by Scarman, see WORKING PAPER NO. 79, *supra* note 53, at 40-52.

97. As Scarman well knew, blasphemy law, reinterpreted in this fashion, would be consistent with the pluralist values of the recently enacted provisions of The Race Relations Act of 1976, 2 Pub. Gen. Acts 1723, ch. 74, § 70, which Scarman was himself instrumental in proposing, and which essentially imposed criminal penalties for incitements to racial hatred. *See* I.A. MACDONALD, RACE RELATIONS-THE NEW LAW 137 (1977). Scarman in fact explicitly drew the analogy between his vision of blasphemy and the Race Relations Act. *Lemon,* 1979 App. Cas. at 665.

not be mutually exclusive concepts. Efforts to establish pluralism will always shade, at one point or another, into assimilationism. The respect for diversity, on which pluralist law is based, may well run contrary to the beliefs of some groups; pluralist attempts to create a legal framework based on the value of toleration may well end up imposing this value on groups who do not share it. Even if diverse groups do share some basic notions of respect and tolerance, the definitive meaning of these values will be given uniform and authoritative interpretation by legal institutions, and hence fail to reflect the various meanings that these values will have to different groups in a heterogeneous society.[98] Indeed, at the most basic level, the definition and recognition of who and what will count as a group within a pluralist legal framework will necessarily rest on assimilationist values. Should Scarman's view of blasphemy become the law of England, for example, English judges would face the uncomfortable, assimilationist task of determining which practices and beliefs would count as "religions," and hence which "feelings" the crime of blasphemy ought to protect.

Pluralist law, then, must at some level remain anchored to assimilationist law; the distinction depends, so to speak, on the length of the chain, on the degree and manner in which the value of diversity penetrates the law. There is a somewhat sharper line of demarcation, however, between pluralism and individualism, as can be illustrated by contemplating what would happen in the United States to any statute that attempted to use the crime of blasphemy in the manner suggested by Lord Scarman. We can learn a great deal about the difference between pluralism and individualism by analyzing why the prospects for such a statute would be so very bleak.

B

One's first thought, of course, is that the religion clauses of the first amendment would flatly bar the enforcement of any blasphemy statute, pluralist or not.[99] Harry Kalven, for example, has written that the "religion clauses" of the first amendment have provided the basis for "a first great principle of consensus," which is that "*In America, there is no her-*

98. That is why the anthropologist Paul Bohannan defines "colonial law" as law that stems from a "unicentric power system" in societies with two or more cultures. Bohannan, *The Differing Realms of Law*, 67 AM. ANTHROPOLOGIST 33, 38-39 (1965). Bohannan's definition implies that pluralist law will always be hegemonic in character. But this implication may or may not be true, depending upon the extent to which a heterogenous society experiences what John Rawls has called "overlapping consensus." The presence of such a consensus may permit assimilationist ground rules for pluralist interaction to in fact serve an expressive rather than hegemonic function. *See supra* notes 12-13 and accompanying text; Rawls, *The Idea of an Overlapping Consensus*, 7 OXFORD J. LEGAL STUD. 1 (1987).

99. For an informed and sensitive discussion of this question, see Note, *supra* note 52.

esy, no blasphemy."[100] The difficulty with this narrow focus on constitutional language, however, is that it ignores the framework of assumptions and values that will necessarily inform the interpretation of that language. The importance of this framework can be illustrated by an examination of the fate of blasphemy laws in the states during the period prior to the 1920's. Although blasphemy prosecutions during that period were challenged as unconstitutional because of state guarantees of religious freedom that were strikingly similar in form to the first amendment,[101] courts uniformly interpreted these state constitutional guarantees as permitting the imposition of criminal penalties for blasphemy.[102]

The first and most influential case was *People v. Ruggles*,[103] in which a defendant in New York was charged with blasphemy for having stated that "*Jesus Christ* was a bastard, and his mother must be a whore."[104] The New York Constitution of the time had not only "discarded religious establishments,"[105] but had also, in order "to guard against that spiritual oppression and intolerance wherewith the bigotry and ambition of weak and wicked priests and princes have scourged mankind," guaranteed "that the free exercise and enjoyment of religious profession and worship, without discrimination or preference, shall for ever hereafter be allowed within this State to all mankind."[106] Nevertheless, the New York Supreme Court, in an opinion by Chief Justice Kent, had no difficulty in upholding the conviction:

> The free, equal, and undisturbed, enjoyment of religious opinion, whatever it may be, and free and decent discussions on any religious subject, is granted and secured; but to revile, with malicious and blasphemous contempt, the religion professed by almost the whole community, is an abuse of that right. Nor are we bound, by any expressions in the constitution, as some have strangely supposed, either not to punish at all, or to punish indiscriminately the like attacks upon the religion of *Mahomet* or of the grand *Lama;* and for this plain reason, that the case assumes that we are a christian people, and the morality of the country is

100. H. Kalven, A Worthy Tradition: Freedom of Speech in America 7 (1988) (emphasis in original).

101. During the period prior to the 1920's, of course, the first amendment had no application to the states. By convention the first case taken to indicate a contrary conclusion is Gitlow v. New York, 268 U.S. 652 (1925).

102. *See* Annotation, *Offense of Blasphemy*, 14 A.L.R. 880, 883-85 (1921). In fact the first reported case to strike down a blasphemy statute was in 1970. *See* State v. West, 9 Md. App. 270, 263 A.2d 602 (1970). Theodore Schroeder, however, has reprinted an unpublished 1895 opinion issued by a lower court in Kentucky sustaining on state constitutional grounds a demurrer to an indictment for blasphemy. T. Schroeder, Constitutional Free Speech Defined and Defended in an Unfinished Argument in a Case of Blasphemy 60-64 (1919).

103. 8 Johns. 290 (N.Y. 1811).

104. *Id.* at 291 (emphasis in original).

105. *Id.* at 296. N.Y. Const. art 38 (1777).

106. N.Y. Const. art. 38 (1777).

deeply ingrafted upon christianity, and not upon the doctrines or worship of those impostors.[107]

Kent distinguished between the formal establishment of religion through the compulsory power of the state, and the voluntary adoption by the "people of this state, in common with the people of this country, [of] the general doctrines of christianity, as the rule of their faith and practice."[108] To "scandalize" Christ was punishable not because it defied established religion, but because it was "a gross violation of decency and good order" that struck "at the root of moral obligation, and weaken[ed] the security of the social ties."[109]

Ruggles set a pattern that would continue for more than 110 years.[110] Prosecutions for blasphemy, in their full assimilationist form, were deemed permissible, notwithstanding constitutional rights of religious freedom. It was not until quite recently that legal professionals have become convinced that prosecutions for blasphemy would violate such constitutional rights. A 1968 conviction for blasphemy in Maryland, for example, was set aside two years later when a Maryland appellate court held that the state's 1723 blasphemy statute was "contrary to the terms of the First Amendment's prohibition of laws respecting an establishment of religion or prohibiting the free exercise thereof."[111] At the time of the Maryland decision, Delaware was in the process of prosecuting for blasphemy two teenagers who had called Jesus Christ a bastard. The teenagers had been jailed and were free on bail pending trial. In light of the Maryland decision, the Delaware attorney general's office decided to drop charges.[112] In 1971 in Pennsylvania, two shopkeepers were charged with blasphemy for displaying a poster reading: "Jesus Christ—Wanted for sedition, criminal anarchy, vagrancy, and conspiracy to overthrow the established government. Dressed poorly; said to be

107. *Ruggles*, 8 Johns. at 295 (emphasis in original).

108. *Id.* at 294, 296.

109. *Id.*

110. *See, e.g.*, State v. Chandler, 2 Del. (2 Harr.) 553 (1837); State v. Mockus, 120 Me. 84, 113 A. 39 (1921); Updegraph v. Commonwealth, 11 Serg. & Rawle 394 (Pa. 1824). Apart from *Ruggles*, the most famous American blasphemy decision was Commonwealth v. Kneeland, 37 Mass. (20 Pick.) 206 (1838), in which Chief Justice Lemuel Shaw upheld a conviction for blasphemy against state constitutional challenge. The *Kneeland* case is discussed in BLASPHEMY IN MASSACHUSETTS: FREEDOM OF CONSCIENCE AND THE ABNER KNEELAND CASE (L. Levy, ed. 1973); Commanger, *The Blasphemy of Abner Kneeland*, 8 NEW ENG. Q. 29 (March 1935). The same blasphemy statute that was at issue in *Kneeland* was also used in 1928 to prosecute Horace Kallen for blasphemy. *Boston Judge Recalls Warrant for Arrest on Statements in Sacco Arrest*, N.Y. Times, Aug. 29, 1928, at 8, col. 1. In addressing a memorial meeting for Sacco and Vanzetti, Kallen "said that 'if Sacco and Vanzetti were anarchists, so was Jesus Christ, Socrates,' and several others." *Id.* Two years previously, the same Massachusetts blasphemy statute had been the basis for a notorious prosecution of Anthony Bimba. *See* Z. CHAFEE, *The* Bimba *Case*, in THE INQUIRING MIND 108 (1974); W. WOLKOVICH, BAY STATE "BLUE" LAWS AND *Bimba* (1973); Note, *supra* note 52, at 708-09.

111. State v. West, 9 Md. App. 270, 276, 263 A.2d 602, 605 (1970).

112. The case is discussed in L. LEVY, *supra* note 52, at 337.

a carpenter by trade; ill-nourished; associates with common working people, unemployed and bums. Alien; said to be a Jew." After the intervention of the American Civil Liberties Union, the county prosecutor asked that the local magistrate drop the charges.[113]

In each of these cases, local attempts to enforce blasphemy statutes were checked by legal professionals who believed that the statutes were contrary to the religious freedom guaranteed by the first amendment. The literal terms of the first amendment could not have dictated this belief, for these terms are not different from those in state constitutions that had consistently been construed to allow the punishment of blasphemy.[114] It is rather that the religion clauses of the first amendment are now interpreted in light of very different assumptions and values than those informing earlier interpretations of equivalent language in state constitutions. It is important, therefore, to explore the values that we bring to contemporary constitutional adjudication. These values are well displayed in the important case of *Cantwell v. Connecticut,*[115] one of the first and most influential decisions to apply the religion clauses of the first amendment to the states.

In that case Jesse Cantwell, a Jehovah's Witness, entered a Catholic neighborhood and played for two Catholic men a phonograph record that contained an attack on all organized religious systems as "instru-

---

113. *Id.* at 337-38.

114. Indeed in 1897 the United States Supreme Court had in dicta interpreted the first amendment in the same manner as state courts had interpreted equivalent state constitutional provisions, stating flatly that the amendment did not extend constitutional protection to "the publication of . . . blasphemous or indecent articles, or other publications injurious to public morals or private reputation." Robertson v. Baldwin, 165 U.S. 275, 281 (1897).

The Court's interpretation was at the time consistent with the opinion of authoritative commentators. Thomas Cooley, for example, had written in 1868 that:

> The constitutional liberty of speech and of the press . . . implies a right to freely utter and publish whatever the citizen may please, and to be protected against any responsibility for the publication, except so far as such publications, from their blasphemy, obscenity, or scandalous character, may be a public offence . . . .

T. Cooley, A Treatise on the Constitutional Limitations which Rest Upon the Legislative Power of the States of the American Union 422 (1868). And Joseph Story, in interpreting the religion clauses of the first amendment, had flatly stated that:

> it is impossible for those who believe in the truth of Christianity, as a divine revelation, to doubt, that it is the especial duty of government to foster and encourage it among all the citizens and subjects. This is a point wholly distinct from that of the right of private judgment in matters of religion, and of the freedom of public worship according to the dictates of one's conscience.

2 J. Story, Commentaries on the Constitution of the United States 661 (3d. ed. 1858). Story stressed that "in a republic, there would seem to be a peculiar propriety in viewing the Christian religion as the great basis, on which it must rest for its support and permanence." *Id.* at 662. He concluded that "[t]he real object of the [first] amendment was, not to countenance, much less to advance Mahometanism, or Judaism, or infidelity, by prostrating Christianity; but to exclude all rivalry among Christian sects, and to prevent any national ecclesiastical establishment . . . ." *Id.* at 664.

115. 310 U.S. 296 (1940).

ments of Satan and injurious to man," and that further singled "out the Roman Catholic Church for strictures couched in terms which naturally would offend not only persons of that persuasion, but all others who respect the honestly held religious faith of their fellows."[116] Cantwell was charged and convicted of the common law crime of inciting breach of the peace.[117]

Chief Justice Kent would certainly have viewed Cantwell's vitriolic attack on organized religion as "an abuse of" the right of free exercise of religion. Indeed in *Ruggles* he said that to construe the guarantee of "free exercise and enjoyment of religious profession and worship" in the New York Constitution "as breaking down the common law barriers against licentious, wanton, and impious attacks upon christianity itself, would be an enormous perversion of its meaning."[118] And Lord Scarman would certainly have deemed Cantwell's conduct to be intolerable "for a successful plural society,"[119] for Cantwell had demonstrated a complete lack of respect for the religious sensibilities of others by gratuitously insulting and offending members of the Catholic religion.

It was open, therefore, to the United States Supreme Court to interpret the first amendment in light of either the assimilationist values of Kent, or the pluralist values that Scarman attempted to use thirty-nine years later to reconstruct the common law crime of blasphemy. But the Court took neither of these paths. Instead it set aside Cantwell's conviction, and offered this important gloss on what it called "the interest of the United States that the free exercise of religion be not prohibited and that freedom to communicate information and opinion be not abridged":[120]

> In the realm of religious faith, and in that of political belief, sharp differences arise. In both fields the tenets of one man may seem the rankest error to his neighbor. To persuade others to his own point of view, the pleader, as we know, at times resorts to exaggeration, to vilification of men who have been, or are, prominent in church or state, and even to false statement. But the people of this nation have ordained in the light of history, that, in spite of the probability of excesses and abuses, these liberties are, in the long view, essential to enlightened opinion and right conduct on the part of the citizens of a democracy. The essential characteristic of these liberties is, that under their shield many types of life, character, opinion and belief can develop unmolested and unobstructed. Nowhere is this shield more necessary than in our own country

116. *Id.* at 309.
117. *Id.* at 300.
118. *People v. Ruggles*, 8 Johns. 290, 296 (N.Y. 1811).
119. *See supra* text accompanying notes 88-98.
120. 310 U.S. at 307.

for a people composed of many races and of many creeds.[121]

According to *Cantwell,* then, the first amendment should be interpreted in a manner consistent with the presence of a heterogeneous society. Kent had brought to his construction of the New York Constitution the assumption that the values of Christianity provided "that moral discipline, and . . . those principles of virtue, which help to bind society together."[122] The Court in *Cantwell,* on the other hand, brought to its reading of the first amendment the assumption that society consists "of many creeds" and is divided by "sharp differences," in which "the tenets of one man may seem the rankest error to his neighbor." The presupposition of social uniformity that underlies Kent's assimilationist vision seems to have vanished from *Cantwell's* account, which is much closer in spirit to the "plural" society described by Scarman. But for Scarman social diversity implied the enactment of pluralist values, so that the law could be used to protect religious differences from "vilification, ridicule, and contempt." For *Cantwell,* on the other hand, the fact of diversity led in exactly the opposite direction, toward the constitutional requirement that the law tolerate "exaggeration," "vilification," and even "excesses and abuses."

It is not difficult to perceive the line that divides *Cantwell* from *Ruggles;* but what distinguishes *Cantwell* from Scarman's pluralist vision? The key lies in the fact that while *Cantwell* focuses its analysis on the religious speaker, Scarman concentrates instead on the offense suffered by the religious audience. There is a deeply significant asymmetry in these approaches: the speaker stands alone, whereas the outrage of the audience is generic. For Scarman the law does not respond to the outrage of offended individuals, but to the common outrage of the members of a religious group whose group identity has been attacked. *Cantwell* explicitly rejects this focus on the group, choosing instead to use the law as a "shield" so that "many types of life, character, opinion and belief can develop unmolested and unobstructed." In essence *Cantwell* requires that established religious groups, who have already developed their distinctive character and beliefs, must suffer offense so that new religious groups can be born.[123] Underlying *Cantwell,* then, lies the classic American commitment to "voluntarism,"[124] to the belief that "religion is . . . a

121. *Id.* at 310.

122. *Ruggles,* 8 Johns. at 294.

123. In 1940, the year in which the Cantwell opinion was issued, the sect of Jehovah's Witnesses was only 68 years old, having been founded in 1872 by Charles Taze Russell in Allegheny, Pennsylvania. E. Gaustad, Historical Atlas of Religion in America 115-16 (1962). In the 1930's, Jehovah's Witnesses began to proselytize actively for new membership, and the sect experienced "sudden progress after 1940, all but eclipsing the development of the first sixty years." *Id.* at 118.

124. *See* P. Miller, The Life of the Mind in America 40-43 (1965).

matter of individual choice."[125]

The contrast between Scarman and *Cantwell* might thus be formulated in this manner: For Lord Scarman religious heterogeneity presupposes a social world in which diverse religious groups already exist as part of a stable and established social fabric, whereas for *Cantwell* religious diversity presupposes instead a social world in which the dynamic of individual choice causes new religious groups continually to evolve. Thus while both Scarman and *Cantwell* recognize the existence of groups, Scarman assumes that the function of law is to protect the integrity of established and stable groups, whereas *Cantwell* assumes that the function of law is to protect the capacity of individuals to form new and different groups. The individual is the locus of value for *Cantwell;* the group is the locus of value for Scarman. The distinction between the two, in short, is that between individualism and pluralism. Unlike the gradient that holds together pluralism and assimilationism, the distinction between *Cantwell* and Scarman is quite sharp, for it turns on the more or less dichotomous determination of whether the law should be used to enforce the norms of groups as against individuals, or to protect instead the prerogatives of individuals as against groups.[126]

In interpreting the Constitution in light of the values and assump-

---

125. R. BELLAH, *supra* note 38, at 225.

126. For a discussion of the tension between pluralism and individualism, see Glazer, *The Constitution and American Diversity,* PUB. INT., Winter 1987, at 10-21; Gordon, *Models of Pluralism: The New American Dilemma,* ANNALS, March 1981, at 179-88.

The sharp break between pluralism and individualism is somewhat surprising, especially given the consensus among social scientists that individual experience is in fact largely social and intimately shaped by group identifications. The reasons for the break can perhaps be illuminated by George Herbert Mead's distinction between the "I" and the "me." Mead believed that the structure of individual identity was at root social in nature. "What makes the organized self is the organization of the attitudes which are common to the group. A person is a personality because he belongs to a community, because he takes over the institutions of that community into his own conduct." G. MEAD, ON SOCIAL PSYCHOLOGY 226 (A. Strauss rev. ed. 1964). But Mead also understood that there is no such thing as a completely "institutionalized individual," *id.* at 239, because of the inherent and irreducible capacity of persons to modify or transcend those aspects of themselves that are socially given. As a consequence, Mead distinguished between the "I" and the "me": "The 'I' is the response of the organism to the attitudes of the others; the 'me' is the organized set of attitudes of others which one himself assumes. The attitudes of the others constitute the organized 'me,' and then one reacts toward that as an 'I.' " *Id.* at 230.

The "I" is spontaneous, unpredictable, and formless; the "me" is structured and static. Mead believed that each was a fundamental and indispensable aspect of the self. He associated the "me" with "social control," and the "I" with "self-expression." *Id.* at 238-40. "Taken together," Mead said, "they constitute a personality as it appears in social experience. The self is essentially a social process going on with these two distinguishable phases." *Id.* at 233.

The sharp contrast between individualist and pluralist law can be understood as flowing from the distinction between these two phases of the self. Pluralist law upholds the values associated with the "me," which is to say with group norms and attitudes that form the structure of personality; whereas individualist law safeguards the values associated with the "I," which is to say with the potential for individual modification and transcendence of that structure. The values of the "me" and of the "I" are necessarily complementary and interdependent, but because they are also in

tions of individualism, *Cantwell* speaks for what unquestionably has become the great tradition of first amendment thought. Of course there have been dissenting voices in that tradition, but it is fair to characterize cases like *Beauharnais* and *Yoder* as ripples on the surface of a deeper and more powerful current of individualist decisions. It is worth pausing for a moment to inquire into the sociological causes of these decisions. Why in the 1930's did we begin to interpret the first amendment to our national Constitution (as distinct from our state constitutions) in light of the principles of individualism? Was it that the natural heterogeneity of American society was more easily visible from a national, rather than a local viewpoint? Or was it instead that the federal enforcement of individualism was integral to the process of forging a distinctively national culture, a culture designed to transcend local and regional identifications? In the answers to these questions lie the roots of our own constitutional perspectives, perspectives that, for example, account for our instinctive rejection of Lord Scarman's proposals for the use of blasphemy law.

If individualism is sharply demarcated from pluralism, it bears a considerably more complex relationship to assimilationism. Paradoxically, individualism and assimilationism are discontinuous and yet interdependent. As Charles Taylor has observed, the concept of "the autonomous, self-determining individual," which lies at the heart of individualism, presupposes a particular "social matrix" and depends for its continuing vitality on "a certain type of culture."[127]

> The crucial point here is this: since the free individual can only maintain his identity within a society/culture of a certain kind, he has to be concerned about the shape of this society/culture as a whole. He cannot . . . be concerned purely with his individual choices and the associations formed from such choices to the neglect of the matrix in which such choices can be open or closed, rich or meager. It is important to him that certain activities and institutions flourish in society. It is even important to him what the moral tone of the whole society is—shocking as it may be to libertarians to raise this issue—because freedom and individual diversity can only flourish in a society where there is a general recognition of their worth. They are threatened by the spread of bigotry, but also by other conceptions of life—for example, those which look on originality, innovation, and diversity as luxuries which society can ill afford given the need for efficiency, productivity, or growth . . . .[128]

Taylor's analysis suggests that at certain points the desires of autono-

---

tension the law must on occasion choose to cast the authority of the state behind one aspect of the self or the other.

127. 2 C. TAYLOR, *Atomism*, in PHILOSOPHY AND THE HUMAN SCIENCES: PHILOSOPHICAL PAPERS 205-09 (1985).

128. *Id.* at 207.

mous individuals may very well clash with the kind of general culture necessary to support autonomous individualism, and at those points individualist law will in effect be transformed into assimilationist law.[129]

This transformation is visible in *Cantwell,* which notes two different assimilationist justifications for the imposition of limitations on individual freedom of speech. The first justification refers to "statements likely to provoke violence and disturbance of good order."[130] *Cantwell* states that "[w]hen clear and present danger of riot, disorder, interference with traffic upon the public streets, or other immediate threat to public safety, peace, or order, appears, the power of the State to prevent or punish is obvious."[131] Thus individual expression can be prevented and punished when it functions as the cause of harms or conduct that can be regulated to protect the assimilationist values of public safety and order. By its evocation of the "clear and present danger" test, *Cantwell* indicates that speech can be penalized only when there is a very strict causal connection between speech and subsequent action or harm. The strictness of the causal nexus is in part designed to maximize the amount of speech constitutionally exempt from the regulation of assimilationist values.

The second limitation on individual expression proposed by *Cantwell* refers to "profane, indecent, or abusive remarks directed to the person of the hearer."[132] *Cantwell* states that "[r]esort to epithets or personal abuse is not in any proper sense communication of information or opinion safeguarded by the Constitution, and its punishment as a criminal act would raise no question under that instrument."[133] This limitation on speech is qualitatively different from the clear and present danger test, for it is grounded on the concept that speech can be regulated because it is itself intrinsically undesirable, regardless of its causal connection to subsequent harms or conduct. *Cantwell* expresses this limitation on speech by reference to a distinction similar to that used in mid-19th-century English blasphemy law. English law distinguished between "sober and temperate" expression, which was addressed to the "judg-

129. Using the perspective of George Herbert Mead, *supra* note 126, we might say that while it is coherent for the law in any particular case to promote the values of the "I" as against the "me," it is incoherent for the law to attempt systematically to disable the "me." This is because the "I" and the "me" are necessarily complementary; neither could exist without the other. It is thus meaningless to speak of the potential for individual transcendence without simultaneously speaking of the structure that is to be transcended. Since the "me" is the internalization of the larger social organization within which the self is situated, laws that constitute and enforce that organization are in essence supportive of the "me." From Mead's perspective, therefore, individualist law will always transform at one point or another into either assimilationist or pluralist law. Of course, law that strives to maximize individualist values will also strive to eliminate particular and unequal restraints on individuals, and hence take the form of assimilationism rather than pluralism.

130. *Cantwell v. Connecticut,* 310 U.S. 296, 309 (1940).

131. *Id.* at 308.

132. *Id.* at 309.

133. *Id.* at 309-10.

ment," and expression infected by a tone of "offence, and insult, and ridicule," which was addressed to "the wild and improper feelings of the human mind."[134] *Cantwell* offers an analogous distinction between speech that communicates "information or opinion," and speech that is "profane, indecent, or abusive."

Just as the style/substance distinction in English blasphemy law did not describe inherent properties of speech, but rather reflected cultural values relating to the "decencies of controversy," so the distinction offered by *Cantwell* should not be understood as describing inherent properties of language, but rather as expressing the cultural values underlying individualism.[135] For *Cantwell* the general culture necessary to sustain autonomous individualism rests on norms of interpersonal respect, and these norms in turn function as assimilationist values that limit the autonomous speech of particular individuals. "Profane, indecent, or abusive" speech violates these norms.

Cantwell' s understanding of these assimilationist norms, however, has been strikingly influenced by *Cantwell'* s underlying individualism. The norms recognized by *Cantwell* differ fundamentally from the assimilationist norms implicit in the English cases. Individuals in the English cases have the right to take offense at communications that insult their particular status as, say, practicing Christians.[136] But the norms of respect upheld in *Cantwell* are quite different, for integral to that decision is the notion that the Constitution prohibits Connecticut from punishing Jesse Cantwell's speech simply because it is outrageous to the Catholicism of his audience. Instead the law can constitutionally intervene to censor only those statements that consist of "abusive remarks directed to the person of the hearer."[137] The specific social status of an audience is immaterial to these kinds of statements, because every person has the right not to be personally abused.

Thus even when it explicitly recognizes assimilationist values that can directly regulate speech, *Cantwell* does so in a manner that follows the logic of individualism to its natural conclusion. *Cantwell* enforces a constitutional symmetry between speaker and audience: it allows the law to redress audience outrage only when that outrage stems from characteristics potentially shared by all individuals, rather than from characteristics that are constitutive of particular social or religious groups.[138] The

134. *See supra* text accompanying note 65.

135. From a strictly logical point of view, "profane, indecent, or abusive remarks" communicate opinion and information, just as do other kinds of statements.

136. This is also true of Scarman's pluralist reformulation of blasphemy law, which would enable individuals in all religious groups to use the law to protect them from insults to their religious beliefs. *See supra* text accompanying notes 89-98.

137. 310 U.S. at 309.

138. The Supreme Court has demonstrated an equally determined universalism in its treatment

assimilationist values underlying *Cantwell* are thus real and palpable, but they are also extremely thin, for there is only so much that we all, as Americans, potentially share in common. The abstract and rather bloodless nature of these values, however, is the price we pay for having a first amendment grounded in individualism, rather than pluralism.

III

It is precisely the abstract nature of these values that is challenged by MacKinnon's and Dworkin's critique of pornography. The censorship of obscenity, as can now plainly be seen, is a paradigmatic expression of assimilationist law, in which the dominant culture in a community is set free to limit individual expression so as to enforce "community standards" and hence define the "tone" and "quality" of its community life.[139] But the pressure of first amendment individualism has forced obscenity law to rest on the kind of thin values which are compatible with that individualism. Obscenity law thus speaks in the abstract language of "prurience,"[140] a vice that is potentially universal and equally dangerous to all individuals. It does not focus at all on the particular outrage inflicted by pornography on women.

Feminists like Dworkin and MacKinnon demand that the law be transformed to take cognizance of that outrage. The problem, however, is that this outrage stems from the characteristics of a specific group (women); it is not the outrage of a generic audience composed of undifferentiated individuals. Dworkin and MacKinnon want the law to recognize that pornography demeans women, not just persons, and in this desire they are like the two Catholic men in *Cantwell* who would seek redress for the specific insult to their Catholicism. The feminist demand for the regulation of pornography is so controversial, in other words, because implicit within it lies the entire difference between pluralism and individualism.

There are several advantages to conceptualizing the pornography controversy in terms of the tension between pluralism and individualism. It focuses analysis on the essential grievance motivating the feminist critique; it does so in a way that minimizes the damage to basic first amendment principles; and it offers the intellectual tools to refine and sharpen

of defamation law; it has conceptualized state libel laws as redressing injuries impairing "the essential dignity and worth of every human being," Gertz v. Robert Welch, Inc., 418 U.S. 323, 341 (1974) (quoting Rosenblatt v. Baer, 393 U.S. 75, 92 (1966) (Stewart, J., concurring)), rather than injuries that would harm merely the honor of particular social groups or roles. *See* Post, *supra* note 13, at 699-719, 722-26.

139. Paris Adult Theatre I v. Slaton, 413 U.S. 49, 58 (1973); Miller v. California, 413 U.S. 15, 33 (1973). As such, of course, obscenity law has always been a thumb in the eye of the first amendment individualist tradition.

140. *Miller*, 413 U.S. at 30.

the exact points in controversy, and so hopefully to expedite a resolution. The first two of these advantages can best be illustrated comparatively, through a brief discussion of three other constitutional understandings of the controversy that are prominent in the current literature.

A

A common justification offered for the suppression of pornography is that it causes discrete acts of sexual violence against individual women. This justification is not theoretically problematic, but its nature and strength depend entirely on the empirical evidence offered in its support. Given its most generous interpretation, the systematic evidence presently available does not demonstrate that pornography automatically leads to sexual violence, but rather that it causes "attitudinal" changes in men which make them more likely to countenance sexual violence against women.[141] For this evidence to justify the censorship of pornography, it must be argued that the relationship between such attitudinal changes and subsequent behavior constitutes a sufficiently close causal nexus as to justify the regulation of pornography.

This is precisely the kind of argument that was traditionally offered to support the regulation of blasphemy. It was contended that blasphemy induced attitudinal changes toward religion that would lead persons to countenance anti-social acts. "Public contumely and ridicule of a prevalent religion . . . threaten the public peace and order by diminishing the power of moral precepts."[142] It is also the kind of argument used by the Supreme Court in the notorious case of *Debs v. United States.*[143] There the Court upheld the conviction of Eugene Debs for delivering an anti-war speech to the state convention of the socialist party of Ohio, on the grounds that the "natural tendency and reasonably probable effect" of the speech would be to induce attitudinal changes in the audience that would increase their willingness to obstruct the recruitment of American forces for World War I.[144]

As these examples illustrate, the government would acquire enormous and intolerable powers of censorship if it were to be given the authority to penalize any speech that would tend to induce in an audience disagreeable attitudinal changes with respect to future conduct. To avoid the potential for such censorship the Supreme Court has held that

141. C. MacKinnon, *supra* note 4, at 187-89; Branit, *supra* note 10, at 456-57; Jacobs, *supra* note 10, at 10-11; Linz, Penrod, & Donnerstein, *The Attorney General's Commission on Pornography: The Gaps Between "Findings" and Facts*, 1987 A.B.F. Res. J. 713, 719-23.

142. 1 C. Tiedeman, A Treatise on State and Federal Control of Persons and Property 201 (1900); *see* State v. Mockus, 120 Me. 84, 94, 113 A. 39, 43 (1921); Updegraph v. Commonwealth, 11 Serg. & Rawle 394, 408-09 (Pa. 1822).

143. 249 U.S. 211 (1919).

144. *Id.* at 216.

speech can only be penalized because of a causal nexus to future overt acts if the speech "is directed to inciting or producing imminent lawless action and is likely to incite or produce such action."[145] Pornography obviously does not meet this test.[146] Given the present state of the evidence, then, the contention that pornography should be generally regulated because of its causal connection to future acts of sexual violence is profoundly at odds with the basic first amendment principle that seeks to circumscribe broad government discretion to curtail speech.[147]

The second justification sometimes offered for the suppression of pornography is the argument that pornography is not speech, but rather "an act of male supremacy."[148] It is contended that "[p]ornography is not expression depicting the subordination of women, but is the *practice of subordination* itself."[149] The power and reach of this argument can be appreciated by calling to mind J.L. Austin's concept of "performative utterances."[150] There are certain occasions when a person's speech makes us think "that he is *doing* something rather than merely *saying* something."[151] Announcing "I do" at a wedding ceremony, for example, is to perform the act of getting married. Performative utterances seem like actions because by common "convention" the acts that they perform are understood to subsist in speech.[152] It may be argued that, in a similar way, certain kinds of social relationships are by convention understood to be constituted in large measure (although not entirely) by speech. Relationships of respect, for example, inherently involve communication, so that to speak disrespectfully is to perform an act of disrespect. From the feminist perspective, pornography is just such a disrespectful act.

This argument can be extended by noting that relationships of inferiority and superiority are also in large measure (although not entirely) constituted by speech. The status of social superiors is established and

145. Brandenburg v. Ohio, 395 U.S. 444, 447 (1969) (per curiam).

146. Emerson, *supra* note 10, at 135.

147. *See* Stone, *supra* note 10, at 475-76. This conclusion also applies to the argument that because "the nature and extent of the link between act and harm are difficult to establish," and because the harm is "potentially severe," "suggestive evidence" of a causal connection between pornography and sexual violence should be sufficient to justify legal censorship. *See* Sunstein, *supra* note 10, at 601. This argument was used by the majority of the Court in Gitlow v. New York, 268 U.S. 652 (1925), to uphold a statute suppressing anarchist speech. The Court noted that the exact causal connection between such speech and the potentially severe harm of revolution was difficult to fix. *Id.* at 669. It is of course possible to argue that the stringent constitutional standards that now apply to most speech should be modified and diluted for pornographic speech. The question, however, is why pornography is, in some constitutionally relevant sense, "different" from other forms of speech. The pluralist/individualist distinction seeks to offer an analytic framework within which this question can be meaningfully addressed.

148. C. MACKINNON, *supra* note 4, at 154; *see id.* at 175-76, 193-94.

149. Brest & Vandenberg, *supra* note 10, at 659 (emphasis in original).

150. J. L. AUSTIN, PHILOSOPHICAL PAPERS 233-52 (3d ed. 1979).

151. *Id.* at 235 (emphasis in original).

152. *Id.* at 237.

confirmed by the tokens of respect that are their due; conversely, the status of social inferiors inheres in part in the disrespect with which they can be treated. Pornography can thus be seen as the practice of subordination because it is the pervasively disrespectful treatment of women. Even if women as a group defy the stigmatizing imputations of pornography, society's countenance of its widespread distribution indicates that this defiance is powerless before the conventional judgment of inferiority that is everywhere pornographically displayed.[153]

There is nothing illogical about this argument; it rests on rather profound insights into the manner in which social relations are constituted by speech as well as by physical actions. In its pure form, however, the argument is incompatible with any viable notion of freedom of expression, for social relations are pervasively comprised by speech.[154] Consider the following three examples, which deal only with relationships of respect: I can, as a literary critic, speak disrespectfully and authoritatively about a new novel; or I can, as an outraged moralist, speak disrespectfully and with great effect about the actions of an

---

153. It is in this sense, I think, that MacKinnon's recurring theme of feminine powerlessness should be understood. "Having power means, among other things, that when someone says, 'This is how it is,' it is taken as being that way." C. MACKINNON, *supra* note 4, at 164. Hence, pornography "*constructs* women and sex," despite the dissent of women; "dissent from it becomes inaudible." *Id.* at 161, 166 (emphasis in original).

154. The very concept of social order, for example, can be understood as constituted by speech. This is nicely illustrated by the remarks of Francis Holt, an English writer who presented the following argument in support of an early form of the style/substance distinction in blasphemy:

> [T]he law does not prohibit reasonable controversy even upon fundamental subjects, so long as it is conducted with a tone of moderation, which shews that argument is the only purpose; the writer abstaining from language and terms which are abusive and passionate, and, therein, indecorous towards the establishment, and offensive to the consciences of individuals.
>
> What is argumentative may be very properly left to be replied to by argument; what is passionate, and therein a disturbance of the proper oeconomy of the state, cannot be so safely passed over to a defence by similar weapons. —Such a sufferance would be the endurance of brawls. When the law is moved against such writers, it is not persecution: it is a defence of the public tranquillity and decency.

F. HOLT, THE LAW OF LIBEL 70-71 (1816). For Holt "public tranquillity" literally subsists in the public observance of rules of "decency"; breaches in decorum are thus equivalent to "brawls." "Passionate" speech is the same as action because Holt understands the social order to inhere in decorum, and decorum to depend upon the verbal exercise of civility and dispassionate reason. Even today the *Corpus Juris Secundum* defines the term "breach of the peace" to include "all violations of the public peace or order, or decorum." 11 C.J.S. *Breach of the Peace* § 1 (1938 & Supp. 1987).

While we may now differ from Holt in our understanding of the particular ways in which the social order is constituted by speech, we nevertheless continue to view speech acts as integral to that order. In Chaplinsky v. New Hampshire, 315 U.S. 568 (1942), for example, the Court justified its conclusion that "fighting" words were unprotected by the first amendment on the grounds that such words "by their very utterance inflict injury." *Id.* at 572. Thirty years later, in Cohen v. California, 403 U.S. 15 (1971), where a defendant was convicted of disturbing the peace for writing "Fuck the Draft" on the back of his jacket, Justice Blackmun could describe "Cohen's absurd and immature antic" as "mainly conduct and little speech." *Id.* at 27 (Blackmun, J., dissenting). Whether or not one agrees with Blackmun's characterization, his point clearly rests upon an intelligible cultural perception.

acquaintance; or I can, as a political partisan, speak disrespectfully and influentially about the character of the President. In each of these examples I have acted disrespectfully, and with devastating consequences to the social standing of the object of my speech. We can argue about whether or not the law should intervene to punish me in any particular case, but surely it goes too far to claim that freedom of speech is not pertinent to any of the examples because they each involve acts rather than communication.

The argument that pornography can be regulated because it is the practice of subordination, rather than speech, thus proves too much to be useful for first amendment purposes. Social relations to a great extent inhere in communications that have the quality of performative utterances,[155] and it would be entirely inconsistent with any modern understanding of the Constitution to remove such communications in wholesale fashion from the purview of the first amendment.

A third justification that has been offered to support the regulation of pornography is that "pornography is more accurately treated as a physical rather than a mental experience" because it contains "neither propositional, emotive, nor artistic content."[156] Pornography lacks "intellectual appeal,"[157] and is "non-rational, almost physical . . . material which is purely designed to excite sexual fantasies, largely as an aid to masturbation."[158] Pornography "thus contains none of the properties that are defined by the technical sense of the word 'speech,' and is thus outside the scope of the Free Speech Principle."[159]

This argument appears inconsistent with the contention that pornography should be regulated because it is the practice of sexual subordination. It is hard to understand how pornography can communicate attitudes of disrespect toward women if it is entirely devoid of propositional, emotive, and artistic content. If one must choose between these two characterizations of pornography, I think that it is more accurate to conclude that pornography does convey specific attitudes toward women, and that it does so in the same manner as any intentional act of communication. The notion that even a "hard-core" pornographic film could be completely empty of content strikes me as fanciful, since at a minimum the film will be understood as attempting to communicate the author's

155. Austin himself was well aware that the "contrast" between performatives and other forms of communication was not at all sharp, and that indeed "stating something is performing an act just as much as is giving an order or giving a warning." J.L. AUSTIN, *supra* note 150, at 246, 251. Ultimately, then, Austin came to the conclusion that "action is . . . usually, at least in part, a matter of convention." *Id.* at 237.

156. F. SCHAUER, FREE SPEECH: A PHILOSOPHICAL ENQUIRY 182-83 (1982).

157. *Id.* at 183.

158. E. BARENDT, FREEDOM OF SPEECH 263 (1985).

159. F. SCHAUER, *supra* note 156, at 183.

perception of what his audience will find sexually arousing. The concept of sexual arousal is of course a complex, substantive matter, filled with implications for the social understanding of gender.

To be fair to the proponents of the argument that pornography lacks all ideational content, however, it should be noted that the argument was originally developed to justify the regulation of obscenity, rather than pornography. Although the argument purports to analyze the intrinsic properties of speech, it is in fact grounded on the same assimilationist values as those that underlie the prohibition of obscenity. The argument's analysis of speech may be fallacious, but its grasp of these values is considerably more formidable.

Like English blasphemy law in the 19th century, the argument turns on the fusion of reason and civility; it rests on a distinction analogous to the opposition between speech addressed to the "judgment," and speech addressed to "the wild and improper feelings of the human mind."[160] "[O]bscenity," so the argument goes in its most explicit form, "pertains, not to the realm of ideas, reason, intellectual content and truth-seeking, but to the realm of passion, desires, cravings and titillation."[161] The implication of the distinction is that obscenity can be regulated because the culture of autonomous individualism depends on reason and is undermined by passion. Reformulated in this way, the argument is a serious attempt to articulate the assimilationist values that necessarily form the foundation of first amendment individualism.[162] But as such the argument ignores the particular concerns raised by Dworkin's and MacKinnon's critique of pornography.

B

These three justifications for the regulation of pornography are a fair sampling of some of the stronger arguments available in the current literature. Yet they all seem deeply unsatisfactory, either because they conflict with basic first amendment principles, or because they miss the essential point of the feminist critique. It is as if commentators are searching for some adequate way to conceptualize the bold new claims presented by the attack on pornography.[163] In fact, however, the structure of these claims should be familiar, for they are analogous to the

160. *See supra* text accompanying note 65.

161. Finnis, *"Reason and Passion": The Constitutional Dialectic of Free Speech and Obscenity*, 116 U. PA. L. REV. 222, 227 (1967); *see* Paris Adult Theatre I v. Slaton, 413 U.S. 49, 67 (1973).

162. For an explicit argument to this effect, see Stanmeyer, *Keeping the Constitutional Republic: Civic Virtue vs. Pornographic Attack*, 14 HASTINGS CONST. L.Q. 561, 585-90 (1987). Politicians have long appreciated the power of this argument. *See, e.g.*, Nixon, *Statement about the Report of the Commission on Obscenity and Pornography, Oct. 24, 1970*, in PUBLIC PAPERS OF THE PRESIDENTS OF THE UNITED STATES: RICHARD NIXON 940-41 (1971).

163. The search is sometimes quite explicit. *See, e.g.*, Sunstein, *supra* note 10, at 602-08.

question of group libel addressed in *Beauharnais.*[164]

In *Beauharnais* the Court held that state law could punish speech calculated to expose ethnic or religious groups to "contempt, derision, or obloquy,"[165] on the grounds that "a man's job and his educational opportunities and the dignity accorded him may depend as much on the reputation of the racial and religious group to which he willy-nilly belongs, as on his own merits."[166] The structure of the Court's reasoning applies equally well to membership in a gender as to membership in a religious or ethnic group. If pornography subjects the group of women to contempt and derision by "eroticiz[ing] dominance and submission or portray[ing] women in a degrading manner as objects to be sexually exploited and manipulated,"[167] the dignity accorded to each woman will suffer, regardless of her personal merits.

Of course as a matter of technical precedent *Beauharnais* comes to us as damaged goods. Its reasoning was crippled by *New York Times Co. v. Sullivan,*[168] and its holding was unmistakably undone by *Philadelphia Newspapers, Inc. v. Hepps.*[169] More importantly, *Beauharnais* depends on the argument that group libel is simply a variant form of individual defamation, and this argument requires that the defendant in a group libel case be given the opportunity to establish the truth of his publication.[170] What is at issue in the feminist critique of pornography, however, is not the falsity of the assertion that women are objects to be sexually exploited, but rather the insult and contempt that is communicated when that assertion is made in a particular way. Pornographically

164. Beauharnais v. Illinois, 343 U.S. 250 (1951); *see* Brigman, *Pornography as Group Libel: The Indianapolis Sex Discrimination Ordinance,* 18 IND. L. REV. 479 (1985); *see also supra* text accompanying notes 30-36.

165. 343 U.S. at 251 (quoting ILL. REV. STAT. ch. 38, § 471 (1949) (repealed 1961)).

166. *Id.* at 263.

167. Jacobs, *supra* note 10, at 24.

168. 376 U.S. 254 (1964). The premise of Frankfurter's opinion in *Beauharnais* was that group libel was a form of defamation and hence completely outside of the purview of the first amendment. 343 U.S. at 258. *Sullivan* exploded this premise, holding that the regulation of "libel can claim no talismanic immunity from constitutional limitations. It must be measured by standards that satisfy the First Amendment." 376 U.S. at 269.

169. 106 S.Ct. 1558 (1986). The burden of proof was placed on the defendant in *Beauharnais* to establish, by way of affirmative defense, not only that "all the facts in the utterance" were true, 343 U.S. 254 n.1, "but also that the publication [was] made 'with good motives and for justifiable ends.'" *Id.* at 265 (quoting ILL. CONST. art. II, § 4). *Hepps,* on the other hand, holds that the first amendment requires that a "plaintiff bear the burden of showing falsity" when a defamation involves a matter of public concern. 106 S.Ct. at 1563.

170. 343 U.S. at 254-56, 258. Ten years earlier David Riesman had stressed this same analogy between group libel and individual defamation. Riesman, *Democracy and Defamation: Control of Group Libel,* 42 COLUM. L. REV. 727, 777-78 (1942). The analogy has been criticized in Arkes, *Civility and Restriction of Speech: Rediscovering the Defamation of Groups,* 1974 SUP. CT. REV. 281, 299-302.

expressed, the assertion is a form of "personal abuse," only it is abuse targeted at a group rather than at an individual addressee.

Because the feminist campaign against pornography aims to suppress a specific message of abuse, some have rejected the purposes of the campaign as "viewpoint discrimination"[171] or "thought control."[172] On one level this objection is easily met. Anti-pornography legislation can effectively be drafted in formally gender-neutral terms and prohibit sexual insult to either men or women. Such a reformulation would be more consistent with the pluralist goal of maintaining respect between competing groups, in this case between the groups of men and women. On a deeper level, however, this reformulation of anti-pornography legislation remains vulnerable to the charge of viewpoint discrimination, for the legislation would still penalize messages of gender insult. It would still contain "an 'approved' view of women, of how they may react to sexual encounters, of how the sexes may relate to each other."[173] When used in this way, however, the charge of viewpoint discrimination applies with equal force to *Cantwell'* s exclusion from first amendment protection of "profane, indecent, or abusive remarks directed to the person of the hearer."[174] *Cantwell* also establishes an "approved" view of how persons should relate to each other and how they should react to personal, religious, or even political disagreements.

The decisive issue, then, is not the presence vel non of viewpoint discrimination, but rather the justification for such discrimination. Reflecting its individualist presuppositions, first amendment law has long asserted that the social costs of viewpoint discrimination are tolerable if they involve only those face-to-face messages that would be deemed universally abusive; it has characterized these messages as "of such slight social value as a step to truth that any benefit that may be derived from them is clearly outweighed by the social interest in order and morality."[175] But first amendment law contains no such confident assertion if the discrimination occurs against those messages that are abusive only to particular groups. As judicial reaction to the feminist anti-pornography campaign illustrates,[176] such discrimination is much more likely to be understood as intolerable viewpoint discrimination, perhaps because of

171. Stone, *supra* note 10, at 467.

172. American Booksellers Ass'n v. Hudnut, 771 F.2d 323, 328 (7th Cir. 1985), *aff'd mem.*, 106 S. Ct. 1172 (1986).

173. *Id.*

174. Cantwell v. Connecticut, 310 U.S. 296, 309 (1940). Of course if one construes the rule of *Cantwell* to turn on the manner of speech, rather than its content, the same point could be made about the regulation of pornography.

175. Chaplinsky v. New Hampshire, 315 U.S. 568, 572 (1942).

176. *See American Booksellers*, 771 F.2d 323.

an instinctive perception that intergroup struggle is a central aspect of our political culture.

The virtue of the distinction between pluralism and individualism is that it forces us to make these different assessments explicit and to subject them to appropriate examination. There are in fact two generic grounds for apprehension concerning the relationship between pluralism and our system of freedom of expression. The first relates to the tenuous nature of group identity in American culture; the second to the distinct kinds of assimilationist values that underlie pluralism and individualism.

Zechariah Chafee noted the first reason for unease long ago when he observed that the ultimate objection to group libel was its potential for strangling public discussion: "Once you start group libel laws, every influential body of men will urge that it has an equal claim to be protected by such legislation. And the wider the protection, the narrower becomes the field for unimpeded discussion of public affairs."[177] Chafee's observation rests on assumptions similar to those that underlie *Cantwell;* he perceives group life in America as dynamic and unstable. Because groups are constantly evolving, the meaning of group identity is ambiguous, and hence there is no natural brake to claims for group protection.[178] That is perhaps why the English are more comfortable than we in using pluralist principles to regulate speech: categories of group identity have in England been made so much more definite by history and tradition.

American perceptions of group identity are exemplified by our ambivalent perception of race, which is for us the paradigmatic example of group identity made distinct through history and tradition. On the one hand we doubt whether a distinct group racial identity should really exist; we sincerely believe that race shouldn't matter and that the law should be color blind. On the other hand, when we acknowledge the existence of that identity, we do so in a way that flattens racial uniqueness into an ethnic culture that is functionally no different from the cultures of other ethnic Americans, like that of the Irish, the Italians, the Scandinavians, and so forth. When we think in terms of pluralism, in other words, even the unique category of race dissolves into a cascade of groups, each forcefully pressing its case to be recognized as the bearer of a valuable ethnic identity. Chafee is right that the first amendment

---

177. Z. CHAFEE, GOVERNMENT AND MASS COMMUNICATIONS 125 (1965).

178. In this regard, I cannot resist noting that the Oriental Rug Retailers of America, a professional association of rug-merchants, has recently demanded an apology from ex-White House Chief-of-Staff Donald Regan for a remark demeaning "rug-merchant type of stuff" before the congressional committee investigating the Iran-Contra arms scandal. The president of the association asserted: "Your statement was thoughtless and implies distrust of all rug merchants, and especially our membership." San Francisco Chronicle, Aug. 7, 1987, at 9, col. 4.

would suffer harm if the law were to be used to regulate expression so as to enforce respect among all such potential groups.

But this conclusion does not settle the question of pornography. It leads instead to the question of whether there is a basis for distinguishing gender groups from all other kinds of groups, or, to put it another way, whether there is a principled manner in which the values of pluralism can be confined to pornography and not applied to expression generally. Catharine MacKinnon has written that "the situation of women is *not really like anything else.*"[179] From a constitutional point of view, much depends on the substantiation of this claim. We have been fairly successful in confining strict scrutiny under the equal protection clause to only a small number of potential groups. The question is whether we can be equally successful in the area of freedom of expression.

The second and ultimately more substantial ground for concern about the relationship between the first amendment and pluralism turns on the kind of assimilationist values that support pluralist law. As the example of *Cantwell* illustrates, individualism tightly circumscribes the assimilationist values that can be used to characterize speech as intrinsically harmful and therefore unprotected. In the individualist realm of the first amendment, assimilationist values are thin and universal, for they must potentially apply to all persons.[180] Such values also tend to be weak, because in order to foster a general culture of autonomous individualism, it is necessary to minimize interference with the expression of autonomous individuals. At the margins the assimilationist values associated with the first amendment authorize censorship of "fighting words," or "personal abuse," or "obscenity." But in the vast majority of cases these values strain to tolerate individual differences. Thus within the realm of the first amendment we say that because "one man's vulgarity is another's lyric,"[181] "uninhibited, robust, and wide-open"[182] discussion of public issues can be attained only by suspending ordinary assimilationist norms of civility and interpersonal respect.[183] Pluralist law, on the other hand, presupposes assimilationist values that are richer and more aggressive. These values not only enable pluralist law to identify which groups deserve legal protection, but also to specify the norms of civility and respect that will obtain between these groups.[184] In this sense pluralism contemplates a far wider and more influential role for assimilationist law than does individualism. For this reason the regula-

179. C. MACKINNON, *supra* note 4, at 166 (emphasis in original).

180. *See supra* text accompanying notes 137-38.

181. Cohen v. California, 403 U.S. 15, 25 (1971).

182. New York Times Co. v. Sullivan, 376 U.S. 254, 270 (1964).

183. Post, *supra* note 13, at 731-39; Post, *Defaming Public Officials: On Doctrine and Legal History,* (Review Essay) 1987 AM. B. FOUND. RES. J. 539, 553-57.

184. *See supra* text accompanying notes 97-98.

tion of pornography proposed by MacKinnon and Dworkin invites the law not only to define and enforce conceptions of group identity within the area of gender, but also to impose norms of respect and civility between genders. Individualist law, in contrast, stresses the value of personal choice, of leaving individuals free to battle over the shape and meaning of gender identity, so that "many types of life, character, opinion, and belief can develop unmolested and unobstructed."[185]

If the pluralist perspective of MacKinnon and Dworkin is perceived to be in tension with the first amendment, it is because we instinctively identify that amendment with the individualist tradition that has evolved since the 1930's. It is hard for us to imagine a system of freedom of expression that does not ultimately embody the value "of assuring individual self-fulfillment."[186] Yet it is precisely this value that MacKinnon and Dworkin call into question. To assess the constitutional implications of their critique, we must distinguish two different meanings to the notion that the regulation of pornography is "in tension" with the first amendment. Consider, first, the kind of constitutional problem that is likely to occur in the drafting of an anti-pornography statute: The pervasiveness of gender relations and the inherent vagueness of the insult to be redressed create the troubling potential of ceding to the government broad and standardless powers of censorship.[187] This potential is "in tension" with the first amendment because it is inconsistent with that distrust of government power to regulate speech which forms the very justification for the amendment.[188]

The argument that pornography should be regulated in order to assure respectful relations between the sexes, however, is not "in tension" with the first amendment in this sense. Instead the argument requires us to engage in a substantive interpretation of the purposes of the amendment, and to inquire whether we value freedom of expression because it furthers individual or group life. As the English example illustrates, either approach is compatible with a system of freedom of expression. The question of which we choose turns on the kind of social world that we want to use the first amendment to help construct. To elect the pluralist option is not to abandon the first amendment, but rather to forsake

185. Cantwell v. Connecticut, 310 U.S. 296, 310 (1940).

186. T. EMERSON, THE SYSTEM OF FREEDOM OF EXPRESSION 6 (1970).

187. On the pervasive quality of subordination in gender relationships, see E. GOFFMAN, GENDER ADVERTISEMENTS 28-51 (1979).

188. At the present time the avoidance of such discretionary powers of censorship strikes me as an essentially technical problem, to be solved by sensitive, craftsmanlike drafting. It would not be unreasonable to proceed on the assumption that by such drafting specifically first amendment concerns can be brought within the range of what we are presently willing to tolerate in the area of obscenity regulation. On the technical difficulties posed by the drafting of group libel statutes, see Z. CHAFEE, *supra* note 110, at 116-30; Tanenhaus, *Group Libel*, 35 CORNELL L.Q. 261, 297-302 (1950).

the individualist assumptions underlying contemporary first amendment law.

The choice between pluralist and individualist interpretations of the first amendment is thus one of high cultural policy, and may well vary from one area of law to another. With regard to the specific matter of pornography, for example, the choice might turn on such considerations as the relationship between individual identity and gender identity, the hegemonic or expressive character of the proposed assimilationist conception of gender roles and rules of civility,[189] the effectiveness and appropriateness of enforcing normative models of gender roles through the public force of the law, and the harms caused by the absence of such enforcement. The question of freedom of expression is certainly pertinent to these inquiries, but I see no reason a priori to believe that it should be dispositive of their resolution.

The ultimate challenge posed by commentators like MacKinnon and Dworkin, then, is not to the system of freedom of expression, but rather to our ingrained individualism. Although equal protection doctrine has begun to reflect pluralist values in the treatment of gender,[190] our allegiance to individualism has remained as strong as ever in the first amendment area, which concerns belief and expression rather than action. The evolving struggle over pornography will test whether that allegiance will continue undiminished, even in the leering face of pornography.

189. *See supra* note 98 and text accompanying notes 12-13.

190. *See, e.g.*, Johnson v. Transportation Agency, 107 S. Ct. 1442 (1987); Williams, *The Equality Crisis: Some Reflections on Culture, Courts, and Feminism*, 7 WOMEN'S RTS. L. REP. 175, 190-200 (1982); *cf.* Fiss, *Groups and the Equal Protection Clause*, 5 PHIL. & PUB. AFF. 107 (1976).

Name Index